The Expositor
(*Atthasālini*)

MLBD

SACRED BOOKS OF THE BUDDHISTS SERIES

Reprinted Under License from **Pali Text Society**

- **A Buddhist Manual of Psychological Ethics** : Translation of the First Book in Abhidhamma Piṭaka entitled Dhammasaṅgaṇī—With Introductory Essay and Notes by *C.A.F. Rhys Davids.*
- **The Book of the Gradual Sayings** : Translation of Anguttara Nikāya, the Fourth Collection of Sutta Piṭaka (**5 Vols.**)—Tr. by *F.L. Woodward* and *E.M. Hare.*
- **The Book of the Kindred Sayings** : Translation of Saṁyutta-Nikāya (**5 Vols.**)—Tr. ,Ed. & Introduction by *C.A.F. Rhys Davids,* Tr. by *F.L. Woodward.*
- **The Collection of the Middle Length Sayings** : Translation of Majjhima Nikāya, the Second Collection of the Sutta Piṭaka containing 152 suttas. (**3 Vols.**)—Tr. from the Pali by *I.B. Horner.*
- **Compendium of Philosophy** : Translation of Abhidhammattha-Saṅgaha)—With Tr., Introductory Essay and Notes by *Shwe Zan-Aung,* Rev. & Ed. by *C.A.F. Rhys Davids.*
- **Culavaṁśa** : Translation from German Translation by Wilhelm Geiger. A Continuation of *Great Chronicle of Ceylon* (Mahāvaṃśa) : (**2 Pts. in One**)—by *C. Mabel Rickmers.*
- **Dialogues of the Buddha** : Dīgha Nikāya, the First Collection of Sutta Piṭaka (**3 Vols.**)—Translation from the Pali by *T.W. Rhys Davids* and *C.A.F. Rhys Davids.*
- **Dictionary of Pali Proper Names (2 Vols.)**—*G.P. Malalasekera.*
- **English-Pali Dictionary** —*Venerable A.P. Buddhadata.*
- **The Expositor** : Translation of Atthaśālinī, Buddhaghoṣa's Commentary on Dhammasaṅgaṇī, the First Book of Abhidhamma Piṭaka—Tr. by *Pe Maung Tin,* Rev. & Ed. by *C.A.F. Rhys Davids.*
- **Conditional Relations [Paṭṭhāna] (2 Pts.)** Part I : Guide, Part II : Translation of Caṭṭasaṅgāyana Text of the Seventh Book of Abhidhamma Piṭaka—Tr. by *U. Narada Mula Patt Thana Sayadow,* Assisted by *U. Thein Nyun.*
- **The Jātaka or Stories of the Buddha's Former Births (6 Vols. in 3 Pts.)**: Translation from the Tenth Book of Khuddaka Nikāya of Sutta Piṭaka—Ed. by *E.B. Cowell,* Tr. by *Robert Chalmers, W.H.D. Rouse, H.T. Francis* and *R.A. Neil.*
- **Pali-English Dictionary**—*T.W. Rhys Davids* and *William Stede.*
- **Pali Metre** : A Contribution to the History of Indian Literature—*A.K. Warder.*
- **Points of Controversy** (Subjects of Discourse) : A Translation of the Kathāvathu from the Fifth Book of Abhidhamma Piṭaka—Tr. by *S.Z. Aung* and *C.A.F. Rhys Davids.*
- **The Sutra of Golden Light** : Translation of Suvarnabhasottamasūtra—*R.E. Emmerick.*

Pali Text Society
Translation Series No. 8,9

THE EXPOSITOR

(*Atthasālinī*)

Buddhaghoṣa's Commentary on the *Dhammasaṅgaṇī*,
The First Book of the *Abhidhamma-Piṭaka*

Translated by

PE MAUNG TIN

Professor of Pāli at the College, Rangoon

Edited and Revised by

MRS. RHYS DAVIDS

Special Lecturer in Philosophy at Manchester University

MOTILAL BANARSIDASS PUBLISHERS
PRIVATE LIMITED • DELHI

First Indian Edition: Delhi, ***2016***
3rt Reprint: Wiltshire, (UK) 2013
First Published: Wiltshire, (UK) 1920 (21)

ISBN: 978-81-208-4036-2

Also available at

MOTILAL BANARSIDASS
41 U.A. Bungalow Road, Jawahar Nagar, Delhi 110 007
8 Mahalaxmi Chamber, 22 Bhulabhai Desai Road, Mumbai 400 026
203 Royapettah High Road, Mylapore, Chennai 600 004
236, 9th Main III Block, Jayanagar, Bengaluru 560 011
8 Camac Street, Kolkata 700 017
Ashok Rajpath, Patna 800 004
Chowk, Varanasi 221 001

MLBD Cataloging-in-Publication Data
The Expositor (Atthasālini)
Translated by Pe Maung Tin,
Edited and Revised by Mrs. Rhys Davids
in *MLBD Sacred Books of the Buddhists Series*
ISBN : 978-81-208-4036-2
Includes Buddhaghoṣa's Commentary on the *Dhammasaṅgaṇī*, the first book of the *Abhidhamma-Piṭaka*, Index
I. Buddhism II. Dhammasaṅgaṇī
III. Abhidhamma-Piṭaka IV. Tin, Pe Maung
V. Mrs. Davids, Rhys

Published by

Motilal Banarsidass Publishers Private Limited
www.mlbd.com • *mlbd@mlbd.com*
Printed by Replika Press Pvt. Ltd.

THE EXPOSITOR

(*Atthasālinī*)

Buddhaghoṣa's Commentary on the *Dhammasaṅgaṇī*,
The First Book of the *Abhidhamma-Piṭaka*

EDITORIAL NOTE

IT is now fully four years since the translation of this important Commentary was begun by Mr. Maung Tin, the representative of the Pali Text Society in Burma. Obstacles confronted him at the commencement, and many difficulties along the way. With a training and a diploma got at Calcutta University, and a proficiency in Pali, Burmese, and English, as well as in Sanskrit and Prakrit, he was anxious to prove himself in the field, yet so lacking in competent labourers, of the ancient classical literature adopted by his native land. Workers in other lands warned him off successively from making more accessible two or three notable works as well as the Atthasālinī, but on this work, not yet begun elsewhere, he took his stand, and during the last year of menace at sea the typescript came over piecemeal in safety. As to the many difficulties in the work itself, there was the lamentable need of revision in the PTS edition of the text, and the many obscurities and elliptical clauses (occurring amid a good deal of unnecessary redundancy) in Buddhaghosa's style. I do not say, nor would the translator claim, that the result is everywhere satisfactory. But we judge that we have made more possible, by this pioneer effort, the production of a really good translation in the future. It is no light effort, all who know the text will agree, for a man to have accomplished the pioneer translation of such a work into a foreign tongue. We should look around for long to find an Englishman capable of such a task. The translator is hoping soon to renew university study at Oxford, and I trust that there and thereafter much good work in Pali literature from his pen will come to aid our knowledge.

Of the Atthasālinī or Aṭṭhasālinī itself I have had my say elsewhere. The many interesting psychological disquisitions in its pages I have also tried to deal with elsewhere, always feeling sorely the need of such a translation as is given below. Here I will only say that the title literally rendered—'abounding in meaning' or (for *attha* has many 'meanings') matter, or profit, etc.—baffled us and 'Expositor' (it should be Expositrix)[1] is a makeshift for which I plead guilty. And I add one more comment.

He has made allusion to terms, in my own 'prentice work on the text (of which this work is the Commentary), the Englishing of which I have since agreed to modify. He has himself altered other terms, and that is quite as it should be. If I ever revise for reprint that now exhausted edition, I shall have other such details to alter. On the word *cetanā*: volition, I have already commented in the Compendium of Philosophy, p. 238, *n*. 3. Another term of great importance in Buddhist thought, and for the translator very elusive, is *rūpa*.

On this term another equally instructive note by Mr. Aung should also be studied (*op. cit.* pp. 271-3). We have followed him in not rendering *rūpa* by 'form.' 'Shape' or 'form' is no doubt the popular and the more archaic sense. If you make a 'likeness,' say a clay model of any person or thing, you would call it his or its *rūpa*. And the primeval factors employed by the creative Brahman in peopling the earth were called 'name' and 'shape' or 'form' (*nāmarūpa*).[2] But for the specialisation required in Abhidhamma these renderings are a little unwieldy. This may be seen more clearly by quoting from the following pages three sentences. '*Rūpa* is that which changes its state' (p. 69). 'The *rūpa* comes into the avenue of the mind-door' (p. 96). 'He develops the path for rebirth in the sphere of *rūpa*' (p. 216). It is fairly clear that no one English word would fit all three cases. They deal, taken in order, with (*a*) something essentially plastic and mutable as distinct from a relatively constant and rigid factor—the 'name' or, according to the Dhammasaṅgaṇī, mind and

---

[1] However, the translator would none of her!

[2] Cf. hereon 'Gestalt' in *Die Weltanschauung der Brāhmaṇa-Texte*, Göttingen, 1919, pp. 102 *f.*, 114, by Hermann Oldenberg—the last contribution, I believe, to our Indological knowledge, by this great scholar whose loss to such studies it will be hard to make good.

Nibbāna[1]; (*b*) that which the organ of sight is said to see[2]; (*c*) a world of intelligent beings that is, for some not obvious reason, called *rūpa*, but which is often called the world of brahmās. Hence we have rendered *rūpa* in (*a*) by 'matter' or 'material quality'; in (*b*) by 'visible object' ('sight' being applicable equally to organ and object of sight and therefore ambiguous); in (*c*) by 'sphere' (or realm) of attenuated matter.'

It is in (*c*) that we really feel the deprivation of the term 'form.' And although I am responsible for the clumsy periphrasis which the translator has been good enough to put up with, I am inclined to think that Pali translators will either revert to 'form,' or keep to the very adaptable word *rūpa*, *rūpalōka*, or use the nearly equivalent term 'Brahmā world.'

To the contradictory *a-rūpa* (p. 267) may be far more easily fitted our terms 'immaterial,' 'incorporeal.' Mental factors are often divided off from corporeal factors by the adjective *arūpino*. And albeit no denizen of any heaven classed as *arūpa* is recorded as having assumed corporeal shape to visit the *rūpaloka* or the lower kāma-worlds (which include the next world and the earth), yet that world was in Buddhist tradition a real Somewhere, described in terms of abstract thought. The world of Form, of the Formless, might still stand, as before, to signify these two departments of the Universe of Being, deriving, for the reader at least, what dignity they may from their capital letters.

But why the clumsy periphrasis 'of attenuated matter'? Well, if neither 'form,' nor *rūpa* be approved, it is evident that neither 'matter,' nor 'visible object' is a more suitable term. *Rūpalōka*, whatever else it mean, does not, in this case, mean a world where matter or material shapes are its typical and preponderant content. Even the denizens—the devas (they are, of course, not 'gods' in any Western sense)—of the world next 'above' earth are shown as less subservient to matter than

---

[1] See *B.P.E.*, p. 341 *f*.

[2] We see directly only extended colour. We see symbolically, by suggestion or inference, much else that we have learned by touch.

we are. They can by an effort of volition transport themselves, mind and body, to this earth and back without inconvenience. But, to appear in that deva-world, a denizen of the 'higher' Rūpa (or Brahmā) world is represented as investing himself at will with a body of 'grosser' material qualities than those that make up his Rūpa-body.[1] This was therefore of a more sublimated, refined, subtle nature. The matter of it was attenuated in density. That this seems to be a Buddhist tradition taught in Burma may be seen from a letter recently received from the translator—I regret that absence on a holiday prevented him from quoting any authority.

'The lower sixteen out of the twenty brahmā worlds are called *rūpa* worlds. And the brahmās of these sixteen worlds are called *rūpāvacarā*,[2] because they are in worlds where *rūpa* arises. They have *rūpa*, but to say that they are so called because of their *rūpa* would not be a correct interpretation, grammatically speaking. Brahmās, it is true, are endowed with *rūpa*, but not with all the twenty-eight forms of rūpa characterizing beings of the *kāmaloka* (or *kāmāvacara*). They are without the *rūpa's* (the material qualities) of femininity, masculinity, the sentient organisms of smell, taste, and touch. And though they are endowed with the elements of extension, heat, and mobility, they differ, even in this respect, from beings of the *kāmaloka*. For instance, a human body is either a present resisting solid, or it is absent. The bodies of brahmās are not so. Cut one with a knife and no harm is done. It is like cutting a flame. Generally speaking, the *rūpa* of brahmās is very refined or sublime, sublimated or, as you render it, attenuated, as distinguished from [the kāmaloka inhabitants on the one hand, and] the *arūpa* or spirit brahmās on the other. Their senses of sight and hearing are highly developed. Theirs it is to own the super-sensitive telepathic faculties entitled *dibbacakkhu*, *dibbasota*.'[3]

In giving no authority for this doubtless hoary Abhidhamma tradition, Mr. Tin leaves me to conclude that *rūpaloka* is so called as a division of the *brahmāloka*. This world by his

---

[1] *Dialogues* ii. 244, 264.
[2] Denizens of the Rūpa sphere.
[3] *Dibba*=*deva*. Usually rendered heavenly or celestial eye and ear.

account is four-fifths *rūpāvacara*, and one-fifth *arūpāvacara*. And that these four-fifths have been distinguished as *rūpa* has nothing to do, comparatively speaking, with the fact or nature of the *rūpa* in the humbler spheres of the earth or the purgatories, or the *sagga*, the next 'bright world' of the better folk who have passed (temporarily) from earth. I note that he uses the word brahmās with a more widely distributed denotation than is the case in either the Dhammasaṅgaṇī (§ 1283), or the Compendium of Philosophy (p. 142), or Childers's Dictionary (*s.v.* Sattaloko). But this is, after all, of little importance. For the tradition he cites, brahmās include all beings, some having a refined corporeality, some being pure spirit, who have passed on either from the 'sagga' of the lower world beyond us, or, through eminent virtue, direct from earth-life.

Future translators will make their choice, as to a name for the former division, between 'world of form,' 'sphere, realm, world of attenuated or subtle matter,' just 'Rūpa,' or some better device. With the term we commend to them two reflections—one concerning the past, one the future. Whence and how did this Buddhist cosmology spring up, whereof we find the several spheres sporadically mentioned already in the Nikāyas,[1] partial classifications of them in the Abhidhamma Piṭaka,[2] and full classification in medieval manuals—*e.g.*, the Compendium of Philosophy (p. 142)? The other reflection, concerning the future—*i.e.*, of human knowledge—is on the need of humanity, in its religion of to-morrow, of a cosmology, soberer and simpler than that built by the ancient mind of Buddhist India, to replace the vast mournful ignorance of the accredited religions of to-day concerning the other-whereness of life, past, present, and future. It was only concerning the future of the Arahant that Gotama drew down the veil of his Avyākata—his 'things unrevealed'—because it was to no good purpose to seek to know.

C. A. F. RHYS DAVIDS.

CHIPSTEAD, SURREY.
June, 1920.

---

[1] *E.g.*, *Dialogues* ii. 39 *f.*; 280, 296; *Majjhima* i. 210; ii. 194; *Kindred Sayings* i. 48; *Pss. of the Sisters*, p. 100 *f.*, etc.

[2] *Dhammasaṅgaṇī*, § 1283; *Vibhaṅga*, last chapter.

PREFACE

In Burma, the Atthasālinī[1] is one of the best known works of Buddhaghosa. It is widely studied by student monks and is freely quoted by authors of Abhidhamma works. It is likely that a European reader, reading through the English translation now offered to the public, will not be favourable in his judgment. The plan of the work itself is enough to prejudice him, while a good knowledge of the cardinal doctrines of the Buddha and Buddhist philosophy is necessary, if Buddhaghosa is to be appreciated. And that is impossible for him unless he is eminently sympathetic towards Buddhist thought. In the present work it is not the aim of Buddhaghosa to expound any particular doctrine; he is only concerned with explaining the meanings of terms that occur in the Dhammasaṅgaṇī. In doing this he has freely scattered the gems of his thought at every opportunity, and has thus enhanced the value of the work. The word-definitions which may be very tedious (and sometimes pointless) to a Western scholar are all-important to the Buddhist student, who must know the meanings of conceptual terms before he can grasp ultimate truths. So one must wade through the word-definitions in this book before getting to the depths of its thought.

Abhidhamma studies have made such strides since Mrs. Rhys Davids translated the first Abhidhamma work—*viz.*, Dhammasaṅgaṇī in 1900—that many of the psychological terms used by her in that translation have been altered by herself in other works in consultation with Mr. S. Z. Aung. I have availed myself of this improvement, and adopted in the present work such terms of the Dhammasaṅgaṇī translation

[1] Burmese scholars invariably spell Aṭṭhasālinī.

as have been approved of by these pioneers of Abhidhamma translation. I have indicated in footnotes other renderings used in that translation. In a few cases I have offered new meanings of my own.

I have nothing to add to what Mrs. Rhys Davids has said, in her Buddhist Psychological Ethics, about the Atthasālinī, its date and importance. But I take this opportunity of recording my appreciation of her scholarship that then enabled her, without aid from Burma, to draw upon the Atthasālinī for her suggestive footnotes. It is no small gain to Abhidhamma scholarship that the first English translator of the first of the Abhidhamma works and the leading Western authority on the subject should, after an interval of twenty years of progressive study, have edited and revised the present translation of the commentary.

The Atthasālinī, from the nature of its contents, is a difficult book to translate. I have therefore tried to be as literal as possible even to the extent of sometimes sacrificing style to clearness. In the course of the translation, I discovered many errors and omissions in the text edited for the Pali Text Society by Professor Edward Müller. I therefore based my translation on two Burmese texts, the one printed by the Sāsanajotika Piṭaka Press, Rangoon, 1913, and the other edited in the well-known Pyigyi-mandaing Press Series by Saya Pye, Aggamahāpaṇḍita. I have derived much help from the two Burmese translations of the Atthasālinī—namely, the Old Nissaya (MS. Bernard Free Library, Rangoon), by Ariyālaṅkāra of the early part of the eighteenth century, and the New Nissaya (printed at Kemmendine, Rangoon, in 1905), by Pyī Sadaw of the middle of the nineteenth century. I have also quoted the following Pali commentaries and sub-commentaries bearing on the Atthasālinī:

1. *Ṭīkā* or *Mūlaṭīkā*, by Ānanda of Ceylon.
2. *Anuṭīkā*, a sub-commentary on the *Mūlaṭīkā*, by Dhammapāla of Ceylon.
3. *Visuddhimagga Ṭīkā* (also called *Paramatthamañjūsā Ṭīkā* or *Mahāṭīkā*), by Dhammapāla of Ceylon.
4. *Sāratthadīpanī*, by Sāriputta of Ceylon.

CONTENTS

BOOKS REFERRED TO

A.—English.

Buddhist Birth Stories (Trübner's Oriental Series). Rhys Davids. London, 1880.

Buddhist India (Story of the Nations Series). Rhys Davids. London, 1903.

BPE=Buddhist Psychological Ethics. A translation of the Dhammasaṅgaṇī. Mrs. Rhys Davids. London, 1900.

Buddhist Psychology (Quest Series). Mrs. Rhys Davids. London, 1914.

Childers's Pali Dictionary. London, 1875.

Compendium of Philosophy. A translation of the Abhidhammatthasaṅgaha. S. Z. Aung and Mrs Rhys Davids. PTS, 1910.

Dialogues of the Buddha. A translation of the Dīgha Nikāya (Sacred Books of the Buddhists). T. W. and Mrs. Rhys Davids. London, 1899, etc.

JPTS=Journal of the Pali Text Society London, 1882, etc.

Kindred Sayings. A translation of the Saṃyutta Nikāya I. Mrs. Rhys Davids. PTS, 1917.

Mahāvaṃsa. Translated by Professor W. Geiger. PTS, 1912.

Points of Controversy. A translation of the Kathāvatthu. S. Z. Aung and Mrs. Rhys Davids. PTS, 1915.

Psalms of the Brethren. A translation of the Theragāthā. Mrs. Rhys Davids. PTS, 1913.

Psalms of the Sisters. A translation of the Therīgāthā. Mrs. Rhys Davids. PTS, 1909.

The Questions of King Milinda. Translated by Rhys Davids. SBE, 1890, etc.

The Religions of India. E. W. Hopkins. London, 1896.

Vinaya Texts. A translation of the greater part of the Vinaya Piṭaka. SBE, 1881, etc.

B.—Pali.

A.=Aṅguttara Nikāya, of the Sutta Piṭaka. PTS, 1885, etc. 5 vols. and index.

Abhidhānapadīpikāsūcī. Colombo, 1893.

D.=Dīgha Nikāya, of the Sutta Piṭaka. PTS, 1889, etc. 3 vols.

Dhp.=Dhammapada, of the Sutta Piṭaka. PTS, 1914.

Dhammapada Commentary. PTS, 1906, etc. 4 vols. and index.

Dhs.=Dhammasaṅgaṇī, of the Abhidhamma Piṭaka. PTS, 1885.

Jātaka. Ed. by V. Fausböll. London, 1877, etc. 6 vols. and index vol.

Kathāvatthu, of the Abhidhamma Piṭaka. PTS, 1894, etc.

M.=Majjhima Nikāya, of the Sutta Piṭaka. PTS, 1887, etc. 3 vols.

Mahāniddesa, of the Sutta Piṭaka. PTS, 1916, etc.

Mahāvaṃsa. PTS, 1908.

Milindapañha. Trenckner. London, 1880.

Pts.=Paṭisambhidāmagga of the Sutta Piṭaka. PTS, 1905-7. 2 vols.

S.=Saṃyutta Nikāya, of the Sutta Piṭaka. PTS, 1884, etc. 5 vols. and index vol.

Sumaṅgala Vilāsinī, Comy. on Dīgha Nikāya. PTS, 1886.

Sn.=Sutta Nipāta, of the Sutta Piṭaka. PTS, 1913.

Udāna, of the Sutta Piṭaka. PTS, 1885.

Vibhaṅga, of the Abhidhamma Piṭaka. PTS, 1904.

Vinaya Piṭaka. Ed. by H. Oldenberg. London, 1879, etc.

Visuddhi Magga. PTS, 1920.

Yamaka, of the Abhidhamma Piṭaka. PTS, 1911, etc.

Unpublished Pali Works.

Papañca Sūdanī, Comy. on Majjhima Nikāya. (P. 188.)

Paṭṭhāna, of the Abhidhamma Piṭaka.

Sumaṅgala Vilāsinī, Comy. on Dīgha Nikāya. (Vol. I. is published by PTS.)

Theragāthā, Comy. on, *v.* Pss. of the Brethren. (P. 77, *n.* 3.)

Udāna Comy.

CONTENTS

PART IX.—DISCOURSE ON IMMORAL CONSCIOUSNESS

PART X.—DISCOURSE ON UNMORAL CONSCIOUSNESS

BOOK II.—MATERIAL QUALITIES (RŪPA)

PART I

PART II.—DISCOURSE ON THE CHAPTER OF THE SUMMARY

THE EXPOSITOR

(*ATTHASĀLINĪ*)

COMMENTARY ON THE DHAMMASAṄGAṆĪ
(COMPENDIUM OF PHENOMENA)

BY

BUDDHAGHOSA

INTRODUCTORY DISCOURSE

Honour be to that Blessed One, the Arahant, the Buddha Supreme

As on all beings his pity, rolled at will
The Sage's insight through all knowable things.
His heart by that world-pitying love inspired,
When, after the Twin Miracle,[1] *he dwelt*
At the high mansion of the Thirty-three,[2]
Throned—like the sun on Mount Yugandhara—
On Paṇḍukambala, his rocky seat,
Under the tree called Pāricchattaka,

---

[1] See *Paṭisambhidāmagga*, i. 125 *f.*; *Jātaka*, i. 77, 88, 193.

[2] *Tidasālaye.* Lit., in the abode of the thrice-ten. *Tidasa,* frequently substituted, in verse, for the more usual *tāvatiṃsa* (*e.g. Therig. ver.* 181; and in prose, *Mil.* 291), is explained by the *Abhidhānaṭīkā* as an elliptical form of *ti-tidasa* = *tāvatiṃsa.* This work sees an alternative explanation in *dasā* = *avatthā,* divisions, namely, of life: birth, development, decease, *or*—according to the *Abhidhānappadīpikāsūcī*—birth, being (*satta*), and destruction (*vināsa*), *dasā* being taken as *parimāṇā* (the three 'measures' of becoming).—*Tr.*

He by that noble insight gave discourse
On the Abhidhamma to the spirits who came,
Led by his mother,[1] *from the myriad worlds,*
And compassed him about on every side.

I bow before the glorious Buddha's feet;
I reverence the Church, and the Good Law.
No evil falls on him who bends the knee
To those Three Jewels. That which the Spirit of spirits
Unto the spirits taught, he afterwards,
The Leader, told it all in form concise[2]
To Sāriputta Elder, when he waited on
The Sage at Anotatta lake.[3] *And what*
The Elder heard, he brought to plains of earth
And taught it to the brethren. And they all
Remembered it. And when the Council met,
By the wise son of the Videhi Dame[4]
It was again rehearsed.
Being besought
By Buddhaghosa,[5] *bhikkhu pure in deed*
And virtue, of subtle insight without taint,
What Abhidhamma from the first hath meant
I shall expound, in many figures shown
And searched at all times by the greatly wise.
The ancient Commentary thereof was sung
By the first Council, Mahākassapa
Their leader, and later again by seers.
Mahinda brought it to the peerless isle,

---

[1] Tradition in Burma makes her reborn as the devī Santussitā. The phrase *mātaraṃ pamukhaṃ katvā* in line 11 may also be construed with the predicate, *sampavattayi*, thus: 'gave a discourse on the Abhidhamma, to the assembly of spirits, *principally* to his mother.'—*Tr.*

[2] *Desetvā nayato,* which may also mean, 'by way of showing the method.'—*Tr.*

[3] A great lake located by tradition in the Himālayas. We have not traced this episode in any other work. Cf. *Vinaya Texts* i. 124.—*Ed.*

[4] Or, 'the sage of wisdom or energy,' Ānanda the Thera. Cf. *Kindred Sayings*, p. 109, *n.* 1; 321.—*Ed.*

[5] Not the Thera, author of this work.—*Tr.*

Ceylon, and in their tongue they wrote the book.[1]
[2] *Rejecting from that ancient scroll the speech*
Of Tambapaṇṇi, I shall here inscribe
On the palmyra-leaf the faultless tongue
That disobeys no rule of holy script,
Illuminate the minds of those who dwell
In the Great Minster, suffering nor taint
Nor base commixture of the heresies,[2]
True meaning of the Abhidhamma show,
And satisfy the wise with chosen words
From expositions of the Sutta-lore.
In the Visuddhimagga I have told
The stations of religious exercise,
Right conduct, super-knowledge, insight true.
These therefore laying by, I shall declare
Precept by precept all the holy script.
Give ear obediently, while I expound
The Abhidhamma-lore,[3] *for it is hard*
To hear such discourse as ye now may hear.

Herein what is meant by 'Abhidhamma'? That which exceeds and is distinguished from the Dhamma (the Suttas). The prefix 'Abhi,' like 'Ati,' is used in the sense of preponderance and distinction, as in such passages as, 'Severe pains overwhelm (*abhikkamantī*) me, brother; and do not abate';[4] and 'of eminent (*abhikkantā*) beauty.'[5] Again: 'Hence when many sunshades and flags are uplifted, the sunshade which excels the rest in size and is of distinguished colour and form is

[1] 450 years after the Parinibbāna, according to Burmese commentators; about 230 years, according to prevailing European computation.—*Tr.*

[2] *Nikāyantaraladdhīhi* = *nikāya*, a 'body' of people, + *antara*, different + *laddhīhi*, with the views. The *Maṇidīpa* says that the two other sects were the Abhayagirivāsī, and the Jetavanavāsī, dwellers at the Abhayagiri monastery, and the Jetavana monastery respectively. Some wrongly translate the expression as 'extreme views of the Nikāyas.'—*Tr.*

[3] *Abhidhammakathaṃ* is short for *Abhidhamma-Aṭṭhakathaṃ*.—*Tr.*

[4] *Saṃyutta* iv. 120.

[5] *Ib.* i. 1. etc.

called *atichattaṃ*, 'the pre-eminent sunshade,' and the flag which is the largest and is replete with various distinguished paints and colours is called *atidhaja*, 'the pre-eminent flag.' And when many princes and gods are gathered together, the prince who is specially distinguished and surpasses others in birth, property, pomp, dominion, and other attainments is called *atirājakumāra*, 'the prince *par excellence*'; and the god who is specially distinguished and surpasses others in age, beauty, dominion, pomp, and other attainments is called *atideva*, or *abhideva*, 'the peerless god.' Similarly Brahmā is called *Atibrahmā*, 'the supreme Brahmā.' Even so this 'dhamma' is called Abhidhamma, because it excels and is distinguished by several qualities from the other Dhamma. In the Suttanta, the five 'aggregates' are classified partially and not fully. In the Abhidhamma they are classified fully by the methods of Suttanta-classification, Abhidhamma-classification, and catechism. Similarly with the twelve sense-organs, the eighteen elements, the Four Truths, the twenty-two controlling faculties, and the twelvefold Causal Genesis. [3] It is only in the *Indriya Vibhaṅga*[1] that there is no Suttanta-classification, and in the Vibhaṅga on Causal Genesis[2] the method of catechism is wanting. In the Suttantas the four Applications in Mindfulness are partially classified, not fully. But in the Abhidhamma they are classified in detail under the three methods. And the same with the Four Supreme Efforts, the Four Steps to Supernormal Potency, the Seven Factors of Wisdom, the Eight-fold Path, the Four Jhānas, the Four Infinitudes, the Five Precepts, the Four Analyses. Of these only in the *Sikkhāpada Vibhaṅga* is there no Suttanta-classification.[3] In the Suttantas knowledge is partially classified, not fully. And so are the Corruptions (*kilesā*). But in the Abhidhamma there is a detailed classification of knowledge after the table of contents has been thus laid down: 'Under the unitary method the basis of knowledge is . . .'[4] and so forth. Likewise the corruptions are classified in many ways

[1] *Vibh.* p. 122 *f.*
[2] *Ib.* p. 135 *f.*
[3] *Ib.* p. 285 *f.*
[4] *Ib.* p. 306 *f.*

beginning with the unitary method.[1] In the Suttantas cosmogony is partially classified, not fully; in the Abhidhamma by the threefold method it is classified fully.[2] Thus is it to be understood that the Abhidhamma exceeds and is distinguished from the Dhamma.

There is a consensus of opinion among teachers that the Abhidhamma is divided into seven books, viz., *Dhammasaṅgaṇī*, *Vibhaṅga*, *Dhātukathā*, *Puggalapaññatti*, *Kathāvatthu*, *Yamaka*, and *Paṭṭhāna*.

But the Vitaṇḍa school[3] say: 'Why bring in *Kathāvatthu*? Was it not settled by Tissa, Moggali's son, two hundred and eighteen years after the Buddha's Parinibbāna? Hence it is [merely] the word of his disciples. Reject it.' [To whom we say:] 'Are there then only six books in the Abhidhamma?' 'I do not say so.' 'What do you say then?' 'Seven books.' 'How do you get the seven?' 'There is a book called *Mahādhammahadaya* (in the Great Commentary); with that I make the seven.' 'In the *Mahādhammahadaya* there is nothing which has not been said already in the *Dhammahadaya Vibhaṅga*.[4] And the remaining catechetical section, which is peculiar to your *Mahādhammahadaya*, is not long enough to make up a treatise by itself. Hence it makes the seven only with the *Kathāvatthu*.' 'Nay, not with the *Kathāvatthu*. [4] There is the *Mahā-Dhātukathā*[5]; with that I make the seven.' 'But there is nothing new in that either.[6] The remaining texts, peculiar to it, are not long enough to make up a treatise. Hence the *Kathāvatthu* makes the seventh.' When the Supreme Buddha, who taught us the seven treatises, came to the *Kathāvatthu*, he began with an eight-faced inquiry

---

[1] *Vibh.* 345 *f.*

[2] *Ib.* 404 *f.*

[3] The Vitaṇḍavādī's are explained by the *Maṇidīpa* to be the sectarians of Abhayagiri and Jetavana of the introductory verses.—*Tr.*

[4] *Vibh.* p. 401 *f.*

[5] Another book compiled in Ceylon. Hence it is uncanonical. The mal-editing in this dialogue in the P.T.S. ed. greatly obscures the meaning.—*Tr.*

[6] Being repeated after such texts as *Dhammahadayavibhaṅga*, *Mahādhammahadaya*, *Dhātukathā*, and *Dhātuvibhaṅga* (*Majjh.* iii. 237).

into the theory of the person (or soul), in four questions each of two fivefold divisions[1] and laid down a table of contents in a text not quite as long as one recital, to be adopted in all the discourses: 'Is the person known in the sense of a real and ultimate fact? Yes. Is the person known in the same way as a real and ultimate fact is known? Nay, that cannot be. Acknowledge your refutation. Is the person not known in the sense of a real and ultimate fact? Nay, it is not known. Is the person unknown in the same way as any real and ultimate fact is known? Nay, it cannot be. Acknowledge your refutation. Is the person known *everywhere* in the sense of a real and ultimate fact? Or is it unknown? Is it known *always* in the sense of a real and ultimate fact? Or is it unknown? Is it known *in everything* in that sense, or is it unknown?'[2] Thus, showing the eight aspects and their respective refutations, the table of contents has been laid down[3] by the Teacher.

Now when he laid down the table of contents he foresaw that, two hundred and eighteen years after his death, Tissa, Moggalī's son, seated in the midst of one thousand bhikkhus, would elaborate the *Kathāvatthu* to the extent of the *Dīgha Nikāya*, bringing together five hundred orthodox and five hundred heterodox Suttas.

So Tissa, Moggalī's son, expounded the book not by his own knowledge but according to the table of contents laid down, as well as by the method given, by the Teacher. Hence[4] the entire book became the word of the Buddha. After which precedent? After the [5] *Madhupiṇḍika-suttanta*[5] and others.[6] In that Suttanta the Blessed one, after laying down heads of a discourse, ended thus: 'Bhikkhu, owing to such causes[7]

---

[1] See *Points of Controversy*, pp. 8–12.

[2] *Ib.* 1 *f.*

[3] Construing *ṭhapitā* with *sa pan'esā* of paragraph 8.

[4] *Iti* = *tasmā*. *Maṇidīpa*.

[5] *Majjhima*, i. 108 *f.*, expounded by Kaccāna.

[6] Such as the *Subhasutta*, *Dīgha*, i. 204 *f.*, expounded by Ānanda, and the *Saṅgītisutta*, *ib.* iii. 207 *f.*, expounded by the Councillors.

[7] *Nidānaṃ*, used in the plural sense of *kāraṇā*.

the factors of prolonged rebirth beset a man.[1] Here if there be nothing to be pleased withal, proud of, or assimilated, then it is the end of the latent bias of lust,' etc.—and then rose from his seat and entered the monastery. The bhikkhus, who received the doctrine, approached Mahākaccāna and questioned him as to the meaning of the heads laid down by the Buddha of the Ten Powers. The Elder, not replying direct to the question, said by way of paying homage to the Buddha: 'Sirs, a person desirous of and seeking pith should bear in mind this simile of pith—the Buddha is like the pith of a tree, his disciples are like the branches and leaves. For, Sirs, the Buddha, who knows all knowable things, discerns all discernible things,[2] is the eye of the world,[3] the wisdom of the world,[4] is like the constituents of wisdom[5] to the world, is like the Ariyan Path[6] to the world, is the speaker and originator of the Four Truths, the expounder of their meaning, the giver of the Deathless, the master of the Law, the Tathāgata.' After thus praising the Teacher he, at the repeated request of the bhikkhus, expounded in great detail the meaning of the heads of discourse laid down by the Buddha and sent them away saying: 'Sirs, if you are willing, approach the Buddha and ask him the meaning. And you should accept what he explains to you, so that if my explanation harmonizes with omniscience you should take it; if not, reject it.' They approached the Buddha and asked him. The Teacher, without referring to any (possibly) ill-spoken words of Kaccāna, raised his neck aloft like a golden drum and filling with breath his noble mouth, graceful as the full-blown lotus, emitted the Brahmā voice,[7] and saying, 'Well done, well done!' to the Elder,

---

[1] Craving, conceit, and wrong view are the three principles which prolong the evolutionary process of a being.—*Tr.*

[2] *Jānaṃ* and *passaṃ* may be taken in two ways; (*a*) as future passive participles—*Jānitabbaṃ passitabbaṃ*, as translated here—and (*b*) as present participles—*jānanto passanto*, in the sense of 'in knowing all things he knows, in seeing all things he sees.'—*Tr.*

[3] Or, 'is the eye of wisdom.' [4] Or, 'is the embodiment of wisdom.'

[5] *Dhamma* = *bodhipakkhiyadhammā*. Cf. *Compendium* 179, *n.* 1.

[6] *Brahma* = *ariya magga*. *Ṭikā*.

[7] See *Dialogues of the Buddha* ii. 263

added: 'Bhikkhus, learned is Mahākaccāna, profoundly wise is Mahākaccāna. If you had asked me the same question, I would have answered exactly as he has done.' Thus since the time when the Teacher gave his approval, the whole Suttanta became the word of the Buddha. And it is the same with the Suttas expounded by Ānanda and others.

Thus in teaching the seven books, when he came to the Kathāvatthu the Buddha laid down the table of contents in the way mentioned above. [6] In doing so he foresaw that two hundred and eighteen years after his death, Tissa, Moggalī's son, seated in the midst of one thousand bhikkhus, would elaborate the *Kathāvatthu* as is stated above. And Tissa, Moggalī's son, expounded the book not by his own knowledge but according to the table of contents laid down, as well as by the method given, by the Teacher. Hence the entire book became the word of the Buddha. Thus the Abhidhamma consists of seven books inclusive of the *Kathāvatthu*.

Now in the first of the seven books, the *Dhammasaṅgaṇī*, there are four divisions, viz., classification of consciousness, of matter, the summary, and the elucidation. In the classification of consciousness, there are eight classes of moral (states) arising in the sensuous universe, twelve classes of immoral (states), sixteen results of good, seven results of evil, eleven inoperatives;[1] five classes of moral states arising in the universe of (attenuated) matter, five results thereof, five corresponding inoperatives; four classes of moral states arising in the immaterial universe, four results thereof, four corresponding inoperatives, four transcendental states,[2] four results thereof: eighty-nine classes in all constituting the divisions of consciousness. It is also called the Chapter on states of consciousness. In extent of utterance, it exceeds six recitals,[3] but is endless and immeasurable when expanded.

Next comes the classification of matter,[4] otherwise known as the Chapter on Matter, in which matter is classified in detail

---

[1] *Kiriyā*. [2] *Lokuttara*. In *B.P.E.* 'higher ideal,' supramundane.

[3] A 'recital' (*bhāṇavāra*) usually consists of 250 stanzas of thirty-two syllables, a stanza consisting of 4 feet of 8 syllables each.—*Tr.*

[4] In *B.P.E.* 'form.'

after the table of contents, laid down under a unitary method, dual method and so on. In extent of utterance it exceeds two recitals, but is endless and immeasurable when expanded.

Next is a summary by way of roots, aggregates, doors, planes of existence, effect or meaning, cause or text, name, sex.

It summarizes roots and aggregates,
And doors, planes of existence, meaning, text,
Name, sex—and therefore is called Summary.

It is also called the Chapter on abstract categories.[1]

In extent of utterance it is exactly three recitals, but is endless and immeasurable when expanded.

Next is a commentarial chapter ending with the couplet of the harmful (and the harmless), and explaining the meaning of the three Piṭakas, which constitute the Buddha's word. [7] Bhikkhus who cannot remember the numerical series in the Great Book have recourse to this section. In extent of utterance it occupies two recitals, but is endless and immeasurable when expanded.

Thus in extent of utterance the entire *Dhammasaṅgaṇī* exceeds thirteen recitals, but is endless and immeasurable when expanded. Such are

The elements of Mind and Matter, and
The sum, the exposition of the whole—
Lore deep and subtle that the Buddha taught.

Immediately following the *Dhammasaṅgaṇī* is the *Vibhaṅga*, consisting of eighteen parts, viz., the classification of (mind and matter into) aggregates, sense-organs, elements, truths, controlling faculties, causal genesis, applications in mindfulness, supreme efforts, steps to supernormal potency, factors of wisdom, paths, jhānas, infinitudes, precepts, analyses, knowledge, the minor subjects and the essence of the Law. Of these, the aggregates are classified by the three methods: Suttanta-classification, Abhidhamma-classification, and catechism. In extent of utterance it occupies five recitals, but is endless and immeasurable when expanded. Next, the sense-

[1] *Nikkhepa.* In *B.P.E.* 'elimination.'

organs and others are classified also by the threefold method. Among them the classification of the sense-organs exceeds one recital in extent of utterance. The classification of the elements occupies two recitals. Likewise that of the Four [Facts or] Truths. There is no Suttanta method in the classification of the controlling faculties. In extent of utterance it exceeds one recital. The classification of the causal genesis occupies six recitals, but there is no catechism. The classification of the applications in mindfulness exceeds one recital. Likewise that of the supreme efforts, steps to supernormal potency, factors of wisdom and paths. The classification of the jhānas occupies two recitals; that of the infinitudes exceeds one. In the classification of the precepts there is no Suttanta method; in extent of utterance it exceeds one recital. [8] Likewise that of the analyses. That of knowledge is subdivided into ten parts. In extent of utterance it occupies three recitals. The classification of the minor subjects is also subdivided into ten parts. In extent of utterance it occupies three recitals. The classification of the 'heart of the Dhamma' is subdivided into three parts and exceeds two recitals in extent of utterance. But all are capable of endless and immeasurable expansion. Thus the *Vibhaṅga* in extent of utterance occupies thirty-five recitals, but when expanded it is endless and immeasurable.

Next comes the book named *Dhātukathā*, which comprises fourteen parts: (1) the grouped and the ungrouped, (2) the ungrouped by the ungrouped, (3) the grouped by the ungrouped, (4) the grouped by the grouped, (5) the ungrouped by the grouped, (6) the associated and the dissociated, (7) the dissociated by the associated, (8) the associated by the dissociated, (9) the associated by the associated, (10) the dissociated by the dissociated, (11) the associated and the dissociated by the grouped, (12) the grouped and the ungrouped by the associated, (13) the associated and the dissociated by the ungrouped, and (14) the grouped and the ungrouped by the dissociated. In extent of utterance it exceeds six recitals, but is endless and immeasurable when expanded.

Next comes the *Puggalapaññatti* under six heads: concepts

of aggregates, of sense-organs, of elements, of realities, of controlling faculties, of the person. In extent of utterance it exceeds five recitals, but is endless and immeasurable when expanded.

Next comes the *Kathāvatthu* bringing together one thousand Suttas: five hundred orthodox and five hundred heterodox. In extent of utterance, as rehearsed at the Councils and not as written now on palm-leaf, it was of the length of the *Dīgha Nikāya*, but it is endless and immeasurable when expanded.

Next comes the *Yamaka*, divided into ten parts: roots, aggregates, sense-organs, elements, truths, coefficients,[1] latent bias, consciousness, doctrine, and controlling faculties. [9] In extent of utterance it occupies one hundred and twenty recitals, but is endless and immeasurable when expanded.

Next comes the Great Book, otherwise called *Paṭṭhāna*, divided into twenty-four parts by way of relations, viz., of root-condition, of object, predominant principles, immediacy, direct immediacy, coexistence, reciprocity, dependence, sufficing condition, pre-existence, post-existence, repetition, kamma, result, nutriment, controlling faculties, jhāna, means, association, dissociation, existence, non-existence, abeyance, absence.

The following points in the *Paṭṭhāna* should be considered: The triplets of 'good,' etc., are twenty-two in number. 'Things (or mental properties) which are root-conditions, or not, down to harmful or harmless'; there are one hundred such couplets in all. 'States either partake of knowledge or not,' to 'are insight into destruction and insight into non-origination': these others are the forty-two Suttanta couplets. Of these the twenty-two triplets and the hundred couplets taught by the omniscient Buddha are the directly spoken words of the Conqueror and form the table of contents for the seven books.

Then whence arose the other forty-two couplets? By whom were they laid down and taught? They originated

---

[1] *I.e.*, of body, speech, and thought. Breath is called *saṅkhāra* because it is accomplished by the body; initial and sustained applications of mind are called *saṅkhārā* because they are accomplished by speech; and the remaining mental coefficients are called *citta-saṅkhārā*.—*Tr.* Cf. *Majjhima*, i. 301 (Vedalla-sutta).—*Ed.*

with Sāriputta, Generalissimo of the Law, having been laid down and taught by him. But he did not lay them down through his own self-evolved knowledge. They have been gathered from the *Eka-Nipāta* and *Duka-Nipāta* of the *Aṅguttara-Nikāya*, the *Saṅgīti* and *Dasuttarasuttantas* of the *Dīgha-Nikāya*, in order to help students of the Abhidhamma in their references to the Suttantas. These triplets and couplets are disposed of in one summarizing chapter. In the remaining chapters the Abhidhamma (proper) is expounded till the couplet of the 'harmful' (and the harmless) is reached.

The supreme Buddha taught in the way of right succession the *Tika-Paṭṭhāna*, based on the twenty-two triplets, and the *Duka-Paṭṭhāna*, based on the hundred couplets. He then taught the *Duka-tika-Paṭṭhāna*, taking the twenty-two triplets and inserting them among the hundred couplets.[1] Then again taking the hundred couplets and inserting them among the twenty-two triplets he taught the *Tika-duka-Paṭṭhāna*. [10] And inserting the triplets among the triplets he taught the *Tika-tika-Paṭṭhāna*. And inserting the couplets among the couplets he taught the *Duka-duka-Paṭṭhāna*. The text says: 'Celebrated and desirable are the Tika, Duka, Dukatika, Tikaduka, Tikatika, and Dukaduka. Profound are these six methods in the way of right succession.' In the converse Paṭṭhāna also the *Tika-Paṭṭhāna* is based on the twenty-two triplets.

The *Duka-Paṭṭhāna* is based on the hundred couplets. The *Dukatika-Paṭṭhāna* has been taught by inserting the twenty-two triplets among the hundred couplets; the *Tikaduka-Paṭṭhāna* by inserting the hundred couplets among the twenty-two triplets; the *Tikatika-Paṭṭhāna* by inserting the triplets among the triplets; the *Dukaduka-Paṭṭhāna* by inserting the couplets among the couplets. Thus in the converse order also the *Paṭṭhāna* is expounded in six ways. And so the text says: 'Celebrated and desirable are the Tika, Duka, Dukatika, Tikaduka, Tikatika, and Dukaduka. Profound are these six methods (of permutation to be understood)

---

1 Combining the twenty-two triplets severally with each couplet.—*Tr.*

in the converse order.' Then again the same six ways have been shown in the combined method of right succession and converse order. Hence the text says: 'Celebrated and desirable are the Tika, Duka, Dukatika, Tikaduka, Tikatika, and Dukaduka. Profound are these six methods in the combined method of right succession and converse order.' Immediately after this the Buddha taught the same six ways in the combined method of the converse order and right succession. Hence the text says: 'Celebrated and desirable are the Tika, Duka, Dukatika, Tikaduka, Tikatika, and Dukatika. Profound are these six methods (of permutation to be understood) in the combined method of the converse order and right succession.' Thus six in the way of right succession, six in reverse order, six in the combined method of right succession and converse order, six in the combined method of the converse order and right succession—the twenty-four universal methods of *Paṭṭhāna* constitute the Great Book.

Now to understand the depth of the Abhidhamma, it must be understood that there are four oceans: the ocean of repeated births, the ocean of waters, the ocean of method, and the ocean of knowledge. Of these,

> '*The unbroken line of organs, elements,*
> *And aggregates—"saṃsāra" is its name.*'

This is the ocean of repeated births. Inasmuch as the ultimate start in birth of these beings is not apparent—whether it was a hundred [11] or a thousand, or a hundred thousand years, or a hundred or a thousand or a hundred thousand cosmic periods ago prior to which they were not, or whether they were born in the time of a certain king or a certain Buddha—prior to which they were not, no limit can be set. 'The ultimate starting-point, bhikkhus, of ignorance before which it did not exist, but after which it came into being is not revealed.'[1] In this way this ocean of repeated births is of an unknown beginning.

And there is the great ocean known as the ocean of waters. It is eighty-four yojanas in depth. There is no measurement

---

[1] *Aṅguttara*, v. 113. Cf. *Saṃyutta Nikāya*, ii 178; iii 149.

of the waters as hundred, thousand, ten thousand, or hundred thousand tins. It is incalculable and immeasurable. Verily it is only reckoned as a mass of water. This is the ocean of waters.

Which is the ocean of method? The three Piṭakas, the word of the Buddha. For in reflecting upon the two Piṭakas, infinite rapturous joy arises in the sons of clansmen who are faithful, abundantly believing and endowed with superior knowledge. Which are the two? The Vinaya and the Abhidhamma. Infinite rapturous joy arises in those bhikkhus who learn the Vinaya text and reflect that it is the province of the Buddhas, and not of others, to lay down the rule for each fault or transgression according to its gravity.

Infinite rapturous joy also arises in the brethren when reflecting on implications of things supernormal, of colours and of good conduct.[1]

Again the bhikkhus, who study the Abhidhamma, experience infinite rapturous joy in reflecting. As though grouping the multitude of stars in the sky (into constellations), the Teacher taught things mental and material, dividing them into various parts and portions—things subtle and abstruse such as the unique[2] content of aggregates, sense-organs, elements, controlling faculties, powers, factors of wisdom, kamma and its result; and the distinction between mind and matter. Consider this story of such an experience. The Elder Mahāgatigamiyatissa [12] crossed over to the opposite shore of India with the intention of paying homage to the Wisdom Tree. Seated on the upper deck of the boat he looked at the great ocean; but neither the thither nor the hither shore appeared to his vision. There appeared only the great ocean, strewn with foam thrown off by the breaking of the billows, and looking like a sheet of silver spread out on a bed of jasmine flowers. He thought to himself: which is more extraordinary

---

[1] See *Uttarimanussadhammasikkhāpadaṃ. Sukkavisaṭṭhi sikkhāpadaṃ*, and *Sañcaritasikkhāpadaṃ*. *Vin.* iii. 92, 113, 139.—*Tr.*

[2] 'Antaraṃ' here can only mean 'unique.' *Ṭīkā*. Cf. Childers's *Dict. s.v.* 'peculiarity,' etc.—*Tr.*

—the heaving of the ocean waves, or the basis of the method of the twenty-four divisions in the Great Book? Then the limits of the great ocean became apparent to him. Indeed, he thought to himself, this ocean is limited, below by the earth, above by the sky, on one side by the mountain encircling the world-system, and on the other by the seashore. But the limits of the universal *Paṭṭhāna* are not apparent. And abundant rapture arose in him, as he reflected on the subtle and abstruse Law. Arresting his rapture and increasing his insight even while he was seated, he threw off all the corruptions, and being established in the topmost Fruition which is Arahantship, he exulted in this song of esctasy:

He is[1] *the true disciple of the Sage*
Who sees, like a bright jewel in his hand,
Root-causes, from which all becoming is—
Lore deep and hard to know, which the Great Sage
Intuited, and all[2] *in order taught.*[3]

This is the ocean of method.

Which is the ocean of knowledge? Omniscience. It is not possible to distinguish the (different) oceans of repeated births, of waters, and of method except by omniscience.

---

[1] Read *attheva* = *atthi eva*.

[2] Nikhilena. If taken as an adjective qualifying the Sage, this word would mean 'free from the five *khilas.*'—*Tr.*

[3] This translation follows the *Ṭīkā*. Other ways of translation are:

'There is the profound and abstruse Paṭṭhāna taught in due order by the Great Sage free from the five "thorns," after intuiting the causal relations of things. And a disciple penetrates it even as one sees a material thing in the palm of one's hand'—*Pyī Sadaw.* 'The Great Sage by his intuition has completely taught in due order things of the present in relation to causes such as condition, and there is the universal Paṭṭhāna, profound and very difficult to understand. The disciple penetrates it as easily as one sees a material thing in the palm of one's hand'—*Maṇidīpa.*

'There are the causal relations completely taught by the Great Sage in due order by his intuition. These causal relations of conditioned things of the present, profound and very difficult to understand, the Buddha's disciple sees as easily as a material thing in the palm of his hand'—*Gaṇṭhipada.*

Hence omniscience is called the ocean of knowledge. Of these four oceans that of method is here intended; for omniscient Buddhas penetrate it.[1] And our Blessed One, seated at the foot of the Wisdom Tree, penetrated it and thought: 'To this has my vision pierced! lo, even to this Law have I reached, who seeking and inquiring for more than a hundred thousand ages, for over four incalculable periods, here seated in this cross-legged posture (as on a throne) have expelled every conceivable corruption.' And he sat on the 'throne' for yet seven days, reflecting on the Law he had penetrated. Then after those seven days, he rose from the throne and stood gazing at it for seven days without blinking his eyes, thinking, 'On this throne I have indeed attained omniscience.' Hence this doubt occurred to the gods: 'Surely to-day Siddhattha [13] must still have something to accomplish, for he has not abandoned attachment to the throne.' The Teacher, knowing their doubt, in order to quiet it, rose immediately into the sky and displayed the Twin Miracle. The miracle performed at the throne under the Wisdom Tree and that performed at the assembly of his relatives and that performed at the assembly of the citizens of Pāṭaliputta[2] were all the same as the Twin Miracle performed at the foot of the white mango-tree in the garden of Kaṇḍa. Thus having displayed the Twin Miracle he descended from the sky and for seven days walked to and fro between the throne and the place where he had stood.

Now not even on a single day during the interval of twenty-one days were rays emitted from the Teacher's body. During the fourth week he sat in a jewel house in the north-west direction. The jewel house here does not mean a house made of the seven jewels but the place where he contemplated the seven books. And while he contemplated the contents of the *Dhammasaṅganī*, his body did not emit rays; and similarly

[1] *Sāvaka's* (disciples or 'hearers') knew it only through the Buddha's preaching.—*Tr.*

[2] The *Ganṭhipada* reads Pādhiyaputta. Since the miracle was performed for the subjugation of this ascetic at an assembly composed of the citizens of Pāṭaliputta, either reading is right.—*Tr.*

with the contemplation of the next five books. But when, coming to the Great Book, he began to contemplate the twenty-four universal causal relations of condition, of presentation, and so on, his omniscience certainly found its opportunity therein. For as the great fish Timiratipiṅgala finds room only in the great ocean eighty-four thousand yojanas in depth, so his omniscience truly finds room only in the Great Book. Rays of six colours—indigo, golden, red, white, tawny, and dazzling—issued from the Teacher's body, as he was contemplating the subtle and abstruse Law by his omniscience which had found such opportunity. The indigo rays issued from his hair and the blue portions of his eyes. Owing to them the surface of the sky appeared as though besprinkled with collyrium powder, or covered with flax and blue lotus-flowers, or like a jewelled fan swaying to and fro, or a piece of dark cloth fully spread out. The golden rays issued from his skin and the golden portions of his eyes. [14] Owing to them the different quarters of the globe shone as though besprinkled with some golden liquid, or overlaid with sheets of gold, or bestrewn with saffron powder and bauhinia-flowers. The red rays issued from his flesh and blood and the red portions of his eyes. Owing to them the quarters of the globe were coloured as though painted with red-lead powder, or besprinkled with the liquid of molten lac, or wrapped round with red blankets, or bestrewn with the shoe-flower, the sea-coral, and *bandhujīvaka* flowers. The white rays issued from his bones, teeth, and the white portions of his eyes. Owing to them the quarters of the globe were bright as though overflowing with streams of milk poured out of silver pots, or overspread with a canopy of silver plates, or like a silver fan swaying to and fro, or as though well covered with such flowers as the wild jasmine, water-lily, chaste flower, jasmine, and coffee-wort. The tawny and dazzling rays issued from the different parts of his body. Thus the six-coloured rays came forth and caught the great mass of earth. The great earth, having a thickness of two hundred and forty thousand yojanas, appeared like a burnished lump of gold. The rays penetrated the earth and caught the water below. The water which supports the earth and has a depth of four hundred and eighty thousand yojanas appeared like gold dust poured out of golden jars. They penetrated the water and caught the atmosphere which, nine hundred and sixty thousand yojanas in thickness, appeared like well-erected columns of gold. Penetrating the atmosphere, they sprang forth into the open space beyond. Going upwards they caught the abodes of the four Regents of the world. Penetrating these, they caught the Tāvatiṃsa, and thence the Yāma, thence the Tusita, thence the Nimmānarati, thence the Paranimmita-vasavattī spheres, and thence the nine Brahmā worlds, thence the Vehapphala, thence the five Pure Abodes, and thence the four Āruppa heavens. Having penetrated the last of these, they sprang into the open space across to the infinite world-systems. In so many of these places, there was no light in the moon, nor in the sun, nor in the host of stars; nowhere was there lustre, neither in the parks, nor in the mansions, nor in the wish-yielding tree, nor in the bodies and ornaments of the gods. Even Great Brahmā, able to diffuse light throughout a billion world-systems, [15] became like a glow-worm at sunrise. There appeared only the mere outline of the moon, the sun, the host of stars, and the parks, mansions, and the wish-yielding tree of the gods. So much space was flooded by the Buddha's rays. Such power is not the potency of resolve nor of culture. But the blood of the Lord of the world became clear as he contemplated such a subtle and abstruse Law. Likewise the physical basis of his thought, and his complexion. The element of colour, produced by the caloric order, born of the mind, steadily established itself with a radius of eighty cubits. In this way, he contemplated for a whole week.

How wide is the Law, contemplated for seven nights and seven days? It is infinite and immeasurable. This, of course, refers to the discourse as thought out in the mind. And it should not be said that the Teacher was unable to finish preaching in a hundred or a thousand or ten thousand years the Law mentally worked out in a week. For subsequently the Tathāgata, seated in the midst of the gods from the ten thousand world-systems, at the Paṇḍukambala stone at the foot of the Pāricchattaka tree in Tāvatiṃsa, making his mother his chief witness, taught the Law, passing from one theme to another[1] in a hundred, a thousand, and a hundred thousand divisions. And infinite and immeasurable was the discourse, which went on ceaselessly for three months with the velocity of a waterfall, or streams of water issuing from water-pots turned mouth downwards. For a speech of the Buddha when thanking his host for entertainment, if elaborated a little, may reach the length of a Dīgha or Majjhima discourse. And a discourse given after a meal to the host of assembled people reaches the length of a discourse in the two great Nikāyas, *Saṃyutta* and *Aṅguttara*. Why should it be so? Because the Buddhas are but slightly occupied with the business of maintaining life, the lips close well, the mouth opens lightly,[2] the tongue is soft, the voice is sweet, the delivery of words is quick.[3] Hence the Law, preached in such a short time, is of the length stated;[4] when it was preached for three months it must have been infinite and immeasurable.

The Elder Ānanda was indeed of wide experience, a student of the Three Piṭakas, and could learn, recite and preach, as he stood, one thousand five hundred stanzas or sixty thousand feet, as easily as though he were gathering creepers and flowers. That was the Elder's single course of exposition. None but the Buddha was able to teach, or attain the distinction of teaching this Elder the actual text, word by word. Even a disciple of such surpassing mindfulness, intelligence [16] and fortitude would not be able to finish learning in a thousand years the sermons preached by the Teacher in three months in the way mentioned above.[5]

But how did the Tathāgata, preaching continuously for three months, sustain the body, which is the issue of grasping

---

[1] Or, 'special or unique themes.' Cf. p. 14, *n*. 2.

[2] Or, 'is well adjusted.' *Mukhādānam* = *mukhavivaraṇaṃ*. *Ṭīkā*.

[3] Uttering 128 words to one of a worldling.

[4] *I.e.*, equal to the Dīgha and Majjhima Nikāyas.

[5] Cf. *Pss. of the Brethren*, p. 354.

and depends on material food? By nourishing it with food.[1] Now each particular interval of time is well marked, well divided and well observed by the Buddhas. Accordingly the Blessed One, in preaching the doctrine in the world of men, looked at the time. He noted that it was the time for going his begging rounds. So he created a Buddha after his own image and thus determined: 'Let this created Buddha hold the robe, the bowl, speak and assume his appearance in such and such a way; let him preach so much of the doctrine.' Then the (true) Buddha took his own bowl and robe and went to Anotatta Lake. The gods offered him a tooth-stick made of Nāga creepers. He used it, bathed in the lake, and stood on the top of the Maṇosilā rock. He put on the well-dyed undergarment and the robe, took the bowl made of blue stone and presented by the four Regents of the world, and went to Uttarakuru. Gathering alms thence he sat on the shore of Anotatta Lake, partook of his meal, and went to a sandalwood forest for the midday rest. Sāriputta, generalissimo of the Law, went there, served the Supreme Buddha, and sat aside. Then to him the Teacher gave the method saying, 'Sāriputta, so much doctrine has been shown.' Thus the giving of the method was to the chief disciple, who was endowed with analytical knowledge, as though the Buddha stood on the edge of the shore and pointed out the ocean with his open hand. To the Elder also the doctrine taught by the Blessed One in hundreds and thousands of methods became very clear. At what time did he, after his midday rest, take up (his bowl and robe) and go to Tāvatiṃsa to preach the Law? He went about the time of showing the Law to the clansmen residents of Sāvatthī who had arrived. Which (spirits) knew of his going (to the world of men) or arrival at Tāvatiṃsa, after showing the Law, and which knew it not? Spirits of greater power knew it; spirits of lesser power knew it not. Why did not these know it? Because there was no difference between the Supreme Buddha and the created Buddha as regards their rays, voices, or words.

[1] Or, 'by relaxing the stiffened muscles and thus equalizing the four postures, walking, sitting, standing, and lying down.' *Ariyālaṅkāra's Nissaya.*

Now Sāriputta, having learnt the Law taught (by the Teacher) preached it to five hundred bhikkhus, his own pupils. The following is their connection with the past. [17] They, so it is said, were born as bats in the time of the Buddha Kassapa. Hanging from (the roof of) a cave, they heard the voice of two bhikkhus reciting the Abhidhamma and grasped a general idea that it was the Law, being unable to distinguish the good from the bad. They passed away with only the general idea suggested by the voice and were reborn in the world of gods. They dwelt there during a whole interval between the death of one Buddha and the appearance of the next, and in the time of this Buddha were reborn as men. Being convinced by the Twin Miracle, they renounced the world in the presence of the Elder who, having learnt the Law taught by the Teacher, preached it to them. Their acquirement of the seven books was simultaneous with the conclusion of the Abhidhamma teaching of the Buddha.

The textual order of the Abhidhamma originated with Sāriputta; the numerical series in the Great Book was also determined by him. In this way the Elder, without spoiling the unique doctrine, laid down the numerical series in order to make it easy to learn, remember, study and teach the Law. Such being the case, was the Elder the very first to understand the Abhidhamma ? Nay, it was the Supreme Buddha who first understood the Abhidhamma. For he, seated on the throne under the Wisdom Tree, penetrated it and became the Buddha and, while seated for seven days in one position on the throne, uttered this song of ecstasy:

Lo ! when appear true doctrines[1] *to the saint*
Zealous and thoughtful, all his doubts dissolve ;
He knows that all Becoming is through Cause.

Lo ! when appear true doctrines to the saint
Zealous and thoughtful, all his doubts dissolve ;
He knows the demolition of all Cause.

---

[1] *Dhammā.* These may mean the four truths, facts, or the 37 factors of enlightenment. *Dhammapāla, Comy. on Udāna.*

Lo! when appear true doctrines to the saint
Zealous and thoughtful, all his doubts dissolve;
And he is as a light unto the world,
Having annihilated Māra's hosts,
Even as the sun illuminates the sky,
Having dispelled the darkness of the night.[1]

These were the first words of the Buddha.

[18] But the students of the Dhammapada say that the following were the first words spoken by the Buddha:

Long I endured the circles of rebirth,
Seeking but finding not the architect.
Rebirth continual is continual pain.
But now have I espied thee, architect!
Behold, thou shalt not build the house again.
Broke are thy beams, thy pinnacle destroyed.
Now to Nibbāna[2] *has my mind attained*
And now in me all craving is destroyed.[3]

The words spoken at the time of the Parinibbāna by the Buddha while lying down between the two *Sāl*-trees were his last:

'Hearken now, bhikkhus, I tell you: Conditioned things are subject to decay; work out your salvation with diligence.'[4]

The good Law pointing to the Deathless and taught (by the Buddha) for forty-five years between these two events, as though he was wreathing a garland of flowers or composing a string of jewel beads, forms his middle sayings. Altogether they form three Piṭakas, five Nikāyas, nine Aṅgas, and eighty-four thousand Khandhas. How so? The entire words of the

---

[1] *Vinaya Texts* i. 18; also translated in *Points of Controversy* 118. Cf. *Comp.*, p. 179.

[2] *Visaṅkhāra.*

[3] *Dhp.* ver. 154; *Pss. of the Brethren* ver. 184, *which ends differently.* In the Introduction to the Jātaka stories, the verses are said to have been uttered by all the Buddhas when they attained omniscience under their Bodhi-tree. Cf. Rhys Davids, *Buddhist Birthstories*, 103 f.—*Ed.*

[4] *Dialogues* ii. 173.

Buddha are divided by way of Piṭaka into three parts: the Vinaya, Sutta and Abhidhamma. Herein both the Pātimokkhas (Bhikkhu and Bhikkhunī) and the two Vibhaṅgas (Bhikkhu and Bhikkhunī), the twenty-two Khandhakas, the sixteen Parivāras, constitute the Vinaya Piṭaka.

The collection of thirty-four suttas beginning with the *Brahmajāla sutta* forms the *Dīgha Nikāya;* the collection of one hundred and fifty-two suttas beginning with the *Mūlapariyāya sutta* forms the *Majjhima Nikāya;* the collection of seven thousand seven hundred and sixty-two suttas beginning with the *Oghataraṇa sutta* forms the *Saṃyutta Nikāya;* the collection of nine thousand five hundred and fifty-seven suttas beginning with the *Cittapariyādāna sutta* forms the *Aṅguttara Nikāya.* Fifteen different treatises[1] to wit, *Khuddakapāṭha, Dhammapada, Udāna, Itivuttaka, Suttanipāta, Vimānavatthu, Petavatthu, Theragāthā-Therīgāthā, Jātaka, Niddesa, Paṭisambhidā, Apadāna, Buddhavaṃsa,* and *Cariyāpiṭaka* form the *Khuddaka Nikāya.* All these constitute the Sutta Piṭaka.

The seven books beginning with *Dhammasaṅgaṇī* form the Abhidhamma Piṭaka.

[19] Herein—

Because it shows precepts and principles,
And governs both the body and the tongue,
Therefore men call this Scripture Vinaya,
For so is Vinaya interpreted.

By 'principles' in this verse are meant the methods of the fivefold Pātimokkha ordinance, of the seven classes of offence beginning with the Pārājika of the Mātikā and of the Vibhaṅga. By 'precepts' are meant the methods of the additional enactments, resulting in the strengthening or the relaxing of the observance of original ordinances. It also regulates the body and the tongue by restraining them from transgression. Therefore on account of its principles and precepts and its regulation of the body and the tongue, it is called Vinaya.

---

[1] Cf. p. 32.

Hence it has been said to facilitate the study of the word-definition:

Because it shows precepts and principles,
And governs both the body and the tongue,
Therefore men call this Scripture Vinaya,
For so is Vinaya interpreted.

Further:

This Scripture shows, expresses, fructifies,
Yields, guards the Good, and is unto the wise
A plumb-line; therefore Sutta[1] *is its name.*

For it shows what is good for the good of self and others. It is well expressed to suit the wishes of the audience. It has been said that it fructifies the Good, as crops fructify their fruit; that it yields the Good as a cow yields milk; and that it well protects and guards the Good. It is a measure to the wise as the plumb-line is to carpenters. And just as flowers strung together are not scattered nor destroyed, so the Good strung together by it does not perish. Hence it has been said, to facilitate the study of the word-definition:

This Scripture shows, expresses, fructifies,
Yields, guards the Good, and is unto the wise
A plumb-line; therefore Sutta is its name.

The word-definition of Abhidhamma has been explained. But here is another:

Because this book shows things that suffer growth,
Of proper attributes, to be revered,
Well-differentiated, and of worth
Surpassing, Abhidhamma is its name.

[20] For the prefix '*abhi*' implies growth, proper attributes, reverence, clear differentiation, and surpassing worth. Thus in such sentences as, 'Sir, severe pains *grow* in me;'[2] it expresses growth. In such sentences as, 'Those are *remarkable*[3] and

[1] Suṭṭa, a string or thread. [2] Cf. p. 3. [3] Abhiññātā.

characterized[1] nights,' it expresses proper attributes. In such sentences as, 'king of kings[2] and conqueror of men,' it expresses reverence. In such sentences as, 'He is able to master the *Abhidhamma* and *Abhivinaya*,'[3] it expresses differentiation; the sentence, that is to say, means, 'He is able to master the Dhamma and the Vinaya without confusing either with the other.' In such phrases as, 'with *surpassing*[4] beauty,' it expresses worth. In the sentence, 'He develops the means for rebirth in the Rūpa-world;[5] he lives diffusing one quarter of the globe with thoughts of love,'[6] things capable of growth are referred to. In such phrases as, 'visible object, audible object,' things of proper attributes are referred to, because they are characterized as objects, etc. And things to be revered are referred to in such phrases as, 'things pertaining to students, things pertaining to adepts, and things transcendental.' In such phrases as, 'this is touch, that is feeling, etc.,' things distinguishable as to their nature are referred to. And things of surpassing worth are referred to in such phrases as, 'states sublime, states immeasurable, states incomparable.' Hence it has been said to facilitate the study of the word-definition :

Because this book shows things that suffer growth, . . . etc.

The term 'Piṭaka' has a common meaning:

By 'Piṭaka' the learned signify
'Study' and 'basket'—with which word compound
These—Sutta, Abhidhamma, Vinaya.

'Piṭaka' is used in the sense of 'study' in such sentences as, 'Let us not [value doctrines] by proficiency[7] in the Piṭaka.'

And it is used in the sense of a 'basket' in such sentences as, 'as if a man were to take a spade and basket and go. . . .'[8]

---

[1] Abhilakkhitā.

[2] Rājābhirājā. *Sutta-Nipāta*, ver. 553.

[3] *Vin.* i. 64.

[4] Abhikkantena. Cf. *Saṃyutta* i. 1, etc.

[5] *Dhs.* § 160.

[6] *Dīgha* i. 250, etc.

[7] *A.* i. 189.

[8] *Majjhima* i. 127.

Wherefore,

By ' Piṭaka ' the learned signify
' Study ' and ' basket '—with which word compound
These—Sutta, Abhidhamma, Vinaya.'

Thus ' Vinaya ' forms a compound with ' Piṭaka ' in its two senses and is called Vinaya-Piṭaka, because of its being at once a study and a basket of meaning. So also do ' Sutta-Piṭaka,' [21] and ' Abhidhamma-Piṭaka.' And having thus understood them, in order again to understand the various aspects of the three Piṭakas,

In them, when need is, let the several kinds
Of sermon, teaching, discourse be explained:
And the profundity of precept-lore
And passion-purging laws. What each attains
In these three studies, how he may succeed,
Wherein he fails, let this too be explained.

To explain and elucidate we add: The three Piṭakas are respectively spoken of as teachings of authority, of popular philosophy, and of metaphysical truths; or as instruction according to misconduct, according to circumstance, and according to states; or again, as discourses of trivial or serious restraint, of the refutation of heretical views, and of the distinction between mind and matter. And herein the Vinaya-Piṭaka, taught generally with authority by the Blessed One who was fit to give authority, is said to be a teaching of authority; the Sutta-Piṭaka, taught generally concerning popular ethics by the Blessed One, who was skilled in popular ethics, is called teachings of popular philosophy; and the Abhidhamma-Piṭaka, taught generally concerning things in their ultimate sense by the Blessed One, who was skilled in ultimate truths, is called teaching in ultimate truths.

Likewise, the first, *i.e.*, Vinaya, instructs grave offenders according to their respective misdeeds, and is called instruction given concerning such: the second, *i.e.*, Sutta-Piṭaka, is adapted to various wishes, latent tendencies, traits of character, resolutions, and is called instruction adapted to circumstance; and the third, *i.e.*, Abhidhamma-Piṭaka, instructs, according to states, those persons who imagine a self in the ultimate sense in mere collocations of things, saying, 'This is I; that is mine,' and is called instruction given in accordance with states.

Similarly, the first is called a discourse of restraint and control, because therein are given discourses on grave or trivial restraint as opposed to transgression. 'Restraint and control' mean restraint big and small, like acts big and small; fruits big and small.[1] The second is called a discourse on the refutation of heretical views, because therein is unrolled the coil of the sixty-two heresies.[2] The third is called a discourse on the distinction between mind and matter, because therein is discourse of that distinction in its ethical connection, etc.

And in the three Piṭakas, the threefold training, the threefold riddance and the fourfold profundity are to be understood: morality treated specially in the Vinaya-Piṭaka is the unique training in virtue; consciousness treated specially in the Suttanta-Piṭaka is the unique training in higher mental training; philosophy treated specially in the Abhidhamma-Piṭaka is the unique training in higher or metaphysical understanding. In the Vinaya-Piṭaka [22] the riddance of transgression due to the corruptions is meant, because morality is opposed to transgressions; in the Suttanta-Piṭaka the riddance of the tyranny of the corruptions is meant, because concentration of thought is inimical to such tyranny; in the Abhidhamma-Piṭaka the riddance of latent bias is meant because understanding is opposed to it. In the first Piṭaka there is a temporary riddance of the corruptions (by means of various factors of morality); in the others their riddance is of the nature of discarding and extirpating by the Path. In the first Piṭaka the riddance is of the corruption of misconduct; in the others it is of the corruption of craving and wrong views. And in each of them, the fourfold profundity,

---

[1] 'Big' restraint includes the Pārājika's and Saṅghādisesa's of the Vinaya (vol. iii.); the rest are 'small.'—*Tr.*

[2] See *Dialogues* i., first Suttanta.

viz., of the doctrine, of the meaning, of the exposition, and of intuition, should be understood.

Herein 'doctrine' (*dhamma*) means the text; 'meaning' (*attha*) the sense of the text; 'exposition' (*desanā*) the verbal preaching of the text which has been borne in mind; and 'penetration' (*paṭivedha*) is the understanding of the text and its meaning as they really are. And in these three Piṭakas, inasmuch as it is difficult for the poor in understanding to comprehend or obtain a firm footing in these four things—just as it is difficult for hares and other small creatures to enter or obtain a firm footing in the great ocean—they are said to be profound. Thus in each Piṭaka the fourfold profundity should be understood.[1] Or again: 'Doctrine' means root-condition; for it has been said[2] that 'knowledge of a cause or condition is the analysis of doctrine.'[3] 'Meaning' is the result of a condition; for it has been said that knowledge of the result of a condition is the analysis of meaning. 'Exposition' means statement* in the sense of verbal expression of the doctrine as it is, or it means a discourse given in the way of right succession or reverse order, in abstract or in detail, etc.

Penetration[4] means comprehending.[5] It is either worldly or transcendental. It penetrates, by way of object and without confusion, into causes according to their effects, into effects according to their causes, into concepts according to circumstances giving rise to such notions. It also implies the irreversibility of the respective characteristics of such and such things (as the five aggregates and Nibbāna), taught in this or that Piṭaka.[6] Now the meaning of such causes and effects

---

[1] The *Anuṭīkā* adds, that 'dhamma' is the original arrangement of words (*saddappabandho*) to be studied and understood with the help of various meanings given to them; that 'desanā' is the subsequent preaching of those words for the understanding of others.

[2] *Vibhaṅga* 293.

[3] Cf. Ledi, as quoted in *Points of Controversy* 380.

* *Abhilāpo.*

[4] The literal meaning of *paṭivedha.—Ed.*

[5] *Abhisamayo.* Cf. *Sum. Vil.* i. 32.

[6] In the first sense, *paṭivedha* has been taken in the active sense. Here it is in the passive.

as things taught under various aspects in the Piṭakas is presented to the intellect of the hearers. Next there is the exposition which elucidates that meaning of things taught under those aspects; then there is intuition, called irreversible penetration of things taught therein, or the irreversible nature of the respective characteristics of things. All this is difficult for the uncultured, who are not well supported by accumulated merit, to grasp or obtain a firm footing, as has been stated above. Thus far [23] this verse:—

In them, when need is, let the several kinds
Of sermon, teaching, discourse be explained,
And the profundity of precept-lore
And passion-purging laws—

has now been explained.

Herein three kinds of study of the three Piṭakas should be considered: study after the manner of one catching a snake, study for the purpose of salvation, and study as of a treasurer. Of these, that study which is badly acquired out of a desire to be vexatious to others, etc.,[1] is like catching a snake. Concerning which it is said: 'Just as, bhikkhus, a person desirous of catching a snake goes out in search of one. He sees a big snake and catches it either by the body or the tail. And the snake turning back bites him on the hand, the arm, or any other part of the body big or small. On that account he dies or suffers pain approaching death. And why? Because, bhikkhus, of his bad catching of the snake. In the same way, bhikkhus, in the religion some good-for-nothing persons improperly study the doctrine in its various branches. Having studied the doctrine they do not intelligently consider the meaning of the text. And the meaning not being considered with understanding, those acquired doctrines do not lend themselves to close insight. These people study the doctrine for the purpose of annoying others or of freeing themselves from the criticism or scoffing of others.* For whatever Good right-

[1] Or, 'to free oneself from the oppression of others.'

* *Itivādappamokkha.*

minded people study the doctrine, that Good these good-for-nothing people do not experience; and the doctrines being badly acquired are conducive to their disadvantage and misery for a long time. Wherefore? Because, bhikkhus, of their being badly acquired.'[1] But that study, which is well acquired by one desirous of fulfilling a body of precepts, etc., and not for the sake of annoying others, is for the sake of salvation, concerning which it is said: 'The doctrines being well acquired conduce to advantage and happiness for a long time. Wherefore? Because, bhikkhus, of their being well acquired.[2] Finally, the saint, who has acquired a complete knowledge of the aggregates, got rid of the corruptions, developed the Path, [24] penetrated the Fruition of Arahantship, realized the Truth of Cessation, and extinguished the intoxicants, studies merely for the purpose of preserving the tradition, and of guarding the lineage of the doctrine. This is the study of the treasurer.

The bhikkhu, who is well practised in the Vinaya, arrives, by fulfilling the precepts, at the three kinds of knowledge, which are fully treated of therein. The bhikkhu, who is well versed in the Suttas, arrives, by his attainment of concentration, at the six branches of super-knowledge, which are fully treated of therein. The bhikkhu, who is well cultivated in the Abhidhamma, arrives, by his attainment of understanding, at the four analyses, which are fully treated of therein. Thus the bhikkhu, who is well trained in the three Piṭakas, in due course arrives at the attainment of the three kinds of knowledge, the six branches of super-knowledge, and the four analyses. But the bhikkhu, who is ill trained in the Vinaya, imagines that there is no fault in the forbidden sensations of touch, because the touch of these is similar to that of blankets and cloaks, etc., which are pleasurable and are permitted by the Buddha. And it has been said:[3] 'I know the doctrine taught

---

[1] Alagaddūpamā-sutta. *Majjhima*, i. 133 f. [2] *Ib.*, 134.

[3] *Majjhima*, i. 130. Ariyālaṅkāra says that Ariṭṭha, a heretic, in some lonely spot gave way to sense-indulgence and, not knowing the Vinaya, said that average men might also be Sotāpanna's, Sakadāgāmī's, or Anāgāmī's, and that Arahants might indulge in the pleasures of the senses.

by the Blessed One, namely, that certain things are inimical (to progress), but that they are incapable of doing any harm to one who uses them in certain ways.' Consequently the bhikkhu arrives at evil practices. The bhikkhu, who is ill trained in the Sutta, gets a wrong idea, not knowing the meaning of such passages as, 'There are, bhikkhus, four persons[1] in the world,' concerning which it has been said, 'Owing to his wrong ideas,[2] he accuses us, harms himself and produces much demerit.' Consequently he arrives at wrong views. The bhikkhu, who is ill trained in the Abhidhamma, makes his mind run to excess in metaphysical abstractions and thinks of the unthinkable. Consequently he gets mental distraction. For it has been said, 'Bhikkhus, there are four unthinkables, things that should not be thought of. Madness or vexation will be the portion of him who does so.'[3] Thus the bhikkhu, who is ill trained in the three Piṭakas, in due course arrives at failure of different sorts, such as evil principles, wrong views, mental derangement.

So far the import of the verse

—— '*what each attains*
In these three studies, how he may succeed,
Wherein he fails, let this too be explained'

has been explained.

Thus the three Piṭakas by the knowledge of the scriptures in various ways are to be known as the Buddha's word.

[25] How are the five Nikāyas grouped? The entire words of the Buddha are divided into *Dīgha Nikāya, Majjhima Nikāya, Saṃyutta, Aṅguttara,* and *Khuddaka Nikāyas.*

---

[1] One who lives for his own good, one who lives for the good of others, one who lives neither for his own nor others' good, one who lives both for his own and others' good. *D.* iii. 232; *M.* i. 341; *A.* ii. 205. This is said by the Buddha as a conventional truth. Not knowing it in the ultimate sense he gets the wrong idea. Discussed in *Points of Controversy*, p. 16.—*Ed.*

[2] Or, 'owing to his wrong nature or conduct,' says the *Sāratthadīpanī*, which also reads *duggahitena dhammena.*

[3] *A.* ii. 80.

Which of these is the *Dīgha Nikāya?* The collection of thirty-four suttas beginning with *Brahmajāla*, forming three divisions.

Suttantas thirty and four in chapters three—
Dīgha Nikāya, first and longest book.

But why is it called *Dīgha Nikāya?* Because it is a group and a location of long suttas, and a group or a location is called Nikāya. 'I do not see, bhikkhus, any other single *group* so varied as the animal group';[1] 'the *abode* of Poṇika princes, of Cikkhalika princes'[2]—these are examples showing the meaning of the term both in the religious and the secular senses. Thus in the remaining Nikāyas also should this definition be understood.

Which is the *Majjhima Nikāya?* The collection of one hundred and fifty-two suttas of medium length beginning with the *Mūlapariyāya-Sutta*, forming fifteen divisions.

Seven score and twelve Suttantas in fifteen
Chapters the Majjhima Nikāya holds.

Which is the *Saṃyutta Nikāya?* The seven thousand seven hundred and sixty-two suttas beginning with the *Oghataraṇa*, and arranged as *Devatāsaṃyutta*, etc.

Seventy-seven hundred suttas, sixty-two
Suttantas, Saṃyutta Nikāya holds.

Which is the *Aṅguttara Nikāya?* The nine thousand five hundred and fifty-seven suttas beginning with *Cittapariyādāna*, arranged by way of an increase of the parts by one at a time.

Nine thousand and five hundred and fifty-seven,
These are the suttas in Aṅguttara.

[26] Which is the *Khuddaka Nikāya?*[3] The whole of the Vinaya-Piṭaka, Abhidhamma-Piṭaka, and the fifteen divisions, as shown above,—beginning with *Khuddakapāṭha*, *Dhammapada*, all the remaining words of the Buddha, excluding the Four Nikāyas.

---

[1] *Saṃyutta*, iii. 152. [2] Not traced. [3] Cf. p. 23.

Save Dīgha and the three Nikāyas named,
The rest of Buddha's word is Khuddaka.

Thus as to Nikāyas there are five.

Which are the 'nine parts'? The entire *Sutta, Geyya, Veyyākaraṇa, Gāthā, Udāna, Itivuttaka, Jātaka, Abbhuta, Vedalla.*[1]

Herein, the dual *Sutta-Vibhaṅga*, the *Niddesa*, the *Khandhakas*, and *Parivāra*, the *Maṅgalasutta, Ratanasutta, Nālakasutta, Tuvaṭakasutta* of the *Sutta-Nipāta*, and any other words of the Tathāgata bearing the name of Sutta should be regarded as Sutta. All the Suttas with verses should be understood as *Geyya*. In particular, all the chapters with verses in the *Saṃyutta-Nikāya* form *Geyya*. The entire Abhidhamma-Piṭaka, Suttas without verses and any other words of the Buddha not included in the eight parts should be understood as *Veyyākaraṇa*,[2] or exposition. *Dhammapada, Theragāthā, Therīgāthā*, those pieces in the *Sutta-Nipāta* not called Sutta, and entirely in verse should be known as *Gāthā*. Eighty-two Suttantas connected with verses due to knowledge and joy should be understood as *Udāna*.

One hundred and twelve Suttantas taught in this wise: 'Thus was it said by the Blessed One,' etc., should be understood as *Itivuttaka* (the 'Thus-said'). Five hundred and fifty birth-stories beginning with the *Apaṇṇaka* constitute the *Jātaka*. All Suttantas connected with wonderful and marvellous things spoken in this wise: 'There are, bhikkhus, four wonderful and marvellous things in Ānanda,'[3] should be understood as *Abbhuta*. All Suttantas in the form of questions asked through repeated attainment of delight and understanding, such as the Suttas: *Cullavedalla, Mahāvedalla, Sammādiṭṭhi, Sakkapañhā, Saṅkhārabhājaniya, Mahāpuṇṇama,*[4]

---

[1] The doctrine as compiled (if not as written) literature is thus enumerated in the Piṭakas, *e.g., Majjhima* i. 133.—*Ed.*

[2] As Geyya means Suttas with verses and Veyyākaraṇa means Suttas without verses, there seems to be no need of a separate part as Suttas, which are neither. In point of fact, Veyyākaraṇa is applied to those Suttas containing questions and answers.—*Tr.*

[3] *Aṅguttara* ii. 132.

[4] *Majjhima* i. 299; 292; 46; *Dīgha* ii. 263; *Majjhima* iii. 99; 15.

etc., should be understood as *Vedalla*. Such are the nine parts.

Which are the eighty-four thousand units of text?

[27] *Eighty-two thousand from the Blessed One,*
Two thousand from the bhikkhu Sāriputta—
Eighty-four thousand dhammas have I learned.[1]

Thus the whole of the Buddha's word is composed of eighty-four thousand units of text. Of these, the Sutta containing one theme[2] forms one unit of text. Where a Sutta contains more than one theme, its units of texts are determined by the number of such themes. In verses each query or question asked forms a unit, and each answer forms another. In the Abhidhamma each trinal or dual classification, as well as each classification of conscious intervals, forms one unit of text. In the Vinaya there are subjects, tables of contents, classification of terms, offence, innocence, interim offence, and division into triplets, wherein each portion should be understood as a unit of text. Such is the division of the Doctrine into eighty-four thousand units of text.

Thus at the time of the Rehearsal at the First Council, held by the five hundred, the company of the self-controlled who recited under the presidency of Mahākassapa did so after previous determination: '[This is the Doctrine, this is the Vinaya];[3] these are the first words, these the middle words, these the later words of the Buddha; this is the Vinaya-Piṭaka, this the Suttanta-Piṭaka, this the Abhidhamma-Piṭaka, this the Dīgha Nikāya. . . . Khuddaka Nikāya; these the nine parts, to wit, the Suttas, etc.; these the eighty-four thousand units of text.' And not only this: the various literary expedients appearing in the three Piṭakas such as the lists of contents (*uddāna*), chapters (*vagga*), elisions (*peyyāla*), sections (*nipāta*) of single, double subjects, etc., groups (*saṃyutta*), fifties (*paññāsa*)—all this having been arranged, was rehearsed in seven months. And at the

[1] Verse spoken by Ānanda to Gopaka Moggallāna. Cf. *Majjhima* iii. 7 *f.*

[2] *Anusandhika. Anusandhi* is a logical sequence of subjects.

[3] Not in P.T.S. ed.—*Ed.*

conclusion of the Rehearsal the great earth quaked (up to the limits of the water) repeatedly, violently, with a vertical upheaval everywhere; and various wonders manifested themselves, as though giving congratulations with well-felt delight at the thought: 'The religion of the Buddha of the Ten Powers has thus, by the Elder Mahākassapa, been made capable of lasting a period of five thousand years.'

Thus as rehearsed at the Council, the Abhidhamma is a Piṭaka by Piṭaka-classification, Khuddaka-Nikāya by Nikāya-classification, [28] Veyyākaraṇa by Part-classification and constitutes two or three thousand units of text by the classification of textual units. One of those bhikkhus who studied the Abhidhamma once sat in the midst of bhikkhus who knew all the five Nikāyas,[1] and quoting the text (*sutta*) from the Abhidhamma taught the Doctrine thus: 'The aggregate of matter is unmoral; of the four (mental) aggregates some are moral, some immoral, and some unmoral. Ten sense-organs are unmoral; the (remaining) two sense-organs may be moral, immoral, or unmoral. Sixteen elements are unmoral; the (remaining) two elements may be moral, immoral, or unmoral. The Fact of the Origination of Ill is immoral; the Fact of the Path is moral; the Fact of Cessation is unmoral; the Fact of Ill may be moral, immoral, or unmoral. Ten controlling powers are unmoral; the controlling power of grief is immoral; the controlling power of (intellect which prompts and inspires us)—"I shall come to know the unknown"—is moral; four controlling powers may be moral or unmoral; six controlling powers may be moral, immoral or unmoral.'[2] A bhikkhu, seated there, asked, 'Preacher, you quote a long text as though you were going to encircle Mount Sineru; what text is it?' 'Abhidhamma text, brother.' 'Why do you quote the Abhidhamma text? Does it not behove you to quote other texts spoken by the Buddha?' (Preacher) 'Brother, by whom was the Abhidhamma taught?' 'Not by the Buddha.'

---

[1] Thus the *Ṭīkā* interprets sabbasāmayikaparisāya. 'Sat in the fourfold assembly' according to the *Gaṇṭhipada*.

[2] *Vibhaṅga*, 62; 73; 90; 112; 125.

(Preacher) 'But did you, brother, study the Vinaya-Piṭaka ?' 'No, brother, I did not.' (Preacher) 'Methinks, because you have not studied the Vinaya-Piṭaka, you say so in ignorance.' 'I have, indeed, brother, studied some Vinaya.' (Preacher) 'Then that has been badly acquired. You must have been seated at one end of the assembly and dozing. A person who leaves the world under such teachers as yourself to give the Refuge-formula, or a person who receives the full ordination under a chapter of such teachers as yourself, who have badly studied the Vinaya, does amiss. And why? Because of this badly "studying some Vinaya." For it has been said by the Buddha:[1] "If without any intention of reviling the Vinaya one were to instigate another, saying, Pray study the Suttas or Gāthās or Abhidhamma first and afterwards you will learn the Vinaya—there is no offence in him." (Again, in the Bhikkhunī Vibhaṅga:[2] "A bhikkhunī is guilty of a minor offence) if she questions on the Abhidhamma or Vinaya after getting permission (to question) on the Suttanta, or on the Suttanta or Vinaya after getting permission (to question) on the Abhidhamma, or on the Suttanta or Abhidhamma after getting permission (to question) on the Vinaya." But you do not know even that much.'[3] With so much refutation was the heretic put down. The *Mahāgosiṅga Sutta* is even a stronger authority (to show that the Abhidhamma is the Buddha's word). For therein when Sāriputta, the Generalissimo of the Law, approached the Teacher to inform him of the reciprocal questions and answers that took place between Mahāmoggallāna and himself, and told how the former had answered, (the Master said) [29] 'Brother Sāriputta, in the religion the talk of two bhikkhus on the Abhidhamma, each asking and answering the other without faltering, is in accord with the Dhamma. Now such a bhikkhu, brother Sāriputta, might enhance the beauty of the Gosiṅga Sāla Forest.'[4] The Teacher, far from saying that bhikkhus, who knew Abhidhamma, were outside his

---

[1] *Vin.* iv. 144.

[2] *Vin.* iv. 344.

[3] Similarly, implies the preacher, there is no offence in me when I say you would do wrong to get ordained.—*Tr.*

[4] *Majjhima.* i. 218.

religion, lifted his drum-like neck and filling (with breath) his mouth, fraught as the full-moon with blessings, emitted his godlike voice congratulating Moggallāna thus: 'Well done, well done, Sāriputta! One should answer rightly as Moggallāna has done; Moggallāna is indeed a preacher of the Dhamma.' And tradition has it that those bhikkhus only who know Abhidhamma are true preachers of the Dhamma; the rest, though they speak on the Dhamma, are not preachers thereof. And why? They, in speaking on the Dhamma, confuse the different kinds of Kamma and of its results, the distinction between mind and matter, and the different kinds of states. The students of Abhidhamma do not thus get confused; hence a bhikkhu who knows Abhidhamma, whether he preaches the Dhamma or not, will be able to answer questions whenever asked. He alone, therefore, is a true preacher of the Dhamma. To this the Teacher referred when he approving said, 'Moggallāna has well replied to questions.' He who prohibits (the teaching of) Abhidhamma gives a blow to the Wheel of the Conqueror, denies omniscience, subverts the Teacher's knowledge full of confidence, deceives the audience, obstructs the path of the Ariyas, manifests himself as advocating one[1] of the eighteen causes of dissension in the Order, is capable of doing acts for which the doer is liable to be excommunicated, or admonished,[2] or scorned (by the Order), and should be dismissed after the particular act of excommunication, admonition, or scorn, and reduced to living on scraps of food.

But if the heretic should say, had Abhidhamma been taught by the Buddha, there would have been an introduction prefatory to it, just as in many thousands of the Suttas the preface generally runs as, 'One day the Blessed One was staying in Rājagaha,' etc., he should be contradicted thus: 'The *Jātaka*, *Suttanipāta*, *Dhammapada*, and so on, have no

---

[1] *Bhedakāravatthu*, viz.: showing what has been spoken by the Buddha as not spoken. The eighteen are given in *Vinaya Texts* iii. 266, § 2.—*Tr.*

[2] See *Vin.* ii. 7 (*Vin. Texts* iii. 343): the Nissayakamma administered to Seyyasaka.

such introductions, and yet they were spoken by the Buddha.'[1] Furthermore he should be told, 'O wise one, this Abhidhamma is the province of the Buddhas, not of others; the descent of the Buddhas, their birth, their attainment of perfect wisdom, their turning of the Wheel of the Law, [30] their performance of the Twin Miracle, their visit to the devas,[2] their preaching in the deva-world, and their descent therefrom are all manifest. It would be unreasonable to steal the Treasure-elephant, or horse of the universal Monarch and yoke it to a cart and drive about, or the Treasure-Wheel and fix it to a hay cart and drive about, or to use the Treasure-jewel capable of shedding light to the distance of a yojana by putting it in a cotton basket —and why? Because they are royal property. Even so Abhidhamma is not the province of others; it is the province of the Buddhas only. Such a discourse as the Abhidhamma can be taught by them only; for their descent is manifest . . . likewise their return from the deva-world. There is, O wise one, no need for an introduction to Abhidhamma.' When this is so stated, the heterodox opponent would be unable to adduce an illustration in support of his cause.

The Elder Tissabhūti, resident at the Central Park, wishing to show that the place of the Great Enlightenment[3] is an introduction to Abhidhamma, quoted the *Padesavihārasutta* —'Bhikkhus, by whatever mode of life I lived after I first attained Buddhahood, I have [these two weeks] lived by that mode of living.'[4] This he expanded: There are ten positions: of the aggregates, the field of sense, the elements, the Truths, the controlling powers, the causal signs, applications of mindfulness, jhāna, mind, and states. Of these the Teacher at the foot of the great Wisdom Tree intuited the five aggregates fully; for three months he lived only by way of the

---

[1] The double negative *na* . . . *na* agrees with the reading in the *Maṇidīpa*. Some read '*atthi, na ca tāni*,' etc.—'they *have* introductions and were *not* spoken by the Buddha.'

[2] Read *tidivokkamo*, so explained in the *Yojanā*. Cf. *Dhammapada Commentary*, iii. 216.

[3] The *Anuṭīkā* takes '*mahābodhinidāno*' to be '*paṭivedhabhūmi*,' the place of intuition, and the *Yojanā*, the Wisdom Tree.

[4] *Saṃyutta*. v 12.

aggregate of feeling.[1] He intuited the twelve sense-organs and the eighteen elements fully; for three months he lived only, by way of feeling, in the field and in the element of mental presentations. He intuited the four Truths fully; for three months he lived only by way of feeling in the Truth of Ill. He intuited the twenty-two controlling faculties fully; for three months he lived only by way of the five emotional indriyas.[2] He fully intuited the chain[3] of the causal genesis; for three months he lived by way of feeling with touch as its cause. He intuited the four applications in mindfulness fully; for three months he lived only by way of feeling to which mindfulness was intensely applied. [31] He intuited the four Jhānas fully; for three months he lived only by way of feeling among the factors of Jhāna. He intuited mind fully; for three months he lived by way of feeling mind only. He intuited (other) states fully; for three months he lived only by way of (one or other of) the triplet of feeling.[4] Thus the Elder set forth an introduction to Abhidhamma by means of the *Padesavihārasutta*.

The Elder Sumanadeva, resident in a village, while translating the Scriptures[5] at the base of the Brazen Palace, thought: 'This heterodox believer, who does not know the introduction (nidāna) to Abhidhamma, is just like one crying (helpless) with uplifted arms in the forest, or like one who has filed a lawsuit without witness.'[6] And in order to show the introduction he said, 'At one time the Blessed One lived among the

[1] S. Z. Aung comments on this: *I.e.*, the Buddha *lived* his thoughts. He *felt* himself identical with himself. In the language of M. Bergson, the Buddha intuited his personality, the real considered by way of aggregate, sense-organ, etc., and actually experienced what he intuited.—*Tr.*

[2] *Vibhaṅga*, 123.

[3] Reading °vaṭṭaṃ.—*Tr.*

[4] Good, bad, indifferent. 'It will be noticed that the feeling by which the Buddha *lived* his thoughts is only a part (*padesa*) of the whole of the object intuited in each case.'—*S. Z. Aung.*

[5] *I.e.*, Abhidhamma and the Commentaries. So Pyī (reading parifor pavattento). Ariyālaṅkāra interprets: 'reciting the Dhamma, to wit, sīla,' etc.

[6] Instead of appealing to us, who can bear testimony to Abhidhamma having an introduction.—*Tr.*

gods on the Paṇḍukambala rock at the foot of the Pāricchattaka tree in Tāvatiṃsa. Then the Blessed One taught Abhidhamma to the Tāvatiṃsa gods thus: 'moral, immoral, and unmoral states of consciousness,' etc.[1]

Whereas in the Sutta discourses there is but one introduction, in Abhidhamma there are two: one on the Career and its Goal, and one on the teaching. Of these the former comprises the events from the time of Dīpaṅkara of the Ten Powers up to the time of attaining the throne under the Wisdom Tree; the latter comprises the events between the last mentioned and the time of turning the Wheel of the Dhamma. Thus for proficiency in the introduction to Abhidhamma, which has both of these, the following questions should be asked: 1. From which source has this Abhidhamma originated? 2. Where has it matured? 3. Where, 4. when, and 5. by whom was it mastered? 6. Where, 7. when, and 8. by whom was it studied? 9. Where, 10. for whose benefit, and 11. for what purpose was it taught? 12. By whom was it accepted? 13. Who are learning it? 14. Who have learnt it? 15. Who know it by heart? 16. Whose word is it? And 17. by whom has it been handed down?

The reply to these is: 1. Faith which urges to enlightenment was the source. 2. In the five hundred and fifty Jātakas. 3. At the foot of the Wisdom Tree. 4. On the full-moonday of Visākha. 5. By the omniscient Buddha. 6. At the foot of the Wisdom Tree. [32] 7. During the seven days spent at the Jewel House. 8. By the omniscient Buddha. 9. Among the Tāvatiṃsa devas. 10. Of the devas. 11. For release from the four Floods. 12. By the devas. 13. Probationers and good worldlings. 14. Saints free from the Intoxicants. 15. Those who lay it to heart. 16. Of the Blessed the Arahant, the Buddha Supreme. 17. By the unbroken line of teachers. It was conveyed up till the time of the third Council by the Elders Sāriputta, Bhaddaji, Sobhita, Piyajāli, Piyapāla, Piyadassī, Kosiyaputta, Siggava, Sandeha, Moggalīputta, Visudatta, Dhammiya,[2] Dāsaka, Sonaka, Revata, and others. After that, it was conveyed by a succes-

[1] *Dhs.* Table of Contents. [2] Or Dhammika—*Pyi.*

sion of their pupils. Thus in India it has been conveyed by an unbroken line of teachers. And to this island of Ceylon subsequently came Mahinda, Iddhiya,[1] Uttiya,[2] Bhaddanāma, and Sambala. These greatly wise ones brought it to this island from India, and thenceforward till to-day it has been conveyed by the line of teachers known as their pupils. Of Abhidhamma thus conveyed, the introduction of the Career and the Goal, from the time of Dīpaṅkara of the Ten Powers till the attainment of the throne under the Wisdom Tree, and the introduction of the Teaching till the turning of the Wheel of the Law will be clear from the tradition:

(Here follows the Dūrenidāna of the Jātaka Commentary, edited by Fausboll, vol. i., pp. 2–47, and translated by Rhys Davids, *Buddhist Birth Stories*, pp. 2–58.)

There in Tusita he surpassed other spirits in ten attributes; he enjoyed celestial pleasure till the end of life [33] for fifty-seven *koṭis* and sixty thousand years by human calculation. The spirits on being informed[3] that he was to come to the end of his life among them in seven days, because of the manifestation of the five portents—namely, the clothes get soiled, the flowers fade,[4] sweat exudes from the armpits, the body becomes uncomely, the spirit cannot remain in his seat—became agitated at the thought 'how empty our heavens will become!' They knew that the Great Being had fulfilled the perfections, and they thought: 'If he should get the Buddhahood now by taking birth in the world of men, then men who do meritorious deeds will pass away, and instead of going out to another world of spirits, will fill our world of spirits.'

(So the Buddha said to Sāriputta):

When I in Tusita abode was called
Santusita, from all the myriad worlds
They came to me with supplicating hands

---

[1] Or Iṭṭiya—*Pyī*. [2] Or Uṭṭiya—*Pyī*.

[3] Pyī supplies '*vattabbe*' after '*pāpuṇissatī ti*.'

[4] They get these clothes and flowers at their rebirth owing to the result of their Kamma.—*Yojanā*.

Saying: Great Hero, now thy time is come.
Enter the womb, and know the Deathless Path,
Bringing salvation unto gods and men.'

Thus requested to be the Buddha, he made the five great observations as to the time, island, locality, family, and life-term of his (future) mother. His resolution having been made, he passed away from Tusita and was reborn in the family of Sakya rajahs, and there in due course reached the prime of life without ever falling off from the full enjoyment of his splendid glory.

The details of his life during this interval should be gathered from such Sutta passages as: 'In the meantime, O Ānanda, the Bodhisat, mindful and knowing, passed away from Tusita heaven and descended into his mother's womb,'[1] and so on, as well as from their commentaries. Enjoying the glory of kingship comparable to that of the gods in the three palaces suitable respectively for the three seasons, one day, when he went out to disport himself in the garden, he saw one after another three divine messengers in the form of an old man, a sick man, and a dead man. He became greatly agitated and turned back. But at the fourth time he saw a monk, and took a fancy to monkhood, thinking, 'It is good to be a monk.' He then proceeded to the garden, spent the day there; and, seated on the bank of the lucky lotus-pond and dressed by the god Vissakamma, who came in the guise of a barber, [34] he heard the news of Rāhula-Bhadda's birth. He conceived a great paternal affection for his son and, thinking that he would cut the bond before it grew stronger, entered the city in the evening.

'*Does not that mother bear a tranquil heart,*
Does not that father bear a tranquil heart,
Does not that spouse, to whom is such a lord?'

Hearing this verse sung by Kisāgotamī, daughter to his aunt,[2] he took off from his neck a necklace of pearls worth a hundred thousand and sent it to her saying: 'She has declared the path of tranquillity to me.' He entered his own mansion,

---

[1] *Majjhima* iii. 119. [2] Pyī takes pitucchā- to mean 'uncle.'

and seated on a glorious couch he saw the physical change that had come over the actresses during sleep. Disgusted at heart he woke up Channa, had his horse Kanthaka brought round, mounted it, and surrounded by spirits from the myriad world-systems went out with Channa on the Great Renunciation. During the remainder of that night he passed the three great kingdoms,[1] became a monk on the banks of the river Anomā, went in due course to Rājagaha. There after going round for alms, while seated in a cave at Mount Paṇḍava, he was offered the kingdom by the king of Magadha, and rejected the offer. However, he gave his promise to the king that he would visit the kingdom after he had attained omniscience. He next approached Āḷāra and Kālāma-Uddaka. Dissatisfied with the special attainments acquired from them, he practised the mighty efforts for six years. On the full-moon day of Visākhā, early in the morning he ate the meal offered by Sujātā in the suburban village of Senāni, floated the golden bowl in the River Nerañjarā, passed the day in various attainments in the dense Great Forest on the bank of the river, and in the evening, taking the eight handfuls of grass offered by the goatherd, Sotthiya, he ascended the consecrated throne under the Wisdom Tree the while his praises were sung by Kāla, the Nāga king, and spread the grass, resolving: 'As long as my mind is not released from the intoxicants through the absence of grasping, I will not change my seat.' And he sat facing the East and, before sunset, dispersed Māra's forces. In the first watch of the night he won insight into former existences, in the middle watch insight into births and deaths, and at the end of the third watch intuited omniscience, adorned with all the qualities of a Buddha, such as the Ten Powers, the Four Confidences, [35] and arrived at the ocean of this Abhidhamma method.

This should be considered as the introduction to Abhidhamma which tells of the Career and the Goal.

He having thus attained Abhidhamma spent seven days in a single sitting posture; seven days in contemplating

[1] Viz. Kapilavatthu, Devadaha, Koliya.—*Ariyālaṅkāra.*

the throne of wisdom without blinking his eyes; seven days in walking to and fro; and in the fourth week he contemplated the self-acquired Abhidhamma.[1] He spent another three weeks at the goatherds' (banyan) tree, the Mucalinda tree, and the Rājāyatana tree.[2] During the eighth week he sat at the foot of the goatherds' banyan tree. Reflecting on the profundity of the Dhamma, he was reluctant to preach it; but when entreated to do so by Sahampati, who came with a retinue of Mahābrahmās from the myriad world-systems, he surveyed the world with the Buddha's eye; and to comply with the wish of Mahābrahmā looked out for disciples, asking to himself. 'To whom shall I first preach the Dhamma ?' He discerned that Āḷāra and Uddaka were dead, but remembering the great services of the group of five monks, he rose from his seat and went to Kāsi-town. He fell in on the way with Upaka the wanderer, with whom he conversed, and on the full-moon day of Āsāḷhi he reached the abode of the group of five monks at the Deer Park at Isipatana. He convinced them (of his own Buddhahood), who were using a term of address[3] unbefitting his new position, and turning the Wheel of the Dhamma he gave to them, headed by the Elder Aññākoṇḍañña, and to the eighteen myriads of Brahmās, the nectar of the Deathless. Thus the introduction to Abhidhamma on the Teaching should be understood as leading up to the turning of the Wheel of the Dhamma.

This is the abstract. The detailed account should be understood from Suttas like *Ariyapariyesanā* and *Pabbajjā*[4] with their commentaries.

These introductions to Abhidhamma on Career and Teaching may be divided into three periods according as the events are distant, not very distant, and proximate. Of these the Distant introduction should be understood as comprising events from Dīpaṅkara till the Tusita abode. From the Tusita abode to the foot of the Wisdom Tree is the Near introduction.

---

[1] *I.e.*, philosophy acquired through intuition.—*Tr.*

[2] The Kingstead Tree. So called because it is supposed to have been the residence of a king of fairies.

[3] Āvuso. [4] *Majjhima* i. 160 *ff.*; *Sutta-Nipāta*, ver. 405-24.

Such a verbal introduction as, 'At one time the Blessed One lived among the Tāvatiṃsa devas on the Paṇḍukambala stone at the foot of the Pāricchattaka tree. There the Blessed One related the Abhidhamma discourse to the Tāvatiṃsa devas'—is the Proximate introduction.

This is the Introductory Discourse.

BOOK I

RISINGS OF CONSCIOUSNESS

PART I—THE TABLE OF CONTENTS

(*MĀTIKĀ*)

CHAPTER I

THE TRIPLETS

[36] Now has arrived the opportunity of discoursing on Abhidhamma according to the agreement made (in the Introductory verse):

> ' *Give ear obediently, while I expound*
> *The Abhidhamma-lore, for it is hard*
> *To hear such discourse as ye now may hear.*'

Now the venerable Abhidhamma consists of seven books beginning with *Dhammasaṅgaṇī*. This book has four divisions: risings of Consciousness, and the rest. The division on risings of Consciousness is twofold: Table of contents and Classification of terms. Of these, the table of contents comes first and is divided into the table of triplets and the table of couplets. Of these, the table of triplets comes first and the triplet headed by moral states is the first therein. In the triplet headed by moral states, the words ' moral states ' are the first. Hence,

> *Ye faithful, with devout and single mind*
> *This subtle Abhidhamma discourse hear.*
> *Thus it begins:*

The triplet of ' moral states, immoral states, unmoral states '[1] is named the moral triplet after the opening

---

[1] *Dhs.* p. 1.

sentence. The triplet of 'states associated with pleasurable feeling, states associated with painful feeling, states associated with feeling neither pleasurable nor painful,' is named the triplet of feeling after the word 'feeling,' common to all the three members. Thus the names of all the triplets and couplets should be understood from either the first term, or the term common to all the members of each.

All these triplets and couplets have been marked off into fifteen divisions—one triplet and fourteen couplets.[1] Six couplets beginning with that of 'states which are conditions, states which are not conditions' may be called the Condition-group, because they stand together like the pericarp of a flower, or a bunch of flowers, by virtue of mutual connection both in text and sense. Next, seven other couplets, beginning with that of 'states with causal relations, states without causal relations,' are not so mutually connected, [37] and are to be understood as the Lesser Intermediate couplets, because they are simply selected as ordinary couplets and placed severally among 'Groups,' and because they are less than the Greater Intermediate ones.

Then the Intoxicant-group (is to be understood) by virtue of six couplets beginning with that of Intoxicants. Similarly with the Fetter-group (which is to be understood) by virtue of the couplet of the Fetters, etc.

And similarly the Knot-group,[2] the Flood-group, the Bond-group, the Hindrance-group are to be understood by virtue of the couplets of the Knots, the Floods, the Bonds, and the Hindrances.

The Reversion-group is to be understood by virtue of five couplets beginning with that of reversion.[3] Thus altogether seven groups should be understood.

Further on come the fourteen Greater Intermediate couplets beginning with that of 'States with object.'

Next follows the Grasping-group of six couplets beginning with that of grasping.

---

[1] *Dhs.* pp. 2–8.

[2] Gantha. In *B.P.E.*: 'The Group of the Ties.'

[3] Parāmāsa. In *B.P.E*: 'The Group on Contagion.'

Thereafter, the Corruption-group of eight couplets beginning with that of the Corruptions.

Then eighteen couplets beginning with that of 'what should be got rid of by means of insight' are called the Final couplets, from being placed at the end of the Abhidhamma table of contents.

But forty-two couplets beginning with that of 'States which partake of knowledge and states which do not partake of knowledge' are called the Suttantika couplets.

Thus all the triplets and couplets have been marked off into fifteen divisions. Thus marked off, they form two portions, according as there is partial treatment or complete treatment. To expand: Of these, nine triplets and seventy-one couplets are termed 'partially treated' because the remaining and partially treated states, mental and material,[1] have still to be taken into account. The remaining thirteen triplets and seventy-one couplets are 'complete' without a remainder. Therein, of the triplets, the nine triplets: those of feeling, initial application of mind, zest, resulting states, the past, and the four object-triplets, are 'partially treated.' Of the couplets are the three at the conclusion of the nine groups beginning with the Condition-group and ending with the Grasping-group.

[38] The four couplets at the end of the Corruption-group; the two Greater Intermediate couplets of 'states associated with consciousness and states dissociated therefrom, and states mixed with consciousness and states unmixed therewith'; the remaining thirty-eight couplets in the Suttantika couplets, with the exception of the four couplets of synonyms, concepts, word-definition, and mind and matter—all these are 'partially treated.' All the remaining triplets and couplets should be regarded as 'complete.'

Now comes the word-by-word comment on the terms in the table of contents, beginning with 'moral states.'

First of all, the word '*kusala*' (moral) means 'of good health,' 'faultless,' 'skilful,' 'productive of happy sentient results,' etc. In such passages as, 'Is your reverence *kusala?*'

---

[1] Which have not been reckoned as triplets or couplets.

'Is your reverence free from ailment?'[1]—*kusala* has the meaning of 'good health.' In such passages as, 'Which, sir, is *kusala* behaviour?' 'Great king, it is conduct that is blameless';[2] and again in, 'Sir, as the Blessed One has taught the Law verily incomparable with respect to *kusala* states'[3]—*kusala* means 'faultless.' In such passages as, 'You are *kusala* at the different parts of a chariot';[4] 'Graceful women who have been trained and are *kusala* in singing and dancing,' etc.[5]—*kusala* means 'skilful.' In such passages as, 'Bhikkhus, (merit flows from) the cause that has built up *kusala* states,'[6] and '(Visual cognition springs into existence) because it has been performed and accumulated by a kamma which is *kusala*'[7]—*kusala* means 'productive of happy results.' Now here, in the phrase 'moral states,' either 'wholesome,' or 'faultless,' or 'productive of happy results' is a suitable meaning.

And the word *dhamma* (state) is used in the sense of 'scriptural text,' 'root-condition,' 'virtue,' 'absence of an entity, living thing,' etc. In such passages as, 'This one studies the *Dhamma*, the Sutta and the Geyya'[8]—*dhamma* means 'the Scriptures.' In such passages as, 'Knowledge of root-conditions is analysis of *dhamma*'[9]—*dhamma* means 'root-condition, or cause.' In such passages as,

> '*Dhamma, adhamma bear not equal fruit:*
> *One leads to Heaven, the other leads to Hell*'—

dhamma means 'virtue,' or 'good quality.'[10]

In such passages as, 'At the time of consciousness coming into existence, there occur *dhammas*';[11] and again, 'he abides watchful over certain *dhammas*'—*dhamma* implies 'absence of an entity or living soul.' [39] And in the Dhammasangaṇī also it is proper to take it in this sense.

---

1 *Dasaratha Jātaka*. *Jāt.* iv., No. 461.
2 *Majjhima* ii. 115.
3 *Dīgha* iii. 102.
4 *Majjhima* ii. 94.
5 *Jāt.* vi. 25.
6 *Dīgha* iii. 58.
7 Commentary on the *Cakkavattisutta*, *Dīgha* iii. 58 *ff.*; *Dhs.* § 43.
8 *Majjhima* i. 133.
9 *Vibhaṅga*, 293.
10 *Theragāthā*, ver. 304.
11 *Majjhima* i. 61.

But to come to word-definitions: *kusala's* are so called in that they cause contemptible things to tremble,[1] to shake, to be disturbed, destroyed. Or, *kusa* are those (vices) which lie in a person under contemptible conditions.[2] And *kusala's* [3] are so called because they lop off, cut off what are known as immoralities (*a-kusala's*). Or, knowledge is called *kusa* [4] because of the reduction or eradication of contemptible things, and *kusala* [5] is so called because things should be taken, grasped, set in motion by that *kusa*. Or just as the *kusa* grass cuts a part of the hand with both edges, so also certain things cut off the corrupt part in two portions, either what has arisen, or what has not arisen. Therefore *kusala's* are so called because they cut off the corruptions like the *kusa* grass.

Dhamma's may be defined as those states which bear their own intrinsic natures, or which are borne by causes-in-relation, or which are borne according to their own characteristics.

'Immoral' (*akusala*) means 'not moral.' Just as the opposite to friendship is enmity, or the opposite to greed, etc., is disinterestedness, etc., so 'immoral' is opposed to moral.

'Unmoral' (*avyākata*) means 'undeclared.' The meaning is that the 'unmoral' cannot be pronounced to be either moral or immoral; it is indeterminate. Of these, moral states or things have the characteristics of 'faultlessness' and 'happy result,' immoral, of 'faultiness' and 'bad result,' and unmoral, of 'no result.'

Have the terms, 'moral' and 'state,' in the opening clause, one and the same meaning, or different meanings? (This query leaves) something (to be said) here.[6] If 'moral' and 'state' had the same meaning, then it would be like saying

---

[1] From *ku*, 'bad,' + $\sqrt{sal}$, 'to tremble,' say the Commentaries.

[2] From *ku*, 'bad,' + $\sqrt{sī}$, to lie.

[3] From *kusa*, so derived + $\sqrt{lū}$, to cut.

[4] From *ku*, 'bad,' + $\sqrt{so}$, to reduce.

[5] From *kusa*, so defined, + $\sqrt{lā}$, to take.

[6] Literally 'And what here?'—a commentarial device adopted to show that the query is incomplete.—*Tr.*

'moral moral.' And if they had different meanings, the triplets and couplets would make sextuplets and quadruplets, and there would be no connection between the terms. To illustrate: If one were to say, 'Moralities, matter, seer,' there would be no (logical) connection between the terms owing to a lack of mutual dependence in thought; so here also there would be an absence of connection (between 'moral' and 'state'). And terms without any connection between the antecedent and the consequent serve no useful purpose. The query would also contradict a later question: 'which states are moral?' For (in this view of different meanings) states can never be identical with moralities; hence the contradiction. But the question: 'which states are moral?' is quite possible.

Another method: If the terms 'state' and 'moral' had the same meaning (*i.e.*, denoted one and the same thing), the terms 'moral,' 'immoral,' and 'unmoral' would have one and the same meaning, because the three terms had the same meaning of 'state.' To expand: The word 'state' coming after 'moral,' etc., has one meaning in the sense of a 'state.' Therefore the (three) words 'moral,' etc., not differing from the thrice following word 'state,' would also have that one meaning; what is moral would be immoral and again unmoral. But if the oneness in the meaning of these three words comprised under 'state' be not accepted, and if it be urged that the word 'state' after 'moral' means [40] one thing, that after 'immoral' means another, and that after 'unmoral' means a third, then it may be said that by 'state' is meant existence; and anything different from existence is non-existent. Therefore existence as denoted by 'state' after 'immoral,' being different from that denoted by the same word after 'moral,' would become non-existent. So also with existence as denoted by 'state' when it comes after 'unmoral.' Moreover, existence as denoted by 'state' after 'moral' would be unreal, on the view that it differs from the other two in meaning. And the words 'moral,' etc., not being different from the word 'state,' which have thus become non-existent, would themselves become non-existent.

All this imaginary objection is not reasonable. And why?

Because the general usage is accomplished by, or in conformity with, convention. For 'usage' is accomplished by conventional signs, through which that 'usage' is accepted by the general consent to express or signify certain meanings. And so in 'moral states,' etc., the word 'state,' preceded by 'moral,' and the word 'moral,' followed by 'state,' have not been accepted by the wise as identical in meaning as in 'moral, moral,' nor as mutually independent in meaning as in 'moralities, matter, seer.' But here in this phrase 'moral states,' etc., the word 'moral' has been accepted as signifying 'faultlessness' and 'happy result'; and 'immoral' as signifying 'faultiness'; and 'unmoral' as signifying 'no result'; and 'state' as signifying 'bearing its own intrinsic nature.'

The word 'state,' uttered immediately after each of these words, reflects its own general meaning on them, inasmuch as they are all 'states' by the general characteristic of bearing their own intrinsic natures, etc. And the words 'moral,' etc., uttered before the word 'state,' reflect their special meaning on it, inasmuch as a 'state' is either moral, immoral, or unmoral. Thus these words being uttered separately indicate their mere meanings, and being uttered in conjunction with 'state,' they all indicate their own general and special meanings. And this usage the wise in the world have accepted. Therefore all that has been said (§§ 96–97) by way of fault-finding regarding identity and difference of meanings is unreasonable.

Thus far for the word-by-word explanation of terms in the triplet beginning with 'moral.' And the same method is to be understood in the remaining triplets and couplets. But henceforward we shall speak merely of what distinguishes those triplets from the foregoing.

The word *sukha* in 'associated with pleasurable feeling,' etc., first of all means 'pleasurable feeling,' 'root of happiness,' 'pleasurable object,' 'condition of happiness,' 'objective station occasioning pleasure,' 'freedom from cares,' and 'Nibbānic happiness,' etc. To expand: In such passages as, 'By getting rid of *sukha*'[1]—*sukha* means 'pleasurable feeling.' In such passages as, '*Sukha* is the appearance of

[1] From Fourth Jhāna formula; cf., *e.g.*, *Dhs.* § 165. . . .

the Buddhas !'[1] '*sukha* is the state of freedom from lust in the world'[2]—*sukha* means 'root of happiness.' [41] In such passages as, 'Mahāli, inasmuch as matter is *sukha*, falls and descends on *sukha*'[3]—*sukha* means 'pleasurable object.' In such passages as, 'Bhikkhus, the word merit is the synonym of *sukha*'[4]—*sukha* means 'condition of happiness.' In such passages as, 'Not easy is it, bhikkhus, to succeed in describing how pleasant are the heavens;'[5] again,

'*They know not bliss who see not Nandana*'[6]—

'bliss' (*sukha*) means 'place occasioning happiness.' In such passages as, 'these states (jhāna) constitute a *sukha* life in this very world'[7] *sukha* means 'freedom from cares.' In such passages as, 'Nibbāna is the highest *sukha*'[8]—*sukha* means 'Nibbānic happiness.' But here 'pleasurable feeling' only is intended.

In such passages as, 'manifest *vedanā* occur to me'—the word *vedanā* should mean 'what is felt.'

The word *dukkha* signifies 'painful feeling,' 'basis of misery,' 'unpleasant object,' 'cause of evils,' 'station of evil as cause,' etc. To illustrate: In such passages as, 'By getting rid of *dukkha*,'[9] *dukkha* means 'painful feeling.' In such passages as, 'Birth is *dukkha*,'[10] *dukkha* means 'basis of misery.' In such passages as, 'Mahāli, inasmuch as matter is *dukkha*, falls and descends on *dukkha*,'[11] *dukkha* means 'painful object.' In such passages as, '*Dukkha* it is to accumulate evil,'[12] *dukkha* means 'cause of misery or ill.' In such passages as, 'Not easy, bhikkhus, is it to succeed in describing how *dukkha* are the purgatories,'[13] *dukkha* means 'place occasioning suffering.' But here

---

[1] *Dhp.* 194. [2] *Udāna* ii. 1. [3] *S.* iii. 69. [4] *A.* iv. 89.

[5] *M.* iii. 172; but upamā replaces akkhānena pāpuṇituṃ. Cf., however, below *n.* 5, where quotation and text *ibidem* agree.—Ed.

[6] *S.* i. 5, 200. [7] Not traced. [8] *Dhp.* 203, 204.

[9] From the formula for Fourth Jhāna; Cf., *e.g.*, *Dhs.* § 165.

[10] *Vin.* i. 10 (*Vin. Texts* i. 95). [11] *S.* iii. 69.

[12] *Dhp.* 117. [13] *M.* iii. 169.

it should be understood to mean only 'painful feeling.' The word-definitions are as follows: That which gives happiness is pleasure or ease; and that which causes misery is pain or ill. That which is neither ill nor pleasure is 'neutral' (*adukkha-m-asukha*), where the letter 'm' is inserted by rules of [philological] combination. All these three kinds are termed 'feeling' because the taste of an object of sense is experienced or enjoyed.

Among them, pleasure has the characteristic of experiencing a desirable object of sense; pain, an undesirable object; that which is neither pain nor pleasure, a (neutral) object opposed to both.

The expression 'associated with' is used with all the three terms. It literally means 'joined equally or together in a variety of ways.' In what ways? 'In ways of a common origin,' etc. [42] (In the *Kathāvatthu* the question:)[1] 'Are there not some states associated with some (other) states?' being answered by 'No,' (the Theravādin goes on:) 'In denying it, are there not some states, accompanied by co-existent states, or mixed with some (other) states, having a common origin, a common cessation, a common basis and a common object of sense?' The meaning of 'association' is thus explained by means of having a common origin and so on. Hence 'associated with' means 'conjoined with in various ways of having a common origin,' etc.

In the triplet of 'results,'[2] the effects of moral and immoral (volitions) which are distinct from each other are called 'results,' a name given to certain mental states which have reached the state of maturity (through distinct causes called moral and immoral volitions).

'States that involve resultant states' mean 'states which bear their own intrinsic nature of causing results.'[3] Just as beings who by their intrinsic nature are liable to birth and old

---

[1] *K.V.* vii. 2 (p. 337; trans. 196). [2] *Dhs.* p. 1.

[3] Vipākadhamma-dhammā, the first 'dhamma' in this expression is synonymous with 'sabhāva,' which is further explained by 'pakatika.' 'Vipākadhammā by itself would mean 'results,' but the whole expression refers to causes effecting those results.—*Tr.*

age are said to be subject to birth and old age, so states by virtue of their producing results should be understood to mean 'state possessing the intrinsic nature of causing results.' The third term (viz., 'states which are neither results nor causes') is said by way of rejecting both.[1]

In the triplet of 'Grasped and favourable to grasping,' 'grasped' means—seized-as-effect by a kamma, attended by craving and wrong view in the act of sensing or thinking of an object. *Upādāniyā* means 'favourable to grasping' because of the connection with grasping by having become objects. The term is applied to objects of grasping. 'Effects grasped and favourable to grasping' (*upādinnupādāniyā*) is a name given to material and mental states born of kamma attended by the 'intoxicants' (*āsava's*). In this way, but in the negative sense, the meaning of the remaining two terms should be understood.

In the triplet of 'Corrupt and corrupting,' 'corrupting' means 'that which corrupts' (*i.e.*, oppresses or torments a being). 'Corrupt' means 'arisen or occurring together with the corruptions.' 'Corruptible' means—capable of becoming corrupt by attending to self as an object, or permanently conjoined with corruption owing to inability to get beyond the state of being objects of corruption. It is a name given to objects of corruption. Corrupt [states][2] which are (at the same time) objects of corruption are called 'corrupt and corruptible.' The remaining two terms should be understood in the same way as in the preceding triplet (*i.e.*, in the negative sense).

[43] In the triplet of 'Initial application of mind,' 'with initial application of mind' means 'occurring together with initial application of mind by virtue of conjunction therewith;' 'with sustained application of mind' means 'occurring with sustained application of mind.' 'With initial and sustained applications of mind' means 'occurring together with both initial and sustained applications of mind.' 'Without initial

---

[1] *I.e.*, 'vipākabhāva,' state of being a result, and 'vipākasabhāva,' a cause possessing the nature of producing results.—*Tr.*

[2] *I.e.*, subject to corruption.—*Tr.*

and sustained applications of mind' means 'devoid of both.' 'Only with sustained application of mind' means 'having the sustained application of mind alone out of the two kinds of application, initial and sustained, as its measure.' The meaning is that such states are not conjoined with initial application over and above the sustained application of mind. 'Without initial and with sustained application of mind only' means 'having the sustained application of mind as its measure without the initial application.'

In the triplet of 'zest,' 'accompanied by zest' means 'gone into a state of having a common origin, etc., with zest,' *i.e.*, 'associated with zest.' The remaining two terms should be explained in the same way.

But in the third and last term 'hedonic indifference' means neutral feeling. It may be verbally defined as 'that which views equably the occurrence of the aspects of pain and pleasure, and may be further amplified thus: 'proceeds under a medium condition by occupying a neutral position.' Thus this triplet is described to show the distinction between pleasure with zest, and pleasure without zest by taking the two terms from the triplet of feeling.

In the triplet of 'insight,' 'by insight' means 'by the path of the stream-winner.' For it is called insight because of the first glimpse of Nibbāna.

But although the 'son-by-adoption'[1] gets as such his first glimpse of Nibbāna, he is as a man come to the presence of the king on a certain business, who sees from far the king going about on elephant-back by a certain route and, on being asked whether he had seen the king, replies that he had not, because his business had not been transacted. In the same way although a man has seen Nibbāna, he cannot be said to have insight, because the corruptions to be got rid of have not been got rid of. That knowledge indeed stands at the point of the Path[2] where the mind turns toward [its goal].

---

[1] On this term (gotrabhū) see *Compendium*, pp. 55, 215. Childers's *Dict.*, *s.v.*

[2] *I.e.*, it occupies the same position in the process of Path-thought as 'adverting' does in an ordinary process of thought.—*Tr.*

'By culture' means 'by the remaining three Paths,' for they arise by virtue of cultivating (or developing) the four Ariyan Truths already seen by the First Path. They do not see anything not already seen previously; hence they are called 'culture' or development. The third term is described by way of rejecting both.

In the immediately following triplet, the expression 'having root-conditions removable by insight' refers to those states the roots of which are so removable. The second phrase should be explained in the same way. But the third term: 'not having root-conditions removable either by insight or by culture' [requires a different treatment. It] must not be understood to mean those states the roots of which are removable neither by insight nor by culture.[1] It must be taken to mean those which have no roots removable either by insight or by culture.[2] [44] Otherwise, unconditional states would not be included. For these contain no roots removable by insight or culture. Moreover, it would imply the removal, by insight or culture, of states other than roots in the conditional states, not of the roots themselves.[3] In point of fact, the expression 'not removable either by insight or by culture' was said with reference to the roots themselves, but not to those other states *which are not roots.* Neither of these interpretations is intended. Therefore the third term 'not having roots removable either by insight or by culture' should be understood to mean those states which *do not have* roots removable either by insight or by culture.

In the triplet of 'leading to accumulation,'[4] 'accumulation' means 'that which is accumulated by kamma and corruptions. It is a name for the processes of rebirth and decease. 'Leading to accumulation' are 'those causes which by being accom-

---

[1] In other words, the phrase should not be rendered by 'having roots not removable by insight nor by culture.'—*Tr.*

[2] In other words, the phrase should be rendered by 'not having roots removable by insight or by culture.'—*Tr.*

[3] The reasoning involved herein is that if roots are not removable something other than roots must be removable.—*Tr.*

[4] *Dhs.* p. 2,

plished go to, or lead a man, in whom they arise, to that round of rebirth.' It is a name for co-intoxicant moral or immoral states. Nibbāna being free from 'cumulation,' which is another word for 'accumulation,' is called 'dispersion.'[1] 'Leading to dispersion' is 'going towards that dispersion which he has made his object.' It is a name for the Ariyan Paths. Or, 'leading to accumulation' are 'those states which go about severally arranging (births and deaths in) a round of destiny like a bricklayer who arranges bricks, layer by layer, in a wall.' 'Leading to dispersion' are those states which go about destroying that very round, like a man who continually removes the bricks as they are laid by the mason. The third term is spoken by way of rejecting both.

In the triplet of 'Appertaining to studentship,' this phrase means 'occurring among the three kinds of study.' These associated states are also called 'appertaining to studentship,' because they belong to the seven stages of study, and because they themselves form the subject of study by reason of the incompleted course of study. From there being no higher study to acquire, certain states are called 'Not appertaining to studentship.' Or, developed states of mature study are called by this name, which is a synonym for the things constituting the Fruition which is Arahantship.[2] The third phrase is used in rejecting both.

In the triplet of 'Limited,' the word 'limited' is applied to a little mass, as in 'a small or little mass of cowdung,'[3] etc., because of its being cut off all round. States which, because of their small power are like little objects, are called 'limited,' a name given to things pertaining to the universe of sense. 'Sublime' means 'having reached greatness,' from ability to discard corruptions, from the abundance of fruition, from the length of duration; or it means 'have been reached by great persons,' *i.e.*, persons with noble intention, energy, impulse, and understanding.

[45] States such as lust, etc., which form a limit are called 'Finite.' 'Infinite' means 'having no such limit either by

---

[1] Namely, of the cumulative round of rebirth.

[2] Viz., the eighth stage.

[3] *Saṃyutta* iii. 144.

way of objects of sense or of association,' or it means 'being opposed to limit.' In the triplet of 'limited objects of sense,' this expression means 'having limited states as objects.' Likewise in the two remaining terms.

In the triplet of 'Low,' this word means 'base' and is applied to immoral states; 'medium' means 'existing midway between low and exalted,' and is applied to the remaining states of the three planes. 'Exalted' has the meanings of 'excellent' and 'unstinted,' and is applied to transcendental states.

In the triplet of 'False,' this word means 'of false nature,' partly by reason of not realizing expectations, such as 'they will bring advantage and happiness to me,' and partly by reason of the reversibility of the beautiful, etc., by their opposites. When giving results of a false nature, certain states are called 'uniform,' as invariably giving the inevitable results immediately after the dissolution of the aggregates.[1] Therefore 'false and uniform' means 'both false in (nature) and uniform (in giving results).' Opposed to what has been said above, 'true' means 'of true nature.' 'True and uniform' means 'true and uniform by way of fructification immediately after themselves.' 'Not uniform' means 'not uniform in both ways.'

In the triplet of 'Object of the Path,' 'Path' means 'that which leads to, *i.e.*, seeks for Nibbāna, or that which goes to Nibbāna destroying the corruptions.' 'Objects of the Path' are 'states having the Path as their object.' 'Conditioned by the Path' means (*a*) 'having the Eightfold Path as their special condition, in causal relation to root-conditions,' or (*b*) 'Conditions associated with, or occurring in, the Path.' Therefore the expression may mean 'having those associated root-conditions in the Path,' or, 'having the root-condition which is the Path,' since right views themselves are at once the Path and the condition. 'Dominated by the Path'

---

[1] *I.e.*, at 'death.' When many acts having such results are done, that only which is strongest gives the result, and not the rest, which are ineffective.—*Ṭīkā.*

means 'having the dominance of the Path by reason of overwhelming (the dominated).'

In the triplet of 'Arisen,' this word means uprisen or happened, *i.e.*, having reached (a state) from the nascent up till the cessant instant. 'Not arisen' means not yet appeared. 'Bound to arise' refers to states which will inevitably arise as part of a completed cause.

In the triplet of 'Past,' this word means passed beyond (*a*) their own characteristics, or (*b*) the momentary states beginning with the nascent instant. By 'future' is meant 'has not yet reached those two conditions.' By 'present' is meant 'uprisen in dependence upon this or that cause.'

In the immediately next triplet, 'their past object' means 'having a past object.' And the same with the remaining two terms.

[46] In the triplet of 'Personal,' this word refers to states which occur after making a locus of selves as though with the understanding 'we shall consider or take things thus existing to be we ourselves.' The word 'personal' (*ajjhatta*) has a fourfold content, namely, personal in field, in self-reference, (just) personal, personal in range.

In such sentences as, 'Ānanda, mind should be well focussed by that bhikkhu as *ajjhatta*, namely, only in that symbol of concentration which has been practised before '[1]; 'inwardly rapt (*ajjhattarato*) and concentrated'[2] *ajjhatta* means 'personal in field.' In such passages as, 'He lives contemplating states, even among states which are pleasing as *ajjhatta*,'[3] *ajjhatta* means 'subjective.' In such passages as 'The six *ajjhattika* sense-organs,'[4] *ajjhatta* means 'personal.' In such passages as, 'This, Ānanda, is the life fully attained by the Tathāgata, to wit, that he, by disregarding all provocative signs and symbols, has reached the *ajjhatta* Void and therein abides,'[5] *ajjhatta* means 'range' in the sense of 'dominion.' The attainment of Fruition is named the dominion of the Buddhas, but here the meaning

---

[1] *Majjhima* iii. 112. [2] *Dīgha* ii. 107. [3] *Ibid.* ii. 301.
[4] *Paṭṭisambhidāmagga* i. 122. [5] *Majjhima* iii. 111.

of 'personal' is intended. Hence states occurring in one's own continuity and pertainng to each individual are to be understood as 'personal.'[1]

But states outside that personality, whether bound up with the controlling faculties or not, are termed 'external.' The third term is spoken by virtue of both.

The immediately following triplet refers to states occurring in the act of attending to just these three kinds of states (*i.e.*, personal, external, externo-personal) as objects.

In the triplet of 'Visible,' states which arise together with sight, *i.e.*, visibility, are termed 'visible.' States which arise together with opposition called 'impact,'* are termed 'reacting.' Some states are termed 'both visible and reacting.' Unseen states are termed 'invisible.' Some invisible states react as described. The third term is used in rejecting both.

So far for the word-by-word commentary on the terms in the table of contents of the triplets.

CHAPTER II

THE COUPLETS

In the table of contents of the couplets we shall comment on those words which have not been found in the triplets.

First and foremost, in the condition-group,[2] *hetu-dhammā* (or *hetū dhammā*) are states called [special] conditions in the sense of roots. [47] The term 'non-condition' is used in

---

[1] 'We, who are but parts existing in such a unique manner by way of inclusion in an individual series of personalities through our characteristic functions of contact, etc., as well as through our sense-organs, etc., constitute the self (attā, kāya), being the totality of (the five aggregates, etc., called) the self-state (attabhāva), which is a whole. The term 'personal' is applied to states which make the self (*i.e.*, the totality of the five aggregates) a locus of parts or selves, or a locus of self-idea as though with this convention, "we shall understand thus," *i.e.*, in the aforesaid sense'—*Pyī Sadaw*.

* Paṭihanana.

[2] Hetu rendered 'cause' in *B.P.E.*; cf. p. 274, *n.* 1; also S. Z. Aung in *Compendium* 279 *f.* *Dhs*. p. 2.

rejecting them. 'Conditional' means 'occurring together with roots by way of association.' 'Unconditional' means 'having no roots which occur in a similar way.' States conjoined with roots by way of a common origin, etc., are termed 'associated with root-conditions.' States disjoined from roots are termed 'dissociated from root-conditions.' Though there is no difference in meaning between the two couplets (viz., the 'conditional' and the 'associated with root-conditions'), they have been thus specified, partly by way of embellishment of the discourse and partly to meet the needs of those persons who thus gain enlightenment. Next, after the last-mentioned couplet, combining the first couplet with the second and the third couplets, the other three couplets are uttered as they ought to be, by virtue of such terms as 'condition' and 'not-condition,' etc. Therein, as the phrase 'conditions as well as conditional states' occurs in the text, so also 'conditions as well as unconditional states' may be formed on analogy; moreover, as 'conditional states but not conditions' occur, so also 'unconditional states but not conditions' may be formed anew. The same method should be followed in conjoining (root-conditions and not-root-conditions) with the couplet of 'associated with root-conditions.'

Though the expression, 'States which are not root-conditions are conditional as well as unconditional' would suffice, an extra phrase was used 'But indeed,' when it was said 'But indeed states which are not root-conditions,' etc., in the text. It may be understood that the following additional meaning is implied by its use. How? Not only states which are not root-conditions (*hetu's*) may be classified as conditional and unconditional, but others also are so classifiable. Nay, more. Not only may the former be so classified, but they may be classified also in other ways. The meaning intended here is: just as states which are not root-conditions are conditional and unconditional, so are states which are root-conditions. Again, just as the former are classified into conditional and unconditional, so may they be classified with 'associated with root-conditions' and 'dissociated from root-conditions.' Such is the extra-signification.

In the couplet of 'Lesser Intermediate,' states which occur together with their own completed cause in a relation are termed 'relative.' States without any causal relation either at the time of genesis or of duration are termed 'absolute' (or non-relative). 'Conditioned'[1] means made by a concurrence of causes-in-relation.' 'Unconditioned means not-made or conditioned.'

States [or bodies] which possess properties of matter in an inseparable state are termed 'material.'[2] States which have no such material properties or qualities are termed 'immaterial.' Or, states possessing matter which has the characteristic of physical change are termed 'material.' Those which are not so changeable are termed 'immaterial.'

In the expression 'worldly phenomena' the round of rebirth is called 'the world' (*loka*), because of its dissolving and crumbling (*lujjana*, etc.). States which are joined to the world by being included therein are termed 'worldly.'[3] [48] To have passed beyond the 'worldly' is to be unworldly, lit., 'ulterior.' Things which have passed beyond the worldly, being not included therein, are termed 'transcendental' (lit., 'ultra-world').[4]

By 'knowable or known by anyone' is meant knowable, etc., by any one of the modes of cognition, visual, etc. The opposite follows, and completes the couplet.

In the Intoxicant-group, 'intoxicants' are 'things which flow,'[5] *i.e.*, flow or arise from the senses and the mind. Or Intoxicants may be defined as things which, as states, 'flow' up to the stage of adoption and which, as in space, 'flow' as far as the topmost plane of existence. The meaning is that they occur keeping these states[6] within that extent of space. The prefix *ā* in *āsava* (intoxicant) is, indeed, used in the sense of 'keeping within.' Or, as the juices of the *madira*[7] fruits, etc., become intoxicants by fermentation for a

---

[1] *Saṅkhata, asaṅkhata. B.P.E.:* 'compound, uncompounded.'

[2] *Dhs.* p. 3 [3] Lokiya. *B.P.E.:* 'mundane.'—*Tr.* [4] Lokuttara.

[5] Like putridity, exuding from a wound.—*Pyī Sadaw.*

[6] Henceforth the text usually takes dhammā (states) as understood.

[7] *Bassia latifolia*, out of which monks are permitted to make sweet decoctions.—*Tr.*

length of time, so certain states which are like these intoxicants are termed *āsava's*. It is customary to call long-fermented *madira* wines, etc., intoxicants. If by long fermentation they are named intoxicants, then these mental states are also worthy of the name. For it has been said: 'No ultimate point of ignorance is apparent, bhikkhus, so that one may say, "once there was no ignorance."'[1] Or, 'intoxicants' are those states which fructify or beget the pains of the ocean of births of long duration. States other than these are not intoxicants. The 'co-intoxicant' states are those which occur together with the arisen intoxicants, with themselves (co-intoxicants) as objects.[2] Those which have no intoxicants (as subjects) are 'non-intoxicant.' The remainder should be understood as explained in the condition-group, but with this difference: In that group the last couplet, to wit, 'But the states which are not root-conditions, indeed, are either conditional or unconditional,' was obtained by placing the second term of the first couplet at the beginning; but here in this group no such final couplet as 'Now the non-intoxicants are with or without intoxicants' has been explicitly stated. Although it has not been so expressed, this couplet and other divisions will be understood as in the foregoing.

In the Fetter-group the states which join or bind in repeated rounds of birth the person in whom they exist are termed 'fetters.' States other than these are termed 'not fetters.' States which, having become objects of sense, help the growth of the fetters by being bound up therewith are termed 'tending to fetters.'[3] This is the name given to the objects, the fetters. Those which are not objects of sense are termed 'not tending to fetters.' [49] The remainder should be understood in the same way as in the condition-group.

In the Knot-group, states which knot or tie in repeated rounds of birth by way of birth and decease the person in whom they exist are termed 'knots.' States other than these

---

[1] *Aṅguttara* v. 113. Ignorance is one of the āsavas.

[2] *Or*, 'The objects of intoxicants occurring together with their subjects are termed co-intoxicants.'—Tr.

[3] Saṃyojaniya. *B.P.E.*: 'favourable to the Fetters.'

are termed 'non-knots.' States which are entangled in, or fastened by, the knots by virtue of being their objects are termed 'liable to knots.' The remainder should be understood in the same way as in the condition-group. The same method of understanding by implications is to be followed in what remains unsaid in the other pairs.

In the Flood-group,[1] states which sink, submerge in repeated rounds of birth the person in whom they exist are termed 'floods.' States which are liable as objects to be overwhelmed by the floods are termed 'subject to floods.' Only[2] those states which are the objects of floods should be taken.

In the Yoke-group, states which yoke to repeated rounds of birth the person in whom they exist are termed 'yokes.' The 'yokeable' should be understood in the same way as in the foregoing.

In the Hindrance-group states which hinder the mind are termed 'hindrances.' 'Liable to be hindered' should be understood in the same way as with the Fetters.

In the Reversion group[3] states which, passing beyond the impermanence, etc., of things as they really are and, by assuming them to be permanent, etc., handle them reversely, are termed 'reversing.' Things which, as objects of sense, are handled in a reverse manner by the 'reversion' are termed 'reversed.'

In the Greater Intermediate couplet, states are termed 'objective'[4] from arising together with objects, because they cannot exist without objects. States which have no objects are termed 'subjective.' 'Consciousness' (*citta*) is so called from thinking (*cit*) of an object, or because it is variegated (*citta, citra*). States which are inseparably joined to the mind are termed 'mental properties.'[5] States which are thoroughly mixed up with consciousness from the nascent stage to the cessant are termed 'mixed with consciousness.' States which

---

[1] *Dhs.* p. 4. [2] Reading eva. P.T.S. ed.: evaṃ.

[3] Parāmāsa-gocchakaṃ. *B.P.E.:* 'Group on Contagion.' *Dhs.* p. 5.

[4] Lit. co-object. *B.P.E.:* 'having a concomitant object of thought.'

[5] Cetasika. *B.P.E.:*—'involved in the life of sense.' *Compendium* —'mental properties.'

though arising simultaneously with consciousness, do so without being thoroughly mixed therewith, are termed 'unmixed with consciousness.'

States by which some things arise are termed 'origin.' Those states which have consciousness for origin are termed 'originated by consciousness.'[1]

States which occur together are termed 'connate.' States which occur together with consciousness are termed 'connate with consciousness.'

States which always follow others are termed 'inevitable successors.' What do they follow? Consciousness. Those which follow consciousness are termed 'mental successors.'

States which are thoroughly mixed with consciousness and are originated by consciousness are termed 'mixed with and originated by consciousness.' [50] States which are thoroughly mixed with, originated by, and co-natal with consciousness are termed 'mixed with, originated by consciousness in co-nativity.' States which are thoroughly mixed with, originated by, and invariably follow consciousness are termed 'mixed with and originated by consciousness in succession.'

All the remaining terms are to be understood by way of contradiction of the terms explained.

By what has been said in the triplet of 'personal' with reference to the six subjective organs of sense, these subjective organs alone are termed 'internal.' States outside of these are termed 'external.'

[States or material qualities] which cling to the Four Essentials,[2] but which are not clung to as are the Essentials, are termed 'derived.' [States] which not only cling, but are also clung to[3] are termed 'underived.'

In the Grasping-group, states which cling strongly (to objects of sense) in the sense of holding fast are termed 'grasping.' States other than these are termed 'non-grasping.'

In the Corruption-group the meaning should be understood in the same way as in the 'corrupt' triplet.

---

[1] *B.P.E.*: 'sprung from thought.'

[2] *B.P.E.*: 'The four great phenomena.'

[3] The word *upādiyanti* is taken in both an active and a passive sense; as *nissayanti* and *nissīyanti*.—*Pyī*.

In the Final Couplets,[1] states which for the most part frequent the abodes of sense are termed *kāmāvacara*. Those that generally frequent the abodes of attenuated matter are termed *rūpāvacara*.[2] Those that frequent the immaterial abodes are termed *arūpāvacara*. This is but an abstract of the Final Couplets. The detailed account will appear hereafter. States which are limited by or included in the round of the triple plane of existence are termed 'Included.' Those not so limited are termed 'Unincluded.' States which, cutting the roots of the rounds of repeated births and making Nibbāna their object, go out from the rounds are termed 'leading out.' Those which do not go out in this manner are termed 'not leading-out.' From the certainty of yielding fruit immediately after decease, or after their own occurrence, states are termed 'certain.'[3] From not being certain in like manner states are termed 'uncertain.'

States which outstrip others are termed 'ulterior.' States which arise together with 'ulterior states' capable of outstripping themselves are termed 'co-ulterior.' Those which have no such ulterior states (beyond themselves) are termed 'incomparable.'

States through which beings bewail are termed 'harm.'[4] Beings overcome by lust and so on bewail in various ways. 'Harm' is the name given to such lust, etc. States which arise together with such harm (as causes of grief) by virtue of association, and a common establishment for riddance in one and the same individual are termed 'harmful.' States which have no such grievous causes are termed 'harmless.'

---

[1] *Dhs.* p. 6.

[2] *B.P.E.*: 'the world of form.' Rūpa may mean (*a*) material, (*b*) visible object. On rūpa as 'attenuated matter,' cf. *Dialogues* ii. 244, 264.—*Ed.*

[3] The five anantariyakammas and niyatamicchādiṭṭhi yield fruit immediately after the next decease. The four Paths yield fruit immediately after their own occurrence. Cf. *Dhs.* § 1290; *Points of Controversy* 275, *n.* 2.

[4] Raṇa = (*a*) reṇu—'dust,' or 'mist' of lust, etc.; (*b*) 'fight, war' against the Paths; (*c*) 'pain' (dukkhavighāta), anguish (upāyāsa) and distress (pariḷāha), which are the fruits of immoralities.—*Ṭīkā*. *B.P.E.*: 'concomitant with war.'

CHAPTER III

SUTTA PHRASES

IN the couplets drawn from the Suttas,[1] states which by virtue of association pertain to wisdom are termed 'partaking of wisdom,' also because they arise as parts and portions of wisdom. Herein eight modes of wisdom, viz., knowledge of insight, potency of the will-power, the six kinds of super-knowledge, belong to wisdom. [51] In the latter sense any one of these eight is wisdom, the rest being considered as parts thereof. Thus wisdom and its associated parts should be understood as 'belonging to wisdom.' But here only states associated with wisdom are meant.

States which by virtue of association belong to ignorance are termed 'belonging to ignorance'; also because they arise as parts and portions of ignorance. Herein ignorance is fourfold: intellectual darkness concealing the Fact of Ill, its origin, its cessation, and the Path leading to cessation.

By the first method, 'belonging to ignorance' also includes states associated with these four modes of ignorance. Any one of these is ignorance, the others being considered as 'belonging to ignorance.' Thus it should be understood that ignorance and states associated therewith 'belong to ignorance.' But here in this couplet only the associated states are meant.

Again, states, which from their powerlessness to overwhelm, their inability to destroy, the darkness of the corruptions, are like lightning flashes, are termed 'lightning-like.' States which, from their ability to destroy the darkness of their corruptions completely, are like the thunderbolt, are termed 'resembling the thunderbolt.'

States established in fools are termed 'foolish.' They are so called figuratively after the customary name of 'fools,' given to persons in whom they are established. From being established in the wise, states are called 'wise.' They are so called figuratively after the customary name of 'wise,' given

---

[1] *Dhs.* p. 7.

to persons in whom they are established. *Or,* 'foolish' from producing folly, 'wise' from producing wisdom.

By 'black' is meant 'dark,' *i.e.*, capable of causing absence of brightness of mind. 'White' means 'capable of causing mental brilliance.' *Or,* because of being the cause of rebirth in miserable planes, states are termed 'black'; and because of being the cause of rebirth in happy abodes, states are termed 'white.'

States which [figuratively] burn both here and hereafter are termed 'burning.' Those which do not so burn are termed 'not burning.'

The three couplets beginning with the 'synonymous' couplet have no difference whatsoever in meaning; the difference is only in the letter. With mere words made their bases, such expressions as 'luck-bringing,' and 'wealth-bringing,'[1] etc., are termed 'synonyms.'

'Etymology' is the derivation of words expressed together with the reason in word-definition as in the example, 'Bhikkhus, *saṅkhārās* are those states which compose what is compound.'[2] The meanings of the derivation are termed *niruttipathā*.

Terms, signifying (one and the same idea) in various ways, *e.g.*, *takka, vitakka, saṅkappa*,[3] are called 'expressions.' The meanings of expressions are termed *paññattipathā*. [52] Of these three couplets, having uttered one couplet (not different in sense from the other two) the motive in uttering the other two should be understood from what has been said in the Condition-group (p. 62).

In the mind and matter group, the term 'mind' (*nāma*) is applied to mental properties, because 'names' once given to them are fixed, or because they bend (*namanti*) objects, or because as objects they bend the mind unto themselves. 'Matter' is that which changes its state or condition.[4] This herein is the abstract; the detailed account will appear in the chapter on the Summary.

---

[1] Lit. luck-increasing. [2] *Saṃyutta* iii. 87.

[3] *I.e.*, calling a single thing, viz., thought, by three names.

[4] (According to heat or cold, etc.) Cf. *op. cit.* iii. 86.

Nescience of the Truths of Ill, etc. is termed 'ignorance.' The wish to live is termed 'craving for existence.'[1]

The 'theories of becoming,' of 'eternalism,' 'non-becoming,'[2] and 'annihilation' refer respectively to the fact of renewed life, eternal life, extinction, and annihilation of life. The process-theories of eternalism, annihilationism, infinity, and finity refer respectively to the views that the soul and the world are eternal, will be annihilated, are infinite, are finite.

The view concerned with the ultimate beginning [of things] is termed 'the view of ultimate beginning.' The view concerned with the ultimate end is analogous.

'Unconscientiousness' is the state of a person who is not ashamed of doing shameful things; it is shamelessness in detail. 'Carelessness of blame' is the state of a person who does not fear what should be feared; it is recklessness in detail. Conscientiousness and discretion are the opposites.

In 'surliness,' etc., a man of conflicting views, who delights in opposition. is devoid of regard for the faith and speaks unpleasant words is said to be 'surly.' The act of such a man is termed 'surly speech'; the state of such a man is termed 'surliness.'

He who has evil friends, such as unbelievers, is termed 'in evil friendship.' 'Suavity' and 'in good friendship' should be understood as the opposite in sense to what has been said.

'The offences' are the five and also the seven classes of offence. 'Proficiency in dealing with the offences' thus declared and in the restoration from these offences [refer to canonical rules].

'Proficiency in attainments' is a name given to discernment of the stages of ecstasy.[3] [53] 'Proficiency in emerging from attainments' is analogous.

'Proficiency in the elements,' . . . 'in attention,' . . . 'in the field of sense,' . . . 'in causal genesis,' . . . 'in occasions' refer respectively to the eighteen elements, to observation of the same, to the organs and objects of sense, to the twelve

---

[1] Lit. 'craving to become.'—*Ed.*

[2] Vibhava-diṭṭhi.

[3] *Or*, 'proficiency in determining the period of jhanic ecstasy induced or entered into.'—*Tr.*

factors in [the formula of] causal genesis, and to what is, or is not the occasion or cause of an event. A cause is described as 'occasion,' because in dependence on it result or fruition is established.

'Uprightness,' 'mildness,' refer to persons so qualified. The state of forbearance in a patient person is termed 'patience'; 'temperance,' the state of one delighting in good (*su-*).

The state of friendliness known as gentleness, causing equal happiness to all, is termed 'amity.' Just as the presence of others leaves no gap around us, so courtesy is a spreading out with things spiritual and material.

The state called 'door-unguardedness as to faculties' refers to lack of restraint of the five controlling powers [or senses] with mind as the sixth. The state of not knowing the measure of the accepting and the partaking of food is 'intemperance in food.' The following couplet should be understood as the contrary of the foregoing.

The state of a person with lapse of memory, known as absence of mind, is termed 'obliviousness.' 'Non-comprehension' is the state of not knowing adequately [or thoroughly].

The faculty which is mindful is termed 'mindfulness'; that which understands adequately is termed 'comprehension.'

'The power of reflection' is the not wavering on account of non-reflection. The strength arisen in one who, with energy as his principal means, develops the seven factors of enlightenment is termed 'the power of culture.'

That which lulls or quiets opposing influences is termed 'calm.'[1] That which sees things in various ways as impermanent, etc., is termed 'insight.' Calm which has taken an object, and again induces calm, becomes the causal symbol for the latter. Similarly for the term 'the mark of support.'[2] [54] That which upholds associated states is termed 'support.' That which does not oscillate about various objects is termed 'balance.'

Moral failure reckoned as non-restraint capable of destroying

---

[1] *Dhs.* p. 8.

[2] Paggaha. *B.P.E.*: 'grasp.'

virtue is termed 'moral depravity.' The failure of views called erroneous opinion capable of destroying right views is termed 'depravity of view.'

Perfection of morality is termed 'moral perfection,'[1] because the morality of one who delights in good deeds perfects or accomplishes virtue. Knowledge which has resulted in perfection of view is termed 'attainment[1] in theory.'

The purity of virtue, namely, virtue which has arrived at a state of extraordinary purity, is termed 'moral purity.' The insight which is capable of reaching purity, *i.e.*, Nibbāna, is termed 'purity of view.' By the sayings:[2] (*a*) 'But now pure views,' as well as (*b*) 'the effort of one who has adequate views,' is meant (*a*) the pure theory which knows that we are owners of our kamma, etc.,[3] and (*b*) the effort associated with that knowledge referring to views adequate to the effort.

The term 'agitation'[4] refers to fear arisen in connection with birth, etc. The causes, namely, birth, etc., productive of agitation, are termed 'occasions for agitation.' By 'the proper effort of the agitated' is meant his adequate exertions. By 'discontent in good states' is meant want of content in the accomplishment thereof. By 'non-retreat in effort' is meant the not stepping back, the not faltering in effort without reaching Arahantship.

'Wisdom' (*vijjā*) is so called because of knowing; 'emancipation' is so called because of being free (from the corruptions).[5]

By 'knowledge in destruction' is meant such knowledge arising in the Ariyan Path as is capable of destroying the corruptions. By 'knowledge in non-origination' is meant such knowledge in the Ariyan Fruition, arisen at the terminus of the Path, as is capable of causing the non-origination of the corruptions, destroyed by this and that Path.

This is the word-by-word commentary on terms in the Table of Contents.

---

[1] *Sampadā*. *B.P.E.*: 'progress.'

[2] *Aṅguttara* i. 95.

[3] *Majjhima* iii. 203.

[4] *Aṅguttara* ii. 115.

[5] *Or*. from directing the mind unrestrainedly towards the object (Nibbāna).—*Yojanā*.

PART II—ANALYSIS OF TERMS

CHAPTER I

OF THE MORAL TRIPLET

Now in order to explain the differences in the states grouped in the Table of Contents already laid down as above, there follows the classification of terms beginning with the question: Which are the moral states ?[1] The first [type of] moral thought, experienced in the universe of sense, has been shown by the words: 'When a sensuous moral thought occurs.' In its exposition, first of all, [55] there are three main sections: the determination of states, the summary, and 'emptiness.' Of these, the determination is twofold: outline and exposition. In the outline there are four divisions: question, exposition of the occasions, outline of states, and conclusion. Of these, 'which states are moral ?' is the question. 'When the sensuous . . . then' is the exposition of the occasion. 'There is touch . . . non-distraction' is the outline of states. 'On that occasion [these], or whatever other mental states there may be, which have arisen in dependence upon (those expressly mentioned):—these states are moral' is the conclusion.

Thus as to the first division, *viz.*, the question: 'which are moral states ?' is a question for the purpose of explanation. To expand: Questions are fivefold: to show something not seen before, to discuss what is already seen, to clear up doubts, to discover opinion, to explain. And this is how they differ: which is a question put to throw light on something not seen before ? The question which is put for gaining knowledge, for seeing, weighing, accomplishing, perceiving, and revealing some point which has not already been understood, seen,

---

[1] *Dhs.* § 1.

weighed, accomplished, perceived, or revealed. What is a question for discussion of views? The point has already been learnt, seen, weighed, accomplished, perceived, and revealed. But the question is put in order to discuss with other wise people. What is a question to clear up doubts? When one has come to misgivings, doubt, dubiety: 'Is it thus, is it not thus, what is it, how is it?' The question is put to remove those doubts. What is a question to discover opinion? The Blessed One in order to discover the opinion of the bhikkhus asks the question: 'What do you think, bhikkhus? Is matter permanent or impermanent?' 'Impermanent, lord.' 'And is that which is impermanent painful or pleasant?' 'Painful, [56] lord.' 'And is it proper to contemplate that state which is impermanent, painful, and reversible as "This is mine, this am I, this is myself"?' 'Nay, lord.'[1] This is the question to discover opinion. What is a question for purposes of explanation? The Blessed One asks the brethren a question in order to explain: 'Bhikkhus, there are four applications in mindfulness. Which are the four?'[2] This is the question for purposes of explanation.

Of these, the first three questions do not arise in the case of the Buddhas. And why? Because for the Buddhas there is nothing, whether conditioned in the three periods of time, or unconditioned and out of time, that has not been known, seen, weighed, accomplished, perceived and revealed. Hence for them there is no question for the illuminating of what is not seen. And there is no need for the Blessed One to discuss what has been intuited by his own knowledge with another monk or brahmin or spirit or Māra or Brahmā. Hence there can arise no question for a comparison of views. Inasmuch as the Blessed One is free from perplexity, has passed beyond doubt, and in all things is devoid of misgivings, there can arise for him no question to clear up doubts. But the other two questions occur to the Blessed One. And of these, the question: 'Which states are moral?' should be understood as having been asked for purposes of explanation.

---

[1] *Majjhima* iii. 19 *f.*

[2] *D.* ii. 290 (slightly different).

Herein by the word 'which,' the question is asked regarding states to be expounded in detail. By the mere words—'States (are) moral,' it is not possible to know how the Blessed One had treated these states, or how they functioned. But when 'which' is uttered, inquiry concerning them is manifest. Hence I have said that the word 'which' refers to the states to be expounded in detail. By the two words 'states . . . moral,' together with the question, the Buddha shows which states are under inquiry. Their meaning has been explained above.

But why, without saying 'moral states,' as in the Table of Contents, is the order reversed as 'states . . . moral'? Because after the discourse, in the Table of Contents, on the distinctions of states, it is for the purpose of showing which states possess those distinctions. In Abhidhamma just states are to be dealt with, but these in turn should be taught in various distinctive aspects, as 'moral' and so forth. Therefore here, in which only states are dealt with, is no popular discourse, and these states should be shown by way of distinctive aspects, and not merely as states in general. For a teaching on states by way of such distinctions carries with it the division of a mass, as well as the higher analytical knowledge.

Having enumerated the different classes of states (in the Table of Contents) as 'moral states' and so on, these states should now be explained by way of their distinctive aspects. [57] To show them by way of distinctions, the order of words has been reversed in 'which states are moral?' For when states have been shown to possess distinctions, it is logical and easy for the understanding to follow up the exposition with another on the distinctions.

Now as to the expression, 'when sensuous moral thought . . .': here he showed consciousness on a given occasion. The Sage first determined the occasion by the state of consciousness; then to show the specific phases of that consciousness, he showed the consciousness as being on a given occasion: 'when a sensuous moral thought, etc.' And why? Because it was by this consciousness [or thought], fixed amid the diversity of occasions by one given occasion, that the Blessed

One undertook the difficult task of enlightening us as to the aspects of the content of that thought on an occasion determined by that thought, the aspects being its continuity, mass, function, object, solidarity.*

Now here is the word-by-word comment on terms in the passage 'when,' etc. 'When' is an indefinite locative. 'Occasion' (*samaya*) denotes the time indefinitely marked by 'when.' Thus far (by these two words) an indefinite time has been shown. The word *samaya*, however:

Means harmony in antecedents, group,
Elimination, moment, penetration,
Condition, acquisition, time, opinion.[1]

E.g., in such passages as, 'Perhaps to-morrow we might approach, having regard to time and *samaya*,'[2] it means 'harmony in antecedents.' In such passages as 'Bhikkhus, there is but one moment, one *samaya* for the practice of the holy life'[3]—*samaya* means 'opportunity.' In such passages as 'Hot *samaya*,' 'fever-*samaya*'[4]—it means 'season.' In such passages as 'a large *samaya* in the great forest'[5]—*samaya* means 'assembly.' In the passage: 'Bhaddāli, you have not discerned the *samaya*: that the Blessed One is staying at Sāvatthī, and will know that the bhikkhu Bhaddāli has not perfected the training in the religion'[6]—*samaya* means 'conditions, *hetu*.' 'At that time a studious wanderer, [58] by name Māna, son of the nun Muṇḍikā, was staying in the Park of Queen Mallikā, surrounded by a fence of fig-trees and containing a hall for discussion in *samaya*'[7]—in such passages *samaya* means 'opinions'—

Whatever 'good' be in the present world,
Whatever 'good' be in the world to come—
He only is called wise who has the skill
To compass abhisamaya *of good*[8]—

---

* Santati (*sic lege* in P.T.S. ed.).

[1] *Sum. V.* i. 31 *f.*

[2] *Dīgha* i. 205.

[3] *Anguttara* iv. 227. Cf. *Saṃyutta* iv. 126; *Jāt.* i. 381.

[4] *Vin.* iv. 117 (*Vin. Texts* i. 44)

[5] *Dīgha* ii. 254.

[6] *Majjh.* i. 438.

[7] *Ib.* ii. 22; *v.l.* Maṇḍikā.

[8] *Saṃyutta* i. 87.

in such passages *samaya* means 'acquisition.' 'By the right *abhisamaya* of conceit he made an end of ill'[1]—in such passages *samaya* means 'elimination.' 'The fact of ill has the sense of oppression, of being conditioned, of burning, of reversibility, of penetrability (*abhisamayaṭṭho*)'[2]—in such passages *samaya* means 'penetration.'

Thus among its many meanings,

> *Time, harmony in antecedents, moment,*
> *Condition, group—these five the wise should note,*
> *These* samaya *here signifies.*

Thus, in the matter of moral consciousness, where 'when sensuous moral thought,' etc., is uttered, these five out of the nine meanings should be understood by the wise.

> *Here 'harmony in antecedents' meaneth*
> *Concurrency of causes: and by 'moment'*
> *The four wheels, the unique 'ninth' is understood.*

To expand: 'Harmony in antecedents' should be understood as the concurrence of causal relations established by their bringing about a common result. Again, the precise ninth moment, declared by the Blessed One in the sentence, 'Bhikkhus, there is but one moment, one opportunity for the practice of the holy life,' should be known as the ninth, the sole moment.[3]

Again, 'Bhikkhus, there are these four wheels wherewith a fourfold wheel of gods and men so endowed rolls on, viz.: dwelling in a suitable place, association with the good, self-control, accumulation of merit in previous existences.'[4] Thus four wheels have been declared, but should be classed as the one moment in the sense of occasion (or conjuncture), for they form the occasion for the production of merit.

Samaya having been shown to mean 'harmony in ante-

---

[1] *Aṅguttara* iv. 8.

[2] *Pṭs.* ii. 106 (but in P.T.S. ed. *abhisamayaṭṭho* is omitted).—*Ed.*

[3] *Aṅguttara* iv. 227. *Pss. of the Brethren* 243, *n.* 1.

[4] *Dīgha* iii. 276; *Aṅguttara* ii. 32.

cedents' and 'moment, or opportunity,' the following is the explanation of the other meanings of the word: 'Time' may be clearly shown as a notion abstracted by mere usage from this or that (event). A collection of states such as 'contact,' etc. may be clearly explained as 'a group' or 'mass.'

To expand: Time is only a concept derived from this or that phenomenon, such as (*a*) states expressed in such phrases as, 'temporal (aspect of) mind,' 'temporal (aspect of) matter'; (*b*) the phenomenal occurrence expressed by such phrases as 'the past' and 'the future'; (*c*) the phenomenal succession in an organism expressed by 'the time of seed-germination' and 'the time of sprouting'; [59] (*d*) the characteristic marks of phenomena expressed by 'the time of genesis' and 'the time of decay'; (*e*) the functions of phenomena expressed by 'the time of feeling,' and 'the time of cognizing'; (*f*) functions of beings expressed by 'the time of bathing' and 'the time of drinking'; (*g*) the modes of posture expressed by 'the time of going' and 'the time of stopping'; (*h*) the revolution of the moon, sun, etc., expressed by 'morning, evening, day, and night'; or (*i*) the grouping of days and nights, etc., into periods expressed by 'half-month,' 'month.' It should be understood that this (abstract time) is a mere concept, because it is not existing by its own nature.

The congeries of states such as contact, feeling, etc., is in our text displayed as 'groups.' *Samaya* having thus been shown to mean also 'time' and 'group,' the other meaning of 'condition' is to be understood: By 'condition' is meant 'causal relation.' That there are several conditions may be understood by way of their 'doors' or relations. To expand: In this connection a cause-in-relation is a condition. The multiplicity of conditions may be understood from their doors or relations. How so? The eye, object, light, attention, etc., are the many causes-in-relation of the sense of sight, etc., arising in the eye-door, etc. In the Great Book (the *Paṭṭhāna*) twenty-four causal relations have been taught, to wit, relation of condition, relation of object, and so forth. Excepting the causal relations of resultants and post-existence, the rest are causes-in-relation of moral states. All these two sets of causes-in-relation are here (*i.e.*, in this connection) meant by the term 'condition.' Thus the multiplicity of conditions should be understood by way of their doors or relations.

It should now be understood that these five meanings of 'harmony of antecedents' and so forth are comprehended under the word *samaya*. But why have all these five meanings instead of any one of them been so comprehended? Because the term is used to show various distinct meanings. To expand: Of these, *samaya* in the sense of 'harmony of antecedents' shows occurrence from many causes. By showing this, the view that there is one single cause[1] is contradicted. By 'harmony of antecedents' is meant the mutual contribution towards the production of a common result. Therefore this also shows that there is no single agent. For when there is a cause (adequate) in its own nature,[2] it is not fitting to look about for another cause. Thus by showing the non-existence of any one cause (the erroneous view) that pain and pleasure are created by oneself[3] is contradicted.

Herein, it may be objected that the expression, 'it shows the occurrence from many causes,' is not proper. [60] And why? Because causes which are not conditions when they exist severally, would not become conditions when they act in harmony. When every one of a hundred blind men cannot see, it is impossible for all the hundred (collectively) to see. This argument is not unreasonable. (The answer is): Causes are said to be in concord when they accomplish a result in common, and not because of the mere combination of various antecedents. And the vision of the blind men is not a result in common. Why? Because of their inability to see though there may be a hundred of them. But vision by the eye, etc., is a result in common, because when the one exists, the other arises in consequence. It is quite clear that though states may be no causes when they are not in concord, they become causes when they are in concord. This may be understood

---

[1] Such as Brahmā, Prajāpati, Purusa, Kāla, or Viṣṇu as creator (issarakāraṇavāda), or nature as cause (pakatikāraṇavāda).—*Ṭikā*.

[2] Such as the sentient organism, *e.g.*, sight and visible object.—*Pyi*.

[3] *Saṃyutta* ii. 22.

by there being no results in the absence of concord and there being results when there is concord. The failure or otherwise of a sense, *e.g.* sight when the sensitive organism is lacking, or not, is clearly proved in this world. This first of all is to show the word *samaya* in the sense of 'harmony of antecedents.'

That 'ninth moment,' which is the inverse of the eight wrong occasions, and the four wheels (of conjuncture), such as 'dwelling in a suitable place,' and so forth, is termed 'moment' in the sense of 'occasion' or 'opportunity.' It does not occur without there being a concurrence of circumstances, such as existence as a human being, the rise of the Buddha, and the stability of the good Law, etc. The difficulty of getting reborn as man, etc., has been shown by the Buddha, in the *Saṃyutta Nikāya*, by the illustration of the blind tortoise, etc.[1] Morality which renders service to transcendental states and is connected with the most subtle moment—subtle, because of the difficulty of getting it—may be said to be difficult of achievement. Thus the word *samaya* in the sense of 'moment' or 'opportunity' makes clear the difficulty of the achievement of good. By thus illustrating opportunity, the negligent life of those who, though they have arrived at the right moment, turn it into a profitless moment, without repeatedly striving to achieve good connected with that moment, is condemned. *Samaya* has thus been shown in the sense of 'moment or opportunity.' Very small is the interval for exercising moral thoughts, and the extreme rarity of such moments may be understood from the Commentary on the Sutta (*of Daḷhadhanuggaha*),[2] where it is said, 'Bhikkhus, there is the speed of this man; greater is the speed of the sun and the moon; greater is the speed of the Yama God who runs before the sun and the moon; swifter yet than that is the perishing of life's activities.'

Here, first of all, the short duration of the physical life-control is described. While (a unit of) matter which has arisen persists, sixteen thought-moments arise and break up. And no

[1] *M.* iii. 169; *S.* v. 455 *f.*

[2] *S.* ii. 266. Note the *v.l.* Yāma°.

illustration can convey the shortness of time they occupy. [61] Hence the Blessed One has said: Bhikkhus, it is no easy matter to illustrate the quickness of thoughts in their changing.[1] Thus the word *samaya* in its sense of time shows the extreme shortness of the time in the occurrence of a moral thought. By this term thus showing the shortness of time, advice has been given exhorting us to great strenuousness and earnestness in intuition,[2] albeit intuition is as difficult for the mind as stringing pearls in the dark by a lightning-flash, because of its extremely short duration. This is the exposition of *samaya* in the sense of time.

Samaya in the sense of 'group' shows the simultaneous occurrence of many states. For an aggregate of states, such as contact, etc., is said to be a 'group'; the consciousness arising in that group of states arises together with those states. Thus the co-occurrence of many states is shown. By this word showing the nature of the group, the occurrence of one 'state' only is contradicted. This is the setting forth of the meaning of *samaya* in the sense of 'group.'

Samaya in the sense of 'condition' shows the occurrence in dependence on another. The phrase 'at what time' connotes the occurrence of something when its condition exists, that is to say, of something on which it depends. By this word showing thus the condition, the conceit of one who believes that states unconditionally follow one's own will[3] is subdued. This is the meaning of *samaya* in the sense of 'condition.'

Thus the phrase *yasmiṃ samaye* when it denotes 'time,' means 'at what time'; when it denotes 'group,' it means 'in what group'; when it denotes 'opportunity,' 'harmony of antecedents,' and 'condition,' it means 'when the opportunity arrives,' 'when there is a concurrence of causes,' and 'when a condition exists,' respectively. *E.g.*, when sensuous moral consciousness springs into being, on an opportunity arriving, a concurrence of causes, or a condition existing, then contact and so forth also arise. Thus should the meaning be under-

---

[1] *Aṅguttara* (henceforth indicated by *A.*) i. 10. [2] Paṭivedha.

[3] *Sa-vasa.* In other words, the theory of absolute free-will is denied.—*Tr.*

stood. Here *samaya* in the sense of time[1] and of group is used in the locative case, *i.e.*, as locality in the sense of basis of things taught here (in Abhidhamma). By the occurrence of *samaya* as opportunity, concurrence of causes, or condition, the occurrence of those states (contact, etc.) is marked. Therefore if understood in these senses, *samaya* in the locative marks state or existence.

By 'sensuous' is meant included in the sensuous states, namely, 'Between the Avīci purgatory below and the Paranimmitavasavatti heaven above,' etc.[2]—concerning which the question and answer are put. [62] Briefly, the literal definition of the term is as follows: sensuous experience is twofold: of basis and of corruption. The latter means passionate desire; the former means the round of the triple plane of existence. Of these the sensuousness of the corruptions is so termed because it desires, and the other, the sensuousness of basis, is so termed because it is desired by, the sensuousness of the corruptions. There are eleven localities, viz.: four purgatories, one world of men and six worlds of spirits, in which this twofold sensuousness prevails. And 'sensuous' is the term applied to them all because 'sensuousness' frequents them, like the battlefield resorted to by soldiers. As the place where armed men resort is called a battlefield because it is specially characterized by them, even though there may be other creatures, unarmed bipeds and quadrupeds, resorting to the same, so though things of other universes such as that of attenuated matter frequent it, the place still continues to be called 'sensuous,' because it has been specially characterized by these modes of sensuous experience. Just as '*rūpa*-sphere' is shortened into '*rūpa*,'[3] so 'sensuous universe' is simply called 'sensuous' by eliding the latter term. Thus 'sensuous universe' means that this (first class of moral) consciousness frequents this eleven-

---

[1] How can time, being a concept, be a basis of things in Abhidhamma? Because states that occur in time marked by consciousness do not exist before or after that time.—*Ṭīkā*.

[2] *Dhs.*, § 1281.

[3] In such phrases as 'he develops the Path for the attainment of *rūpa*.'—*Tr.*

fold localized sensuousness, even though it also frequents the planes of 'attenuated *rūpa*' and of non-*rūpa*. Just as an elephant, which has earned the appellation of 'battle-experienced' from its frequenting the field of battle, continues to be known by that name although it also frequents the town; and just as living creatures whose habitat is land or water, though placed out of their own elements, are still called 'land-traversing' or 'water-traversing,' even so this (class of) consciousness, though occurring elsewhere, should be known as 'sensuous.'

Or (this consciousness is termed) sensuous because its sensuousness frequents, by way of attending to, objects of sense. Certainly it also frequents the universe of attenuated matter and that of non-matter. But a calf is so named because it 'calls' (*vaccha-vadati=vadyati*); and a buffalo is called '*mahisa*' because it lies on the ground (*mahi*). All other animals (although they also make noises and lie on the ground) do not get these names. The application of this illustration should be understood thus.

Or, this class of consciousness is called 'sensuous' because it causes rebirths to frequent the sensuous plane of existence.

By *kusala* is meant (moral) 'good' in the sense of destroying or disturbing contemptible states;[1] *or* in the sense of wholesomeness, faultlessness, and accomplishment by skill. To illustrate: in 'How are you? are you well, sir?' *kusala* is used to mean 'health,' *i.e.*, not being ill or sick or unwell in body. So in mental states it should be understood in the sense of 'health,' *i.e.*, absence of sickness, illness, or disease through the 'corruptions.' [63] Moreover, from the absence of the faultiness, hate, and torments of the 'corruptions,' *kusala* has the sense of 'faultlessness.' Understanding is described as skilfulness. 'Good' has the sense of 'brought about by skilfulness.'

Now consciousness 'associated with knowledge' may be called good (or moral). But how can consciousness 'dissociated from knowledge,' be called by that name?[2] (The

---

[1] Obtained by the scholastic word-play affected at one period by both East and West; *ku*cchitānaṃ *salana*dīhi. This has been anticipated above, p. 48 *f.*—*Ed.*

[2] See *Dhs.* (or *B.P.E.*), §§ 147, 149.

reply is): It is also called good (or moral) by a figure of speech. As a fan made not of palmyra leaves but of mats, etc., is called, figuratively, a palmyra fan from its resemblance thereto, so consciousness though dissociated from knowledge is called good or moral.

But philosophically speaking, 'consciousness associated with knowledge' is called good in the three senses of health, faultlessness, and skill; and that 'dissociated from knowledge' is called good in two senses only. 'Good' as taught by the Jātaka method, by the Bāhitika Sutta method and by the Abhidhamma method[1] is applicable to this consciousness in all three senses.

Moral Good defined by way of characteristic, etc., has faultless, happy results as its characteristic; the destruction of immoralities as its essential property; purity as its recurring manifestation; and rational attention as its proximate cause. *Or*, by being opposed to fault it has the characteristic of faultlessness; the property of purity; the recurring manifestation of desirable results; and the proximate cause of rational attention as said above.

To expand: As regards characteristics, etc., the specific or generic attributes of these, or those states, are termed the 'characteristic' (*lakkhaṇaṃ*).

Essential property (*rasa*) means function or achievement.

Recurring phenomenon (*paccupaṭṭhāna*) means mode of manifestation, or effect.

Immediate occasion (*padaṭṭhānaṃ*) means proximate cause. Thus wherever we speak of characteristics, etc., their mutual difference should be understood in this wise.

By 'consciousness' (*citta*) is meant that which *thinks* of its object, is aware variously. *Or*, inasmuch as this word 'consciousness' is common to all states or classes of consciousness, that which is known as worldly, moral, immoral, or the great inoperative,[2] is termed 'consciousness,' because it arranges itself in a series (*cinoti*, or, its own series or continuity) by way of apperception in a process of thought. And the

---

[1] As shown by the examples quoted on p. 49.—*Ed.*

[2] On this term see below, pt. x., ch. vi.

resultant is also termed 'consciousness' because it is accumulated (*cito*) by kamma and the corruptions.

Moreover, all (four classes) are termed 'consciousness' because they are variegated (*citra*) according to circumstance. The meaning of consciousness may also be understood from its capacity of producing a variety or diversity of effects.

Herein consciousness with lust is one thing, [64] that with hate is another, that with delusion is another, that experienced in the universe of sense is another, and those experienced in the universe of attenuated matter, etc., are others. Different is consciousness with a visible object, with an auditory object, etc.; and in that with visible objects, varied is consciousness of a blue-green object, of a yellow object, etc. And the same is the case with the consciousness of auditory objects.

And of all this consciousness one class is low, another is medium, and a third is exalted. Among the low class again consciousness is different when dominated by desire-to-do, or when dominated by energy, or by investigation. Therefore the variegated nature of consciousness should be understood by way of these characteristics of association, locality, object, the three degrees of comparison and dominance.

Although any single one of these is verily not variegated in itself and by itself in the sense explained thus, it is nevertheless proper to say of any one of them, that it is so called from its variegated character, because it is included in consciousness as making up a variegated whole. Thus far the first explanation of consciousness is from its variegated nature.

How is consciousness (*i.e.*, mind) capable of producing a variety or diversity of effects in action ? There is no art in the world more variegated than the art of painting. In painting, the painter's masterpiece[1] is more artistic than the rest of his pictures. An artistic design occurs to the painters of masterpieces that such and such pictures should be drawn in such and such a way. Through this artistic design there arise operations of the mind (or artistic operations) accomplishing

---

[1] Caraṇa.

such things as sketching the outline, putting on the paint, touching up, and embellishing. Then in the picture known as the masterpiece is effected a certain (central) artistic figure. Then the remaining portion of the picture is completed by the work of planning in mind as, 'Above this figure let this be; underneath, this; on both sides, this.' Thus all classes of arts in the world, specific or generic, are achieved by the mind. And owing to its capacity thus to produce a variety or diversity of effects in action, the mind, which achieves all these arts, is itself artistic like the arts themselves. Nay, it is even more artistic than the art itself, because the latter cannot execute every design perfectly. For that reason the Blessed One has said, 'Bhikkhus, have you seen a masterpiece of painting?' 'Yea, Lord.' 'Bhikkhus, that masterpiece of art is designed by the mind. Indeed, Bhikkhus, the mind is even more artistic than that masterpiece.'[1] Nay, more. All the factors of this diversified sentient organism, such as kamma, feature,* idea, language, etc., in the destinies of spirits, men, denizens of purgatories, lower animals, etc., are also wrought by the mind. Good and bad acts in various deeds, as charity, virtue, cruelty, deceit, etc., are accomplished by the mind. Hence there is a variety of kammas; and owing to this variety of kammas, there is in the various destinies [65] difference of features, *i.e.*, difference in hands, feet, ears,[2] stomachs, necks, faces, etc.; the difference in notion or idea is because of the difference in outward form, expressed by 'this is woman, this is man,' according to the form taken. The difference in the common usage of such terms as 'man,' 'woman' in language, according to ideas, is due to the difference in ideas. Because by virtue of the difference of usage in language, an act, productive (in rebirth) of this or that individuality, is performed (with the wish), 'May I be a woman, a man, a prince, a brahmin,' therefore the difference in effective action (kamma) results from the difference in usage. When the difference of actions effects a (future) existence as prayed for, because it does so through destiny, then from the

---

[1] *Saṃyutta* iii. 151. * *Liṅga.* [2] Not in P.T.S. ed.

difference in kamma results the difference in destiny. By the difference of kammas are manifested the typical or specific difference of animals without feet, of bipeds, etc., in this or that destiny of creatures; the hereditary difference of lowness or highness in the passive side of our existence; the difference of beauty, ugliness, etc., in the features of an individual; and the difference of profit and loss, etc., in worldly conditions. Hence, all the factors of this diversified sentient* organism such as character, outward appearance, idea, language, etc., in such destinies as spirits, men, denizens of purgatories, lower animals, etc., should thus be understood.

This explanation should be understood by a Sutta not rehearsed at the three Councils. For it is there said, ' By the analysis of the various divisions and subdivisions of mutually different kammas arises the determination of the various divisions and subdivisions of mutually different features. By the analysis of the various divisions and subdivisions of mutually different features various divisions and subdivisions of mutually different ideas are determined. By analyzing the various divisions and subdivisions of mutually different ideas, the discrimination of the various divisions and subdivisions of mutually different usages in language is effected. By analyzing the various divisions and subdivisions of mutually different usages in language, the various divisions and subdivisions of mutually different kammas are differentiated. In dependence on the difference in kamma appears the difference in the destiny of beings without legs, with two legs, four legs, many legs, vegetative,[1] spiritual, with perception, without perception, with neither perception nor without perception. Depending on the difference in kamma appears the difference in the births of beings, high and low, base and exalted, happy and miserable. Depending on the difference in kamma appears the difference in the individual features of beings as beautiful or ugly, high-born or low-born, well-built or deformed. Depending on the difference in kamma appears the difference in the worldly conditions of beings as gain and

---

* *Ajjhattikaṃ.*

[1] *Rūpino.*

loss, fame and disgrace, blame and praise, happiness and misery.

Further it has been said:

[66] *From kamma and form form and perceptions come,*
Perceptions differentiation cause
In things, as 'This is woman,' 'This is man.'[1]

By kamma the world moves, by kamma men
Live, and by kamma are all beings bound
As by its pin the rolling chariot wheel.[2]

By kamma one attains glory and praise,
By kamma bondage, ruin, tyranny.
Knowing that kamma bears fruit manifold,
Why say ye, 'In the world no kamma is?'[1]

'O lad, beings have kamma as their property, they are its heirs, are originated by it, are its kin, are sheltered by it. Kamma divides beings into low and exalted.'[3] By this capacity to produce a diversity of effects (in destiny) in a manner detailed above is the diversity of the mind to be understood. For all variations are done by the mind only.

Because a thought, which has no opportunity[4] (of maturing its own effects) or which lacks the remaining conditions,[5] does not produce any of the divers effects, (only) the factors of this manifold sentient organism[6] effected by the (effectual) thought have been declared. The mind is even more diverse than these. Hence the Blessed One has said, 'Bhikkhus, I see no other class so variegated as creatures of the animal kingdom; even more variegated than those creatures, bhikkhus, is the mind.'[7]

In the phrase 'is arisen,'[8] arisen (*uppanna*) has many meanings, as 'existing,' etc. Of these, all that is endowed

---

[1] Not traced. [2] *Sutta-Nipāta*, 654. [3] *Majjhima* iii. 203.

[4] Owing to prohibition by some superior kamma, or because the performer has done it in some place or at some time where no result is given.—*Tr.*

[5] Time, destiny, motive, etc.—*Tr.* [6] Ajjhattikaṃ.

[7] *Saṃyutta* iii. 152. [8] *Dhs.*, § 1.

with (instants of) genesis, decay, and dissolution is termed 'arisen as existing at the present moment.'

The moral and immoral thoughts which have ceased after experiencing their objects and which are therefore known as 'experienced and gone,' as well as the remaining conditioned things which are known as 'become and gone,' because they have ceased after having arrived at the threefold moment of genesis, decay and dissolution, are termed 'arisen as having just gone after becoming.' Because the kamma in such expressions as, 'those kammas done by him in previous existences,' stands, though past, by preventing a different result and by giving occasion to its own result, and because the result though not yet arisen invariably takes place when an opportunity is given, it is called 'arisen as having given rise to a potential opportunity of its own fruition,' or 'arisen as possessing an effected potential opportunity of occurring.'

[67] Immorality not so removed (by the Path) as not to occur in various planes of existence is termed 'arisen as having got a plane for future existence.' Here the difference between 'a plane of existence' and 'a state which has obtained a plane for future existence' should be understood.

'Plane' means the five aggregates of the three planes, which are objects of insight. The body of corruptions fit to arise in those aggregates is said to have 'obtained a plane for future existence.' For that plane is obtainable by this corruption, therefore it (*i.e.*, the body of corruptions) is said to have 'obtained a plane for future existence.' Of these four meanings of *uppanna* described here, that of 'existing at the present' is intended. Herein its word-definition: 'present or existing' is called *uppanna,* because it has arrived at the portal, so to speak, of genesis, etc., after the end of the previous state. This word *uppanna* has many meanings: 'past,' 'getting,' 'uprisen,' 'not discarded,' 'not completely cut off,' 'the totality of the three instants.'[1] In such passages as, 'Bhikkhus, at that time Kakusandha, the Blessed One, the Saint, the Supreme Buddha had *arisen* in the world'[2]—

[1] *I.e.*, the life-*unit* of any living thing—nascent, static, cessant.—*Ed.*

[2] *Saṃyutta* (henceforth indicated by *S.*) ii. 191.

uppanna is used in the sense of 'past.' 'To the elder, Ānanda has *arisen* a superfluous robe'[1]—here *uppanna* means 'getting.' 'Even, bhikkhus, as a strong wind at intervals disperses a great mass of clouds that have *arisen*'[2]—here *uppanna* means 'uprisen.' 'The wandering of the mind which has *arisen* is difficult to remove; (mindfulness on respiration) then and there causes evil, *i.e.*, immoral states, to disappear every time they have *arisen*'[3]—here *uppanna* means 'not discarded.' 'One who cultivates, practises many times the Ariyan Eightfold Path causes at intervals evil, *i.e.*, immoral, states to disappear then and there every time they have *arisen*'[4]—here *uppanna* means 'not cut off.' In the catechism, 'Is a thing arisen in the course of generation? Yes'[5]—*uppanna* has the meaning of 'reached the totality of the three instants.' Here too it means this; so that '(consciousness) has *arisen*'[6] means: 'has reached the totality of the three instants,' 'is existing,' or 'is present.' This is the meaning in brief outline. 'Consciousness has arisen' is the heading of this discourse.

But consciousness does not arise singly. Just as in saying, 'the king has arrived,' it is clear that he does not come alone without his attendants, but comes attended by his retinue, so this consciousness should be understood to have arisen with more than fifty moral (mental) phenomena. But it may be said that consciousness has arisen in the sense of a forerunner. For in worldly phenomena consciousness is the chief, consciousness is the principal, consciousness is the forerunner. [68] In transcendental phenomena, however, understanding is the chief, understanding is the principal, understanding is the forerunner. Hence when the Blessed One came to the explanation of the Vinaya he, in asking a question, did not ask, 'What is your contact, what is your feeling, what is your perception, what is your volition?' but making consciousness the principal, he asked, 'What is your mind, brother?' When answered, 'I have no mind to steal, lord,' the reply is not, 'Abstaining from theft through contact is not an offence, bhikkhu,' etc.,

[1] *Vin. Texts* ii. 213. [2] *S.* v. 50. [3] *A.* iii. 185; *S.* v. 50.
[4] *S.* v. 50. [5] *Yam.* ii. 18. [6] *Dhs.*, § 1

but 'Abstaining from theft in intention is not an offence, bhikkhu.'[1] Not merely in the explanation of the Vinaya, but also in some other lay discourses has he shown mind to be the principal. Even as he said, 'Bhikkhus, whatever states are immoral, pertain to the immoral, take sides with the immoral, all are led by mind; of these states mind arises first.'[2]

'Consciousness leads, rules, makes all modes of mind.
And whoso speaks or acts with evil mind,
Him evil follows as the wheel the ox.
Consciousness leads, rules, makes all modes of mind.
And whoso speaks or acts with a good mind,
Bliss like a faithful shadow follows him.[3]

By mind the world is led, by mind is drawn:
And all men own the sovereignty of mind.'[4]

'Bhikkhu, through mental corruptions beings are corrupted; through mental purity beings are purified.[5] This mind, bhikkhus, is dazzling, and yet it is defiled by foreign corruptions.'[6] 'Householder, when the mind is unguarded, bodily action is unguarded, speech also is unguarded, thought also is unguarded.' . . . Householder, when the mind is guarded . . . malevolent . . . not malevolent . . . saturated with lust . . . not saturated with lust . . . then acts, words and thoughts are in a corresponding state.'[7] Thus in dealing with worldly matters mind is the chief, mind is the principal, mind is the forerunner. Thus it should be understood, [69] and further, that not only one or two of these Suttas, but all are to be taken collectively so that one may support the other.

In asking questions on transcendental matters, one says not 'What contact have you acquired, what feeling, perception, or volition?' but 'Bhikkhu, what understanding have you acquired?—understanding of the first Path or the second or the third or the fourth?' laying stress on understanding as

---

[1] *Vin.* iii. 58. [2] *A.* i. 11. [3] *Dhp.*, ver. 1, 2.
[4] *S.* i. 39. *Cf.* parikassati here, there parikissati.
[5] *A.* i. 10. [6] *S.* iii. 151. [7] *A.* i. 261.

the chief and the principal. No moral states headed by understanding become degraded. But what is the purpose of understanding ? 'Bhikkhus, in the Ariyan disciple endowed with understanding there are established faith which follows it, energy which follows it, and mindfulness and concentration which follow it.'[1]

These and other Suttas should be noted here (as pointing to wisdom or understanding as the principal faculty). Thus when we come to transcendental matters, understanding is the chief, the principal, the forerunner. But we are here discussing secular matters. Hence, making mind the principal, he said, 'consciousness (*i.e.*, mind) has arisen.'

'Accompanied by joy': this means 'gone into the state of a common origin with joy, in the sense of enjoying pleasure like honey.' This word 'accompanied' (*sahagata*) has the meanings of 'corresponding nature,' 'mingled,' 'dependence,' 'object,' 'associated with.' 'This craving produces repeated births and is accompanied by passionate delight'[2]—here *sahagata* means 'of corresponding nature.' The meaning is that craving has become passionate delight. 'This investigation, bhikkhus, is accompanied by idleness, associated with idleness'[3]—here *sahagata* should be known in the sense of 'mingled,' 'mingled with idleness arising at intervals.' 'He develops that factor of wisdom called mindfulness, accompanied by the idea of the skeleton:'[4]—here *sahagata* should be understood as 'dependence.' The meaning is, 'depending on the notion of the skeleton and developing the idea, mindfulness as a factor of wisdom has been obtained.' In the passage, 'He has acquired the attainments accompanied by *rūpa*, or by the immaterial'[5]—*sahagata* is used in the sense of mental 'object.' In the passsage, 'This happiness is accompanied by this zest, [70] is coexistent and associated with it'[6]—*sahagata* is used in the sense of combination. And in this expression, 'accompanied by joy,'

[1] *S.* v. 229. [2] *S.* iii. 158. [3] *S.* v. 280
[4] *S.* v. 131. [5] Not traced.
[6] *Vibh.* 258. . . . As of water and milk.—*Ṭīkā.*

the last meaning is intended. For here 'accompanied by joy' is synonymous with 'thoroughly mixed with joy.'

And this term 'thoroughly mixed with' (*saṃsaṭṭha*) is seen with many meanings, such as 'similar,' 'saturated,' 'companionship,' 'coexistence.' 'Avoiding lean and fat horses *saṃsaṭṭha* horses (in age, appearance and speed) have been yoked '[1]—here the word *saṃsaṭṭha* means 'similar.' 'Ladies, you live *saṃsaṭṭha* with passion '[2]—here it means 'saturated with passion.' 'He lives in association with householders '[3]—here *saṃsaṭṭha* means 'mentally intimate.' 'This happiness is accompanied by this zest, is coexistent, *saṃsaṭṭha* and conjoined with it '—it means 'coexistent.' Here also in 'accompanied by joy '—*saṃsaṭṭha* means 'coexistence in association.' Herein there is no conjoining which is without coexistent, or accompaniment. But the coexistent may or may not be associated and conjoined. For in material and immaterial states which are produced together, matter is coexistent with non-matter, but is not associated or conjoined with it. Likewise non-matter with matter, and matter with matter. But non-matter is always accompanied by, coexistent, associated, and conjoined with non-matter. Bearing this coexistence in a state of mixture, so to speak, and in association—this is meant when it is said, 'accompanied by joy.'

By 'associated with knowledge' is meant 'yoked evenly by way of a common origin,' etc. What should further be said here has been said in the triplet of feeling in the commentary on the Table of Contents. Thus it should be understood that this consciousness is associated (with knowledge) by the characteristics of a common origin, common cessation, common basis, common object. This exposition indicates a maximum limit. But in immaterial existence association without a common basis is obtained.

By this sentence (viz., 'sensuous . . . associated with knowledge'), which class of consciousness is being discussed? That main type in moral (consciousness), experienced in the universe of sense, which is accompanied by joy, thrice-

---

[1] *Jāt.* vi. 22. [2] *Vin.* iv. 240. [3] *Vin.* ii. 4.

conditioned, associated with knowledge, and automatic. By the indefinite question, 'Which states are moral ?' the morals of the four planes of life are taken.[1] By the words, 'sensuous moral thought has arisen,' the moral consciousness of the three (higher) planes is excluded, and only the eightfold sensuous moral consciousness is taken. By the expression, 'accompanied by joy,' that fourfold consciousness which is accompanied by hedonic indifference is excluded from these eight; only the fourfold consciousness accompanied by joy is taken. By the expression 'associated with knowledge,' from these four is excluded the twofold consciousness dissociated from knowledge; [71] only the twofold consciousness associated with knowledge is taken. Automatic (or unprompted)[2] consciousness should not be commented on, as it has not yet been uttered in the text itself. But though it has not been made explicit, yet because the next class of consciousness is said to be consciously prompted, it should be understood that this first type is automatic. For the Supreme Buddha from the very beginning intended to classify this main type of consciousness on this principle, and hence it should here be considered as carried out.

Now in order to show consciousness by way of object he said 'visible or,' etc.; thus the Blessed One in expounding immaterial states shows them by way of basis or object, or both basis and object, or by way of their own function or property.

To expand: In such passages as—'There is contact [having its basis] in the eye, ear . . . in the sense-mind; feeling born of visual contact . . . of sense-mind; visual cognition . . . sense-mind cognition'—immaterial states are shown by way of basis.[3] 'Perception of visible object . . . of ideas; cognition of colour—of ideas'[4]—in such passages they are shown by way of objects. 'Visual cognition arises in dependence upon

---

[1] See *Dhs.* (or *B.P.E.*), §§ 1281–87.

[2] *Asankhāriyabhāvo.* Cf. *B.P.E.* § 146.

[3] In visual contact, etc., the sensitive organ is the basis; in mind-consciousness, etc., the mind-door, as the cause, is the basis.—*Ṭīkā.*

[4] *S.* ii. 251.

sensitive eye and visible object, contact arises from the concourse of these three . . .; mental cognition arises in dependence upon mind-door and object of thought, contact arises from the concourse of the three '[1]—in such passages they are shown by way of basis and object. 'Volitions, bhikkhus, arise through ignorance; rebirth-consciousness arises through volitions '[2]—in such passages they are shown by way of their own functions or properties. But in this place, showing them by way of objects he said, 'visible object or,' etc.

Herein 'visible object' is just one that is past, present, or future arising from four (things);[3] 'audible object' is just one that is sound, past, present, or future, due to two things;[4] 'olfactory object' is odour, past, present or future, due to four (things);[3] 'gustatory object' is taste, past, present, or future, due to four (things);[3] 'tangible object' is touch, past, present, or future, due to four (things).[3] 'Cognizable objects' include (*a*) states due to one, two, three, four, or to none of these causes;[5] (*b*) states past, present, or future; and (*c*) states which cannot be said to be either (*a*) or (*b*), *i.e.*, all states said to be the field of consciousness, but other than those five sensibles already described.[6]

[72] Those who say that 'cognizable object' includes also the five sensibles which have not come into the avenue of the senses should be refuted by the following Sutta, where it is said: 'Mind, brother, is the true refuge (or, co-ordinating resort) of these five sense-faculties, which have several objects and fields of sense, incapable of experiencing one another. Mind experiences their several fields.'[7] Visible objects, etc., are the objective fields of these five sense-faculties; though they are experienced by the mind, it is clear that they are still objects of sight, etc.[8] And further the meaning is rendered

---

[1] *Majjhima* (henceforth indicated by *M.*) i. 11; *S.* iv. 32.

[2] *S.* ii. 2.

[3] Viz., past action, mind, physical inanimate causes, and nutriment.—*Tr.*

[4] Viz., the second and third of the foregoing.—*Tr.*

[5] *E.g.*, old age and impermanence.—*Tr.*

[6] Thus (*c*) refer to concepts and Nibbāna.—*Tr.*

[7] *M.* i. 295.

[8] Hence they are not objects of thought.—*Tr.*

clear from the fact of these sensibles being also the objects of the knowledge given by supernormal vision, etc. For the five objects of sense which have not come into the avenue of the ordinary senses are the objects of supernormal vision, etc., but they are not objects of sense-mind. By what has now been said the determination of objects should be understood.

Of the six objects each comes into the avenues of two 'doors': the visible object (light and colour) comes into the avenue of the mind-door the moment it strikes the sensitive organ, that is to say, it causes vibration of the life-continuum. The case with sound, odour, taste and touch as objects is similar. Just as a bird flying through the sky and alighting on a tree touches the branch of the tree and its shadow strikes the ground, the touching with the branch and the spreading of the shadow taking place in one moment, simultaneously, so the contact with the sensitive organ, etc., by the presented object of sense is simultaneous with its coming into the avenue of the mind-door through its ability to cause the life-continuum to vibrate. After that, the life-continuum is cut off by a process through the eye-door, etc., beginning with 'adverting' and ending with 'determining';[1] immediately after which a state of consciousness of the main type takes place with any one of those objects.

In the purely representative process through the mind-door, however, there is no function of striking the sensitive organ. These objects present themselves naturally by virtue of having been seen, heard, smelt, tasted and touched. How? Some one here below circumambulates a great shrine, which is well plastered, variegated by colours of orpiment, realgar, etc., beset with divers kinds of flags and banners, interlaced with flowers and wreaths, encircled by garlands, so to speak, of lights, illumined by an enchanting glory, and adorned in every respect. On the sixteen platforms he pays homage in the five-fold manner of contact.[2] With clasped hands raised in

---

[1] Cf. *Compendium* 27–30; 126 *f.*

[2] *If standing* by (*a*) keeping the two feet evenly together on the ground, (*b*) keeping the two palms evenly together in contact, (*c*) raising them to the forehead, (*d*) bowing or bending towards an object of

adoration he stands looking upwards [73] with rapture derived from the contemplation of the Buddha. Having thus derived rapture from the contemplation of the Buddha by looking at the shrine, wherever, subsequently, he may have gone and seated himself in places [reserved] for night or day, the well-decorated shrine seems to appear to his eye on reflection, as it did actually at the time when he circumambulated it. Thus, first of all, by previous sight, a visible object comes into the 'avenue.'[1] Hearing the sound of one who with a sweet voice lectures on the doctrine, or who with a sweet voice is merely reciting or reading the Text, wherever, subsequently, he sits thoughtful, the sermon expounded or the text recited is represented at his mind-door, as if it came into the avenue of his ear-door as when he listened and gave his approbation. Thus through previous hearing, the audible object comes into the avenue. Getting a fragrant perfume or flower he offers it with the scent as an object of mind either in his seat or in a shrine; then wherever he afterwards sits down thoughtful, the perfume is as if it came into the avenue of the nose-door as at the time of making the offering. Thus through previous smell the olfactory object comes into the avenue. He enjoys an excellent meal in common with his fellow-monks; subsequently wherever, on getting inferior food, he reflects on his having enjoyed an excellent meal on a certain previous occasion with his fellow-monks, that sapid object is as though it came into the avenue of the tongue-door as at the time when he enjoyed it. Thus the sapid object comes into the avenue through previous experience. He enjoys a soft bed or stool or carpet or covering pleasant to the touch, and subsequently wherever he feels a hard bed, and reflects that he has enjoyed a soft bed

---

adoration, (*e*) finally separating the palms and placing one on each side of the head. *If seated* by (*a*) letting fall the two knees evenly together on the ground, (*b*) letting fall the two elbows evenly together on the ground, (*c*) stretching the two forearms and spreading the palms out, (*d*) keeping them evenly together on the ground, (*e*) placing the head on the back of the two palms.—*Vinayālaṅkāra.*

[1] Āpāthaṃ. Cf. *Vin. Texts* ii. 12; *M.* i. 190. *Bud. Psy.* 66.

on a previous occasion, the tangible object comes into the avenue, as it was actually felt at the time when he enjoyed that pleasurable touch. Thus through previous touch a blanket as tangible object comes into the avenue. Thus in the mind-door as such there is no function of contact with the sensory organism. Through having been seen, heard, smelt, tasted, and touched, these objects should be understood as coming naturally into the avenue.

Now the following is another method of exposition, [74] not mentioned in the (earlier) Commentaries, of the natural representation of objects that have been seen, etc. First and foremost, what is seen, heard, and connected with both—these should be understood as such. Things 'seen' includes what has been seized through the five doors; things 'heard' is what has not been 'seen' directly, but what is learnt by hearsay about the five sensibles.[1] An idea connected with both sources of knowledge is termed 'connected with both.' Thus should it be understood that by virtue of the former these objects (*i.e.*, sensibles) come into the avenue of the mind-door. Herein the representation of them has been described above in five ways. But (as regards the latter class) some one hears that the figure of the Buddha, born of superior merit, is like this and that, that his voice is exceeding sweet, that the scent of certain flowers in a certain place is very delightful, that the taste of certain fruits in a certain place is very sweet, and that the touch of certain coverings, etc., is very pleasant. From mere hearsay, without actual contact with the sensory organs, these sensibles come into the avenue of (or are represented at) the mind-door. Then to such an one consciousness (of that first main type), having for its object that sight or sound described, arises by virtue of faith; or consciousness of the same type with that scent, etc., as its object, arises by virtue of a desire to present such (flowers, fruits, or coverings described) to Ariyans, or by virtue of moral approbation of their being offered by others. Thus these five sensibles come into the avenue at the

---

[1] These two fields might be rendered by 'experience' and 'information.' Cf. *Compendium of Phil.* 37.—*Tr.*

mind-door through what is 'heard.' Lastly, another person has either seen or heard about those things mentioned. To him the thought occurs: 'Of such and such a figure will be the Buddha who will arise in the future.' In this way visible objects, etc., come into the avenue at the mind-door by virtue of their connection with things seen or heard, without actual contact with the sensitive organism. Then to him consciousness (of this first main type), with one or other of the five sensibles as object, arises in the manner described above. Thus it is to be understood that by virtue of the connection with both (experience and information) objects of sight, etc., come into the avenue at the mind-door. This is only a hint.

By virtue of (*a*) (blind) faith, (*b*) approved criticism, (*c*) ratiocination on aspects of things, (*d*) satisfaction at intuition into any reality, etc., the coming into the avenue of visible objects, etc., at the mind-door should be understood in detail. Inasmuch as these objects, which have been represented by faith, criticism, logic, intuition, etc., are both real and unreal, this method has not been adopted in the Commentary. It should be understood that an apperceptional thought[1] having any one of the objects arises through two doors in the manner described. Thus the apperception of a visible object arises at the eye-door and also at the mind-door. The same is the case with apperceptions of sound, etc. Of these doors the apperception of a visible object arising in the mind-door is of three kinds: accomplished by charity, virtue, or culture. [75] Of these again each is of three kinds: deed (body), word, and thought. And the same with apperceptions of sound, etc.

Of these objects, this moral consciousness of the first main type arises having as visible object a certain desirable, pleasing, agreeable, and captivating colour as a sign of beauty in blue-green, yellow, red, or white flowers, raiment, minerals, or metals. 'But is not this desirable object the fundamental cause of greed? How then is this consciousness good?'—(an objector might ask). (The answer is): It has become good by virtue of its being determined, bent,

---

[1] Javanaṃ. Cf. *Compendium of Phil.* 29.

trained, and laid to heart.[1] To expand: A person thinking: 'I ought to do meritorious deeds,' has his mind 'determined' for moral acts, 'bent' only on moral acts by inhibiting immoral acts, well 'trained' by constant practice of good. And has 'laid to heart' through such sufficing conditions as residence in a suitable place, (assistance from or) dependence on good associates, hearing the good Law, merit performed in former existences, etc. Thus by virtue of determination, inclination, training, and idea, there occurs to him a moral thought.

The state of being 'accompanied by joy' should here be understood in virtue of the specific objects before the mind. For this first class of consciousness is accompanied by joy, because a desirable object having arisen, abundance of such factors as faith are reasons for joy. For in those without faith and of wrong views, joy does not arise even when they see the figure of the Tathāgata, which is a truly desirable object. Those, again, who do not see the advantage of producing merit do not experience joy, even though incited by others to do good. Therefore abundance of faith, purity of views, seeing advantage in merit, should be understood as factors of this consciousness in making it accompanied by joy.

Eleven states also conduce to the production of zest (or rapture) as a factor of wisdom, namely, recollection of the Buddha, of the Law, of the Order, of the precepts, of self-sacrifice, of spirits, of peace, avoidance of rough (*i.e.*, ill-tempered) persons, serving meek persons, reflection on a Suttanta which instils faith and a tendency to all this. [76] It is thus that 'accompanied by joy' should be understood. The more detailed account in the *Bojjhaṅgavibhaṅga*[2] will make this clear.

The association with knowledge mentioned in this class of consciousness may be inferred from such causes as kamma (in this existence), birth as determined by past kamma, maturity of the controlling faculties, and distance from the corruptions. For instance, one who preaches the Law to others, teaches the different kinds of blameless arts, manual labour and knowledge,

---

[1] *Abhujita.* [2] *Vibhanga*, p. 227. See also p. 101.—*Ed.*

respectfully asks the preacher to preach the Law, and gives alms of divers kinds with the wish: 'in the future I shall become wise'—to him depending on such kamma, a moral thought (may be said to) arise in association with knowledge. To one born in a world free from ill-will (*i.e.*, the world of attenuated matter) a moral thought associated with knowledge also occurs. To that (spirit) happy therein, sentences of doctrine appear, *e.g.* 'Slow, bhikkhus, is the production of mindfulness; but when it is produced, that person quickly acquires special distinctions'[1]—in this way, in dependence upon rebirth also, a moral thought arises in association with knowledge. Moreover, when a moral thought arises also in dependence on the maturity of faculties, it does so in association with knowledge in those who have arrived at the maturity of those faculties at the wisdom-decade.[2] And when a moral thought arises also in dependence on distance from the corruptions, it does so in association with knowledge in those who have discarded them.

Truly has it been said:

Wisdom[3] *the studious gain, the heedless lose.*

Thus the association of a moral thought with knowledge may be inferred from such causes as kamma, re-birth, the maturity of controlling powers, distance from the corruptions.

Further, there are seven states conducive to investigation of the Law as a factor of enlightenment: frequent questionings (on elements, aggregates, etc.), cleansing of things or substances, equalizing of the faculties, avoiding of unintelligent persons, frequenting of wise persons, reflection on teachings of deep knowledge, inclination (of mind) towards this. For these reasons thought associated with knowledge can also be inferred. The detailed account in the *Bojjhaṅgavibhaṅga* will make this clear.

The main (type of) moral thought which has thus arisen

---

[1] *A.* ii. 185.

[2] Paññādasaka, *i.e.* the ten years (forty to fifty) of maturing wisdom. Cf. *Visuddhi-Magga*, ch. xx.—*Tr.*

[3] Bhūri, lit. abundance.—*Dhp.*, ver. 282.

in association with knowledge is called [77] automatic from its arising without external aid, instigation, or inducement. It has a captivating colour as its object, and arises in three fixed ways, being brought about by charity, virtue, or culture. How? The subject gets either flowers, clothes, or elements [of metals or minerals] such as are blue-green, yellow, red, or white, and bearing in mind a particular colour and thinking, 'This will be my gift of colour,' offers the object to the Three Jewels, namely, the Buddha, etc.; then the consciousness is brought about by charity. For here is a story which I have heard: The treasurer Saṅghamitta (of King Duṭṭhagāmani),[1] it is said, got a dress embroidered with gold and presented it at the great shrine, saying, 'This dress is golden in appearance, the Supreme Buddha also is golden in appearance; the golden cloth suits the Golden One, and it will be our gift of colour.' At such time it is to be understood that the thought is accomplished by charity. But when he gets such a gift and offers it to the Jewels: the Buddha, etc., saying, 'It (*i.e.*, this act of gift) is my family custom, family tradition, family usage, it is my duty,' then the thought is accomplished by virtue.[2] But when he, presenting the three Jewels with such a cloth, establishes the (conviction of) perishing and transience, namely, that 'this colour will perish, will pass away,' then the thought is accomplished by culture.

When the thought, though accomplished by charity, occurs to one who offers the gift to the three Jewels with his own hands, then an act of body accompanies it. When he in offering it to the three Jewels, orders his son, wife, servants, etc., to present it, then there is an act of speech. When he thinks, 'I will make a gift of colour,' referring to the actual object spoken of in various ways, then an act of thought arises. As regards Vinaya exposition, when such words as 'I will give this, I will do this' are spoken, it amounts to a gift by this characteristic of spoken words. But as regards Abhidhamma exposition, a moral thought arises from the time

---

[1] So the *Yojanā*.

[2] *Sīla* is here *cārittasīla*, positive virtue, as opposed to *vārittasīla*, negative morality. Cf. *Visuddhi-Magga*, p. 11.—*Tr.*

when there is thinking in the mind of giving an existing object. It is said [in the Great Commentary] that afterwards by act or speech he will do what is necessary. Thus the consciousness which is accomplished by charity is threefold by virtue of acts of body, speech and thought.

But when, having got an object so spoken of, he offers it to the three Jewels with his own hands according to the traditions of his family, then the act of body is accomplished by virtue. When by family tradition he commands his family to make the offering, then the act of speech is accomplished by virtue. [78] When he thinks of offering as a gift of colour something actually existing according to family custom, family tradition, usage, as his duty, then it is an act of thought. Thus a thought accomplished by virtue is threefold by way of body, speech, and thought. But when he gets the object spoken of and offers it to the three Jewels, and while walking to and fro establishes (the conviction of) perishing and transience, then occurs an act of body accomplished by culture. To him who contemplates as above, accompanied by words, occurs an act of speech (accomplished by culture). To him who so contemplates, without moving the bodily or vocal organs, occurs an act of thought (accomplished by culture). Thus a thought accomplished by culture is threefold by way of body, speech and thought. Thus the Lord of the Law has shown this moral consciousness of a visible object as classified on the threefold basis of meritorious act, as well as by the nine doors of action. The classification applies to audible and other objects. For instance, making a mental object of a captivating sound by a drum or other instrument, this consciousness arises in the three ways as mentioned above. Herein it is not possible to pluck a sound like a bulb or root, and place it in the hand like a stalk of blue lotus and offer it. But a gift of it may be made, together with its basis, *i.e.* the musical instrument. Therefore with the intention of making a gift of sound, he makes a gift of one or other of the instruments, the drum, etc., to the three Jewels, or causes such instruments to be set up; he offers to the religious preachers oil and molasses, etc., as medicine to improve the voice, or announces the sermons and lectures he has arranged;[1] he delivers votes of thanks; then the thought is accomplished by charity. When he does all this ceremony by family custom, etc., as his duty, then it is accomplished by virtue. When, having done all this, he contemplates that such a sound, even though it reaches the Brahmā world, will perish and pass away, then it is accomplished by culture.

Herein, first of all, a thought accomplished by charity becomes an act of body when, taking the drum, etc., he offers them with his own hands, or, though he places them for a perpetual offering, does so with his own hands, or when, with the intention of making a gift of sound, he goes to proclaim the hearing of the Law, to discourse on the Law, or to recite the text.

It is translated into an act of speech when he gives orders: 'Go, friends, make an offering to the three [79] Jewels of this our gift of sound,' and 'place this bheri-drum or this mutiṅga-drum in the precincts of that shrine,' or when he himself proclaims the hearing of the Law, makes a religious speech, or recites the text. But it remains a mere act of thought when, without moving the bodily and vocal organs, he mentally surrenders the actually existing object with the thought, 'I shall make a gift of sounds.' To him who, with the idea that the gift of sound is customary according to his family custom, family tradition, family usage, offers drums, etc., with his own hands or places them in the precincts of the shrine, etc., with his own hands, or gives with his own hands (to the religious preacher) the medicine for the improvement of the voice, or goes, duty bound, to proclaim the hearing of the Law, to discourse on the Law, or recite the text, the thought accomplished by virtue becomes an act of body. To one who gives an order, 'The gift of sound is in accordance with our family custom, family tradition, family usage; go, friends, to the three Jewels, the Buddha, etc., and make an offering'; or to him who himself speaks on the Law, or recites the text as

---

[1] *Upanisinnakakathaṃ karoti* (cf. Upaniṣad). The Commentator (*Ṭīkā*) explains this as: 'recites the Pali text, pronounces religious discourses, delivers lectures.'

a custom of his family, etc., it is translated into an act of speech. To one who thinks: 'The gift of sound is a custom of my family, I will make a gift of it,' and mentally sacrifices the existing object without moving the bodily and vocal organs, it remains a mere act of thought. When going to and fro he establishes (the conviction of) transience and passing away of sound, then the thought accomplished by culture becomes an act of body. To one who accompanies his contemplation with words, but without moving the bodily organs, it becomes an act of speech. But to one who so contemplates the sound in mind only, without moving the bodily and vocal organs, it becomes an act of thought. Thus the Lord of the Law has shown consciousness of an audible object as classified on the threefold basis of meritorious act by means of the nine doors of action.

Selecting, as an object of sense, a captivating scent out of perfumes from roots, etc., a moral thought arises in three fixed ways as said above. Therein when, on getting any one of the scented roots, etc., he, considering it by virtue of the scent and saying, 'my gift of perfume shall take place,' honours the Buddha-Jewel, etc. therewith, then the moral thought is accomplished by charity. All should be understood in detail as was said in the case of a gift of colour. Thus the Lord of the Law has shown consciousness of a scent as an object classified on the threefold basis of meritorious act by means of the nine doors of action.

Making an object of sense of a captivating taste among tastes of roots, etc., a moral thought arises in three fixed ways as was said above. Therein when he gets any object of a captivating taste among roots, etc., [80] and considers it by virtue of the taste, saying, 'my gift of taste shall take place,' and makes an offering, a giving up, then the moral thought is accomplished by charity. All should be understood in detail as was said in the case of a gift of colour.

But here there is a difference in the case of a thought accomplished by virtue. Stories occur in the Great Commentary beginning with that of king Duṭṭhagāmani Abhaya, who ate an excellent meal after offering (the like) to twelve thousand bhikkhus, saying, 'It is not our custom to partake of food without (first) giving it to the Order.' Thus the Lord of the Law has shown consciousness of a taste as an object classified under the threefold basis of meritorious act by means of the nine doors of action.

When the object is something tangible, it consists of the three Great Essentials (or Elements), viz.: extension, heat, mobility. In this connection reference is not to these, but to such things as beds, stools, etc. To expand: When on getting, among furniture, any captivating tangible object he considers it by virtue of the touch and surrenders it with the thought, 'This is my gift of touch,' then the thought is accomplished by charity. All should be understood in detail as was said in the case of a gift of colour. Thus the Lord of the Law has shown consciousness of a tangible object classified under the threefold basis of meritorious act by means of the nine doors of action.

In the case of an object of thought, the six internal sense-organs, the three characteristic marks, the three immaterial aggregates, the fifteen material subtle qualities of matter, Nibbāna and concepts, whether included in the given object or not, form the object of thought. In this oonnection there is reference not to these, but to gifts of food, drink and life. A moral thought with a captivating object from among nutritive substances, etc., arises in the three fixed ways as said above. Therein when he offers butter, ghee, etc., as his gift of food, the eight drinks[1] as a gift of drink, and when as a gift of life he offers a meal by lot, a meal for a party, a meal for the Order, etc., gives medicine to indisposed monks, or gets a physician to attend to the sick, has the net destroyed, the fish-trap broken, the bird-cage spoiled, effects the release of the fettered, prescribes by beat of drum the non-taking of life and does such other acts to protect life, then the thought in question is accomplished by charity. And when by reason of principal or sacred duty he makes these gifts of food, drink, and life because of his family custom, family tradition, family usage, the moral thought under discussion is accomplished by

---

[1] *Vin. Texts* ii. 132.

virtue. When he establishes the conviction of transience and passing away in an object of thought, [81] then the thought in question is accomplished by culture. When with his own hands he makes the gifts of food, drink and life, then the thought accomplished by charity becomes also an act of body. When he does so by ordering his family, then it becomes an act of speech. When, without moving his bodily and vocal organs, he thinks of giving an actually existing object as a gift of food, drink and life, then it becomes an act of thought. But when with his own hands he gives an existing object of various kinds as described above according to the custom or tradition of his family, etc., then the thought accomplished by virtue becomes an act of body. When he does so by ordering his family it becomes an act of speech. When he thinks of giving an existing object of divers kinds as said above according to the custom or tradition of his family, etc., then it becomes an act of thought. When walking to and fro he establishes the conviction of transience and passing away in an object of thought, then the thought accomplished by culture becomes an act of body. To one who establishes by words that conviction without moving his limbs, it becomes an act of speech. Without moving his bodily limbs and vocal organs, to him who in mind only establishes that conviction, it becomes an act of thought. Thus the thought accomplished by culture is threefold by virtue of body, speech, and thought. Thus the Lord of the Law has classified consciousness of an object of thought on the threefold basis of meritorious act by means of the nine doors of action.

This kind of consciousness (viz., the first moral thought of the main type) in connection with various physical bases and various objects of sense has now been elucidated. And it can be obtained by way of various objects of sense also in connection with any subject of discourse. How? Take the robe among the four requisites of a *religieux*—six objects of sense and thought are obtained. For example, the colour of a newly dyed robe is agreeable and comely: this is colour as object. When used it makes a rustling sound—*patta, patta*—it is then an audible object. What scent there is in it of dyestuffs such as bastard sandal wood or aloes, gives odour as object. Taste as an object in a robe may be spoken of figuratively as taste in usage. The pleasant touch there may be in it is tangible object. The pleasurable feeling arising because of the robe is object of thought. In the almsfood an object of taste in the literal sense is obtained. Thus among the four requisites (food, clothing, lodging, medicine) the various objects of sense taking their place, we must classify [our thought] according to charitable giving and so on.

Now of this kind of consciousness the object is a constant concomitant, because without it that consciousness does not arise. But the 'door' is not a constant concomitant. Why? Because of the variableness in previous actions (kamma). Action being not always predictable, the door is equally unpredictable.

PART III—DISCOURSE ON DOORS (OR GATES)

(*DVĀRAKATHĀ*)

CHAPTER I

DOOR OF AN ACT OF BODY

To explain the meaning of this variableness of both *kamma* and door [82], the Great Commentary sets out a discourse on Doors (or Gates).

In this the following subject-heads, viz., the three kinds of action (kamma), three doors of action, five kinds of consciousness, five doors of consciousness, six kinds of contact, six doors of contact, eight [modes of] non-restraint, eight doors of non-restraint, eight [modes of] restraint, eight doors of restraint, ten courses of immoral acts, ten courses of moral acts, have been laid down in the Table of Contents (Pt. I.). Although the three actions are described first in that Table, we may leave these till later and take the three doors of action for classification. Which are the 'three doors of action'? Door of an act of body, door of an act of speech, and door of an act of thought.

In the expression 'act of body,' body is fourfold: that which is grasped at,[1] that which is produced by food, by the caloric order, by mind. Of these, eight material qualities produced by kamma, namely, those beginning with the organ of sight and ending with life-control, and the eight material qualities produced by kamma, viz., the four elements, colour, odour, taste and nourishing essence constitute the body as that which has been 'grasped at' (by desire, etc., attending the kamma in question). These eight qualities born of food constitute the body as produced by food; the same eight born of the caloric order constitute the body as produced by heat; and the same eight born of consciousness constitute the body as produced by mind.

---

[1] Or "laid hold of" (upādiṇṇaka-kāyo). See p. 55.

Of these three doors, 'door of an act of body' is not (the aspect of) body as grasped at by kamma, nor as otherwise produced. But among the eight qualities of body produced by mind, one is (capacity of) intimation, and it is this that is meant by 'door of an act of body.' Concerning that door, it has been said, 'Which quality of body is called body-intimation? It is that particular quality of body which informs, intimates, or communicates in a unique manner, and which aids, supports, or strengthens the body of a person who, with a moral or immoral or unmoral thought, moves forward, or steps back, looks straight ahead or obliquely, bends or extends his limbs.'[1]

To expand: When a thought, 'I will move forward or step back' occurs, it sets up bodily qualities (born of mind). Now there are eight groups of these bodily qualities: the four primaries: extension, cohesion, heat, mobility, and four depending on these: colour, odour, taste, nutritive essence (*ojā*). Among these, mobility strengthens, supports, agitates, moves forward or backward the coexisting physical body. Now in a cognitive process of simple 'adverting' (of attention), when the seven moments of apperception (*javana*) are set up, the first six cause to arise only such [83] mobility as can strengthen and support the coexisting body, but cannot move it. In consequence, however, of this work of the first six moments, the seventh moment sets up mobility able both to move the body forward and backward and to cause the act of looking straight ahead or obliquely, of bending and extending the limbs. Hence there results an act of going or coming or both; (by repetition more than a thousand times) it enables us to say that a man 'has gone a yojana, gone as far as ten yojanas.' As when a cart is drawn by seven yokes, the bullocks at the first yoke are able to bear the yoke but not to turn the wheels. And the same with the bullocks yoked to the second . . . and sixth yokes. But by harnessing bullocks to a seventh yoke a clever driver sitting in the forepart of the cart takes the reins and urges the bullocks with the goad, beginning from the foremost of all; then all the bullocks being of

---

[1] *Dhs.* § 636.

united strength steady the yoke, turn the wheels, draw the cart, enabling us to say that it has gone ten or twenty yojanas. Thus the completeness of this process should be understood.

Now the body produced by consciousness *that* is not 'intimation.' But there is a certain peculiar, unique mode of change in the primaries when set up by mind, through which, as a condition, mobility is able to strengthen, support and agitate the coexistent body. This is intimation. It is not set up by consciousness as are the eight qualities. But as has been said, 'From the decay and death of things that are impermanent, etc., bhikkhus, decay and death is impermanent and conditioned,' etc.;[1] so because of the communicableness of qualities set up by consciousness, intimation may also be said to be produced by consciousness. Because it is a capacity of communicating, it is called 'intimation.' What does it communicate? A certain wish communicable by an act of the body. If anyone stands in the path of the eye, raises his hands or feet, shakes his head or brow, the movements of his hands, etc. are visible. Intimation, however, is not so visible; it is only knowable by mind. For one sees by the eye a colour-surface moving by virtue of the change of position in hands, etc. But by reflecting on it as intimation, one knows it by mind-door-consciousness, thus: 'I imagine that this man wishes me to do this or that act.' For just as during the hot season, where there is water they tie the palm leaves, etc., on the top of a tree in a forest saying, 'By this sign men will know the existence here of water;' or on the door of a liquor-shop they raise a flag; [84] and just as the wind striking the tree blows it about; and the fish disturbing the water, bubbles appear on the surface; just as, again, at the edges of the course where a great flood has been are tangled grasses, leaves and rubbish, and thus in the palm-leaves, in the flag, in the waving foliage, in the bubbles, the grasses, the leaves, and the rubbish, even though they see not the actual objects thought of, men know by mind as follows: 'Here must be water, here liquor, thus the tree must be struck by the wind, there must be fish in the water,

---

[1] *S.* ii. 26.

the flood must have run its course overflowing to this extent,' even so intimation is not visible but knowable. One sees with the eye only the colour-object moving by virtue of change of position in hands,[1] etc. But by reflecting on intimation one knows it by knowing the wish thus: 'Methinks he wishes me to do this or that act.'

And intimation is so called not only because of communicating, but also because of being communicated. Communication by sign is intelligible to others, even to the lower animals. Wherever dogs, foxes, crows and cattle are assembled, and when they see the gesture of striking, on a stick or a stone being seized, they know, 'He wishes to strike us' and flee helter-skelter. There is a time when intimation is not manifest, the object being separated by a wall, enclosure, etc. But though not manifest at that moment to him, yet from its being manifest to those who are in its presence it is called intimation.

When the body set up by mind moves, does the body set up by the other three causes move or not? The latter moves likewise, goes with the former, and invariably follows it. Just as dry sticks, grass, etc., fallen in the flowing water go with the water or stop with it, so should the complete process be understood. Thus intimation among material qualities set up by mind should be understood as a door of an act of body.

By volition manifest in that door one takes life, commits thefts, commits adultery; or else refrains from life-taking, etc.; this volition is said to be an act of body.

There is a heretical view, that body being the door, the volition manifesting itself in that door is an act of body, which should be classed as moral or immoral. But putting this view aside, unmoral acts should also be included, thus making up the triplet.

Herein, as the city-gate stands in the place where it has been made and does not move to and fro even one finger-breadth, and people go about by that door, so while the 'door' does not change place with another, action which arises in this or that door does. Hence the Ancients say:

> *Acts pass through doors, not doors through doors; by doors*
> *One may distinguish well these acts from those.*

[85] Of these a 'door' receives its name from the act and *vice versa*. As the places where consciousness, etc., is set up, are known as the 'door' of consciousness, 'door' of contact, 'door' of non-restraint, 'door' of restraint, so the place where an act of body arises is known by the name of 'door of a bodily act.' And the same with the 'doors' of speech and thought. As a fairy residing in this or that tree gets its name from that tree, as the cotton-tree fairy, the butea-tree fairy, the nimba-tree fairy, or the phandana fairy, so the place where the bodily act arises gets its name of 'door of the bodily act.' And the same with acts of speech and thought.

Of these body is one thing and action another. But from being performed by the body it is called bodily act. Hence the teachers of the Commentaries said:

Work by a needle done is needle-work;
Needle and needle-work are things distinct.
Work by a hatchet done is hatchet-work;
Hatchet and hatchet-work are things distinct.
Work that by man is done is called man's work;
The man and the man's work are things distinct.
An act by body done is body-act;
Body and body-act are things distinct.

(It may be objected that) if this is so, then the doors are not rightly determined, nor the acts. How? In body-intimation, in that it has been said,

'*Acts pass through doors*, . . .'[1]

an act of speech may also arise; therefore to determine body-intimation as 'door of an act of body' (only) is not right. Again, an act of body may arise in speech-intimation; therefore to determine this as an act of body is not right. (We reply) —It is right. And why? Because of frequency and great preponderance. For usually an act of body and not speech or

[1] Whereas in a representative process there is only one kind of adverting to an object of thought at mind-door, in a presentative process, there are two kinds of adverting, first to a sensible external object at the outer door and then to the percept at the inner door.—*Tr.*

thought arises in body-intimation; and therefore intimation by gesture may be called door of an act of body. The acts are rightly determined just as the terms: Brahmin village, mango forest, and iron-wood forest are rightly applied. An act of body arises preponderantly in the body-door, slightly in the vocal door. Therefore from its arising chiefly in the body door, [86] the state of an act of body is (said to be there) accomplished; as we say 'woodmen' for those who frequent the forest, and 'lusty maids' (in general), in the same way are these acts rightly so allocated.[1]

Here ends the Discourse on the door of an act of body.

CHAPTER II

DOOR OF AN ACT OF SPEECH

In this theory of the speech-door, speech may be considered under the three aspects of volition, abstinence and sound. For instance, 'words endowed with four factors, O bhikkhus, are well-spoken, not ill-spoken, faultless and unblamed by the wise'[2]—here speech is voluntary. 'Avoidance of and abstinence from the fourfold misconduct in speech . . . is called right speech'[3]—this is speech by way of abstinence. 'Speech, voice, enunciation, utterance, noise, making noises, speech, articulate speech-sounds'[4]—this is speech as sound. Now of these, 'door of an act of speech' is not the name of speech by way of volition nor of abstinence. But there is a certain intimation accompanying sounds (or words):—this is the door of an act of speech. Concerning this it is said: 'Which is that which is called intimation by speech? That speech, voice, enunciation, utterance, noise, making noises, speech,

---

[1] A village is called Brahmin village, though there are other people than Brahmins in it. Likewise with a mango grove. Brahmins refer to the act of body, village to door; just as the village is full of Brahmins, so the door is of acts.—*Ariyālaṅkāra*. On 'lusty maids' see *Jāt.* iv. 220.—*Ed.*

[2] *Sn.* ver. 78; *S.* i. 189 (cf. *Kindred Sayings* i., p. 239). The 'four' are well-spoken, righteous, kindly and truthful speech.—*Ed.*

[3] *Vibhaṅga* 237.

[4] *Dhs.* § 637.

articulation of one who has a moral, immoral or unmoral thought is called speech. By this speech there is intimation, information, communication; this quality is intimation by speech.'[1] 'I will speak this, I will speak that'—for one thus thinking arises a sound produced by the diffusion of the initial application of mind. This is cognizable, not by the ear, but by the mind. This view is set forth in the Great Commentary. But in the traditional Commentaries on the Suttas, the expression 'sound produced by the diffusion of the initial application of mind' is explained as the sound arisen for one who reflects when he hears the words which, through diffusion of initial application of mind, are muttered in sleep or in swoon. In connection with those words he thinks: 'So that is what you think; so that is what your mind reveals!' and so thinking tells explanatory stories.[2]

In the *Paṭṭhāna* also occurs this sentence, 'Sound born of mind causally relates itself to the sense of hearing by way of an object.' Therefore there is no sound, due to diffusion of initial application of mind, which arises without an impact of intimation, and which is not cognizable by the ear.[3] The thought, 'This will I speak, that will I speak,' sets up the eight material qualities—extension, [87] cohesion, heat, mobility, colour, odour, taste and nutritive essence. Among these, extension produced by consciousness arises impinging on, or striking the element of hardness grasped at by kamma. Sound arises together with that impact between the elements. It is sound set up by consciousness; it is not intimation. But there is a certain unique change (in the primaries set up by consciousness) which is the cause of bringing about the impact of the element, grasped at by kamma, on that set up by mind. This is speech-intimation. This should be followed by what has been said just above, namely: 'This is not produced by consciousness like the eight qualities,' etc.

But here, *i.e.*, in the case of the door of an act of speech, or speech-intimation, if we hear the sound of another calling

---

[1] *Dhs.* § 637. [2] Cf. *Dialogues* i. 278 (Kevaḍḍha Sutta).

[3] Cf. *Points of Controversy* ix. 9.

our name, 'Tissa,' 'Datta,' or 'Mitta,' and think of the intimation, we know it as this: 'Methinks he wishes me to do this or that act.' As in intimation by gesture this also is intelligible to the lower animals. Hearing such sounds as 'come,' 'go,' they know, 'He wishes me to do this, methinks,' and accordingly come or go. But the alternative 'moves or does not move the body produced by three causes' does not hold here. Neither is there the strengthening function (of extension or of impact) produced by the first moment of apperception. It is by the volition which is accomplished in that speech-door that we speak falsehood, calumniate, speak harsh words, frivolous speech, or refrain from all these. This is an act of speech. Henceforward all determination of action and of door should be understood as said above.

Here ends the Discourse on the door of an act of speech.

CHAPTER III

DOOR OF AN ACT OF THOUGHT

In the discourse on the door of an act of thought, mind is considered as fourfold by way of the planes of life.

Of these, the plane of sensuous consciousness is of fifty-four classes; that pertaining to the universe of attenuated matter is of fifteen classes; that pertaining to the immaterial universe is of twelve classes; the transcendental is of eight classes—in all eighty-nine.[1]

Of these, it cannot be said that what is called mind is not mind-door, any more than it can be said that what is volition is not kamma. Just as even the volition associated with the fivefold cognition (*i.e.*, of the five external senses) has been shown in the Great Book to be kamma, even so it should not be said that mind is not mind-door.

Here a question might be asked: what does this (mind-) kamma do? It harmonizes, arranges, co-ordinates, thinks, stimulates and decides. This being so, what does the volition of the fivefold external sense harmonize, arrange, [88] co-ordi-

---

[1] Cf. *Comp. of Phil.* 92.

nate? The co-existent factors. For it harmonizes, arranges, co-ordinates, thinks, stimulates and decides the associated aggregates that are co-existent. This section is generally discoursed on (by teachers) by way of a compendium. What does it amount to? The following is the answer decided upon here:—Mind having twenty-nine phases, which is moral or immoral, and is common to life in the three planes, is the door of an act of thought. The volition which is accomplished in that door, by which we take up covetousness, ill-will, wrong views, or non-covetousness, good-will and right views:—this volition is an act of thought. Henceforward all determination of action and of door should be understood as said above.

Here ends the Discourse on the door of an act of thought. These are the three doors of action.

CHAPTER IV

DISCOURSE ON KAMMA (VOLUNTARY ACTION)

THEY (*i.e.*, the three doors of action) have been shown without first considering the three kammas.[1] We now, making a beginning with these three kammas, shall give a detailed account of the table of contents of the remaining portion of the discourse on the doors.

These are the three kammas: bodily kamma, vocal kamma, mental kamma. And what is this kamma? Volition, as well as some states associated therewith. The following Suttas illustrate that volition is a state of kamma. 'I declare, bhikkhus, that volition is kamma. Having willed, one acts by body, speech and thought.'[2] 'When, Ānanda, there is bodily action, speech or thought, pleasure and pain to the self arise by reason of volition capable of causing an act, speech or thought.'[3] 'Bhikkhus, threefold volition capable of causing an act constitutes the bodily kamma, immoral, increasing pain and having a painful result; fourfold volition capable of causing speech, bhikkhus, constitutes the

---

[1] Cf. above, p. 109.
[2] *A*. iii. 415.
[3] *S*. ii. 39 *f*.; *A*. ii. 157 *f*.

vocal kamma, immoral, etc.; bhikkhus, threefold volition capable of causing thought constitutes the mental kamma, immoral,' etc.[1] Similarly with the bodily, vocal or mental kamma which is moral, increasing pain and having a pleasurable result.[2] 'If, Ānanda, this futile man Samiddhi, on being questioned, were to reply to the Wanderer, Pātaliputta, "Friend Pātaliputta, one who has done a voluntary and pleasurable action by body, speech and thought, experiences pleasure, one who has done a . . . pain-bringing . . . a . . . neutral action . . . experiences neither pleasure nor pain," then the futile man Samiddhi would reply rightly to the Wanderer Pātaliputta, O Ānanda,[3]—these are the Suttas which show first of all that volition is kamma.'

And that states associated with volition are also kamma has been shown by the fourfold classification of kamma. It has been said, 'Bhikkhus, there are four, [89] which I have realized and understood by my own higher (intuitive) knowledge. Which are the four? There is, bhikkhus, kamma which is impure and productive of impurity; there is, bhikkhus, kamma which is pure and productive of purity; there is bhikkhus, kamma which is both impure and pure, and productive of both impurity and purity; there is, bhikkhus, kamma which is neither impure nor pure, productive of neither impurity nor purity, and which, though itself kamma, conduces to the destruction of kammas. And which, bhikkhus, is kamma which is neither impure nor pure, and is productive of neither impurity nor purity? How does it, though itself kamma, lead to the destruction of kammas? The seven factors of wisdom:—mindfulness, etc., may be said to be kamma, which, being neither impure nor pure, productive of neither impurity nor purity, lead to the destruction of kammas.' *The same is repeated substituting the Ariyan eightfold path for the seven factors of wisdom.*[4] Thus these fifteen states, factors of wisdom and of the Path, have been shown by the fourfold classification of kamma.

The twenty-one states, viz., these fifteen together with

---

[1] Not traced.

[2] Sentence omitted in P.T.S. ed.

[3] *Majjhima*, iii. 208 *f.*

[4] *Aṅguttara*, ii. 230 *f.*

the six:—covetousness, ill-will, wrong view, non-covetousness, good-will, right view—should be understood as states associated with volition.

Of these, the transcendental Path may be included in, and classified under, the three forms of kamma (bodily, vocal, mental). To expand: Restraint of the wickedness of transgression by body should be understood as bodily; restraint of the wickedness of transgression in speech, as vocal. Thus right act is bodily kamma and right speech is vocal kamma. When this pair is taken, right living, because it consists of each, is included. Restraint of the wickedness of transgression in thought is mental. This act of thought is fivefold by virtue of (right) view, intention, exertion, mindfulness and concentration. Thus the transcendental Path, if classified, is classifiable under the three forms of kamma. Here comes the subject of inclusion under doors. There is such a thing as kamma which has not run its full course, though movements of bodily and vocal organs may have taken place and though it is generated at the mind-door. [90] Such kammas have been included under doors. Here is an illustration:

He who, thinking 'I will go a-hunting deer,' gets his bow ready, twists[1] the bow-strings, sharpens his spear, eats his meal, arranges his garments—so far he has moved his bodily limbs. After he has roamed the forest the whole day he does not get even a hare or a cat. Does this amount to immoral bodily kamma or not? It does not. And why? From its not having reached the full course of action. It should be understood as a mere misconduct of the body. And the same with such motives for catching fish, etc.

In the case of vocal doors, he gives an order, 'I will go a-hunting; quickly get my bow ready and the rest.' And as before, he does not get anything in the forest. In this case, though there is a movement of the vocal organs, it does not amount to bodily kamma from not having run through the full course of action. [Thus it should be understood as a mere misconduct in speech.][2]

---

[1] *Lege vaṭṭeti.*

[2] Omitted in P.T.S. ed.

But in the case of mind-door there is this distinction: The mere harbouring of criminal intent to kill amounts to kamma, and that by ill-will, not by actual life-taking. For immoral bodily kamma arises in the bodily and vocal doors, but not in the mind-door. Likewise immoral vocal kamma. But immoral mental kamma arises in the three doors. Likewise moral bodily, vocal and mental kammas. How? One who takes life with his own hands, steals what is not given, and commits adultery, commits bodily kamma through the bodily door. Thus, first of all, immoral bodily kamma arises in the body-door. Covetousness, ill-will and wrong view, which are co-existent with those thoughts, pertain to volition and [as bodily kamma] are negligible.[1] To one ordering specifically, "Go, deprive such and such an one of life, steal such and such property,' there is bodily kamma through the vocal door. Thus immoral bodily kamma arises in the vocal door. But covetousness, ill-will, wrong view, which are co-existent with these thoughts, pertain to volition and [as vocal kamma] are negligible. So far the teachers are in commentarial agreement.

But the sectary says that immoral bodily action may arise also in the mind-door. On being pressed to cite any Sutta adopted at the Three Councils, he quotes this Sutta called *Kuḷumpa*:—'Furthermore, [91] bhikkhus, here in this world, someone, recluse or brahmin, who is endowed with supernormal potency and has attained a mastery of his will, repeatedly contemplates with evil intention the embryo of which some woman is pregnant thus: would that that embryo were not born in safety! Thus, bhikkhus, was the infanticide of Kuḷumpa committed.' After quoting this Sutta he says, 'In this way by mere intention the embryo was crushed like a mass of foam. Herein where is the movement of either bodily or vocal organs? It is in the mind-door that this immoral bodily kamma arises.' After saying, 'We shall weigh the meaning of your[2] Sutta,' the teachers weigh it thus: 'You have affirmed the killing of

---

[1] Because there is no directing oneself to what belongs to others, nor is there a command to kill.—*Anuṭīkā*. On 'negligible' (*abbohārikā*) see *Points of Controversy* 361, *n*. 4.

[2] Implying that the Sutta was not adopted at the Councils.—*Tr*.

another by potency [or mental force].' Now potency is tenfold: (1) of resolve, (2) of transformation, (3) accomplished by mind, (4) of diffusion by insight, (5) of the Ariyas, (6) inborn with the result of kamma, (7) of the meritorious, (8) accomplished through art, (9) accomplished by culture, (10) accomplished through industrial processes in this or that work.[1] Of these, to which potency did you refer ?' 'That which is accomplished by culture.' 'What! is there an act of killing another by potency accomplished by culture ?' 'Yes, there is.' [Some teachers say that the act can be done only once. As when a jar full of water is thrown by one wishing to hurt another, the jar is broken and the water is lost, so by potency accomplished by culture the act of killing another can be done only once. Henceforward it is lost.] On this, after declaring that by potency accomplished by culture, the act of killing another is done neither once nor twice, the teachers question the antagonistic speaker on concepts, 'Is potency accomplished by culture moral, immoral or unmoral; associated with a feeling, pleasurable, painful or neutral; connected with both initial and sustained application of mind; connected not with initial, but merely with sustained application of mind; unconnected with both initial and sustained application of mind; experienced in the universe of sense, of attenuated matter or of non-matter ?' The sectary who knows the question will answer thus, 'Potency accomplished by culture is either moral or unmoral, but is associated only with a neutral feeling, is without initial and sustained application of mind, and is only experienced in the universe of attenuated matter.' [He should be asked,] 'In which category of moralities, etc., is the intention of life-taking included ?' If he knows he will reply, 'The intention of life-taking is immoral only, and is connected only with painful feeling, occurs only with initial and sustained application of mind and is experienced only in the universe of sense.' The rejoinder to this is, 'If this be so, your meaning does not harmonize with the triplet of morality, nor [92] with that of feeling,

---

[1] *Pts.* ii. 205 *f.*; *Vis. Mag.* xii.; *Compendium* 60 *f.*

nor with that of initial application of mind, nor with cosmology.' What, then, is such a great Sutta useless?' The orthodox answer is, 'Not useless, but you do not know its meaning.' To explain:—here the expression 'endowed with potency and attained mastery of his will' does not refer to potency accomplished by culture, but to the potency treated of in the Atharvaveda.[1] This is indeed obtainable in this passage. And it is not possible to achieve it without bodily and vocal organ or doors. For those who desire this Atharva potency have to practise for seven days such austerities as eating food without salt, and lying on the *dabba* grass spread on the ground, and on the seventh day have to go through a certain procedure within the cemetery ground by standing, after taking the seventh step, and swinging the hand round and round while repeating certain formulas; then is their work accomplished. Thus this potency cannot be acquired without bodily and vocal doors. And the conclusion which should be arrived at herein is that bodily kamma does not appear at mind-door.

The action of one speaking falsehood, etc., by a sign of the hand is an act of speech, but the door is that of body. Thus an immoral act of speech also arises in the body-door. But covetousness, ill-will and wrong view co-existent with those thoughts pertain to volition, and [as bodily acts] are negligible. But the action of one speaking falsehood, etc., by speech is an act of speech, and the door also is vocal. Thus an immoral act of speech arises in the vocal door. But covetousness, ill-will, wrong view co-existent with those thoughts pertain to volition and [as vocal acts] are negligible. So far the teachers agree.

But the sectary says: 'An immoral act of speech also arises in the mind-door.' On being asked to quote a Sutta adopted at the Three Councils he quotes the *Uposathakkhandha-sutta*:— 'If a bhikkhu, after being thrice summoned to make a confession, would not confess a real offence, which he recollects,

---

[1] Potency spoken of in this, the fourth book of the Veda, is called potency accomplished by art or knowledge (*vijjāmayiddhi*).—*Pyī*.

then he lies knowingly.'[1] In quoting this Sutta he says, 'Thus not confessing his offence, being silent he commits another offence. Herein whence is the movement of his physical limbs or vocal organs ? It is in the mind-door that this immoral act of speech arises.'

He should thus be answered:—'How now ? has your Sutta a meaning to be inferred, or a direct meaning ?' 'My Sutta has a direct meaning.' He should be told, 'Do not say so; we shall weigh the meaning of it,' and he should be questioned, 'What kind of sin is committed by one who knowingly speaks falsehood ?' A well-informed antagonist will say that there is the sin of *dukkaṭa* in conscious falsehood.[2] Further he should be told, [93] 'The body and speech are the two roots of discipline. For all kinds of offence have been declared by the Supreme Buddha with reference to these two doors only. There is no enactment of laws of offence with reference to the mind-door. You are acquainted far too much with the nature of the discipline in that you have enacted laws of offence in matters not enacted by the Teacher. You have accused the Perfect Buddha (of being imperfect); you have given a blow to the Conqueror's sphere of authority.' Having thus put him down with these words, he should be asked the following further question:—

'Does conscious falsehood arise from commission or omission ?' If he is well-informed he will say: 'From omission.' Then he should be confronted with this question, 'What act has been done by one, who does not confess his sin ?' Not seeing any particular act, he would surely be in distress. Hence he should be convinced of the meaning of this Sutta. What will be said is its meaning: what by way of offence is that conscious falsehood, described by the Buddha ? In other words, which kind of offence is it ? It is an offence of *dukkata*, and it is so not on account of the characteristic of false speech,

---

[1] *Vinaya Texts* i. 243 (*Vin.* i. 103).

[2] *Vin. Texts* i. 32. It is really *pācittiya*, but the sectary names that because, for the man who is consciously a liar, *remembers* it and does not confess it, it is *dukkaṭa.*—*Ariyālaṅkāra.*

but by the Buddha's words it should be understood as that offence which arises from omission in the vocal door.

And it has been said,

> *If he should not converse with any man,*
> *Nor even to another use his voice,*
> *He would offend by word and not by deed:—*
> *Of able judges here so runs the rede.*[1]

Thus the right conclusion is that immoral vocal action does not arise in the mind-door.

But when, by moving the limbs, with thought accompanied by covetousness, one takes a [woman's] hands, etc.; with ill-will handles sticks, etc.; with wrong views makes reverence, salutation, worship, preparations for an offering at an altar, saying, 'Khandha,[2] Siva or other (gods) are the highest,' then the act is that of thought and the door is that of body. Thus an immoral act of thought arises in the body-door, but the volition here cannot be called an act of body (lit. is negligible).

When by moving the vocal organs with the thought accompanied by covetousness one covets another's property thinking, 'Would that what belongs to others were mine!'; by ill-will declares, 'Let these beings be killed, imprisoned, cut into pieces, or let them not be'; by wrong view says, 'There is no use in gift, in offering,'[3] etc.; then the act is that of thought and the door is that of speech. Thus an immoral act of thought arises in the speech-door, but the volition herein is not called an act of speech (lit. is negligible).

But when without moving his physical limbs or vocal organs he is seated in seclusion, entertains thoughts accompanied by covetousness, ill-will and wrong view, [94] then the act is that of thought and the door also is that of mind. Thus an immoral mental act arises in the door of mind. But in this place volition and states associated with it arise in the mind-

---

[1] *Vin.* v. 216 *f.*, by which the very faulty reading in the P.T.S. ed. may be corrected.—*Ed.*

[2] *I.e.*, Skanda. On this late Saivite god see Hopkins: *Religions of India*, 410, 414.—*Ed.*

[3] See *Dialogues* i. 73.

door. Thus it should be understood that an immoral act of thought arises in all three doors.

And in what has been said [above], 'Likewise moral bodily, vocal and mental kammas,'[1] this is the method:—When by any cause one who is unable to speak takes the precepts:—'I abstain from life-taking, from theft, from wrong conduct in sensual pleasure,' by mere signs of the hands, then the act is that of body and the door is that of body only. Thus a moral act of body arises in the body-door. And the disinterestedness, love, right views accompanied by those thoughts pertain to volition, but are not called acts of thought.[2] But when he takes those three precepts by word of mouth, then the act is that of body but the door is vocal. Thus a moral act of body arises in the speech-door. And the disinterestedness, etc., accompanied by those thoughts pertain to volition, but are not called acts of thought.[2] But when such precepts are being given, and he takes them without moving his physical limbs or vocal organs, saying mentally:—'I abstain from life-taking, from theft, from wrong conduct in sensual pleasure,' then the act is that of body and the door is mental. Thus a moral act of body arises in the mind-door. And the disinterestedness, etc., accompanied by those thoughts pertain to volition, but are not called acts of thought.[2]

A moral act of speech of one who takes the four precepts of abstention from falsehood, etc., by body, etc., in the way described above should be understood to arise in the three doors. Here also disinterestedness, etc., pertain to volition, but are not called acts of thought.[2] But the action of one moving his physical limbs by thoughts accompanied by disinterestedness, etc., and doing such acts as sweeping the platform of a shrine and honouring the shrine by offerings of scent and flowers, is an act of thought and the door is that of body. Thus a moral act of thought arises in the body-door, but the volition herein is not called an act of thought.[2] Of one who, moving the vocal organs by consciousness accompanied by disinterestedness, etc., says, 'Would that what

---

[1] See above, p. 120, *l*. 6.

[2] Abbohārikā: are negligible.

belongs to others were not mine'; or who with consciousness accompanied by love thinks, 'May all [95] beings be free from enmity, from ill-will, from distress; may they bear themselves happily'; or who by right views thinks, 'There is use in giving,' etc.; the action is that of thought but the door is vocal. Thus a moral act of thought arises in the speech-door, but the volition herein is not called an act of thought—*i.e.*, is negligible. When, without moving the limbs or vocal organs, one seated alone mentally entertains thought accompanied by disinterestedness, etc., the action is that of thought and the door mental. Thus a moral act of thought arises in the mind-door.

But in this place volition and states associated with it arise only in the mind-door. Herein one who says that action in life-taking and theft, instigated by command, is an act of body, and that the door, by virtue of that action, is the body-door, 'preserves' the act, but 'breaks' the door. He who says that the door of falsehood, etc., produced by a sign of the hand is the body-door, and the action, by virtue of that door, is an act of body, 'preserves' the door, but 'breaks' the act. Therefore, with the intention of 'preserving' the act, one should not 'break' the door; nor with that of 'preserving' the door, should one 'break' the act. Action and door should be understood as has been said. Thus speaking one will not 'break' either the action or the door.

Here ends the Discourse on Kamma (action).

CHAPTER V

DISCOURSE ON COURSES OF IMMORAL ACTION

Now in the terms (*a*) 'five external senses,' (*b*) 'five sense-doors,' (*a*) is consciousness on occasion of seeing, hearing, smelling, tasting, touching; (*b*) are the doors of sight, hearing, smell, taste, touch. The volition which arises by virtue of these five doors should be understood as an act neither of body nor of speech, but of thought.

The 'contact' of the eye, of the ear, the nose, the tongue,

the body and the mind are called the 'six contacts.' The 'six doors of contact' are those of eye-contact, ear, nose, tongue, body, and mind-contact. The eight 'non-restraints' are those of the eye, the ear, the nose, the tongue, the sensitive body, the motor-body, speech and mind.

As to their content, these eight non-restraints are reducible to five states, namely: immorality, forgetfulness, absence of knowledge, absence of patience, laziness. Not one of these [96] arises in the five-doored cognitive process till after the [instant of] determining. It arises only in the moment when apperception begins. Unrestrained consciousness arisen in apperception is called non-restraint in five doors. Contact co-existent with sight is called sight-contact and the volition is an act of thought. And that consciousness (*i.e.*, of sight) is called the door of an act of thought. In sight proper there is no fivefold non-restraint; contact co-existent with [the moment of] 'reception' is mind-contact, and the volition is an act of thought. That consciousness (*i.e.*, the receptive) is the door of an act of thought. Herein also there is no fivefold non-restraint. And the same is the case with 'examination' and 'determination.'[1] Contact co-existent with apperception is mind-contact; the volition is an act of thought and that (apperceptional) consciousness is the door of an act of thought. Herein the non-restraint is that of sight, and the same is the method to be adopted in the door of the ear, of the nose, of the tongue, of the sensitive skin. But when mind-door apperception arises, having as object one or other of the objects of sense, resulting in the movement (of body) called body-door simply (*i.e.*, even without the aid of the vocal door), then the contact co-existent with that (apperceptional) consciousness is mind-contact.

Volition is an act leading to deed. But that (apperceptional) consciousness is not usually spoken of[2] as mind-door. (That is to say) because of the arising of (bodily) movement it does not go under the name of mind-door. The non-restraint here is that of the moving body. When such apper-

---

[1] *Cf.* text, p. 271; *Compendium* 28 *f.*

[2] Abbohārika. *Cf.* p. 120.

ception arises, resulting in the movement of the vocal door, pure and simple, without the body-door, then the contact co-existent with that consciousness is mind-contact.

Volition is an act giving rise to speech. But that (apperceptional) consciousness is not usually called mind-door. Because of the arising of the movement (of the vocal organs) it does not go under the name of mind-door. The non-restraint here is that of speech. But when such apperceptive consciousness arises, without the aid of physical limbs and vocal organs, as pure mind-door, then the contact co-existent with that consciousness is mind-contact.

Volition is a mental act; that consciousness is the door of mental act. The non-restraint here is that of mind.

The doors of non-restraint of the eye, of the ear, of the nose, of the tongue, of the sensitive part of the body, of the motor-body, of speech and of mind, by virtue of these eight non-restraints, should be understood as the eight doors of non-restraint.

The eight 'restraints' are those of the eye, the ear, the nose, the tongue, the skin, the moving body, speech and mind. In the ultimate sense they are five principles, namely: virtue, mindfulness, knowledge, patience and energy. None of these [97] arises in conscious processes up to the end of the determination-moment, but only in the moment of apperception. Though arisen in apperception restraint is referred to the doors. The arising of all these restraints should be understood in the same way as by the method described in the case of non-restraints: 'Contact co-existent with visual cognition is eye-contact,' etc. Thus by virtue of these eight restraints, the door of the restraint of the eye and so on should be understood as the eight doors of restraint.

The ten courses of immoral action are life-taking, theft, wrong conduct in sensual pleasure, falsehood, calumnious speech, harsh speech, frivolous talk, covetousness, ill-will, wrong views.

Of these, 'life-taking' means taking life quickly or by violence. Slaughtering or killing of beings is meant. 'Life' here (literally breathing thing), in common parlance, means a being;

in its ultimate sense, living force.[1] And the term 'life-taking' is applied to the bodily and vocal doors of one who is conscious that a being is living, and who produces an effort to cut off the living force in that being. Among animals devoid of virtues (*guṇa*), it is a slight misdeed in the case of a small creature, and a great misdeed in that of a large one. Why? Owing to the greatness of effort, and owing to the great size of the object, even though the effort may be the same. Among men, etc., they being capable of virtue, it entails a small misdeed in the case of a being of small virtue, and a great misdeed in that of a being of great virtue. And it should be understood that when physical virtues are equal, the sin is smaller or greater according as the corruptions and efforts (of the criminal) are weaker or stronger. There are five constituent factors in the crime of murder:—a being, consciousness of there being a living creature, intention of killing, effort and consequent death. And the six means of carrying out the effort are:—one's own hands, instigation, missiles, permanent devices, art and potency. As it will be too lengthy to treat of them here in detail, we shall pass over them as well as other explanations. Those desirous of details should look up the *Sāmantapāsādikā*, the Commentary on the Vinaya.[2]

'Theft' (*adinnādāna*) means the 'taking of what is not given'; the taking of what is another's property, robbery, or the state of being a thief is meant. Here 'not given' applies to property possessed by another. A property concerning which another has arrived at the state of doing whatever he likes, without incurring punishment or blame, is said to belong to another. The intention of stealing, producing the effort to take something [98] with the consciousness that it belongs to another is termed 'theft.' And that entails a small sin if what belongs to another is mean, and a great sin if it be of excellence. And why? Owing to the excellence of the object. If they are of equal value, stealing objects which belong to those distinguished for virtue entails a greater crime than the

---

[1] *Jīvitindriyaṃ.* Or, 'controlling power which is life.'—*Ed.*

[2] Professor J. Takakusu has prepared an edition of this work for the P.T.S.—*Ed.*

theft of objects belonging to one inferior in virtue. There are five constituent factors (in theft):—another's property, awareness that it is so, the thieving mind, effort, and consequent removal—and six means:—taking with one's own hands, etc. One or other of these means may be carried out according to circumstances, in stealing by false measures and weights, by force, by concealment, by design or by forgery. This is an outlined account of theft. The detailed account is in the *Sāmantapāsādikā*.

In the expression 'wrong conduct in sensual pleasures,' 'in sensual pleasures' means 'in matters of sexual intercourse'; 'wrong conduct' means 'base and truly blameworthy conduct.' The characteristic of 'wrong conduct in sensual pleasures' is the volition arising in the body-door, through the unlawful intention of trespassing upon a person to whom one has no right of going. Herein persons to whom men have no right to go are (*a*) ten classes of unmarried women:—a woman under the guardianship (1) of her mother, (2) of her father, (3) of her parents, (4) of her brother, (5) of her sister, (6) of her relations, (7) of her clan, (8) of her spiritual guide, (9) a woman under an engagement and (10) a woman undergoing punishment; and (*b*) ten classes of married women, namely: (1) one bought by wealth, (2) one who becomes a wife through her free-will, or (3) through love of property, or (4) of clothes, (5) one lawfully wedded by parents after the ceremony of dipping the hands of the couple in a bowl of water, (6) one who is taken from the poorer classes, (7) a slave-wife, (8) a servant-wife, (9) a wife captured in war and (10) a mistress kept for a time.

Of these a woman under an engagement and one under punishment together with (*b*) the latter ten:—these twelve it is not allowable for other men to approach. And the sin is smaller or greater according as the forbidden object is devoid of or endowed with virtues, such as the precepts. There are four constituent factors of this crime: the mind to enjoy the forbidden object, the effort to enjoy, devices to obtain, and possession. And only one means: personal experience.

'Lying' is applied to the effort of the body and speech, on

the part of one who is deceitful, to destroy the good of others. The volition setting up the bodily and vocal effort to deceive, with the intention of cheating others, [99] is termed 'false speech.' Another definition:—'lying' is applied to a thing which is not genuine or does not exist, and 'speech' means the representation of that as real, true. The characteristic of 'lying speech or falsehood' is the volition of one desirous of representing to others an untrue thing as true, which sets up a corresponding intimation. It is more or less an offence according as the welfare destroyed is greater or smaller. Or to put it in another way: It is a small offence in laymen if they tell an untruth:—'I have it not'—out of a desire not to give something belonging to themselves; and a great offence if they, as witnesses. perjure themselves in order to cause loss (to others). In recluses it is a small offence if, by way of an ironical joke, on getting but little oil or butter, they say:—'To-day, methinks, a river of oil flows in the village.' It is, however, a great offence in those who say that they have seen something which they have not. There are four constituent factors of this [offence]: an untrue thing, intention to deceive, corresponding effort, the communication of the matter to others. There is only one means: personal action; and that should be understood as the act of deceiving others either by body, or by something connected with the body,[1] or by speech. If by that act another knows that meaning, the volition producing that action is at that moment bound up with the act of lying. In the same way, as one deceives another by deed, by something connected therewith, or by speech, so a person who instigates another, 'Say thus to him,' or who lays a written leaf before another, or who records a permanent writing on walls, etc., to this effect, 'This meaning should be understood thus,' equally deceives others. Therefore it is reasonable to assume that instigation, transmission and permanent records are also involved in this form of immorality. But as the Commentaries have not admitted this, it should be adopted only after a critical examination.

---

[1] As an umbrella or a stick.—*Ariyālankāra.*

'Slander' means calumnious speech which, by being said to another, reduces to nothing the love which that person, or the speaker bears at his own heart to a third person.

A word which makes one's self harsh,[1] or causes another to be harsh, is in itself harsh, neither agreeable to the ear nor appealing to the heart. Such a word is termed 'abuse.'[2]

'Frivolous talk' is speaking senseless, useless things. The volition which is at the root of all speech of this sort, and is named calumnious, etc., is here alone to be understood. The volition of one with a corrupt mind, producing the bodily and vocal effort to sow the seed of discord among others, or to endear oneself to others is termed the volition of calumnious speech. It [100] is a smaller or greater offence, according as the virtue of the person whom he separates is smaller or greater. There are four constituent factors of this crime: (1) Other persons to be divided; (2) the purpose: 'they will be separated,' or the desire to endear oneself to another: 'I shall become dear and intimate'; (3) the corresponding effort; (4) the communication. But when there is no rupture among others, the offence does not amount to a complete course; it does so only when there is a rupture.

By 'harsh speech'[2] is meant the entirely harsh volition which produces a bodily and vocal effort, stabbing another as with a mortal wound.[3] The following story is an illustration: It is related that a certain boy, without listening to his mother's word, went to a forest. The mother, being unable to prevent him, cursed him, saying, 'May a wild she-buffalo chase thee!' And accordingly a she-buffalo appeared in the forest. The boy made an asseveration of truth, 'May what my mother said happen not; what she thought in her mind, may that happen!' The buffalo stood as if there transfixed.[4] Thus though her vocal effort was mortally wounding, yet her speech was not

---

[1] Like the edge of a saw.—*Ṭīkā*.

[2] This paragraph should apparently precede the previous one.

[3] Mamma=maranti anenāti, Yasmiṃ tāḷite na jīvati, taṃ ṭhānaṃ mammaṃ nāma=that place is called 'mamma,' which, being struck, one does not live.—*Yojanā*.

[4] *Maṇḍā viya*; Burm. ed.: baddhā, or bandhā viya.

really harsh, because of her tender heart. For though parents sometimes say thus to their children: 'May thieves cut you up into pieces!' yet they do not wish even a lotus leaf to fall on them. Teachers and spiritual guides sometimes say of their pupils: 'What are we to do with these shameless, reckless lads? Turn them out!' and yet they wish that they may attain and accomplish. But as words are not harsh if the heart be tender, so are they not gentle, just because speech is soft. The words of one desirous of killing: 'Let him sleep in comfort!' are not soft; because of the harshness of thought the words are harsh. Harsh speech is proportionate to the virtue of one concerning whom harsh words are spoken. The three constituent factors of this offence are: Another to be abused, angry thought, and the abuse.

Immoral volition producing the bodily and vocal effort to communicate uselesss things, is termed 'frivolous talk.' Its offence is great or small according as it is practised repeatedly or not. The two constituent factors of this offence are: the inclination towards useless talk—like the stories of the fight of the Bhāratas and of the abduction of Sītā, etc.[1]—and the narration of such themes. But the offence does not run through the full course of action when others [101] do not accept the story; it does so only when they accept it.

'Covetousness' means coveting: a process of inclining towards another's property when confronted with it. It has the characteristic mark of thinking, 'Ah! would this were mine!' As offence it is small or great as in the case of theft. Its two constituent factors are: Another's property, and the bending over of oneself. Though greed for an object which is another's property has arisen, it does not receive the distinction of being a full course of action so long as one does not bend over to it saying, 'Ah, would this were mine!'

That which destroys welfare and happiness is 'ill-will.' It has the characteristic mark of the mental fault of injury to others. The degree of offence is as in the case of harsh speech. Its two constituent factors are: another being, and the thought

---

[1] *Sumangala-Vilāsinī*, i, 76; Rhys Davids, *Buddhist India*, 183.

of doing harm. Mere anger with another being does not reach that distinctive stage of the course of action, so long as there is no destructive thought, such as: 'Would he were cut off and destroyed!'

'Wrong view' is that which sees wrongly by not taking the right view. It has the characteristic of perverted views, such as: 'There is no [use in a] gift.' And the offence is small or great as in the case of frivolous talk, or according as the wrong view is of a temporary or permanent character. Its two constituent factors are: perversion of the manner in which an object should be taken, and its manifestation according to the contrary view held of it. Here the distinctive stage of the course of action is reached by the views: (1) there is no *result* (in a moral act); (2) there are no *causes* (in happening); (3) there is no such thing as (moral) *action*,[1] and not by other views.

As regards these ten courses of immoral action, we may come to decisions respecting them under five aspects, to wit: (1) as ultimate psychological factors, (2) as groups, (3) as objects, (4) as feelings and (5) as roots.[2] (1) The first seven in order out of the courses of action are volitions only; the three beginning with covetousness are factors associated with volition. (2) The first seven and wrong views—these eight are courses of action, not roots. But covetousness and ill-will are both courses of action and roots. Covetousness as a root is the immoral root of greed, ill-will as a root is the immoral root of hate. (3) Life-taking has a conditioned thing for object, from its having the life-force as object. Theft has a living being or a thing for object. Wrong conduct has a conditioned thing for object by virtue of touch, or, as some say, a living being. Falsehood has either a living being or a conditioned thing for object. So has calumnious speech. Harsh speech [102] has only a living being for object. Frivolous talk has either a living being or a conditioned thing for object by way of things seen, heard, felt and thought. So

---

[1] (1) Denies the result of kamma; (2) denies both the cause and the result; (3) denies kamma.—*Tr.* Cf. *Dialogues of the Buddha* i. 73.

[2] Or springs of action, as our tradition would say.—*Ed.*

has covetousness. Ill-will has a living being for object, and wrong views have for object a conditioned thing in the three planes of existence. (4) Life-taking is associated with a painful feeling. For although kings on seeing a thief may say, laughing, 'Go, kill him,' the volition of decision is associated with pain only. Theft may be associated with the three kinds of feeling. He who on seeing another's property takes it with delight has a pleasurable feeling; if he steals it with fright, his feeling is painful; likewise if he does so while he reflects on the consequent fruits. If he takes it with indifference, the feeling is neutral. Wrong conduct is associated with two kinds of feeling, pleasurable and neutral; but in the thought of decision there is no neutral feeling. Falsehood has all three kinds of feeling as with theft; likewise calumnious speech. Harsh speech is associated with a painful feeling; frivolous talk has all three kinds of feeling. To illustrate:—When the story of the abduction of Sītā, or of the fight of the Bhāratas, etc., is recited, and the hearers applaud him and throw up their turbans, etc., there is to the performer a delighted pleasurable feeling. When one who has thus rewarded him comes up later and says: 'Tell us from the beginning,' the narrator is displeased at the idea and thinks: 'Shall I say something irrelevant and miscellaneous or not?' In such a case there is a painful feeling at the time of reciting; if he is indifferent during the recital, then there is a neutral feeling. Covetousness has two feelings, pleasurable and neutral; likewise wrong views. Ill-will has a painful feeling. (5) Life-taking has two roots by virtue of hate and delusion; theft has also two by virtue of hate and delusion or of greed and delusion; wrong conduct also has two by virtue of greed and delusion; likewise falsehood by virtue of either hate and delusion or greed and delusion; likewise calumnious speech and frivolous talk. Harsh speech by virtue of hate and delusion, and covetousness by virtue of delusion, have a single root; likewise ill-will. Wrong view has a double root by virtue of greed and delusion.

Here ends the Discourse on the Courses of Immoral Action.

CHAPTER VI

COURSES OF MORAL ACTION

THE ten courses of moral action are:—abstinence from life-taking, etc., and disinterestedness, good-will and right views.

Of these, life-taking, etc.,[1] have been explained. 'Abstinence' is that by which people abstain from life-taking, etc.; or that which itself abstains; or that which is the mere abstaining. In the passage where it says:—'That avoidance and abstinence from life-taking that there is, at that time, in one who abstains from taking life'[2]—that abstinence which is associated with moral consciousness is threefold: (1) [in spite of] opportunity obtained, (2) because of observance, (3) eradication.

(1) When they who have not undertaken to observe any particular precept, but who, reflecting on their own birth, age, experience, etc., and saying, 'It is not fit for us to do such a bad thing,' do not transgress concerning an object actually met with, the abstinence is to be considered as 'in spite of opportunity,' like that of Cakkana,[3] a lay-disciple in Ceylon. It is said that when he was young his mother suffered from a disease, and the doctor recommended fresh hare-flesh. Cakkana's brother then said to him, 'Go, dear, roam the field,' and sent him. He went there, and at that time a hare came to eat the tender crops. On seeing him it ran with speed, and was caught in the creepers, making the cry kiri! kiri! Cakkana went after the sound, caught the hare and thought, 'I shall make a medicine for mother.' Again he thought, 'It is not proper that for the sake of my mother's life I should take the life of another.' He then freed the hare, saying, 'Go, enjoy grass and water with other hares in the jungle,' and when asked by the brother, 'Well, dear, did you get a hare?' he told him what had happened. For that his brother scolded him.

---

[1] *I.e.,* theft, sexual misconduct, and four kinds of wrong speech. See Ch. V.

[2] *Vibh.* 285.

[3] In Burmese editions, Jaggana.

But he went to the mother's presence and stood averring a truth: 'Since I was born, I declare that I have not intentionally taken the life of any creature.' And straightway the mother recovered.

(2) The abstinence of those who have observed the precepts, both during and after the time-limit, without transgressing against the object even on pain of death, is to be considered as 'by way of observance,' like that of the lay-disciple dwelling in the mountain Uttaravaḍḍhamāna. It is said that, after taking the precepts in the presence of the Elder Piṅgalabuddharakkhita, who dwelt in the Ambariya monastery, he was ploughing his field. His ox got lost. While looking for it he ascended the Uttaravaḍḍhamāna mountain, where a great serpent seized him. He thought, 'I will cut off its head with my sharp axe.' Again he thought, 'It is not proper that I, who have taken the precepts from my teacher of culture, should break them.' And for the third time he thought, 'I will sacrifice my life, but not the precepts,' and threw away in the forest the sharp axe with its shaft from his shoulder. Immediately the boa-constrictor released him and went away.

[104] (3) Abstinence 'by way of eradication' should be understood as that associated with the Ariyan Path. When that Path has once arisen, not even the thought, 'we will kill a creature,' arises in Ariyans. Now, as with immoral states, so with those that are moral, there are five aspects under which decisions respecting them may be reached—namely, (1) as ultimate psychological factors, (2) as groups, (3) as objects, (4) as feeling and (5) as roots.

(1) Of the ten, the first seven are fit to be called volitions as well as abstinences; the last three are factors associated with volition.

(2) The first seven are courses of action and not roots; the last three are courses of action and roots. Disinterestedness, good-will and right view as roots become the moral roots: the opposites of greed, hate and delusion.

(3) These are the same as those of life-taking, etc. For abstention is from (the transgression against) the object to be transgressed against. As the Ariyan Path with Nibbāna as

its object abandons the corruptions, so these courses of action, having the faculty of life, etc., as their object, abandon the wickedness of life-taking and so forth.

(4) All are pleasurable feeling or neutral feeling, for with the attainment of good there is no painful feeling.

(5) The (first) seven are threefold, namely, disinterestedness, love, intelligence, in one abstaining with a consciousness associated with knowledge; twofold in one abstaining with a consciousness dissociated from knowledge. Disinterestedness is twofold in one abstaining with a consciousness associated with knowledge, and single when consciousness is dissociated from knowledge. Disinterestedness by itself is not its own root. Nor is good-will. Right view is twofold, as disinterestedness and as love. These are the ten courses of moral action.

CHAPTER VII

CONCLUSIONS

To the foregoing discussion should be added a consideration of courses of action in connection with self-restraint, etc. Want of self-restraint arisen through the five doors of contact is an immoral mental act. That which has arisen through mind, the door of internal contact, is threefold in action. For when movement of the body-door is reached, it is an immoral act of body; when that of the vocal door is reached, it is an immoral act of speech. When movement of neither is reached, it is an immoral act of thought.

Want of self-restraint which has arisen through the five doors is also only an immoral act of body; that which has arisen through the unrestrained door of the moving body is only an immoral act of body; that which has arisen by the door of speech or by the door of mind [105] is only an immoral act of speech or of thought respectively.[1] The threefold misconduct of body is only an immoral act of body; the fourfold miscon-

[1] The P.T.S ed. has here a different reading.

duct of speech is only an immoral act of speech; the threefold misconduct of mind is only an immoral act of thought.

Self-restraint which has arisen through the five doors of (external) contact is only a moral act of thought; if it has arisen through the door of mental contact, it is threefold in action, as in the case of non-restraint. Self-restraint arisen through the five doors is only a moral act of thought; if it has arisen by the door of the moving body, or through the door of speech, or through the door of mind, it is only a moral act of body, speech, or thought respectively.

Threefold good conduct of body is a moral act; fourfold good conduct of speech is a moral act of speech; threefold good conduct of mind is a moral act of thought.

An immoral act of body does not arise through the five doors of (external) contact, but through the door of mind-contact only; similarly with an immoral act of speech. But an immoral act of thought arises through the six doors of contact. If it results in movement in body and vocal doors, it is an immoral act of body and of speech;[1] not attaining such movement, it is an immoral act of thought. As it does not arise through the contact-door, no immoral act of body takes place through the five unrestrained doors. But it arises through the unrestrained doors of the moving body and the moving vocal organ; it does not arise through the unrestrained door of mind. Nor does an immoral act of speech arise through the five doors when unrestrained; it arises through the door of the moving body when unrestrained and the moving vocal organ; it does not arise through the unrestrained door of mind.

An immoral act of thought arises even through eight unrestrained doors; and the same method holds in moral acts of body, etc., but with this difference:—Immoral acts of body and of speech do not arise through the unrestrained door of mind, but these are not so; without moving bodily limbs or vocal organs, they arise in the self-restrained door of the mind of one who is taking the precepts.

---

[1] "It is mental action in these doors"—*Pyī.*

In such a case moral consciousness in the realm of sense arises through the threefold door of action, and not through the five (external) sense-doors. The feeling, pleasurable, painful, or neutral, is conditioned by eye-contact. It does so by means of the six doors of contact, but not through the eight doors when unrestrained; it arises through the eight doors when restrained; [106] it does not arise through the ten courses of immoral action; it arises through the ten courses of moral action. Therefore, whether this (first main type of moral) consciousness[1] has arisen through the doors of threefold action, or through the six doors of contact, or through the eight restraint-doors, or the ten courses of moral action, it was said with reference to all classes of sensuous consciousness that 'the sensuous moral consciousness that has arisen has either a visible or an audible object, etc., or an idea for its object.'[1]

Here ends the Discourse on 'Doors.'

---

[1] *Dhs.* § 1.

PART IV—OF MORAL CONSCIOUS EXPERIENCE IN THE WORLDS OF SENSE

CHAPTER I

OF THE SUMMARY OF CONSCIOUS STATES

WHATEVER be the object with which consciousness is concerned[1] —in other words, the consciousness in question has arisen concerning, that is, has made an object of, any of the objects of sense or ideas of sense specified above. Up to this clause it might seem as though any one object only among these objects is permitted to this consciousness; so that it (*i.e.*, this consciousness) arises on one occasion in one person attending to a visible object· and again it arises on another occasion in another person with a sound, and so forth as object. But there is no such order as its coming into being in any one existence first with a visible object, afterwards with sound as object. Nor is there any such uniformity as its coming into being first with a blue-green object, afterwards with a yellow object among objects. And it was in order to show that it can arise with *all* objects, and that there is neither order in them nor, in the absence of order, any uniformity in respect of specific sensations, that he said:—' Whatever be the object, etc.' Consciousness arises not only with a certain, say, visible object among these objects, but in reality with any one of them as object. It does not first attend to a visible object and then to sound. It arises with any one of the objects whatsoever by way of passing over one or two or more intermediate terms either in the reverse order or in the way of right succession. Moreover, in the case of a visible object it does not arise with such a uniformity as attending first to a blue-green object, afterwards to a yellow object, but with

[1] *Dhs.* § 1.

any one of them. Such is the meaning. And the same with sound as object. This is one construction of the phrase in question.

Another is as follows:—Consciousness is termed visual, auditory, etc., or cogitative, because it has a visible, audible, etc., object, [107] or has an idea as its object. After having said that such consciousness arises with its corresponding object, he added the phrase 'whatever be the object,' etc. The meaning of this phrase is that consciousness may arise with any one of those objects in the manner explained above. The Great Commentary, however, explains as follows:—'There is nothing *new* implied by the expression "whatever be the object"; what has already been enumerated is to be taken.' And it goes on:—'This expression was used in order to teach that consciousness comes into being with this or that object, *i.e.*, visible object . . . or idea.' Thus much only is in the Great Commentary.

'At that time'[1] is an expression which definitely fixes the time shown indefinitely by the expression 'at what time.' Hence this matter should be regarded thus:—*When moral consciousness in the realm of sense arises, then only there is contact*, etc., down to *absence of distraction*.

Here, just as there is consciousness, so also is there contact, etc. What kind of contact? It is that experienced in the realm of sense; it is moral; it has arisen, and it is accompanied by pleasure—in this way the construction should be made by means of such terms as are obtainable. That the expression, 'as are obtainable,' is used because, in the case of feeling, the phrase, 'accompanied by pleasure' is not obtainable, and in the case of insight, 'associated with knowledge' is not obtainable, is an opinion of teachers[2] out of touch with the Commentaries, and should not be regarded as possessing any value.

But why is contact mentioned here first? Because of its being the first incidence of consciousness on an object, and arises touching the object. Therefore it is mentioned first.

---

[1] *Dhs.* § 1.

[2] Such as Revata.—*Ṭīkā*.

Touching by contact, consciousness experiences by feeling, perceives by perception, wills by volition. Hence it has been said:—'Bhikkhus, touched one feels, touched one perceives, touched one wills.'[1] Further: Just as in a palace a pillar is the strong support to the rest of the structure, just as beams, cross-beams, wing-supports, roof, rafters, cross-rafters, neck-pieces are bound to the pillar, fixed on to the pillar, so is contact a strong support to the co-existent and associated states. It is like the pillar, and the remaining states are like the rest of the structure.

But why, again, is it mentioned first? for the foregoing gives no reason. For of states which have arisen in one conscious moment it is not valid to say that 'this' arises first, 'that' afterwards. The reason is not because contact is a strong support. Contact is just mentioned [108] first in the order of teaching, but it were also permissible to bring it in thus:—There are feeling and contact, perception and contact, volition and contact; there is consciousness and contact, feeling, perception, volition, initial application of mind. In the order of teaching, however, contact is mentioned first. Nor is the sequence of words among the remaining states of any special significance. [Inquiry should be conducted as follows:—] Contact means 'it touches.' It has touching as its *salient characteristic*, impact as its *function*,[2] 'coinciding' (of the physical basis, object and consciousness) as its *manifestation*,[3] and the object which has entered the avenue [of awareness] as *proximate cause*.

Though it is an immaterial state, it proceeds with respect to objects after the mode of 'touching.' Hence touch is its *characteristic*.

There is no impinging on one side of the object [as in physical contact], nevertheless contact causes consciousness and object to be in collision, as visible object and visual organs, sound and hearing; thus impact is its *function;* or it has impact as its *essential property* in the sense of attainment, owing to the

---

[1] *Saṃyutta* iv. 68; words in different order.

[2] Or 'essential property.' Cf. *Comp. of Phil.* 13, 213.

[3] Or 'resulting phenomenon.' *Ibid.*

impact of the physical basis with the mental object. For it is said in the Commentary:—'Contact in the four planes of existence is never without the characteristic of touch with the object; but the function of impact takes place in the five doors. For to sense, or five-door contact is given the name: "having the characteristic of touch," as well as "having the function of impact." But to contact in the mind-door there is only the characteristic of touch, but not the function of impact.' And then this Sutta is quoted: 'As if, sire, two rams were to fight, one ram to represent the eye, the second the visible object; and their collision, contact. And as if, sire, two cymbals were to strike against each other, or two hands were to clap against each other; one hand would represent the eye, the second the visible object, and their collision contact. Thus contact has the characteristic of touch and the function of impact.'[1] Such is the detailed account.

Just as in such phrases as 'seeing a visible object with the eye,'[2] sense-cognition is spoken of by the name of eye, etc., so here it is spoken of as 'eye,' etc. Therefore should the meaning of 'to represent the eye,' etc., be understood as 'to represent visual cognition,' etc. This being so, [109] the function, in the sense of performance, of impact is accomplished, according to this Sutta, in the impact of consciousness with object.

Contact has coinciding as *manifestation*, because it is revealed through its own cause, known as the coinciding of three (basis, object, and consciousness). This is shown here and there by the Sutta-phrase:—'contact is the collision of three.'[3] And in this phrase the meaning is that it is contact because of the collision of the three, but it should not be understood that the mere collision is contact. Thus because it was declared that contact mani-

---

[1] *Milinda* i. 92 *f.*

[2] Quoted in *Dhs.* § 1345.

[3] *Majjhima*, i, 111; *Saṃyutta*, ii, 72; etc. The sense is brought up to the object, there is attention or adverting to the object, the object is prepared, and there is cognition of the object by consciousness.—*Ṭīkā.*

fests itself in this wise, therefore its manifestation is called coinciding. But if manifestation be taken in the sense of effect, contact has feeling as effect. That is, contact produces feeling, causes it to arise. Just as it is the heat in heated lac, and not the coals, or external cause, which produces softness, so albeit there is another cause, viz., the mental object and the basis, it is the consciousness in which feeling inheres which produces it, and not that [external] cause.

Because contact arises by means of suitable attention, or 'adverting,' and through some faculty (*i.e.*, eye, etc.), and immediately in the object that has been prepared by consciousness, therefore contact has as its *proximate cause* an object that has entered the avenue of thought.

'Feeling'[1] is that which feels. It has (1) experiencing as characteristic, (2) enjoying as function, or possessing the desirable portion of an object as function, (3) taste of the mental properties as manifestation, and (4) tranquillity as proximate cause.

(1) There is no such thing as feeling in the four planes of existence without the characteristic of experiencing.

(2) If it be said that the function of enjoying the object is obtained only in pleasurable feeling, we reject that opinion, and say:—'Let it be pleasurable feeling or painful feeling or neutral feeling—all have the function of enjoying (*anubhavana*) the object.'

As regards enjoying the taste of an object, the remaining associated states enjoy it only partially. Of contact there is (the function of) the mere touching, of perception the mere noting or perceiving, of volition the mere co-ordinating (the associated states, or exerting or being active), of consciousness the mere cognizing. But feeling alone, through governance, proficiency, mastery, enjoys the taste of an object. For feeling is like the king, the remaining states are like the cook. As the cook, when he has prepared food of divers tastes, puts it in a basket, seals it, takes it to the king, breaks the seal,

[1] *Dhs.* § 3.

opens the basket, [110] takes the best of all the soup and curries, puts them in a dish, swallows [a portion] to find out whether they are faulty or not, and afterwards offers the food of various excellent tastes to the king, and the king, being lord, expert, and master, eats whatever he likes, even so the mere testing of the food by the cook is like the partial enjoyment of the object by the remaining states, and as the cook tests a portion of the food, so the remaining states enjoy a portion of the object, and as the king, being lord, expert, and master, eats the meal according to his pleasure, so feeling, being lord, expert and master, enjoys the taste of the object, and therefore it is said that enjoyment or experience is its function.

In that second definition[1] feeling is understood as the enjoyment only of the desirable portion of an object 'in any manner' (*i.e.*, by its nature or intention). Thus it is said to have the function of enjoying the desired portion of the object.

(3) The mere presence of feeling, as such, is referred to by calling its manifestation 'tasting a mental property (*cetasika*).'

(4) And inasmuch as a tranquillized body enjoys bliss or happiness, feeling has tranquillity as its proximate cause.

The noting of an object as blue-green, etc., is perception.[2] It has the characteristic of noting and the function of recognizing what has been previously noted. There is no such thing as perception in the four planes of existence without the characteristic of noting. All perceptions have the characteristic of noting. Of them, that perceiving which knows by specialized knowledge has the function of recognizing what has been noted previously. We may see this procedure when the carpenter recognizes a piece of wood which he has marked by specialized knowledge; when we recognize a man by his sectarial mark on the forehead, which we have noted by our specialized knowledge, and say: 'He is so and so'; or when the king's treasurer, in charge of the royal wardrobe,

---

[1] Namely, that only joyful feeling enjoys.—*Pyī*. See preceding page.

[2] *Dhs.* § 4. 'Perception,' 'noting'=saññā, sañjānanā.

having had a label bound on each dress and, being asked to bring a certain one, lights the lamp, enters the jewel chamber, reads the label, and brings the dress. According to another method, perception has the characteristic of noting by an act of general inclusion, and the function of [assigning] 'mark-reasons' for this inclusive noting, as when woodcutters 'perceive' logs, and so forth.

Its manifestation is an inclining [of the attention], as in the case of blind persons who 'see' an elephant.[1] Or, it has briefness as manifestation, like lightning, owing to its inability to penetrate the object.

[111] Its proximate cause is whatever object has appeared, like the perception which arises in young deer mistaking scarecrows for men. Of the perceptions, that which is associated with knowledge follows it, just as, among the elements of extension, etc., with their constituents, the remaining constituents follow the element of extension, etc.[2]

Volition is that which co-ordinates, that is, it binds closely * to itself associated states as objects. This is its characteristic; its function is conation. There is no such thing as volition in the four planes of existence without the characteristic of co-ordinating; all volition has it. But the function of conation is only in moral and immoral states; as regards activity in moral and immoral acts, the remaining associated states play only a restricted part. But volition is exceedingly energetic. It makes a double effort, a double exertion. Hence the Ancients said:

---

[1] Like the blind who imagine an elephant by the particular characteristic of the part touched—*e.g.*, he who has touched the tail says that the elephant is like a broom-handle, and he who has touched the leg says it is like a pestle, etc.—*Pyī*. Or like one who, though now blind, can say what an elephant is like.—*Ariyālaṅkāra*. Cf. *Udāna*, VI. 4.

[2] The element of extension has stability and support as characteristic, yet it cannot appear by itself; it appears with its seven constituents —viz.: colour, odour, taste, essence (*ojā*), moisture, heat, motion. Although this is so, at whatever time its state is stable, it is called extension. Thus the constituents follow the element.—*Ariyālaṅkāra*.

* *Abhisandahati*.

'Volition is like the nature of a landowner,[1] a cultivator who, taking fifty-five strong men, went down to the fields to reap. He was exceedingly energetic and exceedingly strenuous; he doubled his strength, he doubled his effort, and said, "Take your sickles," and so forth, pointed out the portion to be reaped, offered them drink, food, scent, flowers, etc., and took an equal share of the work.' The simile should be thus applied: Volition is like the cultivator; the fifty-five moral states which arise as factors of consciousness are like the fifty-five strong men; like the time of doubling strength, doubling effort by the cultivator is the doubled strength, double effort of volition as regards activity in moral and immoral acts. Thus should conation as its function be understood.

It has directing as manifestation. It arises directing associated states, like the chief disciple, the chief carpenter, etc., who fulfil their own and others' duties. As the chief disciple, seeing the teacher come from afar, himself recites his lessons and makes other pupils recite each his own lesson; when he begins the recitation, the rest follow; and as the head woodcutter, hewing the wood, himself makes other woodcutters do each [112] his own work; for when he begins, the others follow; and as the general, fighting himself, makes other soldiers take part in the battle, for when he begins, the others follow his example without turning back; even so, when volition starts work on its object, it sets associated states to do each its own work. For when it puts forth energy, they also put forth energy. Hence the statement that it accomplishes its own and others' work, like the chief pupil or the head carpenter. It is also evident that it arises by causing associated states to be energetic in such things as recollecting an urgent work, and so forth.

[Mind or] consciousness[2] is that which thinks of its object. A definition of the word has been given.[3] As to its characteristics, etc., cognizing object is its characteristic, forerunning

---

[1] Reading not *vācāriyā*, but *thāvariyā*=*khettasāmi* or landowner. But some read *Pāvāriya*, as the cultivator's name.—*Tr.*

[2] *Dhs.* § 6.

[3] Above, p. 84.

is its function, connecting is its manifestation, a mental and material organism[1] is its proximate cause. There is no such thing as consciousness in the four planes of existence without the characteristic of cognizing. All consciousness has it. But when a 'door' is reached at the place[2] where the 'object' is evolved, consciousness is the forerunner, the precursor. A visible object seen by the eye is cognized by consciousness, etc. . . . an idea known by the mind is cognized by consciousness. For just as the town-guard, seated at cross-roads in the middle of the town, ascertains and notes each comer:—'This is a townsman, this is a stranger,' and so forth, so should this matter be understood. So, too, it was said by the Elder (Nāgasena):—[3] 'Just, sire, as the town-guard, seated at the cross-roads in the middle of the town, would see a man coming from the east, would see a man coming from the west, the south, the north: so, your majesty, the object seen by the eye, the sound heard by the ear, the smell smelt by the nose, the taste tasted by the tongue, the tangible touched by the body, the idea cognized by the mind, is cognized by consciousness.' [113] Therefore it is said to have the function of forerunning.

The consciousness which arises next does so immediately after the preceding consciousness, forming a connected series. Thus it has connection as manifestation.

Where there are all five aggregates, a mental and material organism is always its proximate cause; where there are four aggregates,[4] mind only is its proximate cause. Therefore it is said that mind-and-matter is its proximate cause.

But is this consciousness the same as the former consciousness, or is it different? The same. Then wherefore is that which was previously dealt with mentioned again? This has not been considered in the Commentary. But it is suitable to do so here. The sun and other things, as terms and concepts, derived from material or other data, are

---

[1] Nāmarūpam.

[2] Ṭhāne.

[3] *Milinda* i. 95.

[4] As in ideation.—*Ed.*

actually not different from those data, so that when the sun arises its material quality, viz.: heat, also arises, albeit there is no sun different from the material quality. Consciousness also appears as a derivative from such phenomena as contact, etc.; but actually it is different from them. Hence, when consciousness arises, certainly then it is actually different from contact, etc. To show this meaning the mention of consciousness is repeated, and should thus be regarded.[1]

In such passages as:[2] 'When for the attainment of the Rūpa world one cultivates the path thereto and, aloof from sensualities and from immoral states, by means of the earth-device, attains and abides in the first Jhāna . . . then there arises contact,' etc., he who 'then'—at a fixed time—is practising is not the identical he who is reborn. And therefore in this passage it is only said 'there is contact . . . feeling'; it is not said:[3] he who is practising, *he* is reborn. But in our passage also:—'when moral consciousness . . . arises,' etc.,[4] the consciousness assigned to the given time is not actually identical in its arising with the consciousness which assigned that given time. Hence it is that, when it is said: 'then there is contact, feeling,' it is also said: 'there is consciousness.' And hence the repetition of the word 'consciousness' must be regarded as showing what actually happens.

This is [our] judgment as to the repetition of 'consciousness.' In the section on the outline, the meaning was condensed;[5] in the section of exposition it is detailed. For by the first word consciousness the time has merely been fixed. But in order to show, at the time fixed by consciousness, what states are present, a beginning is made with 'there is contact,' consciousness being also [named as] present; hence the repetition to include that consciousness.

---

[1] The simile holds good so far as the arising goes; the emphasis is on the actual arising of consciousness together with contact, etc., as the sun always rises with, *e.g.*, its rays.—*Tr.* Cf. *Dhs.* § 1, lines 2, 7.

[2] *Dhs.* § 160.

[3] In P.T.S. ed. read *so hotīti na vuttaṃ*.—*Ed.*

[4] *Dhs.* § 1.

[5] P. 84.

[114] In this place, if the word 'that' were not mentioned, it would not be possible in the section of exposition[1] to classify the consciousness (arising) at that time. Thus would its classification suffer. Therefore to classify consciousness in this section it has been repeated.

Or, because in the phrase 'has arisen' this, namely, 'consciousness which has arisen,' is the principal term in the teaching, the Commentary considers that, since consciousness does not arise in isolation, it is not in the word 'arisen' taken by itself, but in conjunction with the fifty-five moral [concomitant] states. And thus 'consciousness' is first used inclusively as involving both itself and these, and secondly as distinct from these and with them classified according to their nature in detail, beginning with 'contact,' consciousness being here considered as one of them.

'Initial application of mind'[2] is literally 'one thinks about,' or a 'thinking about.' It is said to be the prescinding [of the mind].[3] Its [main] *characteristic* is the lifting of consciousness on to the object; having an object, it lifts consciousness up to it. As someone depending on a relative or friend dear to the king ascends the king's palace, so depending on initial application the mind ascends the object. Therefore it has been said that initial application lifts the mind on to the object. And the Elder Nāgasena said that 'initial application of mind has the characteristic of the initial knocking. As, sire, when a drum is struck, it goes on reverberating and emitting a continuous sound, so initial application of mind should be looked upon as the initial stroke; and sustained application of the mind as the after-reverberation and continuous emission of sound.'[4] It has the *function* of impinging, of circumimpinging. By initial application of mind the aspirant is said to strike at and around the object. Its *manifestation* is bringing the mind near to the object.

---

1 *Dhs.* § 6. 2 *Dhs.* § 7.

3 Cf. *Mil.* i. 51, where this characteristic (*ūhana*) is assigned to 'wisdom' (*paññā*).—*Ed.*

4 Cf. *ib.* i. 96, where the simile actually used is a copper vessel, not a drum.—*Ed.*

'Sustained application of mind'[1] is discursive work upon, or traversing of the object. It has threshing out (or contemplation)[2] of object as *characteristic*, the linking of co-existent states to the object as *function*, and continuous binding as *manifestation*. Although there is in some consciousness[3] the non-separation of initial and sustained applications of mind, the former is the first incidence of the mind on the object, as it were the striking of a bell, because it is more gross than, and runs before, (the latter). [115] The latter is the consequent binding of consciousness on the object, as it were the reverberation of the bell, because it is more subtle and of the nature of repeated threshing of the object.

Of the two, initial application of mind possesses vibration.[4] When it first arises, it is as a state of mental thrill, like the flapping of the wings of a bird about to fly up in the air, and like the alighting in front of the lotus of a bee with mind intent on the perfume; sustained application of mind is of a calmer tenour, without much mental thrill, like the planing movement of the wings of a bird in the sky, and the gyrating of the bee about the lotus on which it has alighted. But in the Commentary[5] initial application, as a lifting of the mind on to the object, is likened to the movement of a big bird in the sky, taking the wind with both wings and keeping them steadily in a line. For it advances bent on a single object. Sustained application, on the other hand, should be understood as a state of contemplating which is like the movement of that flying bird flapping its wings to take the wind. For it has been called a threshing of the object. It is a very fitting term to use for a continuous occurrence. The difference between initial and sustained application of mind is plain in the first and second Jhānas.[6] Further, as when a man holds

---

[1] *Dhs.* § 8.

[2] Anumajjana. Morris derived it from *mṛj.*, *J.P.T.S.*, 1886, p. 118.—*Ed.*

[3] *E.g.*, in First Jhāna, fourfold system.

[4] On *vipphāra*, Cf. *Points of Controversy*, 239 § 9.—*Ed.*

[5] *I.e.*, on the Aṅguttara N. i. 171 § 5.—*Ed.*

[6] Fivefold system.

firmly by one hand a dirty copper bowl, and with the other scrubs it with brush (or husk), initial application of mind is like the firmly holding hand, and sustained application of mind the scrubbing hand. So, too, as the potter whirls the wheel by the stroke of the handle and makes the pot, initial application is like the hand pressing the clay down, sustained application the hand turning it to and fro. Again, in making a circle the applying initial application of mind is like the thorn fixed in the middle and the contemplating sustained application of mind the revolving thorn outside.

'Zest,' 'rapture,' is literally that which satisfies, develops.[1] It has satisfaction as *characteristic*, the thrilling of body and mind (or suffusion) as *function*, and elation as *manifestation*. Rapture is of five kinds:—the lesser thrill, momentary rapture, flooding rapture, all-pervading rapture and transporting rapture. Of these, the lesser thrill is only able to raise the hairs of the body; the momentary rapture is like the production of lightning moment by moment; [116] like waves breaking on the seashore, the flooding rapture descends on the body and breaks; the transporting rapture is strong, and lifts the body up to the extent of launching it in the air.

As the Elder Mahātissa residing at Puṇṇavallika on the full-moon day at eventide went into the courtyard of the shrine, saw the moonlight, and turning to the Great Shrine,[2] he called up the transporting rapture, with the Buddha as object of thought, and by virtue of having habitually dwelt upon the vision, at the thought:—'In such an hour, lo! the four assemblies salute the Great Shrine'—on the cemented floor he rose in the sky like a ball with mind entranced, and stood even in the courtyard of the Shrine. Likewise a certain daughter of noble family in Vattakālaka village, the support of Girikaṇḍaka monastery, soared into the sky also by strong transporting rapture when thinking of the Buddha. It is said that her parents, going in the evening to the monastery to hear the Doctrine, said, 'Dear, you are heavily burdened; it is

---

[1] *Dhs.* § 9. Pīṇayatīti pīti.

[2] At Anurādhapura.—*Tr.*

not the time for you to be walking; you are not able. We shall hear the Doctrine, and make merit for you,' and went. Although desirous of going, she was not able to disregard their words, and remained behind in the house. She stood at the door and, looking by moonlight at the courtyard of the Shrine against the sky at Girikaṇḍaka, saw the offering of lamps to the shrine and the four assemblies doing honour to the shrine by garlands and scented perfumes, etc., and circumambulating it, and heard the sound of the mass-chanting of the Brotherhood. Then to her occurred the thought: 'Blessed indeed must be these who can get to the monastery and walk in such a courtyard, and hear such a sweet religious discourse,' and to her, looking at the Shrine rising like a mass of pearls, arose transporting rapture. She soared into the sky, and descended therefrom to the courtyard earlier than her parents, saluted the Shrine, and stood listening to the Doctrine. Then her parents coming asked her: 'Dear, by which way did you come?' 'Dear parents, I came by the sky, and not by the road.' 'Dear, by the sky only saints can go; how could you have come?' Thus questioned, she said, 'As I was standing looking at the shrine in the moonlight, there arose in me a strong rapture while thinking on the Buddha. Then I knew not whether I stood or sat, but I laid hold of a sign, and sprang into the sky, and stood in the courtyard.' So far can transporting rapture work.

[117] When all-pervading rapture arises, the whole body is completely surcharged, blown like a full bladder or like a mountain cavern pouring forth a mighty flood of water. This fivefold rapture, becoming pregnant and maturing, begets the twofold repose of mental factors and of consciousness; repose, becoming pregnant and maturing, begets the twofold bliss, bodily and mental; bliss, becoming pregnant and maturing, begets the threefold concentration:—momentary concentration, access-concentration and ecstatic concentration. Of these, the first two belong here.

Bliss[1] or ease[1] is that which gives pleasure.[2] In whom it

---

[1] *Sukhaṃ*. [2] *Dhs.* § 10.

arises it makes him happy, is its meaning. It is a synonym for joyous feeling. Its *characteristic*, etc., are the same as in feeling.[1] According to another method, bliss or ease has the *characteristic* of being pleasant, the development of associated states as its *function*, and showing favour[2] to the same as its *manifestation*. Although in some kinds of consciousness[3] rapture and bliss are not dissociated, rapture (or zest) is delight in the attaining of the desired object, bliss or ease is the enjoyment of the taste of what is acquired. Where rapture is, there is ease; but where ease is, there is not always rapture. Rapture is classed under the aggregate of mental co-efficients, ease under the aggregate of feeling. Rapture is like a weary traveller in the desert in summer, who hears of, or sees water or a shady wood. Ease is like his enjoying the water or entering the forest shade. For a man who, travelling along the path through a great desert and overcome by the heat, is thirsty and desirous of drink, if he saw a man on the way, would ask, 'Where is water?' The other would say, 'Beyond the wood is a dense forest with a natural lake. Go there, and you will get some.' He hearing these words would be glad and delighted, and as he went would see lotus leaves, etc., fallen on the ground and become more glad and delighted. Going onwards, he would see men with wet clothes and hair, hear the sounds of wild fowl and pea-fowl, etc., see the dense forest of green like a net of jewels growing by the edge of the natural lake, he would see the water lily, the lotus, the white lily, etc., growing in the lake, he would see the clear transparent water, he would be all the more glad and delighted, [118] would descend into the natural lake, bathe and drink at pleasure and, his oppression being allayed, he would eat the fibres and stalks of the lilies, adorn himself with the blue lotus, carry on his shoulders the roots of the mandālaka, ascend from the lake, put on his clothes, dry the bathing cloth in the sun, and in the cool shade where the breeze blew ever so gently lay himself down and say:

---

[1] P. 145 *f*.

[2] Anuggahana. Pyī interprets this as 'repeated grasping'—*i.e.*, of the mental object.

[3] Cf. First Jhāna.—*Tr.*

'O bliss! O bliss!' Thus should this illustration be applied:—The time of gladness and delight from when he heard of the natural lake and the dense forest till he saw the water is like rapture having the manner of gladness and delight at the object in view. The time when, after his bath and drink he laid himself down in the cool shade, saying, 'O bliss! O bliss!' etc., is the sense of ease grown strong,[1] established in that mode of enjoying the taste of the object. In fact, the description (of the two terms) is repeatedly illustrated,[2] and so is the fact that where there is rapture or zest, there also is happiness.

Cittekaggatā[3] is one-pointedness of mind, another name for concentration. Regarding its characteristic, etc., the Commentary has the following:—Concentration has the characteristic of leadership, also of non-distraction. As the dome of a gabled house from binding the remaining constituents of the building is the leader, so concentration is the leader of all those states from their being accomplished by consciousness associated with concentration. Hence has it been said: 'As, your majesty, all the rafters of a gabled house go to the ridgepole, incline towards, meet at the ridgepole, the ridgepole is called the chief among them; so, your majesty, all moral states incline towards concentration, slope towards concentration, take refuge in concentration; concentration is called the chief among them.'[4] And as the king in battle goes wherever the army is giving way, and the army wherever he has gone becomes reinforced and—the hostile army being broken—follows the king,[5] so concentration, from not allowing the co-existent states to be thrown out and scattered, has non-distraction as its characteristic.

---

[1] *Balappattaṃ*. The 'Mandalay' MS. (India Office) has *phalappattaṃ*, 'which has won fruition.'—*Ed.*

[2] As the hearing and seeing of the lake and forest, etc.—*Yojanā*.

[3] *Dhs.* § 11.

[4] *Mil.* i. 60. 'Refuge in' (*samādhippabbhārā*), as in a cave. The three figures occur in the Nikāyas, applied to the sea (*S.* iv. 79) and to Nibbāna (*ib.* 180, etc.). The text of the Burmese translation reads pāmokkha.—*Ed.*

[5] This simile is also in *Mil.*, *ib.*, but is here slightly altered and made more telling.—*Ed.*

Here is another explanation: This concentration, known as one-pointedness of mind, has non-scattering (of itself) or non-distraction (of associated states) as *characteristic*, the welding together of the co-existent states as *function*, as water kneads bath-powder into a paste, and peace of mind or knowledge as *manifestation*. [119] For it has been said: 'He who is concentrated knows, sees according to the truth.'[1] It is distinguished by having ease as *proximate cause*. Like the steadiness of the flame of a lamp in the absence of wind, so should steadfastness of mind be understood.

By it persons or associated states believe, or one believes, or the mere believing—this is *saddhā* (faith).[2] From the overcoming of unfaith, faith is a controlling faculty in the sense of predominance, or in its characteristic of decision it exercises lordship (over associated states). Faith and *indriya*, or controlling faculty, give the compound 'faith-faculty.' It has purifying, or aspiring as its characteristic. As the water-purifying gem of the universal monarch thrown into water causes solids, alluvia, waterweeds and mud to subside and makes the water clear, transparent and undisturbed, so faith arising discards the hindrances, causes the corruptions to subside, purifies the mind and makes it undisturbed; the mind being purified, the aspirant of noble family gives gifts, observes the precepts, performs the sabbath duties and commences his culture. Thus faith should be known to have purifying as its characteristic. Hence has it been said by the venerable Nāgasena: 'As if, your majesty, a universal monarch were to cross a small stream with his fourfold army, and the water would be perturbed, dirty, stirred up and muddy by the elephants, horses, chariots and infantry. And the king, when he had crossed, were to give an order to the men, "Bring me water, I say. I will drink." Now supposing the water-purifying gem of the king would be with them, they would reply, "Even so, lord," and throw the gem into the water. Then at once the solids, alluvia, water-weeds and mud would subside, and the water would become clear, transparent and

---

[1] *A.* v. 3.

[2] *Dhs.* § 12.

undisturbed, and they would offer the water to the king saying, "May the lord drink." As, your majesty, the water, so should the mind be regarded; as those men, so the aspirant; as the solids, alluvia, water-weeds and mud, so the corruptions; as the water-purifying gem, so faith; as the moment when the water-purifying gem is thrown, and the solids, alluvia, etc., subsiding, the water becomes clear, transparent and undisturbed, so, your majesty, faith arising discards the hindrances, [120] and the mind being free from them becomes clear, transparent and undisturbed.'[1]

It is, again, as though a timid crowd stood on both banks of a great river full of all sorts of crocodiles, monsters, sharks, ogres, etc. And a great warrior, the hero of battles, came and inquired, 'Why do you stand still?' And they would reply, 'We dare not cross on account of the dangers.' But he, grasping his sharpened sword and saying, 'Follow me and have no fear,' crossed the river and repelled the oncoming crocodiles, etc. And making it safe for those folk he led them from this bank to that, and from that bank he led them in safety to the hither bank.[2] So faith is the forerunner, the precursor to one who is giving gifts, observing the precepts, performing sabbath duties and commencing culture. Hence has it been said: Faith has purifying and aspiring as its characteristic.

Yet another view:—Faith has confiding as its characteristic; purifying as its function, like the water-purifying gem, or aspiring faith as function, like the crossing of the floods; freedom from pollution or decision as its manifestation; an object worthy of faith or factors of stream-winning[3] as its proximate cause. It should be regarded as at once hand, property and seed.[4]

Viriya is the state of an energetic man, or it is the action of the energetic, or it is that which should be effected, carried

---

[1] *Mil.* i. 54.

[2] Cf. *ibid.* 55, where the danger lies in the river being in flood.—*Ed.*

[3] *D.* iii. 227; *S.* ii. 68-71, etc.

[4] *I.e.*, as emblems of agency, fulfilment, and condition of good thoughts—*Ariyālaṅkāra.*

out by method or suitable means. From its overcoming idleness it is a controlling faculty in the sense of predominance. Or, it exercises government with the characteristic of grasp. Combined with faculty we get the compound: 'energy-faculty.' Its characteristic is strengthening, and grasp, or support. As an old house stands when strengthened by new pillars, so the aspirant, when strengthened by energy, does not fall off. or deteriorate as to moral states. Thus should the characteristic of strengthening be understood. Hence it was said by Nāgasena: 'As, your majesty, when a house is falling one should strengthen it with other pieces of wood; being thus strengthened, the house would not fall, so, your majesty, [121] energy has the characteristic of strengthening; all moral states when strengthened by energy do not fall away.'[1] And as a small army going to battle might be repulsed; then they would tell the king; the king would send a strong reinforcement; the king's army, being thus supported, would defeat the hostile army:—thus energy does not allow associated states to recede, to retreat; it uplifts, supports them. Hence has it been said that energy has the characteristic of supporting.

Another view is that energy has exerting as its characteristic, strengthening the co-existent states as function, and opposition to giving way as manifestation. It has been said: 'He being agitated, makes a rational effort,'[2] hence it has agitation, or the basic condition of making energy as proximate cause. Right energy should be regarded as the root of all attainments.

Sati[3]—by this they remember the object, or one remembers the object, or the mere remembering of the object—this is mindfulness. From overcoming confused memory, it is a faculty in the sense of predominance. It exercises government (over associated states) by the characteristic of '*being present in*,'[4] hence it is a controlling faculty, and hence the

---

[1] *Mil.* i. 57. Viriya and paggāha are in that translation rendered 'perseverance' and 'tension' respectively.—*Ed.*

[2] *Mil.* i. 57; here again the simile is not cited *verbatim.*—*Ed.*

[3] *Dhs.* § 14.

[4] Namely, in any object of the past.—*Pyi.*

compound 'mindfulness-faculty.' Its characteristic is 'not floating away,'[1] and acquirement. As the young treasurer of the king, in charge of the tenfold treasure, both early and late causes the king to take note of and remember the royal possession, so mindfulness takes note of, remembers a moral act. Hence the Elder said: 'As, your majesty, the king's confidential adviser early and late makes the universal monarch remember: so many, lord, are your elephants, so many horses, so many chariots, so much infantry, so much bullion, so much gold, so much property; let your majesty remember it—even so, your majesty, mindfulness does not allow the floating away of moral states, such as the four applications of mindfulness, the four supreme efforts, the four bases of supernatural potency, the five controlling faculties, the five powers, the seven factors of wisdom, the Ariyan eightfold path, calm, insight, knowledge, emancipation, the transcendent states:—thus, your majesty, mindfulness has non-floating away as its characteristic.'[2] And as that jewel, the confidential adviser of the universal monarch, knowing what is disadvantageous and what is advantageous, removes the disadvantageous and promotes the advantageous, so mindfulness, searching well the courses of advantageous and disadvantageous states:—'these are disadvantageous states, misconduct in body,' etc., removes the disadvantageous states, and [122] acquires the advantageous ones:—'these are advantageous states, good conduct as regards body,' etc. Hence the Elder said: 'As, your majesty, that king's jewel, the confidential adviser, knows what is advantageous and what is disadvantageous to the king:—"these are advantageous to the king, those disadvantageous; these are serviceable, those not serviceable"—and then removes the disadvantageous and acquires the advantageous, even so, your majesty, mindfulness as it arises searches well the courses of states, advantageous and disadvantageous:—"these states are advan-

---

[1] Not allowing any floating away, as of a pumpkin in a stream. It does not suffer the object to slip, but keeps it steady as a rock.—*Ṭīkā*.

[2] *Mil.* i. 59. 'Transcendent' (lit. supramundane) states is not in the cited work. It sums up the foregoing 41.—*Ed.*

tageous, those disadvantageous; these states are serviceable, those not serviceable"—and then removes the disadvantageous and acquires the advantageous. Thus, your majesty, mindfulness has acquirement as its characteristic.'[1]

Here is another method: mindfulness has 'not floating away' as its characteristic, unforgetfulness as its function, guarding, or the state of facing the object, as its manifestation, firm perception, or application in mindfulness as regards the body, etc., as proximate cause. It should be regarded as a door-post from being firmly established in the object, and as a door-keeper from guarding the door of the senses.

'Concentration'[2] is that state which sets and places the mind in the object. From overcoming distraction of mind, it is a controlling faculty in the sense of predominance. It exercises government (over associated states) by the characteristic of imperturbability; thus it is a controlling faculty, and gives the compound 'concentration-faculty.' Its characteristic, etc., are those of 'one-pointedness of mind' (p. 156).

Paññā[3] means one understands (*pajānāti*). What does one understand? The Ariyan Facts (or Truths) by the method: This is ill, etc. But in the Great Commentary understanding is defined as 'it causes to know (or understand). What does it cause to know? Impermanence, ill, soullessness.' Through overcoming ignorance, it is a controlling faculty in the sense of predominance. It exercises government (over associated states) by the characteristic of vision, hence it is a controlling faculty and gives the compound 'understanding-faculty.' It has illuminating and understanding as characteristic. As when a lamp burns at night in a four-walled house the darkness ceases, light manifests itself, so understanding has illuminating as its characteristic. There is no illumination equal to the illumination of understanding. To the wise at a single sitting the ten thousand world-spheres appear as of one light. Hence the Elder has said: 'Just as when a man, your majesty,

---

[1] *Mil.* i. 59. [2] *Dhs.* § 15. Samādhi. [3] *Ibid.* § 16.

introduces an oil-lamp into a dark house, the lamp so introduced disperses the darkness, produces light, [123] sheds lustre, makes objects visible, so, your majesty, understanding as it arises dispels the darkness of ignorance, produces the light of wisdom, sheds the lustre of knowledge, makes plain the Ariyan Facts. Thus, your majesty, understanding has illuminating as its characteristic.'[1]

And as a clever surgeon knows which food is suitable, and which is not, so understanding as it arises knows states as moral or immoral, serviceable or unserviceable, low or exalted, black or pure, similar or dissimilar. And this was said by the Generalissimo of the Law (Sāriputta): 'It knows; thus, brother, it is in consequence called understanding. And what does it know? This is ill,' etc.[2] Thus it should be expanded. And thus knowing should be regarded as the characteristic of understanding.

Here is another view:—Understanding has the penetration of intrinsic nature, unfaltering penetration as its characteristic, like the penetration of an arrow shot by a skilled archer; illumination of the object as its function, as it were a lamp; non-perplexity as its proximate cause, as it were a good guide in the forest.

Mind (*mano*)[3] is minding, that is, it discerns (cognizes). But the authors of the Commentary say: like measuring by the *nāḷi* or balancing by a great weight, mind knows the object. It exercises government (over associated states) by the characteristic of measuring, hence it is a controlling faculty, giving the compound 'mind-faculty.' It is just a synonym for consciousness (*citta*) mentioned above.[4]

Sumano, 'joyous,'[5] means that one's mind, being associated with zest and joy, is beautiful; and the state of being joyous is joy. It exercises government (over associated states) by the characteristic of pleasantness, hence it is a controlling faculty, and gives the compound 'joy-faculty.' It is another term for happiness, ease, mentioned above.[6]

---

[1] *Mil.* i. 61. [2] *Majjhima* i. 292. [3] *Dhs.* § 17
[4] P. 148. [5] *Dhs.* § 18. [6] P. 145 *f.*

'Life'[1] is that by which associated states live. It exercises government (over associated states) by the characteristic of ceaseless watching, hence it is a controlling faculty, and gives the compound 'life-faculty.' It is the dominant influence over continuity in [organic] processes. As regards its characteristic, etc., it has the ceaseless watching over states undivided from itself as its characteristic; the processes of such states or co-existent states as function; the placing of them as manifestation; states that have to be kept going as proximate cause. And although there is orderly arrangement in life's essential properties, etc., it watches over those states only in the moment of (their and its) existence, [124] as water over lotuses, etc. And although it watches over them, arisen as its own property, as a nurse over the infant, life goes on only by being bound up with these states that have gone on, as the pilot on the boat. Beyond the cessant instant it does not go on, owing to the non-being both of itself and of the states which should have been kept going. At the cessant instant it does not maintain them, owing to its own destruction, as the spent oil in the wick cannot maintain the flame of the lamp. Its effective power is as its duration.

As to the next five terms,[2] right view conveys the meaning of vision; right intention, that of mental application;[3] right endeavour, that of support; right mindfulness, that of presence (or being at hand); right concentration, that of absence of distraction. As regards word-definitions:—that which sees rightly, or by which beings see objects rightly—this is right view. That which plans rightly, or by which beings plan rightly—this is right intention. That which rightly endeavours, or by which beings rightly endeavour—this is right endeavour. That which remembers rightly, or by

---

[1] *Dhs.* § 19. Jīvitaṃ.

[2] *Dhs.* §§ 20-24. 'Right' (*sammā*) has here the sense of irreversibility and escape from the succession of rebirths.—*Pyī.*

[3] Cf. above, p. 151. Cf. *Dhs.* §§ 7, 21: 'application of mind' and 'intention' are described in identical terms.—*Ed.*

which beings remember objects rightly—this is right mindfulness. That which evenly keeps the consciousness on the object, or by which associated states evenly keep the consciousness on the object—this is right concentration. Again, a praiseworthy or beautiful view is right view. In this way the word-definition should be understood. Their characteristics, etc., have been stated above.

As to the seven 'strengths'[1] 'faith' and so forth have been already described. And 'strength' (*bala*) should be understood in the sense of 'not shaking.' Of these seven, that which does not shake because of unbelief is the strength of faith. It does not shake because of idleness—this is strength of energy. It does not shake because of obliviousness—this is strength of mindfulness. It does not shake because of distraction—this is strength of concentration. It does not shake because of ignorance—this is strength of understanding. It does not shake because of shamelessness—this is strength of conscientiousness. It does not shake because of carelessness of blame—this is strength of fear of blame. Such is the explanation of the meaning by way of both terms.

The first five 'strengths' have been described above as regards their characteristics, etc. In the last pair,[2] conscientiousness is that which abominates or shrinks from. It is a synonym for shame. Fear of blame is [lit.] glowing [*i.e.*, with nervous heat]. It is a synonym for agitation at evil. In the table of contents shame was stated to be the characteristic. In the following detailed discourse will be shown their mutual difference, their origin and how they are influenced. [125] Conscientiousness has a subjective origin, fear of blame has an external cause. Conscientiousness is influenced by the self, fear of blame is influenced by the world. Conscientiousness is rooted in the intrinsic nature of shame, fear of blame in the intrinsic nature of fear. Conscientiousness has the characteristic of respectful obedience, fear of blame that of viewing a fault with timidity and fear. Of the two, conscientiousness

---

[1] *Dhs.* §§ 25-31

[2] *Ibid.* §§ 30, 31.

with its subjective origin arises from four causes: consideration of birth, of age, of heroism, of wide experience. How? 'This evil act is not such as would be done by those of [good] birth; it is such as those of low birth, fishermen and the like, would do; it is not fitting that such as I who am well-born should do it':—thus considering one's birth, and not committing evil such as life-taking, etc., one maintains [a standard of] conscientiousness. Again, 'this evil act is only worthy of boys; it is not fitting that one of my years should do it'—thus considering age, conscientiousness is maintained.' Again, 'this evil act is an act for the weak; it is not fitting that I, who have courage and strength, should do it':—thus considering, one refrains and maintains conscientiousness. Again, 'this evil act is an act for blind fools and not for the wise; it is not fitting that I, endowed with wisdom and wide experience, should do it':—thus considering one's wide experience, one refrains and maintains conscientiousness. Having thus set up conscientiousness by introducing it into the mind, one does not do evil acts, and thus conscientiousness has a subjective origin. How has fear of blame an external origin? 'If you do an evil act, you will get blame among the four assemblies.

The wise will blame you. As the citizen
Shuns all impurity, the good shun you.
How, bhikkhu, will you do that which is wrong?'

Thus considering, one does not do evil owing to fear of blame from without. Thus fear of blame has an external origin.

How is conscientiousness influenced by the self? Take a certain son of noble family [126] who makes self the chief influence, and so refrains from evil:—'It is not fit that such a man as I, who left the world through faith, endowed with wide experience, believing in the ascetic life, should do evil.' Thus is conscientiousness influenced by the self. Hence the Blessed One has said: 'He makes self the chief influence, and abandons immorality, develops morality, abandons faults and develops faultlessness, and keeps himself pure.'[1]

[1] *Aṅguttara* i. 148, slightly different.

How is fear of blame influenced by the world? Here a certain son of noble family makes the world the chief influence and does not do evil. As the Blessed One has said: 'Wide indeed is the world; in the wide world are monks and brahmins of supernormal potency, with clairvoyance and knowledge of others' thoughts. They see afar, although near at hand they are not seen; mentally they know the thoughts of others, me also (he thinks) they will know thus: "Look at this son of noble family. Though he has become a monk by faith, leaving his home for the homeless state, he lives mixed with evil immoral things. There are spirits with supernormal potency, clairvoyance, knowing the thoughts of others. They see afar," etc. Thus he makes the world the chief influence, abandons immorality, develops morality, abandons faults and develops faultlessness, and keeps himself pure.'[1] Thus fear of blame is influenced by the world.

Conscientiousness is rooted in the intrinsic nature of shame, fear of blame in that of dread. Herein shame means the manner of being ashamed, and conscientiousness is rooted in the intrinsic nature of that. Dread means the fear of purgatory, and fear of blame is rooted in the intrinsic nature of that. And both are manifested in the avoiding of evil. For a certain son of noble family, in obeying the calls of nature, on seeing a certain person worthy of respect, would manifest shame, would be ashamed. In the same way, sunken in an internal sense of shame he does not do evil. A certain man frightened by the fear of purgatory does not commit sin. Here is an illustration: As of two iron balls, one being cold and besmeared with dung, the other being hot and burning, a wise man does not catch the cold one from loathing its being smeared with dung, nor the other one for fear of getting burnt. Here the not grasping the cold ball from loathing its being smeared with dung is like the not doing wrong from being sunk in an internal sense of shame. [127] The not grasping the hot ball from fear of being burnt should be considered as the not doing evil from fear of purgatory.

---

[1] *Aṅguttara* i. 148.

Conscientiousness has the characteristic of respectful obedience, fear of blame that of viewing with timidity the fearful aspect of wrong-doing. This duality is manifested in the avoiding of evil. A certain man, indeed, from the four causes of consideration for his high birth, for the dignity of his Teacher, for the greatness of his inheritance, for the honour of his fellow-brethren, produces conscientiousness with the characteristic of respectful obedience and does not do evil. A certain man, from the four causes of self-accusation, of accusation by others, of punishment, of evil destiny, produces fear of blame with the characteristic of viewing with timidity the fearful aspect of wrong-doing and does not do evil. Herein considerations for high birth, etc., and fear of self-accusation, etc., can [as above] be explained in detail.

By this they do not lust, or itself does not lust, or the mere act of not lusting—this is 'absence of greed' (or disinterestedness). And the same for 'absence of hate' and 'of delusion.'[1] Of these three, absence of greed has the characteristic of the mind being free from cupidity for an object of thought, or of its being detached, like a drop of water on a lotus leaf. It has the function of not appropriating, like an emancipated monk, and the manifestation of detachment, like a man fallen into a foul place. Absence of hate has the characteristic of freedom from churlishness or resentment, like an agreeable friend; the function of destroying vexation, or dispelling distress, like sandal wood; the manifestation of being pleasing, like the full moon. Absence of delusion has been explained according to characteristic, etc., in connexion with the term 'faculty of understanding.'[2]

Of these three, again, absence of greed[3] is opposed to the taint of grudging, absence of hate to that of wickedness, absence of delusion to [that of] not developing the moral qualities. And absence of greed is the condition of giving, absence of hate that of virtue, and absence of delusion that of culture. Moreover, through disinterestedness[3] the excessive estimates of the covetous are avoided; through amity the

---

[1] *Dhs.* §§ 32-34. [2] P. 161. [3] Alobho.

one-sidedness of the hater is avoided; through clear-headedness the perversions of delusion are avoided. And, again, when he detects an actual fault, the disinterested man discloses it, for the greedy man hides a fault; similarly, the man of amity discloses a virtue when detected, for the hater [128] effaces a virtue; and the wise man reveals what he finds is really true, while the dull man holds truth false and the false true. And again, through absence of greed one does not feel the pain of separation from that which is beloved, affection being the intrinsic nature of the greedy man as well as inability to bear the pain of separation from the beloved. Through absence of hate one does not feel the pain of association with the unloved, hatred being the intrinsic nature of the man of hate as well as inability to bear the pain of association with the unloved. Through absence of delusion one does not feel the pain of not getting what is desired, such considerations made by one without delusion as: 'How were it possible?'[1] And, again, through absence of greed the pain of rebirth is not experienced, since the former is opposed to craving and the latter has its root in craving. Through absence of hate the pain of old age is not felt, since the keen hater becomes quickly aged. Through absence of delusion the pain of death is not experienced, for verily to die with the mind baffled is a pain which does not come over the undeluded. And, finally, a harmonious life of happy people among laymen is due to absence of greed, among monks to absence of delusion, and among all to absence of hate.

To distinguish:—through absence of greed there is no rebirth in the sphere of the Petas;[2] for verily beings generally are born there through craving, and absence of greed is opposed to craving. Through absence of hate there is no rebirth in purgatory; for verily it is through hate and churlishness that we are reborn in a purgatory resembling hate, and absence of hate is opposed to hate. Through absence of delusion rebirth as a lower animal does not take place; for verily on

[1] Cf. *Dialogues* ii. 177, which has not *labbhati*, but *labbhā*, 'possible'—namely, that that which is impermanent should not decay.—*Ed.*

[2] Ghosts or shades.

account of delusion persons are reborn among the always deluded lower animals, and absence of delusion is opposed to delusion. Of the three, absence of greed inhibits lusting enterprise; absence of hate inhibits separation due to hate; absence of delusion inhibits that indifference which is due to ignorance.[1]

Moreover, according to the order of these three, there are three perceptions: emancipation (associated with the First Jhāna), good-will (associated with love) and non-cruelty (associated with mercy). There are also these three perceptions: the foul, the immeasurable and the elements. Through absence of greed the extreme course of devotion to the pleasure of sense is avoided; through absence of hate the opposite extreme of self-mortification is avoided; and through absence of delusion the Middle Course is reached. Similarly, absence of greed breaks the physical knot of covetousness; absence of hate breaks the physical knot of ill-will; and absence of delusion breaks the remaining pair of knots.[2] Again, the two first applications in mindfulness are accomplished by the power of the preceding two (*i.e.*, absence of greed and of hate); and the two latter applications in mindfulness are accomplished by the power of the last (*i.e.*, absence of delusion). Again, absence of greed is the cause of good health, for the ungreedy man does not resort to what is attractive but unsuitable; hence his good health. [129] Absence of hate is the cause of youthfulness, for the man of no hate, not being burnt by the fire of hate, which brings wrinkles and grey hairs, remains young for a long time. Absence of delusion is the cause of long life, for the undeluded man knows what is advantageous and not advantageous, and avoiding what is not advantageous and practising what is advantageous, lives a long life. Again, absence of greed is the cause of the production of wealth, for wealth is obtained through liberality. Absence of hate is the cause of the production of friends, for through love friends are obtained and not lost. Absence of delusion is the cause of personal attainments, for the undeluded man, doing

---

[1] Cf. *Majjhima* i. 3 with 364; *Visuddhi Magga*, ch. ix.—*Ed.*

[2] Namely, practice of mere ritual and adherence to dogma.—*Dhs.* §§ 1135 *f.*

only that which is good for himself, perfects himself. Again, absence of greed brings about life in deva-heavens, absence of hate brings about life in Brahma-heavens, and absence of delusion brings about the Ariyan life. Moreover, through absence of greed one is at peace[1] among beings and things belonging to one's party, inasmuch as, if disaster befall them, the sorrow which depends on excessive attachment to them is absent. Through absence of hate one is happy among beings and things belonging to a hostile party, inasmuch as in the man of no hate inimical thoughts are absent. Through absence of delusion one is happy among beings and things belonging to a neutral party, inasmuch as for the undeluded there is no excessive attachment to all beings and things belonging to a neutral party. Again, by absence of greed one has insight into impermanence, for the greedy man, owing to his desire for wealth and property, does not regard impermanent conditioned things as impermanent. By absence of hate one has insight into ill, for one inclined to amity has, in possessing, abandoned the acquirement of the basis of vexation and regards conditioned things as ill. By absence of delusion one has insight into soullessness, for the undeluded man is clever in grasping[2] the nature of reality and knows the five aggregates which have no adviser[3] as such. As insight into impermanence, ill and soullessness is brought about by these three states, so they too are brought about by insight into impermanence, ill and soullessness. Through insight into impermanence arises absence of greed; through insight into ill arises absence of hate; through insight into soullessness arises absence of delusion. For who, knowing aright that this is impermanent, would cause affection to arise for the sake of it? Who, knowing conditioned things to be ill, would cause the further ill of anger exceedingly violent to arise for them? And who, knowing things as empty of soul, would again fall into delusion?

---

[1] *Nibbuto;* at peace, because detached.—*Tr.*

[2] In P.T.S. ed. read yathāvagahaṇakusalo.

[3] Cf. *Dialogues* ii. 208, *n.* 1: pariṇāyako.

'Non-covetousness'[1] is that which does not covet others' property.

Good-will[2] is that which does not ruin one's own or another's bodily or mental happiness, worldly or future advantage and good report.

That which sees aright or is a beautiful view:—this is right view.[3] This and the last two terms, viz.: non-covetousness, etc., are other names for absence of greed, hate and delusion. Above, these three were taken by way of roots, here they should be understood by way of courses of action.

The sense of shame (conscientiousness) and fear of blame, taken above[4] as 'strengths,' are here [repeated] in the sense of guardians of the world. For these two states do indeed guard the world, as he said: 'Bhikkhus, these two pure states guard the world. Which are the two? The sense of shame and fear of blame. If, bhikkhus, [130] these two pure states did not guard the world, there would be no regard paid to mother, or mother's sister, or uncle's wife, nor teacher's wife, nor wife of honourable men. The world would be full of promiscuous births, as among goats, sheep, fowls, pigs, dogs and jackals. Because, bhikkhus, these two pure states guard the world, therefore regard is paid to the mother and the rest.'[5]

'Tranquillity of the *kāya*'[6] is the calming of the three groups of mental factors (concomitant with consciousness); tranquillity of consciousness is the calming of mind. *Kāya* here refers to the three aggregates—feeling, perception and mental activities.[7] These two states being taken together have the characteristic of pacifying the suffering of both mental factors and of consciousness; the function of crushing the suffering of both; the manifestation of an unwavering and cool state of both; and have mental factors and consciousness as proxi-

---

[1] *Dhs.* § 35. [2] *Dhs.* § 36. [3] *Dhs.* § 37.

[4] See p. 164 *f.* [5] *Anguttara* i. 51=*Iti-vuttaka* § 42.

[6] *Dhs.* §§ 40, 41.

[7] *Kāya* may mean (1) the body (*S.* i. 156); (2) the tactile sense; (3) bodily action; (4) any group, as here.—*Ed.*

mate cause. They are the opponents of the corruptions, such as distraction, which cause the disturbance of mental factors and of consciousness.

'*Kāya*-lightness' is buoyancy of mental factors; *citta*-lightness is buoyancy of consciousness.[1] They have the characteristic of suppressing the heaviness of the one and the other; the function of crushing heaviness in both; the manifestation of opposition to sluggishness in both, and have mental factors and consciousness as proximate cause. They are the opponents of the corruptions, such as sloth and torpor, which cause heaviness and rigidity in mental factors and consciousness.

'*Kāya*-plasticity' is plasticity of mental factors; *citta*-plasticity is plasticity of consciousness.[2] They have the characteristic of suppressing the rigidity of mental factors and of consciousness; the function of crushing the same in both; the manifestation or effect of setting up no resistance; and have mental factors and consciousness as proximate cause. They are the opponents of the corruptions, such as opinionativeness and conceit, which cause mental rigidity.

'*Kāya*-wieldiness' is wieldiness of mental factors; *citta*-wieldiness is that of mind.[3] They have the characteristic of suppressing unwieldiness in both; the function of crushing the same; the effect of success or attainment of both in making objects of thought; they have mental factors and consciousness as proximate cause; and are the opponents of the remaining hindrances[4] which cause unwieldiness in mental factors and consciousness. [131] They should be regarded as bringing faith in objects of faith, and patient application in works of advantage, and are like purity of gold.

'*Kāya*-fitness' is fitness of mental factors; *citta*-fitness is that of consciousness.[4] They have the characteristic of the freedom of mental factors and of consciousness from illness; the function of crushing illness in both; the manifesta-

---

[1] *Dhs.* §§ 42, 43.
[2] *Ibid.* §§ 44, 45.
[3] *Dhs.* §§ 46, 47.
[4] *Ibid.* §§ 48. 49

tion of freedom from evil; they have mental factors and consciousness as proximate cause, and are the opponents of the corruptions, such as diffidence, which cause illness in both.

'*Kāya*-rectitude' is rectitude of mental factors; *citta*-rectitude is that of consciousness.[1] They have the characteristic of straightness in both; the function of crushing crookedness in both; the manifestation of non-deflection; they have mental factors and mind as proximate cause, and are the opponents of the corruptions, such as deception and craftiness, which cause crookedness in mental factors and consciousness.

'Mindfulness'[2] is that which remembers. 'Comprehension'[3] is that which comprehends. The meaning is to know a thing all round, in different ways. Knowledge of a thing according to its usefulness, its expediency, its scope, and to know it without confusion:—these are its four divisions. For their characteristics, etc., see either term mentioned above as faculties.[4] They are again mentioned in this place under the aspect of serviceableness.

'Calm'[5] is that which calms adverse states, such as sensual desire. 'Insight' is that which views states in their various aspects as impermanent. In meaning it is understanding. The characteristics, etc., of these two have been mentioned above.[6] And here they are given as forming a well-yoked pair.[7]

'Uplift' is that which upholds co-existent states.[8] 'Balance' is the opposite of distraction called excitement.[9] Their characteristics, etc., have been mentioned above.[10] The pair is treated here in order to show the union between energy and concentration.

'Or whatever other immaterial states causally linked there are on that occasion—these are moral'[11] means that these

---

[1] *Dhs.* §§ 50, 51. [2] *Ibid.* § 52. [3] *Ibid.* § 53.

[4] P. 159; 161. [5] *Dhs.* §§ 54, 55. [6] P. 156; 161.

[7] Like an even pair of thoroughbreds drawing in friendly union the carriage of the mind.—*Anuṭīkā.*

[8] Paggāha.—*Dhs.* § 56, or 'grasp' (*B.P.E.*). [9] *Ibid.* § 57.

[10] Under 'energy' and 'concentration,' pp. 158, 161.

[11] *Dhs.* § 1.

fifty states and more (six) which have been explained as 'This is contact,' down to 'This is non-distraction,' in due order of the terms, are not the only (moral states). In point of fact, [132] on the occasion when the first main type of automatic consciousness, accompanied by joy, thrice-conditioned and experienced in the realm of sense arises, there arise on that occasion states other than contact and the rest, but associated with them, each state being produced from its suitable cause, and, by the absence of material quality, in its intrinsic nature incorporeal. And all these states are moral. Having hitherto shown the fifty and more states fixed in the text as factors of consciousness, the King of the Law has indicated nine other states by the phrase 'Or whatever,' etc.

These nine states appear in various passages of the Suttas as desire, resolve, attention, equanimity, pity, sympathy, abstinence from misconduct of body and of speech, and from wrong livelihood. And in this main type of consciousness there is orthodox desire, that is, good in its conational aspect, which is not fixed in the text as a factor of consciousness, but is here included by the 'Or whatever. . . .' Likewise there is resolve, attention, equanimity, and the preparatory stage of amity.[1] This is taken only with absence of hate. There are also the preparatory stages of pity and of sympathy and of hedonic indifference. But this last is taken only with equanimity There are also right speech, right work, right livelihood. This last is not fixed in the text as a factor of consciousness, but is included here in the 'Or whatever.'

Of these nine states these four:—desire, resolve, attention and equanimity—are acquired simultaneously, the rest at different moments. For when by the (first type of) consciousness one abandons wrong speech and by abstinence therefrom fulfils right speech, then the five, to wit, right speech, together with the four beginning with desire, are acquired simultaneously. When one abandons wrong work and by abstinence therefrom fulfils right work, abandons wrong livelihood and by abstinence therefrom fulfils right livelihood, and

---

[1] *I.e.*, which has not reached Jhāna-ecstasy.—*Pyī.*

attains the preparatory stage of pity and of sympathy, then the five, to wit, each of these actions, together with the four beginning with desire, are acquired simultaneously. Passing beyond these five states, one who gives charity, fulfils the precepts and applies himself to work (*i.e.*, stations of religious exercise) acquires the four universal factors. Thus of these nine 'Or whatever' states 'desire' is synonymous with wish to act. Hence its characteristic is wish-to-act, its function is searching for an object, [133] its manifestation, having the object at its disposal, which object is also its proximate cause. In the taking of an object by the mind, desire should be regarded as the stretching forth of the hand.[1]

'Resolution' regarding an object is choice of the same. Its characteristic is determination, its function, opposition to slinking along,[2] its manifestation, unshakableness,[3] its proximate cause, an object fit to be decided. Owing to its unshakable nature it should be regarded as a stone pillar.

'Attention' is a mode of work, working in the mind. It makes mind, so to speak, different from the previous mind. It is of three kinds: Attention which regulates the object, attention which regulates process-consciousness, attention which regulates apperception. Of these, (*a*) that which regulates the object is called attention because it makes [the object] in the mind. It has the characteristic of driving associated states towards the object, the function of joining associated states to the object, the manifestation of facing the object. It is included in the aggregate of mental coefficients, and should be regarded as the charioteer of associated states because it regulates the object. (*b*) Attention which regulates process-consciousness is a synonym for the adverting of mind at the five doors[4]; and (*c*) attention which regulates

---

[1] As by thieves to grasp an object in the dark.—*Pyī.* Cf. Greek ὄρεξις.—*Ed.*

[2] Asaṃsappana. As of an irresolute child thinking, Shall I do it, shall I not do it?—*Ṭīkā.* Cf. *Aṅguttara* v. 288 *f.*, 291.

[3] *Pyī* and P.T.S. edn. read nicchayapaccupaṭṭhāna; but Burmese authorities apparently niccala°.

[4] Or 'presentative consciousness,' (*c*) being 'representative consciousness.'

apperception is a synonym for mind-door-adverting. These two (*b*) (*c*) kinds of attention are not intended here.

'Equanimity' (or balance of mind)[1] is neutrality regarding various states. It has the characteristic of carrying on consciousness and mental properties equally, the function of checking deficiency and excess, or of cutting off partisanship; it has the manifestation of neutrality. By virtue of its indifference regarding consciousness and mental properties it should be regarded as a charioteer who treats with impartiality the well-trained horses he is driving.

'Pity' and 'sympathy' will be explained in the exposition of the Divine States.[2] There is only this difference—pity and sympathy have there attained to ecstasy, and are experienced as in the realm of attenuated matter;[3] here they are experienced in the realm of sense.

'*Kāya*-misconduct-abstinence' means abstinence from misconduct in bodily action. The remaining two sentences are analogous. As regards characteristic, etc., it has been said that each of these three does not trespass nor tread on objects of the other two. They have the function of shrinking from the same; and they have faith, sense of shame, fear of blame, contentment and more, as proximate antecedents. They should be regarded as produced by the averted state of the mind from evil action.

The fifty-six states beginning with contact and the nine 'Or whatever' states form, in this outline section of states, altogether sixty-five groups. Of these, sixty-one sometimes occur in a single moment, and sometimes full sixty. The sixty-one occur on five occasions when they arise in their capacity to fulfil right speech, right work, right livelihood, pity, and sympathy; the sixty occur on a single occasion, quite apart from these five (*i.e.*, in charity or virtue). [134] And excepting the 'Or whatever' states there are fifty-six states mentioned in the text. Moreover, of the fifty-six, by taking what has not been taken, there are fully thirty states, *to wit*:

---

[1] Tatra-majjhattatā is lit. 'there-middleness.'—*Ed.*

[2] *Dhs.* § 251 *f.* and below.

[3] The Rūpa heavens.

the fivefold contact-group,[1] initial application, sustained application, zest, one-pointedness of mind, the five controlling faculties, the two strengths of sense of shame and of fear of blame, the two roots of absence of greed and of absence of hate, the twelve states beginning with repose of mental factors and of mind.[2]

Of these thirty states, eighteen cannot be classified, twelve can be classified. Which are the eighteen? Contact, perception, volition, sustained application, zest, life-faculty, and the twelve beginning with 'repose of mental factors' are unclassifiable. Feeling, consciousness, initial application, one-pointedness of mind, the faculties of faith, energy, mindfulness, understanding, the strengths:—sense of shame, fear of blame, absence of greed, absence of hate—these twelve are classifiable (*sa-vibhattikā*).

Of these, seven states are classified in two places, one in three places, two in four places, one in six places, and one in seven places. How? Consciousness, initial application of mind, faith, sense of shame, fear of blame, absence of greed and absence of hate—these seven are classified in two places. For of these, consciousness (*cittaṃ*) is spoken of as such when it has attained[3] fivefold contact; and as faculty of mind (*mano*) by way of[3] faculties. Initial application is spoken of as such by way of jhāna-factors; and as right intention by way of Path-factors. Faith is spoken of as faculty of faith by way of faculties; and as strength by way of strengths. Sense of shame is spoken of as the strength 'sense of shame' by way of strengths; and as sense of shame under the aspect of the two guardians of the world.[4] And the same with fear of blame. Absence of greed is spoken of as such by way of root;

---

[1] *I.e.*, contact, feeling, perception, volition and consciousness.—*Dhs.* § 1.

[2] The states which have been left out are included in these 30; *e.g.*, 'happy ease' and the 'faculty of joy' are included in 'feeling,' the 'faculty of mind' in 'consciousness,' and the three aspects of Samādhi as well as 'balance' are included in 'one-pointedness of mind,' and so on.—*Ariyālankāra*.

[3] Patvā, having reached, won.

[4] See p. 171.

and as disinterestedness by way of course of action. Absence of hate is spoken of as such by way of root; and as good-will by way of course of action. Thus these seven states are classified in two places. Feeling is spoken of as such by way of the five-fold contact-group, as bliss or ease by way of jhāna-factors, as faculty of joy by way of faculties. Thus one state is classified in three places. Energy is spoken of as faculty of energy by way of faculties, as right endeavour by way of Path-factors, as the strength 'energy' by way of strengths, as 'uplift' by way of the later couplet.[1] Mindfulness is spoken of as faculty of mindfulness by way of faculties, as right mindfulness by way of Path-factors, as the strength 'mindfulness' by way of strengths, [135] as mindfulness by way of the later couplet. Thus two states are classified in four places. Concentration is spoken of as one-pointedness of mind by way of jhāna-factors, as faculty of concentration by way of faculties, as right concentration by way of Path-factors, as the strength 'concentration' by way of strengths, as 'calm and non-distraction' by way of the later couplet. Thus this single state is classified in six places. Understanding is spoken of as the understanding faculty by way of faculties, as 'right views' by way of Path-factors, as the strength 'understanding' by way of strengths, as 'absence of delusion' by way of roots, as right views by way of course of action, as 'comprehension' [by way of the even pair of states, as[2]] 'insight' by way of the later couplet. Thus this single state is classified in seven places.

But if someone should say: —'Therein is nothing new; it only fills up words in various places by taking what has already been taken; it forms a discourse of neither connection nor order, like goods stolen by thieves, an unintelligent discourse, like grass disturbed in the path of a herd of cattle'—he should be checked by our saying, 'Not so!' No discourse of the Buddhas[3] is without connection; there is always a connection. Neither is there an unintelligent discourse. All has been spoken with intelligence. For the supreme Buddha knows

---

[1] See p. 173. [2] Omitted in P.T.S. ed.

[3] Read Buddhānaṃ desanā, and correct what follows *ibid.*

the function of each of the states, knowing which, in making the classification by function, he has classified, each in one place, the eighteen single-functioned states. Knowing the seven states to have a double function, he has classified each in two places. Knowing feeling to have a triple function, he has classified it in three places. Knowing energy and mindfulness to have a fourfold function, he has classified them in four places. Knowing concentration to have a sixfold function, he has classified it in six places. Knowing understanding to have a sevenfold function, he has classified it in seven places.

Here is a simile:—A wise king, they say, goes into solitude and thinks, 'This property, the heritage of royalty, should not be used up anyhow. I will increase the income by suitable arts.' He assembles all his artisans and declares, 'Summon those who know a single art.' Thus summoned, eighteen men stand up. He assigns each his portion and sends them away. When he declares, 'Let those who know two arts come forward,' seven men approach him. To each he entrusts two portions. When he declares, 'Let those who know three arts come forward,' one man approaches him. To him he entrusts three portions. When he declares, 'Let those who know four arts come forward,' two men approach him. To them he entrusts four portions. When he declares, 'Let those who know five arts come forward,' none[1] approaches him. When he declares, 'Let those who know six arts come forward,' one man approaches him. To him he entrusts six portions. When he declares, 'Let those who know seven arts [136] come forward,' one man approaches him. To him he entrusts seven portions. The wise king here is like the incomparable King of the Law, the artisans are like the states which have arisen as factors of consciousness, the increasing of the income by suitable arts is like the classification of the various states according to their functions. And all these states form seventeen groups according to the contact-quintet, jhāna-factors, controlling faculties, Path-factors, strengths, roots, courses of action, guardians of the

[1] P.T.S. ed. should read nāgacchi. Cf. context above.

world, repose, buoyancy, plasticity, wieldiness, fitness, rectitude, mindfulness and comprehension, calm and insight, uplift and non-distraction.

End of the Discourse on the Section of the Summary of Conscious States.

CHAPTER II

DISCOURSE ON THE SECTION OF EXPOSITION

Now in order to show the classification of the fifty-six words which have been fixed as the Text in this Section of the Outline of States, the Section of Exposition has been begun on this wise: 'What on that occasion is contact ?'[1]

The meaning of this question is:—It has been said that on the occasion when the main class of automatic consciousness as experienced in the realm of sense, moral, accompanied by joy and thrice-conditioned, arises, there arises on that occasion contact. And which is that contact ? In this way the meaning of all the following questions should be considered.

'That which on that occasion is contact' refers to that contact which on that occasion arises as a fact of touching. The word in its simple form[2] expresses the intrinsic nature of touch.[3] *Phusanā* is the act of touching. *Samphusanā*, increased by the prefix, is the way of touching [viz.: to unite with the object]. *Samphusitattaṃ* is the state of so touching. And this is the construction: There is on that occasion contact by virtue of touching; there is on that occasion that which is the act of touching; there is that which, on that occasion, is the act of touching to unite with; there is that which, on that occasion, is the state of touching to unite with. *Or* that which, on that occasion, is contact by virtue of touching is, in other different ways, said to be the act of touching, the act of touching to unite with, and the state of touching to

---

[1] *Dhs.* § 2.

[2] *I.e.*, without the aid of prefixes or suffixes.—*Ariyālaṅkāra.*

[3] Or, because it shows the intrinsic nature of touch, free from figures of speech, this word implies an ultimate reality (*sabhāvapadaṃ*), *i.e.*, absence of a living entity.—*Anuṭīkā.*

unite with. This contact there is on that occasion. And the same construction of the words in the expositions of feeling and the rest should be understood.

The following is a decision by classification common to all: In showing the classification of the first main type of consciousness experienced in the realm of sense, the Blessed One [137] has placed the fifty and more words in a table of contents and, taking up each, has made the classification. And they are thus classified according to three causes, are different according to four causes. And in this main type the explanation of the same terms in other ways is twofold. How? They are classified on these three grounds:—the letter, the prefix, and the meaning.

Of these, *e.g.*, 'anger, fuming, irascibility, hate, hating, hatred,[1] is a classification according to the letter.'[2] For here a single thing, that is, anger, is classified according to the letter. In 'application, sustained application, progressive application of mind,'[3] the classification is according to the prefix.[4] In 'erudition, skill, subtlety, criticism, reflection, investigation,'[5] the classification is according to the meaning.

Three kinds of classification are obtained in the exposition of the word contact. *Phassaphusanā* (touch, touching) is a classification according to the letter; *samphusanā* (the touching to unite with) is according to the prefix; *samphusitatta* (the state of touching to unite with) is according to the meaning. In this way the classification in the exposition of all the remaining words should be understood.

Again, they are different for other four reasons:—(1) name, (2) characteristic, (3) function and (4) opposition. (1) Take the passage:—' What on that occasion is ill-will? That which on that occasion is hate, hating '[6] . . . here ill-will and hate are only different names for anger. Thus should the difference in the difference of *names* be regarded.

(2) In the sense of group the five aggregates form one

---

[1] *Dhs.* § 1060.

[2] Vyañjanavasena, *i.e.*, 'verbal form'—*e.g.*, *kodho, kujjhanā*, etc.

[3] *Dhs.* § 8.

[4] Thus *cāro*, augmented by *vi-*, *anu-*.

[5] *Dhs.* § 16

[6] *Ib.* § 419

aggregate. And of these, 'matter' has the characteristic of [changing or] transforming, 'feeling' of experiencing, 'perception' of noting, 'volition' of co-ordinating, 'consciousness' of cognizing. Thus these five aggregates have different characteristics. Thus should the difference according to *characteristic* be understood.

(3) There are four supreme efforts: 'a bhikkhu in this religion sustaining his mind strives for the non-arising of evil, [138] immoral states which have not arisen,' etc.,[1] thus a single thing, that is, energy, by difference in function has arrived at four places, and [thus] difference according to difference in *function* should be understood.

(4) The four bad states: they give weight to anger and not to good states, they give weight to hypocrisy and not to the good Law, they give weight to gain and not to the good Law, they give weight to honours and not to the good Law—in such ways difference according to difference by *opposition* should be understood.

And this fourfold difference is obtained not only in contact, but also in all the fivefold contact-group. Contact, indeed, is the name of contact. . . . Consciousness is the name of consciousness. Thus should the difference be understood by means of the different *names*. And contact has the characteristic of touching, feeling of being experienced, perception of noting, volition of co-ordinating, consciousness of cognizing—thus should be understood the difference in *characteristics*. So contact has the function of touching, feeling of enjoying, perception of noting, volition of co-ordinating, consciousness of cognizing—thus the difference according to different *functions* should be understood. Difference by opposition is not obtained in the fivefold contact-group. But in the exposition of absence of greed or lust, etc., there is this passage: 'Absence of lust, of lusting, of lustfulness'[2]—thus should difference by *opposition* be understood.

---

[1] *B.P.E.*, p. 358 (v.)—viz., (1) prevention of evil, (2) ejection of evil, (3) induction of good, (4) maintenance of good. *Dhs.* § 32.—*Ed.*

[2] *Dhs.* § 32.

Thus, in the exposition of all these words, should the difference obtainable in these four ways be understood.

There is a different twofold explanation: embellishment of the term, and strengthening or intensification.[1] For when *phassa* is uttered once only as if just pressing with the end of a stick, then the word is not decorated, adorned, embellished. When it is repeated as *phassa*, *phusanā*, *samphusanā*, *samphusitatta*, according to the letter, the prefix and the meaning, then there is decoration, adornment, embellishment. As if they were to bathe a young boy, dress him in a beautiful dress, adorn him with flowers, smear his eye (-lids) and make only one mark of vermilion on his forehead, then his forehead-decoration would not be complete unless it were surrounded by various colours and forehead marks were made. Thus should this point be illustrated. This is the word-embellishment. And the repetition by virtue of the letter, the prefix and the sense is known as intensification. As when we say '*brother!*' or '*Reverend Sir!*' or '*ogre,*' or '*snake*' [139] there is no intensification till we repeat—*brother! brother!* and so on, so when *phassa* is uttered once only as if just pressing with the end of a stick, there is no intensification. But when it is repeated as *phassa*, *phusanā*, *samphusanā*, *samphusitatta*, according to the letter, the prefix and the meaning, then there is intensification. Thus this different explanation is twofold, and the meaning everywhere obtainable by that difference in the exposition of the words should be taken into account.

'This contact is on that occasion'[2] means: on the occasion when the first main [type of] moral consciousness experienced in the realm of sense arises, this is the contact that there is on that occasion. This is the elucidation of the exposition of contact. We shall now elucidate only what is special in the exposition of the other words, feeling, and so on. And the rest is to be understood in the same manner as what has been said (with reference to contact).

In the reply, 'That which on that occasion is . . .'[3] [the

---

[1] Pyī reads (*a*) elucidation of one term by another; (*b*) confirmation by means of embellishment or emphasis.

[2] *Dhs.* § 2.

[3] *Ib.* § 3.

neuter gender] '*yaṃ*' ('that which') is used through the influence of the [neuter] word '*sāta*' (happiness),[1] albeit in the question [the feminine gender] '*katamā*' (what) is used:—'what (*katamā*) on that occasion is feeling?'

In 'born of contact with the appropriate element of mind-consciousness'[2] 'appropriate' means 'suitable, fit for pleasantness and pleasure.' For the word '*tajjā*' (appropriate) means 'suitable.' As the Buddha has said: 'He speaks words appropriate and suitable to it.'[3] And the mind-consciousness is said to be appropriate in that it has been produced by visible objects, etc., which render service to pleasure.

'Mind-consciousness' is an element in the sense of being free from an entity; hence 'mind-consciousness.' 'Born of contact' means that it has been produced from, or in contact;[4] hence 'born of contact.'

'Mental' is dependent on the mind. 'Happy' is used in the sense of sweet (like honey).

'That which on that occasion is'—according to the meaning already given—'born of contact with the appropriate element of mind-consciousness, a mental happiness—this is the feeling that there is on that occasion'—on this wise all the terms should be construed.

Now, by the word '*cetasika*' included in the text—'the mental pleasure[5] etc.'—bodily pleasure is inhibited. By the word 'pleasure,' mental ill is inhibited. *Ceto-samphassajaṃ* is born of mind-contact. 'The happy pleasurable feeling' is happy feeling, not unhappy; pleasurable [140] feeling, not painful. The three following words are spoken in the feminine gender.[6] And the meaning is happy feeling, not unhappy; pleasurable feeling, not painful.

In the exposition of perception,[7] 'born of contact with the appropriate element of mind-consciousness' means the perception which is born of contact with the element of mind-consciousness, suitable to the perception that is moral.

---

[1] *B.P.E.*: 'pleasure.' See *n*. 6.

[2] *Dhs.* § 3. *B.P.E.*: 'representative intellection.'

[3] *Majjhima* iii. 163.

[4] *Lege* samphasse.

[5] Sukhaṃ.

[6] Vedanā (feeling) is *f*. gender.

[7] *Dhs.* § 4

Saññā (perception) is the name of a real thing;[1] *sañjānanā* is the act of perceiving by noting; *sañjānitattaṃ* shows the state of having perceived by noting.

The same is to be understood in the exposition of volition.[2]

In the exposition of consciousness,[3] 'consciousness' (*citta*) is so called because of its variegated (*citta*) nature. 'Mind' (*mano*) is so called because it knows the measure of an object. 'Mental action' (*mānasa*) is just 'mind.'

> *The tale of sense-impressions is a snare*
> *That weaves its fetters to and fro in air. . .*[4]

—here *mānasa* (sense-impressions) is [an adjunct of] *mano*.

> *Wherefore should thy disciple, Blessed One,*
> *Delighting in thy Rule, O thou well-known*
> *To men, as undergraduate set term*
> *To life unconsummated in his mind?*[5]

—here 'mind' is Arahantship, but *mānasa* is identical there with *mano*, merely augmented in form.

'Heart' is the same as mind (*citta*). In the passage, 'I will either scatter your mind or break your *heart*,'[6] the breast is meant. In the passage, 'Methinks he chops with a *heart* that knows *hearts*,'[7] the mind is meant. In the passage 'the *vakka* is the *heart*,'[8] the basis of heart is meant. But here the mind is called 'heart' in the sense of inwardness.

Mind also is said to be 'clear' in the sense of 'exceedingly pure,' with reference to the subconscious life-continuum.[9] So the Buddha has said:—'Bhikkhus, the mind is luminous, but is corrupted by adventitious corruptions.'[10] Though immoral, it is called 'clear' because it issues [from subcon-

---

[1] Sabhāva.

[2] *Dhs.* § 5: cetanā. *B.P.E.* 'thinking.' See this corrected, *Compendium*, p. 235 *f.*—*Ed.*

[3] *Dhs.* § 6.

[4] *S.* i. 111 (*Kindred Sayings* i. 140).

[5] *Ib.* 121 (*ib.* 151).

[6] *Ib.* 207 (*ib.* 265).

[7] *Majjhima* i. 32, which reads tacchati. Pyī reads gacchati.

[8] Not traced.

[9] Bhavanga. Cf. *Compendium*, p. 266. *B. Psy.*, pp. 171, 178. 'The Buddhist Philosophy of Change,' *Quest Review*, October, 1917, p. 16.

[10] *Aṅguttara* i. 10.

scious vital conditions] just as a tributary of the Ganges is like the Ganges and a tributary of the Godhāvarī is like the Godhāvarī.

'Mind as organ of mind'—here as [an act of grasping][1] 'mind' (*mano*) is declared to be a sense-organ (*āyatana*). This it shows, not in the sense that *devāyatana* means 'sphere of spirits,' but because *mano* itself is a sphere of sense. The word *āyatana* may mean either abode, mine, meeting-place, [141] birth-place, or reason. To expand:—Among mankind, in such passages as 'the *abode* of the lord,[2] the *abode* of Vāsudeva'[3]—*āyatana* means 'abode.' In such passages as 'an *āyatana* of gold, or of silver,' it means 'mine.' In such religious passages as,

> *In pleasant trysting place the passengers of air*
> *Together flock . . .*[4]

it means 'meeting-place.' And in such passages as: If there be any *āyatana*, then he attains the ability of testifying . . .,[5] it means 'reason' (or ground for).

Here three of these meanings are suitable, viz.: birth-place, meeting-place, reason. For mind is *āyatana* in the sense of birth-place as in the passage:—'states such as "contact" and so on, are born in the mind.'[4] And mind is *āyatana* in the sense of a meeting-place, as in the passage:—'External objects, visible, audible, olfactory, gustatory and tangible assemble there as objects in the mind.'[6] And mind is *āyatana* in the sense of reason (or ground), because of its being the cause-in-relation of the co-existence, etc., of contact and so on.

The meaning of 'faculty of mind' has been discussed.

Viññāṇa is cognizing. *Viññāṇa-khandha* is consciousness as an aggregate. The meaning of *khandha* (aggregate) should be taken as group or mass, etc. 'It goes by the name of a large *khandha* of water'[7]—here *khandha* is used in the sense

---

[1] Manogahanaṃ. The conception of sensation as a grasping, or being seized, is classic in Indian thought. Cf. *B. Psy.* 59.—*Ed.*

[2] Issara.

[3] Cf. *Jāt.* iv. 82.

[4] *Aṅguttara* iii. 43.

[5] *Majjhima* i. 494.

[6] Not traced.

[7] Not traced.

of mass. In such passages as, 'The *khandha* of virtue, or of concentration,'[1] it is used in the sense of good quality. 'The Blessed One saw a large *piece* of wood'[2]—here it is used as mere designation. But in the present connexion it is called 'aggregate' symbolically. For in the sense of mass, one (unit of) consciousness is a part (only) of consciousness. Therefore, as one cutting a portion of a tree is said to 'cut the tree,' so one consciousness, which is only a portion of the aggregate of consciousness, is said symbolically to be the aggregate of consciousness.

Tajjā manoviññāṇadhātu means the element of mind-consciousness suitable to states such as 'contact,' etc. In this expression a single [moment of] consciousness is called by three names: *mano* (mind), in the sense of measuring; *viññāṇa* (consciousness), in the sense of discrimination; *dhātu* (element) in the philosophical sense of ultimate reality, or of absence of a living entity. In this fivefold contact-group, because *phassa* is contact, and is *not* called 'born of contact with the appropriate element of mind-consciousness,' and because consciousness is the element of mind-consciousness (and is *not* called 'born of contact with the appropriate element of mind-consciousness'); therefore in this [142] couplet the expression, 'born of contact with the appropriate element of mind-consciousness' has not been adopted.

But in the terms 'initial application of mind,' etc., although this expression is obtainable, it is not brought out in this exposition of consciousness because it has been cut off. And a difficult thing has been accomplished by the Blessed One, who has brought out the expression after making an individual classification of these states of the fivefold contact group. True, it would be possible to find out by sight, or by smell, or by taste the difference in the colour, smell and taste of a variety of waters or a variety of oils which have been placed in a jar and churned the whole day, yet it would be called a difficult thing to do. But a thing of greater difficulty has been accomplished by the supreme Buddha, who has brought out

---

[1] *Aṅguttara* i. 125 *f*.

[2] *Saṃyutta* iv. 179.

their designation after making an individual classification of the immaterial states, viz., consciousness and its co-efficients which have arisen in one object. Hence it was said by the Elder Nāgasena: 'A difficult thing, your majesty, has been done by the Blessed One.' 'What difficult thing, Venerable Nāgasena, has been done by the Blessed One?' 'A difficult thing, your majesty, has been done by the Blessed One when he declared the determination of these immaterial states, consciousness and its co-efficients, which have arisen in one object, saying this is contact, this is feeling, this is perception, this is volition, this is mind.'

'Give an illustration.' 'As if, your majesty, a certain man were to go down in a boat to sea, and taking some water in the hollow of his hand taste it with the tongue; would he know, your majesty—this is Ganges water, this is Aciravatī water, this is Sarabhū water, this is Mahī water?' 'It would be difficult, venerable Nāgasena.' 'A more difficult thing than that, your majesty, was done when the Blessed One declared the determination of these immaterial states, consciousness and its co-efficients, which have arisen in one object saying, this is contact, this is feeling, this is perception, this is volition, this is mind.'[1]

In the exposition of initial application of mind,[2] this is [called] ap-ply-ing in virtue of 'plying' [the mind with objects]. To what extent is it plied? [*Vitakka*] 'supplies' a pot, a cart, a league, half a league—this is what goes on in 'application.' This is the primary [notion] in the word *takka*. *Vitakka*, 'initial application' in virtue of ap-plying [sup-plying], is an emphatic term for 'plying.'[3]

---

[1] *Milinda* i. 133. B. found this passage very useful, quoting it also in the *Visuddhi Magga*, ch. xvii., and in the *Papañca Sūdanī*. He here omits the Jumna river.—*Ed.*

[2] *Dhs.* § 7.

[3] Takka, Sanskrit tarka, is the Indian term for logic, or dialectic, or reasoning. The root *tark* signifies to turn or twist. We only approach this in our 'controvert' from *wart*, *vṛt*, to turn. Hence it has only been possible (once the decision was made to follow S. Z. Aung's rendering of vitakka) to imitate B.'s play on the word by a parallel play in 'ply.'—*Ed.* B.'s commentators have the following: 'As the draw-

[Among the equivalent terms] 'intention' (*saṅkappa*) conveys the sense of thorough-designing. And 'fixation' is the applying the selective[1] mind to the object. Next [143], 'focussing' is the term for 'fixation,' intensified by a prefix. Then, 'uplift of mind' is the elevating or setting up of consciousness on to an object. And 'right intention' is intention which is praiseworthy, has won to a moral state because of its veracity and progressiveness.

In the exposition of 'investigation,'[2] the [kernel] of the word *cāro* expresses a going-about the object. This is the primary meaning. 'Investigation' indicates general scrutiny. The next terms with prefixes—*anu-upa-vicāro*—indicate order and closeness in the investigation. Next, 'mental adjustment' indicates the mind being fitted to its object as an archer fixes his arrow to the bowstring, and 'examination' is either a sustained consideration, or the opposite of want-of-consideration (*anu-pekkhatā, an-upekkhatā*).

In the next exposition, zest (rapture)[3] is a word of primary meaning. The next two equivalents are developments of the word joy (√*mud*, √*mod*), augmented by their prepositions *ā-*, *pa-*. Or, as the act of blending medicinal herbs, or oils, or hot and cold water is called *mōdanā*, so also zest is a *mōdanā* (blending), because of its making one blend out of co-existent states.

To make merry—this is 'mirth.' To make very merry—this is 'merriment.' They are synonyms for the behaviour of mind in laughing and abundant laughing. 'Felicity' implies wealth, a name for riches. And zest is wealth from being the cause of joy and from its resemblance to wealth. For as joy arises in a rich man on account of his wealth, so it arises in one possessing zest on account of zest. Therefore wealth is a name for zest or rapture which is established in the intrinsic nature of delight. And a rapturous person is said

---

ing, dragging up, withdrawing of water in a pit, so is the *takkanaṃ, ākaḍḍhanaṃ, vitakkanaṃ* of object in consciousness.'—*Ṭīkā*. 'The *vitakka* which arises as if mind were brought to object is really a dragging of object to mind.'—*Anuṭīkā*.

[1] Lit., one-pointed. [2] *Dhs.* § 8. [3] *Ib.* § 9.

to be elated from the exaltation of body and mind. 'Elation' is the state of an elated man. '*Attamanatā*' is one's own delight. The mind of a ruffled or angry man,* from being a proximate cause of ill or pain, is not said to be his own mind; the mind of one who has appeased his anger, from being the proximate cause of happiness or bliss, is said to be his own mind. Hence the term 'one's own delight,' referring to the state of one's own mind. And because it is not the mentality of any other self and is a property of consciousness, therefore we read 'one's own mental delight.'[1]

In the exposition on one-pointedness of mind[2] it stands unshaken in the object—this is 'stability.' The two following words are the same augmented by prepositions. Another explanation is:—It stands combining associated states [144] in the object—this is 'solidity.' It stands having dived and entered into the object—this is 'steadfastness.' In the moral portion four states dive into the object—to wit, faith, mindfulness, concentration, understanding. Hence faith has been said to be the downward plunge, mindfulness to be the non-floating, concentration to be the grounded stand and understanding to be the sounding penetration. And in the immoral portion three states dive into the object—to wit, craving, opinionativeness and ignorance. Hence they are called the down-plungers [or floods]. But one-pointedness of mind is not strong enough to enter (in the immoral portion). As by sprinkling a dusty place with water and smoothing it, the dust subsides only for a short time and again resumes its original condition whenever it is dry, so in the immoral portion, one-pointedness of mind is not strong.[3] And as when we sprinkle a place with water poured from pots and dig it up with spades and cement it by beating, pounding and kneading, an image is reflected there as in a burnished glass, and the reflection is true any moment though a hundred years were to pass, so in moral [consciousness], one-pointedness of mind is strong.

---

* Anabhiraddho. [1] Attamanatā. [2] *Dhs.* § 11.

[3] Yet it is called 'steadfastness,' not because of its strength, but because it is intent on one action—for instance, murder—till that is accomplished.—*Ṭīkā*

'Absence of distraction' is that which is opposed to the 'scattering' which arises by virtue of flurry and perplexity. Consciousness, going [to and fro] through flurry and perplexity, is distracted. But in 'poise' such distraction is absent. By flurry and perplexity consciousness is said to be scattered; it is drawn here and there. But the state of mind called 'unscattered mentality' is just the opposite.

'Calm' is of three kinds—calm of the mind, calm when settling [disputes], calm of all conditioned things. Of these, the first is one-pointedness of mind in the eight attainments. For, owing to one-pointedness of mind the wavering, the trepidation of the mind ceases, stops; therefore it is called calm of the mind. Calm, when settling [disputes] is the seven Vinaya Rules beginning with 'Procedure in presence.'[1] For through those rules cases of dispute are settled, pacified; therefore it is called calm when settling [disputes]. And because all conditioned things, at the advent of Nibbāna, are put to rest and pacified, therefore that Nibbāna is called calm of all conditioned things. It is in this sense that calm of the mind in the exposition of one-pointedness of mind is meant. The 'faculty [controlling power] of concentration' is that which effects governance in the characteristic of concentration. The 'strength of concentration' is that which does not shake through distraction. 'Right concentration' is threefold—irreversible concentration, emancipating concentration,[2] and moral concentration.

[145] In the exposition of the 'faculty of faith'[3]—it is 'faith' as belief in the virtues of the Buddha, etc.; or faith is the habit of believing in the Three Jewels, the Buddha (the Order, the Law). 'Trust' is [the behaviour of mind which] has faith. It dives into the virtues of the Buddha, etc., as though breaking them and entering into them—this is 'confidence.' By this beings have abundant assurance in the virtues of the Buddha, etc.—this is 'assurance.' Or, it itself has great assurance in

---

[1] See *Vinaya Texts* i. 68; iii. 45 *f.* (*S.B.E.* xiii., xviii.). Adhikaraṇa-samatha.

[2] Supply niyyānikasamādhi in P.T.S. text.

[3] *Dhs.* § 12.

them[1]—this is 'assurance.' Now, when a different method of explanation is adopted because of compound terms, as faith-faculty, etc., the classification of terms is made by taking the first member—and this is the rule in the Abhidhamma—therefore the word 'faith' is repeated. Or, here it is not like the term *itthindriya*, which is equivalent to faculty of femininity; this faith *as* a faculty is the term 'faculty of faith.' Thus the word 'faith' has been repeated to show the equality between the two members. And thus the need of repeating the first member in the expositions of all the words is to be understood. It makes government (over associated states) in the characteristic of choosing—this is the 'faculty of faith.' It does not waver on account of unbelief—this is 'strength of faith.'

In the exposition of the 'faculty of energy'[2] the word 'mental' is said to show that energy is always mental. 'Bhikkhus, that which is bodily energy is always energy as a factor of wisdom; that which is mental energy is always energy as a factor of wisdom. Thus energy is outlined.'[3] Thus, in such Suttas, even though this energy may be said to be bodily from its arising in one walking to and fro, etc., yet it is not so called as in the term 'body-consciousness.'[4] Verily there is only mental energy. It is to show this that 'mental' has been said.

By the term 'initial putting forth of energy' (*viriyārambho*) the Blessed One rejects the putting forth of other than energy. For the word *ārambha* (putting forth) comes with the different meanings of kamma, offence, work, energy, cruelty, destruction, etc. For instance:—

Whatever suffering comes to pass, ārambha *is the cause thereof.*
And if ārambha *takes an end, there is no happening of ill:—*[5]

here *ārambha* means [our] kamma.

---

[1] Abhippasādo.
[2] *Dhs.* § 13.
[3] *Saṃyutta* v. 111. P.T.S. ed. there reads āgacchati.
[4] In this term the organ of touch is meant.—*Ed.*
[5] *Sutta-Nipāta,* ver. 744.

'There is both *ārambha* and repentance'[1]:—here it is offence.

Great sacrifices, all the mighty ārambha:
These are not rites that bring a rich result![2]

Here it is the labour over sacrificial pillars, etc.

[146] *Bestir yourselves, rise up, renounce, come forth*
And yield yourselves unto the Buddha's rule![3]

Here 'bestir' (*ārabhatha*) is energy.

'They work against (put to death, *ārabhanti*) creatures with the recluse Gotama's authority'[4]:— here the word means cruelty.

'He refrains from *samārambha* of seeds or plants'[5]:—here it is destruction in the sense of cutting, breaking, etc.

But here the interpretation [of the word] is energy. Hence *viriyārambha* means the putting forth which is energy. *Viriya* indeed has been declared to be *ārambha* by virtue of a putting forth. And this is the primary fact in *viriya*.

Next, 'striving' is by way of escaping from idleness. 'Onward effort' is so called by virtue of reaching a higher and higher place.[6] 'Exertion'[7] is so called by virtue of rising up and keeping going. 'Endeavour' is so called by virtue of special exertion; 'zeal,' of being zealous;[8] 'ardour,' of being exceedingly zealous; 'vigour,' of firmness; 'fortitude,' of bearing consciousness and its concomitants, or of bearing the continuity of morality by unbroken procedure.

Another method of exposition:—This *viriyārambha* is 'striving' in expelling lust, 'onward effort' in cutting the bonds, 'exertion' in escaping from the floods, 'endeavour' in reaching the opposite shore, 'zeal' in being a forerunner, 'ardour' in exceeding the limit, 'vigour' in lifting the bolt

---

1 Not traced.

2 Cf. *S.* i. 15 (*Kindred Sayings* i. 102), which omits the first two words.

3 *Ib.* 157 (*ib.* 195). 4 *Majjhima* i. 368. 5 *Dialogues* i. 5, § 10.

6 Or, stepping over each station of idleness.—*Tr.*

7 Uddhaṃ yamanaṃ niyyāmo (exertion is a striving upward).—*Ṭīkā.*

8 Zeal (*ussāha*) is endurance over against misery, or one's own burden.—*Abhidhānaṭīkā.*

[of ignorance], and 'fortitude' in producing steadfastness. 'Verily, let the skin, veins and bones dry up'[1]—thus by virtue of unfaltering effort at such a time is the 'state of a man of unfaltering effort.' The meaning is firm effort, steadfast effort. Moreover, inasmuch as this energy does not put down the desire-to-do, does not put down, let go, set free the charge to do moral acts, but carries an unflinching mind, therefore it is said to be of 'sustained conation,' 'sustained burden.' Just as if they were to say, 'Get a beast of burden, an ox, to draw a burden from a marshy place not beyond the bullock's strength,' and the bullock, pressing the ground with its knees, were to carry the burden and would not allow it to drop on the ground, so energy lifts up and seizes the burden in the matter of doing moral acts. Hence it is said to be 'support of burden.'

It exercises government (over associated states) in the characteristic of supporting them or carrying out the accepted work—this is 'faculty of energy.' [147] It does not fluctuate on account of idleness—this is 'strength of energy.' 'Right endeavour' is irreversible, emancipating, moral endeavour.

In the exposition of the 'faculty of mindfulness'[2] mindfulness is so called by virtue of calling to mind. This is the primary word. It is 'recollection' by virtue of repeated calling to mind, 'calling back to mind' by virtue of calling to mind as though gone to the presence of the object. These two words merely show increase on account of the preposition. 'Remembrance' (*saraṇatā*) is mental behaviour in remembering. Inasmuch as it is a name for the Three Refuges (*saraṇa*), the word mindfulness is repeated to inhibit that meaning. Here remembrance means mindfulness.

Mindfulness is called 'bearing in mind' from its nature of bearing in mind a lesson heard or learnt; 'non-superficiality' (in the sense of diving or entering into the object) is the state of not letting the object float away. Not as pumpkins and pots, etc., which float on the water and do not sink therein,

---

[1] *Saṃyutta* ii. 28, etc.

[2] *Dhs.* § 14.

does mindfulness sink into the object. Hence it is said to be non-superficiality. From not forgetting a thing done or spoken long ago, mindfulness is called 'non-obliviousness.' It exercises government (over associated states) in the characteristic of presenting or illuminating the object—this is the 'faculty of mindfulness.' It does not fluctuate on account of negligence—this is 'strength of mindfulness.' 'Right mindfulness' is irreversible, emancipating, moral mindfulness.

In the exposition of the 'faculty of understanding'[1] understanding is so called in the sense of knowing plainly, *i.e.*, making plain the meaning of various things. Or, understanding is that which knows states under various aspects as impermanent, etc. This is the primary word. The behaviour of mind in knowing widely is 'wisdom.' That which investigates impermanence, etc., is 'search' (*vicaya*). 'Research' (*pavicaya*) shows increase by means of the preposition. 'Search for doctrine' is that which investigates the doctrine of the Four Truths. Understanding is 'discernment' by virtue of discerning impermanence, etc. By means of the different prepositions understanding is called 'discrimination,' 'differentiation.'

The state of a learned man is 'erudition.' The state of an expert is 'proficiency.' The state of a subtle man is 'subtlety.' 'Criticism' [here] is critical knowledge respecting impermanence and kindred subjects. 'Reflection,' or, in whom it arises it makes him think of impermanence—this is 'reflection.' 'It examines impermanence,' etc.—this is 'examination.' The next term, *bhūrī* (breadth), is a name for the earth; understanding is like the earth in the sense of both subtlety[2] and amplitude; hence 'breadth.' [148] And it has been said that the earth is broad, and that a man endowed with understanding, having richness and abundance like the earth, is of 'broad' understanding. Further, this *bhūrī* is a synonym for under-

---

[1] *Dhs.* § 16.

[2] As the earth, apart from rocks, stones and sand, etc., is called subtle earth (bhūmi saṇhā), so understanding, apart from the rocks of corruptions, is *subtle.—Gaṇṭhi.* Another reading is 'saṇṭhavittaṭṭhena' ='in the sense of stability and amplitude.'

standing, because this delights in the true [or revealed] meaning.[1]

'It slays the corruptions and destroys them, as lightning destroys stone-pillars'—this is 'sagacity'; or, it is 'sagacity' in the sense of quickly grasping and bearing the meaning. Next, 'in whom it arises it bends or inclines him to practise that which is his personal advantage,' or 'it inclines associated states to the penetration of the irreversible characteristic marks'—this is 'guide.' 'It discerns states under various aspects such as impermanence,' etc.—this is 'insight.' 'Comprehension' is that which knows impermanence, etc., in right ways. In order to put the wicked mind which has run off the track on to the right track, understanding urges it, just as a 'goad' urges horses of Sindh who are off the track in order to put them on the right track. It is like a goad, and is called 'incitement.'[2] As a controlling faculty understanding exercises government in the characteristic of 'seeing impermanence,' etc. It does not vacillate through ignorance—this is 'strength of understanding.' As a weapon, in the sense of cutting off the corruptions, understanding is the 'sword of understanding.' In the sense of rising high into the sky like a lofty building it is the 'height of understanding.' In the sense of illuminating it is the 'light of understanding.' In the sense of shedding lustre it is the 'lustre of understanding.' In the sense of being splendid it is the 'splendour of understanding.' For to the Wise Man,[3] possessed of understanding and seated, at one sitting the ten thousand world elements become of one light, one lustre, one splendour. Hence it has been said that understanding is light, etc. In these three words, though the sense is accomplished by any one of them, the teaching is made to meet the inclinations of [various] persons—for instance, in such Suttas as 'Bhikkhus, there are four kinds of light; which are the four ?—the light of the moon, of the sun,

---

[1] An unreproduceable word-play of the 'buried city' species: bhūrīti *bhūte* atthe *ramatī* ti.—*Ed.*

[2] Badly punctuated in P.T.S. ed.

[3] *I.e.*, the Bodhisat.—*Ariyālaṅkāra.*

of fire, and of understanding. These are the four kinds of light. Of these, the light of understanding is the best. Likewise, bhikkhus, the four kinds of lustre . . . of splendour.'[1] For the meaning has been well analyzed in various ways, and others understand it in different ways. The 'treasure of understanding' is meant in the sense of causing, giving, and producing delight,[2] of being worthy of respect (or being varied), of the difficulty of getting, or of manifesting it, of incomparableness, and of being the property of illustrious beings.

Beings are not, on its account, deluded in the object, or itself is not deluded in the object—this is 'non-delusion.' The expression 'search for the doctrine' has been already explained.[3] Why is it repeated ?—in order to show the antithesis between non-delusion [149] and delusion. By that expression non-delusion shows its antithesis to delusion. And non-delusion is not a thing altogether different from delusion; but what is meant here is that the non-delusion known as 'search for the doctrine' is opposed to delusion. Finally, 'right views' are irreversible, emancipating, moral views.

In the exposition of the 'faculty of life'[4] 'that persistence which is in the immaterial states' means the persistence which, in the sense of establishing them, is in the associated immaterial states. For when it is present, the immaterial states occur, go on, continue; hence it is called 'persistence.'[5] This word gives the nature of the faculty of life. And inasmuch as these associated immaterial states—when there is persistence—subsist, occur, maintain themselves, progress, continue, preserve themselves, the terms subsistence, etc., are given. As to the definition of the other terms:—by this the co-existent states subsist—this is 'subsistence'; they occur —this is 'occurrence.' So with 'establishment.' The [stem] vowel in the first word, *yapanā* (occurrence), has been shortened, owing to the influence of scholars.[6] By this the co-

---

[1] *Aṅguttara* ii. 139 *f.* Cf. *S.* i. 14, 47 (*Kindred Sayings* i. 22, 67).

[2] Read rati-kārakaṭṭhena in P.T.S. ed.

[3] Above, p. 195. [4] *Dhs.* § 19.

[5] Āyu. Aya, causative of *i*, to go.—*Ed.*

[6] Yapanā, yāpanā. *B.P.E.*, 'going on, being kept going on.'

existent states progress—this is 'progress'; they continue —this is 'continuance'; they preserve themselves—this is 'preservation'; they live—this is 'life.' It makes government (over associated states) in the characteristic of ceaseless watching over the co-existent states—this is 'the faculty of life.'

In the exposition of the 'strength' called 'sense of shame,'[1] 'that which on that occasion' means 'by which state at the time (of the first type of moral consciousness).' Or, by change of gender (masculine for neuter), 'that state which arises at the time (of the first main type of moral consciousness)'—thus should the meaning be known. '*Hiriyitabbena*' is the instrumentive case used in the sense of employment.[2] The meaning is:—it abominates, loathes misconduct of body and other immoral states fit to be abominated. 'Of bad (states)' means of low (states). 'Of immoral states' means of states not produced by understanding (*i.e.*, produced by ignorance); '*sampattiyā*' is also in the instrumentive case in the sense of employment. The meaning is:—it abominates, loathes the attainment of, the endowment with these immoral states.

In the exposition of the strength called 'fear of blame,'[3] this is in the instrumentive case in the sense of root-condition. [One fears][4] on account of misconduct in deed, word, or thought, where is fear of blame as root-condition, and which is fit to be feared. On account of the attainment of bad states of the kinds stated, and having fear of blame as root-condition—such is the meaning.

In the exposition of 'non-greed'[5] non-greed works by not-lusting. Disinterestedness is that which does not lust. This is a word showing its own nature. 'Not-lusting' is behaviour in not lusting. A person possessed by lust is 'lustful,' the not being which is 'not lustful.' [150] The state of a person not lustful is 'absence of lustfulness.' 'Absence of infatuation' is the opposite to infatuation. The

---

[1] *Dhs.* § 30.

[2] Or, of cause or condition.—*Ṭīkā.*

[3] *Dhs.* § 31.

[4] Consequences—*e.g.*, purgatory.—*Ṭīkā.*

[5] *Dhs.* § 32. Or 'disinterestedness.'

other terms are behaviour in 'not being infatuated,' and the state of one not infatuated.

That which does not covet is 'non-covetousness.' 'Disinterestedness as the root of what is moral' means that root considered as disinterestedness, for this is that root—*i.e.*, cause of moral states. It is moral and a root in the sense of causal relation; hence 'moral root.'

In the exposition of non-hate,[1] 'non-hate' works by not hating. 'It does not hate'—this is non-hate. This is a word showing its own nature. 'Not hating' is behaviour in not hating. The state of a person not hating is 'non-hatred.'

That which, from being opposed to ill-will, is not ill-will is 'good-will.' That which is not spleen from being opposed to the pain of anger is 'absence of spleen.' Non-hate is considered as a moral root—the meaning has already been declared.

In the exposition of 'repose of mental factors,' etc.,[2] because the word *kāyo* means the three aggregates mentioned, therefore it is said, 'Of the aggregate of feeling,' etc. By it those three factors are in repose, freed from suffering, have attained relief—this is 'repose of mental factors.' The second word (*paṭipassaddhi*—composure) has been increased by the preposition. 'Calming' is the behaviour of mind in calming. The second word (*paṭipassambhanā*—tranquillizing) has been increased by the preposition. By the endowment of repose, the state of the three aggregates which have been tranquillized is 'tranquillity.' All these words describe the composure of suffering caused by the corruptions of the three aggregates. By the second method[3] the composure of the suffering of the aggregate of consciousness is described.

Ease in change[4] is buoyant behaviour, the lightly changing in those three factors, their state in thus changing. As has been said, it is the capacity for quickly revolving. 'Non-sluggishness' is a word contrasting with heaviness. It means the being not-burdened. 'Non-inertia' is the not being stiff[5]

---

[1] *Dhs* § 33. [2] *Ib.* § 40 *ff.* [3] *Ib.* § 41. [4] *Ib.* § 42.

[5] Like a python that has swallowed an iron stick.—*Pyi*

owing to the absence of the burden of sloth and torpor. These describe buoyancy of behaviour in the three aggregates. By the second section[1] buoyancy of behaviour in the aggregate of consciousness is described.

[151] 'Plasticity' means soft state. Herein fine smoothness is called soft. The state of that is 'suavity.' 'Non-roughness' means the state of being not rough. 'Non-rigidity' means the state of being not rigid (hard). Here also the plasticity of the three aggregates and that of the aggregate of consciousness are discussed consecutively.[2]

'Wieldiness'[3] means soundness of action. Serviceableness for moral action is the meaning. The remaining pair of words (*kammaññattaṃ kammaññabhāvo*—tractableness, pliancy) have been increased in verbal form.[4] Here again the three aggregates and consciousness are taken consecutively.

'Fitness'[5] means the fitting state. Absence of disease and sickness is the meaning. The remaining pair of words have been increased in verbal form, and here also is consecutive description.

'Rectitude'[6] is the upright state. The state of procedure with an upright behaviour is the meaning. The state of the three upright aggregates and of the aggregate of consciousness is 'rectitude.' 'Non-deflection' is opposed to crookedness in flow, as of ox-urine; 'non-crookedness,' to that of the crescent moon; 'non-twist' to that of a ploughshare.

---

[1] *Dhs.* § 43.

[2] The absence of resistance in acting morally on the part of these states, which are not devoid of buoyancy, like those associated with delusion, is 'plasticity' (muditā). The plasticity of immaterial states, from resemblance to matter, etc., which are said to be plastic on account of non-resistance, is 'suavity' (maddavatā).—*Ṭīkā*.

[3] *Dhs.* § 46 *f.*

[4] The mind, exceedingly soft (mudu), being wet with craving, is unwieldy for moral action, like powdered gold. The mind, very rigid with conceit, etc., is unwieldy, like unheated gold. The mind which is soft to the right extent for morality is wieldy, like properly tempered gold. Thus wieldiness depends on the right softness.—*Ṭīkā*.

[5] *Dhs.* § 48 *f.*

[6] *Ib.* § 50.

He who, having done evil, says, 'I have not done it,' is said to be crooked like ox-urine from having proceeded and backed out. He who, while doing evil, says, 'I fear evil,' is said to be crooked like the crescent moon from being crooked in general. He who, while doing evil, says: 'Who may not fear evil ?' is said to be crooked like the ploughshare from being but slightly crooked. Or again, whoever has the three doors of action impure is said to be crooked 'like ox-urine'; whoever has any two doors of action impure is said to be crooked 'like the crescent moon'; and whoever has one door of action impure is said to be crooked like the ploughshare. But the reciters of the Dīgha-Nikāya say: One, who in the whole of his life practises the twenty-one things not to be pursued[1] and the six things not to be practised[2] is said to be crooked like ox-urine. One who during the first portion of his life fulfils the four Purity Precepts,[3] abominates evil, is sensitive, is observant of the precepts, and is like the preceding person [152] in the middle and last portions of his life is said to be crooked like the crescent moon. One who during the first and middle portions of his life fulfils the four Purity Precepts, abominates evil, is sensitive, is observant of the precepts, and is like the preceding two types of persons in the last portion of his life is said to be crooked like the

---

[1] The *Ṭīkā* has the following enumeration of these: doctoring, carrying messages, going on (other) errands, excision of tumours and abscesses, anointing scars, giving emetics or aperients, cooking secretions, preparing oil for the eyes (why are these five not included in the first ?), giving of bamboos, leaves, flowers, fruits, bath-powder, toothpicks, water for face-bathing, medical powders, or chalk; cajolery, idle talk (lit. pea-soup talk), petting children. Cf. a partly identical list in *Milinda* 370.

[2] These are: *vesiyāgocara*, asking alms from a prostitute's house through friendship; *vidhavagocara*, or from a divorced woman's house; *thullakumārīgocara*, or from an old maid's house; *paṇḍakagocara*, or from an eunuch's house; *pāṇāgāragocara*, or from the house of dealers in drink; *bhikkhunīgocara*, or from nuns' premises.—*Ṭīkā*.

[3] *I.e.*, restraint according to the Pātimokkha (*Vin. Texts* i. 1-69), restraint of sense and other faculties, purity of livelihood, restraint connected with the four requisites. Cf. *Vis. Magga.* ch. i.

ploughshare. And the state of a man crooked by virtue of the corruptions is called 'deflection,' 'crookedness,' 'twist.' By way of opposition to these, non-deflection, etc., have been discussed. The teaching given has been determined by the aggregates. For the non-deflection, etc., are of the aggregates and not of the person. Thus by means of all these terms behaviour in straightness of the three aggregates and of the aggregate of consciousness has been consecutively discussed—that is to say, of these immaterial states in the absence of the corruptions.

Now in the words 'Or whatever' this section of the conclusion has already been discussed. By it the exposition in brief of the 'Or-whatever' states shown in the section of the outline of states is now finished.

End of the Discourse on the Section of the Exposition.

CHAPTER III

ON THE SECTION OF THE SUMMARY[1]

THUS far is finished the section of the determination of states adorned by its eight divisions, to wit, four in the section of outline (questions, exposition of occasion, outline of states,[2] conclusion) and the same four in the section of exposition. Now the section of the summary is begun with, 'On that occasion there are four aggregates.'[3] It is threefold by virtue of outline, exposition and further exposition. Of these, 'Now on that occasion there are four aggregates,' etc., gives the outline. 'What on that occasion are the four aggregates?' etc., is the exposition. 'What on that occasion is the aggregate of feeling?' etc., is the further exposition.

Of these, in the section of the outline, there are twenty-three portions beginning with the four aggregates. Their meaning should be taken thus:

At what time the first main type of moral consciousness,

---

[1] Saṅgaha. *Dhs.* §§ 58-120.

[2] *Dhs.* § 58 *ff.* (koṭṭhāsavāra), etc.

[3] Reading in P.T.S. ed. dhammuddeso as before.—*Tr.*

experienced in the realm of sense, arises, those states exceeding fifty[1] which, excepting the 'Or whatever,' have been included in the text, and which have arisen at that time as factors of consciousness—all these being gathered together make four aggregates in the sense of groups: [153] two sense-organs in the sense of '*āyatana*' given above, two elements in the sense of intrinsic nature, emptiness of self, absence of a living entity. Further, three of these states are called nutriments in the sense of causal relation. The rest are not nutriments.

What then? Are these fifty-three (other than the three nutriments) in a causal relation either one with another, or with matter originated by themselves, or are they not? [They are.] But the 'three nutriment' states, in one way[2] or another,[3] as causes surpass the fifty-three states; hence they are spoken of as nutriments. How? To whatever present states the remaining [factors of] mind and mentals are causal relations, to those three contact also, as a nutriment, is in causal relation and sustains [or induces] the three feelings. The volition of mind as a nutriment is also in causal relation to them and sustains the three existences. Consciousness as a nutriment is also in causal relation to them and sustains the organism of mind and matter in reconception. (Thus as nutriments they surpass the fifty-three states.)

But is not this [consciousness as nutriment] merely a result, while this first main type of consciousness is a moral consciousness? [We reply:—] Although it is a moral consciousness, it has been called consciousness as nutriment because of its resemblance to the consciousness which is a result. Or, these three states are called nutriments in the sense of strengthening the associated states, as material food strengthens the body. Hence it is said: 'The immaterial nutriments are causally related, as nutriments, to their associated states and to the material qualities produced by them.'[4]

---

[1] Fifty-six in all.

[2] They render service as co-existent states. This is the expansion of *tathā* (*Ṭīkā*).

[3] This is the expansion of *aññathā* (*Anuṭīkā*).

[4] *Paṭṭhāna.*

Another explanation:—Because they are in a special causal relation in the subjective continuity, material food and the three states are said to be nutriments. Material food is specially correlated to the material body of beings who partake of it; so is contact to feeling in the immaterial group; so is mental volition to consciousness, and consciousness to the dual organism. As the Blessed One has said, 'Just as, bhikkhus, this body is established on material food, stands in dependence on it, does not stand without it, so from contact as cause arises feeling, from feeling as cause arise activities, from activities as cause arises consciousness, from consciousness as cause arises the mental and material organism.'[1]

Next, eight states are controlling faculties, in the sense of dominant influence and not the rest. Hence it is here said: 'there are eight controlling faculties.' Again, five states are Jhāna-factors, in the sense of viewing the object closely. Hence it is here said: 'there is fivefold Jhāna.' [154] Next, five states are Path-factors, in the sense of means of escape from the round of existence, and of being the condition of reaching Nibbāna. Hence it is here said: 'there is a fivefold Path.' For although the Path is eightfold, yet, in the worldly consciousness,[2] the three abstinences[3] are not obtained at one and the same instant. Therefore it is said to be fivefold only. But [it may be objected] there is this scripture: 'The Path by which they came is a phrase for the Eightfold Ariyan Path.'[4] In this Sutta the Path of insight preceding the Transcendental Path is eightfold, just as the latter is eightfold. Now, since the mundane Path, as implied by the term 'path by which they came,' is eightfold, should it not be eightfold here also?

Nay, it should not be. This Suttanta teaching is [carried out by] expounding. In this way he said, for instance,

---

[1] Not traced. Cf. *Saṃyutta* v. 64 *f*.

[2] As represented in this first main type.—*Ariyālaṅkāra*.

[3] A scholastic term for the factors in the Eightfold Path called 'right speech, action and livelihood. Abstinence from the opposites of these.' —*Compendium*, p. 97, *n*. 2.—*Ed*.

[4] *Saṃyutta* iv. 195.

'Verily, before this happened, his bodily acts, vocal acts and life were quite pure.'[1] But this [Abhidhamma] is bare teaching without exposition. In the worldly consciousness the three abstinences are not[2] obtained at one and the same instant, and therefore the Path is said to be fivefold.

Seven states are 'strengths' in the sense of not shaking[3]; three states are root-conditions in the sense of roots; one state is contact in the sense of touching the object; one state is feeling in the sense of experiencing the object; one state is perception in the sense of noting the object; one state is volition in the sense of planning; one state is consciousness in the sense of (*a*) being aware and (*b*) being variegated; one state is the aggregate of feeling[4] in the sense of a group and experiencing the object[5]; one state is the aggregate of perception in the sense of a group and noting the object; one state is the aggregate of mental co-efficients in the sense of a group and planning; one state is the aggregate of consciousness in the sense of a group and being aware and variegated; one state is the sense-organ of mind in the sense of knowing the object and an abode, as was said above; one state is the controlling faculty of mind in the sense of knowing and being dominant; one state is the element of mind-consciousness in the sense of knowing and of being intrinsic in nature, void [of personality] and without a living entity. The remaining states are not like this last. Moreover, excepting consciousness, all the remaining states form one sphere of (mental) states according to the meanings already given; and one state is the element of (mental) states. By the section of the conclusion: 'or whatever at that time,' the 'or-whatevers' discussed above are taken here also. So everywhere should also the 'or-whatevers' be taken. [155] After this section we shall not discuss at such length. And in the sections of the exposition and further exposition the meaning should be understood as given above.

End of the Section of the Summary, otherwise called the Section of Groups.

---

[1] *Majjhima* iii. 289. [2] *Sic lege* in P.T.S. ed. [3] *Dhs.* §§ 95 *ff.*
[4] *Sic lege* in P.T.S. ed. [5] *Dhs.* §§ 112-120.

CHAPTER IV

OF THE SECTION ON THE VOID, OR EMPTINESS[1]

Now, 'At that time there are states,' thus the section of the Void begins. It stands in two ways—outline and exposition.

In the former section, with the words, 'states there are,' there are twenty portions, but in none of them is there a division made, as above, into four, two, three. And why? Because such a division was made in the section of the summary. The states classified there are spoken of here. And here there are only states; no permanent being, no soul is known.[2] These (fifty-six states) are mere states without essence, without a guiding principle. And it is to show the emptiness of this that they are stated here also. Therefore the meaning should here be thus regarded.

At what time the first main type of moral consciousness experienced in the realm of sense arises, at that time, by virtue of being factors in consciousness, the fifty and more states which have arisen are ultimate things. There is nothing else whatever, neither a being, nor an individuality, nor a man, nor a person. Likewise they are aggregates in the sense of groups. Thus by the former method the connexion of the matter should be understood in all the words.

And because there is no Jhāna factor different from Jhāna, no Path-factor different from the Path, therefore here it is said merely: 'there is Jhāna, there is the Path.' There is Jhāna in the sense of viewing the object closely; there is Path in the sense of condition [for getting Nibbāna]; there is no other, neither a being nor an individuality—thus should the connexion of the meaning be understood in all the words. The meaning of the section of the exposition is evident.

Here ends the section of the Void.

Here ends the Commentary on the First Type of Consciousness set forth as adorned with the three main sections.

---

[1] *Dhs.* § 121.

[2] *Bhāvo ti satto, yo koci vā attho.—Ṭīkā.*

CHAPTER V

THE SECOND TYPE OF CONSCIOUSNESS

Now to show the second class of consciousness, etc., the beginning is thus: 'which are the states?'[1] In all of them the main sections should be understood as given in the first class.

[156] And not only the main sections, but the meaning of all the words which have been analogously stated in the first type of consciousness should be understood in the manner already given. After this second class of consciousness we shall comment on new words only.

In the exposition of the second class, '*sasaṅkhārena*'[2] is a new word, meaning 'with *saṅkhāra*.' The import is 'with external plan, effort, instigation, expedient, totality of causes.' By what totality of causes, viz., an object, etc., the first main type of consciousness arises, with that instigation, that expedient the second type arises. Thus should its arising be understood. For instance, in this dispensation a certain bhikkhu, dwelling in a border monastery, when the time has arrived to sweep the courtyard of the shrine, or to attend to the Elder or to listen to the Law, thinks thus: 'It is too far to go and come back. I will not go.' He thinks again, 'It is improper for a bhikkhu not to sweep the courtyard, not to attend to the Elder, not to listen to the Law. I will go,' and goes. Now whether it is from self-instigation, or whether he has been admonished by another pointing out the disadvantage in not doing one's duty, etc., and the advantage in doing it, or whether he has done his duty by being impelled thereto by such words as, 'Come and do this,' his moral consciousness is said to have arisen by external plan, by the totality of causes.

---

[1] *Dhs.* § 146.

[2] *Dhs.* § 147.

CHAPTER VI

THE THIRD TYPE OF CONSCIOUSNESS

In the third class of consciousness *ñāṇavippayutta* means 'dissociated from knowledge.' This consciousness also takes pleasure in the object, but here there is no discriminating knowledge. It should be regarded as the consciousness arising in young boys who, when they see and greet a bhikkhu, say, 'This is my Elder,' and show respect when saluting the shrine and listening to the Law. But in the text here understanding is lacking in seven places.[1] The remaining contents need no comment.

CHAPTER VII

THE FOURTH TYPE OF CONSCIOUSNESS.[2]

In the fourth class of consciousness also the same method should be taken. Because it is said to be with external plan, we may regard it as obtained, *e.g.*, at such a time when parents catch hold of young boys by the head and make them pay homage to the shrine, etc., and the boys, although it was not their aim, do so with pleasure.

CHAPTER VIII

THE FIFTH, SIXTH, SEVENTH, AND EIGHTH TYPES OF CONSCIOUSNESS[3]

In the fifth class of consciousness, *upekkhāsahagata* means 'accompanied by hedonic indifference.' [157] For this fifth class is neutral towards the object, and there is also a discriminating knowledge. It is stated here in the text that in fivefold Jhāna there is indifference, in the eight controlling faculties there is indifference. Accordingly, in the exposition of all

---

[1] *I.e.*, understanding as controlling faculty, strength, path, root, course of action, and one of the pairs is omitted. Cf. *Dhs.* §§ 16, 20, 29, 34, 37, 53, 55.—*Tr.*

[2] *Ib.* §§ 148 *f.*

[3] *Ib.* §§ 150 *f.*

hedonistic terms, neutral feeling has been discussed in a doctrine which eliminates both the happy and the unhappy, the pleasurable and the painful. The state of indifference as a controlling faculty should be understood as making government (over associated states) in the characteristic of neutrality.

In one place, in the serial order of words, 'rapture' is wanting. Therefore the states established in the text as factors of consciousness are only fifty-five. It is with reference to these fifty-five states that the decision in all the groups in all the sections should be understood. The sixth, seventh and eighth classes of consciousness should be understood in the same way as the second, third and fourth. For in these classes there is only change of feeling and lack of rapture. And the remainder of the words, together with the manner of arising, is like the second, third and fourth classes of consciousness. Again, when the preamble of Pity and Sympathy[1] [is being practised], these classes, according to the Great Commentary, arise.

Now these are the eight types of moral consciousness experienced in the realm of sense. And all of them should be set forth by the ten bases of meritorious acts. How? Bases of meritorious acts, consisting of (1) charity, (2) of virtue, (3) of culture, (4) of respect for elders,[2] (5) of dutifulness,[2] (6) of sharing of one's merit, (7) of thanksgiving, (8) of teaching, (9) of listening to the Law, (10) of rectification of opinion—these are the ten bases of meritorious acts.

Of these, (1) charity is the charitable meritorious act, which is the basis of various advantages. And the same holds good with the remaining words; for instance, when one has made a gift of the four requisites, such as a robe, or of any object of sense, or of the ten bases of giving, such as food, etc., the volition that arises in the giver on the three occasions of producing the articles prior to the gift, of making the gift, and of recollection with a joyful heart after the gift, is the basis of charitable meritorious action.

(2) The volition that arises in one who takes the fivefold

---

[1] Cf. *Dhs.* §§ 258-61.

[2] *Sahagataṃ* has no meaning here except 'accompanied by intimation through act and speech [of respect for elders and of dutifulness].'—*Pyi.*

precept, the eightfold precept or the tenfold precept; or who goes to the monastery thinking, 'I will become a recluse'; who becomes a recluse and reflects, 'I have fulfilled my wish, I am indeed a recluse; that is good and well done'; who observes the Pātimokkha and reflects on the four requisites, such as a robe, etc.; who guards the eye-door, etc., regarding objects of sense which have presented themselves; [158] who purifies his mode of life—all such volition is the basis of virtuous meritorious action.

(3) In one who cultivates himself, regarding both the eye as impermanent, ill and selfless, and the other senses and the mind, also visible and other sense-objects, objects of thought, sense-cognition with mental cognition, sense-contact, feeling born of sense-contact, perception of sense-objects, old age and death all in the same way as is taught in analytical knowledge[1] by the path of insight, all his volitions that have not attained ecstasy in the thirty-eight objects of consciousness[2] constitute the basis of meritorious action in culture.

(4) Respect as a basis of meritorious action should be known in such acts as going to meet an elderly person, taking his bowl and robe for him, saluting him, showing him the way.

(5) Dutifulness as basis of meritorious action should be known in those acts by which we carry out duties great and small towards our elders, when, for instance, we take the bowl from a bhikkhu who has been seen to enter the village for alms and fill it with food in the village, and present it to him, or go quickly and take the bowl, etc., on hearing the summons, 'Go and bring the bhikkhus' bowl.'[3]

(6) The sharing of one's merit as basis of meritorious action should be recognized in the case of one who, having made a gift and an offering of perfume, etc., gives part of his merit thus: 'Let this share be for such an one!' or, 'Let it be for all beings!' What then, will there be loss of merit to him who thus shares what he has attained? No. As when from a burning lamp

---

[1] Paṭisambhidā.

[2] Viz., 40 Kammaṭṭhānas *minus* āloka and ākāsa. Cf. *Compend.* 202 *f.*

[3] Reading bhikkhūnaṃ pattaṃ. P.T.S. ed. reads: 'Go, bhikkhu, and fetch that bowl.'

a thousand lamps were lit, it would not be said that the original lamp was exhausted; the latter light, being one with the former [added] lights, becomes increased, thus there is no decrease in our sharing what we have attained; on the contrary, there is an increase. Thus it should be understood.

(7) Thanksgiving as basis of meritorious action is to be understood as giving thanks with the words, 'Good, well done!' when, for instance, others share their merit with us, or when they perform another meritorious act.

(8) From a desire for gain, thinking, 'Thus they will know me to be a preacher,' someone preaches a sermon. That sermon is not of much fruit. One who makes the attainment of emancipation the chief motive, not a desire for honour, and so preaches to others the doctrine in which he is proficient—this is the basis of meritorious action consisting of teaching.

(9) One who listens to the doctrine, thinking, 'They will take me, thus listening, for one of the faithful'—this does not yield much fruit. Another, out of the softness of heart, suffusing good,[1] listens, thinking, 'There will be much fruit for me.' This is the basis of meritorious action consisting of listening to the Doctrine.

[159] (10) To correct one's own views is the basis of meritorious action of rectified opinion. But the reciters of the *Dīgha-Nikāya* say that rectified opinion is the characteristic of assurance respecting all things.[2] For by it there is much fruit to one doing any sort of merit.

Of these bases of meritorious action, (1) charity arises with the thought 'I will give charity,' when he is making the gift, and when he reflects 'I have given it.' Thus the three volitions—preliminary volition, volition at the time of making the gift, subsequent volition—become one, and constitute the basis of meritorious act consisting of charity.

(2) That which consists of virtue also arises with the thought, 'I will fulfil the precepts,' when he is fulfilling them, and when he reflects: 'I have fulfilled the precepts.' All the

---

[1] Either to himself or others.—*Pyī*.

[2] *I.e.*, all courses of moral action, or bases of meritorious action.—*Pyī*.

three volitions, becoming one, constitute the basis of meritorious act consisting of virtue.

So for the remaining eight.

In the Suttas there are only three bases of meritorious action —charity, virtue and culture. The other bases should be understood as included in these three. Respect and dutifulness are thus included in that which consists of virtue. Sharing of merit and thanksgiving[1] are included in that which consists of charity; teaching, hearing the Law and rectification of opinion in that which consists of culture. Rectification of opinion, in the doctrine of those teachers who say that it has the characteristic of assurance in all the bases, is comprehended in the three bases of charity, virtue and culture. Thus these bases of meritorious act form three in abstract and are ten when expanded.

Now, as to these bases, when we think 'I will give in charity,' thought works by one or other of those eight classes of moral consciousness experienced in the realm of sense; in making the gift we give by one of them; in reflecting 'I have given charity,' we reflect by one of them; in thinking 'I will fulfil the precepts,' we think by one of them; in fulfilling the precepts we fulfil by one of them; in reflecting 'I will develop culture,' we think by one of them; in developing it, we develop by one of them; in reflecting 'I have developed culture,' we reflect by one of them. [160] In thinking 'I will pay homage to my elders,' in paying it, in reflecting 'I have paid it,' we think, reverence, and reflect by them. In thinking 'I will do my duty by the body,' in doing it, in reflecting 'I have done it,' we think and reflect by them. In thinking 'I will share my merit,' in doing it, in reflecting 'I have shared it'; in thinking 'I will give thanks for a gift of merit by another, or for the merit acquired by others'; in giving thanks; in reflecting 'I have given thanks,' we work by those eight classes. In thinking 'I will preach the doctrine'; in preaching

[1] This is included in charity because, as a loving giver, sacrificing a faultless thing, rejoices at the gain of another, so one who gives thanks rejoices at another's possessions.—*Ṭīkā*.

it; in reflecting 'I have preached it,' we think, preach, reflect by them. In thinking 'I will listen to the doctrine'; in doing so; in reflecting 'I have listened,' we do likewise. Likewise in thinking 'I will rectify my opinion.' But in rectifying our opinion we do so only by one or other of the four main classes of moral consciousness associated with knowledge. In reflecting 'I have rectified my opinion,' we do so by one or other of all the eight.

In this connexion[1] there are four Infinites, to wit, (1) space, (2) world-systems, (3) groups of sentient beings, (4) the knowledge of a Buddha.

(1) There is, indeed, no limit to space reckoned as so many hundreds, thousands, or hundred thousands of yojanas to east, west, north, or south. If an iron peak of the size of Mount Meru were to be thrown downwards, dividing the earth in twain, it would go on falling and would not get a footing. Thus infinite is space.

(2) There is no limit to the world-systems reckoning by hundreds or thousands of yojanas. If the four [161] Great Brahmās, born in the Akaniṭṭha mansion, endowed with speed, and capable of traversing a hundred thousand world-systems during the time that a light arrow shot by a strong archer would take to travel across the shadow of a palmyra tree, were with such speed to run in order to see the limit of the world-systems, they would pass away without accomplishing their purpose. Thus the world-systems are infinite.

(3) In so many world-systems there is no limit to beings, belonging to land and water. Thus infinite are the groups of beings.

(4) More infinite than these is a Buddha's knowledge.

Thus of the countless beings in the countless world-systems, many kinds of moral consciousness experienced in the realm of sense, accompanied by joy, associated with knowledge, and with external aid, arise to one and many to many. And all of these in the sense of being experienced in the realm

[1] Or place, *ṭhāne*, explained by the commentaries as referring to the Great Commentary.—*Tr.*

of sense, of being accompanied by joy, of being associated with knowledge, of being without external aid, may be classified in one group—namely, the main class of consciousness accompanied by joy, thrice-conditioned and automatic. And the same with the main class of consciousness 'with external aid,' and so on down to the eighth class, accompanied by hedonic indifference, dissociated from knowledge, twice-conditioned, with external aid. Now, all these classes of moral consciousness experienced in the realm of sense, arising in the countless beings in the countless world-systems, the Supreme Buddha, as though weighing them in a great balance, or measuring them by putting them in a measure, has classified by means of his omniscience, and has shown them to be eight, making them into eight similar groups. Again, in this connexion[1] the striving for merit has been taken in six ways. There is merit done by one's own nature, merit done after the example of another, merit done by one's own hands, merit done by ordering (another), merit done with knowledge of the result of kamma, merit done without knowledge of the result of kamma.[2] And anyone working merit by any of the first four methods does so by one or other of these eight classes of moral consciousness. One working merit by the fifth does so by the four classes 'associated with knowledge'; one working it by the sixth does so by the four classes 'dissociated from knowledge.'

Further, in this connexion the four purities of gift have been reckoned, to wit: lawful acquisition of the requisites, greatness or nobleness of volition, properties of the basis,[3] consummate virtue. Of these, requisites obtained through righteousness and equity are lawful requisites. [162] Greatness of volition is his who gives with faith and confidence in kamma and its result. The state of freedom from the Four Intoxicants is fulfilment of right virtues in the recipient. The state of the saint purged of the intoxicants, when he emerges from jhāna, is

---

[1] See preceding note.

[2] Or, merit done with comprehensive knowledge and that done without it.—*Tr.*

[3] *I.e.*, virtue in the recipient.—*Tr.*

consummate virtue. The moral consciousness experienced in the realm of sense of one who is able to make gifts connecting these four factors yields fruit even in this bodily existence, like that of Puṇṇakaseṭṭhi, Kāḷavalliya, Sumana the flower-seller, etc.

Considered in abstract, the whole of this moral consciousness experienced in the realm of sense is one, being grouped as consciousness (*citta*) in the sense of knowing the object and of being varied. By way of feeling it is twofold: accompanied by joy, or by hedonic indifference. By way of teaching showing the classification of knowledge it is fourfold: (*a*) type of consciousness, without external aid, accompanied by joy, associated with knowledge; and type of consciousness, without external aid, accompanied by hedonic indifference, associated with knowledge;[1] (*b*) the same associated with knowledge and with external aid; (*c*) the same without external aid and dissociated from knowledge; and (*d*) the same with external aid and dissociated from knowledge. Thus it is according to the teaching on the classification of knowledge. Thus in this fourfold division there are eight kinds of moral consciousness, to wit, four without external aid and four with external aid considered under this head. Knowing these truly, the Blessed One, the omniscient, most excellent of leaders, best of sages has declared, taught, regulated, established, discussed, analyzed, and expounded them.

End of the Exposition of Moral Consciousness in the world of sense-experience, [a portion] of 'The Expositor,' the Commentary on the 'Compendium of States.'

[1] In the sense of association with knowledge and of being without external aid, these two are one.—*Tr.*

PART V—DISCOURSE ON MORAL CONSCIOUSNESS IN THE REALM OF ATTENUATED MATTER[1]

CHAPTER I

JHĀNA—THE FOURFOLD SYSTEM

Now the beginning of this division: 'Which are the states that are moral?'[2] proceeds to show the nature of moral consciousness in the realm of attenuated matter. In the reply, by [attenuated] matter, life under those conditions is meant. 'That he may attain to'—*i.e.*, may obtain rebirth, renewed existence, be produced there. 'Way thereto'—*i.e.*, a means. The import is:—He traces out, seeks after, engenders, effects that rebirth. And this is what has been said: 'He develops the path (*magga*) by means of which there is birth, existence, production in that sphere of life.' What then? By this path is there assuredly rebirth in that sphere? Not so. By such utterances as 'Bhikkhus, develop [ecstatic] concentration; in such a state one knows, one sees as things really are,'[3] we see that there is a transcending even of that sphere by penetration [of insight]. Nevertheless, for rebirth in that sphere there is no path other than this. [163] Hence the words:—'he develops the path for rebirth in the sphere of attenuated matter.'

In its meaning, this path is volition, or states associated

---

[1] *Rūpāvacara*, lit. sphere of matter or material qualities, *or* sphere where rūpa's or objects of sight are the principal medium of experience.—*Comp.*, p. 12. Actually, the material environment and the corporeal frames in those realms seem to have been as varied in kind as in the lower planes of the Kāmāvacara 'heavens,' but more refined or sublimated. Cf., *e.g.*, *Dialogues* ii. 244, § 17. Rendered 'form' in *B.P.E.*, whereon cf. *Comp.* 271.—*Ed.*

[2] *Dhs.* §§ 160 *ff.*

[3] *Saṃyutta* iii. 13; v. 414.

with volition, or both. In the passage: 'Sāriputta, I know purgatory and the path leading to purgatory,'[1] the 'path' is the volition [the will that leads thereto]. In the lines:

Faith, modesty and meritorious giving—
These are the things that men of worth pursue;
This, say they, is the path celestial;
Hereby we pass into the deva-world,[2]

states associated with volition are the 'path.' Volition and states associated with volition are the 'path' in the *Saṅkhārūpapatti Sutta*, etc.:—'This, bhikkhus, is the path, this is the way.'[3] In the present connection, from its being said to be jhāna, the states associated with volition are intended. And inasmuch as volition in jhāna drags in rebirth, therefore both volition and the associated states increase.

'Develops'[4] means to beget, produce, increase. This is the meaning of *bhāvanā* here. Elsewhere the meaning is different according to the preposition, as *sambhāvanā*, *paribhāvanā*, *vibhāvanā*. Of these, *sambhāvanā* means religious confidence, thus:—'In my Order, Udāyi, my disciples *believe* in the higher ethics, knowing that the recluse Gotama is virtuous and is endowed with the higher ethics.'[5] 'Concentration *perfected by* virtue is of much fruit, of great advantage; understanding *perfected by* concentration is of much fruit, of great advantage; the mind *perfected by* understanding is well freed from the Intoxicants'[6]—here *paribhāvanā* means perfecting. *Vibhāvanā* means disappearance in: 'cause matter, cause feeling, perception, activities, consciousness to disappear.'[7]

Again, *bhāvanā* is used in the sense of producing and increasing, *e.g.*:—'Udāyi, I have preached to the disciples

---

[1] *Majjhima* i. 73.

[2] *Anguttara* iv. 236. Burmese texts, for *diviyaṃ* (*celestial*) read *viriyaṃ*. Cf. *Points of Controversy*, 199.

[3] *Majjhima* iii. 100.

[4] *B.P.E.*: 'cultivates' (*bhāveti*). Cf. *B. Psy.* 107 *n.* 1, 133, 158.

[5] *Majjhima* ii. 9.

[6] *Dīgha* ii. 81 (*Dialogues* ii. 85 *f.*).

[7] Not traced.

the practice according to which they develop the four applications in mindfulness.'[1] And such is its meaning here also. Hence it has been said that *bhāveti* means to beget, produce, increase. But why is the teaching here on the moral consciousness of the realm of attenuated matter initiated by the personal agent, and not by taking the conscious state (*dhamma*), as in the exposition of the moral consciousness of the sensuous realm? [164] Because it should be accomplished by practice. For the moral consciousness of this realm is to be accomplished by one or other of the four Modes of Progressive Practice.[2] It does not arise without progressive practice like that of the sensuous realm. And progress arises when there is a person to attain it. To show this meaning the Blessed One, in giving the teaching introducing first the person, has said: 'he develops the path for rebirth in the Rūpa sphere.'

Next, the phrase 'aloof, indeed, from sensuous desires'[3] means being separated from, being without, having parted from the pleasures of sense. And the word 'indeed' (*eva*) here is to be understood as having the meaning of assurance.[4] Because it has this meaning the Blessed One shows the opposition of the First Jhāna to the pleasures of sense which do not exist in the interval when one has attained it (First Jhāna), and its attainment only by the rejecting of them. How? When thus, by being aloof from sensuous desires, assurance is given, this meaning is made clear:—as where darkness exists, there is no lamp-light, so this Jhāna does not arise in the presence of sensuous desires, which, indeed, are opposed to it. As by abandoning the hither bank, the thither bank is obtained, so by abandoning sensuous desires this Jhāna is attained. Therefore he made this a matter of assurance.

Herein one might object: 'But why is this "indeed" spoken with the preceding term (*i.e.*, sensuous desires) and not with the following term (*i.e.*, immoral states)? What? should one live attaining to this Jhāna without being aloof from immoral states?' Not thus should the matter be understood.

---

[1] *Majjhima* ii. 11.
[2] *Dhs.* §§ 176 *ff*.
[3] *Dhs.* § 160.
[4] Niyamattho.

Eva, it is true, is spoken with the preceding term, because jhāna is an escape from sensuous desires; and jhāna is that because it has passed beyond all sensuous conditions, and is opposed to the lust of sense-desires. Accordingly he said: 'From sensuous desires this [jhāna] is the escape, this is the exit.'[1] Yet the word 'indeed' may also be used with the following term, as it is in 'Indeed, bhikkhus, in my dispensation . . . the first class of recluse is to be found, the second class of recluse is to be found.'[2] For it is not possible to live in the attainment of this jhāna without being aloof from those immoral states, known as the Hindrances, which are so different from it. Thus assurance should be understood in both the terms. And although, in this pair of terms, by the common word 'aloof' all kinds of aloofness are included, such as that of the corresponding part and so on, yet here only aloofness of body, aloofness of mind and by aloofness arrest [of the Hindrances] are to be understood.

By the term 'sense-desires' the desires based on objects of sense are referred to, as in the *Mahāniddesa*:—'What are the desires based on objects, delightful and lovely?'[3] And in the *Mahāniddesa* and the *Vibhaṅga* these are said to be sense-desires of our lower nature,[4] *e.g.*, 'The desire that is will, [165] lust, lust of the will, lustful intentions.'[5] All the sense-desires of our lower nature also should be understood as included. This being so, the meaning of 'aloof indeed from sensualities' ought also to be 'aloof indeed from sense-desires based on objects,' by which bodily aloofness is meant.

[In the next clause:—] 'aloof from immoral states,' the proper meaning is 'separated from the sense-desires based on our lower nature, or all immoral states,' by which mental aloofness is expressed.

By the former clause (*i.e.*, aloof indeed from sense-desires), because it has been said to be aloof from the sense-desires

---

[1] *Dīgha* iii. 275 (vii.).
[2] *Anguttara* ii. 238.
[3] *Mahā-Niddesa* 1.
[4] Specified as the ten *kilesa's*. On this term see *B.P.E.*, p. 327 *f.*
[5] *Vibhanga* 256.

based on objects, therefore it is clear that the pleasure of enjoying such sense-desires has been given up. By the second clause (*i.e.*, aloof from immoral states), because it has been said to be aloof from the sense-desires based on our lower nature, it is clear that the bliss of jhāna-emancipation has been comprehended.[1] Thus from their being said to be aloof from sense-desires based on objects and on our lower nature, by the first of the two phrases is shown clearly the relinquishment of the basis of the lower nature itself, by the second, that of our lower nature; by the first, the giving up of frivolity,[2] by the second, that of foolishness; by the first is shown the purity of motive, by the second, the nourishment of the wish (for Nibbāna).[3]

Thus far, in the clause 'from sense-desires,' we have the method for the portion including sense-desires based on objects. In the portion including sense-desires of our lower nature, 'sensuous desires,' variously considered as will, lust, etc., is the will of those desires. This sensuous desire, though included among immoral states, is taken separately, as being opposed to jhāna in the same way as it is said in the *Vibhaṅga*:—'Herein what is the sensuous desire which is the will thereof?'[4] Or it is taken in the first phrase as being sensuous desires of our lower nature, and in the second phrase as being included in things immoral. And the plural 'from sense-desires,' not the singular, is used to show its manifold nature. And although other states are immoral, only the Hindrances are spoken of as showing the opposition to, hostility of the higher jhāna factors in the same way as is said in the *Vibhaṅga*:—'Herein which are the immoral states? Sensuous desire,' etc.[5] For it is said that the Hindrances are opposed to the jhāna-factors, which are hostile to them and dispel and destroy them.

---

[1] This sentence is omitted in the P.T.S. ed.—*Ed.*

[2] *I.e.*, to lust after any and every visible object met with.—*Pyi.*

[3] By being pure from the corruptions.—*Ṭikā*. Or, *āsayaposana* means the fulfilment of one's wish, which consists in the accomplishment, by means of good deeds done in former existences, of antecedent conditions for the development of jhāna.—*Anuṭīkā.*

[4] Cf. *Vibhaṅga, loc. cit.*

[5] *Ibid.*

Likewise it is said, in the *Peṭakopadesa*,[1] that concentration is opposed to sensuous desire, rapture to ill-will, initial application of mind to sloth and torpor, bliss to flurry and worry, sustained application of mind to perplexity. Thus the former clause —' aloof indeed from sensualities '—expresses separation from, by the discarding of, sensuous desire, the latter clause—' aloof from immoral states '—separation from the five Hindrances. And if we include what has not been [explicitly] included, the separation by discarding is stated, in the first and second clauses, respectively, of sensuous desire and of the remaining Hindrances; of greed (one of the three immoral roots, with the five pleasures of sense for object) and of hate and delusion [the other immoral roots] with the bases of vexation, etc. [166] for object; of sensuality as ' flood,' ' bond,' ' intoxicant,' ' grasping,' ' the physical knot ' of covetousness, the lust of desire as ' a fetter ' among the ' floods,' etc., and of the remaining floods, bonds, intoxicants, graspings, knots and fetters of craving and states associated with it, and of ignorance and states associated with it; and also of the eight states of consciousness associated with greed and of the remaining four immoral states of consciousness.

So much, then, for the setting forth of the meaning of ' aloof indeed from sensualities and aloof from immoral states.' Now, having so far shown the factor eliminated in the First Jhāna, the clause—' with initial and with sustained application of mind '—is next stated to show the factors associated with it.

In this phrase jhāna is said to arise, together with initial and sustained application, classified according to the characteristics, etc., already given above [in connection with the realm of sense, a mental state which] has arrived at the realm of attenuated matter through association with ecstasy. It has been said that, as a tree is found with its flowers and fruits, so this Jhāna occurs with initial and sustained application. And in the *Vibhaṅga*, the teaching, as determined in a personal way, is given thus:—' One is endowed with, possessed of, this

[1] Here called ' Peṭake.'

initial application, this sustained application,' etc.[1] But the meaning there is to be understood as in this passage.

In the term 'born of solitude' the meaning is separation, solitude, freedom from the Hindrances. Or it means 'solitary,' 'separated.' The group of states associated with jhāna and separated from the Hindrances is the meaning. And 'born of solitude' is born from that solitude, or in that solitude.

Next, 'full of rapture-bliss':—these terms have been set forth above. Of the fivefold rapture this is the 'all-pervading rapture,'[2] which, being the root of ecstatic concentration, goes on increasing and has reached association with concentration. This is the rapture meant here. And this rapture and this bliss are obtainable in this jhāna; hence it is said to be 'full of rapture and bliss.' *Pītisukhaṃ* means rapture and bliss, like 'Dhamma-Vinaya,' etc. There is the rapture and bliss born of solitude of, or in, this jhāna; hence 'born of solitude, full of rapture-bliss.' For verily as the jhāna is born of solitude, so in it the rapture and bliss are also born of solitude and are obtainable in it. Therefore it is proper to say 'born of solitude and full of rapture-bliss' as one term. But in the *Vibhaṅga* it has been said in this way: 'This bliss is accompanied by this rapture,' etc.[3] The meaning, however, is to be understood as in this passage.

[167] 'First Jhāna'—this is the numerical order. 'First' is the first to have arisen[4]; and also that it is the first to be entered into. But this last meaning is not a sure characteristic. For an aspirant who is of practised self-control, and has attained the eight attainments, is able to enter into jhāna from the beginning to the end, and from the end to the beginning, and also to fall into it at intermediate stages. Thus this jhāna is first in the sense of arising first.

Jhāna is twofold: that which (views or) examines closely the object and that which examines closely the characteristic marks. Of these two, 'object-scrutinizing' jhāna examines

---

[1] *Vibhaṅga* 257, l. 12 *f.*

[2] See above, p. 153.

[3] *Vibhaṅga* 258.

[4] Uppannan ti. Or, to be attained.

closely those devices [for self-hypnotism][1] as mental objects. Insight, the Path and Fruition are called 'characteristic-examining jhāna.' Of these three, insight is so called from its examining closely the characteristics of impermanence, etc. Because the work to be done by insight is accomplished through the Path, the Path is also so called. And because Fruition examines closely the Truth of cessation, and possesses the characteristic of truth, it also is called 'characteristic-examining jhāna.' Of these two kinds of jhāna, the 'object-examining' mode is here intended. Hence, from its examining the object and extinguishing the opposing Hindrances,[2] jhāna is to be thus understood.

'Having attained' is said to mean 'having approached,' 'having reached,' or, 'having fulfilled,' 'having accomplished.' In the *Vibhaṅga*, 'having attained' is said to mean the getting, gaining, attainment, full attainment, touching, realizing, fulfilling of the First Jhāna.[3] There the meaning is to be understood in the same way.

'He lives' means to be endowed with the Jhāna, the various kinds of which have been distinguished above by the mode of behaviour corresponding to that Jhāna, and to accomplish the progress or function, continuance, preservation, maintenance, regulation, living of a personality. Indeed, it has been said in the *Vibhaṅga*, that 'he lives' means to progress, continue, preserve, maintain, regulate, live.[4] Hence 'he lives.'

In the term 'earth-device,' the circular [portion of] earth is called earth-device as representing the entire earth. The image of the mark, or the after-image obtained in dependence on that disc of earth, is also called the 'earth-device'; so also is the jhāna obtained in that image. Of these three meanings, the last is to be understood here. The meaning in abstract is that he is living in the attainment of the First Jhāna known as that of the earth-device. [168] With this earth-

---

[1] See *B.P.E.*, p. 43, *n.* 4, 57.

[2] On this, as preceding Jhāna, cf. *Dialogues* i. 82-84; *Compendium* 54.—*Ed.*

[3] *Loc. cit.* [4] *Vibhanga, loc. cit.* B.P.E., 'abides in (viharati).'

device, what ought to be done by a clansman's son who has done the preamble, induced the fourfold and fivefold Jhānas, increased insight with jhāna as proximate cause, and who is desirous of attaining Arahantship? At first, having purified the Four Precepts of restraint known as the *Pātimokkha*, restraint of controlling faculties, purity of life and dependence on requisites; he should establish himself in the sublimer Precepts; he should cut off any impediment, which exists in him, among the ten impediments beginning[1] with 'house-life'; he should approach that good friend, who gives him stations of exercise; he should study that exercise befitting his own practice among the thirty-eight stations of exercise as given in the Text,[2] and if the earth-device is suitable he should take that up; he should reject an unsuitable monastery,[3] living in one that is suitable for his jhāna culture; he should sever the minor impediments; and by not slackening the arrangement of the entire process of culture, comprising the different stages of preamble, guarding of the image, avoiding of the seven unsuitable things, pursuing the seven suitable things, and proficiency in the tenfold ecstasy, he should practise with a view to the attainment of jhāna.

This is an abstract; the detailed account is to be learnt from the account given in the *Visuddhi-Magga*.[4] The same remark holds good in the case of the following Jhānas. The entire process of culture of all the stations of exercise has been detailed in the *Visuddhi-Magga*, where the method of all the Commentaries has been followed. What good is there in repeating what has been said in various places? We shall therefore not explain it in detail again. Without spoiling the meaning, we shall without break give the explanation of the Pali Text in order due, without repeating ourselves.

Finally, the phrase 'at that time' means the time of his life when he has attained the First Jhāna. 'There is contact . . . there is non-distraction'—these are the fifty-six states, the various kinds of which have been distinguished as to the order

---

[1] *Mahā-Niddesa*, 156.
[2] *Compendium*, 202.
[3] Reading gahetvā bhāvanāya na anurūpaṃ . . .
[4] Chs. iii *ff*.

of terms in the first class of moral consciousness of the realm of sense. In reality, only these are of the realm of sense. Those discussed here, as to plane, are sublime and experienced in the realm of attenuated matter. This is the distinction here. The remaining words are the same. But here are obtained the four 'Or-whatever' states beginning with will.[1] The sections of the Groups and of the Void have been explained.

End of the First Jhāna.

CHAPTER II

THE SECOND JHĀNA[2]

In the exposition of the Second Jhāna, the clause:—'from the suppression of initial and sustained application' [169] means 'owing to the suppression, the transcending of these two: initial application and sustained application, they not being manifested from the moment when Second Jhāna begins.' Not only are all the mental factors of First Jhāna not present in Second Jhāna, but even those that are present—contact, and so on—are different. It is through the transcending of the gross element that there is the attainment of other Jhānas, the second from the First and so on. And it should be understood that it was to show this meaning that the words 'from the suppression of initial and sustained application' were said.

'Subjective' (*ajjhatta*) here means 'personal.' But in the *Vibhaṅga* just this is said:—'"Subjective" means self-referring.'[3] And because 'personal' is intended, therefore that which is one's own, produced in one's continuity, is to be here understood.

Next, 'tranquillizing':—faith is said to be tranquillizing. Through connection with it, the jhāna also is said to be tranquillizing, as a cloth when steeped in indigo is called indigo. Or, because this jhāna tranquillizes the mind owing to its union with faith and the suppression of the disturbing initial

[1] Or 'desire-to-do' (*chanda*).

[2] *Dhs.* § 161.

[3] *Vibhanga* 258—*paccattaṃ*; 'personal' is *niyakaṃ*. Cf. below.—*Ed.*

and sustained application, therefore it is called 'tranquillizing.' In this second sense the construction is to be understood as 'the tranquillizing of mind.'

In the former sense, 'of mind' is to be construed as 'with supreme exaltation,' this being the connected meaning:—alone (*lit.* one, *eko*) it rises above (*udeti*)—this is *ekôdi* (exalted). 'No longer overgrown by initial and sustained application, it rises up at the top, as the best' is the meaning; for in the world what is best is also called unique (*eko*). Or, it may also be said that,[1] as deprived of initial and sustained application, it rises up (*udeti*) single, or companionless; hence 'rising alone.' Or, again, it raises associated states, or causes them to rise. 'One' in the sense of 'best,' and exalted in the sense of 'raising,' give us *ekodī*:—'supremely exalted'—which is a synonym for concentration. And this Second Jhāna develops this exaltation, therefore it is called *ekodībhāva*—'pre-eminent,' 'single,' 'best to produce associated states.' And as it is of mind and not of an entity, or a living principle, it has been said to be 'unique exaltation of mind (*cetaso*).'

[It may here be objected:—] is not this faith and this concentration called 'uniquely exalting' present in First Jhāna also? Why *this* tranquillizing only, and unique exaltation of mind? The answer is:—That First Jhāna, being disturbed by initial and sustained application, is not *quite* clear, but is like water full of big and small waves, therefore [170] it is not said to be tranquillizing, though there be faith in it. And because it is not *quite* clear, concentration in it is not well manifested,[2] therefore unique exaltation is not ascribed to it. But in the Second Jhāna, owing to the non-existence of the impediments of initial and sustained application, faith, having got its opportunity, is strong, and concentration, by attaining intimate alliance with strong faith, is manifested. Therefore in this way should the formula be understood.

In the *Vibhaṅga* only this much is said, that tranquillity is faith, believing, confiding, assuring; and that unique exalta-

---

[1] Reading iti pi vattuṃ vaṭṭati.

[2] Like fish in muddy water.—*Ṭīkā*.

tion of mind is [defined as right concentration:—] 'that mental persistence . . . right concentration, which, etc.'[1] The explanation given above, however, should be understood as not going against, but indeed coinciding, concurring with the meaning given in the *Vibhaṅga*.

'Without initial and sustained application.' From being removed by culture, there is no initial application in this Jhāna; hence 'without initial application.' Similarly, it is 'without sustained application.' And in the *Vibhaṅga* it has been said that this initial application and this sustained application are calmed, quieted, suppressed, terminated, exterminated, destroyed, completely destroyed, dried up, quite dried up, finished; hence 'without initial and sustained application.'[2]

Here it may be said:—Is not this meaning determined by the phrase 'from the suppression of initial and sustained application'? Then why is it repeated as 'without initial and sustained application'? True, this latter meaning has already been determined. Yet the repetition does not show merely the meaning of the former phrase. Have we not said, that from the transcending of the gross factor there is the attainment of other Jhānas beyond the First?[3] To show this, it is said that the Second Jhāna tranquillizes the mind because of the suppression of initial and sustained application, and not because of the slough of our lower nature (as at the moment of access). Because of the suppression of initial and sustained application it develops unique exaltation, and not, like the access in jhāna, because of the removal of the Hindrances, and also not, like the First Jhāna, because of the manifestation of the factors. Thus this phrase shows the condition of tranquillity and unique exaltation. Moreover this Second Jhāna is without initial and sustained application, because they are suppressed, unlike the third and fourth Jhānas, and visual cognition, etc., which are without initial and sustained application, because they do not exist. Thus

---

[1] *Vibhaṅga* 258, l. 10. The abbreviated definition there is given in full, *ibid.* 217, and in this work is discussed on p. 157 *f.*

[2] *Loc. cit.*

[3] Supra, p. 225.

it also shows the effect, and not merely the fact of the non-existence of initial and sustained application. But the phrase 'without initial and sustained application' merely shows their non-existence. Therefore, having said the former phrase, we may also say this latter phrase.

'Born of concentration' means born of the concentration of the First Jhāna, or of the associated concentration. [171] Of the two, although the First Jhāna is also born of the associated concentration, yet only the Second Jhāna is worthy of being called concentration, from its freedom from the disturbing initial and sustained application, from being quite unshakable and from being well clarified. Therefore, to speak its praises, it is said to be born of concentration.

'Full of rapture-bliss'—this is as said above. 'Second' is by numerical sequence. The meaning also is that he enters into this Second Jhāna.

[In the list:—] 'At that time there is contact,' etc.—this being fivefold Jhāna, the words 'initial and sustained application' have been left out; so in the fivefold Path the words 'right intention' have been left out. By their influence the decision as to the classifiable and unclassifiable terms should be understood.

In the section of the Groups[1] also occur the threefold Jhāna and the fourfold Path. The rest is the same as in the first Jhānas.

End of the Second Jhāna.

CHAPTER III

THE THIRD JHĀNA

In the exposition of the Third Jhāna,[2] in the clause 'because of distaste for rapture,' the distaste is the revulsion from, or transcending of, the kind of rapture mentioned. The word 'and' between the two words, rapture and distaste, has

[1] Cf. above section, pp. 202-5.

[2] *Dhs.* § 163.

simply a conjunctive meaning. It combines the suppression of rapture with that of initial and sustained application.

When the work of suppression only is added, then the construction should be understood as 'because of distaste for rapture, nay more, because of its suppression.' And in this construction distaste has the meaning of 'revulsion from. Therefore the meaning should be taken as 'because of revulsion from, and suppression of, rapture.' But when the suppression of initial and sustained application is added, then the construction should be understood as 'because of distaste for rapture, nay more, because of the suppression of initial and sustained application.' And in this construction distaste has the meaning of 'transcending.' Therefore the meaning should be taken as 'because of the transcending of rapture and of the suppression of initial and sustained application.'

Although the initial and the sustained application has been suppressed even in the Second Jhāna, the suppression of both has been said to show the way to, and to extol the praises of, the Third Jhāna. For when 'because of the suppression of initial and sustained application' is said, is not the meaning plain that the suppression is the way to this Jhāna? And albeit they are not removed in the Third Ariyan Path, yet the five lower [172] Fetters beginning with the theory of individuality are said to be removed by way of extolling the Path, so that those striving for its attainment may put forth effort. Even although they have not been suppressed, their removal has been mentioned for purposes of commendation. Hence the meaning has been said to be 'from the transcending of rapture and from the suppression of initial and sustained application.'

In 'one lives indifferent,' 'indifferent' means he looks on disinterestedly; the meaning is: he looks evenly, not taking any side.[1] One who is possessed of the Third Jhāna is called indifferent from being endowed with that indifference, pure, abundant, and strong.

---

[1] *I.e.*, from any feeling of pleasure or pain.—*Pyī*.

Indifference is of ten kinds: (1) sixfold, (2) of the Divine States, (3) of the Factors of Wisdom, (4) of energy, (5) of complexes of activity, (6) of feeling, (7) of insight, (8) of equanimity, (9) of jhāna, and (10) of purity. (1) Of these, 'the bhikkhu who in this life is purged of the Intoxicants sees with the eye a visible object, and is neither joyful nor sad, but lives indifferent, mindful and comprehending.'[1] Thus the indifference which comes to such a saint, in such a way that he does not abandon the pure original state, when the six kinds of objects, whether desirable or undesirable, are presented at the six doors, is known as the sixfold indifference. (2) The indifference which takes up the neutral position regarding beings[2] thus: 'He continues to diffuse one quarter [of any region] with a mind accompanied by equanimity'[3] is known as that of the Divine States. (3) The indifference arising with the mode of neutrality among co-existent states thus: 'He develops indifference as a factor of wisdom and dependent on detachment'[4] is known as that of the Factors of Wisdom. (4) The indifference which arises thus in the text: 'The indifference which from time to time attends to the [so-called] "mark of indifference,"'[5] and is neither too intense nor too slack, is known as that of energy. (5) The indifference which is a state of equanimity derived from the estimate that the Hindrances, etc. [are to be put away], in such texts as 'How many kinds of equanimity arise by means of concentration, how many by means of insight? Eight arise by means of concentration; ten by means of insight'[6] is known as that of the complexes. (6) The indifference which

---

[1] *Aṅguttara* ii. 198.

[2] Viz., that they are 'owned by their kamma.'—*Pyī*. Cf. *Majjhima* iii. 203.

[3] *Dialogues* i. 318, etc.

[4] *Saṃyutta* iv. 367; v. 91.

[5] 'Neutral energy,' being free from contraction and expansion, is called indifference, and this, under the aspect of such neutrality, is called the 'mark of indifference,' because it is a condition of the production of similar energy.—*Ṭīkā*.

[6] *Pts*. i. 64. *I.e.*, by means of the eight worldly attainments (*samāpatti*) and by means of the ten composed of the Four Paths, Four Fruitions—the Void and the Signless.—*Ṭīkā*.

is neither painful nor pleasurable, as in 'When sensuous moral consciousness arises accompanied by indifference,'[1] is known as that of feeling. (7) The indifference which arises as equanimity in respect of [intellectual] investigation, thus: 'He puts aside the "is," the "has come to be," and acquires indifference,'[2] [173] is known as that of insight. (8) The indifference which balances co-existent states equally, and which comes among the 'Or whatever states,' beginning with will, is known as that of equanimity. (9) The indifference which comes as 'He lives indifferent,'[3] and which does not beget partisanship with the bliss, excellent though it may be, of the Third Jhāna, is known as that of jhāna. (10) The indifference which comes as 'indifference of the Fourth Jhāna in its utter purity of mindfulness,'[4] and which is purified of all opposing states, and has no business in their suppression, is known as that of purity.

Of these, the sixfold indifference and that of the Divine States, of the Factors of Wisdom, of equanimity, of jhāna, and of purity are one in sense, as being equanimity. But they are distinguished under six heads owing to the different states or conditions corresponding to the classification, though there is only one kind of being, just as in boys, lads, elders, generals, kings, etc. Therefore among them, where there is the sixfold indifference, there is nothing of the Factor of Wisdom, etc. And where there is the indifference which is a Factor of Wisdom there is no sixfold indifference, etc.

As these six are one in sense, so is the indifference of the (mental) complexes and of insight one in sense—namely, understanding, which is twofold in function. As a man, holding a stick cleft like a goat's hoof, searches for a snake, which has entered the house late in the day, and seeing it lying on the heap of husks, looks down, thinking, 'Is it a snake, or not?'

---

[1] *Dhs.* §§ 150, 156.

[2] As to the five aggregates. Not traced. He becomes indifferent on contemplating the three characteristics of the five aggregates, just as a man is no longer curious when he is satisfied that a snake is poisonous by seeing the three rings on the neck.—*Tīkā.*

[3] *Dhs.* § 163. [4] *Dhs.* § 163.

but on seeing the three rings on the neck is no more doubtful, but becomes indifferent as to search, so the aspirant, who has worked at insight, on seeing the three characteristic signs by means of insight, becomes indifferent as to search for the impermanence, etc., of the complexes. This is the indifference of insight.

As when the man firmly catches hold of the snake by his goat's-hoof-cleft stick and, seeking to release it, thinking, 'How shall I free it, so that I may not hurt it and I myself be not bitten?' becomes indifferent as to catching it, so from looking upon the three existences as though on fire, as a result of his seeing the three characteristic signs, a man becomes indifferent as to seizing the complexes. This is the indifference of the complexes. Thus when the indifference of insight is accomplished that of the complexes is also accomplished. In this way the twofold function of neutrality consists in searching and seizing. [174] But the indifference of energy and that of feeling are different from each other and from the others.

Thus, of the ten kinds, it is the indifference of jhāna that is here intended. It has the characteristic of middleness, the function of not enjoying (even the excellent bliss of the Third Jhāna), the manifestation of absence of activity, the proximate cause of distaste for rapture.

Here one might object: 'Is not this jhāna-indifference the same in sense as that equanimity-indifference, which is obtainable in the First and Second Jhānas? If so, then, in those two Jhānas also, it should be said that "he abides indifferent." Why has this not been said?'

Because there is no distinct function. Indeed, the function of equanimity is not distinct in the First and Second Jhānas, because it is overwhelmed by initial application, etc. But in the Third Jhāna, because it is not overwhelmed by initial and sustained application and rapture, it has lifted up its head, so to speak, and has a positive distinct function. Here ends the full explanation of the sentence 'He abides indifferent.'

Now as to 'mindful and comprehending,' we think or

remember and are 'mindful.' We know fully and are 'comprehending.' Thus the mindfulness and the comprehension are stated in connexion with the person.

Of these, mindfulness has the characteristic of remembering, the function of opposition to forgetfulness, the manifestation of watchfulness; comprehension has the characteristic of opposition to delusion, the function of overcoming doubt, or of bringing a work to completion, and the manifestation of examination. Although this phrase is obtainable in the preceding Jhānas—indeed, to one of forgetful memory and without comprehension there does not arise even the access stage of jhāna, much less ecstasy—yet from their grossness the process of consciousness is easy, like the movement of a man on the earth, and in them the function of being mindful and comprehending is not revealed. But from the putting away of the gross factor and the fineness of this Third Jhāna, it is desirable that the process of consciousness be maintained by the function of being mindful and comprehending like the movement of a man on the edges of razors. Hence it has been mentioned here only.

Is there anything more to say ? As the suckling calf, being removed from the cow and left unguarded, again approaches the cow, so the blissful ease of the Third Jhāna, being removed from rapture, if unguarded by mindfulness and comprehension, would again approach rapture and be associated with it. Indeed, beings long for happiness; and the blissful ease of the Third Jhāna is exceedingly sweet, than which there is no greater bliss. But owing to the power of mindfulness and comprehension, there is no longing present for this bliss, and this condition does not change. It is to show this distinctive meaning that the phrase has here been said.

Now in the clause 'he experiences blissful ease by the mental factors,' [175] although to one endowed with the Third Jhāna there is no thought of such experience, yet he may experience that bliss which is associated with his mental factors, or, though he has emerged from jhāna, he may still experience that bodily bliss, because his material body has been suffused by the exceedingly refined mind-born matter produced by that associated bliss. Hence the phrase has been said to show this meaning.

Now in the clause 'of which the Ariyans declare: he, indifferent and mindful, abides in blissful ease,' the meaning is that by reason of, on account of, the Third Jhāna the Ariyans, that is, the Buddhas, etc., declare, point out, designate, establish, reveal, disclose, explain, set forth, praise a person who has mastered that jhāna.

And how? [By saying:] 'he indifferent and mindful abides in blissful ease,' and having entered into the Third Jhāna he so abides—thus should the sequence in the meaning be understood. But why do they praise him so? Because he is worthy of praise. To expand: Because he is indifferent even in the Third Jhāna which has reached the perfection of bliss of exceeding sweetness, because he is not dragged along by the contagion of the bliss of it, and is mindful with an established mindfulness, so that rapture may not arise, and because he experiences by his mental factors that bliss which is not corrupt and which gives delight to, and is followed by, the Ariyans, therefore is he worthy of praise. Him praiseworthy the Ariyans praise, setting forth his merits as the condition of their praise: 'Indifferent and mindful he abides in blissful ease.'

'Third' is by numerical sequence; this is the Third Jhāna he enters into.

In 'at that time there is contact,' etc., in the fivefold Jhāna the word 'rapture' is wanting, and by its influence the decision of the terms, both classifiable and unclassifiable, should be understood.

In the section also of the Groups mention of the twofold Jhāna is made. The rest is the same as in the Second Jhāna.

End of the Third Jhāna.

CHAPTER IV

THE FOURTH JHĀNA

In the exposition of the Fourth Jhāna, the clause 'from the putting away of pleasure and from the putting away of pain'[1] means the putting away of pleasure and pain in the mental factors.

'Previous' means that the putting away of pleasure and pain took place before, and not at the moment of the Fourth Jhāna.

The clause 'from the passing away of joy and grief,' namely, of mental pleasure and mental pain, has been said [176] because of the previous passing away, the putting away of these two. When are they put away? At the 'access'-moments[2] of the four Jhānas. For joy is put away at the access-moment of the Fourth Jhāna; pain, grief and pleasure are put away [respectively] at the access-moments of the First, Second and Third Jhānas. Thus, although they have not been stated according to the sequence of their removal, yet their removal should be understood even by the sequence of the summary of controlling faculties both in the *Indriya-Vibhaṅga*[3] and here.

But if they are put away at the access-moments preceding this or that Jhāna, then why is it said [that their cessation is *in* the Jhānas themselves] thus: 'Where does the uprisen controlling faculty of pain cease completely? Bhikkhus, in this case the bhikkhu, aloof indeed from sense-desires . . . enters into and abides in the First Jhāna. Here the controlling faculty of pain which has arisen ceases completely. . . . Where do the controlling faculties of grief, . . . of pleasure, . . . and of joy which have arisen cease completely? Bhikkhus, in this case the bhikkhu from the putting away of joy . . . enters into and abides in the Fourth Jhāna. Here the controlling faculty of joy which has arisen ceases completely.'[4]

---

[1] *Dhs.* § 165.

[2] On this term see *Comp. of Phil.* 55.

[3] *Vibhanga* 122.

[4] *Saṃy.* v. 213 *f.*

This is said because of their complete cessation. For in the Jhānas their cessation is completed, not merely begun; at the access-moments their cessation is not completed. True, though there is cessation in the access to the First Jhāna, with a different adverting of the mind, yet there the controlling faculty of pain may be produced through contact with gad-flies, mosquitoes, etc., or by falling on to an uneven seat; but there is no such production within the ecstasy; or this controlling faculty of pain which ceases at the access does not thoroughly cease, because it is not killed by its opposite (faculty). But within the ecstasy, owing to the diffusion of rapture, the whole body is surcharged with pleasure. And the controlling faculty of pain of the pleasure-suffused body has thoroughly ceased, being killed by its opposite. Moreover, although it has been put away, the controlling faculty of grief may arise at the access to the Second Jhāna with a different adverting of the mind. Why does this arise when there is bodily suffering and mental distress, with initial and sustained application of mind as its cause, and does not arise in the absence of initial and sustained application? Where it arises, it does so when there is initial and sustained application; and at the access to the Second Jhāna initial and sustained applications have not been put away; hence the possibility of its arising. But there is no such possibility owing to the removal of the cause in the Second Jhāna. Similarly, although it has been put away, the controlling faculty of pleasure may arise at the access to the Third Jhāna in one whose body has been suffused by refined matter produced by rapture; but it may not arise in the Third Jhāna itself, because rapture, the cause of pleasure, has completely ceased therein.

[177] Similarly, although it has been put away, the controlling faculty of joy may arise at the access to the Fourth Jhāna because it is near and has not been well transcended, owing to the non-existence of indifference which has attained to ecstasy; but it may not arise in the Fourth Jhāna itself. Hence in various places the word 'complete' has been taken as 'Here the uprisen controlling faculty of pain ceases *completely*.'

Why [it may be objected] are these feelings, which have thus been put away at the access to the various Jhānas, gathered together in the Fourth Jhāna ?

For the purpose of apprehending them easily. In other words:—in 'neither painful nor pleasurable' this neutral feeling is [revealed as] subtle and hard to understand. It is not possible to apprehend it easily. Therefore, as, in order to catch a vicious bull that may not be caught by approaching it anyhow, the cowherd brings together all the cows in a pen, lets them out one by one, and, when the bull comes out in its turn, orders its capture: 'catch it!' so the Blessed One, to make easy the comprehending of the neutral feeling, has brought forth all the feelings. By showing all the feelings it is possible to comprehend neutral feeling as that which is neither pleasure nor pain, neither joy nor grief.

Further, these feelings should be understood to have been stated to show the cause of the mental emancipation of the Fourth Jhāna, which is neutral feeling. The preceding Jhānas which have put away pleasure and pain are indeed the causes of this mental emancipation. As has been said: 'Four, Sir, are the causes of the attainment of mental emancipation which is neutral feeling. In this case, Sir, a bhikkhu from the putting away of pleasure . . . enters into and abides in the Fourth Jhāna. These, Sir, are the four causes of the attainment of mental emancipation, which is neutral feeling.'[1]

As, although they are put away elsewhere, the errors of individuality, etc., are said to be put away in the Third Path with a view to extol its praises, so, in order to praise the Fourth Jhāna, these feelings should be understood to be mentioned in connection with it. Or they should be understood to be mentioned to show the great remoteness of lust and hate here, owing to the destruction of their causes. For as to these pleasure is the cause of joy, joy of lust, pain of grief, grief of hate. And by the destruction of pleasure, etc., lust and hate are destroyed with their causes. Thus they are very distant.[2]

---

[1] *Majjhima* i. 296.

[2] From the Fourth Jhāna.—*Ṭīkā*.

The clause 'neither pain nor pleasure' means not pain by the absence of pain; not pleasure by the absence of pleasure. By this the Buddha shows the third [kind of] feeling as opposed to pain and pleasure, and not merely the absence of pain and pleasure. The third feeling is neither pain nor pleasure, and is also called hedonic indifference. [178] It has the characteristic of enjoying an object midway between the desirable and the undesirable, the function of middleness, the manifestation of not being apparent, the proximate cause of the cessation of pleasure.

Then as to the clause:—'Purity of mindfulness born of indifference,' in this Jhāna, because of the purity of the mindfulness which has been produced, mindfulness is pure. Such purity is made by indifference, not by any other; hence this Jhāna is called 'purity of mindfulness, born of indifference.'

In the *Vibhaṅga* it has been said that mindfulness is cleansed,[1] purified and burnished by indifference; hence 'purity of mindfulness born of indifference.' That indifference by which there is here purity of mindfulness should be understood as equanimity. And not merely mindfulness has been purified by indifference, but also the associated states have been purified. The teaching, however, has put mindfulness at the head.

Although this indifference exists also in the first three Jhānas, yet as the crescent moon, being overpowered by the sun by day, and not getting the favourable night which makes it cool and renders service to it, is not clear, not radiant, though it exists by day, so the crescent moon of equanimity, being overpowered by the night of opposing states, such as initial application of mind, and not getting the favourable night of indifferent feeling, is not clear in the first three Jhānas, even though in them it is present. And when indifference is not clear, the co-existent states, such as mindfulness, like the light of the indistinct crescent moon by day, are not clear. Therefore in the three Jhānas not one is said to be 'purity of mindfulness born of indifference.' But in the Fourth Jhāna the crescent moon of equanimity, not being overpowered by the might

---

[1] Or 'diffused,' reading *visadā* for *vivaṭā*.—*Tr.*

of opposing states, such as initial application of mind, and getting the favourable night of indifferent feeling, is exceedingly clear. Owing to its clearness the co-existent states, such as mindfulness, like the light of the clear crescent moon, become clear, radiant. Hence the Fourth Jhāna is said to be 'purity of mindfulness born of indifference.'

'Fourth' is by numerical sequence; he enters into this Jhāna as fourth.

In 'there is contact,' etc., in the fivefold contact, indifferent feeling should be understood as the only 'feeling.'

Moreover, in the fivefold Jhāna, in the eight controlling faculties [179], this has been said: 'There is indifference; there is the controlling faculty of indifference.' The remaining words, wanting in the Third, are also wanting in the Fourth Jhāna.

In the section of the Groups also, the Jhāna should be understood to be twofold by virtue of indifference and one-pointedness of mind. All the remaining words are the same as in the Third Jhāna.

End of the Fourfold system.

CHAPTER V

THE FIVEFOLD SYSTEM

Now with the words:—'which are the states that are moral,'[1] the fivefold system begins.

Why [is there a fivefold system]? There are two reasons:— [to satisfy some] persons' inclinations, and to adorn the teaching. To expand:—In the assembled gathering of the spirits, to some spirits only initial application of mind appeared gross, and sustained application of mind, rapture, pleasure, one-pointedness of mind appeared good. To them in a fitting manner the Teacher divided the fourfold Second Jhāna as without initial, and with only sustained, application. To some spirits sustained application appeared gross, and rapture, pleasure and one-pointedness of mind appeared good. To

[1] *Dhs.* § 167.

them in a fitting manner he classified the threefold Third Jhāna. To some spirits rapture appeared gross and pleasure and one-pointedness of mind appeared good. To them in a fitting manner he classified the twofold Fourth Jhāna. To some spirits pleasure appeared gross and indifference and one-pointedness of mind appeared good. To them in a fitting manner he classified the twofold Fifth Jhāna. Thus far for [the appeal to different] personal inclinations. Again, those conditions of the Law by which, because they have been thoroughly penetrated, the teaching is adorned—those conditions were thoroughly penetrated by the Tathāgata. Hence, because of the vastness of his knowledge, the Teacher, who is skilful in arranging his teaching, and who has attained the [art of] embellishing it, fixes that teaching by whatever factor that has come to hand, and in any way he chooses. Thus here he has classified a First Jhāna of five factors, a fourfold Second Jhāna 'without initial and with only sustained application of mind,' a threefold Third Jhāna, a twofold Fourth Jhāna and a twofold Fifth Jhāna. This we have called embellishing the teaching.

Further, the Blessed One taught three kinds of concentration in the Suttanta passage: 'Bhikkhus, the three kinds of concentration are: with initial and sustained application of mind, without initial and with only sustained application, without initial and without sustained application.'[1] Of these, that with initial and sustained application, and that without initial and sustained application have been classified and shown above; [180] but not that concentration without initial and with only sustained application. And it should be understood that the Fivefold System has been begun to show that concentration.

In the list:—'contact,' and so on, belonging to the exposition of the second Jhāna of the Fivefold System,[2] only 'initial application of mind' is wanting. And in the section of the Groups this also is special: 'There is the fourfold Jhāna, there is the fourfold Path.' All the rest are the same as in

---

[1] *Aṅguttara* iv 310 *f*. Cf. *Saṃyutta* iv. 360, 362; *Questions of Milinda* ii. 222.

[2] *Dhs.* § 161.

the First Jhāna. And the Second, Third and Fourth Jhānas in the Fourfold System are the Third, Fourth and Fifth Jhānas here. It is to show the order of their attainment that this system should be understood.

It is said that a minister's son came to town from the district to attend on the king. He saw the king for one day only, then wasted all his wealth by the vice of drink. One day, when he was drunk, they stripped off his clothes, covered him with worn-out mats and hauled him out of the liquor-shop. A certain man who could read the signs on a man's limbs saw him asleep on a rubbish heap and came to this conclusion: 'This man will be a protection to the people; he ought to be looked after.' So he had him bathed with powdered earth, had him clothed in a pair of thick robes, had him again bathed in scented water, had him dressed in a suit of fine clothes, made him ascend his palace, fed him with delicious food, gave him to the care of his servants, saying: 'Tend him,' and went away. Then they brought him to bed, and, in order to prevent his going to the liquor-shop, four strong men stood pressing his hands and feet: one of the servants shampooed his feet, a second took a fan and fanned him, a third sat playing the lute and singing. By getting to bed fatigue left him and he slept awhile. On waking he was unable to bear the pressure on his hands and feet, and threatened them, saying, 'Who presses my hands and feet? Go away!' They went away at the first word. Then again he slept awhile, and on waking, being unable to bear the shampooing of his feet, said: 'Who shampoos my feet? Go away!' The man went away at the first word. Then again he slept awhile, and on waking, being unable to bear the wind of the fan, he said: 'Who is this? Go away!' The man went away at the first word. Again he slept awhile, and on waking, being as unable to bear the sound of music as if it were a dart in his ear, threatened the musician, who also went away at the first word. [181] Then in due course the nuisance of fatigue, pressing, shampooing, fanning, and music being removed, he slept soundly, rose and went into the presence of the king. And the king gave him high authority. He became a helper of the people.

In this simile, the minister's son who comes to ruin by drink represents a householder of the clansmen who has in many ways come to loss and ruin. The reader of signs on the limbs represents the Tathāgata. The conclusion that this man will be a helper of the people, and that he is worthy of attendance, represents the resolution of the Tathāgata that such and such an one will be a helper of the people, and that he is worthy of ordination. The cleansing of the minister's son by powdered earth is the clansman's attainment of ordination. The former's being wrapped in thick robes is the latter's putting on the dress of the ten moral precepts; again, as the bath of the former in perfumed water, so is the latter's bath in the perfumed water of the Pātimokkha self-restraint, etc.; as the former's dressing in a suit of fine clothes is the latter's dressing in the fine clothes of the fulfilment of the purity of the said precepts. Again, as the ascending into the palace by the former dressed in fine clothes, so is the ascending into the palace of concentration and culture by the latter dressed in the fine cloth of the purity of virtue. Then the partaking of delicious food by the one is as the partaking of the deathlessness of such states as mindfulness and comprehension, which renders service to concentration. Again, as the putting to bed of the one by the attendants after his meal, so is the putting of the other to the 'access'-Jhāna by initial application of mind, etc. Again, as the group of four men who pressed the hands and feet of the minister's son in order to prevent his going to the liquor-shop, so is the emancipated initial application of mind which presses the mind on the object to prevent its going in the direction of sensuous perceptions. The shampooer of the one represents the sustained application of the other, causing the repeated contemplation of the object by the mind. As he who produces a breeze by fanning, so is rapture bringing coolness to the mind. As the musician gratifying the ear, so is joy gratifying the mind. As the former's going off to sleep in bed for awhile getting rid of fatigue, so is the latter's approach to the First Jhāna getting rid of the fatigue of the hindrances through dependence upon 'access'-jhāna. Then, as to the former's inability to bear the pressure on his hands and feet on his waking from sleep, his threatening the men, and his subsequent sleep awhile after their departure, [182] so is the seeing defect in initial application of mind through inability to bear its pressing on the mind, when he rises from the First Jhāna, and his subsequent approach to the Second Jhāna, initial application being removed, and with only sustained application. The threatening the shampooers of feet, etc., one by one, through inability to bear the shampooing, as said in due course above at his waking from repeated sleep, and his going off to sleep awhile at their departure should be regarded as the other's seeing defect in sustained application of mind, etc., one by one, through inability to bear them with their defects already mentioned on his rising repeatedly from the Second Jhāna, etc., and his repeated approach, these faults being removed to the Third Jhāna without initial and sustained application, the Fourth Jhāna free from rapture and the Fifth Jhāna where joy has been put away. As the rising from sleep, going to the king's presence and attaining to authority should be understood the attainment of Arahantship by the clansman who has risen from the Fifth Jhāna and followed the Path of Insight. And as the attaining to power by the minister's son and his being a helper to many a man should be understood the attaining to Arahantship by the clansman, and his being a helper to many. For all this it is that he is called the incomparable field of merit.[1]

End of the Fivefold System.

CHAPTER VI

THE FOURFOLD PROGRESS

By so much has the double classification, called the Ninefold Scheme, comprising the fourfold and fivefold systems, been set forth. But in its contents this classification should be

[1] *Saṃyutta* i. 220, etc. (*Kindred Sayings* 282).

known as the Fivefold Jhāna, the fourfold system being included in the fivefold system.

Now because this jhāna is accomplished also with a certain rate of progress, therefore, in order to show the classification of progress, the text again begins with 'which are the states that are moral ?'[1]

Herein, when this jhāna has a painful progress, we get the clause 'progress being painful'; when there is sluggish intuition, we get 'intuition being sluggish.' Thus there are three names to this jhāna, to wit: 'painful progress,' 'sluggish intuition,' and 'earth-device.' And the same method is observed in 'painful progress, quick intuition.'[2]

Herein, from the first resolve till the access of the particular jhāna arises, the jhāna-development which occurs is called progress. And the insight which occurs from the access till the ecstasy is called intuition.[3] And this progress is painful to some. The meaning is that, [183] from the abundant production of such opposing states as the Hindrances, it is difficult, not pleasant to carry on. To some, from there being no such opposition, it is easy.

To some, again, intuition is sluggish, weak and of slow occurrence; to others it is quick, strong and of swift occurrence. Hence he who from the beginning, in discarding his lower nature, does so with fatigue, painfully, by means of external aid, of instigation, to him progress is painful. And he who, having discarded the lower nature, abiding round about the ecstasy, takes long to attain to the manifestation of the jhāna-factors, is of sluggish intuition. He who quickly attains to the manifestation of the jhāna-factor is of quick intuition. He who in discarding the lower nature does so with ease, without fatigue, is one to whom progress is easy.

Details concerning what is fitting and is not fitting, preliminary works such as cutting off the impediments, skilfulness in ecstasy, etc., have been explained[4] in the exposition of mental

---

[1] *Dhs.* § 176.
[2] *Ib.* § 177.
[3] *Abhiññā*, more lit. superknowledge.—*Ed.*
[4] Vis. Mag. p. 90 *f.*

culture in the *Visuddhi Magga*. Of them, he who pursues what is not fitting is of painful progress and sluggish intuition. He who pursues what is fitting is of easy progress and quick intuition. And he who in the preliminary stage to access pursues what is not fitting, and in the subsequent stage to access pursues what is fitting, or who in the preliminary stage pursues what is fitting, and in the subsequent stage pursues what is not fitting, is of mixed progress and intuition. Further, the progress of one who, without accomplishing the preliminary work of cutting off the impediments, applies himself to culture is painful. The reverse is easy progress. Again, the intuition of one who does not perfect skilfulness in ecstasy is sluggish; and it is quick in one who perfects skilfulness in ecstasy.

Moreover, the classification according to craving and ignorance, and the chief reason of calm and insight should be understood. To expand: To one overcome by craving the progress is painful; to one not overcome by craving it is easy. And to one overcome by ignorance the intuition is sluggish; to one not so overcome it is quick. And he who has no past conditions for calm makes painful progress; one who has such makes easy progress. And one who has no past conditions for insight is of sluggish intuition; one who has such is of quick intuition.

Classification by virtue of our lower nature and controlling faculties should also be understood. To expand: To one whose nature is acutely corrupt and whose controlling faculty is soft, progress is painful and intuition sluggish. But to one of keen controlling faculty, intuition is quick. To one with a mild lower nature and soft controlling faculty, progress is easy and intuition sluggish. But to one of keen controlling faculty intuition is quick. Thus in progress and intuition the person who attains to jhāna [184] by means of painful progress and sluggish intuition, that jhāna is said to be of painful progress and sluggish intuition. In the remaining Jhānas also the same method is to be understood. In these progress should be understood as [lying] in the arrest either of that mindfulness of which it is said thus: 'The mindfulness corresponding to that [of the first Jhānas][1] is firmly established, understanding partakes of firmness'; or of the desire for the various Jhānas. The intuition in abiding round about the ecstasy of one who has attained to the access of these Jhānas is also to be understood [as here involved].

And the progress and the intuition are just according to how they come.[2] In other words, the Second Jhāna which arises following the attainment of a First Jhāna, where progress is painful and intuition sluggish, is even like the First Jhāna (its condition). And the same with the Third and Fourth Jhānas.

As in the fourfold method, so in the fivefold method the progress should be understood as of four kinds. Thus we get in all nine groups of four combinations with respect to progress. In these, according to the text, there are thirty-six classes of consciousness. Actually, however, from the inclusion of the fourfold method in the fivefold method, there are only twenty classes of consciousness.

End of the fourfold Progress.

CHAPTER VII

THE FOUR OBJECTS OF THOUGHT

Now because this Jhāna is fourfold by object-classification, as well as by progress-classification, therefore, to show the former classification, we have again the beginning: 'which are the states that are moral?'[3]

In this clause:—'limited and with a limited object of

---

[1] Tadanudhammatā=false mindfulness as an aggregate (khandha) associated with craving which lusts after the various Jhānas. *Or* that mindfulness which bears the various Jhānas and which is not free from lusting after them.—*Ṭīkā*.

[2] *I.e.*, the progress of the Second and other Jhānas depends sometimes, but not always, on the attainment of the First Jhāna.—*Ṭīkā*.

[3] *Dhs.* § 181.

thought'—'limited' refers to that Jhāna which has not been practised and is not able to become a cause of the next higher Jhāna. Again, that Jhāna which arises in respect of an object of the size of a small sieve, or the cover of a cooking-pot, and which has a small object, is said to be 'with a limited object of thought.'

That Jhāna [on the other hand] which has been practised and well developed, and is able to become the cause of the next higher Jhāna, is called 'immeasurable.'[1] That Jhāna which arises in respect of an extensive object and which has an immeasurable object due to its growth in size is said to be 'with an immeasurable object of thought.' And from the combination of the characteristics already mentioned the combined method should be understood. Thus in respect of objects also the four ninefold methods have been discussed. And the classes of consciousness here are the same in number as in the preceding fourfold progress.

End of the fourfold Object of Thought.

CHAPTER VIII

THE SIXTEENFOLD COMBINATION

Now in order to show the sixteenfold method of combined object and progress [185] we have again in the beginning:—'which are the states that are moral?'[2] Therein the jhāna spoken of in the first system is low for four reasons: painfulness of progress, sluggishness of intuition, limitedness, limitedness of object. The jhāna spoken of in the sixteenth method is exalted for four reasons: ease of progress, quickness of intuition, immeasurableness, immeasurableness of object. In the remaining fourteen methods the lowness and exaltedness should be known for one, two and three reasons.

---

[1] *Dhs.* § 182.

[2] *Ib.* § 186

CHAPTER IX

DISCOURSE ON THE DEVICES (OR ARTIFICES, *KASIṆA*)

BUT why was this method taught? Because it led to the production of jhāna. To expand: the supreme Buddha, in connection with the 'earth-device,' taught schematized[1] jhāna by the fourfold and the fivefold methods; likewise schematized progress and object. Of the two jhāna-series also, to those spirits who were able to understand schematized jhāna by the earth-device as it is taught by the fourfold method, this fourfold method was taught in a fitting manner. To those spirits who were able to understand it as it was taught by the fivefold method, the fivefold method was taught in a fitting manner. To those spirits who were able to understand it as it is taught by the fourfold method, with schematized progress and object, the fourfold method in bare progress and bare object was taught in a fitting manner. To those spirits who were able to understand it as it was taught by the fivefold method, the fivefold method was taught in a fitting manner. Thus the teaching has been taught above with reference to people's [various] inclinations.

And the Supreme Buddha, who was capable of adorning the teaching, had divided the four branches of analytical knowledge, and had a clear knowledge of the ten 'strengths,' the four grounds of confidence, etc., was able, owing to his having well penetrated the irreversible functions and characteristics[2] of states, and his skill in concepts of things, to fix the teaching by any method whatever. Therefore, by means of his proficiency in elaborating the teaching, he made a discourse on the bare fourfold method in connection with the 'earth-artifice.' And because those persons who bring up jhāna cannot do so without object and progress, therefore, because it is certain to produce jhāna, this sixteenfold method was set forth.

---

[1] Suddhika-, lit. pur-ish. Cf. *Points of Controversy*, 14, *n*. 2.

[2] Or, the characteristics known in their own irreversible nature.—*Yojanā*.

So far the bare set of nine, the four progress sets of nine, the four object-sets of nine, these sixteen sets of nine, in all, twenty-five sets of nine, have been set forth. In each set of nine are two methods, namely, the fourfold and the fivefold methods. Thus there are fifty methods. In the text are two hundred and twenty-five kinds of jhāna-consciousness: one hundred in the twenty-five fourfold methods, [186] one hundred and twenty-five in the fivefold methods. But from the fourfold method being included in the fivefold method, there are only one hundred and twenty-five modes of consciousness. And of these two hundred and twenty-five modes of consciousness which are in the text, in the exposition of each are three main sections beginning with the determination of states. But they have been abridged after the schematized method in each exposition had been shown.

End of the Earth-device.

CHAPTER X

THE OTHER DEVICES[1]

Now inasmuch as these Jhānas arise also through the water-device, etc., in order to show these devices we have again as opening question, 'Which are the states that are moral?'[2] In them the textual method, elucidation of meaning, classes of consciousness and abridgment of sections are all to be understood as given under the earth-device. But the whole of this method of culture, beginning with the preamble of the device, has been set forth in the *Visuddhi Magga*.[3]

In the *Mahāsakuludāyi-Sutta*[4] ten devices are mentioned. Of them, the 'consciousness'-device is the same as the sublime consciousness produced with respect to space, and as the attainment of the sphere of infinite consciousness produced after the preamble of the sublime consciousness. Thus it follows the

---

[1] Or artifices (*kasiṇa*)—namely, for inducing jhāna.

[2] *Dhs.* § 203. [3] Chs. iv., v. [4] *M.* ii. 14.

teaching on the immaterial in all its aspects. Hence it is not mentioned in this place. And the 'space'-device is the same as the space obtained by separating the device, as the aggregate produced by making that space the object, as that separated space which ought to be taken as the mark in any hole in a wall, etc., and as the Fourth and Fifth Jhānas produced by making that separated space the object.

Of these two, the first method (of space separated from the device and the aggregate) follows the teaching on the immaterial; the last method (including the remainder) follows the teaching on the Rūpa realm. Thus, owing to its mixed nature, it has not been mentioned in the teaching on the material realm. The jhāna produced in the separated space, however, is the path to the attainment of the Rūpa planes. Hence it should be taken into account. But in it only the Fourth and Fifth Jhānas arise, but not the Immaterial Jhāna. Why? Because the separation of the device is not obtained. For though it is repeatedly separated, it remains just space, and thus in it the separation of the device is not obtained.[1] Therefore the jhāna which arises from it is conducive to a happy abode under present conditions; is a basis of super-knowledge, of insight, but not of cessation. But here graduated cessation is not obtained as far as the Fifth Jhāna; [187] on the contrary, it is a basis of the round of births. And as this Jhāna (of separated space) is the basis of super-knowledge, so also are the Jhānas arising in the previous device. But in these Jhānas their distinction lies in their being bases of cessation. All that remains to be said on the space-device has been said in the *Visuddhi Magga*.[2]

By the aspirant who wishes for the potency of transformation, such as 'being one yet many,'[3] and producing the eight attainments in the previous eight devices, the mind should be tamed in these fourteen ways: (1) in the way of right succession of the devices; (2) in the reverse order of the devices; (3) in the way of right succession and the reverse order of the devices; (4) in the way of right succession of the Jhānas;

---

[1] Reading *na labbhati*. [2] Ch. v. [3] *Dialogues* i. 88.

(5) in the reverse order of the Jhānas; (6) in the way of right succession and the reverse order of the Jhānas; (7) by passing over Jhānas; (8) by passing over devices; (9) by passing over Jhānas and devices; (10) by change of factors; (11) change of objects; (12) change of factors and objects; (13) specification of factors; (14) specification of objects. The detailed discourse is given in the *Visuddhi Magga*.[1]

It is impossible that the aspirant as a beginner, without such a previously developed culture, taming his mind in the fourteen ways, should fulfil by any means the potency of transformation. For the preamble of the device is burdensome to the beginner; one in a hundred, a thousand, might be able to perform it. To him who has performed the preamble of the device the production of the mark is burdensome; one in a hundred, a thousand, might be able to produce it. When the mark has been produced, the attainment of ecstasy after increasing the mark is burdensome; one in a hundred, a thousand, might be able to attain it. To one who has attained ecstasy the taming of the mind in the fourteen ways is burdensome; one in a hundred, a thousand, might be able to tame it. To one who has tamed the mind in the fourteen ways, the potency of transformation is burdensome; one in a hundred, a thousand, might be able to acquire it. To one who has attained the potency of transformation, quickness of intuition* is burdensome; one in a hundred, a thousand, might be able to get it, like the Elder Rakkhita of eight years' full ordination among the thirty thousand elders of supernormal potency, who had come to minister to the sick Elder Mahārohanagutta at the Therambatthala.[2] The story has been told in the *Visuddhi Magga*.

End of the Discourse on the Devices.

---

[1] Ch. xii: 'Iddhividhā-niddeso.' * *Khippanisanti.*

[2] *I.e.*, the mango tree where Mahinda first alighted in Ceylon.—*Yojanā*. See *Mahāvaṃsa*, xxxvi. 106. Name of one of the peaks of the Missaka mountain in Ceylon *Sāmantapāsādikā*. *J.P.T.S.*, 1888, 7.

CHAPTER XI

DISCOURSE ON THE POSITIONS OF MASTERY

HAVING shown thus the moral consciousness of the realm of attenuated matter in the eight devices, because there occurs more of the same among those eight devices which are called the Position of Mastery,[1] [188] a system which is dissimilar in culture, though similar in object, it is here set forth once more with the beginning, 'Which are the states that are moral?'[2]

Therein 'not perceiving material quality in himself' means devoid of the perception of the preamble in his own bodily frame, either from not getting it, or from not wishing it.

'Sees material qualities external to himself' means, from having performed the preamble externally in the eight devices, he sees with jhāna-eyes the external objects of these eight devices by virtue of the preamble and the ecstasy.

'Limited' means not growing.

In 'having mastered them': just as a man of vigorous digestion getting a spoonful of food makes a lump of it and swallows it, saying, 'Call that eating anything?' so a person of transcendent and clear knowledge masters the device-objects and attains jhāna, saying, 'What is there to attain in this limited object? This is not burdensome to me.' The meaning is that he produces ecstasy together with the production of the image of the mark in this limited object.

And by 'I know, I see,' his former correct ideas are stated. But in the Four Nikāya Commentaries[3] it is said that by this sentence his correct ideas are meant, and that they are indeed the correct ideas of him who has arisen from, and is not still within, the attainment.

'Immeasurable'[4] means growing in size. In 'having mastered,' just as a great eater getting a plate of food will

---

1 Abhibhāyatana is jhāna with an overpowering (abhibhū) preamble, or knowledge as cause (āyatana), or jhāna with an abode or locus (āyatana) called the object to be overpowered (abhibhavitabbaṃ Abhibhāyatana).—*Tīkā*.

2 *Dhs.* § 204.

3 *Āgam'aṭṭhakathesu.*

4 *Dhs.* § 212.

not look at it because of his large appetite, saying, 'Let another come! let another come! what will this one plate do for me?' so a person of transcending and clear knowledge masters those immeasurable objects and attains jhāna, saying, 'What is there to attain in this immeasurable object? This is not burdensome to me in making one-pointedness of mind.' The meaning is that he produces ecstasy together with the production of the image of the mark in the immeasurable object.

'Limited, limited object; immeasurable, limited object': here in this object-couplet of the first and second positions of mastery,[1] because the word 'limited' is mentioned, the immeasurableness of object has not been included. In the second method of the following third and fourth positions of mastery,[2] because the word 'immeasurable' is mentioned, the limitedness of object has not been included. But in the Great Commentary it is said that, in this place, the objects have been taken by twos, not by fours. [189] And why? Because if the four objects were taken, the teaching would be sixteenfold. And the sixteenfold teaching has already been uttered at length by the Teacher, as though he was scattering sesamum seeds on a mat. It is his wish to make an eightfold discourse in this place. Hence the objects have been taken by twos.

'Beautiful or ugly'[3] means pure or impure colours. Pure objects of blue-green, etc., indeed, are called beautiful, and impure objects of blue-green, etc., are called ugly. Thus it is here intended. But it is said in the Nikāya Commentaries that these positions of mastery have been shown as beautiful or ugly by way of limited and immeasurable. But in these four devices the limited comes by virtue of the frequency of initial application of mind, the immeasurable by virtue of the frequency of delusion, the beautiful by virtue of the frequency of hate, the ugly by virtue of the frequency of lust. For to these persons walking in initial application,[4] etc., these devices, limited, etc., are suitable. And this suita-

---

[1] *Dhs.* §§ 204-224. [2] *Ib.* §§ 225-245. [3] *Ib.* § 244.

[4] P.T.S. ed. omits part of this sentence.—*Tr.*

bility has been declared at length in the exposition of conduct in the *Visuddhi Magga.*[1]

But why, without saying 'a man perceiving material quality in himself sees external forms limited,' etc., is it said here in the four positions of mastery, 'without perceiving material quality in himself'? Because his own body is not to be mastered. For there, as well as here, it is only external objects that are to be mastered; hence they should always be mentioned. Thus in both places they have been declared. And the expression: 'without perceiving material quality in himself,' is merely an embellishment of the discourse by the Teacher. This, so far, is an exposition of the new terms in the four positions of mastery.

Moreover, schematized method and classification by progress are to be understood in each position of mastery in the same way as was said in connection with the earth-device, except that here the fourfold object is the object-couplet; and the sixteenfold method is the eightfold. The rest is the same. Thus here in each position of mastery are fifteen sets of nine: one scheme of nine, four progress-sets of nine, two object-sets of nine, eight sets of nine in the combination of object and progress. Thus in the four positions of mastery the (15 × 4) full sixty sets of nine should be understood.

[190] In the fifth and other positions of mastery the term 'blue-green'[2] has been used as summarizing all such devices. The term 'indigo colours' is said in speaking of blue-green as colour. The term 'indigo appearances' is said by way of blue-green in appearance. Objects of opaque blue-green are seen without the faintest sign of a flaw, and unbroken in colour—so it is stated. 'Shimmering indigo' is said with reference to their radiance, meaning irradiating, associated with, indigo. It shows the special purity of colour of these four 'positions of mastery.'[3]

In 'yellow,' etc., also the meaning is to be understood in the same way. And one taking up the blue-green device here seizes the mark (of upholding and its image) in a blue

---

[1] P. 101 *f.*: *Cariyā-niddesa.* [2] *Dhs.* §§ 246 *f.*

[3] P.T.S. ed. omits half the sentence.—*Tr.*

(-green) flower, or cloth, or colour-element. The work of the device, the preamble, the arrangement of the ecstasy—all has been discussed at length in the *Visuddhi Magga*.

And as in the earth device, so here twenty-five sets of nine should be understood in each position of mastery.

End of the Discourse on the Positions of Mastery.

CHAPTER XII

DISCOURSE ON THE DELIVERANCES

Now because this moral consciousness of the realm of attenuated matter arises, not merely as positions of mastery, by mastering the positions called objects, but also as deliverance, therefore, in showing that method, again the beginning has been made with 'Which are the states that are moral ?'[1]

Now in what sense should 'deliverance' be understood ? In the sense of *adhimuccana*. And what does this mean ? *Adhimuccana* means being 'well freed' from opposing states, or it means sustained attention by way of taking delight in the object. It is said to be the occurrence in the object[2] without oppression and without hesitation, like the sleep of a child on the hip of the father with its limbs, big and small, quite free. It is to show the moral consciousness of the realm of attenuated matter with such characteristics, and as having attained to deliverance, that this method has been begun.

Therein 'one having material qualities' (*rūpī*) refers to the possession of material quality (*rūpaṃ*), which means the *rūpajhāna*, produced with reference to the hairs, etc., of one's own body. For in doing the preamble of blue-green as to one's own body, one does it with reference to the hair, or the bile, or the pupil of the eye. In doing the preamble of yellow, it is done with reference to the fat, the skin, [191] or the yellow spot of the eyes. In doing the preamble of red, it is done

---

[1] *Dhs.* § 248. [2] Or, 'procedure in connection with the object.'

with reference to the flesh, the blood, the tongue, the palms of the hands and feet, or the red of the eyes. In doing the preamble of white, it is done with reference to the bones, the teeth, the nails, or the white of the eye. Thus it is with reference to a person who has done the preamble, and is possessed of the jhāna induced, that this has been said.

'Sees visible objects' means he sees with jhāna-vision the external device-objects, blue-green, etc., also. By this sentence the jhāna-attainment is shown with reference to the devices of both the internal and the external bases.

'Unaware of his own material qualities.'[1] The meaning is to be without the jhāna produced with reference to one's own hairs, etc. By this phrase is shown the state of the jhāna obtained through external [objects] by performing the preamble externally.

By the phrase 'How beautiful!'[2] the Jhānas are shown in colour-devices, such as blue-green, of thorough purity. In such jhāna it is true that there is no discernment of the beautiful within (*anto*) the ecstasy. Nevertheless, one who, maintaining as object of his thought a thoroughly pure and beautiful device, may abide in the attainment of First Jhāna, with the thought, 'How beautiful!' and of the other Jhānas likewise. Such an one is indicated in the teaching.

Now in the *Paṭisambhidā-magga* [the question is asked]:[3]— 'By the mere laying to heart that "it is beautiful!" how is there deliverance?[4] Here in this case the bhikkhu continues to diffuse one quarter of a [given] region with thoughts of love. . . . Owing to this culture in love, persons become free from aversion. Again, he continues to diffuse one quarter of a [given] region with thoughts of pity, of sympathy . . . of indifference. Owing to this culture in . . . indifference, persons become free from aversion. Thus he lays to heart that it is beautiful. And for this reason there is deliverance.'

But here, because it is dealt with further on in the text of the Divine States,[5] that method has been rejected, and

---

[1] *Dhs.* § 249. [2] *Ib.* § 250. [3] *Pṭs.* ii. 39.

[4] P.T.S.: *adhimatto ; v.l. adhimokkho*, for *adhimutto*. [5] *Dhs.* § 251.

only the æsthetic deliverance by way of the colours, very blue-green, very yellow, very red, very white, pure blue-green, pure yellow, pure red and pure white, has been allowed. Thus the jhāna of the realm of attenuated matter is said to be device, or position of mastery, or deliverance. For this jhāna is called 'device' in the sense of the entirety of the object, 'position of mastery' in the sense of mastering the object, 'deliverance' in the sense of bending towards or attending to the object, or of being set free from opposing states. [192] Of these, be it known that the teaching of the device was uttered as Ābhidhamma, but the other two discourses on position of mastery and deliverance were uttered as Suttanta teaching (*Dīgha* ii, 110 *f.*).

This, so far, is the exposition of the new terms. Moreover, taking twenty-five in each deliverance, as in the Earth-device, seventy-five sets of nine should be understood.

End of the Discourse on the Deliverances.

CHAPTER XIII

THE DIVINE STATES

Now to show the moral consciousness of the realm of attenuated matter occurring by way of the Divine States of love, etc., again the beginning is made with 'What are the states that are moral?'[1]

Therein 'accompanied by love' means possessed of love. And the same with the following 'accompanied by pity,' etc. Now by whatever arrangement one practises and lives in the attainment of the Jhānas accompanied by love, etc., all that arrangement of culture has been explained at length in the *Visuddhi Magga*.[2] The meaning of the remaining text should be understood by the method given in the earth-device. It is only in the earth-device that there are twenty-five sets of nine. Here in the first three of the Divine States

---

[1] *Dhs.* § 251. 'Divine' = brahma-. [2] Chapter IX.

are twenty-five sets of seven by virtue of threefold and fourfold jhāna. In hedonic indifference by virtue of fourfold jhāna there is a single set of twenty-five. In pity and sympathy, these two together with the four, to wit, will and the rest, are obtained as 'or whatevers' (p. 174). And here painfulness of progress, etc., should be understood by discarding ill-will from love, cruelty from pity, dislike from sympathy, lust and hatred from hedonic indifference.

Whereas the limitedness of object is by having not many beings as object, immeasurableness is by having many beings as object. This is the distinction. The remainder is the same as in the earth-device.

Now that these four divine (*brahma-*) states as taught by the Best of Brahmās [the Buddha] have been understood by way of the Text, the following particular comments concerning them should be known. Thus: of love, pity, sympathy, equanimity, 'love' means 'one loves.'[1] It signifies 'one wishes well.' Or love is so called because it goes on concerning a loved one (*mettā, mitte*), or because of the state of being a loved one.

That which makes[2] the heart of the good quiver at the pain of others is pity. Or it crushes,[3] destroys the pain of others, thus it is [193] pity. Or it is pity because it is scattered over[4] the afflicted, stretched out over them by diffusion.

(Thirdly) sympathetic joy (*muditā*) means those endowed therewith, or with the co-existent states, rejoice, or one's self rejoices, or just 'rejoicing.' (Fourthly) 'may they be without enmity!'—thus, by the removal of such ill-will, one contemplates with disinterestedness by attaining to a condition of centrality—this is hedonic indifference.

As to characteristic marks, etc., first among them, *love* has the characteristic of being a procedure of modes of beneficence;

---

[1] *Mettā* (love) is thus derived from $\sqrt{mid}$—to love. It is implied that it is a *dhamma* that loves, and not a person; therefore the view of the heresy of the self is inhibited.—*Visuddhi Magga Ṭīkā.*

[2] *I.e., karuṇā* (pity) is derived from $\sqrt{kar}$—to make.—*Tr.*

[3] *I.e.,* the derivation is from $\sqrt{kī}$—to destroy, kill.—*Tr.*

[4] The derivation is from $\sqrt{kir}$—to scatter.—*Tr.*

the function or property of bringing good; the manifestation or effect of taking hatred away; the proximate cause of seeing the lovableness of beings. Its consummation is the quieting of ill-will; its failure is the production of lust. *Pity* has the characteristic of evolving the mode of removing pain; the property of not being able to bear [seeing] others suffer; the manifestation of kindness; the proximate cause of seeing the need of those overcome by pain. Its consummation is the quieting of cruelty; its failure is the production of sorrow. *Sympathy* has the characteristic of gladness; its property is the absence of envying; its manifestation is the destruction of disaffection; its proximate cause is seeing the prosperous state of other beings. Its consummation is the quieting of dislike; its failure is the production of derision. *Equanimity* has the characteristic of evolving the mode of centrality as regards beings; its function is appreciation of others; its manifestation is quieting both aversion and sycophancy; its proximate cause is seeing the heritage of the occurring kamma as 'Beings are the property of their kamma. By its influence they will attain to pleasure, or be free from pain, or not fall from the prosperity already acquired.'[1] Its consummation is the quieting of aversion and of sycophancy; its failure is the production of a profane and unintelligent indifference.[2]

These four Divine States have the bliss of insight and the attainment of a happy existence as their common result. Their several results are the destruction of ill-will, etc. Love, for instance, has the destruction of ill-will as result. The others have the destruction of cruelty, of dislike, and of lust as respective results. As it has been said: 'Friends, that mental emancipation called love is the escape from ill-will . . . that mental emancipation called pity is the escape from cruelty. . . that mental emancipation called sympathetic joy is the escape from dislike . . . that mental emancipation called equanimity is the escape from lust.'[3]

---

[1] Cf. *Vis.-Magga*, ch. ix.

[2] *I.e.*, absence of knowledge (*aññāṇa*), may also be taken to be devoid of joy and grief.—*Mūlaṭīkā*. Cf. another pseudo-equanimity in *Majjhima* i. 364.—*Ed.*

[3] *Aṅguttara* iii. 291.

Each of them has two enemies, near and distant. To expand: of the Divine State of love the near enemy is lust, because, like love, it sees merits. It is like a foe lurking near a man. Quickly it finds access. Hence love should be well protected from lust. Ill-will is its distant enemy. From its dissimilarity in nature it is like a man's foe dwelling in a mountain fastness, etc. [194] Hence love should be cultivated secure from ill-will. It is impossible that one should cultivate love and at the same time get angry.

As to pity, one who views visible objects, desirable, lovable, endearing, delightful, associated with craving, objects which have not been obtained *as* not obtained, or who remembers what has been obtained formerly as now past, ceased, changed, is filled with the sorrow called worldly (or profane).[1] This, because it also contemplates adversity, is the near enemy of the Divine State of pity. From its dissimilarity in nature cruelty is the distant enemy. Hence pity should be cultivated secure from cruelty. It is impossible that one should cultivate pity and at the same time strike with the hand, etc.

As to sympathy, one who views visible objects, desirable, etc., is filled with the joy called worldly. This, because it also contemplates prosperity, is the near enemy of the Divine State of sympathy. From its dissimilarity in nature dislike is its distant enemy. Hence sympathy should be cultivated secure from it. It is impossible that one should be sympathetic and at the same time be discontented with secluded monasteries or with the higher moral states.[2]

The fool who has seen a visible object and who is deluded, an average man who has not overcome the limits of his lower nature and the result of former births, who does not see the evils of all conditioned things, is unacquainted with the teaching—this average man is filled with such indifference as is not able to transcend the visible object. Hence it is called worldly (or profane), and is mere delusion. Owing to its similarity in not considering faults and merits, it is the near enemy of

---

[1] Gehasita is lit. domestic, of the 'house-life.'—*Ed.* Kāma, being the abode of craving, is called *geha.*—*Pyi.* Cf. *Milinda* i. 71.

[2] Adhikusaladhammesu. Omitted in P.T.S. ed.

the Divine State of equanimity. From their dissimilarity in nature, both lust and aversion are its distant enemies. Hence equanimity should be cultivated secure from them. It is impossible that one should cultivate equanimity, and at the same time be enamoured with, or hurt another.

Of all of these four Divine States, will, *i.e.*, the will-to-do, is the beginning; the discarding of the Hindrances is the middle; ecstasy is the end. [195] One being or many beings as concepts are the objects of those states. There is development of the object on attaining to the 'access' or the 'ecstasy.' This is the order of the development:—As a good cultivator marks off the portion to be ploughed, and then ploughs it, so, marking off one dwelling, one should develop love towards the beings therein on this wise: 'May the beings in this dwelling be free from enmity!'

Having made the mind soft and workable as to one dwelling, two dwellings should be marked off, then in order three, four, five, six, seven, eight, nine, ten dwellings, a highway, half a village, the whole village, a district, a kingdom, one quarter of the globe—thus a world-system and more should be marked off, and love should be developed as to the beings in them. Likewise pity, and the rest. This herein is the order in the development of the object.

And just as concentration on the immaterial may be considered as the result of the devices, concentration on the sphere of neither perception nor non-perception as the result of concentration on the immaterial, the attainment of fruition as the result of insight, the attainment of cessation as the result of calm and insight, so here equanimity is the result of the preceding three Divine States.

As without raising the pillars and hoisting the cross-beams and wall-plates it is not possible to place aloft the peak and the rafters, so without the Third Jhāna obtainable in the first [three Divine States] it is not possible to develop the fourth state, even though that state does not arise in dependence on the Third Jhāna produced in the devices, owing to dissimilarity of the objects.

[Herein one might ponder in this wise:—]' Why are love,

pity, sympathy and indifference called the Divine States? why are there four? what is their order? And why in the *Vibhaṅga* are they called the "Immeasurables"?'[1]

First, they are to be understood as divine in the sense of 'best' (or highest—*settha*), and by their faultless nature. For these states are best as constituting a superlative mode of conduct towards others. And as Brahmā divinities live with faultless thoughts, so aspirants associated with these four states live like the Brahmās. Thus because of the meaning of 'divine' and of their faultless nature, they are called the Divine States.

There are Four Powers leading to Purity;
These are the Modes that start with Amity.
Limit unto their onward sweep is none.
By range as the Immeas'rables they're known.[2]

Namely, inasmuch as love is the way to purity for him who abounds in ill-will, as pity is the way if he abound in cruelty, sympathy if he abound in repulsion, equanimity if he abound in lust; again, because the fourfold work of the mind in relation to others is the conveyance of good, the removal of harm, [196] gladness over their success, and absence of preoccupation; and inasmuch as he who practises the Immeasurables should cultivate the four states towards all beings like a mother, who in midst of four sons, one a babe, one ailing, one adolescent, one managing his own affairs, desires for the babe growth, for the sick riddance of illness, for the adolescent persistence in the good things of adolescence, and is in no way anxious for the son who manages his own affairs, therefore is the order of the influences leading to Purity thus.

And because a person desirous of cultivating them should first practise them on beings by way of working good, and love has the characteristic of proceeding by way of working advantage; and because he then, pondering* on what he has seen or heard, of beings praying for welfare when overcome by

---

[1] *Vibhaṅga*, ch. xiii. [2] *Visuddhi-magga*, ch. ix.

* *Sambhāvetvā.*

sufferings, should practise them by way of taking away suffering, and pity has the characteristic of proceeding by way of taking away suffering; next because he, seeing the prosperity of those beings who had prayed for welfare and the removal of suffering, should practise them by way of rejoicing at prosperity, and sympathy has the characteristic of profuse gladness; and lastly, because he should practise them by the mode of centrality called equanimity, owing to there being no work to be done, and equanimity having the characteristic of proceeding by the mode of centrality, therefore love has been mentioned first by way of working good, etc., then pity, sympathy, equanimity—thus the order should be understood.

And because all of them arise in an immeasurable field, therefore are they called the Immeasurables. For beings without limit constitute their field. 'Though it be but a single being, in such a portion should love, etc., be developed,' thus without making any limit they evolve by way of thoroughgoing diffusion. Hence it has been said that they are four by reason of the way to purity, etc.; their order is by reason of the modes of working good; and they are also called the Immeasurables as arising with respect to an immeasurable field of objects.

And of these having the characteristic of immeasurableness in their field of objects, the first three are of the Third and Fourth Jhānas.[1] Why? Because they are not dissociated from joy. But why should they not be dissociated from joy? Because of their being the escape of such qualities as ill-will, which spring from melancholy. The last Divine State is of the remaining (Fifth) Jhāna. Why? Because of association with neutral feeling. For the Divine State of equanimity which arises in the mode of centrality [197] does not arise without neutral feeling.

End of the Discourse on the Divine States.

---

[1] Fivefold system.

CHAPTER XIV

THE DISCOURSE ON THE FOUL

Now in order to show a class of moral consciousness of the realm of attenuated matter[1] certainly beneficial to beings who walk in lust and which proceeds by virtue of each of the Jhānas among [certain] various objects, once more we have the beginning 'which are the states that are moral?'[2]

Herein 'accompanied by the perception of a swollen thing,' 'swollen' is said of a corpse bloated by degrees from the time of the loss of life onwards, like a bather's inflated bag. Or, 'swollen thing' refers to its loathsomeness from its abominable state, and is a synonym for such a corpse. 'Discoloured thing' is a corpse of a predominating blue-green colour, mixed with white and red; or just a corpse of blue-green colour corrupted from its original state; or it is a corpse discoloured and loathsome from its abominable state. It is an equivalent term for a corpse of a red colour in the fleshy parts, white where matter gathers, and generally of a blue-green colour in blue-green parts, as though covered by a blue-green sheet. 'Festering thing' is a corpse with matter flowing in lacerated places; or it is a corpse loathsome from its abominable state and is festering. It is an equivalent term for such a corpse. 'Fissured thing' is a corpse split in two, or a corpse fissured and loathsome from its abominable state. It is an equivalent term for a corpse cut in the middle. 'Mangled thing' is a corpse torn here and there in various ways by dogs and jackals, etc., or it is a corpse mangled and loathsome from its abominable state. It is an equivalent term for such a corpse. 'Dismembered thing' is a corpse of which the parts have been scattered, or it is just a dismembered corpse and loathsome from its abominable state. It is an equivalent term for a corpse dismembered here and there, in one place a hand, in another a leg, in a third place the head. 'Cut and dismembered thing' is a corpse cut in pieces and dismembered in the way just given, a name for a corpse cut by a knife

---

[1] Rūpāvacara.

[2] *Dhs.* § 263.

in the limbs, big and small, after the pattern of a crow's foot [198] and dismembered in the above sense. 'Bloody thing' is that which scatters, pours out blood, causing it to trickle here and there—an equivalent term for a corpse besmeared with trickling blood. 'Worm-foul' is worm-infested. It pours forth worms; hence a name for a corpse full of worms. 'Bone' refers to skeleton, or to its being loathsome from its abominable state. It is an equivalent term both for a group of bones linked like a chain, and for a single bone.

And these foul things are the names both of the marks (of upholding and image of the mark[1]) arisen in dependence on them, and also of the Jhānas obtained with reference to the marks. Therein the perception arisen by way of ecstasy with reference to the mark of a swollen corpse is the 'perception of the swollen thing.' And 'accompanied by the perception of the swollen thing' is in the sense of association with such perception. So for the perception of the other nine.

Whatever arrangement for practice should be said here has been said in all respects in the *Visuddhi Magga*.[2] The remaining exposition of the text should be understood by the method given above. But, as in the Divine State of equanimity alone, by virtue of the Fourth Jhāna, there are twenty-five sets of one, so here by virtue of the First Jhāna in each foul thing there are twenty-five sets of one. And the Jhāna having as its object the mark produced in a limited part of the swollen corpse should be understood as having a limited object from its inability to develop the foul object; and that in respect of a large portion of the swollen corpse should be understood as having an infinite object. So for the remaining nine.

Thus the 'Impurities' the Man of virtue pure,
By [Sakka] thousand-eyed extolled, of Tenfold Power,
Named as conditions of this Jhāna and of that.[3]

Now that we know all the foul things according to the method of the text, this particular discourse on them should

---

[1] Cf. *Compendium* 54. [2] Chapter vi.

[3] *Ib.* p 193. Cf. *Dialogues*, Sta xxi., esp. p. 320.

further be learnt. For he who has attained Jhāna, with reference to any one whatsoever of the ten 'foul things' becomes sober in behaviour, because, like a passionless saint, he has well discarded lust. 'And this being so, this classification of the "foul" has been declared, and is to be understood by virtue of the corpse developing its intrinsic nature,[1] and of the different kinds of lustful behaviour. To expand: a corpse which has arrived at the loathsome state may also reach the intrinsic nature of the swollen corpse or of any of the others: discoloured corpse, etc. [199] Thus the mark of upholding, "this is the loathsomeness of the swollen corpse; this is the loathsomeness of the discoloured corpse," etc., should be caught in whatever corpse he is able to catch it. Thus the tenfold classification of the Foul should be understood by virtue of the corpse developing its intrinsic nature.

'And of them, in particular, the swollen corpse, as making clear the decay of the form of the body, is suitable for one lusting after the form of the body. The discoloured corpse, as making clear the decay of the beauty of skin, is suitable for one lusting after the complexion of the body. The festering corpse, as making clear the stench connected with the sores of the body, is suitable for one lusting after the smell of the body produced by means of flowers, perfumes, etc. The fissured corpse, as making clear the existence of a hollow within, is suitable for one lusting after the solid state (of limbs) in the body. The mangled corpse, as making clear the decay in the perfection of the fulness of flesh, is suitable for one lusting after the fulness of flesh in such parts of the body as the breasts, etc. The dismembered corpse, as making clear the scattering of the limbs, big and small, is suitable for one lusting after their gracefulness. The cut and scattered corpse, as making clear the change that has come over the different joints, is suitable for one lusting after the perfection of the joints, of the body. The bloody corpse, as making clear the abominable state of

---

[1] *Vis. Mag.* 193 *f.* The *V. M. Ṭīkā* says that the body, under insight, is regarded in its intrinsic nature like a disguised ogre seen in his true nature. Some read *sarīrasabhāva-vipatti-vasena*—'by virtue of the false manifestation of the intrinsic nature of the body.'—*Tr.*

being besmeared with blood, is suitable for one lusting after beauty produced by adornment. The worm-foul corpse, as making clear the state of the body in common with various kinds of worms, is suitable for one lusting after the idea that the body is his own. The skeleton, as making clear the abominable state of the bones of the body, is suitable for one lusting after the perfection of the teeth. Thus it should be understood that the classification of the Foul has been declared to be tenfold also by means of the different kinds of lustful behaviour.

'And because, in this tenfold classification of the Foul, just as in a river of swift current with flowing waters a boat is steady by means of the rudder, and cannot stop without the help of the rudder, so from the weakness of the object[1] the mind is collected by the strength of initial application of mind, without which it cannot be steady; therefore here is obtainable the First Jhāna (with initial application of mind), and not the Second and other Jhānas. Though there is abomination, yet because he has seen benefit in this foul object: "surely by such progress I shall be freed from old age and death," and because of the removal of the torments of the hindrances, rapturous joy arises in him, like the flower-rubbish remover [200] who feels joy over the rubbish heap in seeing benefit, and thinks: "Now I shall get much wages," and like the sick man at the alleviation of the misery of sickness when vomiting and purging.

'The foul thing, though tenfold, is one in characteristic, which is the impure, evil-smelling, disgusting and abominable state. Not only in the dead body does it appear with this characteristic, but, as in the case of the Elder Mahātissa, resident at Mount Cetiya, seeing the teeth of a laughing woman, and of the attendant novice of the Elder Saṅgharakkhita looking up at the king on an elephant's back, it may also appear in a living body. Indeed, the living body is as foul as the dead body. But in the former the characteristic of the foul, being covered by temporary adornments, does not appear.'

End of the Discourse on the Foul.

---

[1] The inability of the object to draw the concentration of the mind on itself owing to its abominable state is its weakness.—*Pyī.*

But is this all the ecstasy belonging to the [consciousness of the] realm of attenuated matter, beginning with the earth-device and ending in the perception of the skeleton ? Or is there something more ? Yes, there is. There is the respiration-Jhāna, and the culture of mindfulness regarding the body, which have not been spoken of here. Why not ? The respiration-Jhāna is included in the air-device; the culture of mindfulness regarding the body arisen by virtue of the fourfold and fivefold Jhānas with reference to the hair, etc., is included in the colour-devices; the mindfulness regarding the body produced by virtue of the Jhānas attending to the abomination in the thirty-two parts of the body, and that of the Jhāna attending to the colours of the nine[1] sorts of corpses in the charnel field is included in the ten foul things. Thus all the ecstasies of [consciousness connected with] the realm of attenuated matter have been included here.

End of the Discourse on moral consciousness of the realm of attenuated matter.

---

[1] As, one-day-old, two-day-old, etc.—*Tr.*

PART VI—MORAL CONSCIOUSNESS OF THE IMMATERIAL WORLD

Now to show the moral consciousness of the immaterial realm, again the beginning runs:—'which are the states that are moral ?'[1]

Here, in the phrase:—'for the attainment of the immaterial abodes,' '*arūpa*' is the immaterial 'abode'; and the term 'immaterial uprising' means rebirth in the immaterial abode. 'He cultivates the path' means he produces and develops the means, condition, cause. 'Wholly' means 'in all respects'; or 'of all, without remainder.'

[Beyond all] 'perceptions of material qualities'[2] (*rūpa-saññānaṃ*) means the aforesaid Jhānas [201] of the realm of attenuated matter and the registered objects (in the 'devices'). Such Jhāna is symbolized by the designation 'matter' (or 'material,' *rūpa*). Such is the case in the foregoing phrases 'aware of his bodily frame he sees material objects';[3] again, 'externally he sees objects beautiful or ugly.'[4] Hence in this passage 'perception of material qualities,' that is, perception with respect to material qualities is an equivalent term for such Jhāna of the realm of attenuated matter symbolized by the perception. That such Jhāna is called 'matter-perceptioned' (*rūpa-saññaṃ*) means that 'matter' (material quality) is a name for it, and should be understood as an equivalent term for the devices and the registered mental objects.

'By having passed beyond,' namely, through distaste for and cessation. What is this saying? It means he, having attained, abides in [the Jhāna of] the infinity of space conditioned by distaste and cessation, to wit, the distaste for,

---

[1] *Dhs.* § 265.

[2] *B.P.E.*, 'consciousness of form.'

[3] *Ib.* § 248.

[4] *Ib.* § 223.

and cessation in all respects of, all perceptions of material qualities, of those which are known as the fifteen perceptions of jhāna by virtue of moral, of resultant and of inoperative consciousness, and of those which are known as the eight perceptions of object by virtue of the earth-device, etc. It is not possible to live in the attainment of that without wholly passing beyond the perception of matter. And on this point, because one lusting after the object cannot possibly transcend such perception, and because when the perceptions are transcended the object is transcended, therefore without speaking of the latter process the *Vibhaṅga* mentions only the transcending of the perception:—'Herein, what is the perception of matter? To one who has reached the attainment of the realm of attenuated matter, or who is born in a material abode, or to one who lives in happiness under present conditions, there are perception, the perceiving, the state of having perceived. These are called perceptions of matter. There is the passing beyond, the surpassing, the transcending of these perceptions. Hence it has been said "by wholly passing beyond all perceptions of form."'[1] And because these attainments are to be acquired by transcending 'object,' and not a single object as in the First Jhāna, etc., therefore this exposition of the meaning has been made also by way of transcending 'object.'

'By the dying out of the perception of impact'[2]:—the perception, that is, which is produced by the impact between eye, etc., as physical bases, and visible things, etc., as objects, is called the perception of impact. It is an equivalent term for the perceptions of visible things, etc. As he said:—'The perceptions of visible object, of sound, smell, taste, tangible object—these are called the perceptions of impact.'[3] The stated clause implies, by the dying out, putting away, not arising, not occurring of the whole ten impact-perceptions, of the five good results and five bad results. [202] Surely [it may be said] these are not obtained by one who has attained to the First and other Jhānas, since, at the time of attaining these, consciousness is not arising by way of the five doors.

---

[1] *Vibhaṅga* 261. [2] *Dhs.* § 265. [3] *Vibhaṅga* 261.

Nevertheless, just as pleasure and pain are mentioned in the Fourth Jhāna and just as the theory of individuality, etc., is mentioned in the Third Path,[1] although they are removed at another stage, so these impact-perceptions are to be understood as mentioned here by way of praising this jhāna, so that people may strive for it. Or, although they are not obtained by one who has attained the [consciousness of] the realm of attenuated matter, it is not because they have been removed; for the culture of the jhāna of that realm is not conducive to distaste for matter; rather the occurrence of these impact-perceptions is in conjunction with matter. But this culture of 'the immaterial' is conducive to distaste for matter. Hence it is proper to speak of their removal here. It is proper not only to speak of them, but also to bear in mind that they have actually been removed. Verily, it has been said by the Blessed One that, because of the non-removal of these impact-perceptions prior to the jhāna of the immaterial, sound is a thorn to one attaining the First Jhāna.[2] But owing to their removal, here the imperturbability of the immaterial attainments and peacefulness of emancipation have been declared. And when Kāḷāma Āḷāra entered on the attainment of 'the immaterial,' he did not see, nor did he hear the sound of five hundred carts passing close by him.[3]

'By not attending to perceptions of difference' means either 'to perceptions going on in a different field,' or 'to perceptions of differences' (or multiformity). This term 'perception of difference' is mentioned for two reasons:—The *Vibhaṅga* analyzes it as follows:—'What herein is perception of difference? The perception, perceiving, state of having perceived, in one who has not attained jhāna and who is endowed with the datum of mind, or with that of mental awareness—these are called perceptions of difference.'[4] In other words, the perception of such an one, comprising

---

[1] The Path of 'the Never-Returner, for whom the five lower Fetters are done away with.'—*Points of Controversy*, 74. The 'theory of individuality' or soul was the first Fetter.

[2] *Points of Controversy*, 331, quoting *Aṅguttara* v. 133-35.

[3] *Dialogues* ii. 141 *f*.

[4] *Vibhaṅga*, p. 261 *f*.

the data of his mind and mental awareness, goes on in a field of diverse nature with reference to difference in sights, sounds and so on. In the next place, there are forty-four [classes of perceptions] which are mutually unlike, being diverse in their intrinsic nature. These are the eight classes of moral perceptions,[1] the twelve immoral, the eleven of moral results, the two of immoral results, and the eleven 'inoperative'—all of the realm of sensuous experience. And the 'entire inattention to these perceptions of difference' implies not adverting to, not considering, not reflecting upon. And because he does not advert in mind to them, does not attend to, does not reflect upon them, [203] therefore the expression [commented on] was used.

And because the preceding perceptions of matter and of impact do not exist in the immaterial plane produced by this jhāna, much less in that plane at the time of abiding in the attainment of this jhāna, therefore is their non-existence said thus to be due to the two causes of transcending and dying out. But among the different perceptions, because twenty-seven perceptions, to wit, eight moral perceptions of the sensuous realm, nine inoperative perceptions, ten immoral perceptions exist in the plane produced by this jhāna, therefore the cause of not attending to them was mentioned. And because one abiding in the attainment of this jhāna in that plane of existence does so by not attending to those perceptions, one who attends to them has not attained the jhāna.

Briefly, 'by passing beyond the perceptions of matter' implies the removal of all states of the realm of attenuated matter. 'By the dying out of the perceptions of impact, by inattention to perceptions of difference,' implies the removal of, and inattention to, all consciousness and mental properties of the sensuous realm.

Thus by these three clauses:—transcending the perceptions of matter, the dying out of the ten perceptions of impact, the not attending to the forty-four different perceptions, the Blessed One has spoken the praises of the attainment of the

[1] As discussed above, Part IV., pp. 141 *ff*. The remainder are discussed in succession below.

infinity of space. For what reason? For the purpose of rousing the audience to activity and to persuade them, lest some unlearned people should say: 'The Teacher declared, "Get the attainment of the infinity of space." But what is the use, what is the benefit of this?' To prevent them from so speaking, he praised this attainment in such wise. For they, hearing its praises extolled, will reflect thus: 'So calm, they say, is this attainment and so exalted; we will get it.' Then they will endeavour to get it. And he has praised it to them for the purpose of persuasion, like a dealer in molasses [who is called a dealer] in 'visakaṇṭaka.'[1] He, it is said, took in a cart hard molasses, soft molasses, lumps of molasses, treacle, etc., went to the border village and shouted, 'Buy visakaṇṭaka, buy visakaṇṭaka!' (*lit.:* poison-thorn). The villagers, hearing him, shut the doors of their houses and made the children run away, saying, 'Poison is cruel; he who eats it dies; a thorn pierces, kills you. Both are cruel; what is the use of them?' Seeing this circumstance, the merchant thought, 'They are unskilled as to names in vogue, [204] these villagers. I will make them buy the toffee by a stratagem.' So he shouted, 'Buy a very sweet thing, buy a very delicious thing; hard molasses, soft molasses, treacle may be got at a low price, even for bad farthings, for bad pennies,' etc. Hearing him, the villagers, glad and delighted, came out and bought them, giving him much money. Now here, like the shout of the merchant's 'Buy visakaṇṭaka!' is the saying of the Blessed One, 'Produce the attainment of the infinity of space'; like the thought of the villagers: 'Both are cruel; what is the use?' is the thought of the audience:—'The Blessed One has told us to produce the sphere of the infinity of space. What benefit is there? We do not know its merits.' Then, like the words of the merchant, 'Buy a very sweet thing,' etc., is the Blessed One's showing the benefit, beginning with the transcending of the perceptions of matter. As the villagers giving much money and taking the molasses, so is the thought:—by hearing of the benefit, those whose hearts

[1] A name for a species of sugar. *Abhidhānapadīpikā.* Cf. our 'bull's eyes,' or the Lancashire equivalent 'humbugs.'—*Ed.*

have been persuaded will make a great endeavour to get this attainment. Thus the Blessed One has spoken for the purpose of producing endeavour and so as to persuade.

[Next we have] 'accompanied by the space-infinitude-realm-perception.' Here 'infinite' means 'it has no end.' 'Space-infinitude realm' means realm of infinite space or of infinitude of space, in the sense of abode of the associated jhāna,* like a spirit-realm of spirits. It is an equivalent term for the space separated off by the [space]-device. 'Accompanied by the perception of the sphere of infinite space' means accompanied by the perception which has reached ecstasy with reference to infinite space as object. But the words given elsewhere —'Infinite is space!'[1]— are not included here in reference to space as being either infinite or limited. Why? When it is infinite it cannot be taken to be limited, when limited it cannot be infinite. This being so, the fourfold object would not be complete and the discourse would not be sixteenfold. And it was the Supreme Buddha's wish to make the discourse in this place sixteenfold. Hence without saying 'infinite' or 'limited' he said 'accompanied by the perception of the sphere of the infinity of space.' Indeed, by this expression, both the words are included, the fourfold object is completed, and the discourse becomes sixteenfold. The meaning of the remaining text should be understood as said above.

And in this jhāna, sorrow at the destruction of desire for the Fourth Jhāna of the realm of attenuated matter makes [205] progress painful.[2] Sluggishness of entrance into ecstasy, on the part of one who has destroyed desire, makes intuition sluggish. The reverse should be understood as easy progress and quick intuition. And the jhāna which arises in space divided off by a limited device is called 'limited object,' that

---

* *Ākāsānañca.*

[1] When this Jhāna is stated as a stage of Deliverance (fourth in the eight), the formula runs thus (instead of as in the *Dhs.*): 'thinking "space is infinite!" he reaches and remains in,' etc. *Dialogues* ii. 119. Cf. *B.P.E.* 71, *n.*

[2] Cf. above, p. 246, The Four Objects of Thought.'

which arises in space divided off by an extensive device is called 'immeasurable object.' As in the divine state of equanimity, so here also by virtue of the Fourth Jhāna there are twenty-five sets of one, and as here, so also in the following Jhānas. And we shall explain only what is specific in these latter.

In the next stage, to the clause 'by passing beyond the sphere of infinite space,'[1] the previous method should be applied, showing both the realm of infinite space, in the sense of abode, and the jhāna to be so called. Both are united in the one term, and show that by not proceeding with them, by not attending to them, both the jhāna and its object are transcended, and he attains and abides in the sphere of infinite consciousness.

In the clause 'accompanied by the perception of the consciousness-infinitude-sphere,' infinite means that in attending to it, one thinks there is no end to it. 'Infinitude' is just 'infinite.' Instead of using *viññāṇānañcaṃ* for 'consciousness-infinitude,' the shorter term (*viññāṇāñcaṃ*) has been used, an instance of the elision of a syllable. This consciousness is the sphere, in the sense of abode, of this perception—hence 'the sphere of infinite consciousness.' 'Accompanied by the perception of the sphere of infinite consciousness' means accompanied by the perception arising with reference to that sphere of infinite consciousness. It is a name for the jhāna which has as its object consciousness as proceeding in space. In this jhāna, from the pain of the destruction of desire for the attainment of the sphere of infinite space, progress should be understood as painful; from a sluggish entrance into ecstasy on the part of one who has destroyed one's desire, a sluggish intuition should be understood. The reverse should be understood as easy progress and quick intuition. 'Limitedness of the object' should be understood as procedure with reference to attainment which has for its object space divided off in a limited 'device'. The reverse should be understood as the immeasurableness of object.

The rest is the same as in the preceding Jhāna.

---

[1] *Dhs.* § 266.

In the clause:—' by passing beyond the sphere of infinite consciousness '[1] the previous method should be applied, showing both the sphere of infinite consciousness, in the sense of abode, and the jhāna to be so called. Both are united in the one term, and [206] show that by not proceeding with them, by not attending to them, both the jhāna and its object are transcended, and one attains and abides in the sphere of nothingness.

In the clause ' accompanied by the perception of the sphere of nothingness,' here ' nothing ' signifies ' there is nothing of it.' The statement is, that not even disruption remains of it. Nothingness is the state of having nothing left, an equivalent term for the disappearance of the consciousness of the sphere of infinite space. ' Sphere of nothingness ' is the sphere, in the sense of abode, of the perception of that nothingness. ' Accompanied by the perception of the sphere of nothingness ' means accompanied by the perception proceeding with reference to that sphere of nothingness, and is a name for the jhāna having as its object the disappearance of consciousness proceeding with reference to space.

In this jhāna, where there is pain from the destruction of desire for the attainment of the sphere of infinite consciousness, progress is painful; where there is sluggishness of entrance into ecstasy on the part of one who has destroyed one's desire, intuition is sluggish. The reverse should be understood as easy progress and quick intuition. ' Limitedness of object ' should be understood as being the object, the disappearance of the consciousness proceeding with reference to space divided off by a limited device. The reverse should be understood as immeasurableness of object. The rest is the same as the first.

In the phrase:—' by passing beyond the sphere of nothingness,'[2] by applying the previous method, the jhāna with the sphere (in the sense of abode) of nothingness is shown to be itself called the sphere of nothingness; so also, by the aforesaid method, is its object. Both are united in the one term, and show that, by not proceeding with them, by not attending to them, both the jhāna and its object are transcended, and

---

[1] *Dhs.* § 267. [2] *Ib.* § 268.

one attains and abides in the sphere of neither perception nor non-perception.

In the clause:—'accompanied by the perception (idea) of the sphere of neither perception nor non-perception,' the jhāna is so called because of the real existence of such perception. In order to show this perception and its progress* arising in one who practises accordingly, the *Vibhaṅga* elaborates the phrase, 'neither perceptual nor non-perceptual,' and says that 'one attends to the sphere of nothingness as peace, [207] and cultivates the attainment of the residuum of mental coefficients; therefore it is said to be neither perceptual nor non-perceptual.'[1] In that text the sentence 'attends . . . as peace' means that he attends to the sphere of nothingness as peace from the peacefulness of the object, thinking:—'Verily this attainment is peace; since it will hold with non-existence itself as its object.' If he attends to it as peace, he is no longer in a state of desire for [further] attainment when he would be thinking, 'How can I transcend this?' His mind is considering its peace, but as to regarding, contemplating, attending how 'I shall attain, I shall sustain, I shall emerge from, I shall reflect upon [what I have gone through],' he does nothing of all this. Why? Because the sphere of neither perception nor non-perception is more peaceful, more excellent than the sphere of nothingness. As a king riding his elephant in great state, and going about the city streets, might see craftsmen such as carvers in ivory, tightly swathed in one garment, their heads covered with another, their limbs besprinkled with ivory dust, making various forms out of ivory, etc. And he, being pleased with their skill, might say: 'O sirs, how clever are these masters who can do such things!' But the thought does not arise in him: 'Good indeed would it be were I to give up my kingdom and become such a craftsman!' And why is that? Because of the great advantage of the glory of kingship. Now just as the king goes past the craftsmen, so although the aspirant attends to that attainment as peace, he does not consider, ponder, attend thus: 'I will attain it, sustain it, emerge from it, reflect

* *Taṃ tāva.*

[1] *Vibh.* 263. Cf. *Sum. V.* on *D.* ii. 69, § 33.

upon it.' Attending to it as peace by the previous method, he arrives at exceedingly subtle perception with the attainment of ecstasy. By means of that perception he becomes neither perceptive nor non-perceptive. And he is said to have cultivated the attainment of the residuum of mental coefficients, that is, the fourth 'immaterial' attainment of mental coefficients of exceeding subtleness.

Now in order to show the meaning of that sphere of neither perception nor non-perception, which by virtue of the thus acquired perception is so called, the states of mind and mental properties are here stated of one who has entered into that sphere of consciousness, or of one who is born in that plane of existence,[1] or of one who lives in happiness under present conditions. Of these three the states of mind and mental properties of one who has entered on that conscious experience are here intended. The literal definition is that, owing to the absence of gross perception and the presence of subtle perception in this jhāna, with its associated states, there is neither perception nor is there the absence of perception. This jhāna of neither perception nor non-perception is [classed as] a sphere included in the [conscious] 'spheres' of mind and of ideas, [208] hence the name 'sphere of neither perception nor non-perception.' Or, again, the perception here is non-perceptual in so far as it is incapable of effective functioning; and owing to the presence of the subtle residuum of mental coefficients it is not non-perceptual—hence 'neither perception nor non-perception.' And 'sphere of neither perception nor non-perception' means that it is a sphere in the sense of abode of the remaining states.

And not only perception is of such a kind. Feeling also is neither feeling nor non-feeling, consciousness also is neither consciousness nor non-consciousness, contact also is neither contact nor non-contact. It should be understood that this discourse has been made with perception as representative of the other associated states.

---

[1] The four 'immaterial' Jhānas were supposed to be tastes of the presumably normal consciousness experienced, respectively, by one reborn on the four planes of the immaterial worlds.—*Ed.*

This meaning can be made plain by the similes of oil for besmearing bowls, etc. It is said that a novice besmeared a bowl with oil and put it by. At the time of drinking rice gruel the Elder said to him, 'Bring the bowl.' He answered: 'There is oil in the bowl, sir.' Then, when the Elder said, 'Novice, fetch it; we will fill an oil-tube,' he answered, 'There is no oil, sir.' In this simile, as from the said [quantum] of oil inside, there is oil in the sense of the bowl's being unfit for rice gruel, and yet there is not sufficient oil for the filling of the oil-tube, even so that perception, from its incapacity for effective functioning, is not perception, and from the presence of the subtle residuum of mental coefficients is not non-perception.

But what is the function of perception here? The noting of the object, and the engendering of repulsion through extraordinary insight. As the element of heat cannot perform its function of burning in cold water, so this perception cannot manifest the function of noting. And in the remaining attainments it is not possible to engender repulsion through extraordinary[1] insight as perception can. Indeed, a bhikkhu, who has not accomplished his contemplation in other groups [of exercises], cannot attain to repulsion after he has grasped the groups of the sphere of neither perception nor non-perception, albeit perhaps the venerable Sāriputta, or a greatly wise man of matured insight like Sāriputta might be able to. 'These states (of neither perception nor non-perception) not having been, have come to be; having become, they perish'—thus he might be able by way of contemplating the group as a whole, but not by means of insight into individual states. Such is the subtleness of this attainment.

As by the simile of oil for besmearing the bowl, so by the following simile of water in one's path this meaning is to be made plain. [209] They say a novice, going on a journey ahead of his Elder, saw a little water and said, 'Water, Sir; take off your shoes.' Then when the Elder said, 'If so, bring the bathing cloth; we will bathe,' he replied, 'There is no water.' In this simile, as there is water in the sense of being

[1] Read *visesa-* for *visaya-*.

just enough to wet the shoes, and no water in the sense of being enough for bathing, so this perception from its incapacity for effective function is not perception, and from the presence of the subtle residuum of mental coefficients is not non-perception. Not only by these, but also by other fitting similes, should this meaning be made clear.

'Accompanied by the perception of the sphere of neither perception nor non-perception' means accompanied by this perception which proceeds in, or which is the sphere of, neither perception nor non-perception. It is an equivalent term for jhāna which has the attainment of the sphere of nothingness for object. Where there is pain at the destruction of desire for the attainment of the sphere of nothingness, progress here is painful; where there is sluggishness of entrance into ecstasy on the part of one who has destroyed desire, intuition is sluggish. The reverse should be understood as easy progress and quick intuition. 'Limitedness of the object' should be understood as referring to attainment when space is divided off in a limited device as object. The reverse should be understood as the immeasurableness of object. The rest is the same as the first.

The fourfold consciousness of immaterial spheres
Th' incomparable Lord hath [here] declared. And now
That these we've learnt, we must go on to know thereof
Some teaching in detail. These four do come to pass
If one transcend th' object experienced. But the wise
Believe the jhāna qualities are not surpassed.

Of the four attainments, the first is from transcending the image of the mark or the device-object, the second is from transcending space, the third is from transcending the consciousness proceeding with reference to space, the fourth is from transcending the disappearance of consciousness proceeding with reference to space. Thus these four immaterial attainments should be understood in all respects to have transcended the object. But in them the wise do not hold with the transcending of the factors. In them there is no transcending of the factors as in the attainments of the realm of attenuated matter, because in all of them there are just two jhāna-factors: hedonic indifference and one-pointedness of mind. Yet though there is no transcending of the factors, the subsequent attainments here (in the immaterial) are more exalted than the preceding.

Here each latter one is nobler: understand
The similes of dress and storeys thus:—

[210] As in the lowest storey of a four-storeyed palace there might be available the highest of the five pleasures of sense in the form of celestial dancing, singing, music, fragrant scent, garlands, sweet drinks and eatables, couches, etc.; in the second storey the pleasures available might be higher than those in the first; those in the third storey might be higher still; those in the fourth storey might be the highest of all; although herein the four are all palace-storeys, and there is no distinction in them as such, yet owing to the difference in the performance of the pleasures, the higher storey is more excellent than the lower. . . .

And as a woman might possess two garments of a texture four, three, two, or one in weight, spun thick, soft, very soft, most soft, and of the same dimensions in length and breadth; although herein the four garments are the same in length and breadth, and there is no difference in respect of size, yet the last named are more excellent than the former as regards the coarseness or smoothness of touch, fineness of texture and value, so also in these four immaterial attainments, although there are only two factors: indifference and one-pointedness of mind, yet owing to the distinction in culture and the degree of excellence of the factors, the subsequent attainments here are more exalted. Thus they are of graduated excellence.

Where a pavilion stands with filth around
One clinging hangs, another on him leans.
Another stands without and leaning not.
On him a fourth man leans. The wise should see
In these four men those Four respectively.[1]

[1] See *Visuddhi-magga*, chap. x. 'Āruppaniddeso.'

This is how the meaning is connected:—They say that there was a pavilion in an unclean place. A certain man on arriving there, loathing the dirt, hung on to the pavilion with both hands and remained there as though fixed. Another man having come remained leaning on the first man who had hung on to the pavilion. Then a third man having come thought, 'He who hangs on to the pavilion and he who leans on him—both of them are badly situated. Their fall with the fall of the pavilior is certain. Now I stand outside,' and stood apart without depending on them. Then a fourth man came, and considered the unsafe position of the man who hung on to the pavilion, and of the man who leant on him, and considering the safe position of the man who stood apart stood leaning on him.

Herein the device of marked off space should be regarded as the pavilion in an unclean place; the sphere of infinite space, with space for object and a contempt for the device-object, as the man who, loathing the impurity, hung on to the pavilion; [211] the sphere of infinite consciousness arising in dependence on the sphere of infinite space, with space for object, as the man who leant on him who hung on to the pavilion; the sphere of nothingness, which does not make the sphere of infinite space its object, but has the absence (of the first immaterial consciousness) for its object, as the man who thought of the unsafe position of both those men, and who without leaning on him who hung on to the pavilion stood apart; the sphere of neither perception nor non-perception proceeding in dependence on the sphere of nothingness, established in the exterior position called the absence of the (first immaterial) consciousness, as the man who thought of the unsafe positions of the men who hung on to the pavilion and of the man who leant on him, and who, considering the man who stood without as 'he is well placed!' stood leaning on him.

Though this be so,

'This' takes just 'that' as object, for it finds
No other; even so, that they may live,
Men [take] a king whose faults lie bare to view.

'This' sphere of neither perception nor non-perception takes 'that' sphere of nothingness for its object for want of another, in spite of the latter's fault of having the sphere of infinite consciousness as its 'near enemy.' Like what? Like the people who, for the sake of their livelihood, lean upon the king though they see his faults. For although the people see his faults, to wit, 'his conduct is harsh,' they would not get their livelihood save under this king who, though unrestrained, harsh in act, speech and thought, is lord of all the quarters of the country. Even so this sphere of neither perception nor non-perception takes that sphere of nothingness for its object, in spite of its fault, from inability to get any other. Still,

Who climbs a stairway grasps the stairway rail;
Who climbs a hill sees steadfastly the peak;
Who climbs a rock may seek a kneehold firm;
So doth a man just on this jhāna lean,
And as he leans upon it, carries on.

End of the Discourse on the Immaterial Moral Consciousness.

PART VII—DISCOURSE ON MORAL CONSCIOUSNESS AS THREE-PLANED

Now, in order to show all the moral consciousness of the three planes of existence as divided into 'low,' etc., again the beginning is made with, 'Which are the states that are moral?'[1] Herein 'low' should be understood as 'base' (or paltry) by way of putting forth (or heaping up). [212] 'Medium' is a state between low and high or (excellent). 'Exalted' means led up to *ex*-treme *alt*itude or supreme state[2]; the meaning is 'excellent.'

They are to be understood as referring to putting forth effort. When, at the moment of putting forth any effort, desire, energy, awareness, or investigation is low, that [moral consciousness] is known as 'low.' When these four states are medium, and again exalted, it is medium and exalted respectively. That moral consciousness which is put forth, with desire in the sense of will-to-do as its principal, its chief, its leader, is said to be dominated by desire as coming from such dominant influence. And the same with the dominant influence of energy, and the other two factors.

Halting at this place, we should count the methods thus:— One method the foremost classification of all, one low, one medium, one exalted, one method dominated by desire-to-do —these are the five methods in moral consciousness dominated by desire-to-do. So also there are five methods in each of the dominant influences of energy, etc., and four times five gives twenty. Or, the first is the bare method; the low, etc., amount to three more; four are the dominant influences of desire-

---

[1] *Dhs.* §§ 269-76.

[2] A 'buried city' word-play only—*pa*-dhānaṃ bhāvaṃ *nītaṃ* paṇītaṃ.—*Ed*

[to-do]; twelve are these four considered as low, medium and exalted, in all twenty methods. Where are these twenty great methods classified? They are classified in the chapter entitled 'Low Triplet' of the Great Book.[1] And in this place, taking the middle group from the Low Triplet, three portions as low, medium, exalted should be made. From these three, excepting the middle group, and taking the low and the exalted, sets of nine portions should be made. For in low moral consciousness there are low, medium, exalted; and in the exalted moral consciousness there are low, medium, exalted. Likewise in the low, by low moral consciousness there are low, medium, exalted; likewise in the low, by the medium moral consciousness; and likewise in the low, by the exalted moral consciousness. This is one set of nine.

In the exalted, by low moral consciousness, there are also low, medium, exalted; likewise in the exalted, by medium moral consciousness; and likewise in the exalted, by exalted moral consciousness. This is the second set of nine. The two sets make eighteen doors of action.[2] [213] From being

---

[1] *Paṭṭhāna.* The 'Low Triplet' is one of the chapters in the First Book, or Tika-paṭṭhāna.—*Ed.*

[2] In the middle group of the Low Triplet those moral thoughts which, with their results, are produced by way of gifts, etc., which depend on the round of rebirths, are done as 'low': those which, with their results, are produced by way of gifts, etc., which depend on the release from the round of rebirths, are done as 'exalted'; those which give no results are done as 'medium.' Of these three groups, excepting the middle group, because of its not giving results and taking the other two, nine kinds of moral consciousness certainly depending on the round of rebirths, and nine kinds depending on the release from the round of rebirths, form eighteen doors of action. These actions are also doors in the sense of being causes of the various results, hence doors of actions. Or the Buddha has declared the consciousness in various places to be so many doors of action: or the body-intimation, etc., to be doors of action. And the eighteen princes should be known according to their actions to be the worthless nine from the standpoint of sanctity consisting of the 'low by the low' trio, etc., and the worthy nine consisting of the 'exalted by the exalted' trio, etc. Likewise the priests, etc., and the devas. The forty-eight family customs are their different customs.—*Ṭikā.*

Or, that which is done without reverence is low; that which is done

developed by, and by virtue of them, eighteen princes, eighteen priests, eighteen merchants, eighteen workmen and forty-eight family customs[1] should be understood. But among these three-planed moral thoughts, that of the realm of sense is thrice-conditioned by way of association with and dissociation from knowledge; it is also twice-conditioned; that of attenuated matter and the immaterial realms is thrice-conditioned only, and associated with knowledge. And of them the moral consciousness of the sensuous realm arises, together with or without the dominant influence; that of attenuated matter and of the immaterial realm is replete with the dominant influence. And of them, in the moral consciousness of the sensuous realm, two dominant influences, viz.; object and co-existence, are obtained; in the other two realms the dominant influence of object is not obtained, only that of co-existence is obtained. In the text 'moral consciousness of the sensuous realm arising . . . with the dominant influence of awareness (*citta*),'[2] awareness as the dominant influence is said by way of associated states. On the other hand, owing to the absence of the union of two types of consciousness, awareness cannot be the dominant influence of an associated consciousness. And the same with desire, etc., as dominant influences.

---

with indifference is medium; that which is done with reverence is exalted. Or, that which is done for the sake of some worldly gain is low; out of a desire for a meritorious result is medium; from a sense of propriety by one established in Ariyanship is exalted. Or that which occurs through lust for the fulfilment of existence is low; out of a desire for absence of greed is medium; for the good of others is exalted. A limited moral consciousness is low; that which is done by measure is medium; that which is done in excess is exalted. The moral consciousness which is just obtainable among the sublime morals is low; that which has not been exceedingly well cultivated is medium; that which is well cultivated and acquired by men of control is exalted.—*Anuṭīkā*.

[1] Leaving out the low by the medium trio from the set of nine beginning with the low by the low trio, a set of six is obtained. Leaving out the exalted by the medium trio from the set of nine beginning with the exalted by the exalted trio, a set of six is obtained. These two give 12, which with the 4 'castes' make 48 family customs.—*Tr.*

[2] *Dhs.* § 269.

But if morality arises in one who is aware and who, making any consciousness the principal, the chief, has put forth another moral consciousness:—'it will arise in me,' some hold that his first consciousness should be called the dominant influence of awareness, and the second, as coming from such dominant influence, should be said to be dominated by it. This method, however, does not appear in the Text, nor in the Commentary. Hence the state of being the dominant influence is to be understood by the method given.

In these nineteen main methods are the types of consciousness of the extent given in the first main method, as formulated, with the sets of nine and the sections of the text. Therefore among the types of consciousness 'associated with knowledge' according to the extent given, the twentyfold classification of 'consciousness,' 'set of nine,' 'section' should be understood. Among the four types 'dissociated from knowledge,' the sixteenfold classification of the same should be reckoned. This is known as the Particular Discourse on the moral consciouness of the three planes.

End of 'Moral Consciousness as Three-planed.'

APPENDIX

SOME PALI WORDS DISCUSSED IN THE COMMENTARIES

(Indicated by an asterisk in the Translation. The figures in brackets refer to the page of the Expositor)

Ajjhattikaṃ (87)=indriyabaddhasantānaṃ.—*Ṭīkā.*

Anabhiraddho (190)=anabhirato, kuddho.—*Yojanā.*

Abhilāpo (28): etena desanā ti paññattī ti etaṃ vacanaṃ dhammaniruttābhilāpanaṃ sandhāya vuttaṃ.—*Ṭīkā.*

Abhisandahati (147)=pabandhati.—*Ṭīkā,*=sampayuttadhamme sakasakakicce paṭṭhapeti.—*Anuṭīkā.*

Ākāsānañca (274): ākāsānanta=ākāsānantya=ākāsānanca=ākāsānaṃca=ākāsānañca.—*Pyī.*

Itivādappamokkha (29): iti evam etāya paripattiyā vādappamokkhānisaṃsa. *Or,* so so vādo iti vādo iti vādappa mokkha.—*Sāratthadīpanī.*

Khippanisanti (251)=khippadassanaṃ khippābhiññatā (nisanti *is from* sam—*to look*).—*Ṭīkā.*

Taṃ tāva (277): tan ti taṃ saññā paṭipadaṃ; yathāvuttasaññaṃ tassāca adhigamūpāyan ti attho.—*Visuddhimagga Ṭīkā.*

Paṭihanana (61)=paṭimukhībhāva.—*Ṭīkā.*

Liṅga (86)=saṇṭhāna.—*Ṭīkā.*

Santati (*continuity*) (76) means the solidarity of individual mass by virtue of the continuous procedure of past moments of consciousness (like a chain of moving ants). Samūha (*mass*) means the solidarity of things such as contact, etc. Kicca (*function*) means the solidarity of single moments of consciousness having the same characteristics or states of single moments of consciousness by virtue of the resemblance of functions. Ārammaṇa (*object*) means the solidarity of single moments of consciousness by virtue of the aspect of difference between consciousness and object.—*Pyī.*

Sambhāvetvā (262): vā ti imāya paṭipattiyā ayaṃ nirayādisu nibbatteyyā ti parikappetvā vā.—*Visuddhi-magga Ṭīkā.*

PART VIII—DISCOURSE ON THE TRANSCENDENTAL[1]

CHAPTER I

THE FIRST PATH

HAVING thus shown the moral consciousness productive of prosperity in the three forms of rebirth, now to show the transcendental moral consciousness for the transcending of all rebirth,[2] again a beginning is made with 'which are the states that are moral?'[3]

Herein in what sense is it 'transcendental'? [214] Because it crosses the world, it crosses over the world, passing beyond the world it stands overpowering it.

'He cultivates[4] the Jhāna' means he evolves, produces, develops the ecstatic Jhāna of one momentary flash of consciousness.

Because it goes forth from the world, from the round of rebirths, this Jhāna is called 'going out.' Or, a person goes forth by means of it; hence it is called 'going out.' The

---

[1] Lit., supramundane (*lōkuttara*). *B.P.E.* 82 : 'engaged upon the higher ideal.'

[2] *Bhava-*; forms of rebirth—lit., [re-]becoming.

[3] *Dhs.* § 277.

[4] *Bhāveti*. Cf. above, p. 217.

person who is endowed with that, comprehending (the Fact of) Ill goes forth, abandoning the cause (of Ill) goes forth, realizing the (Fact of) cessation goes forth, evolving the Path goes forth.

Again, this is not like that which is known as 'leading to accumulation,'[1] which heaps up and increases decease and rebirth in the round of rebirths by the moral consciousness of the three planes of existence. But this is even as, when one man having heaped up a stockade eighteen cubits high, another man taking a large hammer were to go on knocking down and demolishing what had been heaped up. So it sets about pulling down and demolishing decease and rebirth heaped up by the three-planed moral consciousness, by bringing about a deficiency in the causes thereof; hence it is 'leading to dispersion for the putting away of [wrong] views.'

In the phrase 'for the putting away of [wrong] views,' views are called 'view-gone-things,' just as we say 'muck-gone-thing,' 'dung-gone-thing,' for muck, dung, etc.[2] Or, from being included among the sixty-two false views, they *go* to be included among 'the *views*'—hence 'view-gone-things.' Or, the course of these states is the *course* of the *view*—hence the term. Similar in course and procedure to the view is the meaning. Which are they? (The theory of individuality),[3] doubt, practice of mere rite and ritual, and the immoral states of lust, hate, and delusion leading to perdition, together with the associated states. It is they that are said to be similar in course to [false] views from the nature of their procedure till the evolution of the First Path. Thus the sixty-two false views and also these immoral states are 'view-gone-things.'

Of these view-gone-things, 'for the putting away' means in order to remove by extirpation.

'The first' is [in order] of counting, and also the first to be called up.

---

[1] Cf. above, p. 57 *f.*

[2] The suffix 'gatāni' has no meaning.—*Tr.*

[3] *Pyī* omits.

'Stage' (*bhūmi*):—in such phrases as 'of the uncovered *bhūmi*' the great earth is called *bhūmi*; in such phrases as 'in the pleasurable *bhūmi* in the realm of sense-desire' a state of consciousness is called *bhūmi*. But here the fruition of the religious life is intended; it is called *bhūmi* because it is the ground (or soil) for associated states, which are dependent on it. Or it is so called because, although it transcends the world, it itself arises, unlike Nibbāna, the unmanifested. 'For the attainment' of that First Stage should be understood to mean for the winning, the getting of the first Fruition of the religious life called the Fruition of Stream-winning. [215] 'Aloof from' means separated by way of extirpation, being without.

Now although the transcendental Jhāna is not accomplished without progress, yet out of a desire not only to [state but to] emphasize here that it goes with progress, [the Buddha,] abandoning the simple formula referred to 'painful progress, sluggish intuition,' etc.[1] Where that person who, in discarding the lower nature from the outset, does so with pain, by external aid, or instigation, and with fatigue, progress is painful. And he who, having discarded the lower nature, in living the life of insight, attains to the manifestation of the Path only after a long time, intuition is sluggish. Thus, any unspecified occasion (when the lower nature is discarded) is known as of painful progress and sluggish intuition. Of which occasion do they approve? That occasion[2] when the lower nature which revives after having been discarded once, and twice, on the third occasion remains discarded, and is brought to complete severance by means of the Path—of that they approve. It has been given the name of painful progress and sluggish intuition. With so much the matter is clear. Therefore the explanation here should be understood from the beginning thus:

That person, who, in comprehending the four Great Primaries [or Essentials], comprehends derived matter, comprehends the immaterial, but in comprehending the material

---

[1] Cf. above, p. 242 *f*.

[2] According to the Teachers.

and the immaterial, is able to do so with pain, difficulty and fatigue—to him progress is painful. And to him who has comprehended the material and the immaterial in his life of insight, if there be sluggishness in the manifestion of the Path, intuition is sluggish. He who having comprehended (without difficulty) the material and the immaterial in determining [the complex of] mind-matter, does so with pain, difficulty and fatigue, and who, having so determined that [complex], in living the life of insight, is able to produce the Path only after a long time, is of painful progress and sluggish intuition.

Another man who, having determined the [complex of] mind-matter in comprehending the causal relations, does so being fatigued with pain and difficulty, and who, having comprehended the causal relations in living the life of insight, produces the Path only after a long time, [216] is also of painful progress and sluggish intuition.

Another man who, having comprehended the causal relations, in penetrating the characteristic signs (of impermanence, etc.) does so fatigued, with pain and difficulty, and who, living the life of insight, has penetrated the characteristic signs, produces the Path only after a long time, also shows painful progress and sluggish intuition. Another man who, having penetrated the characteristic signs—his insight being sharp, valiant, clear, transporting—in laying hold of the uprisen desire for insight, does so fatigued with pain and difficulty, and who, having laid hold of that desire, lives the life of insight, but produces the Path only after a long time, also shows painful progress and sluggish intuition. They,[1] approving of this section, have given it the name of painful progress and sluggish intuition. In this way should the following three stages of progress be understood.

In the list 'contact, etc.,' four terms:—'the controlling faculty of believing "I shall come to know the unknown," right speech, right action, right livelihood'—are extra.[2] The terms 'path-factor,'[3] etc., also are extra, occurring in the

---

[1] The Teachers.

[2] Cf. *B.P.E.*, § 277, *n*. 2.

[3] *Dhs.* § 283. *B.P.E.*: 'Path component.'

sections of the Exposition and in the expositions of 'initial application of mind,' etc. The rest are all as said above.[1] But the state of being transcendental by way of 'stages' (or planes) is here a distinctive feature.

Of them the faculty of believing 'I shall come to know the unknown'[2] is the controlling faculty which has arisen, by means of former reflection, in one who practises accordingly, 'I shall know the unknown deathless path, the doctrine of the Four Truths, in the continual stream of becoming, of unknown beginning.' Its characteristic, etc., should be known by the method given above in the controlling faculty of understanding.[3]

'Right speech' is beautiful or praiseworthy speech, a name for abstinence from wrong speech by the complete severance of misconduct in speech. It has comprehension[4] as its characteristic, abstaining (from wrong speech) as its function, the putting away of wrong speech as its manifestation.

'Right action' is beautiful or praiseworthy action, a name for abstinence from life-taking, and so on, by the complete severance of wrong action. Its characteristic is the production of, or striving after, or the rousing of associated states for good action, its function is abstinence (from wrong action), its manifestation is the putting away of wrong action.

'Right livelihood' is beautiful or praiseworthy livelihood, a name for abstinence from wrong livelihood. It has purification[5] as its characteristic, suitable maintenance of life [217] as its function, the putting away of wrong livelihood as its manifestation. Or, the characteristic, etc., here are to be understood by what has been said on the three abstinences.[6]

Thus, by virtue of these three states the Path mentioned above as fivefold should here be understood as the eightfold Path. The absence [of these Path-factors], and likewise the absence of pity and sympathy among the 'Or-whatever-

---

[1] Cf. above, p. 142 *f.*

[2] *Dhs.* § 296.

[3] Cf. above, p. 161.

[4] *I.e.*, of associated states, or of the listener.

[5] *I.e.*, of the living being, of associated states, or of life.

[6] See above, p. 174 *f.*

states,'[1] should be noted, for those three factors occur in the text here, and pity and sympathy have a being for object, whereas these transcendental states have Nibbāna for object; hence those two are not included here. So far for the distinctive meaning in the section of the Summary. In the section of the Exposition the terms 'Path-factor' and 'Path-included' mean respectively 'a portion of the Path,' and included in, connected with, the Path as a thing included in the forest is forest-included.

In 'rapture as a factor of perfect wisdom (or of full enlightenment)'[2] the expression means that rapture is the factor of perfect wisdom. Herein, 'factor of wisdom' (*bodhi*) may also be taken to mean factor of one who has wisdom (*bodhī*, or who is enlightened). The Ariyan disciple is enlightened by means of the harmony of the seven constituent states of mindfulness, investigation of the Law, energy, rapture, repose, concentration and equanimity. This arises at the moment [when we experience] supramundane things, and is opposed to the various perils of mental contraction and distraction, fixity and struggle, indulgence in sensual pleasures and devotion to self-torture, and addiction to the speculations of annihilation and eternalism, etc. It is this harmony of states, at the moment when the transcendental state arises, that is called *bodhi* (enlightenment, knowledge). And the verb *bujjhati* (to be awake, enlightened, to know) implies a rising from the slumber of the continuum of the lower nature, or a penetrating the Ariyan Truths, or a realizing Nibbāna. The factor of such *bodhi*, called the harmony of states, is 'the Wisdom-factor,' like Jhāna-factor, Paṭh-factor, etc. The Ariyan disciple who is enlightened by means of such harmony of states as has been described is said to have *bodhi*. The potential parts of this *bodhi* are 'factors of wisdom (or enlightenment),' like the factors of an army, or of a chariot. Hence the Commentarial Teachers have said: 'Wisdom-factors are the [potential] parts of a person who is being enlightened.'

---

[1] *Ibid.* [2] *Dhs.* § 285.

Further, in what sense are they Wisdom-factors? Because they conduce to enlightenment, because they are enlightened, [218] because they are fittingly enlightened, because they are penetratively enlightened, because they are rightly enlightened. Thus by this analytic method also may the meaning of 'Wisdom-factor' be known.

Again, 'factor of perfect wisdom' is a praiseworthy or beautiful factor of wisdom. And 'rapture as a factor of perfect wisdom' means that rapture itself is a factor of perfect wisdom. In the expositions of one-pointedness of mind, etc.,[1] where the term occurs the meaning is to be understood in the same way.

'Of those states'[2] means, of those states of the Four Truths which at that time become intuited. 'That are unknown' means, although these states (the Four Truths) are now known by means of the First Path, yet, as a man having come to a monastery where he has never been before, and being seated in the middle of it would say with reference to his not having gone there before, 'I have come to a place I have never been to,' and being decorated with flowers that he has never before been decorated with, and being dressed in a dress that he has never before worn, and having eaten a meal that he has never before enjoyed would say, with reference to his new experiences, 'I have eaten a meal not enjoyed before,' and so on; so here also, because these states had never before come into this given person's experience, therefore the word 'unknown' is said. And the same with [the equivalents] 'undiscerned,' etc.

Of these terms, 'undiscerned' means 'not discerned before this with the eye of wisdom'; 'unattained' means 'not attained in the sense of access'; 'not understood' means 'not made clear by knowledge or insight'; 'unrealized' means 'not brought right before the eyes.'

'For the realization' means 'for the purpose of bringing right before the eyes.' And as the full construction is made with this word, so ought it to be carried out with the others—

---

[1] *Ib.* §§ 287-95.   [2] *Ib.* § 296.

namely, for the purpose of knowing the unknown, of discerning the undiscerned, of attaining the unattained, of understanding what is not understood.

In 'from the fourfold misconduct of speech,'[1] speech should be known as vocal intimation. Conduct spoiled by any of the three faults (lust, hate, delusion) is misconduct. Misconduct produced from, or accomplished by speech is misconduct of speech. 'Avoidance' (*ārati*) means one delights in being away from this fourfold misconduct of speech. 'Abstinence' (*virati*) means one delights in being without them. 'Renouncement' (*paṭivirati*) means, being turned away from them, one delights in being without them. Or we may see in each prefix an added emphasis. The whole three are synonyms for refraining. 'Abstention' (*veramaṇī*) means it kills, destroys enmity. This also is a synonym for refraining.

[219] Moreover, one speaking falsehood, etc., by any volition is said to commit misconduct of speech. When the abstinence belonging to this supramundane Path has arisen, it does not allow the commission of such an act, it cuts off the course of action (*i.e.*, volition), hence the term 'to leave uncommitted.' Similarly it does not allow the doing of such an act, it cuts off the course of action, hence 'to leave undone.' And he who commits the fourfold misconduct of speech by any volition is said to transgress. When the abstinence belonging to this supramundane Path has arisen, it does not allow such transgression, hence 'non-transgression.' 'Non-trespassing the boundary (*anatikkamo velā*)'—in such passages as 'at that *time*,'[2] *velā* means 'time.' In 'he lives at Uruvelā,'[3] *velā* means 'heap,' [namely, of sand (*uru*)]. In 'being steady by nature he does not pass beyond the *boundary*,'[4] *velā* means 'boundary.' Here also it means 'boundary.' The fourfold good conduct of speech is intended to be the boundary, because it is not to be trespassed. So he who commits the fourfold misconduct of speech by any volition is said to trespass over the boundary. When the

---

[1] *Ib.* § 299.
[2] *Saṃyutta* i. 76, § 6 *passim.*
[3] *Ib.* 103 *f.*
[4] Not traced.

abstinence belonging to this supramundane Path has arisen, it does not allow (this volition) to trespass over the boundary —hence 'not to trespass over the boundary.' Or, *velā* means it destroys (*velāyati*). What does it destroy? The fourfold misconduct of speech, from destroying which it is called *velā*. And *anatikkamo* means it does not get beyond a person's prosperity and happiness. Thus is the meaning to be understood by these two words. Finally, 'to destroy the causeway,' that is 'he breaks down the causeway.' The meaning is that it destroys the base, the cause of the fourfold misconduct of speech; for that condition is here intended by causeway. This is the definition of the word:—the condition, such as lust, etc., of the fourfold misconduct of speech ties, makes a person to be bound in the round of rebirths—hence 'cause-way-breaking,' *i.e.*, abstinence which breaks up misconduct in speech.[1] Moreover, this abstinence called right speech is obtained in a variety of conscious experience previous to the Path; for by one thought one abstains from speaking falsehood, by another from calumnious speech, etc. But it is obtained in one conscious experience at the moment of the supramundane Path; for there arises only one abstinence cutting off the base of the fourfold volition of misconduct of speech and fulfilling the Path-factor. 'From misconduct of body' means from evil practices such as life-taking, etc., produced on account of, or accomplished by the body. The remainder is to be understood by the previous method.

And this abstinence called right action[2] is obtained in a variety of conscious experience previous to the Path; for by one thought [220] one abstains from life-taking, by another from theft and wrong behaviour. But it is obtained in one conscious experience at the moment of the supramundane Path; for there arises only one abstinence cutting off the base of the threefold volition of misconduct of body and fulfilling the Path-factor.

With respect to the 'leaving undone' in the exposition of

---

[1] The word-play here cannot be reproduced in English. *Setu*—dyke, or causeway, or 'bund'—is made a derivative from *Si*, to bind.—*Ed.*

[2] *Dhs.* § 300.

right livelihood[1] one maintaining a wrong livelihood by any volition is said to be continuing the practice (of wrong livelihood). But when the abstinence belonging to this supramundane Path has arisen it does not allow (this volition) to keep up the practice; hence 'leaving undone.' In this way the construction should be understood. And there is no such separate thing as 'livelihood.' It is understood, together with speech and action, from being part and parcel of them. But by way of a constant dependence on the four requisites,[2] it has been taken out from them and so taught. This being so, right livelihood has no [separate] function of its own, and does not complete the eight path-factors [by any new increment]. Wherefore it behoves this method to make a 'function' for 'right livelihood,' and to let the eight path-factors be completed. For livelihood, in failing, fails at the doors of body and speech; it cannot fail at the mind-door. In succeeding, it succeeds at these two doors; it cannot succeed at the mind-door. And transgression at the body-door is, or is not conditioned by livelihood. Likewise at the vocal door. In this respect, kings and ministers, addicted to amusement and displaying their bravery, indulge in deer-hunting, or highway robbery, or adultery. This is an immoral act of body; abstinence therefrom is right action. Whatever fourfold misconduct of speech people commit that is not conditioned by livelihood is an immoral act of speech; abstinence therefrom is right speech. And for the sake of livelihood, whatever creatures hunters, fishermen, etc., may kill, whatever theft people may commit, however they may wrongly behave themselves (in sensual pleasures)—this is known as wrong livelihood; abstinence therefrom is known as right livelihood. After taking a bribe, whatever lies they may speak, whatever calumnious speech they may utter, harsh speech, or frivolous talk—this is known as wrong livelihood; abstinence therefrom is known as right livelihood. And Mahāsīva the Elder has said: 'Transgression in the doors of body and speech,

---

[1] *Dhs.* § 301.

[2] The four life-necessaries for the religieux—food, clothing, lodging, medicine.—*Ed.*

[221] whether conditioned or not by livelihood, is counted as an immoral act of body and of speech. Abstinence therefrom is said to be right action and right speech.' When the pupils asked, 'Where does livelihood come in?' he replied, 'The enjoyment of the four requisites, which have been produced in dependence upon the threefold hypocrisy[1] is livelihood.' But this is the height of wrong livelihood, abstinence from which is known as right livelihood. This right livelihood is obtainable in the various conscious experiences previous to the Path. For by one conscious experience one abstains from the transgression in the door of body; by another, from that in the door of speech. But it is obtained in one moment of consciousness at the moment of the transcendental path; for then there arises only one abstinence, cutting off the base of the volition of wickedness called wrong livelihood, produced by way of the seven courses of action[2] in the doors of body and of speech, and fulfilling the path-factor. This is the distinction in the Section of the exposition.

Among the controlling faculties the faculty of believing, 'I shall come to know the unknown,' and among the path-factors right speech, etc., are additions. Through these [additions] nine controlling faculties and the [full] Eightfold Path are declared in the section of the Summary.[3]

The section of 'Emptiness' retains its original form.[4] So far the Progress formula is different. Farther on the teaching is divided into the Emptiness formula, the Empty-Progress, the 'Unhankered-after' and the Unhankered-after Progress.[5] Of these, Empty is the name of the supramundane Path, given for the three reasons: of arrival, of its own merits and of the object. How? In the Order a bhikkhu, being

---

[1] The threefold hypocrisy produced by evil desires is wearing of coarse raiment, boasting of one's saintly qualities, behaving as though one had attained holiness.—*Ṭīkā*.

[2] Misconduct, threefold by act, fourfold by speech.

[3] *Dhs.* § 337; *B.P.E.* § 337*a*. *I.e.*, one more faculty in addition to those named in §§ 58, 74.

[4] *Ib.* §§ 344, 345; cf. §§ 132-45 (title), where the P.T.S. ed. apparently omits the word suññataṃ.

[5] *Ib.* §§ 344-57.

convinced of the non-existence of an absolute soul, views complexes as soulless. But because, by merely viewing them as soulless, the genesis of the Path is not obtained, it behoves him to view them also as impermanent and as ill, therefore he practises the contemplation of the threefold discernment of impermanence, ill and soullessness. Still his insight leading to emergence[1] views the complexes of the three planes, as Empty. This insight is known as Emptiness. Standing in the place of 'that which tends to arrive,' it gives the name of Emptiness to its own path. Thus the Path gets the name of Emptiness because [this concept tends to] arrive.

And because the path is void of lust, etc., therefore it gets the name of Emptiness by means of its own merits. Nibbāna also, from being void of lust, etc., is called Emptiness. Because it arises with Nibbāna for object the Path gets the name of Emptiness from its object. [222] Of these three reasons it gets its name from its own merits, and also from the object by means of the Suttanta or explanatory method of teaching. Abhidhamma discourse is teaching without such a method. Therefore, here 'Emptiness' gets its name, not from its own merits, nor from the object, but from the fact of its arrival; for arrival is the principal[2] and is twofold: of insight, of the Path. Of these, the insight-arrival is the principal where the Path has arrived; the Path-arrival is the principal where fruition has arrived. Here, owing to the arrival of the Path, the insight-arrival is the principal.

In 'the Undesired,'[3] 'undesired' is a name of the Path,

---

[1] The insight which views conditioned things with indifference. It occurs together with the stage called adaptation (anuloma), and is called insight leading to transcendence. Because it views conditioned things as empty, it is called 'emptiness' (suññatā). Because it views them as ill, or because in it craving is dried up, it is called undesired, unhankered after.—*Ṭīkā*.

The word transcend-ence, henceforward occurring frequently, is lit., standing up away from: v-uṭṭhāti—*i.e.*, rising from. It is translated 'transcending,' *or* 'emerging from.'—*Ed.*

[2] Some read dhuvaṃ: 'certain,' 'assured,' for dhuraṃ: 'principal.'

[3] *Dhs.* § 351. *B.P.E.*: 'unhankered after.' Cf. *Compendium* ix., § 9. Apaṇihita is from (a)pra-ni-dhā: 'not to lay down toward.' Not aimed at, or aspired to. Cf. *A.* i. 8; *S.* iv. 302.—*Ed.*

which gets it for three reasons. How? Here a bhikkhu, being convinced from the beginning of the Truth of ill, views complexes as ill. But because, by merely viewing them as ill, the emergence of the Path is not obtained, it behoves him to view them also as impermanent and selfless, therefore he practises the contemplation of the threefold discernment as impermanent, ill and selfless. Still his insight leading to emergence dries up, destroys and relinquishes the desire for the complexes of the three planes. This insight is known as 'the undesired.' Standing in the place of that which tends to arrive, it gives the name of Undesired to its own Path. Thus the Path gets its name of Undesired because the concept tends to arrive. And because, in the Path, the desire of lust, hate and delusion does not exist, therefore it gets the name of Undesired by means of its own merits. Nibbāna also, from the absence of those desires, is called the Undesired. From arising with Nibbāna as its object, the Path gets the name of Undesired. Of these three reasons, etc. (*continue as in preceding paragraph*).

[223] To the objection:—but are not 'Emptiness, Signless, Undesired' three names of the Path? As the Buddha has said, 'Bhikkhus, there are three Deliverances: that of Emptiness, of the Signless, of the Undesired.'[1] Why of the three are the two taken here, and not the Signless?—we reply:—From the absence of the arrival. For the insight of the 'Signless' is not able by itself to stand in the place of arrival and to give the name to its own path. Nevertheless, the Buddha Supreme declared the insight of the 'Signless' to his own son, Rāhula the Elder:

Study the signless, and abandon pride's
Deep-hidden bias; so by conquering
Thy pride thou mayest know tranquillity.[2]

For insight severs the signs of permanence, stability, bliss, self.[3] Hence it is spoken of as the Signless. Yet, although

---

[1] *Pṭs*. ii. 35.

[2] Ascribed to Abhirūpanandā. Pss. of the Sisters, ver. 20, and to Ānanda addressing Vangīsa, Pss. of the Brethren, ver. 1226. But cf. *S*. iii. 135 *f*.; *A*. ii. 165.—*Ed*.

[3] Reading attanimittaṃ.

it severs the sign, it itself frequents states which are signs; thus it occurs with the sign. Therefore it itself is not able to stand at the place of arrival and give the name to its own path.

A further view: The Abhidhamma is the teaching of things in the ultimate sense. And in the ultimate sense there is a deficiency in the conditions producing the Signless Path. How ? The deliverance called Signless has been declared by way of the discernment of impermanence. And by means of that deliverance the controlling faculty of faith is excessive. Owing to its not being a Path-factor, it is not able, in the ultimate sense, to give the name to its own path. Of the other two, the deliverance called 'empty' has been declared by way of the discernment of soullessness, and the deliverance called 'undesired' has been declared by way of the discernment of ill. Of them, by means of the deliverance called 'empty,' the controlling faculty of understanding is excessive; by means of the deliverance called 'undesired' the controlling faculty of concentration is excessive. These controlling faculties, being factors of the Ariyan Path,[1] are able in the ultimate sense to give the name to their own paths. In other words, in the triplet of the object of the Path,[1] also, in the classification of the states as the dominant influence of the Path, because desire-to-do and consciousness, at the time of their being dominant influences, are not Path-factors, the state of their being dominant influences of the Path is not stated. Thus should this be understood. This is the decision of the opinion of a certain teacher apart from the Commentary.

[224] Thus in all respects the insight of 'the Signless' is not able by itself, standing at the place of arrival, to give a name to its own Path; hence a Path of the 'Signless' has not been included. But some have said that such a Path, although it does not get the name from its arrival, gets it, by the Suttanta expositions, from its own merits and from its object. They should be refuted thus:—If the 'Signless path' gets its

---

[1] *Dhs.* §§ 1031-3.

name from its own merits and from the object, then the Empty and the Undesired paths also should here, in the Abhidhamma, get their names from their own merits and from their objects. But they do not. And why? Because this [sort of] path gets its name for two reasons:—from its essential property and from opposing; in other words, from its intrinsic nature and because of something rejected. Now the paths called Empty and Undesired get their names from their own intrinsic natures and from opposing. They are void of lust, etc., and without the desires springing from lust, etc.; thus they get their names from their own intrinsic nature. And Emptiness is opposed to the (false) conviction of the soul and the Undesired to desire; thus they get the name from opposing. But the Signless Path, owing to the absence of the signs, etc., of lust, of permanence, gets its name from its intrinsic nature, but not from opposing; for it is not opposed to the discernment of impermanence, which has the signs of the complexes as its object, and which stands in conformity to it; thus in all respects, by Abhidhamma exposition, there is no Signless Path. But by the Suttanta exposition it is brought out and shown. For on any given occasion there is the emergence of the Path, the three characteristic signs[1] present themselves, as if by a single act of 'adverting.' There is no simultaneous presentation of the three, yet it is said so, to show when the station of religious exercise is manifested. Indeed, from the outset, let there be anywhere a conviction [of the mind], then insight making for emergence, as it emerges, gives the name of its own path to whatever sign it has grasped, placing it at the point of arrival by just that sign. How? Because of the disposition here or there respecting any one of the three Signs, the rule is that the other two Signs are seen also, for when one Sign alone is seen, there is no emergence of the path. Hence the bhikkhu [225] who is convinced as to impermanence, emerges not solely as to that, but also as to the other two; similarly if he start with either of these two.

---

[1] Impermanence, ill, soullessness.

Of the three Paths, the Path of one emerging by means of impermanence is the Signless; that of one emerging by means of ill is the Undesired; that of one emerging by means of soullessness is the Empty. Thus by the Suttanta expositions[1] it has been brought out and shown. But (to object:) what has insight leading to emergence for its object? The three characteristics. What is called a characteristic is the same as a concept, and is not a state that can be said to be limited or sublime, etc. And whoso discerns the three characteristics as impermanence, ill, soullessness, to him the five aggregates become like a corpse tied to his neck. Knowledge, having the complexes as its object, emerges from them. So a bhikkhu, desirous of buying a bowl, might see one brought by a bowl-merchant, and glad and delighted would think, 'I will take it.' On examining it he might see holes, whereupon he loses all attachment, not for the holes, but for the bowl. Similarly, noting the three characteristics [the student] has no further attachment for conditioned things. He transcends any such thing by means of knowledge, having such thing as object.

The simile of the robe may be similarly applied.

Thus the Blessed One, in classifying transcendental jhāna, brought out the two methods of the fourfold and fivefold jhāna in the 'progress' formula, as well as progress in the [idea of] emptiness and the 'undesired' in those corresponding formulas respectively. Why did he so bring them out? To meet individual inclinations and to adorn his discourse, both of which reasons are to be understood as stated above. So in the words 'he cultivates transcendental jhāna'[2] we find the two methods, by way of fourfold and fivefold jhāna, in the 'progress' formula, as also in the rest. Thus in all the five portions ten methods have been classified. Hereon the following is the special [comment]:—

Subjective and objective with respect
To matter, th' immaterial, the five,
The interchange of factors eight and seven,
The sign, the progress, the chief influence.

---

[1] *Pṭs.* ii., Vimokkhakathā, esp. p. 64. [2] *Dhs.* §§ 277 *ff.*

Namely, in the transcendental Path, being convinced of one's own person one transcends it [226]; being so convinced one transcends that which is objective; being convinced of the objective one transcends that; being convinced of matter one transcends that; so convinced one transcends the immaterial; being convinced of the immaterial one transcends that; being so convinced, one transcends matter. At one stroke one transcends the five aggregates. As to 'the interchange of factors eight and seven,' this Path is both eightfold and sevenfold; the Factors of Wisdom also are seven or six; jhāna is fivefold, four- three-, or twofold:—thus should the mutability of factors eight, seven, etc., be understood. And as to 'the sign, the progress, the chief influence,' 'sign' is that which is transcended; the other terms refer to the steadiness or unsteadiness of progress, and to the dominant influence.

As regards the sentence—'being convinced of his own person he transcends it'—this refers to one who from the outset is subjectively convinced as to the five aggregates, and being so convinced considers them as impermanent, liable to suffering, void of soul. But inasmuch as by this purely subjective view there is no emergence of the Path, and it behoves him to consider also that which is objective, he considers the aggregates of another person, and so, with regard to things not affecting his own desires, he considers them also as impermanent, etc. Now he contemplates his subjective self, now that which is objective. When he thus contemplates his own person, his insight unites with the Path. And so, being convinced as to his own person, he transcends it. But if his insight unites with the Path when he is contemplating the objective, then he is convinced as to the subjective and transcends the objective. Similarly when he is convinced as to an objective personality and transcends both it and his own personality.

Another man from the outset is convinced of matter and, being so convinced, defines elemental matter and derived matter, and views them as impermanent, etc. But because by just this formulated view of matter there is no emergence of the path, and it behoves him to view the immaterial as well, therefore [227] he defines feeling, perception, mental co-efficients, consciousness, which have arisen by making matter the object, saying 'This is not material,' and views them as impermanent, etc. Now he contemplates matter, and now non-matter. When he thus contemplates matter, his insight unites with the Path. So being convinced of matter he is said to emerge therefrom. If, on the other hand, when he contemplates non-matter, his insight unites with the Path, he is said to be convinced of matter and to transcend non-matter. And the same with his being convinced of non-matter and transcending both that and matter. 'Whatever has the nature ot coming to be, has the nature of passing away'[1]—thus being convinced at the time of transcending, he is known to transcend at one stroke the five aggregates.

This is the insight of a bhikkhu of sharp insight and great understanding. As if folk were to offer a man aching with hunger a bowl full of food of divers excellent tastes and put a lump of ordure in the middle. And he were to scrape the curry with his hand, and seeing the lump were to ask, 'What is this?' and on being told, would not have any inclination for the food or the bowl, saying, 'Fie! Fie! take it away,' so should the application of this simile be understood. As the time of rejoicing on seeing the bowl full of food, so is the time when the bhikkhu, then a foolish average man, grasps the five aggregates as '*I am* the five aggregates; *mine* are they.' As the time of seeing the lump of ordure, so is the time of noting the three characteristics. As the time of having no inclination for the food or the bowl is the time when the bhikkhu of sharp insight and great understanding transcends at one stroke the five aggregates, saying, 'Whatever has the nature of coming to be has the nature of passing away.'

As regards

The interchange of factors eight and seven,

---

[1] *Vinaya Texts* i. 97, § 29.

it should be understood in accordance with the change of factors classified above. For the insight of indifference to conditioned things fixes the distinction among the wisdom-factors, the Path-factors, and the Jhāna-factors of the Ariyan Path. But some Elders say that the basic jhāna does so; others say that the aggregates which are the objects of insight do so; others say that individual inclination does so. Concerning these doctrines it should be understood that this previous insight leading to transcendence, also called indifference to conditioned things, fixes that distinction.

Here is the discourse in regular succession: The Path arisen in one of dry insight[1] [228] by the fixing as insight, and the Path arisen without making a base of the Jhāna of one who has acquired the attainment, and the Path produced by making a base of the First Jhāna and contemplating particular conditioned things (*i.e.*, other than the basic Jhāna) are of the First Jhāna. In all of them there are seven Wisdom-factors, eight Path-factors, five Jhāna-factors. Their previous insight is accompanied by joy and by indifference and, at the time of emerging after attaining to the state of indifference to conditioned things, is accompanied by joy only. In the five-fold method, in the Paths produced by making a base of the Second, Third, Fourth Jhānas, the jhāna in due course has four, three, two factors. But in all the Paths there are seven Path-factors, in the Fourth jhāna six Wisdom-factors. This distinction is due to the fixing of the basic jhāna and of insight, for their previous insight is accompanied by joy and indifference, but the insight leading to transcendence is accompanied by joy only. But in the Path produced by making the Fifth Jhāna the basis by way of indifference and one-pointedness of mind, there are two Jhāna-factors; the Wisdom-factors and Path-factors are six and seven respectively. This distinction also is due to the double fixing (of basic jhāna and of insight). In this method the previous insight is accompanied by joy and indifference; that leading to transcendence is accompanied by indifference only. And the same with the

[1] Cf. *Compendium*, pp. 55, 75.

Path produced by making the immaterial Jhānas the basis. Thus the attainment, emerging in proximity to the Path produced by contemplating any conditioned things whatever after emerging from the basic jhāna, makes the Path similar to itself, as the colour of the ground is similar to that of the iguana.

In the second doctrine of the Elders, the Path produced by emerging from any attainment, and contemplating any states of attainment, is similar to that attainment—that is, to the contemplated attainment. But if we contemplate states of the sensuous sphere, we are in the First Jhāna. Here also the fixing as insight is to be understood by the method stated.

[229] In the third doctrine of the Elders, the Path produced by contemplating any jhāna states, when any jhāna is made the basis, in accordance with one's wish: 'O if I could attain to the Path with seven factors, with eight factors!' resembles that particular jhāna. Yet without the basic jhāna, or the contemplated jhāna, the resemblance thereto is not accomplished by the mere wish. This meaning is intended to be shown by the *Nandakovāda Sutta*.[1] For there it is said:—'Bhikkhus, as on the fifteenth, the Sabbath day, people have no doubt, no misgivings whether the moon will be deficient or full, but are quite sure that it will be full, so, bhikkhus, those bhikkhunīs are delighted at Nandaka's sermon on the Law, and have their intentions fulfilled. Bhikkhus, of those five hundred bhikkhunīs, even she who is the most backward is a "Stream-winner," not liable to suffer in purgatory, assured, and bound for enlightenment.' For among them she who has in her the sufficient cause of the fruition of Stream-winning, has her intentions fulfilled by just that fruition; and so for the three higher fruitions.[2] Thus the path produced by contemplating any jhāna states, making any jhāna the basis in accordance with one's wish, resembles that jhāna.

Yet without the basic jhāna or the contemplated jhāna the resemblance thereto is not accomplished by the mere wish. Here also the fixing of insight is to be understood by the said

---

[1] *Majjhima* iii. 270 *f.*, esp. 277.

[2] Of once-returning, never-returning, Arahantship

method. To the Elder Tipiṭaka-Cūḷanāga,[1] holder of the doctrine [that the basic jhāna alone fixes it], his pupils said, 'Reverend sir, let the basic jhāna, where it is present, fix it [as you say]. But where it is absent—that is, in the immaterial existence—what fixes it?' 'There also the basic jhāna fixes it, my friends. For the bhikkhu who has attained the eight attainments makes a basis of the First Jhāna, produces the Path and Fruition of Stream-winning, does not fall away from the jhāna, and when his hour comes is reborn in the immaterial worlds. Emerging from the attainment of the Fruition of Stream-winning of the First Jhāna, he establishes insight and produces the upper three Paths and Fruitions. These are only of the First Jhāna; the same is true for the Paths and Fruitions of the Second Jhāna, etc. [230] In the immaterial consciousness[2] there arise the threefold, fourfold Jhānas, which are transcendental, not worldly. So, my friends, there also the basic jhāna fixes it.' 'Reverend sir, the question has been well explained.'

The Elder Mahādatta, resident at Moravāpi, held the doctrine that aggregates, which are the objects of insight, fix it, in that the Path, which emerges after contemplating any aggregate, resembles that aggregate. His pupils said to him: 'Reverend sir, in your doctrine a flaw appears. According to it the bhikkhu who has emerged after contemplating matter, would have a Path resembling matter and undeclared.[3] He who has transcended, after comprehending rightly the sphere of neither perception nor non-perception, would have a Path resembling that, and have attained to the state of that sphere.' 'Friends, it is not so; for the transcendental Path is never known not to attain ecstasy. Hence one who has transcended, after contemplating, matter has a Path of eight factors accom-

---

[1] This name means 'Little-wonderman knowing by heart the Three Piṭakas.' See below, p. 354. The name may have served to distinguish him from the Cūḷanāga, who accompanied Mahinda to Ceylon. *Sāmantapāsādikā*, p. 313.—*Ed.*

[2] *I.e.*, consciousness such as he would have in the Arūpa worlds. —*Ed.*

[3] *Avyākata*. *I.e.*, unmoral.

panied by joy; he who also has transcended, after contemplating, the sphere of neither perception nor non-perception has no Path resembling that sphere in every respect, but has a Path of seven factors accompanied by indifference.'

[Students] quoted the doctrine of the Elder Tipiṭaka-Cūḷābhaya, that personal inclination fixed it, and told it to the Elder Tipiṭaka-Cūḷanāga. He replied: 'Whoso has the basic jhāna can let personal inclination fix it for him; but whoso has it not, what inclination can avail to fix it for him? It would be like one who looks for interest when he has no capital.'[1] They told that utterance to the Elder Tipiṭaka-Cūḷābhaya, who replied: 'Friends, that doctrine of mine that the personal inclination fixes it, was said with reference to one possessed of the basic jhāna.' As it has been understood with reference to one possessed of the basic jhāna, so should it be understood with reference to one possessed of the contemplated jhāna. For the path produced in him who, emerging from the Fifth Jhāna, is contemplating the First Jhāna, etc., becomes, in the doctrine of the first Elder, of the First Jhāna, and of the First Jhāna and the rest in the doctrine of the second Elder. Thus the two doctrines oppose each other. In the third doctrine it becomes of whatever jhāna among the Jhānas is desired; thus those two doctrines do not clash with this, and the inclination is beneficial. The three Elders, then, were clever, experienced, and full of intelligence. [231] On that account the teachers have made a text of their doctrines. In this commentary just the meaning in point has been brought out, and it has been shown that only insight fixes the three doctrines.

Now as regards

The sign, the progress, the chief influence,

at the time of the production of the Path, since there is 'a change of factors,' whence does adoption[2] rise, and whence the Path? Adoption emerges from the sign (*i.e.*, the object

---

[1] For *Nibbānassa* read *niddhanassa* . . . (P.T.S. ed.)—*Ed.*

[2] *Gotrabhu*, or 'becoming kin'—namely, to the spiritual consciousness of Buddhas and their elect followers, the moment preceding Jhāna-ecstasy. Cf. *Compendium*, p. 215.—*Tr.*

of insight), and is not able to cut off the process (of states in the round of re-births); for it emerges from one side. The Path emerges from the sign, and cuts off the process; for it emerges from both sides. This is the manner of their production:—On whatever occasion there is emergence of the Path, on that occasion the adaptation[1] is not once, nor for the fifth time. For adaptation at the first occurrence does not get the causal relation called 'repetition.' At the fifth time, owing to its nearness to the life-continuum, it trembles,[2] for at the fifth time the apperception is known to have fallen (in strength).[3] Hence it is neither at the first nor the fifth time. But to one of great understanding there are two adaptations, thirdly, adoption, fourthly, Path-consciousness, [then] three fruitional consciousnesses, after which comes the lapse into the (subconscious) life-continuum. To one of medium understanding there are three adaptations, [then] (4) adoption, (5) path-consciousness, [then] two fruitional [movements of] consciousness, after which is the lapse into the life-continuum. To one of inferior understanding there are four adaptations, then (5) adoption, then (6) Path-consciousness, then (7) fruitional consciousness, after which is the lapse into the life-continuum. Of these three persons (the emergence of the Path) ought to be said concerning the person of medium understanding and not concerning persons of great, or of inferior understanding. For on whatever occasion there is emergence of the path, on that occasion the element of mind-consciousness, inoperative, unconditional and accompanied by indifference, becomes 'adverting' of the mind-door, and makes the aggregates of the field of insight its object, setting the life-continuum in motion. Taking the aggregates taken by that adverting, there immediately arises the first insight of adaptation with apperception. This occurs among those aggregates as impermanent, ill or soulless, [232] dispels the gross darkness covering the Four Truths and ceases, revealing the

---

[1] *Anuloma*, the stage preceding 'adoption.'

[2] And so is unable to be the cause of 'adoption.'—*Ṭīkā*.

[3] Just as a man's strength fails in old age.

more clearly the three characteristics. Immediately afterwards arises the second adaptation. Of these two, the first is devoid of the causal relation of repetition, and renders service to the second, which is sharp, valiant, clear, and which, occurring even in that object (of the field of insight) in that manner (*i.e.*, of being impermanent, ill, soulless), dispels the darkness of medium density covering the Four Truths and revealing all the more clearly the three characteristics, ceases. Immediately afterwards arises the third adaptation, to which the second renders service. From its acquirement of the causal relation of repetition, it is sharp, valiant, clear, occurs in that object in that manner, completely dispels the residuum of darkness of slight density covering the Four Truths, reveals all the more clearly the three characteristics and ceases. So when, by the three adaptations the darkness covering the Truths is dispelled, there immediately arises the insight of adoption making Nibbāna its object.[1]

Here is an illustration: They say a certain man who had eyes to see, went forth at night saying, 'I will observe the conjunction of the stars,' and looked up to see the moon, which from being covered by clouds did not appear to him. Then a wind came and dispersed the densest clouds, another wind the lighter clouds and a third wind the thinnest of the clouds; so that he saw the moon in the sky clear of clouds and observed the conjunction of the stars. Herein, the darkness of our lower nature, dense, thick, medium, thin, covering the Truths, is like the three clouds; the three kinds of adaptation-consciousness are like the three winds; the insight of adoption is like the seeing man; Nibbāna is like the moon; the dispelling of the darkness covering the Truths by each adaptation-consciousness is like the dispersing of the three clouds one by one by the winds; [233] the making of pure Nibbāna the object of the insight of adoption when the darkness covering the facts disperses is like the seeing by the man of the pure moon in the sky clear of clouds. As the three winds are able only to disperse the clouds covering the moon and not to see the

---

[1] *Compendium, loc. cit.*

moon, so the adaptations are able only to dispel the darkness covering the Truths, and not to make Nibbāna the object. As the man is able to see the moon, but not to disperse the clouds, so the insight of adoption is able to make Nibbāna the object, but not to dispel the darkness of our lower nature. Thus adaptation has conditioned things for its object and adoption has Nibbāna for its object.

For were adoption to take the object taken by adaptation, a subsequent adaptation would follow it;[1] and so there would not be just the rise of the Path. But the insight of adoption, not taking the object of adaptation, does not allow the reproduction of adaptation. And although it itself is not adverting, it stands at the place of the adverting consciousness and, as though giving a sign to the Path, 'Arise thus!' ceases. And the Path, not letting go the sign given, follows it without a break, and arises piercing and bursting the mass of greed, hate and delusion never before pierced and burst.

Here is an illustration: They say an archer had a hundred planks placed at a height of one hundred bowlengths, and wrapping his face with a cloth fixed an arrow and stood in a car. Another man rolled the car, and when the planks came facing the archer, made a sign with a stick. The archer, not letting go the sign of the stick, shot the arrow and pierced the planks. Herein the insight of adoption is like the sign of the stick; the insight of the Path is like the archer; The making Nibbāna the object and the piercing and bursting of the mass of greed, hate and delusion, never before pierced and burst, by the insight of the Path at the sign given by the insight of adoption, is like the archer's piercing the planks by not letting go the sign of the stick.[2]

[234] This bursting of the mass of greed, etc., is also called the complete destruction of the causeway, the extirpation of the ground that had been got. Indeed, the Path has only one function:—to reject latent evil tendencies.[3] In rejecting

---

[1] Namely, by our lower nature for rebirth. 'Adoption' (gotrabhū) will have become 'adaptation' (anuloma).—*Tr.*

[2] *Vis. Magga*, p. 674.

[3] The seven anusaya's. *Compendium*, p. 176.—*Tr.*

latent tendencies one is said to emerge from the (five aggregates as) sign and to cut off their proceeding. The sign is the sign of matter, feeling, perception, mental co-efficients, consciousness; the process is the continual round of these five aggregates and is twofold: grasped at, not grasped at. Of these two, the teachers, saying that the shadow of the emergence of the path from the process not grasped at was seen, affirmed that it emerged from such an occurrence.

By the path of stream-winning five kinds of consciousness—four associated with false views and one accompanied by doubt—are put away. These five kinds of consciousness produce matter, which is called the material aggregate not grasped at, they themselves being called the conscious aggregate; feeling, perception, and mental co-efficients associated with them are called the three immaterial aggregates. Concerning these, if the path of stream-winning were not cultivated by the stream-winner, these five kinds of consciousness would break out among the six objects of sense. But the path of stream-winning preventing this, and destroying the causeway so that it cannot arise again, is said to emerge from the 'not grasped at.'

By the path of Once-returning six kinds of consciousness, four dissociated from false views, two accompanied by grief—namely, gross sense-desire and ill-will—are put away. By the path of Never-returning the same six kinds—namely, subtler sense-desire and ill-will—are put away. By the path of Arahantship, five kinds of immoral consciousness—four dissociated from views and one accompanied by distraction—are put away. In this, if those three paths were not cultivated by Ariyans, these kinds of immoral consciousness would break out among the six objects of sense. But the three paths preventing this, and destroying the causeway so that it cannot emerge again, were said to emerge from the 'not grasped at.'

The teachers also said, that when the shadow of the emerging from the process grasped at was seen, [235] it emerged from such process. For if the stream-winner were not to cultivate the path of stream-winning, the process of the aggregates grasped at would go on in the continual stream of becoming the beginning whereof is unknown prior to seven rebirths. *And why? Because of the existence of the conditions of the process. But in point of fact the path of stream-winning arising severs these five corruptions—three fetters, latent bias of wrong view, latent bias of doubt. Now (that the path of stream-winning has arisen), whence for the stream-winner could the process of the aggregates grasped at go on in that continual stream of becoming the beginning whereof is unknown prior to seven rebirths?* So the path of stream-winning bringing about the discontinuity of the aggregates grasped at is said to emerge from the 'grasped at.'

If the Once-returner were not to cultivate the path of Once-returning, the process of the 'grasped at' would go on in the five rebirths, after the next two. And why? Because of the existence of the conditions of the procedure. But in point of fact the path of Once-returning arising severs these four corruptions: gross fetters of sense-desires and of aversion, gross latent bias of sense-desires and gross latent bias of aversion. Now (that the path of Once-returning has risen), whence for the Once-returner could the process of the aggregates grasped at go on in five existences excepting two? So the path of Once-returning bringing about the discontinuity of the aggregates grasped at is said to emerge from the 'grasped at.'

If the Never-returner were not to cultivate the path of Never-returning, the process of the aggregates grasped at would go on in the second existence after the next. And why? Because of the existence of the conditions of the process. But in point of fact the path of Never-returning arising severs these four corruptions:—the subtle fetters of sense-desires and of aversion, the subtle latent bias of sense-desire, the subtle latent bias of aversion. Now (that the path of Never-returning has arisen), whence for the Never-returner could the process of the aggregates grasped at go on in the next rebirth save one? So the path of Never-returning bringing about the discontinuity of the aggregates grasped at is said to rise from that which is 'grasped at.'

If the Arahant were not to cultivate the path of Arahant-

— Omitted in P.T.S. ed.—*Ed.*

ship, the process of the aggregates grasped at would go on in material and immaterial existences. And why? Because of the existence of the conditions of the process. But in point of fact the path of Arahantship arising severs these eight corruptions:—lust of material existence, lust of immaterial existence, conceit, distraction, ignorance, the latent bias of conceit, the latent bias of lust of existence, the latent bias of ignorance. Now (that the path of Arahantship has arisen), whence for the Arahant could the process of the aggregates grasped at go on in a new existence? So the path of Arahantship [236] bringing about the discontinuity of the aggregates grasped at is said to emerge from the 'grasped at.' And of these the path of Stream-winning emerges from existence in purgatory, the Path of Once-returning emerges from one portion of the happy tendency of sensuous existence, the path of never-returning emerges from sensuous existence, the path of Arahantship emerges from material and immaterial existences, also from all existences. So say the teachers. And this is the text for the elucidation of this meaning (*i.e.*, of emergence from the process of the 'grasped at').

It is owing to the cessation of constructive consciousness[1] by the insight belonging to the Path of Stream-winning that whatever mind and matter may have arisen in the continual stream of becoming, the beginning whereof is unknown prior to seven rebirths, they cease, are suppressed, terminated, calmed in that Path. It is owing to the cessation of constructive consciousness by the insight belonging to the Path of Once-returning that whatever mind and matter may have arisen in the last five existences save two, they cease, are suppressed, terminated, calmed in that Path. It is owing to the cessation of constructive consciousness by the insight belonging to the Path of Never-returning that whatever mind and matter may have arisen in the two last existences save one, they cease, are suppressed, terminated, calmed in that Path. It is owing to the cessation of constructive consciousness by the insight

[1] Which gives result in purgatory and in happy tendencies beyond the seventh rebirth.—*Tr.*

belonging to the Path of Arahantship that whatever mind and matter may have arisen in the material or immaterial element, they cease, are suppressed, terminated, calmed in that Path. This is the text. But, together with the cessation of the last consciousness of the Arahant who has entered on the utter passing away without leaving any residue of life, understanding, mindfulness, mind and matter cease, are suppressed, terminated, calmed. So far is the decision regarding the sign.

As regards 'the progress, the chief influence,' does the progress waver or not ? It wavers. To expand: the four paths for the Tathāgata and Sāriputta the Elder were of easy progress and quick intuition. The first path of Mahāmoggallāna the Elder was of easy progress and quick intuition, the upper three paths were of painful progress but quick intuition. And why ? From oppression by drowsiness. They say that the supreme Buddha looked after the Elder, as though he were a child, for seven days; and one day the Elder sat dosing. Then the teacher said, 'Moggallāna, Moggallāna, are you sleepy with heavy eyelids, brahmin ?' The progress of a disciple who had attained to such superknowledge wavered. [237] Will not, then, the progress of others waver ? Verily, of one bhikkhu, the four paths are of painful progress and sluggish intuition, of another are of painful progress and quick intuition, of another they are of easy progress and sluggish intuition, of another, of easy progress and quick intuition. Of some one the first path is of painful progress and sluggish intuition, the second path is of painful progress and quick intuition, the third path is of easy progress and sluggish intuition, the fourth path is of easy progress and quick intuition. And the dominant influence wavers like the progress. For, of one bhikkhu the four paths are dominated by desire-to-do, of another by energy, of another by consciousness, of another by investigation. And of one the first path is dominated by desire-to-do, the second by energy, the third by consciousness, the fourth by investigation.[1]

---

[1] The text here has *Pakiṇṇakakathā niṭṭhitā* (end of the discourse on particulars), but it is not obvious where this discourse begins.

Now[1] because, in cultivating the transcendental moral consciousness [the student] cultivates not merely the Jhāna, in the sense of closely examining the object, but also the path in the sense of escape from the round of rebirths, the application in mindfulness in the sense of having the mental object present, the supreme efforts in the sense of making effort, the bases of supernormal potency in the sense of accomplishing, the controlling faculty in the sense of dominant influence, the strength in the sense of not shaking, the factor of wisdom in the sense of being enlightened, the fact in the sense of being true, the calm in the sense of non-distraction, the idea in the sense of emptiness, the aggregate in the sense of a group, the sense-organ in the sense of exerting, the element in the sense of emptiness, intrinsic nature, and absence of a living entity, the nutriment in the sense of causal relation, the contact in the sense of touching, the feeling in the sense of experiencing, the perception in the sense of noting, the volition in the sense of co-ordinating, the consciousness in the sense of cognizing, therefore, in order to explain these nineteen terms, a beginning is once more made with, 'which are the states that are moral?'[2] So with the meaning: 'he cultivates this also, he cultivates that also,' twenty methods have been shown by way of personal inclination and of adorning the discourse. To expand: In the company of devas seated to listen to the Law, [238] whichever devas know in the course of the preaching the spiritual in the sense of closely examining the object, to them in a fitting manner it has been preached as Jhāna . . . those devas who know, in the course of the preaching, consciousness in the sense of cognizing, to them in a fitting manner it has been preached as consciousness. This is personal inclination.

Furthermore, the supreme Buddha, on account of his true enlightenment and because of his ten powers, four grounds of confidence, four analyses, six kinds of special knowledge, can fix and preach the discourse as he wishes. If he so desires,

---

[1] Some read vibhāv-ento, -eti, for bhāv-ento, -eti, thus altering the meaning into 'Now because, in explaining transcendental moral consciousness, the teacher explained,' etc.—*Tr.*

[2] *Dhs.* § 358.

he can preach it as the transcendental Jhāna in the sense of closely examining the object, as the transcendental Path in the sense of escape . . . as the transcendental consciousness in the sense of cognizing. Of them, as where the transcendental Jhāna is described, ten methods have been classified, so with the Path, etc. Thus in twenty places two hundred methods have been classified.

Now, in order to show the classification of the dominant influence once more a beginning is made with ‘which are the states that are moral ?’[1] wherein the transcendental Jhāna produced by making desire-to-act the principal, the chief, the forerunner is known as dominated by desire-to-act. And the same with the rest. Thus in the preceding formulated method there are two hundred methods, and there are two hundred each in those dominated by desire-to-act, etc. Thus the king of the Law has shown the First Path in classifying it by a thousand methods.

End of the First Path.

CHAPTER II

THE SEÇOND PATH

Now, in order to show the Second Path, and so on, again a beginning is made with ‘which are the states that are moral ?’[2] Herein ‘for the diminution of sense-desire and ill-will’ means in order to diminish the strength of these corruptions. Here the diminution should be understood to take place in two ways: by occasional production and by feebleness in breaking out. For to the Once-returner the lower nature does not arise frequently as in the majority who follow the round of rebirths. It arises occasionally like the sparse blades of grass in an imperfectly mown field. And when it does arise it does not arise crushing, spreading, covering, [239] making darkness, as in the case of the people who follow the round of rebirths.

[1] *Dhs.* §§ 359-64.

[2] *Ib.* § 362.

But being put away by the two Paths, it becomes very weak and is attenuated in form like a film of cloud and a fly's wing. Some Elders say on this point, 'to the Once-returner the lower nature arises thick and strong, although it may only arise after a long interval. For verily, he has sons and daughters.' This saying is not material. For sons and daughters are due to the mere exercise of bodily functions. But the lower nature, being put away by the two paths, lacks strength. Hence the diminution of the Once-returner's lower nature should be understood as due to the two reasons of occasional production and feebleness of power. 'Of the second' is second by way of calculation and of the second production. 'For the attainment of the stage' means for the purpose of getting the fruition of religious life. And so for the Third and the Fourth Paths. We shall speak only of what is specially distinctive. 'The controlling faculty of perfected knowledge' is the knowing controlling faculty, said to be that controlling faculty which knows, without passing beyond the limit of knowledge made by the first Path, the four facts known by that Path.

In the section of the exposition also its meaning is to be understood in the same way. In the section of the groups also, together with it are nine controlling faculties. The rest is to be understood by the previous method.

CHAPTER III

THE THIRD AND FOURTH PATHS

In the Third Path[1] 'for the complete putting away' means for the purpose of entirely putting away those 'Fetters' which have been diminished by the path of Once-returning.

In the Fourth Path[2] 'for the complete putting away of lust for the material, for the immaterial, conceit, distraction, ignorance' means for the purpose of entirely putting away these five upper 'Fetters.' Of these, lust for the material is

---

[1] *Dhs.* § 363. [2] *Ib.* § 364.

lust and desire for material existence. Lust for the immaterial means lust and desire for immaterial existence. Conceit is that which is killed by the Path of Arahantship. [240] So are distraction and ignorance. In these two Paths also the ninth controlling faculty is perfected knowledge.[1]

In all the paths, by the due order of terms, there are altogether sixty terms. With the four absolute factors they make sixty-four. Undivided they are thirty-three. The sections of the groups and 'Emptiness' remain the same. And there are one thousand methods in each of these in the second Path, etc., as in the first. Thus the king of the Law has shown the four Paths classifying them by four thousand methods.

In the *Saccavibhaṅga*[2] transcendental points of sixty thousand methods have been set down by way of these four Paths (or these one thousand methods), so also there have been set down similar points of twenty thousand methods in the *Satipaṭṭhāna Vibhaṅga*, of twenty thousand methods in the *Sammappadhāna Vibhaṅga*, of thirty-two thousand methods in the *Iddhippāda Vibhaṅga*, of thirty-two thousand methods in the *Bojjhaṅga Vibhaṅga*, or twenty-eight thousand methods in the *Maggavibhaṅga*. But in the *Dhammasaṅgaṇī* four thousand methods in the four Paths have been set down. Out of the four paths in the first Path of the first Jhāna eight factors have been classified. Likewise in the second, etc.

In the first Path right view abandons wrong view; hence it, with right intention, etc., should be understood in the sense of abandoning the opposite. This being so, because the sixty-two heresies[3] have been abandoned by the first Path, there would be no heresy to be abandoned by the three higher Paths. How, then, can right view be mentioned in them ?[4] As whether there is poison or not, an antidote is called antidote, so whether there is wrong view or not, right view is called right view. If this were so, right view would be a mere

---

[1] *B.P.E.* § 364*a*. Cf. *Iti-vuttaka*, p. 53.

[2] *Vibhanga*, ch. iv., vii.-xi. [3] Described in *Dialogues*, i. 27-55.

[4] Reading *kathaṃ* for *kataṃ*.

name and have no function in the three higher Paths, and the path-factors would not be fulfilled; hence it is proper that right view be made to have its function and the path-factors be fulfilled. But in the three higher Paths right view should be shown to have its function by fixing according to what is obtainable. To expand: There is a certain conceit to be killed by the three higher Paths. It has its locus in heresy. Right view abandons that conceit. Hence it is right view. For in the path of Stream-winning right view abandons wrong view. Moreover, the Stream-winner has a conceit which is to be killed by the path of Once-returning, and which has its locus in heresy. Right view abandons that conceit. Hence it is right view. Only the Stream-winner has an intention which is co-existent with seven [of the twelve] kinds of immoral consciousness,[1] by which there take place movements of the vocal organs, of the physical limbs, enjoyment of the requisites, [241] the co-existent[2] endeavour, the intrinsic nature of unmindfulness, the co-existent[2] one-pointedness of mind. These states [beginning with intention] are called wrong intention, etc. In the Path of Once-returning right intention, etc., are so called by the putting away of those states, wrong intention, etc. So, in the Path of Once-returning, the eight factors of the Path come by performing their own functions.

The Once-returner has a conceit which has to be killed by the path of Never-returning, and which has its locus in heresy. Only to the Once-returner intention, etc., as co-existent with seven kinds of immoral consciousness [are known as wrong intention, etc.]. By the putting away of these the performance of their own functions by the eight factors in the path of Never-returning should be understood.

The Never-returner has a conceit which has to be killed by the path of Arahantship and which has its locus in heresy. But intention, etc., co-existent with five kinds of immoral consciousness,[3] which only the Never-returner has, are known

---

[1] Read: satta akusala . . . Namely, four kinds dissociated from false views, two rooted in hate, and one connected with distraction.—*Tr.*

[2] Co-existent with those seven kinds.—*Pyī.*

[3] Namely, four dissociated from false views and distraction.—*Pyī.*

as wrong intention, etc. By the putting away of these wrong states, the performance of their own functions by the eight factors in the path of Arahantship should be understood.

The first out of the four Paths discerns the Four Truths, which are also discerned by the three higher Paths. The latter do not discern anything not discerned by the first. This discourse is one generally accepted among the teachers. But the sectary[1] says, that in them one does see what has not been discerned by the first Path. He should be asked, 'Which controlling faculty in the first Path do you single out [as functioning herein]?' If he knows, he will reply, 'The controlling faculty of believing, "I shall come to know the unknown."'[2] And when he is asked, 'Which controlling faculty in the three higher Paths will you classify?' he will reply, 'The controlling faculty of perfected knowledge.'[3] He should be told, 'If one sees something which has not been discerned by the first Path, you must classify the controlling faculty of believing, "I shall come to know the unknown" [which is peculiar to the First Path], under the three higher Paths also, so that it may meet the question.' He would again ask, 'Does another path put away other corruptions, or those already put away?' When he is told, 'Another path puts away other corruptions,' he says further, 'If another path puts away other corruptions not yet put away, then one also [by it] sees Truths unseen by the first Path.' He should be asked, 'How many Truths are there?' If he knows, he will answer, 'Four.' He should be told, 'In your doctrine sixteen "truths" would arise. You see truths unseen even by the Buddhas. You are a seer of many "truths." Do not take such a view. There is nothing new in seeing the Truths. But one puts away corruptions not yet put away.'

[242] In this matter of nothing being new in seeing the Truths, the simile of the basket has been taken:—They say that a certain man kept four treasure-baskets in a grand treasure-room. At night some business in connection with them arising, he opened the door, lit a lamp and, when the darkness

---

[1] Vitaṇḍavādins. Cf. *Dialogues* i. 14, *n.* 3; 167 *f; and above*, 5, *n.* 3.

[2] *Dhs.* § 296. *Above*, p. 295.

[3] See *above*, p. 320.

was dispersed by the lamp and the baskets were visible, he did the business, shut the door and went away, and darkness was spread abroad again. A second time and a third time he did likewise. When, for the fourth time, the door was opened and he was looking to find the baskets invisible in the darkness, behold ! the sun arose. When through the brightness of the sun the darkness disappeared, he did his business with the baskets and went away. In this simile the four baskets are like the four Truths; the time of the opening of the door for some business with them is like the time of the putting forth of insight for the Path of Stream-winning; the darkness is like the obscurity covering the Truths; the light of the lamp is the light of the Path of Stream-winning; the manifestation of the baskets to the men on the disappearance of the darkness is like the manifestation of the Truths to the insight of the Path. And the Truths manifested to the insight of the Path are manifested to the person endowed with the Path. The time of his going away after doing his business with the baskets is like the time of cessation of the Path of Stream-winning after it has done its part in putting away corruptions. The spreading of darkness again is like the obscurity yet covering the Truths and to be killed by the three higher Paths. On the second occasion the time of the opening of the door is like the time of putting forth insight of the Path of Once-returning; the light of the lamp is like that of the Path of Once-returning; the time of departure after doing the business of the baskets is like the time of cessation of the Path of Once-returning after it has done its part in putting away the corruptions; the spreading of darkness again is like the obscurity still covering the Truths and to be killed by the two higher Paths. On the third occasion the time of opening the door is like the time of putting forth insight of the Path of Never-returning; the light of the lamp is like that of the Path of Never-returning; the time of departure after doing the business of the baskets is like the time of cessation of the Path of Never-returning after it has done its part in putting away the corruptions; the spreading of darkness again is like the obscurity covering the Truths and

to be killed by the higher Path of Arahantship. On the fourth occasion the time of opening the door is like the time of putting forth the insight of the Path of Arahantship; the rising of the sun is like the production of the Path of Arahantship; the disappearance of darkness is like the dispelling of the obscurity covering the Truths by the Path of Arahantship; [243] the manifestation of the baskets to the man at the disappearance of darkness is like the manifestation of the Four Truths to the insight of the Path of Arahantship; and the Truths manifested to the insight are manifested to the person; the time of departure after the business with the baskets is like the casting off of all the corruptions by the Path of Arahantship; the time of the occurrence of light since sunrise is like the non-obscurity of the darkness covering the Truths since the production of the Path of Arahantship. So far the simile shows that nothing new is added after the Truths are seen. For the three higher Paths discern in them *only* what has been discerned (by the first Path).

As regards 'another Path puts away other corruptions,' the simile of the soap has been taken:—A certain man gave dirty clothes to the washerman, who applied the three kinds of soap consisting of saline soil, potash and dung powder. When he had ascertained that these alkalines were dissolved, he washed the clothes in the water and removed the grossest dirt. Then knowing them to be not yet altogether cleansed, he applied the three soaps a second time, washed them in the water and removed the finer dirt. Then knowing them to be still not altogether clean, he applied the soaps for the third time, washed them in the water and removed the finest dirt. Then knowing them to be not yet altogether cleansed, he applied the soaps for the fourth time, washed them in the water, removed all the dirt from within their texture, and returned them to the owner, who put them in a scented chest and wore them at will. Here the dirty clothes are like the mind following after the corruptions; the time of applying the three kinds of soap is like the time of producing work in the threefold discernment; the removal of the grossest dirt after the washing is the casting off of five corruptions by the Path of Stream-winning. The re-application of the soaps for the second time is the procedure of work in the threefold discernment which knows the mind to be not yet altogether cleansed; the removal of the finer dirt than in the first case is like the casting off of the pair of gross 'Fetters' by the path of Once-returning; the re-application of the three soaps when it is known that the clothes are not yet [244] altogether cleansed, is like the procedure of work in the threefold discernment which knows the mind to be not yet altogether cleansed; the removal of the still finer dirt is like the casting off of the pair of subtle 'Fetters' by the Path of Never-returning. The re-application of the soaps when it is known that the clothes are not yet altogether cleansed is like the procedure of work in the threefold discernment which knows that the mind is not yet altogether cleansed; the removal of dirt from within the texture by a subsequent washing is like the casting off of the eight corruptions by the Path of Arahantship; the wearing at any desired moment of the clean clothes resembling silver plates and kept in a scented chest, is the living at any desired moment of the life of fruitional attainment by the cleansed mind purged of the 'intoxicants.' Thus runs the simile. 'Friends, as the garment is old and dirty, and the owners gave it to the washerman, who kneaded and soaked it in the three kinds of soap: consisting of saline earth, potash and dung powder, and washed it in clean water; although it became clean, exceedingly clean, a very subtle smell of salt earth, or potash, or dung powder remained unremoved in it; the washerman returned it to the owner, who kept it in a chest perfumed with scent; and the subtle residuum of the smell of salt earth, or potash, or dung powder was completely removed—so, friends, although the Ariyan disciple has put away the five lower "Fetters," there is in him a subtle residuum from among the five grasping aggregates of the conceit of "I am," of the desire[1] for "I am," of the latent bias of "I am."'[2] Subsequently he lives in the discernment of the rise and fall of the

[1] According to the *Ṭīkā* 'desire' (*chando*) here = craving (*taṇhā*), and the latent bias is in the form of craving and of conceit.

[2] *Saṃyutta* iii. 131.

five grasping aggregates. And to him who so lives discerning that 'these are material qualities,' 'this is the origin of them,' 'this is the end of them,' 'this is feeling' . . . 'this is perception' . . . 'these are mental co-efficients' . . . 'this is consciousness,' 'this is the origin of consciousness,' 'this is the end of consciousness,' that subtle residuum, which is his from among the five grasping aggregates of the conceit of 'I am,' of the craving for 'I am,' of the latent bias of craving and conceit of 'I am' is completely removed. [245] Of the four Paths the Path of Stream-winning has put away, by way of factors of consciousness, five immoral kinds of consciousness, together with the evil states arising; the Path of Once-returning has diminished, by way of factors of consciousness, two classes of consciousness accompanied by grief, together with the evil states arising; the Path of Never-returning has put away the same two kinds of consciousness together with the associated states; the Path of Arahantship has put away, by way of factors of consciousness, five kinds of immoral consciousness together with the evil states arising. From the time when these two kinds of immoral consciousness are put away there is no such thing as a corruption which may arise again in the Arahant by way of a factor of consciousness.

Here is an illustration:—They say a great king placed guards at the frontier country and lived at the capital in the enjoyment of kingship. Then the frontier country rose in rebellion. At that time a dozen robber chiefs together with many thousands of men plundered the kingdom. Officials from the frontier country sent word to the king:—'Your Majesty, the frontier country has risen.' The king sent back a message, 'Catch the robbers without hesitating. I will reward your work.' At the first engagement the official forces killed five robber-chiefs together with many thousands of men. The remaining seven took each his own followers and entered the mountains. The officials informed the king of the occurrence. The king sent them treasure, saying, 'I will reward your work; catch the robbers.' At the second engagement the ministers defeated two robber-chiefs and reduced the strength of their followers, who all fled and entered the mountains. The king was informed of that occurrence and again sent them treasure, saying, 'Catch them without delay!' At the third engagement the official forces killed the two chiefs together with their companions, and informed the king of the occurrence. Again the king sent them treasure, saying, 'Catch the remainder without delay.' At the fourth engagement the official forces killed the five chiefs with their followers. There was no one going by the name of a robber after the death of those twelve chiefs. The districts were secure from danger and the people lived dancing their children on their breast so to speak. And the king surrounded by the victorious heroes [246] enjoyed great glory in a magnificent palace. Here the great king is like the King of the Law; the officials living in the frontier country are like the religious aspirants; the twelve robber-chiefs are like the twelve kinds of immoral consciousness;[1] their many thousands of companions are like the evil states arising by way of the factors of consciousness; the time of information of the revolt of the frontier country is like the time of telling the teacher when the corruptions arise with reference to an object:—'Reverend sir, in me corruptions have arisen'; the giving of treasure with the message, 'Catch the thieves without delay!' is like the announcement of a station of religious exercise by the King of the Law: 'Bhikkhu, put down the corruptions'; the time of killing the five robber-chiefs with their followers is like putting away the five kinds of immoral consciousness with their associates by the Path of Stream-winning; the renewed reporting of procedure to the king is like telling the supreme Buddha the merits acquired; the giving again of treasure, saying, 'Catch the rest,' is like the announcement of the insight of the Path of Once-returning by the Blessed One; the reduction of the strength of the two robber-chiefs with their followers at the second engagement is like the diminution of the two kinds of consciousness of melancholy with their associates by the Path of Once-returning; the renewed reporting of procedure to the king is like telling the Teacher the merits acquired; the

---

[1] See *below*, Part IX.

giving again of treasure, saying, 'Catch the thieves without delay,' is like the announcement of the insight of the Path of Never-returning by the Blessed One; the killing of the two robber-chiefs with their followers at the third engagement is like putting away the two kinds of consciousness with their associates by the Path of Never-returning; the renewed reporting of procedure to the king is like telling the Tathāgata the merits acquired; the giving again of treasure, saying, 'Catch them without delay,' is like the announcement of the insight of the Path of Arahantship by the Blessed One; the time of security of the district after the destruction of the five robber-chiefs with their followers at the fourth engagement is like the impossibility of an immoral state arising again by way of a factor of consciousness after the putting away of the twelve kinds of immoral consciousness, when the remaining five kinds of immoral consciousness with their associates are put away by the Path of Arahantship; the enjoyment of great glory in a magnificent palace by the king surrounded by the victorious heroes is like [247] the enjoyment of the bliss of whichever of the three kinds of fruitional attainment he prefers —the 'Emptiness,' the 'Signless,' the 'Undesired'—by the King of the Law surrounded by the Arahants.

Here ends the Exposition of the term 'moral consciousness.'

PART IX—DISCOURSE ON IMMORAL CONSCIOUSNESS

CHAPTER I

DISCOURSE ON THE SECTION OF THE SUMMARY OF STATES

Now in order to show the classification of the term 'immoral state' a beginning has been made with, 'Which are the states that are immoral?'[1] Herein the different sections of the determination of states, etc., and the decision of the meanings of terms already mentioned above are to be understood in the way given above. And we shall explain just what is special here and there to this discourse.

Herein, in the determination of the occasion, because there is no series of planes of the immoral as there is of the moral, therefore this immoral consciousness, though it certainly is of the realm of sense, is not said to be so.[2] As regards the phrase 'associated with opinions,' *diṭṭhi* (opinions) is the same as *diṭṭhi-gataṁ*, like *gūthagataṃ*, *muttagataṃ*, etc. Or, from there being no species to be understood, it is simply 'opinions,' and *diṭṭhigatasampayuttaṃ* means simply associated with opinions (or views). The origin of this wrong view called *diṭṭhi-gata* should be known to be due to these reasons:—the hearing of evil doctrine, evil friendship, the desire not to see Ariyans, unsystematic thought; in other words: of those doctrines which are associated with erroneous views, such hearing being preceded by much vain imagining, by a want of centrality of mind and a lack of scrutiny; evil friendship said to be the companionship with evil friends who have failed in the true doctrine; the desire not to see Ariyans such as the Buddhas and good men; unskilfulness in the Ariyan Law of different

[1] *Dhs.* § 365. [2] Following the M. reading in P.T.S. ed.—*Ed.*

kinds, such as the four applications of mindfulness, etc.; the absence of discipline or the destruction of restraint with respect to the Ariyan Law (divided into the restraint taught in the Pātimokkha, the controlling faculties, mindfulness, knowledge, elimination) and the doctrine of good men; and addiction to tumultuous festivities by means of unsystematic thought developed by the foregoing reasons. That this consciousness is automatic should be considered in the way mentioned above.[1]

[248] In the section of the summary of states,[2] 'contact' is co-existent with an immoral consciousness. And the same with 'feeling,' etc. Thus their being immoral is what alone distinguishes them from the former states.

The 'one-pointedness of mind' is the steadiness of mind free from distraction when taking life, etc. Indeed, men concentrating the mind are not distracted and let fall unerring weapons on the bodies of creatures. Being well concentrated they steal others' property. With mind [governed by] a single function they fall into wrong behaviour. So there is one-pointedness of mind in the occurrence of immorality.

'Wrong view' is untrue view; or, from being held amiss, a false view is a wrong view. A view loathed by the wise as bringing disadvantage is also a wrong view. And the same with 'wrong intention,' etc. Further, by it associated states see wrongly, or itself sees wrongly; or it is the mere act of wrong seeing—thus it is wrong view. It has unwise conviction as characteristic; perversion as function; wrong conviction as manifestation; the desire not to see the Ariyans as proximate cause. It should be regarded as the highest fault. In 'wrong intention,' etc., only the term 'wrong' is distinctive. The remainder should be understood in the same way as under the head of moral consciousness.

As regards 'the strength called unconscientiousness, strength called fearlessness of blame,' the meaning of 'strength' will be made plain in the section of the exposition. And in the others, 'unconscientious' means that it is not modest, or does not abominate; the state of immodesty or of not abominating is

[1] Pp. 207; also 102; 215.

[2] *Dhs.* § 365.

unconscientiousness. No fear of blame is fearlessness of blame. Of them unconscientiousness has the characteristic of not abominating misconduct of the body, etc., or of absence of shame. Fearlessness of blame has the characteristic of not being diffident on account of misconduct oi the body, etc., or of absence of confusion. Unconscientiousness as a strength is strength of unconscientiousness. Recklessness of blame as a strength is strength of recklessness of blame. This is the meaning in abstract. The detailed account is to be understood as opposed to what has been said above.[1]

By it associated states lust, or itself lusts, or the mere act of lusting—[249] such is 'greed' (or lust). By it associated states are deluded, or itself is deluded, or just the being deluded —this is 'delusion.' Of them, greed has the characteristic of grasping the object like sticky lime; the function of clinging like a piece of flesh thrown into a hot pan; the manifestation of not letting go like a taint of lampblack; the proximate cause of viewing the fetter-like states as enjoyment. Growing into a river of craving, it takes away beings to purgatory as a river of swift current carries any object fallen into it to the great ocean. Thus it should be regarded.

'Delusion' has the characteristic of blindness or opposition to knowledge; the essence of non-penetration, or the function of covering the intrinsic nature of the object; the manifestation of being opposed to right conduct or causing blindness; the proximate cause of unwise attention; and should be regarded as the root of all immoralities.

By it they covet, or itself covets, or the mere coveting—this is 'covetousness.' It has the characteristic of a desire to make others' prosperity one's own; the function of seeking with such desire; the manifestation of gazing at others' prosperity; the proximate cause of a great fancy for others' prosperity. Indeed, it appears only as gazing at the prosperity of others, and arises when there is a great fancy for the same. It should be regarded as the outstretched hand of the mind for others' prosperity.

---

[1] Cf. p. 198.

In 'there is calm,' etc., calm is due to the suppression of distraction in other objects. It lifts or supports the mind in the occurrence of immorality—this is 'support.' 'Non-distraction' means it is not distracted.

In this consciousness faith, mindfulness, wisdom and the six pairs have not been taken. And why? There is no faith in an unbelieving mind, therefore that has not been taken. What! Do men of false opinions not believe in their own teachers? They do. But that is not faith; it is a mere acquiescence in words; in the real sense it is either indiscrimination (that is, delusion) [250] or opinion. And there is no mindfulness in a mind unguarded by mindfulness, therefore that has not been taken. What! Do men of false opinions not remember an act done by themselves? They do. But that is not mindfulness. The procedure of immoral consciousness is due to such mere mode of remembering. Therefore mindfulness has not been taken. Then why is it said, 'wrong mindfulness' in the Sutta?[1] In the Sutta the discourse is made by the explanatory method so as to complete the 'Wrong Path' and the notion 'wrongness,' because of the immoral aggregates being exempt from and opposed to mindfulness. But in the absolute method (of Abhidhamma) in immoral consciousness there is no mindfulness; therefore it has not been taken. And in the consciousness causing blindness and folly there is no wisdom, therefore that has not been taken. Is there no deceptive knowledge in men of false opinions? There is. But it is not knowledge; it is trickery (*māyā*), which in the real sense is craving. Moreover, this consciousness is connected with torment, slow, heavy, rough, stiff, unwieldy, unhealthy, bent and crooked. Hence faith and the six pairs [repose of mind and of mental factors] have not been taken.

Having by so many terms in due order shown the thirty-two terms established in the text as factors of consciousness, now to show the 'or-whatever' states, he said 'or-whatever states on that occasion.' Herein the meaning is to be understood

---

[1] *E.g.*, *Dīgha* iii. 254, 287, etc.; *Majjhima* i. 118, iii. 77, etc., etc.

thus:—in all immoral consciousness are ten states, to wit: desire-to-do, resolve, attention ,conceit, envy, meanness, sloth and torpor, flurry and worry, which come in the Sutta, appear in Sutta passages. These states are spoken of in the Commentary as 'or-whatever' states. But in this consciousness desire-to-do, resolve, attention and excitement—these four states called 'the unfailing factors' are the 'or-whatever,' of which the first three should be understood in the way given above. There they are moral; here immoral. Moreover, the other state is the state of the excited mind—hence excitement or flurry. It has mental excitement as characteristic like wind-tossed water; wavering as function, like a flag waving in the wind; whirling as manifestation like scattered ashes struck by a stone; unsystematic thought owing to mental excitement as proximate cause; and it should be regarded as mental distraction over an object of excitement. Thus there are in all thirty-six terms of states [251] in this section of the summary of states—thirty-two beginning with contact and the four 'or-whatevers.' Leaving out the four unfailing factors only thirty-two come in the text; but here by taking what has not been taken, the fivefold contact-group, initial application, sustained application, zest, one-pointedness of mind, controlling faculty of energy, controlling faculty of vitality, wrong views, strengths: unconscientiousness and fearlessness of blame, greed, delusion—thus there are sixteen states.

Of these sixteen states seven occur under a single category, nine occur under different categories. Which are the seven ?—contact, perception, volition, sustained application of mind, zest, life-controlling faculty, delusion—these seven states occur under a single category. Feeling, consciousness, initial application of mind, one-pointedness of mind, energy-controlling faculty, wrong view, strength of unconscientiousness, strength of fearlessness of blame and greed—these nine states occur under different categories. Of them, six states are referred to two categories, one to three, one to four, one to six categories. And how ? Consciousness, initial application of mind, wrong view, the 'strengths': unconscientiousness and fearlessness of blame, and greed—these six are referred to two categories. To expand:—First: consciousness by way of the fivefold contact-group is called consciousness; by way of the controlling faculties it is called controlling faculty of mind. Initial application of mind by way of jhāna-factors is called initial application of mind, by way of the Path-factors is called wrong intention. Wrong view is called so in the Path-factors and courses of action. The 'strength': unconscientiousness, is called so by way of the 'strengths,' and unconscientiousness by way of 'world-destroying pair.' And the same with fearlessness of blame also. Greed is called so by way of the pair of conditions, and covetousness by way of the course of action. Thus these six are referred to two categories. And feeling is called so by way of the fivefold contact-group, bliss by way of jhāna-factors, and the controlling faculty of joy by way of the controlling faculties—thus one state is referred to three categories. And energy is called the controlling faculty of energy by way of the controlling faculties, wrong endeavour by way of the Path-factors, 'strength' of energy by way of the 'strengths,' and support by way of the Final Pairs[1]—thus one state is referred to four categories. And concentration is called one-pointedness of mind by way of jhāna-factors, concentration-controlling faculty by way of the controlling faculties, wrong concentration by way of the Path-factors: the 'strength': concentration by way of the 'strengths,' [252] calm by way of the Final Pairs by virtue of the unitary method in the second couplet,[2] and non-distraction in the third—thus one state is classified in six places. All these states form nine groups by virtue of the fivefold contact-group, jhāna-factor, controlling faculty, strength, Path-factor, root, course of action, world-destroying factor, Final Pairs. What ought to have been said in the section of the outline of states has been said in the exposition of the first moral consciousness.

End of the Discourse on the Section of the Outline of States.

---

[1] *Dhs.* §§ 1254 *f.*

[2] Cf. *Dhs.* § 1355 *f.*; §§ 54, 57. *B.P.E.*: 'composure' and 'balance.'

CHAPTER II

THE FIRST TYPE OF IMMORAL CONSCIOUSNESS

In the section of the exposition,[1] in the exposition of one-pointedness of mind, the double expression, 'solidity and steadfastness,' is synonymous with stability. But that expression which has been said in the exposition of moral consciousness, to wit, 'It stands having dived and entered into the object,'[2] does not count here. True, in the immoral consciousness, it has been shown above that the one-pointedness of mind present is weak. Such meaning as non-scattering is the opposite of scattering, produced by way of distraction and perplexity is not obtained here. But that which does not disperse co-existent states is non-scattering; that which is not distracted is non-distraction; by way of the immoral one-pointedness of mind the state of mind is non-scattering. It does not tremble through the co-existent states—this is strength of concentration. Because the concentrating or fixing on the object is perverted, the concentration is false. Thus the meaning should here be understood.

In the exposition of the controlling faculty of energy[3] the method given above—namely, 'striving in expelling lust'[4]—is not obtained here. Only in the sense of not trembling because of the co-existent states is the 'strength' called energy to be understood.

In the exposition of wrong views[5] in the sense of not viewing justly, such views are called *diṭṭhigata* (*gone to views*), from being included in the sixty-two heretical views.[6] The meaning of this word has been discussed above. Just 'opinion' as being something difficult to get beyond is meant by 'view as jungle,' like a jungle of grass, of forest, of mountain. Just 'opinion' as being something dangerous and fearsome is meant by 'view as wilderness,' like a wilderness infested by thieves and wild beasts, of sand, waterless, without food. As something crushing or boring through the right view and being

---

[1] *Dhs.* § 375. [2] Cf. p. 194. [3] *Ib.* § 376.
[4] Cf. p. 193. [5] *Ib.* § 381. [6] Cf. *above*, p. 321.

contrary to it is meant by 'opinion as a disorder.' For wrong views when they arise pierce right views, and go counter to them. The changing and wavering of views from the holding at one time the Eternalistic, and at another time the Annihilationistic standpoint is meant by 'opinion as a scuffling.' A man of opinions is not able to stand by one view, follows at one time the Eternalistic and at another time the Annihilationistic view. Opinion as holding captive is meant by 'fetter' in the term 'opinion as a fetter.' It seizes the object firmly as crocodiles, etc., seize a man—thus it is called 'grip'; and 'fixity,' because it establishes itself. For a false view or opinion from the strength of its procedure establishes itself and seizes. By way of permanence, etc., it convinces—hence the term 'conviction' (or 'tendency'). Passing over the intrinsic nature of things, it considers them perversely, as permanent, etc.—this is 'perversion.' It is a vile path, because it brings disadvantage; or, it is the way to vile places of suffering—hence the term 'by-path.' From being not the right path, it is a 'wrong path.' For just as one who is gone astray, although he holds that this is the path to such a village, does not arrive at the village, so a man of false opinions, although he holds that this is the path to a happy destiny, cannot get there; hence from being not the right path it is a wrong path. From its false nature it is wrongness. (Just as people may appear to be crossing at the ferry), fools frequently cross over at an opinion or view from their merely wandering to and fro at it—thus it is a 'ford.' It is a ford, an abode of disadvantages—thus it is a 'fording-place' (*titthāyatana*), or in the sense of the birth-place, dwelling-place (*āyatana*) of heretics (*tittha*) it is *titthāyatana*. That state or intrinsic nature which is an inverted grasp is *vipariyesagāha;* or it is grasp (*gāha*) on account of the object being inverted; thus it is *vipariyesagāha*. Perverted grasp is the meaning.

In the expositions of unconscientiousness and recklessness of blame, the meaning is to be understood contrary to what has been said in conscientiousness and fear of blame. And the 'strength' called unconscientiousness-with-recklessness of blame is to be understood in the sense of not trembling because of co-existent states.

In the expositions of greed and delusion,[1] 'greed' means 'is greedy.' 'Being greedy' is the mode of greed; 'greedy' is consciousness associated with greed, or a person with such consciousness; 'greediness' is the state of the greedy mind or person. 'Infatuation' is excessive lust. 'Being infatuated' refers to its mode. 'Infatuation' is the state of an infatuated mind or person. 'Covetousness' means coveting. It has been explained under 'greed.' [254] 'Immoral root' means immoral *plus* root, root of immoral things.

'Lack of knowledge' and 'of vision' is the opposite of knowledge and vision. 'Lack of comprehension' means the not getting at, not coming up to things when confronted with them. Co-ordination of things[2] is judgment; 'want of judgment' is the opposite; 'lack of enlightenment' is the not connecting them with impermanence, ill, soullessness; perceiving in an unreal, distorted way is also 'lack of enlightenment.' 'Lack of penetration' is not penetrating the doctrine of the 'Four Truths.' 'Lack of grasp' is the not comprehending even a single fact of external experience under the general law of impermanence, etc. Does not probe into a matter—this is 'lack of thorough grasp.' Does not contemplate impartially (evenly)—this is 'lack of impartial regard.'[3] Does not take a view based on the nature of things—this is 'non-reflection.' There is not one single act among moral and immoral acts that this delusion visualizes, owing to its perverting and failing to comprehend the intrinsic nature—this is 'non-visualization.'[4] Or, such delusion cannot itself perform the visualization of any such action—this is non-visualization. That delusion destructive of the pure continuity of consciousness, which by its absence would remain pure and cleansed, is 'destructive of purity.' The state of

---

[1] *Dhs.* §§ 389, 390.

[2] Lit. perceiving things as fit (*anurūpato . . . anubodho; sic lege*).

[3] Lit. of even regard.

[4] Lit. [absence of] work of bringing before the eyes.

being foolish is 'folly.' Is deluded—this is 'delusion.' Excessive delusion is 'vagueness.' That which is deluded all round is 'obfuscation.' What is not knowledge by being opposed to it is 'ignorance.' The meanings of the next words, 'flood,' 'bond,' have been given. Continually lies latent in the sense of being firmly fixed—this is 'bias.' Besets and subjugates the mind—this is 'bursting forth.'[1] Cannot go in the direction of benefit owing to not acquiring benefit; it lags—this is a 'barrier'; it limps is the meaning. Or in the sense of being difficult to open or lift it is a bar. For as an iron bar called *mahāpaligha* is difficult to lift, so is this delusion like the bar; hence a 'bar.' The rest is clear in meaning.

[255] The sections of the Summary and Emptiness are to be understood in sense by the method given above.

End of the First Kind of Immoral Consciousness.

CHAPTER III

THE SECOND AND FOLLOWING TYPES OF CONSCIOUSNESS

In the second class of consciousness,[2] the expression 'with external aid'[3] is the only variant. The meaning of that also has been discussed above. But further, although [as in the first class] this consciousness arises in one who with joy lets his sense-experience evoke greed, and who [erroneously] regards such notions as 'a being,' 'a person' [as something ultimately true], yet inasmuch as it may also arise 'through external aid' —*i.e.*, be deliberately, methodically [brought about]—at such a time this class of consciousness is to be understood as coming to pass. Thus, when the son of a noble family asks in marriage a maiden of heretical views, and they will not give her, saying, 'You have different views,' other relatives cause them to give her to him, opposing them by saying, 'This [young man] will do whatever work you do.' And in company with these

[1] Cf. *Points of Controversy*, p. 288 (*pariyuṭṭhānaṃ*).

[2] *Dhs.* § 399.

[3] *B.P.E.*: 'prompted by a conscious motive.'

heretical people, he goes to the heretics, and at first there is only a difference of opinion, but as time goes on, the doings of these heretics become acceptable, and he accepts the heretical views, saying, 'They are pleasing to me.'

Moreover, in this class, among the 'or-whatever' states, sloth and torpor are additional features. Of these the one is the state of being slothful, the other is the state of being torpid. Absence of striving, difficulty through inability, is the meaning. The compound 'sloth-torpor' is sloth *plus* torpor; of which sloth has the absence of, or opposition to striving as characteristic, destruction of energy as function, sinking of associated states as manifestation; torpor has unwieldiness as characteristic, closing the doors of consciousness as function,[1] shrinking in taking the object, or drowsiness as manifestation; and both have unsystematic thought, in not arousing oneself from discontent[2] and laziness [or indulgence], as proximate cause.

End of the Second Type of Consciousness.

The Third class of consciousness arises in one who with joy lets his sense-experience evoke greed, who does not [erroneously] regard such notions as 'a being,' 'a person' [as something ultimately true], who goes to look at cock-fights, wrestling, boxing, dancing, theatres. etc., or is devoted to [256] listening to pleasant sounds, and so on [for the other senses]. Here there are five factors unfailing[3] together with conceit.. Herein conceit is fancying (deeming, vain imagining). It has haughtiness as characteristic, self-praise as function, desire to [advertise self like] a banner as manifestation, greed dissociated from opinionativeness as proximate cause, and should be regarded as [a form of] lunacy.

End of the Third Type of Consciousness,

---

[1] Reading *odahanarasaṃ*. *Onahanarasaṃ* would mean 'binding of associated states.'—*Tr*.

[2] Namely, in quiet settlements, calm, insight, etc.—*Pyī*.

[3] See above, p. 334.

When at the above-mentioned places (cock-fights and so on) people spit on one's head, scatter the dust off their feet, then in those who, to avoid the spittle and dust, strenuously look to themselves at intervals, as well as in those who look through this and that aperture when a royal procession goes forth or a festive party moves along, this fourth consciousness arises. In it are seven [of the ten] 'or-whatevers,'[1] together with sloth and torpor. In both this class and the next wrong view is wanting. Excepṭing this the enumeration of states is to be understood by the other classes.

End of the Fourth Type of Consciousness.

The fifth class arises in one who being neutral as to feeling lets his sense experience evoke greed, and who [erroneously] regards such notions as 'a being,' 'a person,' etc., as ultimately true. In it indifferent feeling is in place of joy; zest is wanting. All the rest is like the first class of consciousness.

End of the Fifth Type of Consciousness.

The sixth, seventh, eighth classes of consciousness are to be understood in the same way as the second, third and fourth by changing the feeling and leaving out zest.

In these eight classes of consciousness, accompanied by greed, two dominant influences of co-existence and of object are to be understood.

The ninth class arises in one who with gloom lets his sense-experience evoke aversion. In the determination of the occasion of this consciousness, 'gloomy' refers to a mind depraved by hate, or a mind contemptible through having base feeling. The state of such a mind is gloom (or moroseness). 'Accompanied by gloom' means morose.[2] It impinges on the object without affection—this is aversion.

[1] See above, p. 334.

[2] *Dhs.* § 413.

'Associated with aversion' means accompanied thereby. [257] In the summary of states, in three places, morose [or gloomy] feeling of grief occurs where the meaning of the term feeling has been explained; likewise the terms painful and gloomy.

With reference to characteristics, etc., gloom has the experiencing of an undesirable object as characteristic, making use of the undesirable in this or that manner as function, mental ailing as manifestation, and assuredly the heart-basis as proximate cause.

Hate and ill-will have been discussed in connection with roots and courses of action, just as greed and covetousness have been mentioned in the first class of consciousness. 'Hate' may be defined as 'by it [associated states] offend [the object],' or 'itself is offensive,' or as mere offending. It has flying into anger or churlishness as characteristic, like a smitten snake; spreading of itself, or writhing as when poison takes effect, as function; *or*, burning that on which it depends[1] as function, like a jungle-fire; offending or injuring as manifestation, like a foe who has got his chance; having the grounds of vexation as proximate cause, like urine mixed with poison.

By it the mind reaches the putrid state:—this is 'malignity,'[2] or, it ruins the practice of the Vinaya, the attainment of beauty, of benefit, of bliss, etc.—this is ill-will. In meaning it is just *doso* (the preceding term).

And in this ninth kind of consciousness are twenty-nine terms in order due, making fourteen by taking what has not been taken. By virtue of them the difference between the groups, classifiable and unclassifiable, is to be understood.

Of the 'or-whatevers,' desire-to-do, resolve, attention and distraction are constant. But these arise as groups of five with the presence of one or other of the three:—envy, meanness and worry. These three are thus known as inconstant 'or-whatever' states. Of these 'envy' is that which envies.[3] It has the characteristic of envying, of not enduring the

[1] The heart or physical base (*hadaya-vatthu*).—*Pyī*.

[2] *Dhs.* § 419.

[3] *Ib.* § 1121.

prosperity of others, the function of taking no delight in such prosperity, the manifestation of turning one's face from such prosperity, the proximate cause being such prosperity; and it should be regarded as a fetter.

'Meanness'[1] is the state of being mean. It has, as characteristic, the concealing of one's property, either attained or about to be attained; the not enduring the sharing of one's property in common with others, as function; the shrinking from such sharing, or niggardliness or sour feeling* [258] as manifestation; one's own property as proximate cause; and it should be regarded as mental ugliness.

A contemptible act is *kukata;* the state of [a displeased mind, produced by making] such an act [its object] is 'worry' (*kukkucca*).[2] It has repentance as characteristic, sorrow at deeds of commission and omission as function, regret as manifestation, deeds of commission and omission as proximate cause, and it should be regarded as a state of bondage.

So much of what is distinctive is there in the section of the outline.

In the exposition of feeling,[3] in the section of the exposition, 'unhappy' should be known as the opposite of happy.

In the exposition of hate,[4] that which offends or hates is 'hate.' 'Hating' is the act or mode of offending. 'Hatred' is the state of the offending mind or person. Offence in the sense of forsaking nature[5] is 'disordered temper.' 'Upsetting' is the act or mode of such offending. That which opposes is 'opposition.' That which opposes repeatedly is 'hostility.' This is said of the mode of the opposing or hostile [person or mind]. The rough, hard-hearted person is 'churlish.' The state of such an one is 'churlishness.' On account of this fault not a word is well-chosen, but is ill-spoken, not completed—this is 'abruptness.' In anger there is no finished speech, or even if speech during anger is so, it is without measure. For *asuropa* others read *assuropa* 'dropping tears,' because of tears being shed. This view is not reasonable, because a

---

[1] *Dhs.* § 1122.

[2] Cf. *B.P.E.*, p. 312, *n.* 4.

[4] *Ib.* § 418.

* *Kaṭukañcukatā.*

[3] *Dhs.* § 415.

[5] *Pakatibhāvo.*

happy person may also shed tears. As to the term *anattamanatā*, there is no mentality of self because of opposition to mentality of self, as explained above. But because this is of the mind only, and not of a being,[1] therefore it has been said to be 'of the mind.' Here, as well as in the sections of the Compendium and Emptiness, the remainder should be understood by the method given above.

The Tenth Type of Consciousness.

The tenth, because it is induced 'by external aid,' arises in one urged by others, one who remembers the offence of another, one who by himself keeps remembering others' offences and gets angry. In this class of consciousness also are twenty-nine terms in order due; but they make fourteen terms by taking what has not been taken. And in the 'or-whatevers' sloth and torpor also are obtained. Therefore in this consciousness are these six:—to wit, four unfailing factors and sloth and torpor, without envy, meanness and worry. At the time when envy, etc., arise, seven 'or-whatevers' at any one moment arise together with one or other among them. All that remains in all the sections is just like the ninth kind of consciousness. But in these two kinds of consciousness where dejection is a factor, [259] only the co-existent dominance is obtained; object-dominance is not obtained,[2] for anger does not care or have respect for anything.

The Eleventh Type of Consciousness.

The eleventh kind of consciousness arises when misgiving is aroused in one who as to feeling is indifferent with regard to the six objects of sense. In determining the occasion of this sort of consciousness, we find a new phrase:—'associated with doubt.'[3] In the outline of states only the expression, 'there is doubt,' is distinctive. Here doubt means exclusion from the cure[4] [of knowledge]. Or, one investigating the intrinsic nature by means of it suffers pain and fatigue (*kicchati*)—thus it is doubt. It has shifting about as characteristic, mental

[1] Satto, ultimate persistent entity, soul.

[2] See above. p. 284.

[3] *Dhs.* §§ 422–25.

[4] Cikicchā, omitted in P.T.S. ed.

wavering as function, indecision or uncertainty in grasp as manifestation, unsystematic thought as proximate cause, and it should be regarded as a danger to attainment.

There are twenty-three terms in order due in this consciousness; by taking what has not been taken they make fourteen. By way of them the determination of the groups classifiable and unclassifiable is to be understood. These two, attention and distraction, are the only 'or-whatevers.'

In the exposition of one-pointedness of mind,[1] because this 'distraction' is weak, and because, in the eleventh class, there is just a mere static instant[2] of the mind, therefore without saying 'solidity,' etc., just one term—'stability of mind'—is stated. On this account, in the section of the outline also, 'the controlling faculty of concentration,' etc., are not given.

In the exposition of perplexity or doubt, 'doubt' (*kaṅkhā*) is the act of doubting. A previous doubt is said to induce a subsequent doubt; or the term is one of manner or mode. Consciousness imbued with doubt is 'dubious' from the arising of doubt, and of such the state is 'dubiety.' Puzzlement is 'not intelligence.'[3] 'Perplexity' has been explained. In the sense of wavering already given it sways to and fro—'swaying between two.' Because of hindering attainment it is like a path branching in two—a 'double path.' 'Fluctuation' is the inability to establish anything in one mode, thus, 'Is this state permanent, or is it impermanent?' [260] Because of the inability to 'comprehend,' there is 'uncertainty of grasp.' 'Evasion' is the being unable to decide, receding from the object. 'Hesitation' is the being unable to plunge in. 'Not plunging in' is the inability to plunge right in. 'Mental rigidity' is the inability to proceed as deciding respecting the object. Stiffness is the meaning. For perplexity having arisen makes the mind stiff, But because on arising it takes the object and, so to speak, scratches the mind, therefore it is called 'mental scarifying.' The rest in all the sections is evident.

---

[1] *Dhs.* § 424.

[2] Some read idaṁ cittaṁ dubbalaṁ, ettha pavatti ṭhitimattam eva, 'this consciousness is weak and there is just the mere static procedure.'

[3] Read Vimati ti na mati.

The Twelfth Type of Consciousness.

In the determination of the occasion of the twelfth kind the phrase 'associated with distraction'[1] occurs. This sort of consciousness—namely, being hedonically neutral as to sense—becomes distracted. In the 'summary of states' distraction here comes in place of perplexity (or doubt). In the order of terms there are twenty-eight terms, which make fourteen by adding what has not been taken. It is through these that the arrangement of the groups, classifiable and unclassifiable, is to be understood. Two 'or-whatevers' are present:—resolve and attention.

In the exposition of 'distraction,'[2] in the Exposition section, 'of mind' means excluding a being or a man (as ultimate entity). 'Distraction' is the mode of mind when excited, flurried. 'Disquietude' is unquiet. 'Agitation' is a throwing about of mind. 'Turmoil of mind' is a reeling condition like the swaying of a moving vehicle, or an ox, etc. By this expression fluctuating about one object only is intended; for distraction wavers as to one object, doubt as to various objects. The rest in all the sections should be understood by the method above given.

Now in these two classes of consciousness, this is the specific distinction. On being asked, 'How many kinds of consciousness roll off from an object?' these two, 'associated with distraction' and 'accompanied by doubt,' should be stated. Of these the latter [261] invariably rolls off; the former, when it has obtained a footing in the acquirement of resolve, rolls off at stages. Just as if two stones, one round and the other rectangular, were to roll down an inclination, the round stone would roll down right away, the rectangular stone would roll with intervals of stopping, so should the application of this simile be understood.

In all these twelve classes of consciousness the classification of 'low,' etc.,[3] has not been brought out, because all of them

[1] *Dhs.* § 427. [2] *Ib.* § 429. [3] Cf. above, p. 284.

are low. The dominant influence[1] of co-existence, although obtainable, has not been brought out, because the method has already been shown above. But in these twelve, owing to the absence of knowledge, there is no such thing as the dominance of investigation. In the last two classes a different dominant influence (from that of investigation) might have been brought out, but it (*i.e.*, that of co-existence) is also absent, because it does not arise with any co-existent state as the principal in desire-to-act, etc., and because of the inhibition in the *Paṭṭhāna*. But when action is put forth by these twelve classes of immoral consciousness, excepting the one accompanied by distraction, the remaining eleven involve rebirth. When the kind that is accompanied by doubt, being weak and without obtaining resolve, involves rebirth, why does not the one accompanied by distraction, which is strong and has obtained resolve, do so? Because of its not being a state 'removable by the path of insight.'[2] Did it carry rebirth, it would come in the division named 'removable by the path of insight.' (But it does not so come), hence, excepting it, the remaining eleven involve rebirth. Moreover when action is put forth by any of the eleven, there is rebirth in the four places of suffering by that volition, and rebirth is got by the unconditioned element of mind-cognition accompanied by indifference as an immoral result. And there would also be a getting of rebirth in the four places of suffering by the kind of consciousness accompanied by distraction. If so, there should then be removal by the path of insight. But because there is to this kind of consciousness no getting of rebirth in purgatory, therefore it does not come in that Division.

End of the explanation of the expression, Immoral States.

---

[1] Cf. above, p. 284. [2] Cf. p. 57.

PART X—DISCOURSE ON UNMORAL CONSCIOUSNESS

CHAPTER I

DUALITY IN AWARENESS OF MIND

Now the analysis and exposition of the term 'unmoral' begins at the question, 'Which are the states that are unmoral ?'[1] Unmoral [consciousness] is then shown as fourfold—namely, with respect to result, inoperative action, matter and Nibbāna'. That question is stated to show resultant unmoral consciousness, the moral result in that, the limited result in that, the unconditioned element in that,[2] as well as the fivefold sense-awareness therein,[2] and visual awareness by 'door'-process thereïn. [262] And the statement: '. . . because moral kamma has been wrought on the sensuous plane . . .' is to show genesis in that (visual awareness) by kammas specifically caused, thus excluding reference to such general conditions as 'door,' 'object,' etc.

Here '. . . has been wrought' refers to the act as a cause; 'has been stored up' refers to the heaping up, the development,* as cause. 'Visual awareness' is cognition by sight as a cause, or cognition proceeding from, or seated in the eye. This holds for the other senses. In visual awareness, the 'characteristic' is being aware of a visible object by dependence upon the sense of sight, the 'function' is the taking as object merely the visible form, the 'manifestation' is the state of confronting the visible object, the 'proximate cause' is the disappearance of the inoperative element of 'mind' with regard to the visible object. The other modes of sense-awareness may be similarly defined. Here taken in order are ten terms, or, by omitting what has already been taken, seven. Of the seven, two only are classifiable. Of these, consciousness is classified with respect to two

---

[1] *Dhs.* § 431. [2] Clauses omitted in P.T.S. ed. * Upacitattā.

occasions—namely, by way of the fivefold contact-group and of controlling faculty; feeling with respect to three occasions —by way of the fivefold contact-group, of Jhāna-factor and of controlling faculty. Of groups also there are these three; there is only one 'or-whatever'—to wiṭ, attention.

In the section of the Exposition, visual awareness as 'clear'[1] is said with reference to basis. For consciousness, when moral, is known to be clear by its own purity, when immoral, by the results in the life-continuum, and when resultant, by the clearness of the basis.

In the exposition of one-pointedness of mind,[2] 'stability of thought'—thus much of the term is stated. For this consciousness also is weak; in it just the static instant is obtained; it is not able to reach solidity, steadfastness.

In the section of the Summary, the Jhāna-factors and Path-factors have not been brought out, because the Jhāna is consummated by[3] initial application of mind and the Path is consummated by a moral condition. Originally without conscious initial application the Jhāna-factor is not obtained, neither, in consciousness morally unconditioned, are the Path-factors obtained. [263] Therefore in this kind of consciousness neither of these factors has been brought out. In it has been classified the fourfold aggregate of mental co-efficients (contact, volition, one-pointedness of mind, life-controlling faculty). The section of Emptiness is clear as to its meaning.[4] The expositions of auditory awareness, etc., should be understood in the same way.

Indifference has been assigned to any cognition by way of sense; but pleasure, only to the sense of touch. Herein is this distinction, which should be understood with reference to impact. In the four doors—eye, ear, nose, tongue—only derived matter strikesor impinges on derived matter. When this takes place, the resisting friction is not strong; there is just the mere touch, as when four lumps of cotton placed on four anvils are struck by cotton lumps. Feeling takes up the

---

[1] *Dhs.* § 436. [2] *Ib.* § 438.

[3] °Pacchimakaṁ. Some read °pamāṇaṁ, 'measured by.'

[4] Or remains the same.

middle (neutral) position. But in the door of the bodily surface the external great essential itself as the object strikes the internal sentient organism and impinges on the [internal] great essentials which are the cause of [internal] sensory stimulation. As when the cotton lump, placed on top of the anvils, is struck with a hammer, the hammer breaks through the cotton and 'takes' the anvil, and the friction is strong, so the friction of the impact is strong.[1] With reference to a desirable object, intimation by act arises, accompanied by pleasure; with reference to an undesirable object, it is accompanied by pain. And the basis, door, object of these five classes of consciousness are constant. In the fivefold cognition of sense there is no such thing as the shifting of the basis, etc. For the moral resultant, visual cognition, making the sensitive eye the basis, and accomplishing the function of seeing visible objects sprung from four causes and desirable or fairly desirable, stands at the eye-door and becomes a 'result.' The auditory and other cognitions, making the sensitive ear, etc., the basis, and accomplishing the function of hearing, smelling, tasting or touching, in sounds, etc., desirable or fairly desirable, stand at the ear-door, etc., and become results. But of these objects sound springs from two causes (thought and the caloric order).

In the exposition of the mind-element,[2] mind, in the sense of intrinsic nature, emptiness, absence of a living entity, and element make up this compound. It has the characteristic of knowing visible or other objects immediately after visual or other cognition respectively, the function of receiving visible and other objects, the manifestation of the state of such reception, the proximate cause of the absence of visual and other cognition. [264] Here, in the section of the outline of states, are twelve terms; by taking what has not been taken there are nine, of which seven are unclassifiable, two classifiable. Resolve and attention are the two 'or-whatevers.' The exposition of initial application of mind defines it as a setting on to the object. But because the consciousness in

---

[1] Cf. *Comp. of Phil.* 231 *f.*

[2] *Dhs.* §§ 455 *ff.*

question is neither moral nor immoral, therefore it is not said to be 'right intention, or wrong intention.' In the section of the Summary, the Jhāna-factor, although obtainable, has fallen into the stream of the fivefold sense-cognition; hence it has not been brought out. And the Path-factor is not even obtained.[1] The section of Emptiness is evident. The basis of this consciousness is constant and is the heart-basis. The door and object are not constants. Of these, though the door and the object may be shifted, yet the locus is one; for this consciousness has receptiveness for function[2]—namely, in the five objects at the five doors—where, after being receptive, it becomes a result. When visual and other cognitions of moral results cease, it receives those visible and other objects which have reached their loci, and been produced immediately after the cognitions.

In theexpositions of the element of mind-cognition[3]the term, rapture, in the first element of mind-cognition is an additional feature. Feeling also is joyful feeling. Because this first element arises only with respect to a desirable object therefore it is joyful feeling. The second element arises with respect to a desirable neutral object, therefore in it is indifferent feeling. The terms are the same as those in the exposition of the mind-element. In both, because the elements of mind-cognition have fallen into the stream of the fivefold sense-cognition, the Jhāna-factors have not been brought out, nor have the Path-factors, because they are unobtainable. The remainder in all the sections should be understood by the method given above. But as to characteristics, etc., this twofold element of mind-cognition with unconditional resultant has the characteristic of knowing the six sense-objects, the function of receptiveness, etc., the manifestation of such a state of receiving, etc., the proximate cause of the heart-basis.

Of the two elements, the first becomes a result on two occasions:—when this resultant mind-element, coming imme-

---

[1] Reading, for *pana*, pi na.

[2] Reading ekaṃ, sampaṭi°.

[3] *Dhs.* §§ 469 *ff*.

[4] *Ib.* § 455.

diately after such sense-cognition as is a moral resultant in the five doors, and receiving the object of such cognition, ceases, it stands in the five doors and becomes a result, accomplishing the act of receiving with respect to that very object. And it becomes a result as the registration (or retention) with respect to a vivid object at the six doors. [265] How? When a boat goes across a fierce current, the water is cleft and follows the boat a little distance, and then goes along with the current. So when at the six doors the vivid object, being deceitful, presents itself, apperception takes place; after this happens, there comes the turn for the subconscious life-continuum. But this consciousness, not allowing this turn, seizes the object which was seized by apperception, arises in the first or second conscious interval, and descends even into the life-continuum. Or similarly, when a herd of cattle cross a stream—so the simile might be expanded. Thus this element of mind-cognition, from seizing that object seized by apperception, results in an act of registration.

And the second becomes a result on five occasions. How? At the time when the blind, the deaf, the foolish, the mad, a hermaphrodite, or a neuter takes conception in the world of men, such consciousness takes effect as conception; after that as long as such a person lives, it takes effect as life-continuum; in the fivefold-object-process with respect to the moderately desirable, it takes effect as receiving, in a vivid object at the six doors, at the moment of death, registration and decease respectively. Thus it results on five occasions.

End of the Twofold element of mind-cognition.

CHAPTER II

DISCOURSE ON THE MORAL RESULT OF THE SENSUOUS REALM

Now to show the eight main kinds of resultant consciousness, once more a beginning is made with, 'Which are the states that are unmoral?'[1] Herein, since the method has already

[1] *Dhs.* § 498.

been given in the text, all the sections have been abridged. Their meaning should be understood by the method given above. But herein, to show such distinctions as there are, it is stated that 'the absence of greed is an unmoral root.' As to such terms as are not stated, they should be understood thus: the divisions into door of kamma, course of kamma, basis of meritorious act[1], described under the moralities of the sensuous realm, do not obtain here. And why? Because here we deal with consciousness where there is no production of intimation, no giving of result, no arising as a meritorious act, such as charity, etc. [266] Among the 'or-whatevers,' the pity and sympathy given above are not among the results, owing to their having a being as object. For the results of consciousness in the sensuous realm are really concerned with limited objects. And it is not only pity and sympathy that are here absent, the 'abstinences' are also absent. For, of course, the five precepts are [not unmoral, but] moral.

Here also the arrangement of classes of consciousness as automatic and non-automatic by means of moral thought and different causes should be understood as obtaining. The result of automatic moral consciousness is automatic, but of non-automatic moral consciousness, it is non-automatic. Moreover, that result which arises from such causes as potent objects is automatic; the other arisen from such other causes as weak objects is non-automatic. In the division also into low, etc., these units of resultant consciousness are not known as 'low,' 'medium,' 'exalted,' because they are not accomplished as such by desire-to-do or other dominant influence.[2] But the result of low moral consciousness is low, that of medium moral consciousness is medium, and that of exalted moral consciousness is exalted. Here there are no dominant influences. And why? Because they are unfit to be produced with desire-to-do, etc., as the principal. All the remainder is as has been said in the eight classes of moral consciousness.

Now we have to understand the occasion when the results

---

[1] See above, pp. 209 *ff.*

[2] P. 284.

of these eight main classes of resultant consciousness take effect. This is on four occasions:—conception, life-continuum, decease, registration. How? They take effect as conception in the case of meritorious, twice-conditioned, or thrice-conditioned persons among men and devas of the sensuous realm. Next, subsequent to conception, they become the life-continuum for sixty, eighty, or even an incalculable number of years, for the whole life-cycle; thirdly, registration at the six doors in the case of a vivid object; and lastly, decease at the moment of death. Thus on four occasions they take effect.

All those who are about to be Buddhas, at the time of taking their last conception, do so by means of the great units of resultant consciousness, accompanied by joy, thrice-conditioned and automatic. And that conception-consciousness is the result of a prior consciousness of love. But [in their case] the incalculably long lifetime [conferred] in that conception is reversed as to time. Mahāsiva the Elder said: 'Consciousness accompanied by indifference is stronger than that which is accompanied by joy; it is by the former that Bodhisats take conception; conceived by that, they have noble aspirations, they do not hanker even after celestial objects, they are like Tipiṭaka-Cūḷanāga the Elder and others.' [267] But the Great Commentary, rejecting this view, thus, 'This idea is merely the Elder's fancy,' goes on to say: 'The beneficent work of omniscient Bodhisats is powerful;[1] therefore Bodhisats take conception by a consciousness, which in its early phase was love, was a moral resultant of experience in the world of sense, is accompanied by joy, is thrice-conditioned and automatic.'

Now a table of contents should be drawn up for the discourse of elucidating results. So far the Elder Tipiṭaka-Cūḷanāga has said: 'By one moral volition sixteen kinds of resultant consciousness arise. In this (by virtue of twice-conditioned conception) there are the twelve kinds[2] of results, and (by virtue of unconditioned conception) the eightfold unconditioned

---

[1] Cf. *Jātaka* i. 172.—*Ed.*

[2] Maggo.

result.' But Mahādatta the Elder, [known as] Moravāpīvāsin,[1] has said: 'By one moral volition arise twelve kinds of resultant consciousness. In this (by virtue of the twice-conditioned conception) are the ten kinds[2] of results, and, by virtue of unconditioned conception, the eightfold unconditioned result.' Elder Tipiṭaka-Mahādhammarakkhita said, 'By one moral volition arise *ten* kinds of resultant consciousness. In this, by virtue of unconditioned conception, there is the eightfold unconditioned result.' On this occasion they took up the 'Sāketa query.' In Sāketa the devotees, assembled in hall, raised the query:—'When by one volition kamma is put forth, is there one conception only, or different conceptions?'[3] Being unable to decide it, they went and asked the Abhidhamma Elders, who convinced them by saying, 'Just as from one mango seed only one sprout issues forth, so there is only one conception.' Then one day they raised the query thus:—'When kamma is put forth by different volitions, are there different conceptions[3] or is there one only?' And being unable to decide it they asked the Elders, who convinced them by saying, 'Just as when many mango seeds are sown, many sprouts issue forth, so are there many conceptions.'

Furthermore, on this occasion there was drawn up what is known as the declaration of [karmic] preponderance. Namely:—these [reborn] beings abound in greed, hate and delusion, as well as in the severally opposite tendencies. [Let us call the former *G*, *H*, *D;* the latter *g*, *h*, *d.—Ed.*] Now what determines the abundance? Previous conditions. Variation is determined just at the moment when kamma is exerted. How so? When, at such a moment, *G* only in the kamma is strong, *g* is weak, *h* and *d* are strong, *H*, *D* are weak, then the weak *g* is unable to cancel[4] the strong *G*, but *h*, *d*, being strong, [268] are able to cancel *H*, *D*. Hence the being, born through conception given by such kamma, is of strong appetites, of sanguine[5] habit, good tempered, intelligent and keen as adamant in wit.

---

[1] Dweller at the Peacock's Pond.

[2] Maggo.

[3] *I.e.*, of living beings in rebirth.—*Ed.*

[4] Lit. possess (*pariyādātuṃ*).

[5] Lit. happy going (*sukha-sīlo*).

If, on the other hand, when kamma is put forth, both *G*, *H* are strong, and *g*, *h* are weak, *d* is strong, *D* is weak, then by the foregoing method the resultant being has strong appetites and dislikes, but is intelligent and keen as adamant in wit, as was Elder Dattābhaya. When *G*, *D* are strong, and the rest weak, the resultant, by the preceding method, is lustful, dull, but is amiable and gentle of disposition. Furthermore, when *G*, *H*, *D*, at that moment, are strong, the rest *g*, *h*, *d* weak, by the foregoing method, the resultant is strong in appetites and dislikes, and is dull in intelligence. Again, when, at that moment, *g*, *H*, *D* are strong, *G*, *h*, *d* weak, he will be fairly free from lust, and not carried away even by the sight of divine objects, but he will be full of enmity and dull of intelligence. Again, when *G*, *h*, *D* at that moment are strong, and the rest weak, he, by the foregoing method, will be greedy and amiable, but dull. Again, when *g*, *H*, *d* are strong, and the rest weak, he, by the foregoing method, will be not greedy or intelligent, and full of dislikes. Finally, when *g*, *h*, *d*, at that moment, are strong, and *G*, *H*, *D* are weak, the resultant being will be disinterested, amiable and wise as was Elder Mahā-Sangharakkhita.

Furthermore on that occasion the declaration as to root-conditions was drawn up[1]:—Thrice-conditioned kamma gives a result which may be thrice-conditioned, twice-conditioned, or unconditioned. Twice-conditioned kamma does not give thrice-conditioned result, but gives the others. By thrice-conditioned kamma conception may be thrice-conditioned, or twice-conditioned, but not unconditioned; by twice-conditioned kamma, it may be twice-conditioned or unconditioned, but not thrice-conditioned. Automatic moral consciousness gives a result which may be automatic[2] or non-automatic. [269] Non-automatic moral consciousness gives a result which may be non-automatic or automatic. Feeling must vary according to the object. Registration must be determined by apperception.[3]

---

[1] The reader is reminded that 'root-conditions' refer to the foregoing six: *G, H, D, g, h, d.*—*Ed.*

[2] See above, p. 353; cf. 373. [3] See *Compendium*, p. 126 *f.*

Now in the doctrine of this and that Elder, sixteen kinds (of results), etc., should be understood.

To expand: In the case of a being who has taken conception by the first main class of resultant consciousness, similar to the first class of sensuous moral consciousness, and, after issuing from the womb, has become able to acquire a certain status of restraint and non-restraint, when a desired object has presented itself at the door of his eye, and before the adverting door-consciousness has affected the subconscious life-continuum, there is no measure of the object and its passing. Why is it thus? Because of the weakness of the object. This is one of the occasions without effect.

Again, when adverting by the five doors does agitate the life-continuum, but has not yet reached determination, it persists in the interval, visually cognizing, or receiving, or examining, and it is impossible that it should turn back. Reaching determination, one or two moments of consciousness arise; then, getting the causal relation of repetition, and persisting as apperception, it again lapses into subconsciousness. This act of perception is also of the kind where the object is weak, and is obtained when we say, 'It was as if I saw,' or 'I heard.' This is another occasion without effect.

Again, when another person attending on occasion of sense agitates my subconscious life-continuum, processes of cognition arise,[1] apperception takes place. But whereas registration should occur at the conclusion of apperception, before registration arises, apperception lapses into the subconscious life-continuum. To illustrate this:—Just as in constructing an embankment in the river, and in directing the water to a great channel, the water first flows over and fills the fields on both sides of the bank and flooding, runs along crab-passages, etc., then flows into the full river, so herein. The time when the water flows [only] in the river [270] is like that of the proceeding of the subconscious life-continuum. The time of constructing the embankment is like that of the adverting by a sense-door agitating the life-continuum. The time of

[1] Lit. processed cognitions (*vīthicittāni*).

water flowing into the great channel is the occurrence of the process of perception. The filling of the fields on both sides of the bank is like apperception. The flowing back of the water into the river after running along crab-passages, etc., is the relapse into the life-continuum after apperception has taken place, before registration arises. Thus there is no means of computing the act of consciousness descending into the life-continuum. This consciousness is also of the kind described owing to the weakness of the object. It is the third occasion without effect.

But now, if a vivid object is presented, visual or other cognitions arise when adverting by the five doors agitates the life-continuum, and a unit of the first kind of moral consciousness of the sensuous realm becomes apperception at the stage of apperception, and coming into play six or seven times, gives the turn to registration, then this registration being at the same time established, the main type of *resultant* consciousness, similar to that unit of moral consciousness, is established. This resultant consciousness gets two names:—'root of life-continuum,' from its resemblance to conception-consciousness, and 'registration,' because [like the act of registration] it seizes the object which was seized by the apperception.

On this occasion four kinds of resultant consciousness:—visual cognition, reception, examination, registration—are counted as results. And when the second class of moral consciousness becomes apperception, then the second kind of resultant consciousness resembling it is established as registration. This second kind of resultant consciousness, in that it does not resemble conception-consciousness, gets two names:—'adventitious life-continuum' and 'registration'—by the former method. Together with it the four preceding kinds of [resultant] consciousness make five. And when the third class of moral consciousness becomes apperception, then the third kind of resultant consciousness resembling it stands as registration. By the said method this consciousness gets two names:—'adventitious life-continuum' and 'registration.' Together with it the preceding five kinds of consciousness make six. And when the fourth class of moral consciousness becomes apperception, then the fourth kind of resultant consciousness resembling it stands as registration. This consciousness by the said method gets the same two names. [271] Together with it the preceding six kinds of consciousness make seven.

Next, when at the eye-door a moderately desirable object is presented, in that object also by the said method three ineffective occasions may happen. But because [in this case] feeling is interchangeable with the object, therefore over that object there is examination accompanied by indifference. At the conclusion of any of the four main classes of moral apperceptions, accompanied by indifference, each of the corresponding four main kinds of resultant consciousness accompanied by indifference stands as registration. And these four kinds of consciousness by the said method get two names:—'adventitious life-continuum' and 'registration,'—and are called the posterior life-continuum. Thus these five kinds of consciousness together with the preceding seven make twelve. So there are twelve at the eye-door and in each of the other doors of ear, etc., making fully sixty kinds of resultant consciousness [having respect to each sense]. So by one volition, when kamma is put forth, full sixty kinds of consciousness can arise. However, by taking only what has not been taken, twelve in the eye-door and the four cognitions—auditory, olfactory, gustatory and tactile—make sixteen.

In this connection the [consulting Elders] adopted the parable of the mango:—A certain man with his head covered went to sleep at the foot of a fruiting mango-tree. Then a ripe mango loosened from the stalk fell to the ground, grazing his ear. Awakened by that sound, he opened his eyes and looked; then stretching out his hand he took the fruit, squeezed it, smelt it, and ate it. Herein, the time of his sleeping at the foot of the mango-tree is as when we are subconsciously alive; the instant of the ripe mango falling from its stalk grazing his ear is like the instant of the object striking the sentient organism; the time of awaking through the sound is like that of adverting by the five doors agitating the subconscious life-continuum; the time of the man's opening his eyes and looking is like that of accomplishing the function of seeing through visual cognition; the time of stretching out his hand and taking the mango is as that of the resultant mind-element receiving the object; the time of taking it and squeezing it is as that of the resultant element of mind-cognition examining the object; the time of smelling it is as that of the inoperative element of mind-cognition determining the object; [272] the time of eating it is as that of apperception enjoying the taste of the object. What does this simile signify? The function of the object striking the sentient organism. When this happens there is the function of adverting by the five doors just agitating the life-continuum, the function of just the seeing by visual cognition, of just the receiving of the object by the resultant mind-element, of just the examining of the object by the resultant element of mind-cognition, of just the determining of the object by the inoperative element of mind-cognition. But verily only the apperception enjoys the taste of the object. This is what it signifies. And in the production of this consciousness there is no doer or instigator saying, 'Be thou life-continuum, be thou adverting, be thou the vision, be thou the reception, be thou the examination, be thou the determination, be thou apperception.'

Once more: on that occasion they adopted the fivefold order [of the cosmos]:—Germinal, Caloric, Moral, Natural-phenomenal, Psychical.[1] Of these, the Germinal order [reveals] a giving of this and that similar modes of fruition to this or that seed, as in the gram's top shoots sprouting to the north, the southern creeper growing round a tree from the right, the sunflower's facing the sun, the Māluva creeper growing towards a tree, the holes occurring in the top of the cocoanut.

The Caloric order is the simultaneous blossoming, fructifying and sprouting of such and such trees at such and such seasons.

Thrice-conditioned kamma gives thrice-conditioned, twice-conditioned, unconditioned result; twice-conditioned kamma

---

[1] Cf. the editor's *Buddhism* (1912), p. 118 *f.* (I regret I overlooked this interesting historical reference.) Cf. also Ledi Sayadaw's discussion in 'Expositions,' *Buddhist Review*, London, 1916.—*Ed.*

gives twice-conditioned, unconditioned result, not thrice-conditioned result—this giving of suitable results by various kammas is the Moral Order. And there is another moral order according as the result resembles the kamma. To show this meaning they tell the story:—In the time of the supreme Buddha a village near the gate of Sāvatthī was burnt down, a blazing wisp of hay therefrom rose up and caught the neck of a crow flying in the sky. The crow, screeching, fell to the ground and died. In the ocean, too, a certain ship got aground. They, not seeing any obstruction from below, cast lots; the unlucky number fell into the hand of the captain's wife. They then said: 'Owing to one woman let not all perish; we must throw her into the water.' The captain, saying 'I cannot bear to see her floating in the water,' tied a pot of sand to her neck and had her thrown. At that moment the ship moved off like an arrow shot from a bow. A certain bhikkhu lived in a cave. A huge mountain peak fell and closed up the entrance. On the seventh day of itself it moved away.

They told these three stories together to the perfect Buddha, as he sat in the Jetavana preaching the Doctrine. The Teacher said, 'This kamma was not the work of others; it was done by the crow itself,' etc., and he showed the related past:—The crow in a previous existence was a man, who, being unable to tame a vicious ox, tied a bundle of straw to its neck and set it on fire, and the ox died. Now that action did not allow the crow to escape [even though] he flew into the sky. That woman in a previous existence was also a woman. A dog was devoted to her, and when she went to the forest went and came back with her. Men scoffed at her with: 'There goes our dog-mistress.'[1] She felt ashamed and, being unable to restrain the dog, tied a pot of sand to its neck and threw it into the water. That action did not allow the woman to escape in mid-ocean. That bhikkhu in a previous existence was a cowherd. When an iguana entered a hole he closed the entrance by a handful of broken twigs, and on the seventh day himself came and opened it. The iguana came out

---

[1] Luddhikā. *Pyī* reads luddako, 'hunter-dog.'

trembling. Through pity he spared its life. That action did not allow that bhikkhu to escape even when he had entered a mountain cave and sat there. Thus connecting these three stories he spoke this verse:—

> *Not to the sky nor to mid-ocean, nor*
> [274] *By hieing him to any cavern of the hills,*
> *Nor is there any spot in all the earth*
> *Where he could stand so that he might escape*
> *From deed of wickedness that he had wrought.*[1]

This also is known as the Moral Order.

Other such stories might also be told.

Bodhisats taking conception, being born of a mother, their final enlightenment, as Tathāgata turning the wheel of Dhamma, the surrender of life and utter passing away:—the world-earthquake at each is of the Dhamma-Order.

And when an object strikes the sentient organism there is no doer or instigator to say, 'Be thou adverting,' etc. From the time the object strikes the sentient organism; each according to its own nature adverting by the five doors agitates the life-continuum, visual cognition accomplishes the function of seeing, the resultant mind-element accomplishes the function of receiving, the resultant mind-cognition-element that of examining, the inoperative mind-cognition-element that of determining, apperception enjoys the taste of the object:—all this is understood as the Psychical Order.

When, by thrice-conditioned and non-automatic moral consciousness, and also by automatic or non-automatic moral consciousness accompanied by indifference kamma is wrought, and similar resultant consciousness comes in the re-conception obtained, the same method holds good. But in the two classes of consciousness accompanied by indifference, procedure, having first been shown by way of a fairly desirable object, should afterwards be shown by way of a desirable object. Thus in each door are twelve, making sixty in all. By taking what has not been taken sixteen kinds of resultant consciousness arise.

---

[1] *Dhp.* 127.

In this connection they took the simile of the five machines for squeezing sugar-cane. Suppose, they said, that when sugar-cane is squeezed, eleven mechanics come out from one village, and seeing a plantation, know that it is ripe. Going up to the owner they announced that [275] they were mechanics for squeezing sugar-cane. He said, 'I am just looking for you,' and took them to the sugar-cane shed. There the eleven set up the machine and said, 'We are eleven; we ought to get another man; hire one.' The owner replied, 'I will be your mate,' entered the hut and became their mate. When each had done his work, when he who boiled the molasses had boiled the cane-juice, and it had been rolled into balls, and the owner after weighing it had given to each, and each had taken his due, and they had made over the shed to the owner, and in this way had done their work in four other sheds, they departed.

Now the five machines in the five huts are like the five sentient organs; the five plantations are the five kinds of objects. The eleven itinerant mechanics are the eleven kinds of resultant consciousness; the five owners of plantations are the five classes of sense-cognition; the time of the collaboration of the twelve men, inclusive of the owner in the first hut and the taking by each of his due, corresponds to the eleven kinds of resultant consciousness working in union with visual cognition, and accomplishing each its own function with regard to the visible object at the eye-door; the time of the owner's taking over the shed corresponds to the door of visual cognition not being transferred. The collaboration of the twelve men in the second, third, fourth, fifth sheds, and each taking his due, corresponds to the eleven kinds of resultant consciousness working in union with other sense-cognitions, and each accomplishing its function with regard to the other kinds of sense-object at the respective doors. To this extent is re-conception thrice conditioned by kamma which has three conditions. The foregoing covers also all twice-conditioned re-conception due to similar kamma.

We will now take kamma which was conditioned by two 'roots' only. This results in re-conception conditioned by two 'roots.' When kamma is wrought by double-rooted consciousness which is accompanied by joy and is automatic, in the case of one who has taken re-conception by means of the similar doubly-conditioned resultant consciousness, [276] those three ineffectual occasions may arise at the eye-door, by the said method, when a desirable object is presented. At the conclusion of a unit of twice-conditioned, automatic apperception accompanied by joy, arises registration resembling it and termed 'sub-consciousness of conditions.' But if apperception is not automatic, the registering is termed 'adventitious sub-consciousness.' After either of the apperceptions which are accompanied by indifference concerning a fairly desirable object arise two moments of registration resembling them. Here, making eight at each door, are full forty kinds of consciousness. But by taking what has not been taken, eight at the eye-door with the four cognitions by way of ear, etc., make twelve. Thus by one volition, when kamma is wrought, there arise twelve kinds of resultant consciousness. The mango simile and the discourse on the fivefold order are as before.

The same method should be applied in the case of one who has taken re-conception by the resultant consciousness resembling the remaining three kinds of consciousness which have two roots. But on this occasion, in the parable of the sugar-cane-press, seven mechanics are desired. When by the seven the press is set up, it is to be understood that the owner makes the eighth, in accordance with what has been said. To this extent is re-conception twice-conditioned by kamma, which has two conditions (or roots).

Next the discourse on re-conception which is without 'roots.' When kamma is wrought by one or other of the four twice-conditioned kinds of moral consciousness, it is not right to say that in the case of one who has obtained re-conception by consciousness, which is a moral resultant, is accompanied by indifference and sense-mind cognition without root-conditions, his re-conception will be like that kamma. As a matter of fact, the kamma is twice-conditioned, the re-conception is unconditioned by roots.

When a moderately desirable object is presented at the eye-door of a grown-up being, the [possibility of the] three ineffectual occasions should be understood by the foregoing method. But at the conclusion of any apperception among the four kinds of twice-conditioned moral consciousness, the unconditioned consciousness persists as registration and gets two names:—root-subconsciousness and registration. Thus here in the eye-door, visual cognition as well as reception is accompanied by indifference. Examination also and registration are accompanied by indifference. Hence, not taking one out of these two, there are reckoned three kinds of consciousness. And in the desirable object examination and registration are accompanied by joy. Taking one of these two, the three foregoing kinds of consciousness make four. Thus, making fours in the five doors when kamma is exerted by one volition, there arise twenty kinds of resultant consciousness. [277] Nevertheless, by taking what has not been taken, the four kinds of consciousness at the eye-door with the four cognitions of the other senses make eight. This is called the unconditioned set of eight. It is experienced among mankind, and is a process obtainable among the four planes of suffering. Indeed, when Mahāmoggallāna the Elder created a lotus in purgatory, and, seated in the pericarp, gave a religious discourse to the denizens of purgatory, in them as they looked at the Elder arose such visual cognition as was a moral resultant; as they listened to his voice, they had such auditory cognition as was a moral resultant; when they smelt the odour of his robe, as the Elder was going away after sitting for the midday rest in the sandalwood forest, there arose in them olfactory cognition which was a moral resultant; at the time of giving water, after he had caused rain to fall to quench the purgatorial fire, there arose gustatory cognition which was a moral resultant; at the production of a softly wafting breeze there arose tactile cognition, which was a moral resultant. Thus the unconditioned set of eight:—five kinds of sense-consciousness, one [phase of] reception, two examinations—is obtained. Reconception in the case of serpents, Supaṇṇa birds, Petas who have pavilions, is by immoral result, but in the process moral result is given. So it is with the state-elephants, horses, etc., of a universal monarch.

Thus far the path of discourse on moral apperception regarding desirable and moderately desirable objects.

When, in respect of a desirable object, the four kinds of immoral consciousness which are accompanied by joy have reached apperception, then there is registration, which is consciousness without roots, accompanied by joy, and is a moral resultant. When, in respect of a moderately desirable object, these four, associated with greed and accompanied by indifference, have apperceived, then there is registration which is consciousness without roots, accompanied by indifference, and is a moral resultant.

And what has been said as to registration being necessarily determined by apperception should be understood to have been said with reference to moral consciousness. Which registration arises (when it does arise) immediately after an apperception which is accompanied by melancholy? Consciousness of the element of sense-mind-cognition, which is an immoral resultant and unconditioned. Which state fixes this apperception as moral or immoral? [The phase of] adverting, and also that of determining. Indeed, when the adverting and the determining are wisely and methodically done, the apperception is unlikely to be immoral, and [278] *vice versa.*

In the case of a desirable object contemplated by the subject with misgiving and excitement, what sort of registration is there? Whether he feels misgiving and excitement, or not, registration, in the case of a desirable object, is just moral resultant consciousness, without roots and joyful; in the case of a moderately desirable object it is the same, but accompanied by indifference instead of joy.

The exposition here given in outline is called the Theory of Mahā-Dhammarakkhita the Elder. When, namely, apperception accompanied by joy takes place, five moments of registration, and when it is accompanied by indifference, six moments of registration should be sought.

Now suppose that one who was reborn with a joyous

nature produces Jhāna, but in the process is careless and loses it. Reflection brings the thought:—'Lost for me are the excellent conditions!' And through remorse melancholy arises. What registration does he get? For in the Paṭṭhāna, it is forbidden [to posit] melancholy immediately after joy, and the converse. Should we not also find, in that book, that when there has been apperception concerning a sublime state of consciousness, it is also forbiden [to posit] registration?

There arises an element of sense-mind-cognition which is unconditioned, accompanied by indifference, and a resultant either moral or immoral. What adverting has such a state? It has no adverting function any more than there is one in the subconscious continuum. Granted that such advertings arise from tendency, habit or practice,[1] how does such sense-mind-cognition arise? Just as in the following psychic attainments: —the sphere of neither perception nor non-perception when it is in the causal relation of contiguity to trance, the consciousness in one who has emerged from trance, of fruition attained, the consciousness of the Ariyan Path, consciousness of fruition after a path—these states arise albeit there is no tendency, habit, or practice, even so such sense-mind-cognition may arise without them either. For consciousness may arise without adverting, but not without object. If so, which then is the object of that element of sense-mind-cognition? One or other of the limited states, such as visible objects, etc. For of these states, whatever object is presented, at whatever time, this consciousness arises referring to that object.

Now [279] to illustrate all these kinds of consciousness, there is this special illustrative method:—Cob-web, door-keeper, village child, mango, sugar-cane squeezing, born-blind and cripple, object-seizing, sufficing condition, purpose.

Among these 'cob-web' should be understood thus:—A certain highway spider (which waits in the path of insects)[2] spreads his web in five places, makes his net, and sleeps in the middle of it. When an insect, grasshopper or fly comes in contact with the web spread in the first place, he bestirs

---

[1] See the exposition of natural psychic law in *Milinda* i. 89, with the same terms.—*Ed.*

[2] Thus the *Yojanā*.

himself from his bed, comes out, goes along the web, kills the insect, drinks its marrow, again returns to the web and sleeps. He does likewise when the webs in the second place, etc., are touched. Herein like the webs spread in five places are the five sentient organs: like the spider sleeping in the middle is consciousness; like the moment when the web is touched by the insect, etc., is the moment when the sentient organism is struck by the object; like the stirring of the spider sleeping in the middle is the adverting by the five doors setting life-continuum in motion after the object which has struck the sentient organ has been seized; like the passage along the web is the occurrence of the cognitive process; like the drinking of the marrow after piercing the head is the time when apperception takes place in the object; like the sleep in the middle after his return is the procedure of consciousness depending on the heart-basis. What does this parable signify? That when an object strikes the sentient organism, the unit of consciousness depending on the physical basis of the heart arises before the unit depending on the sentient basis. This is what it signifies; and this also:—Each object reaches the avenue of thought by two doors.[1]

'Door-keeper' should be understood thus:—A certain king went to bed and fell asleep. His attendant sat shampooing his feet; a deaf door-keeper stood at the door. Three guards stood in a row. Then a certain man resident at a border village, bringing a present, came and knocked at the door. The deaf door-keeper did not hear the sound. He who shampooed the king's feet gave a sign, by which the door-keeper opened the door and looked. The first guard took the present and handed it to the second guard, who gave it to the third, who in turn offered it to the king. The king partook of it. [280] Herein apperception should be regarded as the king; adverting as he who shampooed the feet; visual cognition as the blind door-keeper; the three phases of thought-process beginning with reception as the three guards; the striking of the sentient organism by the object as the knocking at the door by the

[1] External sense and sense-mind.

resident of the border village who brought the present; the adverting by the five doors, setting life-continuum in motion, as the giving of the sign by him who shampooed the feet; the time of visual cognition accomplishing the function of sight with respect to object as the time of opening the door by the deaf door-keeper at the given sign; the resultant mind-element receiving the object as the taking of the present by the first guard; the resultant element of mind-cognition examining the object as the first guard giving it to the second; the element of inoperative mind-cognition determining the object as the second giving it to the third; the making over to apperception by determination as the third offering it to the king; apperception enjoying the essential property of the object as the king enjoying it. What does this parable signify? Just the functions of object striking the sentient organism; of the five-door-adverting setting the life-continuum in motion; of visual cognition, etc., seeing, receiving, examining, determining. But verily only apperception enjoys the essential property of the object.

'Village child' should be understood thus:—Many village lads were playing with dust in the middle of the road. A coin hit the hand of one of them. 'What is this that has hit my hand?' he said. Then one boy said, 'It is a white thing.' Another grasped it firmly together with the dust; another said, 'It's broad and square.' Another said, 'This is a kahāpaṇa[1].' Then he took it and gave it to his mother, who used it in some [jewellery] work. Herein, like the many boys playing and sitting in the middle of the road, is the procedure of the subconscious life-continuum; like the coin striking the hand is the object striking the sentient organism; like the asking, 'What is this?' is the five-door-adverting setting the life-continuum in motion after seizing the object; like the saying, 'It is white,' is the visual cognition accomplishing the function of seeing; like the grasping it firmly together with the dust is the [281] resultant mind-element receiving the object; like the saying, 'It's a broad square thing,' is the

---

[1] On the kahāpaṇa, a square coin, see *J.R.A.S.*, 1901, 877 *f.*; Rhys-Davids, *Buddhist India*, 100 —*Ed.*

resultant mind-cognition-element examining the object; like the saying, 'This is a kahāpaṇa,' is the inoperative mind-cognition-element determining the object; like the mother making it into some jewellery is apperception enjoying the essential property of the object. 'What does this simile signify?' The five-door-adverting sets the life-continuum in motion without seeing it; the resultant mind-element receives it without seeing it; the resultant mind-cognition-element examines it without seeing it; the inoperative mind-cognition-element determines it without seeing it; apperception enjoys the essential property of the object without seeing it. But verily only visual cognition accomplishes the function of seeing. This is what it signifies.

'Mango, sugar-cane-squeezing'—this refers to the mango-parable and that of the owner of the sugar-cane shed parable told above (pp. 359, 363).

'Born-blind and cripple' should be understood thus:—Both of them sat in a hall at the city-gate. The cripple said, 'Oh, blind one, why do you get shrivelled up by frequenting this place? In such and such another place there's plenty of food, plenty of drink. Does it not behove you to go there and live in ease?' 'You have been the first to tell me so. Is it not up to *you* to go there and live in ease?' 'I have no legs to go with.' 'Nor have I eyes to see.' 'If so, there are your legs and my eyes.' And both agreed, saying, 'All right.' The blind made the cripple mount his shoulder where the latter sat, putting his left arm round the other's head, and with his right hand marking the road: 'In this place a root stands blocking the way. In this place is a rock. Give up the left and take the right-hand path. Give up the right and take the left.' Thus, by the association both of the blind man's legs and the cripple's eyes, they went to the place they wanted and lived in ease. Herein, like the blind man is the material body; like the cripple is the immaterial body; like the want of preparedness on the part of the blind to go without the cripple to another place [282] is the inability of matter to take, seize, vibrate without the immaterial. Like the want of preparedness to go to another place on the part of the cripple without the blind man is the inability of the immaterial, where life is conditioned by the five aggregates, to proceed without matter. Like the going to the desired place by the association of both and their living in ease is the manifestation of procedure in all functions by the mutual association of material and immaterial phenomena. Thus this problem is stated with reference to the fivefold aggregate.[1]

'Object-seizing' should be understood thus:—The eye seizes the visible object; the ear seizes audible objects, and so on.

'Sufficing condition, result' should be understood thus:—Because of a sufficing condition and because of result or motive. Of these, given four conditions—to wit, the visual organ unimpaired, access of visible objects to the line of vision, dependence on light, and attention—then visual cognition arises with its concomitant phenomena. For instance, the eye of a dead man is 'impaired.' The sight of a living man, which is extinguished or impeded by bile, phlegm or blood, being unable to cause visual cognition, is said to be impaired; that which can be such a cause is unimpaired. So for the ear, etc. And although the eye may not be impaired, yet when externally the object does not come into the line of vision, visual cognition does not arise. And although that object may come into the line of vision, when there is no basis[2] of light visual cognition does not arise. And although there may be light, yet when the five-door-adverting does not agitate the life-continuum, visual cognition does not arise; it arises only when the life-continuum is agitated. Visual cognition thus arising arises together with the associated states. Thus given these four conditions visual cognition arises.

Given the same four conditions, and substituting space for light and sounds for visible objects, auditory cognition arises, together with its associated states. Herein, 'dependence on space' means that auditory cognition arises only when this dependence is obtained; it cannot arise without it. Indeed, it cannot arise in one who has the aural orifice closed. The

---

[1] *Visuddhi-Magga*, p. 596.

[2] Or medium (sannissaya).—*Ed.* Cf. *M.* :, 190.

rest is to be understood by the foregoing method. And so also in the following cognitions. We shall speak of just what is special to each sense.

The same four conditions are necessary for the arising of olfactory cognition, substituting the element of mobility for that of space. [283] Here 'dependence on the element of mobility' means that olfactory cognition arises only when this element enters the nostril, and cannot arise without it.

The same four conditions are necessary for the arising of gustatory cognition, substituting the element of cohesion (or moisture) for that of mobility. Here, 'dependence on the element of cohesion' means that gustatory cognition arises only when this element wetting the tongue is obtained; it does not arise without it. Indeed, it does not arise in those whose tongue is dry, even though dried food be placed on the tongue.

The same four conditions are necessary for the arising of tactile cognition, but 'element of extension' must be substituted for that of cohesion. Here 'dependence on the element of extension' means that tactile cognition arises only when dependence on this element as a condition of tactile sensitivity is obtained; it does not arise without it. Indeed, in the door of touch, externally the 'great Essential'[1] as object stimulates the internal sensitive surface, and impinges on the great essentials [composing it] which are the causes of its sensitivity.

The same four conditions are necessary for the arising of sense-mind[2] cognition, but 'dependence on the heart-basis' must be substituted for 'element of extension.' Here 'sense-mind' is the consciousness of the [subconscious] life-continuum. When it ceases, or when it is weakened, it cannot cause 'adverting' and is said to be impaired. When unimpaired, it can cause adverting. 'Access of cognizable things to the line [of sense-mind]' means access of such as objects of thought. 'Dependence on the heart-basis' means that thought arises only when such dependence is obtained and cannot arise without it. This problem also is stated as refer-

---

[1] See below, Book II, Ch. II.

[2] Mano.

ring to [life as conditioned by] the fivefold aggregate. 'Attention' as one of the conditions means that it arises only when the element of inoperative mind-cognition sets the life-continuum in motion. So far this is the exposition of the term 'sufficing condition.'

'Purpose' is to be understood thus: Eye is for the purpose or function of seeing, ear of hearing, nose of smelling, tongue of tasting, bodily surface of touching, [284] mind of cognizing. The eye's seeing is its purpose [or aim]. *This* is accomplished by *that*. So with the other senses [and the sensorium or sense-mind]. Thus far, in the doctrine of Tipiṭaka-Cūḷanāga the Elder,[1] the sixteenfold scheme is finished, together with the twelvefold scheme and the unconditioned set of eight.

Now the doctrine of Moravāpivāsī-Mahādatta the Elder is a discourse on the twelvefold scheme, wherein the Sāketa query, the declarations of abundance and of conditions are evident. But this Elder, seeing a flaw in the theory of automatic moral kamma giving non-automatic result, says that automatic moral kamma gives only automatic result, not non-automatic, and that non-automatic kamma gives only non-automatic result, not automatic. And this Elder does not speak of fixing consciousness by apperception, but of fixing feeling by object. On that account in his doctrine, in bringing out result, there is obtained what is called the twelvefold scheme, wherein are included the tenfold scheme and the unconditioned set of eight.

In the twelvefold scheme this is the method:—Let kamma be exerted by a consciousness that is accompanied by joy, thrice-conditioned[2] and automatic, in an adult who has taken re-conception by means of the resultant similar to that consciousness. Then, when a desirable object reaches the line of vision in the eye-door, there arises one of the three ineffectual occasions described above. In his case, supposing his consciousness be one of thirteen kinds:—four that are moral accompanied by joy, four that are immoral, five that are inoperative—then, when registration supervenes after apperception, a [phase of]

---

[1] See above, p. 354 *f*. [2] *I.e.*, having three 'roots.'

consciousness becomes established which is accompanied by joy, is automatic, and has three root-conditions, or two. Thus, when he is seeing, his [units of] consciousness may be reckoned as five:—three of visual cognition, two of registration.

Assuming that feeling changes with the object, there arises in him one or other of the twelve kinds of consciousness which are accompanied by indifference—namely, four that are moral, four immoral, and four inoperative. This consciousness arises after apperception as registration—a registration which is resultant, accompanied by indifference, is automatic, and has three, or only two root-conditions. Thus, when he is seeing, his units of consciousness may now be reckoned as three:—an examining accompanied by indifference and these two [forms of] registration. These with the foregoing five make [285] eight. As many are reckoned in each of the other four senses. Hence when kamma is exerted by one volition full forty kinds of consciousness may arise. But by taking what has not been taken there are twelve:—eight in the eye-door and the other four cognitions, auditory, etc.

Here in the discourse on the twelvefold resultant, the remarks on 'subconsciousness of conditions' and 'adventitious subconsciousness,'[1] the mango-parable,[2] and the discourse on the 'fivefold cosmic order,'[3] are to be understood in the same way. When kamma is exerted by consciousness which is accompanied by joy, thrice-conditioned, non-automatic and moral, and also by consciousness which is accompanied by indifference, thrice-conditioned, automatic and non-automatic, the same method is to be understood. And the press-parable[4] on this occasion is evident.

So far the occasion:—'thrice-conditioned conception takes place by thrice-conditioned kamma' has been discussed. And the occasion:—'twice-conditioned conception takes place by thrice-conditioned kamma' remains inexplicit.

Now comes the discourse that by twice-conditioned kamma arises twice-conditioned re-conception. To expand: Suppose kamma is exerted by consciousness, accompanied by joy, twice

---

[1] See p. 358.
[2] See p. 359.
[3] See p. 360.
[4] See p. 363.

conditioned, automatic, in an adult who has taken re-conception by a resultant similar to that consciousness. When at the eye-door a desirable object is presented there may be those three ineffectual occasions after the said fashion. But in twice-conditioned consciousness there is no work of apperception. Therefore one or other of these eight kinds of consciousness:—four that are moral accompanied by joy, four that are immoral, at the conclusion of apperception, arises as registration, which is twice-conditioned, accompanied by joy, and automatic. Thus in him four kinds of consciousness:—the three phases of cognition (visual, etc.) and this phase of registration—are reckoned.

And one or other of the eight—four, namely, which are accompanied by indifference and are moral, concerning a moderately desirable object, and four which are immoral, at the conclusion of apperception—becomes registration which is twice-conditioned, accompanied by indifference and automatic. Thus in him two kinds of consciousness:—examining, accompanied by indifference, and this registration are reckoned. These, together with the foregoing four, make six. In each of the other doors are also six. Thus when kamma is exerted by one volition, there arise full thirty kinds of consciousness. But by taking what has not been taken there are ten:—six eye-door and the other four sense-cognitions. The mango-parable and the discourse on the fivefold cosmic order are evident. And the cane-press parable on this occasion does not obtain, and therefore is not given. [286] When kamma is exerted by consciousness which is accompanied by joy, is twice-conditioned, non-automatic and is moral, or is accompanied by indifference, is twice-conditioned, and either automatic or non-automatic, the same method is to be understood.

We have now discussed the case when 'twice-conditioned conception takes place by twice-conditioned kamma.' And the occasion:—'unconditioned conception takes place'—is to be understood thus:—When kamma is exerted by the four kinds of consciousness which are dissociated from knowledge as moral, and when re-conception has been got in which the element of mind-cognition is moral, resultant, unconditioned and accompanied by indifference, it should not be said that re-conception is similar to the kamma. Speaking by the said method, and beginning with this phrase:—'by the four kinds of consciousness dissociated from knowledge as moral,'—the consciousness which arises concerning a desirable, and concerning a moderately desirable object should be understood. In this Elder's doctrine, namely, mass-apperception[1] takes place. The remaining discourse:—'which state fixes this apperception for purposes of morality and immorality?'[2]—should all be understood by the method given above.

With this, in the doctrine of Moravāpivāsī-Mahādatta the Elder, the discourse of the twelvefold resultant scheme finishes, together with the tenfold scheme and the unconditioned set of eight.

Now, in the doctrine of Mahādhammarakkhita the Elder, the discourse is on the tenfold scheme, wherein the Sāketa query and the declaration of preponderance[3] are evident. But in the statement of conditions this is special:—Thrice-conditioned kamma gives thrice-conditioned result, and twice-conditioned result and unconditioned result. Twice-conditioned kamma does not give the thrice-conditioned result, but gives the others. By thrice-conditioned kamma conception is thrice-conditioned and also twice-conditioned, not unconditioned. By twice-conditioned kamma conception is twice-conditioned and unconditioned, not thrice-conditioned. Automatic kamma gives automatic result, not non-automatic; and non-automatic kamma gives non-automatic result, not automatic. Feeling should be [considered as] changed with object; apperception takes place in masses. From the beginning units of consciousness are to be spoken of.

Wherein this is the method:—An individual exerts kamma by the first class of moral consciousness, takes re-conception only by the first kind of resultant consciousness. This re-conception is similar to the previous kamma. To the adult,

---

[1] Piṇḍajavanaṃ. ? Unanalyzed, unclassified thought.—*Tr.*

[2] See above, p. 366.

[3] See above, p. 355.

when a desirable object is presented at the eye-door, three ineffectual occasions by the said method may arise. Then to him one or other of the thirteen [287] apperceptions, accompanied by joy mentioned above, becomes at the conclusion of apperception the first kind of resultant consciousness, being registration which goes under the two names of 'subconsciousness of conditions' and 'registration.' Thus to him four kinds of consciousness:—the three cognitions (visual, etc.) and this registration—are thus reckoned. In a moderately desirable object, one or other of the twelve apperceptions accompanied by indifference by the above-said method becomes established, at the conclusion of apperception, as a registration-consciousness, accompanied by indifference, thrice-conditioned, and automatic. This also goes under the names of 'adventitious life-continuum' and 'registration.' Thus to him two units of consciousness:—examining accompanied by indifference and this registration—are reckoned. These two, together with the foregoing four, make six. Thus, when kamma is exerted by one volition in the five doors, full thirty kinds of consciousness arise. But by taking what has not been taken there are ten:—six in the eye-door and the four cognitions, auditory, etc. The mango-parable and the discourse on the cosmic orders are evident. Likewise, though kamma is exerted by the second, third, fourth classes of moral consciousness, there are only so many kinds of resultant consciousness. Also when kamma is exerted by the four classes of consciousness which are accompanied by indifference, the same method should be understood. But in the latter case, first the moderately desirable object should be shown, afterwards feeling should be changed with the [changes in the] desirable object. The mango-parable and the discourse on the cosmic orders are evident. The cane-press-parable is not obtained. In moral consciousness, beginning with, 'when kamma is exerted by any of the four classes which are dissociated from knowledge,' all should be expanded and the unconditioned set of eight be stated. Thus far, in the doctrine of Mahādhammarakkhita the Elder, the tenfold scheme finishes together with the unconditioned set of eight.

But of these three Elders whose doctrine should be accepted?

Not anyone's unreservedly. But in the doctrine of all of them what is fitting should be accepted. In the first doctrine the automatic and non-automatic arrangement is intended to serve a division in causal relations. Therefore by taking in it the non-automatic result which has arisen through weak conditions of automatic moral consciousness, and the automatic result which has arisen through strong conditions of non-automatic moral consciousness, leaving out the obtainable inoperative apperceptions, and fixing (*a*) the registration by means of moral apperception and registration, and (*b*) feeling by means of the object, [288] the sixteenfold scheme has been drawn up for the use of probationers and average persons. And at the conclusion of immoral apperception, that registration which is an unconditioned result has been shown in that doctrine, but not in the two others. Therefore that unconditioned registration included in it and the conditioned resultant included in the other two—all this is obtained here also, wherein this is the method:—When in the intervals of moral apperceptions immoral apperception takes place, then the conditioned registration at its conclusion, being similar to the apperception practised at the conclusion of the moral consciousness, is fitting. When immoral apperception takes place uninterruptedly, then the registration which is without root-conditions is fitting. Thus much of what is fitting in the first doctrine should be taken.

But in the second doctrine, the automatic and non-automatic arrangement is intended on moral grounds. For this reason, taking the automatic resultant of automatic moral consciousness, and the non-automatic resultant of non-automatic moral consciousness, without fixing registration by apperception, [we should consider] the entire twelvefold scheme as stated with reference to the total apperception worthy of arising in probationers, adepts, and average persons And in it, at the conclusion of thrice-conditioned apperception, thrice-conditioned registration is fitting; at the conclusion of twice-conditioned apperception, twice-conditioned registration is fitting; at the conclusion of unconditioned apperception, unconditioned registration is fitting. Nevertheless, it has not been drawn up as classifying them. Thus in the second doctrine what is fitting should be accepted.

In the third doctrine also the automatic and non-automatic arrangement on moral grounds only is intended. But because of the expression, 'thrice-conditioned kamma yields results thrice-conditioned, twice-conditioned, and unconditioned;[1] twice-conditioned kamma yields results twice-conditioned and unconditioned,' in one who has taken automatic, thrice-conditioned re-conception, registration should be also automatic and twice-conditioned. Without showing this, the registration has been shown as similar to the condition (of productive kamma). The mention of this registration does not fit in with the foregoing view of the statement of the producing condition. [That expression was said by the Elder] only for the purpose of setting forth the tenfold scheme. However, the other (automatic, twice-conditioned registration) should also be obtained. Thus in the third doctrine also what is fitting should be accepted.

And all this and all the discourse on registration is said with reference to the results of kamma as productive of re-conception. However, because of the expression [in the Paṭṭhāna], 'conditioned life-continuum is in the causal relation of contiguity to unconditioned life-continuum,' registration which is conditioned resultant arises also in one who has taken unconditioned re-conception by means of manifold kamma. The order of its arising will be evident in the *Paṭṭhāna*.

End of the Discourse on Moral Resultants in the Realm of Sense-Experience.

[289] CHAPTER III

DISCOURSE ON RESULTANTS IN THE REALM OF ATTENUATED MATTER AND IN THE IMMATERIAL REALM

Now to show the resultant of the material and immaterial realms, once more a beginning is made with 'which are the states that are unmoral?'[2]

---

[1] *I.e.*, without 'roots' (hetu). [2] *Dhs.* §§ 499-504.

Herein, because the resultant of the sensuous realm is both like and unlike its own moral consciousness, therefore it has not been classified as simply a sequel similar to that moral consciousness. But in the case of these two realms—of Rūpa and Arūpa—the results of kamma are like the moral consciousness in each, just as the shadows of elephants, horses, mountains, etc., resemble these. Therefore it has been classified on this principle. Again, kamma of the sensuous realm gives result at one time or another; but the kamma of the Rūpa and Arūpa realms, being unobstructed, gives result in the second individuality. Therefore it has been classified as having a similar sequel to the moral consciousness [which caused it]. The rest should be understood by the methods given under 'moral consciousness.' But this is special:—In the divisions into progress, etc., and the state of being low, exalted, or medium, resultants should be understood as coming by jhāna. Moreover, under 'predominant influences'[1] these conscious resultants being unproducible are not taken in that connection.

End of the Discourse on Resultants in the Realm of Attenuated Matter and the Immaterial Realm.

CHAPTER IV

DISCOURSE ON TRANSCENDENTAL[2] RESULT

Transcendental results, because they resemble the causal transcendental moral consciousness, have also been classified as having a similar course to morality. And because the moral consciousness on all three planes stores up and increases the round of births by means of decease and conception, therefore concerning it 'having been wrought and stored up'[3] is said. But the transcendental disperses what has been stored up; of itself it pulls down what through decease and rebirth has been piled up. Hence here 'having been worked and cultivated' has been said, instead of 'having been wrought and stored up.'

---

[1] See p. 284. [2] *Dhs.* § 505. Cf. above, p. 289*f.* [3] *Dhs.* § 431.

In the 'Void,' etc., the Path gets this name for three reasons. —by way of attainment, of one's merits, of the object. This expression has been expanded above under the subject-head of 'moral consciousness.'[1] Of the three reasons, the name is obtained 'by way of one's merits' and also 'of the object' in the Suttanta explanations. For this kind of teaching is explanatory. But Abhidhamma discourse is teaching without explanation. Therefore in the Abhidhamma the name is not obtained because of one's merits and of the object, but only by way of attainment.

Now attainment is certain, and is twofold: insight-arrival and Path-arrival. Of these two, where the path has been reached, insight-arrival is certain; [290] where its Fruition has been reached, Path-arrival is certain, as has been said above. We are now dealing with the occasion of the attainment of fruition, hence that the attainment of the Path is certain must here be taken as understood.

It is said also that this Path as attainment gets the name of the Void or Empty, and is called the Signless and the Undesired because of its own merits and of the object. Therefore itself occupying the goal of Path-arrival, it gives the three names to its own fruition. How? This Path called Emptiness, which has got its name by means of just the fact of arrival, itself occupies the place of arrival, and gives the name to its own fruition—namely, 'Emptiness.' The empty, signless Path itself occupies the goal of arrival, and in giving the name to its own fruition, gives the name 'Signless.' The empty, undesired path itself occupies the goal of arrival and in giving the name to its own fruition gives 'the Signless.' And these three names are obtained, in this way, with respect to fruitional consciousness only, immediately after the Path, and not when attainment of fruition is subsequently resorted to. And subsequently it is possible to discern by the threefold insight of impermanence, suffering and no soul. Then in that person, by virtue of much insight arisen, come to pass the three fruitions called the Signless, the Undesired and Emptiness.

---

[1] See p. 206.

And of them those kinds of knowledge, such as insight into impermanence, with conditioned things for object, are called the knowledges of adoption.[1] And that which was said on the 'empty' Path should be understood as obtaining on the 'undesired' Path also. This Path which has also got its name only by means of just the fact of arrival, itself occupies the goal of arrival, and in giving the name to its own fruition gives 'the Undesired.' The undesired, signless Path itself occupies the goal of arrival and . . . gives 'the Signless.' The undesired empty Path similarly gives 'Emptiness.' And these three names are obtained in this way only at fruitional consciousness immediately after the Path, and not when attainment of fruition is subsequently resorted to. Thus in this exposition of resultants, the kinds of resultant consciousness are to be taken as treble those of the [causal] moral consciousness.

But whereas moral activities of the three planes are not able to make their own results get a dominant influence, transcendental moral activities can do this. And why? In the former the time of putting forth activities is different from the time for yielding result. On this account they are not able to make their own results get a dominant influence. But transcendental activities, before the faith, energy, mindfulness, concentration, and wisdom which occur in the transcendental Path have ceased, get the result immediately after the Path without fail and without opposition. For this reason they are able to make their results get a dominant influence. Just as where a small fire has sprung up, the creation of heat comes to an end as soon as the fire has been extinguished, and nothing else is wanted; and just as when a big blazing mass of fire set round with dried cow-dung is extinguished, the creation of heat does not come at once to an end; so in the three-plane moral activities the kamma-moment is as different from the resultant moment as is the extinction of the fire and the heat in the case of the small fire. Therefore it is not able to make its own result get a dominant influence. But in transcen-

[1] See above, p. 310, *n*. 2. *Pyī* reads 'adaptation.'

dental activities, before faith, etc., have ceased, fruition arises immediately after the path. Therefore it causes its own result to get a dominant influence. For this reason the Ancients have said, 'Except in the transcendental, there is no dominant influence in the resultant.'

In the exposition of the Fourth Fruition, 'the controlling faculty of one of perfected knowledge'[1] refers to that of [the saint] whose knowledge has been perfected, and has performed its function in respect of the Four Truths. Or it is a controlling faculty through the accomplishing of control within the states of consciousness that arise, possessed by those who have perfected knowledge, those, namely, who have completed what was to be done in the matter of the Four Truths, who have come to know, who have penetrated the Four Truths. [292] In the section of the exposition of the expression, 'of those of perfected knowledge,' means, of those who having come to know [so] endure. 'States'[2] mean inner [subjective] associated states. 'Perfected knowledge' means having come to know.[3] 'Insight, understanding' and so on have already been explained. 'Path-factor, Path-included' =the factor of the Path arising in fruition and included in that Path.

There is something else to be said. In this transcendental result this is distinctive:—One of these three controlling faculties goes to one objective, one goes to six objectives, one goes to one objective. To expand: The faculty of believing 'I shall come to know the unknown' goes to one objective, viz., the Path of Stream-winning. The faculty of perfected knowledge goes to six objectives: the three lower Fruitions and the three higher Paths. The faculty of a person of perfected knowledge goes to one objective—viz., the fruition of Arahantship. In all, the paths and fruitions amount to eight [multiplying]eight controlling faculties. Thus sixty-four transcendental

---

[1] *Dhs.* § 555. The 'section' referred to just below is the answer to the question.

[2] In *B.P.E.*, § 555, for 'doctrines' read states.

[3] *Ā-jānanā. Jānanā* means 'coming to know.' Cf. *connaître* and *savoir;* we have no such equivalents.—*Ed.*

controlling faculties have been accounted for. But textually[1] Paths and Fruits are multiplied by nine, making seventy-two controlling faculties. 'Path-factor' is said with reference to the Path and also to Fruition. So also is the term 'factor of Enlightenment.' 'Avoidance, abstinence' refer to the moment when the Path is realized, and the moment when Fruition is realized. 'Path' means just 'being in the Path,' but fruition is so named with reference to the Path.[2] It is proper to say that a factor of fruition is included in fruition. In the Path the condition of one about to be enlightened as to the four Facts is the factor of Enlightenment. In the Fruition it is the condition of one who has known the four Facts. In the Path avoidance and abstinence are so called by virtue of [the exercise of] avoiding and abstaining. In the Fruition they are so called by virtue of having avoided, having abstained.

End of the Discourse on Transcendental Result.

CHAPTER V

DISCOURSE ON IMMORAL RESULT

These seven kinds of consciousness when they constitute immoral results—namely, visual, auditory, olfactory, gustatory, and tactile cognitions, one sense-mind-element and one sense-mind-cognition-element, by text and in sense—resemble the corresponding kinds of moral resultant consciousness described above. The latter, of course, have moral kamma for cause; the immoral resultants have immoral kamma for cause. And the former arise concerning desirable and moderately desirable objects, the latter concerning undesirable and moderately undesirable objects. In the former tactile cognition is accompanied by pleasure, in the latter it is accompanied by pain. [293]In the former the element of mind-cognition, accompanied

[1] Pāḷito.

[2] *I.e.*, becau e of resembling the path (*Ṭīkā*).

by indifference causing rebirth among men of one born blind, yields result on five occasions. But here in the latter consciousness, when kamma is exerted by the elevenfold immoral consciousness, it causes re-conception in the four spheres of evil doom,[1] making either kamma, kamma-symbol, or tendency-symbol the object, and gives result. Starting from the occasion of the second consciousness, it becomes (1) life-continuum while life lasts, (2, 3) examination in the five thought-processes with undesirable and moderately undesirable objects, (4) registration in the six doors when the object is vivid, and (5) decease at the time of death. Thus it gives result on five occasions.

End of the Discourse on Immoral Result.

CHAPTER VI

THE ELEMENT OF INOPERATIVE SENSE-MIND CONSCIOUSNESS

Now to show by classifying unmoral consciousness [called] 'inoperative,' a beginning is once more made with 'which are the states that are unmoral ?'[2] Here 'inoperative' means the mere acting or doing of a function. In all inoperative consciousness that which has not attained the apperceptional state is fruitless like a plant with a wind-snapped flower; that which has reached the apperceptional state is fruitless like the flower of an uprooted tree. Nevertheless, because of procedure in accomplishing this and that function, there is the mere doing, hence [the activity] is called 'inoperative.'[3] The phrase 'neither moral nor immoral,' etc., means that, owing to the absence of the moral condition called the moral root, it is not moral; owing to the absence of the immoral condition called the immoral root, it is not immoral. Owing to the absence of moral and immoral causes of wise and unwise attention, it is said to be neither moral nor immoral. Owing

---

[1] Purgatory, Asuras, Petas, and animals.

[2] *Dhs.* § 566. Cf. *Compendium*, p. 149 *f.*

[3] Or ineffectual.—*Ed.*

to the absence of the productive condition called moral and immoral, it is not result of kamma.

In the exposition of one-pointedness of mind,[1] here the mere static procedure is obtained. In these seventeen modes of consciousness, the five cognitions as moral and as unmoral, the three mind-elements, the three mind-cognition elements, consciousness accompanied by perplexity, [the terms] solidity, steadfastness, etc., are not obtained because of weakness. Excepting the occasion of its genesis, elsewhere all the rest should be understood by the method given in the exposition of the resultant mind-element.[2] [294] Namely, that resultant consciousness arises immediately after the five cognitions. But this inoperative consciousness arises before all thought-processes, when the thought-process arises on occasion of an object in the five doors. How? In the eye-door among desirable, moderately desirable, undesirable, moderately undesirable objects, when any one visible object strikes the sentient organism, it seizes this and that object and arises as the precursor by virtue of adverting and setting the life-continuum in motion. In the ear-door, etc., the same method should be understood.

End of the Element of Inoperative Sense-Mind Consciousness.

CHAPTER VII

CONCLUSION

THE element of mind-cognition arising . . . 'accompanied by joy'[3] means that this consciousness is the special property of one purged of the 'Intoxicants,' is not shared in common with others, and is obtainable in the six doors. To expand: In the eye-door seeing a suitable place for religious application, the Arahant is joyful at this thought. In the ear-door he becomes joyful at this kind of thought:—'when they, being

---

[1] *Ib.* § 570.   [2] See above, p. 358.   [3] *Dhs.* § 576.

seized by excessive greed, are making a great noise in the market-place, such frivolous craving of lust have I put away.' In the door of smell, joy arises when he is offering odours and flowers at a shrine. In the door of taste, joy arises when, after acquiring savoury alms and distributing them, he partakes of them and thinks: 'Surely I have fulfilled the duties of courtesy!' In the door of tactile activities joy arises at the consciousness, 'Surely I have completed the minor duties!' So far it is thus obtained in the five doors.

Moreover, in the mind-door joy arises with reference to past and future objects. For instance:—reflecting on the reason of some act done in the time of the lad Jotipāla,[1] of the King Makhādeva,[2] of the ascetic Kaṇha[3] and others, the Tathāgata manifested a smile. And that reflection is a function of the knowledge of former existence and of omniscience, at the conclusion of the practice of which this laughter-producing consciousness arises. The Tathāgata smiled at the thought:—'in future Tantissara the silent Buddha, Mudiṅga [295] the silent Buddha will arise.' That reflection is the function of the knowledge of the future and of omniscience, at the conclusion of the practice of which the laughter-producing consciousness arises. And in the section of the exposition of such consciousness, 'one-pointedness of mind' should be brought and placed as the 'strength' of concentration, because it is stronger than the other kinds of consciousness without root conditions. Energy also should be placed as the 'strength' of energy. But in the section of the outline, because the 'strengths' of concentration and energy do not occur, the pair are not called 'strengths' in the sense of completion or fulness of strength.[4] And because this consciousness is neither moral nor immoral, therefore it has not been placed as 'strength.' And because it certainly is not strength, therefore in the section of the Summary also it has not been said 'there are two strengths.' In the exposition of the unconditioned[5]

---

[1] *M.* ii. 45. [2] *Ib.* 74. [3] *Jāt.* iv. 6 *f.*

[4] Because of the absence of root to the unconditioned consciousness, there is no firmness or stability; hence the strength is not complete. —*Ṭīkā.* [5] *I.e.*, without 'roots.' Some read 'conditioned.'

mind-cognition-element accompanied by joy, all the rest should be understood by the said method.

In the phrase 'accompanied by indifference,'[1] this consciousness (of adverting at the mind-door) is common to all beings in the three planes who are endowed with mind. In such it cannot fail to arise. It must arise. And in arising there is determination in the five doors, adverting in mind-door. And the six kinds of knowledge not so held in common seize the very object seized by this consciousness. It is called the 'great elephant.' There is no object it does not seize. Which is that consciousness which, not being omniscience, is seized by omniscience? This consciousness. Of it the rest should be understood by the method given in the foregoing consciousness. There, however, from there being rapture the aggregate of the mental co-efficients has been classified as ninefold. Here from being without rapture the aggregate of the mental co-efficients has been classified as eightfold.

Now because the eight main types of consciousness arise as moral in [a saint] purged of the 'Intoxicants,' whatever kinds of inoperative consciousness are produced should therefore be understood by the method given in the exposition of moral consciousness. Here laughter-producing consciousness should be placed and included. How many are these? Thirteen. For average persons laugh at eight kinds of consciousness accompanied by joy: four moral, and four immoral. Probationers laugh at six kinds of consciousness: four moral accompanied by joy, and two immoral dissociated from error and accompanied by joy. Arahants laugh at five accompanied by joy, and inoperative.

[296] In the expositions of inoperative consciousness in the Rūpa and Arūpa realms,[2] the phrase 'easeful living under present conditions' means the mere happy living in this very individuality, in the present. For the Arahant, any attainment won while he is yet at the stage of the average man is of moral [value] while he is winning it and inoperative when it is won. When he becomes Arahant, that attainment be-

---

[1] *Dhs.* § 576. [2] *Dhs.* §§ 577-82.

comes inoperative only. All the rest should be understood by the method given in the exposition of moral consciousness, because of the resemblance to such consciousness.

End of the Discourse of the Book on Risings of Consciousness, in the 'Expositor,' the Commentary on the Compendium of States of Consciousness.

BOOK II

MATERIAL QUALITIES (RŪPA)

CHAPTER I

MATTER AS UNMORAL

WITH the foregoing completion of the comments on conscious states the subject of the Unmoral is still unfinished. Once more comes the question: 'Which are the states that are unmoral?'[1]—the object being now a classification of a section on the 'material' [in consciousness]. Under genesis of consciousness above, the unmoral as resultant consciousness and as inoperative consciousness has been exhaustively classified. The 'unmorals' which are material, and the 'unmorals' which are Nibbāna have not been classified. It was to show these that he grouped the unmoral under four heads, and began by speaking of (1) 'the resultants of moral and immoral states.'

The foregoing 'moral and immoral states' all belong to the four planes; so far then the unmoral as resultant has been delimitated by the two terms 'moral resultant' and 'immoral resultant.' But because the whole of that 'unmoral as resultant' is either of the sensuous sphere, or of one of the other spheres, therefore it has been set forth as included in [the consciousness of] the given sphere by the method adopted in each case. But again, because as consciousness it is [definable as] one or other of the four mental aggregates, therefore it is shown as comprised under these. Yet again, besides these three methods:—moral-immoral consciousness, plane [or sphere] of consciousness and associated aggregates—

[1] *Dhs.* § 583.

he showed the unmoral as inoperative [297] in the terms 'those states which are inoperative.' Here the three planes and the four aggregates might have been alluded to. But these were dealt with in what had preceded. In this way the treatment has been arranged.

Now in showing forth the unmoral that is yet to be classified, he said, 'all matter and unconditioned element,' etc. Herein, by the term 'all matter' twenty-five material qualities and ninety-six material species have been taken without remainder. By the expression 'and unconditioned element' nothing but Nibbāna has been designated. By thus much the term 'unmoral state' is completely accounted for.

CHAPTER II

THE FOUR GREAT ESSENTIALS

WHY has the expression, 'In this connection what is "all matter"?' been chosen? In the preceding chapters the unmoral as matter has been mentioned only in the abstract. Now to classify and show it in detail by way of sets of one and more up to eleven this expression has been chosen. The meaning is:—in the two terms given: 'all matter' and 'unconditioned element,' what is the former? In showing this he named the four great essentials, etc. Here four is the numerical limit precluding more or less than four.

The word 'and' has the sense of inclusion by which the four great essentials are not the only material things; there are others. Thus it includes derived matter. The 'great essentials' or 'phenomena' are so-called for such reasons as the manifestation of their greatness. For they are called 'great essentials' [or primaries] because of the manifestation of their greatness, because of the illusory resemblances they show in phenomena, the immensity of their maintenance (*parihāro*), the immensity of their metamorphoses, their vast elementality. Of these terms the first means that they are manifested as vast in a continuity that is 'grasped at' and in a continuity that is 'not grasped at.' The continuity 'not grasped at' should thus be understood:—

One world-system in length and breadth is 1203,450 yojanas.[1]

[298] *Thirty-six hundred thousand yojanas,*
Ten thousand, fifty, and three hundred make
The world's whole round, wherein lies this our earth,
In thickness four and twenty nahutas.[2]
In thickness eight and forty nahutas[2]

---

[1] The yojana itself is a disputed quantity. In the oldest books it seems to have been between seven and eight miles.—*Ed.*

[2] Nahuta = 10,000, here, presumably, 'of yojanas.'

The wind-girt water flows, and the wind climbs
For six and ninety myriad yojanas
Unto the lower æther. Even thus
Is told the measure of the Universe.
Sineru, highest of the mountain peaks,
Sinks four and eighty thousand yojanas
In the great deep, and to that height ascends.
To half this measure sink and rise these seven
In due succession named:—Yugandhara,
And Isadhara, Karavīka Range,
Sudassana, and Mount Nemindhara,
Vinataka, and Assakaṇṇa's mass.
These seven celestial ranges, beautified
With many gems, compass Sineru round.
There dwell Great Regents, Yakkhas, deities.
Himăvā stands five hundred yojanas
In height (three thousand are its length and breadth),
Crowned with its four and eighty thousand peaks.
This island Jambudīpa has been named
After the Jambu tree, which others name
Năga, whose trunk is fifteen yojanas
In girth. The trunk and the outspreading arms
Are fifty yojanas in length. It shades
A hundred; and a hundred is its height.

And the dimensions of the Jambu are the dimensions of the variegated trumpet-flower of the Asŭras, the silk-cotton tree of the Garuḷas, the kadamba tree of Aparayoga, the wish-yielding tree of the Uttarakurus, the acacia of Pubbavideha, and the coral tree in Tāvatiṃsa.

[299] Hence the Ancients said:—

Kadamba, and devas' Pāricchattaka,
Pātali, Kappa, Jambu, Simbali,
Sirīsa seventh.
The great world's rocky rim sinks in the deep
Eighty-two thousand yojanas, its height
Identical, encircling the whole world.

In continuity 'grasped-at,'[1] such material forms as the bodies of fish, turtle, deva, demon, etc., are big in appearance. As it was said by the Blessed One:—'Bhikkhus, in the great ocean are creatures one hundred yojanas in size.'[2]

'From illusory resemblance in phenomena' means, just as the juggler shows water which is not a gem as a gem, a stone which is not gold as gold, and himself not being an ogre,[3] nor a bird, as ogre or as bird, so these forms, not being indigo, may appear as indigo-coloured derived matter, not being yellow, nor red, nor white, as derived matter of these colours. Thus because of their illusory resemblances to the juggler's counterfeiting are they called 'great phenomena.' As such great essentials of Yakkhas and the like who seize any being are not found inside that being, nor outside, but just exist in dependence upon him, so these material forms are not found standing mutually inside or outside; they just exist depending one on the other. Thus because they have unimaginable footing, and resemble the counterfeiting of phenomena by Yakkhas, etc., they are called 'great phenomena.'

Again, the great essentials are like ogresses. As these by seductive transformations of their external appearance, and hiding their own fearfulness, deceive people, so they, by means of lovely skin and complexion in the bodies of women, men, etc., and of lovely contour of limbs, big and small, and of lovely gestures of hands, feet, fingers, eyebrows, hiding their own various intrinsic characteristics of harshness, and so on, deceive fools and do not allow them to see their real nature. Thus owing also to their similarity to the illusory phenomena of ogresses in counterfeiting, they are 'great phenomena.'

[300] 'From maintenance' means, because they are maintained by great or many causes. These material forms, namely, from being daily maintained occur as essentials through abundance of food, covering, etc.; hence the name.

'From the immensity of their metamorphoses' means, because of the great changes [undergone by] the elements in material forms 'grasped-at' as well as not 'grasped-at.'

---

[1] Below, p. 437, *n.* 1. [2] *Vin. Texts*, iii, 302. [3] *I.e.*, Yakkha.

Of these the vastness of the change in the underived is manifested at the destruction of a world-cycle; that of the derived is manifested when the elements are disturbed.

When heat consumes this world, the flame of fire
Leaps upward even to the Brahmā world.
When angry waters whelm the universe,
The whole world of ten myriad koṭis falls.
When perturbation of the element
Of motion overwhelms the universe,
The whole world of ten myriad koṭis falls.
As bodies that the kaṭṭhamukha bites
Stiffen, so bodies from the tottering
Of the extension-element, grow stiff
As though they entered kaṭṭhamukha's mouth.
As bodies that the pūtimukha bites
Grow putrid, bodies from the tottering
Of the cohesion element will rot
As though they entered pūtimukha's mouth.
As bodies that the aggimukha bites
Grow hot, so bodies from the tottering
Of the heat-element wax also hot
As though they entered Aggimukha's mouth.
As bodies that the satthamukha bites
Are cut up, bodies from the tottering
Of the element of motion are cut up
As though they entered satthamukha's mouth.

Such mighty changes are implied in the name 'great essentials' or phenomena.

'Because of the vastness of their "becoming"':—that is, these [elemental forms], as existing, require mighty effort to cope with them, and on this account are called Great Essentials. For such reasons are they called 'great essentials.'

'The derivative matter of the four great essentials'—here the possessive case is in the sense of the ablative. The meaning is, matter which has proceeded in dependence on, is derived from, has not let go the four great essentials. This is what is called 'all matter,' and comprises four great essentials, and twenty-three derived material things shown in due order. Thus this scheme of twenty-seven kinds constitutes 'all matter.'

[301] Now to show that matter in detail, he said, 'all matter is not a condition,' etc., laying down the table of contents by means of unitary, and so on, up to elevenfold compendia. Herein to the term 'all matter' should be applied all the terms, thus: 'All matter is not-a-condition, all matter is unconditioned.'[1] And all these forty-three terms, beginning with 'not-a-condition,' are shown briefly. Of them forty terms have been placed in due order by taking them from the Table of Contents; at the conclusion there are three terms not from the Table of Contents. Thus so far in the first compendium a specification of the Text should alone be understood. And so also in the second compendium, etc.

Now in the second there are one hundred and four couplets, of which fourteen, stated at the outset as 'there is matter derived, there is matter underived,'[2] are known as special cases, from the absence of mutual connection. The following twenty-five couplets, beginning with 'There is matter which is the basis of eye-contact,' are called basis-couplets, because they proceed by investigating what is basis and what is not. Following them, twenty-five couplets, beginning with 'There is matter which is the object of eye-contact,' are called object-couplets, because they proceed by investigating what is object and what is not. Following them, ten couplets, beginning with 'There is matter which is the organ of eye,' are called sense-organ couplets because they arise by investigating what is organ and what not. Following them, ten couplets, beginning with 'There is matter which is the element of eye,' are called element-couplets, because they proceed by investigating what is element and what is not. Following them, eight couplets, beginning with 'There is matter which is the controlling faculty of eye,' are called controlling faculty-couplets, because they proceed by investigating what is controlling-faculty and what is not. Following them, twelve couplets, beginning

[1] *I.e.*, without the 6 hetu's (p. 61 *f*.).

[2] *Dhs.* § 585.

with 'There is matter which is body-intimation,' are called refined matter-couplets, because they proceed by investigating what is refined and what is unrefined matter. This is the specification of the Text in the second compendium.

In the third compendium[1] are one hundred and three triplets. Here connecting one personal couplet, from among fourteen particular couplets given in the second compendium, with the remaining thirteen, we find thirteen special triplets laid down by the method beginning with, 'That which is personal matter is derived, that which is external matter [302] is derived and not derived.' Subsequently, connecting that personal couplet with the remaining couplets, the remaining triplets have been laid down by the method beginning with, 'That which is external matter is not the basis of eye-contact, that which is personal matter is the basis and not the basis of eye-contact.' Their names and number should be understood by virtue of basis-couplets, etc. This is the specification of the Text in the third compendium.

In the fourth compendium[2] are twenty-two quadruplets. With the exception of the last all these have been stated by taking into account the tabulated qualities of matter in connection with:—'There is matter that is derived . . . is underived.' How? By taking, in the twofold compendium, each of whatever three couplets there are from the beginning among particular couplets and connecting it with five and five couplets by the method beginning with, 'That matter which is derived is "grasped at" and not "grasped at,"' fifteen quadruplets have been laid down at first, having their root in those three couplets. Now because the fourth couplet about matter as 'visible' is not connected, in the absence of *sense*, of *serial order*, of *emphasis*, with the following couplets by the method beginning 'That matter which is visible is reacting, non-reacting,' or with the preceding couplets by the method beginning with 'It is derived, underived';—owing to the absence of *sense* thus 'It is not that the visible is unimpinging or underived'; owing to the absence of *serial*

---

[1] *Dhs.* § 586. [2] *Ib.* § 587.

order thus, 'the visible is grasped at and not grasped at'; owing to the absence of *emphasis* (all the couplets are connected only with the following couplets), this is the serial order here. With the preceding couplets it is absent. When there is the absence of what is 'grasped at' and not 'grasped at,' the absence of serial order does not matter; hence one should say that the construction should be with the 'grasped at,' etc.; it should not be made owing to the absence of distinction. Indeed the terms 'grasped at,' etc., have been connected with this visible couplet. In that construction, when it is said, 'Either the "grasped at" is visible, or the visible is "grasped at,"' there is no distinction. Therefore without contemplating that fourth couplet and connecting each two couplets, which are connected by the method beginning with 'That matter which is impinging is a controlling faculty, not a controlling faculty; that matter which is non-impinging is a controlling faculty, not a controlling faculty,' together with the three following couplets beginning with [303] 'There is matter impinging,' six quadruplets have been laid down.

And as this fourth couplet does not undergo connection, so also the initial couplet is not connected with it. Why? Because underived matter is invisible. To expand: This initial couplet being connected with the fourth:—'That matter which is not derived is visible, invisible'—does not undergo connection. Therefore passing over that fourth couplet, it has been connected with the fifth. So whichever couplet is connected with any other couplet, it should be understood that it does not undergo connection. Such is the specification of the Text in the fourth compendium.

The seven following compendia, beginning with the fivefold, are not mutually mixed. Such should be considered as the specification of the Text in the entire table of contents.

Now to classify and show the meaning of that Table of Contents, the beginning is 'no matter is a condition.'[1] But why herein has the question not been put:—'what is that "all matter" not any of which is a condition?' Because

---

[1] *Hetu. Dhs.* § 595. *I.e.*, the 6 hetus are immaterial.—*Ed.*

the subject is not divided. In such couplets, etc., as, 'there is derived matter; there is not derived matter,' there is partial inclusion, but here there is not such distinction as 'condition, not condition' and 'conditioned, unconditioned.' Therefore the classification has been made without a query. And the meaning is: 'all'—that is, without remainder; 'matter':—that is, the word which shows, expresses, names, characterizes the state of being affected by external objects; 'not any condition':—that is, an expression indicating the emphatic rejection[1] of the condition.[2]

Herein condition is fourfold:—root-condition, causal condition, chief condition, common condition. Of these, that which includes the 'three moral conditions, three immoral conditions, three unmoral conditions' is root-condition. 'Now, bhikkhu, the four great essentials are the condition, the cause in the designation of the material aggregate'[3]—here we have *hetu* (condition) in the general sense of causal relation (*paccaya*). In the following phrases *hetu* means chief condition:—a desirable object is the chief (thing) in a good result, an undesirable object in a bad result. As he said:—[304] 'He understands as it really has come to be, [namely,] as to occasion and condition, the result of the acquiring of kamma, past, future, and present.'[4]

'This is the condition, this is the cause of kamma-activities,[5] to wit, ignorance':[6]—here ignorance, being the common condition of those activities, distributes the causal state, and this is *hetu* as 'condition held in common.' As the cause of both what is sweet and what is bitter is an essential property of the extended and the cohesive, so the condition of both good and bad kammic activities is ignorance. In this place the interpretation of *hetu* is root-condition. Having thus fixed the import of the conditioned state of matter laid down in the Table of Contents as, 'states which are conditions,

---

1 Read sāvadhāraṇa- for sādhāraṇa-.

2 *I.e.*, a *hetu*, or 'spring of conduct,' moral or immoral.—*Ed.*

3 *S.* iii. 101.

4 *S.* v. 304; *A.* iii. 417.

5 *Sankhārā.*

6 *S.* ii., 1 *ff.*

states which are not conditions,'[1] he now says 'not any condition,' rejecting such a state. In this way, in all the terms, the statements as to rejection and non-rejection should be understood.[2] And the definition of all the terms has been given in the commentary on the Table of Contents.[3]

'Related to a cause' means: matter sprung from kamma is caused by kamma, that sprung from nutriments, etc., is caused by nutriments, etc. Thus by virtue of the said four causes of matter should the meaning be understood.

'Just matter'[4] rejects the immaterial state referred to in the table of contents[5] as 'material states, immaterial states.' 'Arisen by means of the six modes of [sense-] cognition' means that only matter as now present should be understood by means of all the six modes of cognition. That is fixed by the cognition of the five senses, but these cognitions do not cognize the past and the future; only sense-mind-cognition does that; it falls into the stream of the fivefold cognition and goes along with it. It is impermanent in that it becomes and perishes; it is overpowered by old age because of its having such nature; or, because in the material body old age is evident, therefore it is said to be 'overpowered by old age.'[6]

'Compendium of matter under a single aspect'[7]:—the word aspect (*vidhā*) is found affixed to the terms conceit, appearance, portion. '*Conceit* at the thought, "I am the better man"'; '*conceit* at the thought, "I am equal,"' etc.[8]—thus *vidhā* is a mode of conceit. 'What *sort* of a person do they call virtuous, wise?' etc.—here *vidhā* means the apparent. [305] For of the term, 'what sort,' the meaning is 'what is he like?' 'The basis of knowledge as one portion,' etc.[9]—here *vidhā* means portion. Here also aspect means portion.

The word 'compendium' (*sangaha*) also is fourfold by way of co-birth, similar birthplace, similar work and calculation. In the passages:—'May all princes come, all priests come, all merchants come, all workmen come!'[10] and 'Visākha, these

---

[1] *Dhs.*, p. 2.
[2] *Ib.* § 595.
[3] Above, p. 61 *f.*
[4] *B.P.E.*, p. 168, *n.* 4.
[5] *Dhs.*, p. 3, *l.* 3.
[6] *Ib.* § 584 (end).
[7] *B.P.E.:* 'category of Form considered by way of single attributes.'
[8] *Dhs.* § 1116.
[9] *Vibh.* 306 *f.*
[10] Not traced.

three states: right speech, right work, right livelihood are comprised in the aggregate of virtue '[1]:—such compendium is comprising under similarity in kind. In the following all are comprised as one in origin as though it were said, 'Let all of one kind come! Let all people of Kosala, of Magadha, of Bhārukaccha come!' and 'Visākha, these three states: right endeavour, right mindfulness, right concentration are comprised in the merit of concentration.'[2] Thus this compendium means similarity in source, as though it were said, 'Let all men bred in one place come.' In the following:—'Let all elephant-riders, horsemen, charioteers, come!' and 'Visākha, these two states: right view, right intention are comprised under the aggregate of wisdom,'[3]—this is compendium as work. And all these are classed together on account of their own work. In the following:—'Under what reckoned aggregate does the organ of sight go? That of the material aggregate. Verily it is so. Wherefore, indeed, dear sir, the organ of sight is comprised under the material aggregate'[4]—here compendium is a summary. The meaning is, reckoning matter by one specimen. And the same everywhere.

---

[1] *Majjhima N.* i. 301. [2] *Ib.* [3] *Ib.*

[4] Not traced. The diction is that of the *Kathāvatthu* (*Points of Controversy*). The matter is the subject of *Dhātukathā*, cf. i., § 17.—*Ed.*

CHAPTER III

DERIVED MATERIAL QUALITIES

Now in the twofold and following compendia[1] he said, 'What is the material quality that is derived?' and so forth, thus showing the term-analysis preceded by the query, because distinctions were revealed, viz.: 'There is matter derived . . . not derived.' Here 'derived' is 'it grasps.'[2] The meaning is: grasping the great essentials, not letting go,[3] such (derived forms) proceed in dependence upon them.

[306] Now in showing that [derived matter] according to its variety, he said, 'Organ of sight, etc.' Having thus briefly pointed out derived matter under twenty-three aspects, and then in showing it at length, he said, 'What is that matter which is organ of sight?'[4] wherein 'eye' is twofold:—eye of flesh and eye of insight. Of these eye of insight is fivefold according to this division:—Buddha eye, all-seeing eye, eye of knowledge, clairvoyant eye, and eye of the Dhamma. Of these, the passage:—'Bhikkhus, in surveying the world with the eye of a *Buddha*, I saw beings with but little dust of corruption in their eyes . . . beings docile and indocile,'[5] refers to the 'Buddha eye.' 'Omniscience is called the *all-seeing eye*'[6] —this is the all-seeing eye. '*Vision arose, knowledge arose*'[7]— this is the eye of knowledge. 'Bhikkhus, with *clarified spiritual eye* indeed I saw'[8]—this is the psychic eye. 'In that very seat, the pure, unstained *eye of the Dhamma* arose'[9]—'this is the Dhamma eye, comprising the first three Paths.

Again, the eye of the flesh is twofold: viz., as compound

---

1 *Dhs.* § 596. 2 Burm. text: upādāyati.

3 Read in P.T.S. ed. amuñcitvā. Cf. above, p. 395.

4 *Dhs.* §§ 597-600.

5 *M.* i. 169; cf. *Dialogues* ii. 32; *Kindred Sayings* i. 174; *Vinaya Texts* i. 88.

6 Not traced. 7 *Dialogues* ii. 26. 8 *S.* ii. 213.

9 Cf. *Dialogues* i. 95.

organ and as sentient organ. Of these, a lump of flesh is situated in the cavity of the eye, bound by the bone of the cavity of the eye below, by the bone of the brow above, by the eye-peaks on both sides, by the brain inside, by the eyelashes outside. It has fourteen constituents: briefly, the four elements, colour, odour, taste, nutritive essence, collocation, appearance, life, nature, sensitive skin, sentient eye. In detail, there are the four elements and the following six which depend on them:—colour, odour, taste, nutritive essence, appearance, and collocation. These ten, in that they spring from four causes, make forty. Four, to wit, life, nature, sensitive skin, sentient eye, spring solely from kamma. Thus [307] these forty-four material qualities make forty-four constituents. Although the world perceives the eye as white, as [of a certain] bigness, extension, width, they do not know the real sentient eye, but only the physical basis thereof. That lump of flesh situated in the cavity of the eye is bound to the brain by sinewy threads. Therein are white, black, red, extension, cohesion, heat, and mobility. The eye is white from the abundance of phlegm, black from that of bile, red from that of blood, rigid from that of the element of extension, fluid from that of cohesion, hot from that of heat, and oscillating from that of mobility. Such is the compound organ of the eye. And that sentient organ situated in and bound to it is called the sentient eye as derived from the four great essentials. In[1] the circle of vision where arise images of the bodies of men standing, right in front, in the middle of the black disc surrounded by white circles of the constituent organism, it [the sentient organ] permeates the ocular membranes as sprinkled oil permeates seven cotton wicks. And it is served by the four elements doing the functions of sustaining, binding, maturing, and vibrating, just as a princely boy is tended by four nurses doing the functions of holding, bathing, dressing and fanning him. And being upheld by the caloric order, by thought and nutriment, and guarded by life and attended by colour, odour, taste, etc., the organ, no

---

[1] *Visuddhi Magga*, p. 445.

bigger in size than the head of a louse, stands duly fulfilling the nature of the basis and the door of visual cognition, etc. As it has been said by the 'General of the Dhamma':—

> *That organ of the visual sense, by which*
> *Objects are apprehended, is a small*
> *And subtle thing, and like a louse's head.*[1]

The term *cakkhāyatanaṃ* means 'sense of sight.'[2] In the phrase 'that eye which is the sentient organ derived from the four great essentials,' the possessive case is used in the sense of purpose. The sentient organ arises grasping the four great essentials is the meaning. By this expression he takes only the sentient organ and rejects the remaining visual organism. But in the *Indriyagocara* Sutta[3] the sentient organ arising as derived from one great essential, [308] which is the element of extension, is well upheld by the other three great essentials: cohesion, heat, and mobility. In the *Catuparivatta* Sutta[4] the sentient organ arising as derived from the two great essentials of the elements of extension and of cohesion, is well upheld by the two great essentials of heat and mobility. These two sayings have been made by way of explanation, and this Suttanta-like discourse is an explanatory teaching. The sentient organ arising as derived from the four great essentials is true of any one and also of any two of them. In this way is the teaching in the two Suttas. But the Abhidhamma is teaching without explanation. Therefore it is here said, 'the sentient organ derived from the four great essentials.'

Because it is grasped by foolish folk, as 'this body or this collection of the five aggregates is my *self*,' therefore both the bodily frame and the fivefold aggregate is called 'self-state' (*attabhāva*, *i.e.*, personality).

'Included in personality' is comprised in and depending on just that.

'Invisible':—what cannot be seen by visual cognition.

'Reacting':—reaction, friction is here produced.

---

[1] Not traced.
[2] *Dhs.* § 597.
[3] No such named Sutta as this is known.
[4] ? *S.* iii. 59; cf. *S.* ii. 103.

'By which,' etc.:—that is to say, in brief, this eye by which as cause a given person 'has' in the past 'seen' the visible object specified, or, now proceeding, 'sees' it, or in future 'will see' it. If the eye be intact, he 'may see' such visible object as comes into focus, or he 'may have seen' a past object with a sight that is past. He sees a present thing by a present [eye]; he will see a future thing by a future [eye]. If the given object come into the focus of the eye, he 'may see' it by the eye:—here the phrase is conditional.

'Moreover this is sight,' refers to direction of vision.

'And this is visual sense,' refers to source and collocation.

'And this is visual element,' refers to emptiness of essence, of entity.

'And this is controlling faculty of sight,' refers to the setting up of control as an essential characteristic in vision.

'And this is a world,' refers to its transience, perishableness.

'And this is a door,' refers to its being an entry.

'And this is ocean'—because it cannot be filled.

'And this is lucent'—because it is very pure.

'And this is a field,' refers to origin of contact, etc.

'And this is a basis,' refers to its fixed seat. It guides the subject showing what is level and not level—this is meant by the term 'guide,' and in that sense also it is 'guidance.'

[309] 'And this is the hither shore,' refers to its being included in individuality.[1]

'And this is an empty village,' refers to its being common to many and to the absence of a possessor.[2]

So far by joining these fourteen epithets beginning with 'moreover this is sight,' with the four terms beginning with 'he has seen,' the four methods of specification have been expounded. How? 'By that eye invisible and reacting he has seen a thing visible and reacting. And this is sight—and this is empty village'—such visible thing is the visual sense. This is one method. So should the rest be understood.

Now because a visible object strikes the sentient visual organ even when there is no desire to see, as when lightning flashes,

[1] *I.e.*, existence in the three planes. [2] *S.* iv. 174.

etc., therefore to show that mode the second section of the exposition was begun. Here 'on which eye'[1] means, on the eye which is in the locative case, 'visible object' being in the nominative case. 'Has impinged' shows the meaning of the past, 'impinges' that of the present, 'will impinge' that of the future, 'may impinge' that of possibility. To expand:—Past object impinges on past eye, present object on present eye, future object on future eye; should that object reach the avenue of eye, it would impinge on the eye:—this is the meaning of possibility. But in reality only in striking the sentient organ is the visible object said to impinge. Here also, according to the foregoing method, four methods of specifying should be understood.

Now to show the case of one who by his own wish has brought the eye close to a visible object with a desire to see, so that eye impinges on object, the third section of the exposition was begun. Its meaning is clear. Now here the eye in receiving the object is said to 'impinge on it.'[2] Here also by the foregoing method the four methods of specifying should be understood.

[310] In what follows, ten sections in all are shown, five by way of showing the arising of the five modes of sense-contact, and five by way of showing the arising as in connection with their objects.

In these sections 'depending on eye'[3] means, making eye the cause. 'Concerning a visible object' means, on account of,[4] relating to, because of, a visible object. By this is shown the correlation of visible object, namely, contact, etc., having the basis in the sentient organ, and being related to it by 'priority'; also what is included under 'process of apperception through the door of the eye' is related to it by 'object as dominant' and 'object as sufficient cause.'[5]

---

[1] *Dhs.* § 598. [2] *Dhs.* § 599. [3] *Dhs.* § 600.

[4] Lit. 'having arrived at'; *āgamma*, the other synonyms being *ārabbha*, *sandhāya*, *paṭicca*.—*Ed.*

[5] 'Priority,' modes of 'object,' 'dominance,' 'sufficient cause' constitute the tenth, second, third and ninth of the twenty-four relations between things taught in the Paṭṭhāna. Cf. *Compendium*, p. 192 *f.*—*Ed.*

In the other five sections the term *rūpārammaṇo*[1] means that [mind] has a visible thing as its object, correlation being shown merely by the relation of 'object.' The fourfold method of specifying should be understood in these ten sections, as in the foregoing three sections.

Thus thirteen sections of exposition have been shown, to wit, the preceding three to show in various ways that the eye, which has been brought out in the question 'What is that matter which is the organ of sight?'[2] is this sort of state, and these ten. And in each of them, because four methods of specifying are obtained, they have been shown as elaborated into fifty-two methods (13 × 4). And the same with the following expositions also. Here only their specific differences are to be considered.

Sotaṃ means hearing[3] (or ear). In the interior of the compound organ of the interior of the ear, at a spot shaped like a finger-ring and fringed by tender, tawny hairs, tended by the elements of which the different kinds have been mentioned, sustained by the caloric order, by mind, by nutriment, guarded by life,[4] attended by colour, etc., it stands duly fulfilling the nature of the basis and door of auditory cognition, etc.

Ghanaṃ is smelling.[5] In the interior of the compound organ of the nose, at a spot shaped like a goat's hoof, tended, supported, guarded, attended [as aforesaid], [311] it stands duly fulfilling the nature of the basis and door of olfactory cognition, etc.

'Tongue'[6] is so called in the sense of tasting flavours.[7] Above the middle of the compound organ of the tongue, at a spot shaped like the upper part of a torn lotus leaf, it stands duly fulfilling the nature of the basis and door of gustatory cognition, etc.

---

1 This is in a section of the text of the *Dhammasangaṇi* omitted in the P.T.S. ed. § 600, just before *cakkhuṃ p'etaṃ*. The ten sections in the one § 600 are brought out in *B.P.E.*, p. 177 *f.*—*Ed.*

2 *Dhs.* § 597.

3 *Dhs.* § 601.

4 Āyunā. *I.e.*, jīvitindriyaṃ.—*Pyi.*

5 *Dhs.* § 605.

6 *Dhs.* § 609.

7 Sāyana may also mean 'being pleasant.'—*Tr.*

But in this body, wherever there is a matter grasped at the 'body as field of touch'[1] everywhere becomes [the object of] service, sustenance, protection, attendance, as said above. Like oil diffusing over cotton-rag, it stands duly fulfilling the nature of basis and of door of bodily cognition, etc.

What has been said is special [to the sense in question]. The rest of the text and the meaning should be understood by the method given in the exposition of sight. For here the terms 'ear,' etc., are simply substituted for the term 'eye'; the terms 'sound,' etc., for the term 'visible object'; the terms 'has heard,' etc., for the terms 'has seen,' etc. Owing to the absence of this pair of terms, 'guide, guidance,' there are [only] twelve sets of similes. The rest everywhere is as has been said.

It may be objected that if in this body, wherever there is matter grasped at, the tactile sense stands everywhere like oil in cotton-rag, then there will be a mixing of characteristics.

Nay, there would be no such thing. Why? Because of the absence of any other species of object. But, it may be said, even if this is so, the tactile sense would not 'stand everywhere.' True, in the ultimate (or metaphysical) sense it is not everywhere. But the expression (stands everywhere) is used because it is impossible to set forth the variety in the tactile sense by breaking it up. It is impossible to separate tastes, etc., of material things like particles of sand, and so they are said to be mutually diffused; ultimately, too, there is no taste 'in' material things (if there were, there would be a 'taste-seizing' whenever there was a sight-seizing). Even so the tactile sense is not everywhere in an ultimate sense; and it is not absent because of the impossibility of breaking it up. Hence it is that no mixing of characteristics comes to pass.

[312] Moreover, the determining of characteristics, etc., prevents such mixing. For the eye has the characteristic

---

[1] *Dhs.* § 613. *Kāyo* (body) does duty also for 'sense-organ of touch,' or 'skin-sensibility.'

of sentience for phenomena[1] worthy of directly impinging on the object, or of sentience sprung from action caused by a desire to see the object. It has the function of drawing consciousness towards the objects; it has the localizing of visual cognition as its manifestation; it has the being produced by action caused by a desire to see as proximate cause. The ear has the characteristic of sentience for phenomena worthy of directly impinging on sounds, or of sentience sprung from action caused by a desire to hear sounds; it has the function of drawing consciousness towards sounds; it has the localizing of auditory cognition as its manifestation; and it has a proximate cause as above. The nose and the tongue (or smell and taste), and lastly the body or tactile sense may be analogously defined.

But some say that eye is a sentient surface for phenomena having excess of heat; that ear, nose, tongue are sentient surfaces for phenomena having excess of mobility, extension, cohesion; that body is a sentient surface for all phenomena. Others, again, in the case of the last four senses, assign sentience as follows:—space-element, mobility, cohesion, extension.

Such persons should be asked: Adduce your Sutta! Surely they will never find such a Sutta.

But some of these give as their reason that object-seizing is aided by visible objects which are qualities of heat,[2] so for the other senses. They should be answered:—

'Who has said [313] that visible objects are qualities of heat, and so on?' Nay, it is not permissible to say, of indivisible phenomena, this is a quality of that. Should they say: 'Just as you assigned the functions of sustaining, etc., on the part of extension, etc., owing to the excess of this and that phenomenon among the various supports,[3] so should you agree to this expression, "visible objects, etc., are qualities

---

[1] *Bhūtappasādo.* The *Ṭīkā* understands by *bhūta-*, *mahābhūtā*. See also below, p. 410.—*Tr.*

[2] For instance, light as a quality of lamp-fire aids the seizing of the visible object by the eye; sound as a quality of mobility aids the seizing of the audible object by the ear, etc.—*Tr.*

[3] *I.e.*, the material objects sprung from the four elements.—*Tr.*

of elements" from seeing the excess in visible and other sense-objects when in those supports there is preponderance of heat,'[1] etc.

They should be answered thus:—If the smell in cotton with a preponderance of extension is greater than that of liquor fermented with a preponderance of cohesion, and if the colour of cold water be inferior to that of hot water with an excess of heat—if these were so, we should agree to your expression. But since these two instances cannot happen, therefore you should give up the special reasoning regarding those phenomena which are bases. As in one group, although there is no distinction of phenomena, the tastes of visible and other objects are unlike each other, so even though there is no other special reason, the visual and other sentient organs are unlike each other. What is that reason which is not mutually common? The reason of the distinction among the senses is just kamma. Therefore from the difference of kamma, and not from that of phenomena, the difference in these is to be understood. For if phenomena were different [in kind], there would be no sentient organ. Hence the ancient [thinkers] said: 'The sentient organ is [sentient] of phenomena similar [to itself], not of dissimilar.'[2]

And so among these sentient organs, because they are distinct and because of the differences of kamma, eye and ear seize the object before they have come into physical contact with it. This is because consciousness arises in an object which does not adhere to its own basis.[3] Nose, tongue, and tactile sense seize their object while in physical contact with themselves. This is because consciousness arises in objects which adhere to their own basis. But in the Commentary the object is said to have attained [contact] because it has reached the 'sense-avenue.' The colour of the discs of the moon and sun situated above forty-two thousand yojanas away strikes the sentient visual organ. That colour,

---

[1] Such as the blazing and dazzling colour of fire, audible sound of wind, good taste in earth, sweet taste in water.

[2] Cf. the Greek theorem: Knowledge is of like by like, *e.g.*, in Aristotle's *De Anima* i. 2. 5.

[3] Namely, one of the great essentials.—*Pyī*.

although it appears to be far, is known to be in physical contact. Because it has such a range, the eye is said to have attained range-contact. The changes in the body of men cutting down trees at a distance and of washermen washing clothes appears as far off. But sound striking the sentient ear by an elemental series is [relatively] slow of ascertainment.

[314] Although [in the Commentary] it is said that 'the object is said to be in physical contact because it has reached the sense-avenue,' yet the colour of the disc of the moon, etc., appears as not in physical contact[1] and at a distance. And if sound also should come slowly, having arisen from far, it should be heard after some time. Coming by serial impact and striking the sentient organ of the ear, its direction might not be evident. Hence eye and ear have an object not in physical contact, and are like the snake, etc. As a snake takes no delight outside [its range] in places which have been scoured and swept, but is delighted when, at resting time, it has entered a place of refuse, a lair of grass and leaves, an ant-hill, and secures mental quietude, so also the eye prefers broken-up effects. It does not delight in burnished, gilded walls and the like, it does not even wish to look at them, but it delights in [surfaces] variegated with pictures and beautified with flowers and creepers, etc. Indeed, in such places, when the eye does not suffice, folk wanting to look open mouths as well. Again, the crocodile[2] going out, does not see what there is to seize, but goes after food with eyes shut. But when it has dived into the water a hundred fathoms deep and entered its den and laid itself down, then its mind becomes quieted and it sleeps at ease. So, too, [the sense of] hearing desires a 'den'; it entertains a wish for the cavity of the ear which is dependent on space. The space in the ear-cavity is the cause of hearing a sound. And open space also is operative when [a bhikkhu] is reciting within [a cave]. The sound does not break through the roof of the cave and come out, but going out by the doors and windows strikes the sensitive ear in an

[1] Read *asampatto* in P.T.S. ed.

[2] *Suṃsumāro,* usually rendered crocodile.—*Ed.*

elemental series. Immediately, then, those seated at the back of the cave know that so-and-so is reciting If such be the case,—it may be said—then there is physical contact [with object]. But has this ear such an object? Yes, it has. If so (the objection is) when drums, etc., are struck from far there should be no knowledge that the sound is distant. But there is such knowledge. For when the sensitive ear is struck by sound, there is such and such a variety of knowledge as—distant sound, near sound, sound from the further bank, sound from the hither bank. Such knowledge is natural law. What is this natural law? Wherever there is a cavity, [315] from that comes hearing, like the seeing of the (distant) moon and sun, etc. Such is the absence of physical contact in hearing.

The bird does not delight in a tree or the ground, but when it rises into the sky and goes beyond a stone's throw or two, it gets a feeling of security. So also the nose desires space, and has for object odour dependent on wind.[1] Indeed, cattle at the first showers of rain keep smelling at the earth, and turning up their muzzles to the sky breathe in the wind. And when a fragrant lump is taken in the fingers and smelt no smell is got when breath is not inhaled. Again, a dog in wandering about does not see a safe place, but is harassed by the throwing of stones, etc. But when it enters the village and scratches up ash at an oven-door and lies down, it finds ease—so is it with the tongue. This, too, desires 'a village' and has for object the taste dependent on the watery element. Thus even when a bhikkhu's duties have been done during the three[2] watches of the night, and he early in the morning, taking bowl and robe, has to enter the village, he is not able to discern the taste of dry food unwetted by the saliva.

Again, the jackal does not find delight in roaming about till it eats human flesh at the cemetery for non-cremation, and lying down it gets ease. So the tactile sense also desires

---

[1] Wind which takes the odour is the sufficing condition, yet by common usage the odour is called the sufficing condition of [the sensed] wind.—*Ṭīkā.*

[2] P.T.S. ed.: read *ti-yāma°* for *niyāma°*.

matter grasped at, and takes a tangible object dependent on the extension element. Thus, persons getting no other matter 'grasped at,' will when lying down put the head on the palm of the hands. Internal and external extension is the cause of the tactile sense seizing the object. Thus it is not possible to know the hardness or softness of a bed well spread out or of fruits placed in the hand without sitting down on the one or pressing the other. Hence internal and external extension is the cause in the tactile cognition of the tactile organ.

Of these senses, too, [as in sight and hearing] specifying of characteristics, etc.,[1] reveals an absence of intermixture. For the characteristic, function, manifestation, proximate cause, desired object, and bases of the sentient visual organ are different [316] from those of the other sentient organs, hence the senses are not mixed. And, further, these similes illustrate the absence of intermixture:—just as although the shadow of uplifted banners of five colours seems to be blended in one, yet the shadow of each does not mix with that of the others; as although, when a lamp that is lit, has a cotton wick of five colours, the flame seems to be blended in one, yet the individual flame of the fibre of each cotton does not mix with that of the other, so these five organs, although they meet in one individuality, yet do not mix with each other. Not only they but also the remaining material objects, etc., are unmixed. For in this body are three portions: lower body, middle body, upper body. Of these, from the navel downwards is the lower body, in which are forty-four material qualities: body-decad, sex-decad,[2] eight material things sprung from nutriment, eight from the caloric order and eight from mind. From the navel upward till the wind-pipe is the middle body in which are fifty-four material qualities: body-decad, sex-decad, basis-decad, three sets of eight sprung from nutriment, etc. From the wind-pipe upward is the upper body wherein are eighty-four

[1] See above, p. 405.

[2] On 'decads,' see *Compendium*, pp. 164, 250 *f.*

material qualities: eye-decad, ear-decad, nose-decad, tongue-decad, touch-decad, sex-decad, the three sets of eight sprung from nutriment, etc. Among these, this decad, to wit, the four great essentials as causes of the sentient organ, together with colour, odour, taste, nutritive essence, life-controlling faculty, the sentient organ is called the eye-decad by virtue of its absolutely indivisible pre-determined material qualities. The remaining decads are to be understood in the same way. Among them the material qualities in the lower body do not mix with those in the middle and upper bodies; and the material qualities in the remaining two bodies do not mix with those in the lower. As although at eventide the shadows of the mountain and of trees seem to be one yet they are mutually unmixed, so although in these three parts of the [same] body, the forty-four, fifty-four, and eighty-four material qualities appear as one, they are mutually unmixed.

In the exposition of 'visible object'[1] colour is just 'coloured appearance'; or it shines—hence appearance. 'Evident to visual cognition' is the meaning [317] of the compound term. 'Visible' is [literally] co-vision; the meaning is, it is to be seen by visual cognition. 'Reacting' is [literally] co-reaction; the meaning is, producing the friction of impact. Among blue-or-green things,[2] etc., the colour of 'blue-or-green' (*nīla*) is like the clitoria, 'yellow' is like the bauhinia, 'red' is like the bandhujīvaka, 'white' is like the morning star, 'black' is like burnt coal, 'crimson' is like the sindhu-vāra, kaṇavīra flowers. In the Cūḷahaṃsa Jātaka[3] *hari* is used for golden:—'O Sumukha, thou golden-coloured one, depart

[1] *Dhs.* § 617.

[2] On this curious colour-blindness in Indian vision, see *B.P.E.*, p. 62, *n.* 1. Dr. Edridge Green, author of *Colour-blindness and Colour-perception,* would call such vision tetrachromic (seeing but four colours in the spectrum). It regards 'blue as a greenish-violet, and calls it violet or green, according to its proximity to one of these colours.' See *Strand Magazine*, Dec., 1909: 'Colour-blindness and its Dangers.' —*Ed.*

[3] Called (in the Fausböll edition) Mahāvaṃsa Jātaka (v. 359, 89), which follows the Cūḷahaṃsa.—*Ed.*

if thou wilt.' But in what follows *jātarūpa* is rendered by golden, hence here *hari* is dark green. These seven terms of colour have been pointed out merely with respect to their nature, without taking into account the substance itself. *Harivaṇṇa* is the colour of a dark-green leaf. *Ambaṅkura-vaṇṇa* is like the colour of a mango-shoot. These two terms have been pointed out by taking into account the substance.

The twelve terms beginning with 'long' have been pointed out by common usage. This is accomplished by reference and by juxtaposition. For the terms 'long,' etc., are accomplished by mutual reference. The terms 'circular,' etc., are accomplished by juxtaposition. Among them with reference to what is short, 'long' is so-called as being higher than that; 'short' is so-called as being lower than 'long.' With reference to what is big, a thing smaller than that is 'little,' with reference to which a greater thing is 'big.' 'Circular' is shaped like a wheel; 'oval' like an egg. 'Square' is bounded by four sides. And the same should be understood with six sides, etc. 'Sloping' (low-lying) is bent down, 'high-lying' (upland) is raised up. Among these expressions, because it is possible to know 'long,' etc., also by touch, but not 'blue-green,' etc., therefore in reality 'long' is not directly[1] a visible object, neither is 'short,' and similar terms. What we call 'long,' 'short' is relative to (dependent on) this or that, has such and such a position, and it is to be understood here as mentioned in accordance with this or that conventional usage.

The pair of terms 'shady' and 'glowing' have been mutually divided. 'Light' and 'dim' likewise. 'Cloudy,' 'frosty,' 'smoky,' 'dusty' are shown as [referring to] four substances. Of these *abbhā* is cloudy, *mahikā* is snow or frost. By these four terms the colours of clouds, etc., have been shown. By 'like the disc of the moon in colour,' etc., the radiant [318] colours of the moon, etc., have been shown; their difference as objects should be understood thus: Made of gold, roofed with silver, forty-nine yojanas in length and breadth, the moon is the mansion of the moon god. Made

---

[1] *Na nippariyāyena.* Or, 'is only figuratively. . . .'—*Ed.*

of gold, roofed with crystal fifty yojanas in length and breadth, the sun is the mansion of the sun god. The mansions of various gods are made of the seven gems, and are seven, eight, ten, twelve yojanas in length and breadth. These are the constellations. Of these the moon is below, the sun is above. Between the two is one yojana. From the lower edge of the moon to the upper end of the sun is one hundred yojanas. The constellations of the stars march on both sides. The moon is sluggish in his course, the sun is quick, the constellations are the fastest of all. At times they are in front, at times behind the moon and the sun.

'Mirror' is a disc made of copper. 'Gem' means, all the various gems except the cat's eye, as *jotirasa*, etc. 'Shell' is of the ocean. 'Pearl' is ocean and other pearls. 'Cat's eye' is a jewel of the bamboo colour. *Jātarūpa* is 'gold' of the colour of the Master's complexion. For the Master has a golden complexion, for which *suvaṇṇa* (literally, 'fine colour') is also used. 'Silver' stands for the coin (or *kahāpaṇa*).[1] *Māsakas* of copper, wood, lac are in common use and are all included here. By the expression 'or whatever other,' excepting the visible object enumerated in the Text, all remaining objects of different colours, such as cups or shutters, rough cloth, mildew, etc., are included.

Thus all visible objects, though of different sorts, such as blue-green, etc., are not specifically divided as regards their characteristics, etc. For all this matter has the characteristic of striking the eye, the function or property of being in the relation of object to visual cognition, the manifestation of being the field of visual cognition, the proximate cause of the four great essentials. Likewise all derived matter has the four great essentials as proximate cause. But where (in other sense-cognition, etc.) there are different features, of that we shall speak. Where there are none the method used in the exposition of sight should be understood. [319] The difference is simply that there the exposition begins with sight, here it begins with visible object. And there there are four-

---

[1] See above, p. 369, *n*. A kahāpaṇa might be of any metal.

teen similes beginning with 'it is eye'; here there are three beginning with 'it is matter.' The rest is the same. For as thirteen sections have been said to specify the eye by elaborating them in four methods, here they are also given.

In the exposition of sound,[1] 'sound of drum' is the sound of big drums. The other three terms denote sounds of tabors, conches, and tom-toms. 'Song-sound' is sound of singing. 'Musical sound' includes all other sounds of stringed instruments, such as the lute, etc. 'Sound of cymbals' is the sound of copper and wooden clappers. 'Manual sound' is the sound of clapping hands. 'Noise of people' is the sound of the incoherent articulations of an assembled multitude. 'Sound of concussion of things' is the sound of trees rubbing against each other; of bells and gongs. Wind-sound is that of blowing wind; water-sound is that of water flowing or driven by wind; 'human sound' is that of men talking, etc.; and all such sound except this is 'non-human sound.'[2]

By this last pair of terms all sounds are exhausted. Nevertheless sound not mentioned in the Text and produced by splitting bamboos, tearing cloth, etc., is included under the category of 'or whatever. . . .'

Although sounds have been distinguished [in the Text] as, *e.g.*, of a big drum, they have not been differentiated as regards salient characteristics, etc. As to these, all sounds have the characteristic of striking the ear, the function-and-property of being the object of auditory cognition, the manifestation of being the field or object of auditory cognition. The rest should be understood by the method used in the exposition of sight. Here also the thirteen sections elaborated in the four methods are given. Their meaning may be known by the first exposition. Hence it is not expanded.

In the exposition of the field of odours,[3] 'odour of roots' is odour produced by any root. And the same with 'odour

---

[1] *Dhs.* §§ 621-24.

[2] Amanussā may mean infra-human beings, as in *Mil.*, p. 207, where they are opposed to devatā (spirits, gods). Here, however, they are used in a more general sense as logical contradictories.—*Ed.*

[3] *Dhs.* §§ 625-28.

of sap,' etc. Odour of vegetables, etc., uncooked or badly cooked, is 'raw odour'; that of fish, shell-fish, rotten flesh, stale butter, etc., is 'putrid odour.' [320] 'Pleasant odour' is desirable smell. 'Unpleasant odour' is undesirable smell.

By these two last terms all odours are exhausted. Nevertheless all odours not mentioned in the Text, such as that of mildew, cloth, etc., are included under the category of the 'or whatever. . . .'

Though odours have been distinguished by such classes as odour of roots, etc., they have not been differentiated as regards salient characteristics, etc. As to these, all odours have the characteristic of striking the sense of smell, the property of being the object of olfactory cognition, the manifestation of being the field of the same. The rest should be understood by the method used in the exposition of sight. Here also are given the thirteen sections elaborated in fifty-two methods. Their meaning is evident.

In the exposition of objects of taste,[1] 'taste of roots' is taste produced by any root. And the same with 'taste of stems,' etc. 'Sour' tastes are buttermilk, etc. 'Sweet' is really ghee from cow's milk, etc., but honey is connected with astringency and after standing long becomes astringent. Raw sugar is connected with alkaline and after standing long becomes alkaline. But butter after standing long, although it loses colour and smell, does not lose its taste, hence it only is genuinely sweet. 'Bitter' is as nimb leaves, etc.; 'pungent' is as ginger, pepper; 'saline' is as sea-salt; 'alkaline' is as a brinjal sprout or tender fruit. 'Acrid' is as the jujube; 'astringent' is as myrobalan, etc. All these tastes involve reference to the substance,[2] but here it is to be understood that, by the names 'sour,' etc., a sapid object has this or that substance.[2] 'Nice' is desirable taste; 'nauseous' is undesirable taste. By these two expressions all tastes are exhausted. Nevertheless, those not included in the text, such as those of a stone, a wall, a cloth, etc., are included under the category of the 'or whatever. . . .'

---

[1] *Dhs.* §§ 629-32.

[2] Or base (vatthu).

And though it is distinguished under these classes, yet the object of taste has not been differentiated as regards salient characteristic, etc. As to that, all tastes have the characteristic of striking the tongue,[1] the property of being the object of gustatory cognition, the manifestation of being the field of the same. The rest should be understood by the method used in the exposition of sight. [321] Here, also, as there the thirteen sections elaborated in fifty-two methods are given.

In the exposition of the feminine controlling faculty,[2] 'that which' is an expression showing the reason. The meaning here is:—'by whatever cause a woman has feminine features,' etc., where 'feature' is shape. To expand: The shape of a woman's hands, feet, neck, breast, etc., is not like that of a man's. The female lower body is broad, the upper body is less broad. The hands and feet are small, the mouth is small. 'Mark' is recognizable sign. The female breast is prominent. The face is without beard or moustache. The dressing of the hair, the wearing of the clothes are also unlike those of a man. 'Occupation' is action. Thus in youth women play with tiny shallow baskets, pestles and mortars, variegated dolls, and weave string with clay-fibre. 'Deportment' is mode of going or gait, etc. Thus there is a want of assertion in women's walking, standing, lying down, sitting, eating, swallowing. Indeed when a man of that description is seen, folk say, 'He walks, stands, etc., like a woman.' 'Feminine in condition and being'—these two have one meaning: the nature of woman, which is born of kamma and produced at the instant of conception. But feminine features, etc., are not the female controlling faculty; they are produced in course of process because of that faculty. When there is seed the tree grows because of the seed, and is replete with branch and twig and stands filling the sky; so when there is the feminine controlling faculty called femininity, feminine features, etc., come to be. The feminine controlling faculty should be regarded as the seed; as

---

[1] Cf. *Vis. Magga*, pp. 446, 447. There, too, the palate plays no part in the organ of taste.

[2] *Dhs.* § 633.

the tree stands growing and filling the sky because of the seed, so the feminine features, etc., arise in course of procedure because of that faculty. Herein the controlling faculty is not known by visual cognition but only by mind-cognition. But feminine features, etc., are known by visual as well as by mind-cognition. 'This is that matter which is the feminine controlling faculty' means 'such matter is not as the eye-controlling faculty, etc., are in the male.' By natural law the controlling faculty of a woman is of the woman only.

And the same [322] with the masculine controlling faculty.[1] Masculine features, etc., should be understood as the opposite of the feminine. For the shape of the hands, feet, neck, breast, etc., of a man is unlike the shape of those of a woman. For a man's upper body is broad, the lower body is less broad; his hands and feet are large, the face is large, the breast-flesh is less full; beard and moustaches grow. Hair-dressing and the wearing of clothes are not like those of women. In youth they play with chariots and ploughs, etc., make sandbanks and dig ponds. There is assertion in their walking, etc. When a woman is seen taking long strides, etc., folk say 'she walks like a man.' The rest is the same as was said of the feminine controlling faculty.

Of these two controlling faculties the feminine has the characteristic (of knowing)[2] the state of a woman, the function of showing 'this is woman,' the manifestation which is the cause of femininity in feature, mark, occupation, deportment. The masculine controlling faculty has the characteristic of (knowing)[2] the state of man, the function of showing 'this is man,' the manifestation which is the cause of masculinity in feature, etc. Both came into being during the procedure of the first inhabitants of this cycle, subsequently they arise at conception. Matter coming into being at conception fluctuates during procedure and changes its features; and matter coming into being during procedure does likewise; as has been said: 'At that time in a certain bhikkhu the features of a woman were revealed; at that time in a certain female

[1] *Dhs.* § 634. [2] So *Ṭīkā*.

bhikkhu the features of a man were revealed.'[1] Of the two, the masculine sex is superior, the feminine is inferior. Therefore the former disappears through grossly immoral conduct; the latter may be brought about by weak morality. But in disappearing, the latter does so by weak immorality, the former may be brought about by strong morality. Thus both disappear through immorality and may be brought about by morality.

Does a hermaphrodite possess one controlling faculty or two? One, and that is feminine to a female hermaphrodite and masculine to a male hermaphrodite. This being so, there should be no existence of the latter sort of hermaphrodite. For the female controlling faculty is said to be the reason of the characteristic-mark (*vyañjana*).[2] Then has the male hermaphrodite no controlling faculty? In such the female controlling faculty is not the reason of the characteristic-mark, [323] because of its invariable absence. For when in a female hermaphrodite a lustful thought for a woman arises, then the masculine characteristic-mark is manifested, and the feminine characteristic-mark is hidden and concealed; and *vice versa*. And if in such people the controlling faculty was the cause of the latter characteristic-mark, then always there would be a persistence of both characteristic-marks. But in reality there is no such persistence Hence it is to be understood that in a hermaphrodite the controlling faculty is not the reason for the characteristic-mark. (What then is the reason?)—Lustful thought, friend of (past) kamma, is the reason. And because there is only the one controlling faculty in a hermaphrodite, therefore the female hermaphrodite herself becomes pregnant and causes another to become pregnant; the male hermaphrodite causes another to become pregnant but himself does not become so.

In the exposition of the controlling faculty of life,[3] what should be said has already been said above under the immaterial controlling faculty of life.[4] There it was simply said 'that

---

[1] *Vin.* iii. 35.

[2] Such as features and marks.—*Tr.*

[3] *Dhs.* § 635.

[4] See above p. 197. *Dhs.* § 19.

which is of those immaterial states':—here, because of the material nature of the faculty, the only textual difference is 'that which is of those material states.' And its characteristic, etc., should be understood thus: The controlling faculty of life has the characteristic of watching over co-existent material objects, their procedure as function, their persistence as manifestation, the thing which ought to be maintained as proximate cause.

In the exposition of body-intimation,[1] here intimation in the first place is the making known one's own state by [overt] bodily action, both by animals to men and by men to animals, in accordance with a [certain] disposition of the body; thus that state by which such a disposition is made known. Itself intimates in the same way, or again, by such a disposition one's self is made known—this also is intimation. The kind of intimation called body-intimation is the agitating of the body recognized in such sayings as 'self-restraint in action is excellent.' A meaning is made known by bodily gestures, and thus one's self is made known.

In the words 'of a moral thought,' etc., reference is made to the nine kinds of moral consciousness:—eight of the sensuous realm and one concerning super-knowledge; 'or of an immoral thought' by means of the twelve kinds of immoral consciousness; 'or of an unmoral thought' by means of the eleven kinds of inoperative consciousness: eight great inoperative, two limited inoperative, one sensuous inoperative which has attained to super-knowledge. Other kinds of consciousness than these do not produce intimation. [324] But there is intimation by means of not more than these kinds to probationers, adepts, and average persons. Thus by way of these three terms, moral, immoral, unmoral, etc., intimation has been shown as a causal condition.

Now to show such intimation by means of six terms as result the Text goes on:—'of one advancing.' Because advancing and other acts arise by virtue of intimation, they are called results of intimation. Of these, 'of one advancing' is of

---

[1] *Dhs.* § 636.

one carrying the body forward; 'of one receding' is of one bringing the body backward; 'of one looking ahead' is of one looking straight; 'of one glancing around' is of one looking sideways here and there; 'of one retracting an arm' is of one bending in the joints; 'of one stretching it out' is of one stretching out the joints.

Now to show intimation by means of six terms in its intrinsic nature the Text goes on:—*kāyassa thambhanā;* wherein *kāyassa* is, 'of the body.' *Thambhanā* is stiffening, making stiff the body. Increasing it by the preposition, *saṃ*, he said, *santhambhanā;* this may mean a stiffening of greater strength. *Santhambhitatta* is the state of a well-stiffened body. Next, *viññatti* is intimation; *viññāpana* is the act or mode of intimating. The state of being intimated is *viññāpitattaṃ*. Anything here to be added has been said above in the discourse on Doors.[1]

Likewise in speech-intimation[2]. But the meaning of the term 'speech-intimation,' and of the terms in the exposition, has not been stated in the discourse on Doors, and should be understood thus:—those who make known their own state by speech—including men with animals and animals with men—this state is made known in accordance with a [certain] disposition of speech. Grasping the significance of words, oneself is intimated—thus it is intimation. The kind of intimation called speech-intimating is an agitating of the voice recognized in such sayings as 'self-restraint in speech is excellent,' etc. It is a way of intimating one's intention by the sound of speech. Again, from intimating oneself in this way intimation is made by means of speech. In 'speech,' 'voice,' etc., the sound which is uttered by a person is 'voice'; 'speech' is that which is uttered, emitted. 'Utterance' is a significant sentence. It is that sentence which is the means of expression of those desirous to know and to make known. That which is uttered is 'enunciation.' 'Noise' is that which is sounded. 'Work or act' is that which is done. 'Noise-work' is making noise. Noise made in various ways [325] is the meaning.

---

[1] See Part III., p. 109. [2] *Dhs.* § 637.

'Articulate speech' is special forms of speech, which is no mere jangle, but is speech with a specified signification; or vocal utterance so divided as to convey a meaning. The word 'speech' has been shown by means of all these terms.

Now to show that intimation intrinsically, in three modes, by virtue of the terms 'intimation,' etc. (their meaning having been given above), and by joining them with that 'speech,' it is said 'that intimation by that speech,' etc. The meaning is plain from what has been said above.

Now among modes of consciousness producing intimation for the purpose of not causing delusion, thirty-two, twenty-six, nineteen, and sixteen should be understood as particularized. Thirty-two modes of consciousness cause material qualities to arise, and strengthen the postures and give birth to the twofold intimation. Twenty-six modes of consciousness do not give birth to intimation only, but make the other two [processes also]. Nineteen modes of consciousness produce only matter, and do not make the other two. Sixteen modes of consciousness do not make any one of the three. Of all these modes of consciousness, thirty-two are the eight moral types analyzed above and the twelve immoral from the sensuous realm, ten from those that are inoperative, the consciousness of super-knowledge in probationers and average persons, and that of [saints] purged of the intoxicants. The twenty-six are five moral types, and five inoperative from the material realm, four moral and four inoperative from the immaterial realm, the four [stages of] path-consciousness, the four of fruitional consciousness. The nineteen are eleven from the sensuous moral resultants, two from the immoral resultants, inoperative mind-element from inoperative consciousness, five modes of resultant consciousness from the material realm. The sixteen are the ten cognitions, the rebirth-consciousness of all beings, decease-consciousness of [saints] purged of the intoxicants, four immaterial resultants. Thus these sixteen thoughts are not effective in either matter, posture, or intimation. Many other thoughts in the immaterial sphere do not produce matter from having failed to get an opportunity, but such as do produce body-intimation are speech-intimation.

In the exposition of space-element[1] 'space' is that which is not 'scratched,' not scratched off, which is not possible to scratch, cut, or break. With affix *gata* (gone-to) the meaning is the same, as in *khelagata* (saliva), etc.; or it may be taken as *ā-kāsagata*, an 'unscratched' place. 'Sky' is that which is not struck (*a-ghaṃ*); not strikable is the meaning. *Aghagataṁ* is the same. 'Vacuum' (*vivara*) is in the sense of a hole; also *vivaragataṃ*. By 'untouched by the four great essentials' the unentangled space-element untouched by these is stated. And starting with its characteristic, space-element has the characteristic of delimitating material objects, the function of showing their boundaries, the manifestation of showing their limits, state of being untouched by the four great essentials and of being their holes and openings as manifestation, the separated objects as proximate cause. It is that of which in the separated groups we say 'this is above, this is below, this is across.'

The following expositions[2] of 'buoyancy of matter,' etc., should be understood by the method given above on 'buoyancy of thought,' etc.[3] But here as to characteristic, etc., buoyancy of matter has non-sluggishness as its characteristic, removing the heaviness of material objects as its function, quickness of change as its manifestation, buoyant matter as its proximate cause. Next 'plasticity of matter' has non-rigidity as characteristic, removing the rigidity of material objects as function, absence of opposition in all acts due to its own plasticity as manifestation, plastic matter as proximate cause. 'Wieldiness of matter' has workableness suitable or favourable to bodily actions as characteristic, removal of non-workableness as function, non-weakness as manifestation, workable matter as proximate cause.

These three do not[4] abandon each other. Yet though this be so [they are mutually distinguishable]. That change of matter which is buoyancy of matter is buoyancy of material

---

[1] *Dhs.* § 638. [2] *Dhs.* §§ 639-46. [3] See p. 199 *f.*

[4] Supply *na* in P.T.S. ed., p. 326.

objects, non-sluggishness and the special kind of change which is as the quick movement of one free from ailment, and is produced from the opposite cause to that perturbation of the elements which makes the sluggishness of matter. That change of matter which is plasticity of matter is plasticity of objects like that of well-pounded leather, is distinguished by tractableness, suavity in all special works, and is produced from the opposite cause to that perturbation of the elements which makes the rigidity of matter. That change of matter which is wieldiness of matter is wieldiness of material objects like that of well-polished gold, is distinguished by suitableness for all bodily works, [327] and is produced from the opposite cause to the perturbation of the elements which makes unsuitableness. Thus their difference should be understood. And kamma is not able to make them; only nutriment, [thought, and the caloric order][1] can do so. Thus ascetics[2] say, 'To-day we have agreeable food; our body is light, plastic, wieldy'; 'to-day we have suitable weather'; 'to-day our mind is one-pointed, our body is light, plastic, and wieldy.'

In the exposition of integration and continuity,[3] 'of organs,' *i.e.*, of ten and a half[4] sense-organs of matter, 'accumulation' is production or genesis. 'That is the integration of matter' means, 'that accumulation of organs of repeated production.' The meaning is growth. 'That which is integration of matter is the continuity of matter' means, 'the excess of growth during procedure over the growth of material things thus started is continuity of matter. The meaning is procedure. 'Accumulation' should be understood as genesis, as when water issues from a hole dug in the river bank; integration as growth, as when the hole is full of water; continuity as continuous proceeding, as when the water overflows. What does this exposition signity? By sense-organ accumulating is implied,

---

[1] Text has 'nutriment, etc.' [2] *Yogino.* [3] *Dhs.* §§ 642-43.

[4] *I.e.*, five organs of eye, ear, nose, tongue, body, and five of visible object, sound, odour, taste, tangible object, and the sixteen subtle material qualities, forming a *portion* (half) of sixty-nine principles which are reckoned as the *dhammāyatana* or organ of the cognizable object. See *Compendium*, p. 184.—*Tr.*

and by accumulation sense-organ. Both have been stated.[1] And what does the mention of both imply ? The accumulation integration, production, growth of the four continued material things is mentioned. In the real sense both integration and continuity are synonyms of the production of matter. Yet so as to make clear the difference in the mode of production, he makes the teaching in the Outline as [distinguishing between] integration and continuity. Having done so, because there is, in a real sense, no difference in these two words, therefore in the exposition he said, 'That which is accumulation of organs is integration of matter,' 'That which is integration of matter is continuity of matter.' That arising of sense which is said to be accumulation is called integration of matter; further, the subsequent arising of sense is called, in the sense of upper growth, integration of matter, and also continuity of matter.[2] And because both these, integration and continuity, are synonyms of the production of matter therefore (of them) integration of matter has the characteristic of accumulation, the function of making material things rise at the beginning, leading them, or the fulness of matter as manifestation, integrated matter as proximate cause. Continuity has the characteristic of continuous occurrence, the function of linking or binding without a break, unbroken series as manifestation, matter bound without a break as proximate cause.

In the exposition of decay,[3] 'decay' is getting old; [328] this indicates its *intrinsic* nature. The mode of decaying is 'ageing.' The three terms beginning with 'decrepitude' indicate function after the lapse of time. The two last, 'shrinkage in life and maturity of faculties,' indicate the nature of decay. The word itself 'decay' shows what it naturally is; hence the exposition states its nature. By the word 'ageing' mode is shown; hence this exposition indicates the manner of decay. By the word 'decrepitude' is shown

---

[1] Also accumulation is the characteristic and sense-organ is the possessor of the characteristic. Hence they are relative and mentioned together.—*Ṭīkā*.

[2] This sentence is not in the P.T.S. ed.—*Tr*.

[3] *Dhs*. § 644.

the function which is the reason[1] for the broken state of teeth, nails, etc., in process of time. By 'hoariness' is shown the function which is the reason for the greyness of hair on the head and body. By 'wrinkles' is shown the function which is the reason for the wrinkled state in the skin making the flesh fade. Hence these three terms indicate the function of decay in process of time. By showing these changes decay is manifested. As a path taken by water or by fire is clear from the broken and scattered state, or from the charred state of the grass, the trees, etc., but the path itself is not the water or the fire, so the path of decay is clear by decrepitude, etc., in teeth and so on. It might be taken with open eyes; but decrepitude, etc., are not decay, which, indeed, is not [a thing] cognizable by the eye. And decay has been shown by the resultant nature known as the very evident wasting of life and maturity of the controlling faculties of sight, etc., in process of time by these terms:—'shrinkage in life and maturity of faculties.' Hence these two last expressions indicate the resultant nature of this decay. Because the life of a being who has reached decay shortens, therefore decay is said to be the shrinkage in life by a figure of speech. Moreover, the faculties, such as sight, etc., capable of easily seizing their own object, however subtle, and which are clear in youth, are mature in one who has attained to decay; they are disturbed, not distinct, and not capable of seizing their own object however gross. Hence decay is said to be the maturity of faculties by a figure of speech. And all this decay so indicated is twofold:—evident and hidden. Decay is called evident in material states from the sight of brokenness, etc., in teeth and so on; it is called hidden in immaterial states from our not seeing such change. Again it is twofold as uninterrupted and interrupted. Decay is called uninterrupted from the difficulty of knowing the distinction in colour, etc., from stage to stage, as in the decay of gems, gold, silver, coral, moon, sun, etc., of beings in the decade of infancy, etc., of flowers, fruits, sprouts, etc., [329] of inanimate things; decay without

---

[1] Reading °*kāraṇa*°.

interruption is the meaning. And decay is called interrupted when it is easy to know the distinction in colour, etc., from stage to stage in the aforesaid things other than gems, gold, silver, etc. As to characteristics, etc., the decay of matter has the characteristic of maturity of matter; leading (to disruption) as function; want of a fresh state, though not devoid of its intrinsic nature, as manifestation, like rotten paddy; the maturing matter as proximate cause.

In the exposition of impermanence,[1] 'destruction' is the becoming destroyed; 'passing away' is the process of so passing; 'break-up' is dissolving. And because after attaining [its own nature], matter undergoes loss, destruction, breaks up, therefore it is with respect to that nature that it undergoes destruction, passing away, dissolution. The term being increased by the preposition *pari-*, 'break-up' is called 'total dissolution' (*paribheda*). In the sense of not existing after having become, it is not permanent, that is, 'impermanent.' The state of such matter being impermanent is 'impermanence.' 'Disappearance,' *i.e.*, matter disappears. When it has reached death, the material qualities disappear and become invisible; not matter only, but all the five aggregates disappear. Hence by the impermanence of every one of the five aggregates, just this is the characteristic. Fully defined, impermanence of matter has the characteristic of complete dissolution, the merging of matter as function, destruction and evanescence as manifestation, matter undergoing dissolution as proximate cause. Above, birth is implicated and decay also; in this place death is implicated. Thus these three states are to beings so constituted like enemies with uplifted swords. For as [any] three foes of a man go about seeking for an opportunity, and one would say, 'Let it be my business to draw him out and bring him to the forest,' the second would say, 'Let it be my business to strike and fell him to the ground, once he is brought to the forest,' the third would say, 'Let it be my business from the time of his falling to the ground till his head is cut off with the sword,' so are these [three stages of life].

---

[1] *Dhs.* § 645.

For birth is like the enemy who draws him to enter the forest; because he has come to birth in this or that place. Decay is like the enemy who strikes and fells him to earth when he has reached the forest, because the aggregates produced are weak, dependent on others, lying down on a couch. Death is like the enemy who [330] with a sword cuts off the head of him when he is fallen to the ground, because the aggregates, having attained to decay, are come to destruction of life.

In the exposition of solid food,[1] 'solid' means it is made into an eatable morsel. Food (nutriment) means, it is 'taken into.' It is made into a morsel and swallowed down, is the meaning; the fetching-hither (*ā-hāra*) of matter. 'Boiled rice,' etc., is said to bring out the name by the substance, and again, to show its different kinds by the substance. For the nutritive substances implied herein are twelve, beginning with boiled rice and ending with syrup. Roots, etc., not mentioned in the Text are included in the 'or whatever.' Now in order to show these roots, fruits, etc., as things eatable, it has been said: 'in whatever region,' etc. Herein what is to be eaten and enjoyed by the mouth is *mukhāsiya*, what is to be torn by the teeth is *vikhādanaṁ*, to be swallowed by the throat is *galajjhoharaṇiyaṁ*. Now 'stomach-filling' is said to show that substance by virtue of function. For the substance swallowed, such as roots and fruits, etc., as well as boiled rice, sour gruel, etc., fills the stomach. This is the function of the substance.

By all the foregoing terms nutriment is shown together with the substance. Now to show the real nutritive essence extracted from the conceptual, the expression 'by which nutritive essence beings maintain themselves' is said. Of these, which is the function of the substance and which of the nutritive essence? The removal of risk and preservation respectively are their functions. For the substance removes risk and is not able to preserve. The nutritive essence preserves and is not able to remove risk. Being together, the two are able both to preserve and to remove risk. What is this risk? Heat born of kamma. For when there is no substance such as boiled rice in the stomach, that heat arises

---

[1] *Dhs.* § 646.

and seizes the stomach-walls and causes the being to cry out thus, 'I am hungry; give me food.' When it has eaten, the heat releases the stomach-walls and seizes the substance. Then the person is quieted in mind. For as a hungry demon seizes him who enters the shade of the tree, binds him with spirit-chains and, rejoicing in his own abode, comes when hungry and bites him on the head, so that the person cries out till those who hear the sound come from various places, saying: 'Here is someone in trouble!' [331] and the demon devouring everyone that comes rejoices in his own abode, so should the application of this simile be understood. For like the hungry demon is the heat born of kamma; like the being kept bound in spirit-chains is the stomach-wall; like the men who keep coming is the substance of boiled rice, etc.; like the descent from the tree and bite on the head is the release of the substance and seizure of the stomach-wall by the heat produced by kamma; like the bitten man's cries is the saying, 'Give me food'; like the rejoicing over the abode after tearing and eating every man that comes at that alarm is the quietude of mind when the stomach-wall is released, and the substance seized by the kamma-born heat.

Herein the nutritive essence in gross substance is weak, in the subtle substance strong. For after eating coarse grain, etc., one becomes hungry again after a brief interval. But to one who has partaken of butter, etc., food is no more welcome for the rest of the day. And here the grossness and subtleness should be understood with varying reference. Thus the nutriment of peafowl is subtle as compared with that of crocodiles. These are said to swallow stones and digest them in their stomach; peafowl eat such creatures as snakes and scorpions. And the nutriment of hyenas is subtle as compared with that of peafowl, for they are said to eat horns and bones discarded for three years, and which become soft as bulbs and roots the moment they are wetted by their saliva. The nutriment of elephants is subtle as compared with that of hyenas, for they eat leaves of various trees, etc. More subtle yet than that is the nutriment of the gayal, the wild ox, deer, etc., which eat the pithless leaves of various trees, etc. More subtle than that is the nutriment of cattle, which eat grass, wet and dry. More subtle still is the nutriment of hares, more subtle still is that of birds, more still that of frontier people, more still that of village pensioners, more still that of kings and ministers, more still that of universal monarchs, more still that of earth spirits, more still that of the four firmament-guardians, each being more subtle than the last, as far as the Yāma and Paranimittavasavatti spirits, [332] whose nutriment attains perfect subtlety.

As to its characteristic, etc., solid food has the characteristic of nutritive essence, the function of fetching matter [to the eater], of sustaining matter as its manifestation, of substance to be swallowed as proximate cause.

In the exposition of 'not derived'[1] as derived matter clings to, but is not clung to by, another, so this non-derived matter not only clings to, but it also is verily clung to.[2] 'The tangible' is what may be known when touched. The compound term in the Text is 'that which is tangible' *plus* 'object of sense.' The compound term 'cohesion-element'[2] is that which is 'cohesion' and 'element' in the sense of a nature which is not entity, is void [of self].

Now because three kinds of material things may be touched and known, therefore to classify and show them it is said, 'Which is that matter which is tangible object?'[3] (1) The element of extension, which has the characteristic of hardness, being the fulcrum[4] [of co-existent states] as function, receiving them as manifestation. (2) The element of heat, which has the characteristic of heat, maturing as function, the gift of softening [co-existent states] as manifestation. (3) The element of mobility, which has the characteristic of strengthening, impelling as function, bringing near and over as manifestation. And the first [named] element, that of cohesion, has trickling as characteristic, breeding [of co-existent states] as function, gathering them together as manifestation. Each of these four has the remaining three as its proximate cause.

---

[1] *Dhs.* § 647. [2] So *Pyī* reads. [3] *Dhs.* §§ 648-51.

[4] Or platform (*patiṭṭhānā*-).

'Hard' means rigid, 'soft' means not rigid. 'Smooth' means polished, 'rough' means harsh. 'Pleasurable contact' means desirable touch causing pleasurable feeling; 'painful contact' means undesirable touch causing painful feeling. 'Heavy' means weighty, 'light' means not heavy. And here by means of these terms: 'hard, soft, smooth, rough, heavy, light,' the element 'extension' is analyzed. When this body is accompanied by the life-controlling faculty, by the element of heat, by consciousness, then it becomes lighter, softer, [333] more wieldy. In the Text (Sutta) 'light' and 'soft' concern only the element of extension. But the pair of terms: 'pleasant contact and painful contact,' belongs to the analysis of the three great essentials, viz.: extension, heat, mobility. For whereas the element of extension has a pleasurable touch, as well as a painful touch, so also have the elements of heat and mobility. To them the element of extension with a pleasurable touch, when a lad with soft and tender hands shampoos one's feet, makes this kind of speech, 'Dear, press on, press on, dear!' The element of heat with a pleasurable touch, when in the cold season someone takes a warming-pan and warms one's limbs, makes this kind of speech, 'Dear, foment [them]!' The element of mobility with a pleasurable touch, when in the hot season a dutiful lad fans us with a fan, makes this kind of speech, 'Dear, fan away, fan, dear!' On the other hand, when a lad with hard hands presses one's feet, it is as though the bones would break, and he gets told to go away. If the warming-pan were brought in the hot season, one would be told to take it away. In the cold season if one were fanned by a fan, it would be said, 'Take it away, don't fan!' Thus should the pleasurable and painful touch of these be understood.

Thirteen sections adorned each with four methods as follows:—'such a tangible, invisible and reacting,' etc., are to be understood by the method given in visible object, etc., above. Do these three great essentials reach the avenue of the senses simultaneously or severally? Simultaneously. And do they being thus presented strike the sentient body or not? They do. Making them the object, does bodily cognition arise at one stroke or not? It does not. For the object becomes such by virtue of deliberate inclination or of intrusion. Of these [alternatives] deliberate inclination should be understood thus:—when the bowl is filled with food and brought, one who takes up a lump and examines whether it is hard or soft, is considering only the element of extension, though there may be heat as well as mobility present. One who investigates by putting the hand in hot water, is considering only the element of heat, though extension and mobility are present. One who lets the wind beat upon the body by opening the window in the hot season, is considering, while the wind beats gently and softly, [334] only the element of mobility, though extension and heat are present. Thus the [mental] object is made by deliberate consideration. But he who slips, or knocks his head against a tree, or in eating bites on a stone takes as his mental object only the element of extension, on account of its intrusiveness, though where he slipped, etc., heat and mobility were present. One treading on fire makes only the element of heat his object, owing to its intrusiveness, although extension and mobility are present therein. When a strong wind blows striking the ear as if to make one deaf, although extension and heat are present therein, the element of mobility alone is made the object owing to its intrusiveness. The tactile cognition of one who [deliberately] makes any element the object of thought does not arise at once. The touch of one pierced by a bundle of pins is stimulated at once. But wherever the sensitive surface is intrusive, there tactile cognition arises, and wherever the impact is strong, there it arises first. On bathing a wound with a fowl's feather, a filament may touch the sensitive surface, but tactile cognition arises only there where the sensitive surface is obtruded. And wherever the impact is strong, one makes the object by intrusion, and by intrusion tactile cognition is said to arise.

But how does the mind shift from an object? In one of two ways:—by one's wish, or by excess of [a new] object. To expand:—one who goes to festivities held in honour of monasteries, etc., with the express wish of paying homage to the various shrines, to bhikkhus, images, and of seeing the works of carving and painting, and when he has paid his respects and seen one shrine or image, has a desire to pay homage to, and see another, and goes off. This is shifting by one's wish. And one who stands gazing at a great shrine like a silver mountain peak, when subsequently a full orchestra begins to play, releases the visible object and shifts to the audible object; when flowers or scents possessing a delightful odour are brought, he releases the audible object and shifts to the olfactory object. Thus the mind is said to shift owing to excess of [a new] object.

[335] In the exposition of the element of cohesion[1] 'liquid'[2] is the natural word, whether it be *āpo* or *āpagata*; 'moist' is by way of being fluid, whether it be *sineha* or *sinehagata*. 'Cohesiveness of matter' is the cohering condition of the essential matter, such as the element of extension, etc. For the element of cohesion binds together iron, etc., in masses, makes them rigid. Because they are so bound, they are called rigid. Similarly in the case of stones, mountains, palm-seeds, elephant-tusks, ox-horns, etc. All such things the element of cohesion binds, and makes rigid; they are rigid because of its binding.

Is the element of extension the basis of the remaining elements by being in contact with them, or not? In other words, does the element of cohesion in binding the remaining elements, bind by being in contact, or not? In the first place, the element of extension is the basis of that cohesion without being in contact with it; but is the basis of the elements of heat and mobility by being in contact with them. But the element of cohesion binds the three others without being in contact with them. Otherwise it would be called tangible object. And the same is true of the elements of heat and of mobility in performing their own functions with regard to the remaining two. For the element of heat touches that of

---

[1] *Dhs.* § 652.

[2] *Āpo* (water, liquid) has in philosophic terminology assumed the meaning of *bandhanatta*, cohesiveness.—*Ed.*

extension and cooks it. Yet the latter does not burn by the intrinsic nature of heat. Did it do so, it would be defined as having the characteristic of being hot. And the element of heat touches that of cohesion and dries it up, yet the latter does not dry up by the intrinsic nature of heat. Did it do so, it would be defined as having the characteristic of being hot. And the element of heat touches that of mobility and heats it, yet the latter does not become heated by the intrinsic nature of heat. Did it do so, it would be defined as having the characteristic of being hot. And the element of mobility touches that of extension and strengthens it, and it does the same to the element of heat; [336] but it strengthens the element of cohesion without being in contact. When a lump of raw sugar is made by cooking sugar-cane juice, is the element of cohesion rigid or not? Not rigid. For it has the characteristic of flowing, it is the element of extension which has that of hardness. And the deficient cohesion becomes an excessive extension. Indeed, it abandons its status of fluidity, but not its characteristic [of flowing]. Though the lump of raw sugar is reduced or pounded, the element of extension is not pounded. Indeed the element has the characteristic of being hard; that of cohesion has the characteristic of flowing. And the deficient extension becomes excessive cohesion. It abandons its status of being in the form of a lump, but not its own characteristic. For there is alteration in state (by way of deficiency and excess) of the four Great Essentials;[1] but there is no such thing as alteration of characteristics. The absence of such alteration of the characteristic is shown in the *Aṭṭhānaparikappa Sutta*: 'Verily, Ānanda, of the elements of extension . . . of cohesion, these four great essentials might alter their characteristic sooner than it were possible for the Ariyan disciple endowed with assured faith in the Buddha to alter.'[2] For this is the meaning:—Ānanda, the element of extension with the characteristic of being hard might change

---

[1] Such as the becoming fluid or soft of the hard molasses and the becoming hard of fluids.

[2] *Anguttara* i. 222.

and be called the element of cohesion with the characteristic of flowing; but there would be no change in the Ariyan disciple. Thus is impossibility of change mentioned in the Sutta.

The meaning of the terms 'grasped-at,'[1] etc., in the following expositions of 'matter which is grasped at,'[2] should be understood by the method given in the discourse on the Table of Contents.

The organs of sight, etc., have been treated at length above. We shall here speak only of what is distinctive in them. In the exposition of the 'grasped-at,' the sense organs are mentioned solely from this aspect of 'being grasped at.' And because objects of sense are also grasped-at, therefore they, having been shown briefly under 'or whatever,' have again been expanded by the method beginning with 'matter through kamma having been wrought.' In this way the meaning in all the 'or-whatevers' should be understood.

But why, in both expositions, have decay and impermanence not been taken as 'due to kamma having been wrought,' and 'not due to kamma having been wrought'? Why are they taken only in the expositions of the 'not-grasped-at,' etc.?[3] [337] In 'not due to kamma having been wrought,' matter sprung from another cause than kamma has been taken. In 'due to kamma having been wrought' only matter sprung from kamma has been taken. And these two, decay and impermanence, do not arise either from kamma,[4] or from any other matter-producing cause. Therefore they have not been taken. That they do not so arise will be clear later. And by such expressions as 'not-grasped-at,' etc., both the state of springing from kamma, etc., has been rejected, and the state of springing from another cause has not been granted. Hence in that exposition these two have not been taken.

In the exposition of 'sprung from [or originated by] consciousness,'[5] because the pair of terms, 'body-intimation, speech-intimation,' appears with reference to phenomena solely

---

[1] *Upādiṇṇa* :—'issue of grasping,' *B.P.E.*, p. 201; 323, *n.* 1. See *Compendium*, p. 159, *n.* 6.

[2] *Dhs.* §§ 653 *ff.*

[3] *Dhs.* § 656.

[4] *Points of Controversy*, 207 *f.*

[5] *Dhs.* § 667.

originated by consciousness, therefore it is mentioned here. In an ultimate sense, however, only the phenomena on which these two intimations depend are originated by consciousness. As it is from depending on such phenomena that decay-and-death of impermanent matter is called impermanence, so does this twofold intimation become known as 'originated by consciousness.'

The same method should be understood in the exposition of the term 'connate with consciousness.'[1] Inasmuch as they appear as consciousness, therefore this pair of questions has been asked. There is, however, not a [genuine] arising connate with consciousness as is the case with the phenomena and also with feeling, etc.

And the same with 'consequent on consciousness.'[2] Inasmuch as [such matter] appears as consciousness, therefore this pair [of opposites] is so called.

'Gross'[3] means thick, that which may be seized by impact of the sensitive surface, because it has become the basis and the object of thought. 'Subtle'[4] should be understood as the contradictory of what has been said.

'Remote'[5]:—[an object may be] far even though it stand near. This is when there is a difficulty of cognizing, because it is not to be seized by way of impact. The other term 'near' [may apply to an object] though it stand far. This is when there is ease of cognizing, because it may be seized by way of impact.

The expositions of sight, etc.,[6] are to be understood at length by the method given above.

[338] So far this is what is distinctive in the twofold summary[7] of matter.

The threefold summary[8] is clear in meaning.

At the end of the fourfold summary, owing to the absence of divisions in the last term in 'what is seen,' etc., omitting

---

[1] *Dhs.* § 669. *B.P.E.*:—'comes into being together with thought.'
[2] *Dhs.* § 671. *B.P.E.*:—'consecutive to thought.'
[3] *Dhs.* § 675. [4] *Dhs.* § 676. [5] *Dhs.* § 677.
[6] *Dhs.* §§ 695-741. [7] *Dhs.* §§ 653-741. [8] *Dhs.* §§ 742-876.

the query from the beginning it is said: 'The visible object is a thing seen, the audible object is a thing heard.'[1] Herein it is possible to see by looking at the visible object with the eye—thus it becomes 'a thing seen.' It is possible to cognize by hearing sound-organ by the ear—thus it becomes 'a thing heard.' The three fields of odour, taste, and touch, when they have been reached by nose, tongue, and body, become 'considered' (*mutaṁ*)[2] as something to be seized and considered in the sense of being known. It is said to be 'considered' by reason of the arising of knowledge when there has been contact. Thus it is said also in the Commentary. All matter should be known by means of mind-cognition—thus it becomes known as 'cognized by mind.'

In the exposition of the fivefold compendium[3] 'hard' is rigid. *Khara* (rough) is also *kharagata;* 'harsh' is the meaning. The other two terms also indicate intrinsic nature. 'Personal' is belonging to self. 'External' is outside. 'Grasped at' is originated by kamma. Generally, however, only matter established in the body is implied. Indeed, whether such matter is grasped at, or not, all is known as 'grasped-at' by virtue of being taken, seized, and wrongly handled.

Tejogata[4] is matter with the characteristic of heat (*tejo*) included in (*gata*) all kinds of heat or organic energy. Or, heat has 'gone' to the state of heat—hence *tejogata*. 'Scorching heat' (*usmā*) is a mode of heat. *Usmāgata* is gone to such a state of scorching heat, and is the name for the mode of scorching heat. *Usuma* is strong heat. That which has gone to such a state is *usumagata*. 'Mobility'[5] is going without stopping. Mobility having *gone* to such a state is *vāyogata*. 'Inflation' is the firm state of matter like that of the lotus stalk, leather-bag, etc., when filled with air.

[339] Owing to the absence of the differentiation of the concluding term of the three compendia beginning with the sixfold, the exposition has been made without putting the query from the outset. Herein 'possible to know by visual

---

1 *Dhs.* § 961.
2 Mutaṃ: 'imagined.' *B.P.E.*, p. 239.
3 *Dhs.* §§ 962-66.
4 *Dhs.* § 964.
5 *Dhs.* § 965.

cognition' is meant by 'cognizable by eye.'[1] 'Cognizable by mind,' *i.e.*, possible to be known by mind-cognition. It is possible to know specifically by the 'threefold element of mind.'[2] In 'all matter,' this is said because there is no such thing as any kind of matter not cognizable by the element of mind-cognition. Indeed, the Supreme Buddha is never known to have missed the right occasion on which to use method when he came to Abhidhamma. The right occasion to use the method is so-called owing to the absence of any kind of matter uncognizable by the element of mind-cognition. Hence in using the method he said 'all matter.'

'Pleasurable contact'[3] is cause of attainment of pleasurable feeling. 'Painful contact'=cause of attainment of painful feeling. In these two expressions this method has been given because the tangible object is the condition[4] of pleasure and pain.

And in the ninefold aspect[5] the method has been given owing to the existence of matter called the controlling faculty. Owing to such matter being with and without reaction, the method has been given under the tenfold aspect.[6]

In the elevenfold aspect[7] ten and a half organs have been classified. Their sections of expositions should be understood at length by the method given above. The remainder everywhere is clear in meaning.

And in order not to get confused with respect to these material forms, this particularization should be considered:—

Combination, origination, predetermination, conditioning.

Herein combination is the taking all that matter in groups or collectively, amounting to twenty-five; from organ of sight down to material food, tangible objects, element of cohesion. These together with the basic matter make twenty-six. [340] There is no matter other than these forms. But some[8] say: There is the material quality of torpor. They

---

[1] *Dhs.* § 967. [2] *Dhs.* § 969. [3] *Dhs.* § 970.

[4] Sabbhavato. (Or, reading sabbhāvato)—owing to the existence or manifestation of pleasure and pain having a tangible object.—Tr.

[5] *Dhs.* § 971. [6] *Dhs.* § 974. [7] *Dhs.* § 978.

[8] The dwellers at Abhayagiri.—*Pyī*.

should be told after this sort:—'Surely you are the Sage, the Buddha Supreme, in whom are no hindrances!' and checked thus: 'There is no such thing.' Others say that there are twenty-seven kinds of material things with the material quality of power, twenty-eight with that of collocation, twenty-nine with that of birth, or up to thirty with that of disease. These teachers should be refuted by the non-existence of these [added material qualities] being shown in turn. When the element of mobility is taken, the material quality of power is taken also; there is no other. The material quality of collocation is taken with the element of cohesion, that of birth with integration and continuity, that of disease with decay and impermanence; there is no other. Diseases of the ear and so forth are merely an element originated by misfitting causes; no other disease is present. Hence collectively there are only twenty-six material qualities.[1]

'Origination.' How many qualities of matter have how many origins? Ten material qualities have one origin, one has two origins, three have three origins, nine have four, two have none. Of these, eight, viz.: sentient organ of sight down to the life-controlling faculty verily have their origin in kamma. The pair called body-and speech-intimation verily originate from consciousness. Thus ten have a single origin. Sound [object of hearing] originating from the caloric [*i.e.*, physical] order and consciousness is the one which has two origins. Among sounds, unintelligible sounds originate from the caloric order, intelligible sounds originate from consciousness. Three material qualities:—buoyancy, pliancy, wieldiness originate from the caloric order, consciousness and nutriment. Thus three have three origins. The rest of the nine originate both from these three sources and from kamma. Thus nine have four sources. And decay and impermanence do not originate from any one of these four sources, and thus are the two which have no origin. And why? Because they are not born. Verily they are not born. And why? Because of the maturity and breaking-up of that matter which has been

[1] Cf. *Compendium*, pt. vi.

produced, for all that is material or immaterial which has arisen breaks up. [341] Verily this is to be accepted. For there is no thing arisen, material or immaterial, which does not undergo loss. But as long as it does not break up, there is a process of maturity; hence the expression, 'because of the ripening and dissolution of that matter which has been produced,' is accomplished. And if these [two material qualities] were produced, they would also mature and break up. Maturity does not mature, breaking-up is not broken up. Hence because of the maturing and breaking up of matter which has been produced, this pair of material qualities has not been produced.

Here this objection might be raised:—As in the expositions beginning with 'from kamma having been wrought,' by the expression, 'integration of matter, continuity of matter,' the expression 'birth is born' has been accepted, so the expression, 'let maturity mature, let breaking-up break up,' ought to have been accepted. (Reply):—In those expositions, 'birth is born,' etc., has not been accepted However, whatever states come into birth through kamma, etc., because of their having been reborn,[1] the common phrase of birth being the cause of such states has been granted. But in the ultimate sense birth does not come into being. To one who is being born, the mere [fact of] rebirth comes into being.

Here the objection might be raised:—'Just as birth acquires the common usage of being called both the cause of rebirth of these states and rebirth, so maturity and breaking-up also acquire those names by common usage. But then it should also be granted that this pair of material qualities has kamma, etc., for origin.' (Reply) Maturity and breaking-up do not get that common usage. And why? From their absence at the moment when the productive cause is powerful. For there is power to productive causes only at the moment of the production of a state to be produced; none subsequent to that. And birth appearing at the moment of states about to undergo rebirth by means of productive

---

[1] Abhinibbatti:—*B.P.E.*, p. 271, 're-created.'

causes, acquires by common usage the name both of being their causes and of being rebirth, birth being present at that moment. The other pair (decay and impermanence) being absent at that moment, [such common usage is not acquired], it may not be said that they come into being. Should you imagine that this pair does come into being from the statement, 'Bhikkhus, decay and death are impermanent, conditioned, arisen from a cause,'[1] it is not so. In the Sutta the teaching is explanatory. For in this passage the pair has been said to be dependent in origination by way of explanation, because of the decay and death of states which are of dependent origination. 'If so, the three:— [birth, decay, death]—not coming into being [342] are, like the hare's horn, non-existent. Thus they are permanent like Nibbāna'—is not the case, because they happen bound up with the bases. For when the bases appear—extension and the rest—the trio (birth, etc.) is revealed. Hence it cannot be said that these three are not. They are. They are also revealed in the absence of the bases. Hence they are not permanent. And it was in order to prevent a wrong conviction that this was said: 'Bhikkhus, decay and death are impermanent, conditioned, arisen from a cause.' Thus by such and other methods [we show that] these two qualities of matter have not sprung from any source.

Moreover, the word 'origin' has different implications. In the Table of Contents we have matter (1) born of kamma, (2) caused by kamma, (3) originating in the caloric order caused by kamma, (4) originating in nutriment, (5) caused by nutriment, (6) originating in the caloric order caused by nutriment, (7) originating in the caloric order, (8) caused by the caloric order, (9) originating in the caloric order caused by the caloric order, (10) originating in consciousness, (11) caused by consciousness, (12) originating in the caloric order caused by consciousness. Of these the eightfold matter beginning with the visual organ together with the heart-basis is matter born of kamma (1). Hair, beard, elephant-tusk, horse-tail, yak's tail—such matter is caused by kamma (2). The Wheel-treasure,[2] the

---

[1] *S.* ii., 26. [2] *Dialogues* ii. 202 *f.*

mansions and gardens of devas, are matter originating in the caloric order and kamma (3). The formula of eight originating from nutriment refers to matter originating in nutriment (4). Material food is the cause of two continuities of matter, of that originated by nutriment and of that which is grasped at. Being the producer of the first, it is a cause; being the guardian of matter born of kamma, it is a cause. This matter born of kamma watched over by nutriment is known as matter caused by nutriment (5). To one who lives on disagreeable food and goes about in the sun arise freckles, moles, leprosy, etc., which originate from the caloric order caused by nutriment (6). The formula of eight originating in the caloric order is called so (7). The caloric order present in this group produces another eightfold group, said to be caused by the caloric order (8). [343] The caloric order present in this other eightfold group produces still another eightfold group, originating in the caloric order which is caused by caloric order (9). Thus the caloric order is able to impinge on three continuities of matter, but not more. It is proper to disclose this meaning also by what is not grasped at. Clouds are said to originate in the caloric order. Torrents of rain are said to be caused by the caloric order. And when rain falls, seeds grow, earth sends out odour, mountains appear blue-green, the ocean increases:—such matter is said to originate in the caloric order caused by the caloric order (9). The formula of the eightfold group originating in consciousness is said to 'originate in consciousness' (10). This material body of pre-existence defined thus, 'posterior mental states and mentals are in the relation of posteriority to this prior body,' is caused by consciousness (11). In the sky, in the firmament, he depicts an elephant, a horse, a chariot, various army forces:—this 'originates in the caloric order caused by consciousness' (12).

'Predetermined.' Fifteen material qualities are called predetermined, ten are unpredetermined.[1] If there were

[1] Parinipphannan ti. This term is stated thus as if it were in the text; but it is not in the P.T.S. ed. The translator, now in England, has not access to the Burm. text. In a dual (positive, negative) list of material attributes in the Visuddhi-Magga, p. 450, Buddhaghosa includes this pair of terms. Cf. *Points of Controversy*, pp. 368, 396.—*Ed*.

unpredetermined material qualities, they would be called unconditioned. And the bodily change of these determined material qualities is called body-intimation; change in speech is speech-intimation. Space-element is [any] opening or cavity. Buoyancy is lightness; plasticity is softness; wieldiness is workableness; integration is coming into being; continuity is a proceeding; decay is mode of wearing out; impermanence is process of having become [then] not being. Thus all matter is 'predetermined and conditioned.'

End of the elucidation of the chapter on Material Qualities, in the Expositor, the Commentary on the Summary of States.

PART II—DISCOURSE ON THE CHAPTER OF THE SUMMARY

CHAPTER I

THE TRIPLETS

HITHERTO the 'moral triplet' has been expanded by the word-classifying method of all states, moral and so on. And because that method also holds good in the remaining triplets and couplets—for as here, in the moral triplet, it has been noted by the wise, so it is possible for the wise to note it in all the triplets and couplets in serial order thus, 'Which are the states associated with a pleasurable feeling? [344] These are the states associated with a pleasurable feeling'—therefore, the detailed teaching being omitted in order to show the classification of states in all the triplets and couplets by another method neither too concise nor too detailed, the chapter on the Summary beginning with, 'Which are the states that are moral?'[1] has been begun. The chapter on the states of consciousness is a detailed discourse; that on the commentary is a concise discourse. But the chapter on the summary, concise with reference to that of the states of consciousness, is detailed with reference to that of the commentary. Hence it is of the nature of being neither too concise nor too detailed. It should be known as the chapter on the Summary, because it leaves out the detailed discourse, as well as for the reason mentioned above (in the Introductory Discourse).[2] For it has been said:—

It summarizes roots and aggregates,
And 'doors,' planes of existence, meaning, text,
Name, sex—and therefore is called Summary.

This chapter, namely, on the Summary is taught by summarizing (*a*) roots by the method beginning with 'The three moral

[1] *Dhs.* § 981.

[2] P. 9.

roots,'[1] (*b*) aggregates by the method beginning with 'That is the associated aggregate of feeling,' (*c*) doors by the method beginning with 'Bodily kamma originating from it.' Kamma arisen in the body-door is called body-kamma. It has been shown by summarizing planes of existence by the method beginning with 'in a pleasurable soil [or plane] in the sensuous realm.'[2] And from being shown here and there by way of meaning, text, name, and sex (or form), it is shown by summarizing meaning, etc. There, in the exposition of moral consciousness,[3] in the first place, the word 'three' limits the calculation. States which are moral and roots are moral *roots*, or, they are roots in the sense of rendering service by being the condition, source, production, origin, and birth of moral states; hence 'moral roots.' Thus, having shown them by way of meaning[4] (or intrinsic nature),[5] now to show them by way of their [specific] names, he has said, 'non-greed, non-hate, non-delusion.' Because thus far there is nothing moral freed from a root, therefore by bringing all the four-planed moral [consciousness] under the three roots the King of the Law has shown this.

[345] 'That is associated':—that is, associated with non-greed, etc. Here, in the aggregate of the mental co-efficients[6] associated with non-greed are also counted non-hate and non-delusion. With the remaining two in [similar] association also, the same method should be understood. The King of the Law has shown this by exhausting again the four-planed moral consciousness in association with the associated fourth aggregate.

'That is originated,' *i.e.*, originating in non-greed, etc. In this way also the King of the Law has shown this by exhausting even that four-planed moral consciousness in connection with the three doors of action. Thus far moral consciousness has been shown by being exhausted in three respects.

For immoral consciousness also the same method should be

---

[1] *Dhs.* § 981. [2] *Dhs.* § 984. [3] *Dhs.* § 981.

[4] *Phalattha.—Ṭīkā.* [5] *Sabhāvattha.—Anuṭīkā.*

[6] The fourth, or *sankhārakkhandha*.

understood. Indeed, of the twelve types of immoral consciousness not one is free from a root. The King of the Law has shown this by exhausting it by means of the root.

There is no immorality above that associated fourth aggregate. Hence the King of the Law has shown by exhausting those twelve types of immoral consciousness only by way of the fourth aggregate.

But because the procedure of those classes of immoral consciousness is by way of bodily, vocal, and mental action, therefore the King of the Law has shown them exhaustively by way of those doors of action.

Moreover, here, in the exposition of immoral consciousness,[1] the passage 'corruptions which are united therewith' should be understood thus:—'united' means persisting in one consciousness or person. That which persists in one consciousness is called 'united in co-existence,' that which persists in one person is called 'united in removal.' It persists with greed, etc., hence is called united therewith; or, it is called united because it persists in one consciousness together with another state, such as contact (other than greed, etc.), shown in various passages.

Of these, union in co-existence is implied in the following passages:—'which are the states that are corrupt and corrupting?' in the corrupt and corruptible triplet;[2] 'which are the states that are base?' in the base or low triplet;[3] 'which are the states that are moral?' in this moral triplet; [346] 'which are the states that are corrupt?' etc., in the corruption group;[4] 'which are the states that are harmful?' in the harmful couplet.[5]

And union in removal comes in the following passages:—'these are the three fetters—corruptions' in the triplet of 'removable-by-insight';[6] again, 'these three—corruptions' in the triplet of 'having-root-conditions-removable-by-insight';[7] also 'the three fetters—have root conditions removable by insight' in the same triplet; and 'herein which

---

[1] *Dhs.* § 982. [2] *Dhs.* § 993. [3] *Dhs.* § 1025.
[4] *Dhs.* § 1243. [5] *Dhs.* § 1294. [6] *Dhs.* § 1002.
[7] *Dhs.* § 1010.

are—the corruptions ?' in the *Vibhanga* chapter on the 'Right Efforts.'[1]

The exposition of the term 'unmoral'[2] is clear in meaning. In this triplet [teachers have] said that three characteristics, three concepts, space obtained by separating the device,[3] open space, object of nothingness, attainment of cessation are not obtained.

In the exposition of the triplet of feeling[4], in 'pleasurable soil,'[5] pleasurable feeling is called pleasurable soil in the same way as soils are called red or coppery and black. As when we say sugar-soil, rice-soil, we mean the localities where sugar and rice thrive, such consciousness as is an occasion for the arising of pleasure is called 'pleasurable soil.' That sort of consciousness is here implied. And because that feeling arises in the sensuous realm as well as in the other two realms of life, [347] to show its specific kind it is said, 'in the sensuous realm,' etc. 'The pleasurable feeling itself excepted':—*i.e.*, excepting that pleasurable feeling which is in the pleasurable 'soil.' 'Associated therewith,' *i.e.*, associated with that excepted pleasurable feeling. In the remaining pair of terms also the meaning should be understood in the same way.

In this triplet we get neither all three feelings, nor anything material, nor Nibbāna. For this triplet is said to be free from these four features which are not got in the moral triplet.

Now in the following triplets and couplets what might have been said by way of text and meaning, all in the order of the terms, has been said in the discourse on the Table of Contents and in the exposition of moral and other consciousness. But wherever there is any specific difference, we shall speak of just that.

In those triplets and couplets, taking first the resultant triplet,[6] although material [resultant] states as well as immaterial states have their origin in action (*kamma*), yet they, from being without an object, are not like that action. But

---

[1] *Vibhanga*, p. 209.
[2] *Dhs.* § 983.
[3] Kasiṇa. See above, p. 248.
[4] *Dhs.* §§ 984-86.
[5] *B.P.E.*, p. 252, *n.* 1.
[6] *Dhs.* §§ 987-89.

immaterial [resultant] states which have a mental object, because they resemble the action, have been likened, as results, to fruit which resembles the seed. When rice seed is sown, the shoot, leaves, etc., although coming out are not called *rice fruit*, but when the rice ear is ripe, mature, then the rice which is like the seed is called rice fruit. And the shoot, leaves, etc., are said to be produced from, born of, the seed. Similarly it is fitting to call matter 'kamma'-born or 'grasped-at.'

In the triplet on 'grasped at,'[1] although the body and mind in [the personality of] saints may cause others to grasp at [things desired], as when it is said, 'Our senior uncle, the Elder!' 'Our junior uncle, the Elder!' still a saint has not himself seized, or wrongly handled, or grasped at the Paths, the Fruits or Nibbāna. As a heated iron ball is not the cause of flies sitting thereon, so the plenitude of spiritual heat in Path, Fruit, Nibbāna is not the cause of anyone else seizing through [his own] craving, conceit, or wrong views.

Hence it has been said, 'These are the states which are neither grasped at, nor favourable to grasping.' And the same with those which are neither corrupt nor corruptible.[2]

Those states, because they do not occur in the moral triplet, together with the sustained application of mind, which is co-existent with the initial application, do not occur in the triplet of initial application of mind.[3]

[348] In the triplet of the 'rapture-accompanied,'[4] rapture, pleasure, indifference, giving their nature to the states co-existent with themselves, themselves become regressive.[5] In this triplet, states of consciousness accompanied by grief, bodily cognition accompanied by pain, indifferent feeling, matter, Nibbāna—nothing of all these is obtained. For this triplet is said to be free from the content not occurring in the moral triplet and these five features.

In the triplet, 'removable-by-insight,'[6] 'fetters' are bonds; 'theory of individuality' is a view arising with respect to the

---

[1] *Dhs.* §§ 990-92. [2] *Dhs.* § 995. [3] *Dhs.* §§ 996-97.
[4] *Dhs.* § 999. [5] Piṭṭhivaṭṭakā. [6] *Dhs.* § 1002.

body in the sense of existing, and called the fivefold aggregate, or, itself appearing as the view arising with respect to that body.

That it is possible to purify by (mere) rules, that it is possible to purify by (mere) rites, that it is possible to purify by rule and ritual:—observance thus taken is called 'wrong observance (or handling) of mere rule and ritual.' 'Here'[1] is an indeclinable, signifying place. Sometimes it is said to refer to the world, as when [the Buddha] said, 'Here in the world the Tathāgata appears.'[2] Sometimes it is said to refer to the dispensation or religion, as when he said, 'In just this dispensation the first monk, the second monk. . . .'[3] Sometimes it is used to refer to a place, as when [the Buddha] said:—

'Here as I stood a deva, I obtained
Another life, as thou, good sir, shouldst know.'[4]

Sometimes it is used merely to fill up a half-line, as when he said, 'Here as I ate, bhikkhus, I was not prevented.'[5]

Here it is used for the world.

In 'ignorant average man,' 'ignorant' should be known as 'owing to the absence of access to the Scriptures, and of the higher attainment of the Path and Fruition.' For to whomsoever, owing to the absence of learning by heart, catechism thereon and deduction therefrom regarding the aggregates, elements, sense-organs, the causal mode, the application of mindfulness, etc., there is no attainment of that learning which represses opinionativeness, nor any access, owing to the non-attainment of what should be attained by conduct, such a person, from the absence of such access and such attainment, should be known as 'ignorant':—

One of the 'manyfolk' is he who brings about
A multiplicity of things, 'mid manyfolk engulfed.[6]

[349] For he who is ignorant is called ['average' or]

---

[1] *Dhs.* § 1003. [2] *Dīgha* i. 62, etc.
[3] *Anguttara* ii. 238. Cf. *ib.*, *n.* 1; *Dīgha* ii. 151; *Points of Controversy.*
[4] Not traced. [5] Not traced. Br. text reads *apavārito.* Tr.
[6] *Sumangala-Vilāsinī* i. 59.

'common' for such reasons as the production of corruptions, many and of various sorts, as has been said: 'He produces many corruptions: they have many views of individuality unremoved; they look to the face of many teachers; they have not got clear of all tendencies; they construct many and various complexities; they are borne along by many and various floods; they are anxious with many and various anxieties; they burn with many and various heart-burnings; with the manifold five desires of sense they are enamoured, swallowed up, cleaving to, attached to, hung up on them, hanging from them, obstructed by them; by the various five hindrances they are enwrapped, muffled up, stifled, closed in, covered up, cramped; or from being engulfed among persons, passing the bounds of calculation, of low practices [or principles] turned away from the Ariyan Law—such are "common."' Or counted as 'separated from,' 'unmixed with' the Ariyan folk possessed of the qualities of virtue, learning, etc.—thus 'average.' By these two terms the 'ignorant average' man [is denoted]:—

> *The Buddha, kinsman of the sun, hath seen,*
> *In common folk two species : one is blind,*
> *The other class is good at heart.*[1]

Thus two sorts of average men have been named, of whom the blind average man is here meant:—'Who perceives not the Ariyans.' From being far (*āra*) from the corruptions, not urging (*iriya*) the world to behave to unbeneficial purpose, urging beneficial behaviour, worthy of being resorted to by the world of men and devas:—Buddhas. silent Buddhas, Buddhas' disciples—are they called 'Ariyans.'[2] Or, only the Buddhas herein are Ariyans. As has been said: 'Bhikkhus, in the world of men and devas the Tathāgata is the Ariyan.'[3]

'Good men'=silent Buddhas, Tathāgatas, disciples. Be-

---

[1] *Sumangala-Vilāsinī* i. 59.

[2] The commentarial word-play here is untranslatable. It pieces Ariyā out of *āra*, far, *iriya*, urging, etc. Cf. *Anguttara* iv. 145; *Majjhima* i. 280.

[3] Not traced.

cause they from being yoked with transcendental virtues are lovely men, therefore are they 'good men.' [350] Or, all of them are said to be twofold: Ariyans and good men. For Buddhas are both Ariyans and good men; so also silent Buddhas and Buddhas' disciples; as it is said:—

> '*He of a grateful heart, of cultured mind,*
> *Firm in devotion, and a virtuous friend,*
> *Who carefully doth tend the many needs*
> *Of them that ail, is called by mortals "good."*'

Indeed, by so much of the text: 'Firm in devotion, and a virtuous friend' is the Buddhas' disciple declared; by 'grateful, etc.,' are the silent Buddhas and Buddhas declared. Now that person, who is not used to perceiving these Ariyans, and does not consider it right to do so, should be known as 'one who perceives not the Ariyans.' And there are two kinds: he who does not perceive them by the eye, and he who does not perceive them by insight. Of them the latter is here meant. Ariyans are both seen and not seen when the carnal or the psychic eye merely seizes on outward complexion, and is unable to take Ariyanship as object. Dogs and jackals, etc., see Ariyans by the eye, but are not perceivers of the Ariyans.

Hereon this story:—One who left the world in his old age, who was a supporter of an Elder, purged of the intoxicants, resident at Mount Cittala, while walking about for alms one day with the Elder, carrying the Elder's bowl and robe behind him, asked, 'Sir, what are the Ariyans like?' The Elder said: 'Friend, even though in this religion some old man goes about together with the Ariyans, taking their bowl and robe, and does the greater and lesser duties towards them, he does not know them. Friend, Ariyans are difficult to know.' Though this was said, he did not understand the hint. Therefore seeing is not by the eye but by insight, as he said: 'Vakkali, what good to thee is this [my] visible foul body? Verily, Vakkali, he who sees the Law sees me.'[1]

[1] *Saṃyutta* iii. 120; *Pss. of the Brethren*, p. 198.

Hence not seeing the characteristic signs of impermanence, etc., seen by the Ariyans with insight, not arriving at the Law arrived at by the Ariyans, not seeing Ariyanship or the states which bring about Ariyanship, he, though he sees by the eye, should be known 'to perceive not the Ariyans.'

[351] 'Who comprehends not the Ariyan doctrines':— is unskilled in the Ariyan doctrines such as the different kinds of application of mindfulness, etc.

'Who is not trained according to the Ariyan doctrines.' Discipline here is twofold; each of which is fivefold. Owing to the absence of that discipline this average man is called 'untrained.' For this discipline is twofold, of restraint, namely, and of elimination, each of which is fivefold. Discipline of restraint is fivefold thus:—restraint by virtue, mindfulness, insight, patience, and effort. Discipline of elimination is fivefold thus:—elimination of the factor in question, discarding, extirpating, composure, escape. With these one is filled, replete, endowed with this Pātimokkha restraint—this is restraint by virtue. One guards the eye-controlling-faculty, arrives at restraint in the sight-controlling-faculty—this is restraint by mindfulness.

The currents flowing in the world, O Ajita,
Said the Exalted One, these may
By mindfulness be checked, this the restraint I teach,
By insight they may be shut in[1]—

this is restraint by insight. Endurance of cold and heat—this is restraint by patience. Not consenting to the uprisen lustful thought—this is restraint by effort. And all this restraint is called restraint and discipline, from the restraining and eliminating of bodily misconduct, etc., which ought to be restrained and eliminated by each for himself. So far should the discipline of restraint be understood to be fivefold.

And owing to opposition among the different kinds of insights and knowledges, such as the distinction of mind from matter, there is elimination of this and that disad-

---

[1] *Sutta-Nipāta*, ver. 1035.

vantage by means of this and that insight and knowledge like the removal of darkness by lamplight. Elimination, namely, of the theory of individuality by means of determining mind and matter, [352] of the views as to what are not conditions, and what are uneven conditions by means of insight grasping the cause, of the doubtful state by means of insight transcending doubt subsequent to the preceding insight, of such attachment to a view as I, mine, by means of insight contemplating the group of mind and matter, of imagining what is not the path to be the path by means of determining the right path and the wrong path, of the annihilationistic view by means of discernment of genesis, of the eternalistic view by means of discernment of transience, of imagining no danger in danger by means of discernment of peril, of the perception of infatuation by means of the discernment of evil, of the perception of delight by means of insight into disgust, of the desire not to be free by means of knowledge of a desire to be free, of want of indifference by means of knowledge of indifference, of opposition in causal genesis[1] and in Nibbāna by adaptation, of the signs of things-in-the-making by adoption—this is elimination of the factor in question. And that elimination, like smiting away weeds on the water's surface with a pot,[2] of these and those hindrances, etc., by way of hindering their procedure by means of concentration in the different kinds of access, this is known as elimination by discarding. Elimination by means of the certain non-occurrence of the group of corruptions belonging to the 'uprising' [of Ill][3] and spoken of in this way, 'for the sake of eliminating [wrong] views in one's own life-continuum' on the part of one who is in this or that Path, cultivating the four Ariyan Paths, is called elimination by the removal called extirpation. That tranquillizing the lower nature at the moment of Fruition is called elimination by composure. That Nibbāna which has eliminated all conditioned things owing to detachment from all conditioned things is called elimination by escape.

---

[1] *Dhammaṭṭhiti*. Cf. *Points of Controversy*, p. 386 *f*.

[2] Cf. Childers' Dictionary *sub v.* Vikkhambanaṃ.—*Ed.*

[3] Samudayapakkhikassa. Cf. the second Ariyan 'Truth.'—*Ed.*

And because all this is called elimination in the sense of giving-up, and discipline in the sense of suppressing, therefore it is called elimination-discipline. Or, all this is so called from the production of this and that discipline in one who eliminates this and that. Thus it should be understood under five heads. Thus because it, in brief twofold and analysed as tenfold, does not exist in an ignorant average man, because he breaks down restraint and does not eliminate what should be eliminated, therefore from the absence of such discipline such an one is called 'untrained.'

[353] And the same method is to be understood in 'who perceives not good men, who comprehends not, nor is trained according to the doctrine of good men.' For there is no difference in meaning, as it has been said:—'Whatever Ariyans there are, are called good men; whatever good men there are, are called Ariyans. Whatever is the doctrine of Ariyans is the doctrine of good men; whatever is the doctrine of good men is the doctrine of Ariyans. Whatever Ariyan disciplines there are, are the disciplines of good men; whatever disciplines of good men there are, are disciplines of Ariyans. Ariyans and good men, doctrines of Ariyans and doctrines of good men, disciplines of Ariyans and disciplines of good men—they are mutually interchangeable, they are one, of one meaning, identical, partake of an identical nature, correspond in sense, and each is even the other.'[1]

Regarding 'He views material qualities as the self'[2]—here in this world someone looks upon material qualities as the self: 'That which is corporeal is I, I am that matter.' Thus he looks upon matter and self not as two. As he views the flame and the colour as one, 'That which is the flame of a burning oil-lamp is the colour, that which is the colour is the flame,' so here he views matter as the self, owing to wrong views. 'Or the self to be possessed of matter':—taking the immaterial to be the self, he views it as having matter, as a tree has a shadow. 'Or matter in the self':—taking the

[1] Not traced.

[2] Cf. *B.P.E.*, p. 259, for the different renderings of this and the following phrases in this paragraph.

immaterial to be the self, he views matter as in the self, like scent in a flower. 'Or the self in matter':—taking the immaterial to be the self, he sees the self as in matter, like a gem in a casket. And the same with feeling, etc.[1]

Hereby 'he views matter as the self,' bare matter only has been spoken of as the self. In these seven places: viz., 'he views the self as possessed of matter, or matter as in the self, or the self as in matter, feeling, perception, complexes, consciousness as the self,' the immaterial has been spoken of as the self.

[354] In twelve places by way of threes in the four aggregates, viz., 'or the self as having feeling, or feeling as in the self, or the self as in feeling,' mixed matter and non-matter have been spoken of as the self. In five places: 'he views matter as the self, feeling, perception, complexes, consciousness as the self,' the annihilationistic view is stated. Thus here are fifteen views concerning being and five concerning non-being. All of them are to be considered as blocking the way to the Path, as not blocking the way to happy rebirth, and as that which is to be slain by the First Path.

'He doubts the Teacher,'[2] that is, as regards the Teacher's body, or qualities, or both. In doubting that body he doubts:—'Is there, or is there not a [human] body adorned with the thirty-two excellent characteristic signs?' In doubting those qualities, he doubts:—'Is there, or is there not omniscience capable of knowing the past, present, and future?' In doubting both, he doubts:—'Is there, or is there not a Buddha who is endowed with the colouring of eighty minor signs and a halo of glory, who has penetrated omniscience, is capable of knowing all knowable things, and who is the world-saviour?' Thus, because of his doubting the Buddha's personality and qualities he is said to doubt both. 'Is perplexed':—being unable to decide as to the object of thought, he wearies, he suffers. 'Is not resolved':—he does not get decision as to the object. 'Is not calm':—he is not able to free the mind

---

[1] *I.e.*, with the other four constituent factors of personality.

[2] *Dhs.* § 1004.

from perturbation and calm it, and is not calm regarding qualities.[1]

In 'he doubts the doctrine,' etc., he is said to doubt the doctrine thus: 'Are there, or are there not the four Ariyan Paths which eliminate the lower nature, the four Fruitions of the religious life, which tranquillize the lower nature? Is there, or is there not the great deathless Nibbāna, related by way of object to the Paths, and Fruition?' as well as, 'Does the doctrine lead out of the round of births or not?'

[355] He is said to doubt the Order thus: 'Four persons in the Paths, four in the Fruitions—these are that treasure which is the Order; do they exist, or not?' also, 'Is this Order well-behaved or ill-behaved?' also, 'Is there, or is there not any resulting fruit of a gift to the Order?'

He is said to doubt the Training thus: 'Are there the three stages of training, or not?'[2]

'The past':—past aggregate, element, sense-organ. 'The future' are the corresponding future [states of consciousness]. Of these, regarding past aggregates, etc., he is said to doubt the past thus: 'Have there been, or not these past aggregates?' etc. Regarding those of the future he is said to doubt the future thus: 'Are there any, or are there not any in the future?' In doubting 'both,' he is said to doubt the past and the future.

In doubting thus: 'Is there, or is there not the round of the twelve causes?' he is said to doubt these causally generated states. Herein the word-definition is: 'The causes of these states, decay and death, etc., are specifically assignable causes.' 'Specifically assignable causality' is the state of such assignable causes. The two expressions are identical, and are synonyms here of birth, etc. Birth and the rest of the series are said to be causally generated in the sense 'come to pass because of, in consequence of.' Or, he doubts the specifically assignable causation of states which are causally generated.

'By mere rule of morality':—by ascetic habits called 'bovine,' etc.[3] 'By ritual,' *i.e.*, by ascetic conduct called

---

[1] Cf. P.T.S. ed., p. 354, *n.* 10.

[2] *Anguttara* i. 236 *f.;* Editor's *Buddhism*, 1912, ch. viii.

[3] Cf. *B.P.E.*, p. 260, *n.* 4. *Dialogues* iii. 11 *f.*

'bovine,' etc. 'By rule and ritual':—by both. 'Purity' is purity from corruption, or Nibbāna as the ultimate purity.

'United therewith,'[1] here chiefly the corruptions as collectively eliminable.[2] And the Text accepts two:—the corruptions of dogmatism and perplexity. The other eight:—greed, hate, delusion, conceit, sloth, excitement, shamelessness, fearlessness of blame, which are not included should be referred to and explained. For here when dogmatism and perplexity are removed, all the eight beginning with greed, which lead to purgatory and being united in elimination, are eliminated. And union in co-existence should be brought out and explained. [356] Thus, five kinds of consciousness:—four accompanied by dogmatism and one accompanied by perplexity—are removed by the [first, or] stream-winning Path. Of these, when the two kinds of automatic consciousness of dogmatism are eliminated, these corruptions, viz., greed, delusion, excitement, shamelessness, recklessness, which are co-existent therewith are removed by means of such union in co-existence. The remaining corruptions of dogmatism and of perplexity are removed by means of union in elimination. And when the modes of non-automatic consciousness associated with dogmatism are eliminated, these corruptions, viz., greed, delusion, sloth, excitement, shamelessness, recklessness, co-existent therewith, are eliminated by means of union in co-existence. The remaining corruptions of dogmatism and of perplexity are eliminated by means of union in elimination. So union in co-existence is obtained only in union in elimination. This they [the teachers] have brought out and explained.

'Associated *therewith*':—associated with those eight united corruptions. Or, this should be shown as association with each corruption separately, as with 'that greed,' with 'that hate.' Of them, when greed is taken, this group of corruptions, the aggregate of mental co-efficients, viz.: delusion, conceit, sloth, excitement, shamelessness, recklessness, is called greed-

---

[1] *Dhs.* § 1006.

[2] *I.e.*, Corruptions established as removable in a single individual. —*Tr.*

associated. When hate is taken, this group of corruptions, viz.: delusion, sloth, excitement, shamelessness, recklessness, is called hate-associated. When delusion is taken, this group of corruptions, viz.: greed, hate, conceit, sloth, excitement, shamelessness, recklessness, is called delusion-associated. When conceit is taken, this group of corruptions co-risen therewith, viz., greed, delusion, sloth, excitement, shamelessness, recklessness is called conceit-associated. In this way the state associated with 'that sloth,' 'that excitement,' 'that shamelessness,' 'that recklessness' is said to be associated therewith. Thus should the connection be made.

'Originated thereby' means sprung from, or originated by 'that greed' . . . 'that recklessness.'

In 'these are the states eliminable by insight' the Stream-winning Path is called 'insight,' by which they should be put away—such is the meaning. But why is the Path known as insight? Because in it Nibbāna is first seen. But does not 'Adoption' see it first of all? [357] It does. But having seen it, one does not do what is necessary in the elimination of the Fetters, hence it should not be said that 'it sees.' A man of the provinces, although he may have seen the king at some place, says: 'Neither to-day have I seen the king,' because he has not offered his presents, nor accomplished his business. This is an illustration.

'The remaining greed' is what remains from that which has been put away by insight. And the same with hate and delusion, etc. For it is by insight only that those which lead to purgatory are put away. It is to show about the other [corruptions] that this: 'the remaining greed,' etc., has been said. 'United,' etc., refers to the five[1] corruptions united by association with, as well as by elimination of, those three corruptions adopted in the text.

'Neither by insight nor by culture'[2] is said with reference to the fact that [certain things] are not to be put away by this or that Path, as are the Fetters, etc. That elimination of

---

[1] Conceit, sloth, excitement, shamelessness, recklessness.—*Tr.*

[2] *Dhs.* § 1008.

moral, immoral, and unmoral [kamma] which was admitted [above] in such dicta as 'whatever mind-and-body may have arisen in the ageless round of rebirth, save in the seven [last] lives,[1] here cease to be,'[2] by the insight of the First Path, by the cessation of that consciousness which prepares [new birth], —that elimination [we repeat] is to be understood as said with respect to this explanation, namely, that because of those Paths not being cultivated, such [personalities] as might arise are eliminated because of the elimination of corruptions having sufficing conditions [in the past eventually bringing about that elimination].

In the triplet of 'having root-conditions removable by insight,'[3] having concluded that these are the states which have root-conditions removable by insight, again the expression 'three Fetters,' etc., is said in order to show, after pointing out what is to be eliminated, the conditions and states with conditions by a state of union. Although in the expression 'with conditions removable' these states are comprehended, viz., 'Among these conditions to be removed by insight delusion accompanied by greed is conditional with it; delusion accompanied by hate is conditional with it; and greed, hate are conditional with delusion,' yet delusion accompanied by perplexity, owing to the absence of another associated condition, is called just condition, and it is not accompanied by a condition. It is to show the elimination of this delusion that the above expression has been said.

[358] In the second answer, to show the elimination of delusion accompanied by excitement, 'these are the states having root-conditions to be removed by culture'[4] has been said. For delusion makes states associated with itself 'coconditional' and becomes regressive.[5] Owing to the

---

[1] Cf. *Points of Controversy*, p. 77, *n*. 3; 268, 271.

[2] Cf. *Dialogues* i. 283, and cf. above p. 316; also *Visuddhi Magga*, 674 *f*. On p. 316, for 'the beginning whereof is unknown, prior to seven rebirths,' read as above.—*Ed.*

[3] *Dhs*. § 1009.

[4] *Dhs*. § 1011.

[5] Piṭṭhivaṭṭako. See p. 450.

absence of another associated condition like 'delusion accompanied by perplexity,' delusion is not included in the expression 'condition to be removed.'

In the third answer, 'all other states good,, etc.' the immoral has been included for the purpose of including delusion accompanied by perplexity and distraction, so these delusions, from the absence of the associated condition, are not called 'having root-conditions to be removed.'

In the triplet 'with limited objects'[1]:—'with reference to' means having made a mental object. For whether they are themselves limited or sublime, the states arisen, by making limited states the object, are 'with limited objects'; those arisen by taking sublime objects are 'with sublime objects'; those arisen by taking immeasurable objects are 'with immeasurable objects.' But these last are also limited and sublime as well as immeasurable.

In the triplet on wrongfulness, 'immediate'[2] means giving results without intervening [time]. This is an equivalent term for such acts as matricide, etc. Indeed, when one such act is done, another act is not able, by ejecting it, to find opportunity for its own result. For even the action of one who all his lifetime gives the four requisites to the Order, with the Buddha as the head, lodged to its full capacity in a monastery which he may have caused to be built, with golden shrines of the size of Mount Meru and jewelled walls as ample as a world-system, cannot inhibit the [immediate] result of these acts. 'And that wrong view which is assured': *i.e.*, one or other of the assuredly wrong views of those who do not believe in cause, deny the efficacy of action, are nihilists. The person who has adopted and maintains them even a hundred or a thousand Buddhas are not able to enlighten.

In the triplet of 'with the Path as mental object,'[3] 'in connection with the Ariyan Path,' means making the transcendental Path the mental object. And these states with the Path as object may be either limited or sublime.

[359] In the exposition of 'conditioned by the Path,'[4] by

[1] *Dhs.* § 1022. [2] *Dhs.* § 1028. Cf. *Points of Controversy*, pp. 268, 274.
[3] *Dhs.* § 1031. [4] *Dhs.* § 1032.

the first formula the state of aggregates as accompanied by conditions is shown, the aggregates being associated with the Path by means of condition in the sense of causal relation.[1] By the second formula is shown the state of being accompanied by conditions of the remaining Paths, the condition being called right views and being the Path itself. By the third formula is shown the state of being accompanied by conditions, the state, namely, of right views got by means of conditions arisen in the Path.

'Making the dominant influence'[2] means making the object of thought the dominant influence. And verily such states are limited. For the dominant influence of the mental object is obtained at the time when Ariyan disciples attaching importance to their own Path reflect on it. But although the Ariyan disciple reflects on and gives importance to another person's Path by means of his knowledge of the thoughts of another, he does not attach the same importance to it as to the Path attained by himself. Does he attach importance or not to the Path of the Tathāgata after seeing him do the Twin Miracle? He does, but not as if it were to his own Path. And the same meaning is to be understood in, 'The saint attaches importance to no state except the Path, Fruition and Nibbāna.' 'With investigation as the dominant influence':—this is said to show the co-existent influence. For to one who, cultivating the Path, makes conation the chief, conation is called the dominant influence and not the Path. The remaining states also are said to have conation and not the Path as the dominant influence; and the same with sense-consciousness also. But to one who in cultivating the Path makes investigation the chief, investigation as well as the Path is the dominant influence. The remaining states are said to have the Path as the dominant influence. And the same with energy also.

In the exposition of the 'arisen' triplet[3]: 'are born' means 'come to be' Such terms as 'become' are synonyms,

---

[1] Paccay'aṭṭhena hetunā. 'Condition,' as always, refers to the six 'springs of action.' See next chapter.—*Ed.*

[2] *Dhs.* § 1034. [3] *Dhs.* § 1035.

all meaning 'having got an intrinsic nature.' For the states which are said to be 'born' are said to 'have become' from attaining an intrinsic nature, 'have been gotten' from union with a cause, 'have attained renewed existence' from having attained to the characteristics of such. Increasing the term by the preposition (*abhi*) they are said to 'have fully attained rebirth.' 'Made manifest' is being made evident. [360] 'Have arisen,' *i.e.*, from the past uprisen. Increasing the term by the preposition *sam*, they are said to be 'ever coming to pass.' 'Have uprisen,' *i.e.*, in the sense of coming to be, they persist 'upward.' 'Have supervened,' *i.e.*, they have happened owing to union with causes. The reason in the repetition of 'have arisen' should be understood by the said method. 'Included among things that have arisen' means counted as a portion of those arisen states. 'Matter, feeling, perception, complexes, consciousness'—this signifies the intrinsic nature of these arisen states. The exposition in the second reply of 'not arisen' should be understood as the negating of the foregoing. The exposition of the third reply is clear in meaning.

And this triplet has been shown to be complete by virtue of the two times (past and future). Indeed the ripening of kamma which has got its opportunity is twofold:—that which has 'reached the moment' and that which has not. The first is said to 'have arisen'; the second may arise immediately after the thought [which is the kamma], or not till the expiration of a hundred thousand ages. But owing to its having an enduring causal relation, it is not non-existent, but has become [a series of] potentially arising states. As he said: —'Granted, Poṭṭhapāda, that there is an incorporeal "soul" compact of ideas, even then for this person his arisen ideas are no longer the same when they cease.'[1] Thus here, when

[1] *Dīgha* i. 187; *Dialogues* i. 253. I venture to think the translation has missed the meaning of aññā . . . aññā (cf. Latin *alter* . . . *alter*); also *Saṃyutta* ii. 20, 95. On 'potentially arising,' cf. 60: 'bound to arise' (uppādino). *B.P.E.*, p. 270, *n.* 4; *Points of Controversy*, p. 242, where the old terminology also seems to need the scientific *mot juste*.—*Ed.*

during life in this sensuous realm consciousness concerning the immaterial plane arises, although the original subconscious continuum ceases, yet, when [in its turn] that [higher] consciousness ceases, the latter will certainly arise. Thus the self, if reckoned as incorporeal, is not counted as non-existent, but is become a potential [series of] states. In this way the results of kamma are twofold.

Now if all moral and immoral kamma which have been put forth were to give a result, there would be no opportunity for any other state. But such kamma is twofold:—its result is either a constant or not. The five kinds of kamma having immediate result,[1] the eight Attainments, the four Ariyan Paths:—such kamma is said to have a constant result. [361] And the result is either instantaneous, or not. In the former case it is said to have 'arisen'; in the latter not arisen. Whether the ripening of that twofold kamma arise immediately after the [kamma-] thought, or at the expiration of a hundred thousand cycles, it is not said to be non-arisen because of the meaning of a constant causal relation; it is known as potentially 'arising states.' The Path of Metteyya, the future Buddha, is said to be non-arisen; its Fruition to be 'potentially arising states.'

In the exposition of the 'past' triplet,[2] 'past' means having got beyond the three moments.[3] 'Ceased,' *i.e.*, has reached cessation. 'Dissolved,' *i.e.*, gone to destruction, departed. 'Changed,' *i.e.*, transformed by abandoning the original nature. 'Terminated' means gone to the term called cessation. The term 'exterminated' has been reinforced by the prefix *abhi*. 'Dissolved after having arisen,' *i.e.*, departed after having come to be. The reason for the repetition of the word 'past' has been given above. In the following terms ['future,' etc.] the same method is to be understood. 'Included among things that are past,' *i.e.*, reckoned to be a portion of the past. Which are these past states? 'Matter,

---

[1] See p. 462, *n.* 2. [2] *Dhs.* § 1038.

[3] Viz., genesis, 'stasis' and passing away. Cf. *Anguttara* i. 152; *Points of Controversy*, p. 374.—*Ed.*

feeling, perception, complexes, consciousness.' And the same with the terms 'future,' etc.

In the exposition of the triplet of 'with the past as object of thought'[1]:—in the passage 'with reference to past states,' only limited and sublime states should be understood. For these arise concerning the past.

In the exposition of the 'personal' triplet[2]:—by the pair of terms, 'for these or for those [beings],' all beings are comprised. Both 'personal' and 'self-referable' are synonyms of one's own personality. 'One's own,' *i.e.*, become of one's self. 'Individual,' *i.e.*, belonging to each person severally. 'Grasped at,' *i.e.*, established in the bodies of beings. They may, indeed, be born of kamma, or not. But by virtue of grasping, seizure, wrong handling, 'grasped at' is here said. 'For other beings,'[3] *i.e.*, for all remaining beings excepting one's self. 'For other persons' is merely its synonym. The rest is even as has been said above. 'Both those,'[4] *i.e.*, both [personal and external].[5]

In the first term of 'having the personal as object of thought,'[6] limited and sublime states should be understood. [362] In the second, immeasurable states should also be understood. In the third, only the limited and sublime should be understood. But the immeasurable do not make at one time the external, at another time the personal their object.

The exposition of the triplet of 'visible states' is clear.

CHAPTER II

COUPLETS AND OTHER GROUPS

AMONG the coupled [propositions], in the exposition of 'absence of hate'[7]:—'having love'[8] is exercising love, 'loving' is the method of exercising love; 'lovingness' is the state

---

[1] *Dhs.* § 1041. [2] *Dhs.* § 1044. [3] *Dhs.* § 1045.
[4] *Dhs.* § 1046. [5] *Pyi.* [6] *Dhs.* § 1047.
[7] *Dhs.* § 1056. [8] Mettī. Cf. *B.P.E.*, p. 275, *n.* 2.

of heart which is endowed with love, is productive of love.[1] 'Tender care,' *i.e.*, watchful, meaning 'one protects.' Tenderly caring is the method of such care. 'Tender carefulness' is the state of tenderly caring. 'Beneficence' is seeking [to do] good. 'Compassion' is exercising compassion. And by all these terms that love, too, which [in Jhāna] has reached access and ecstasy is included. By the remaining terms absence of hate that is either worldly or transcendental is described.

In the exposition of absence of delusion[2]:—'insight[3] into Ill' means insight into the Fact of Ill. And the same with 'the origin of Ill,' etc. And of these, 'insight into Ill' occurs in hearing, contemplation, intuition, and reflection. Likewise 'origin of Ill.' But 'insight into cessation' occurs only in hearing, intuition, and reflection. Likewise 'insight into the Way.'[4] 'Former things,' *i.e.*, in the past portion; 'latter things,' *i.e.*, in the future portion; 'former and latter,' *i.e.*, in both. 'The assignable causation of states causally generated' means—this is the cause; that is the effect;[5] depending on this cause that result has been produced. Thus it is insight into causes and effects.

Next, in the exposition of 'greed,'[6] the following is the meaning of terms not hitherto mentioned.

'Passion' is the exercise of lusting. 'Infatuation' has the sense of strongly lusting. 'Seduction' is the repeatedly leading beings in the fields of sense. 'Compliance' is to comply with, *i.e.*, following after one's desires. 'Delight' [refers to this, that] by greed beings in any existence feel delight, or greed itself is a delighting in. In 'passionate delight' we get the first term combined with delight. Craving once arisen as to an object is 'delight'; arisen repeatedly, it is 'passionate delight.' 'Infatuation of mind' means that the term described above is not of a permanent being, but only of consciousness. 'Wanting' means that by greed objects

---

[1] Br. ed. reads mettāya ayitassa.—*Tr.*

[2] *Dhs.* § 1057.

[3] Ñāṇaṃ. *B.P.E.*:—knowledge.

[4] Paṭipadā. Cf. the Fourth 'Truth.'

[5] See, in P.T.S. ed. (p. 362), *n.* 13.

[6] *Dhs.* § 1059.

are wished for. 'Languishing' means that, through the strength of the lower nature, creatures languish with greed. 'Devouring' is to grasp by swallowing and finishing. 'Greediness' means that by greed beings become greedy, practise greed. Or greediness has the sense of 'thickness,' as we speak of a forest being thick (or dense). The next term is [the same] increased by the prefix *pali-*, or it may mean omnivorous[1] greediness. 'Cleaving' means that by greed one clings, or hangs on to. Greed is 'slough' in the sense of submerging, 'longing' in the sense of drawing towards. As it is said 'longing draws this man to and fro for rebirth in this or that plane.' 'Illusion'[2] means deception. 'Genitrix'—because greed gives birth to beings in the round of life renewed. As it is said:—

Desire begets a man ; his mind a-wandering goes.

'Progenitrix,' [the prefix *sañ-* indicating greed's] enchaining [*saṃyojamānā*] beings in that round by suffering. 'Seamstress' as sewing, for as a tailor sews cloth to cloth, so greed sews, stitches beings in that round by way of decease and re-conception; hence seamstress is said with the meaning of sewing. 'She who ensnares,' *i.e.*, craving has a net of manifold sense-experience, or a net quivering and far-fixed. 'Flowing stream,' as drawing along by a swift current, or as wetness. For it is said:—

Joys wet and viscid come to sons of men.[3]

Both [adjectives] are here meant.

'*Visattikā*'[4] is spread out, diffused, extensive, compelling, deceptive, misleading, poison-bearing, poison-rooted, poison-

---

[1] Lit. greediness in every respect.

[2] *Māyā*. *B.P.E.*: 'trickery' (because in the Suttas the word occurs usually in connection with the conjurer's craft).—*Ed.*

[3] *Dhammapada*, ver. 341.

[4] This word was apparently a crux to the Commentator. He usually connects it either with *saj*, *satta*, to cling to, clung, or with *visa*, poison. Cf. *Kindred Sayings* i. 2, *n.* 6. Here he adduces other sources with a brave and generous disregard of sound etymology, his mind intent only on a constraining exegesis.—*Ed.*

fruited, poison-enjoying, permeates; *or*, that craving is spread out, extended over sights, sounds, odours, tastes, tangibles, ideas, over family, over a multitude. The word 'thread' refers to loss and disaster as if [greed] were a string securing fish-baskets.[1] As it is said:—'The thread, bhikkhus, is an allegory of passionate delight.'[2] 'Diffused' means spread out over objects of sense. 'She who urges,' *i.e.*, greed makes beings toil to get this and that. 'Consort,' *i.e.*, as a comrade, greed suffers us not to pine; she does not suffer beings to pine on the round of life renewed; wherever they are reborn she, like a dear companion, fills them with pleasure. Wherefore it is said:—

The man mated with craving wanders long
Through life and death, nor does he get beyond
His travels thus—reborn then otherwise.[3]

'Aiming' is setting [the mind] upon. 'Guiding to rebirth,' *i.e.*, the rope to rebirth; for by greed, as cattle bound at the neck by a rope, beings are led whithersoever it desires. 'A forest'—in that greed wins its way to, haunts, remains stuck in, this or that object. Or as begging.[4] 'Jungle,' which [in Pali] is the same with an extra syllable.[5] Or whereas a forest is likened to strong craving as being a jungle where obnoxious trees[6] have grown up, *vanatha* means, as dense undergrowth, a yet stronger craving. As it is said:—

Cut ye the forest, brethren, not the tree,
Peril and fear are from the forest born.
Cutting away forest and undergrowth,
So shall ye be [free and] dis-forested.[7]

'Intimacy' is consorting with,[8] meaning intercourse. [365] Of the two kinds, intimacy of natural desire and of [fraternal]

---

[1] So *Ṭikā*. Cf. our 'lobster pots.'
[2] Not traced.
[3] *Sutta Nipāta*, ver. 740.
[4] This is so unintelligible, that the *v. l. yāti*, 'going,' is possibly right.—*Ed.*
[5] *Vana, vanatha*.
[6] The Burm. MSS. read dukkhānam for rukkhānam.
[7] *Dhammapada*, ver. 283.
[8] In Pali one term with different inflections.

love, the former is here meant. 'Fondness' is attachment. 'Longing for' is the exercise of taking up [one's heart's] abode. And this, too, is said:—'Thine, O king, are those four and eighty thousand cities, the chief of which is the royal city of Kusāvatī. For these, O king, let desire awaken! Quicken thy longing after life!'[1] That is, make [them thy heart's] abode. 'Connection,' as of kindred, *i.e.*, greed connects us with individual objects of thought, or is individually akin in the sense of a relative, for in the sense of a constant dependence there is no relative to equal craving. 'Appetite,' *i.e.*, from [greed's] consumption[2] of the mind's objects, meaning both a spreading itself over them and partaking of them without gaining satisfaction. 'Wanting' signifies the function, 'cupidity' the corresponding state.

Now to show the objective of that craving the following nine terms have been said, wherein taking the meaning of *āsā* to be 'appetite,' we get yearning for visible and other objects. Of these the first five refer to pleasures of sense, the sixth refers to greed for the 'requisites,'[3] and is said especially for recluses. The three following terms refer to the bases of a layman's insatiableness. For to them there is nothing more dear than wealth, sons, life.

'This belongs to me, this is mine,' 'such a man has given me this, this has not been given me'—thus greed makes [people] mutter, hence 'mumbling' (*jappā*), and the following two terms increased by means of the prefixes. Following these, begun so as to classify the next two by a different way, 'mumbling' is again said, followed by the 'act of muttering' and the 'state of muttering.' 'Self-indulgent' means a repeated plundering, hauling along in the fields of sense, followed by [inflections signifying] self-indulgence, self-indulging, state of one who is given to self-indulgence.

'Fluster' is the name of that craving by means of which people go about agitated in places where anything is to be

---

[1] *Dialogues* i. 223 *f.*

[2] Āsā, āsanato.

[3] Parikkhāra; the recluse's necessities, food, lodging, clothing, medicines.—*Tr.*

gained, like dogs wagging their tails. Greed is keenly desirous of what is agreeable, *i.e.*, of objects, the state of being such is 'keen desire.' [366] Passion for what is improper, such as for a mother, or aunt, etc., is 'incestuous passion.' Greed which is strong, although arisen concerning what is proper, is 'lawless greed.' Or, from such expressions as 'passion,' 'lawless,' whether proper or not, the lustful desire arisen is called 'incestuous passion' in the sense of being unrighteous, and 'lawless greed' in the sense of being irregular. 'Hankering-after,' *i.e.*, desiring objects. Such an act is a 'hungering.' 'Entreating' is a wishing for things. 'Envying' is the act of envying. Earnest entreating is 'imploring.'

Craving for the pleasures of the five senses is 'sensuous craving.' 'Craving for rebirth' is 'craving for existence, material and immaterial.'[1] 'Craving for non-existence' is desire not to be reborn, called the annihilationistic view. 'Craving for material form' is craving for a purely material existence. 'Craving for the immaterial' is craving for immaterial existence. 'Passion for opinions' is accompanied by the annihilationistic view.[2] 'Craving for cessation' is craving for the annihilationistic view. Craving for sights is craving for things seen. And so on for sounds, odours, etc.

The meaning of 'flood,' etc., has been discussed.[3] As 'obstruction' greed blocks the moral states. As covering [them] it is [called] 'covering.'[4] As 'bondage,' it binds beings in the round of births. Approaching the mind greed corrupts it, makes it corrupt, and so is 'depravity.' As 'latent bias' greed lies chronically in us as a strong [tendency]. As 'obsession' greed breaks forth as it arises in the mind.[5] It seizes on the turn of good [conduct] by not suffering it

---

[1] 'Rebirth,' 'existence,' is *bhava*, lit. becoming.—*Ed.*

[2] We should have expected to find here the opposite, namely, eternalistic view.—*Ed.*

[3] See above, p. 65.

[4] The renderings 'counterfeiting' and *B.P.E.*, p. 281, are not tenable. —*Ed.*

[5] Pariyuṭṭhāna. Cf. *Points of Controversy*, p. 288. S. Z. Aung's rendering 'obsession' is not a sufficiently aggressive term, but must serve.—*Ed.*

to arise—such is the meaning. In 'Thieves plundered the wayfarer, drunkards plundered the wayfarer,' etc., it is implied that they seized the way. So here also 'obsession' is to be understood in the sense of taking possession.

[Greed is] like a 'creeper' in the sense of enveloping. Where also it comes as,

'*The creeper rears itself, and stands erect.*'[1]

this craving is spoken of as a creeper. [Next] as 'avarice,' because it wants divers things; as the 'root of ill,' that is, of the ills of life renewed in rebirth; 'source of ill' refers also to those ills; so does 'production of ill.'

[Greed is as] a snare, because it binds. 'Māra-snare' is the snare [used by] Māra. It is as a fish-hook, because it is hard to disgorge, and it is the fish-hook [used by] Māra. It is 'Māra's domain,' because, overcome by it, beings cannot get past it; Māra assumes authority over them. [367] It is a 'stream'[2] in the sense of flowing, a 'leash,' because by craving beings are firmly bound and led, as dogs are whither you will; and as hard to fill, craving is even as the 'ocean.'

In the exposition of hate[3]:—'he has done me harm,' *i.e.*, has worked my disadvantage.[4] In this way the meaning in all this [group of] terms is to be understood. 'Or when vexation (springs up) groundlessly' means anger without reason; for example, someone gets angry saying 'it rains too much,' 'it does not rain,' 'the sun shines too much,' 'it does not shine'; gets angry when the wind blows, when it does not blow, gets angry at being unable to sweep away the Bodhi leaves, at being unable to put on his robe; he gets angry with the wind, in slipping he gets angry with a tree-stump—in such connection is the expression said. And on nine of the ten occasions mentioned above [in the text], because they concern people, each is divisible into [harm or benefit] of thought, word, and deed. But the unreasonable vexation arising concerning things is

---

[1] *Dhammapada*, ver. 340.

[2] The Br. text reads *sandana.*

[3] *Dhs.* § 1060.

[4] Avaḍḍhim me akāsi, 'he has wrought me dis-growth.'—*Ed.*

not so divisible. 'Vexation of spirit' is mental vexation. More strong than that is 'resentment.' 'Repugnance' is the exercise of resistance. 'Hostility,' that of opposing. 'Ill-temper' is getting angry. In 'irritation,' 'indignation,' the terms are intensified by means of the prefixes (*pa, sam*) 'Hate' is offending (or spoiling). In 'antipathy,' 'abhorrence,' the terms are increased by means of the prefixes. 'Mental disorder' means upsetting of mind. 'Detestation' is [hate] corrupting the mind as it arises. 'Anger' is the getting angry. The mode of getting angry is 'fuming.' The state of one angry is 'wrath.' Now to show the aforesaid method 'hate, hating,' etc., were said in the exposition of immoral consciousness.[1] Hence in what is here said of hate, 'all such' states as have been described as 'vexation of mind' down to 'wrath,' whatever state was said above in the former method on 'hate, hating,' etc.—were said to be hate. In this way is the connection here to be made. For by doing so the fault of repetition is avoided.

[368] The exposition of delusion[2] should be understood in the opposite way to what has been said in that of non-delusion, and in every respect will be made plain in the commentary on the *Vibhanga*.[3]

'States which by those [six condition-] states have [one or more of] them as concomitants,'[4] that is, whatever other states, whether they are themselves among the six, or not, these are 'conditioned' (*sahetukā*). So for the contradictory term, 'unconditioned.' Here 'condition' is just condition. Where two or where three conditions arise together, the term 'condition' applies. But where delusion accompanied by perplexity and distraction arises, the condition-state (delusion) is itself unaccompanied by other conditions (*ahetuko*). So also for the exposition of the couplet of states 'associated with a condition.'[5]

---

[1] See p. 336.
[2] *Dhs.* § 1061.
[3] The *Sammoha-Vinodanī*. A first edition of this work in Roman letter is shortly to be issued by the Pali Text Society.
[4] *Dhs.* § 1073-74. Cf. above, p. 61 *f.*
[5] *Dhs.* § 1095.

In the exposition of the couplet on conditioned [states],[1] the phrase 'that state which is [not causally related], just that state . . .'[2] and which refers to the 'unconditioned element' mentioned in the previous couplet, is used in the singular number. But in that previous couplet, because the question is set forth in the plural, the answer follows the lead given by the question and is also given in the plural:—'these states are not causally related.'[3] This applies also to the following answer:—'these are the states that are visible.'[4]

In the exposition of the couplet of 'cognizable in one way'[5] . . . 'cognizable by sight' means to be known by the visual sense. And the same also with the rest of the terms. And herein 'cognizable in one way' means to be known either by the visual or by the auditory sense. 'Not cognizable in another way' means not to be known either by visual or auditory sense. This being so, inasmuch as it was said above, in the Table of Contents, that the couplet is formed owing to the difference in the meaning of the two terms, the couplet does not take the form:—'those states that are cognizable by sight are not cognizable by hearing.' But taking the meaning to be that visible objects are cognizable by sight, but sounds are not, this single couplet takes this form:—'Those states that are cognizable by sight are not cognizable by hearing; conversely, states that are cognizable by hearing are not cognizable by sight.' Thus making the couplets four by four with each [of the five] controlling sense-faculties as basis, a set of twenty couplets is to be understood.

[369] What then? is there no such specific cognizing by the *sensus communis* (*mano*)? Is it on that account that there is not a couplet concerning this? There *is* such cognizing, but it is left implicit, there being here no complete specification. For there is no complete specification as to what is not cognizable by sight. So in the case of 'mind'-cognition, there is here no couplet because there is no [explicit]

---

[1] *Dhs.* § 1085.

[2] *Ib.* § 1086. The translation (*B.P.E.*) does not quite reproduce the emphasis in this one reply.

[3] *Dhs.* § 1084. [4] *Ib.* § 1087. [5] *Ib.* § 1095.

specification. Nevertheless, it is meant that there are things cognizable in one way, not in another way, by mind-cognition. Hence, though this is not stated, it should be understood according to what is obtained [in consciousness].

So far only states of the sensuous plane are cognizable by some and not by other states of the sensuous plane, as amounting to mind-cognition. States of the plane of attenuated matter and others also are cognizable by some, and not by other states of the sensuous plane. Even states of the sensuous plane are cognizable by some and not by other states of the plane of attenuated matter also; by means of which even states of the plane of attenuated matter and others also are cognizable in some cases and not in others. But states of the sensuous plane, of that of attenuated matter, of the Unincluded are not cognizable by states of the immaterial plane. And states of the immaterial plane are cognizable by some and not by other states of the immaterial plane, of which even some are cognizable and others are not by means of states of the immaterial plane. States of the sensuous plane and others are not cognizable by the Unincluded. Again [states of] the Unincluded, from being not cognizable by Nibbāna, are cognizable by some and not by other states of the Unincluded. And of these, from being not cognizable by Path and Fruition, some are cognizable and others are not cognizable by the Unincluded. Thus it should be known by virtue of what is obtained [in conscious experience].[1]

In the exposition of the Intoxicants,[2] the lust of the five pleasures of sense is called the 'intoxicant of sensuality.' Passionate desire for life in a heaven of attenuated matter, and of immaterial existence, longing for Jhāna, lust coexistent with an eternalistic view are called the 'intoxicant of rebirth,' as being desire applied to rebirth. The sixty-two heresies are known as the 'intoxicant of views.' Lack of knowledge regarding eight points[3] is the intoxicant of ignorance.

---

[1] The P.T.S. ed. does not contain this sentence.

[2] *Dhs.* § 1096. Āsavā. See above, p. 48.

[3] Namely, the Four Truths, the past, the future, or both, and causal genesis.

In order to prevent confusion, the Intoxicants, as they occur here and there [in the Canon], should be considered under one or more heads. Thus as to their meaning they are as one in the sense of 'long fermentation.' In the Vinaya[1] two heads are accepted:—the restraint of intoxicants in the present life, destruction of them in future lives. In the Suttanta, there is first a threefold division:—*e.g.*, in the Saḷāyatana Sutta[2]:—'There are these three intoxicants, friend—sensuality, rebirth, ignorance.' Then a fivefold division in the Nibbedhika Sutta[3]:—'Bhikkhus, there are intoxicants leading to purgatory, [370] to the animal kingdom, to the Peta kingdom, to human life, to celestial life.' In the Āhuneyya Sutta[4] there are six categories:—'Bhikkhus, there are intoxicants to be eliminated by restraint, by habit, by endurance, by avoidance, by suppression, by culture.' In the Sabbāsava Sutta[5] these six with the addition of 'eliminated by insight' make seven. But here they are presented as four. And the definition of them is as follows:—desires belonging to sense *plus* 'intoxicant' make 'sensuality-intoxicant.'

The intoxicant concerned with Rūpa and Arūpa rebirth, dual as due to [previous] kamma and [subsequent] happening, is rebirth-intoxicant. The opinion-intoxicant is just opinions. The ignorance-intoxicant is just ignorance.

'Concerning desires,'[6] *i.e.*, the desires of the five senses. 'Sensual desire' is desire so called, not [just] conation, or righteous desire. 'Sensual passion,' *i.e.*, sense-desire as just desiring and lusting after. 'Sensual delight,' *i.e.*, sense-desire as just desiring and delighting in. And understanding sense-desire thus in all the terms, we get, besides, craving, fondness, fever in the sense of burning, languishing, rapacity in the sense of swallowing, consummating. 'This is called,' namely, the sensuality-intoxicant analyzed in eight terms.

'Concerning rebirths'[7]:—'desire for rebirth' is desire which

---

[1] *Vinaya* iii. 21; v. 143, 223.

[2] *Saṃyutta* iv. 256; cf. Sammādiṭṭhi Sutta, *M.* i. 55; *A.* i. 167.

[3] *A.* iii. 410, 414.

[4] *Ibid.* 387.

[5] *M.* i. 7 *f.*

[6] *Dhs.* § 1097.

[7] *Dhs.* § 1098.

arises by way of aspiring to rebirth in Rūpa and Arūpa forms of life. By this method the other terms should be understood.

That 'the world is eternal' is the view held in ten ways to be the 'Eternalistic view.' Here it is held that the five aggregates are 'the world,' and that this world is eternal, everlasting, is for all times. [371] 'Not eternal' is the view arising as the 'Annihilationistic view' of one who holds that this same world is annihilated, perishes. 'Finite' belongs to the theory that 'the world is finite,' held by one who judges, that the states of consciousness such as he would get on the plane of attenuated matter, or that of immaterial life, and has now got within a limited Jhāna-device[1]—one the size of a winnowing basket or shallow cup—are 'the world,' a world finite by the limits of the device. This finite view is both Eternalistic and Annihilationistic. The theory that 'the world is infinite,' is that of one who holds that the states of consciousness such as he would get on the plane of attenuated matter, or that of immaterial life, and has now got through taking a very ample device and attained to the symbol in that device, are 'the world,' a world that is endless according to the limits of the device. This is both Eternalistic and Annihilationistic

That 'the living soul is the same as the body' is the theory held on Annihilationistic lines that since the soul belongs to a merely dissoluble body, it is annihilated when the body is annihilated. In the next clause, since the soul is held to be other than the body, when the body is annihilated, the soul is not annihilated, is a theory on Eternalistic lines.

In the four following views about the Tathāgata, the first, that he as a permanent entity[2] is [reborn] after death is Eternalistic; the second, that he is not [reborn] is Annihilationistic; the third, of one who holds he both is and is not, is semi-Eternalistic; the fourth, of one who holds he neither is nor is not, is the Eel-wriggling theory.[3]

These are 'the states that are the intoxicants,' thus making

---

[1] See above, p. 248 *f.*

[2] *Satto.* Cf. *Points of Controversy.*

[3] See *Dialogues* i. 40.

that of sensuality and of rebirth one as modes of lusting,[1]—the intoxicants are three states in brief and four when expanded.

But—[it may be asked]—is the passionate desire which arises for a mansion, a wish-yielding tree, ornaments, etc., just an intoxicant of sensuality or not? It is not. And why?—because lust of the five senses is put away of the brahma-devas here, *i.e.*, in this plane of desire. Now that passionate desire, when it is ranked in the Condition-group,[2] is known as 'the condition that is greed'; when it is ranked in the Knot-group[3] it is known as the 'bodily knot of covetousness'; in the Corruption-group[4] it is known as 'the corruption that is greed.' But is passionate desire when co-existent with dogmatism known as the intoxication of sensuality, or not? It is not. It is called the lust of dogmatism. Thus it is said: 'Gifts made to a person lusting with the lust of dogmatism are not of much fruit, [372] nor of great advantage.'[5]

Moreover, it is proper to take these drugs or intoxicants in the order of the Corruptions as well as that of the Paths. In the order of the Corruptions, the intoxicant of sensuality is eliminated by the [third] Path of Never-returning, that of rebirth by the Path of Arahantship, that of dogmatism by the Stream-winning Path, that of ignorance by the Path of Arahantship. In the order of the Paths, the intoxicant of dogmatism is put away by the Stream-winning Path, that of sensuality by the Never-returning Path, that of rebirth and of ignorance by the Path of Arahantship.

Among the Fetters in the exposition of 'conceit,'[6] 'conceit at the thought—I am the better man' is the conceit arising thus: In the scale of perfection I am the better man. 'Conceit at the thought—I am as good as they' is the conceit arising thus: In the sense of equality I am as good. 'Conceit at the thought—I am inferior' is the conceit arising thus: In the sense of baseness I am inferior. Thus these three kinds of conceit of superiority, equality, inferiority arise in three sorts of men. For in the superior man the three may arise:—

[1] Br. text: of 'becoming.'
[2] P. 474.
[3] P. 64 *f*.
[4] P. 55.
[5] Not traced.
[6] *Dhs.* § 1116.

I am superior, equal, inferior. Likewise in the equal and the inferior man. In the superior man the conceit of superiority is alone a real conceit, the others are not real. In the equal man the conceit of equality, in the inferior man the conceit of inferiority is alone real. What does this signify? That in one man the three kinds of conceit may arise. But in the *Khuddakavatthu Vibhaṅga*, in the classification of the first conceit,[1] it is said that one conceit occurs in three men.

'Conceit,' 'overweening,' and 'conceitedness' signify mode and state. 'Loftiness' is in the sense of rising upwards or of springing over others. 'Haughtiness,' *i.e.*, in whom conceit arises, him it lifts up, keeps upraised. 'Flaunting a flag' is in the sense of swelling above others. 'Assumption' means uplifting; conceit favours the mind all round. Of many flags the flag which rises above others is called a banner. So conceit arising repeatedly in the sense of excelling with reference to subsequent conceits is like a banner. That mind which desires the banner is said to be desirous of the banner (*i.e.*, self-advertisement). Such a state is 'desire for self-advertisement.' And that is of the heart, not of a real self; hence 'desire of the heart for self-advertisement.' Indeed, the heart associated with conceit wants a banner, and its state is reckoned as banner-conceit.

[373] In the exposition of envy,[2] 'envy at the gains, honour, reverence, affection, salutation, worship accruing to others' is that envy which has the characteristic of not enduring, or of grumbling at, the prosperity of others, saying concerning others' gains, etc., 'What is the use to these people of all this?' etc. Herein 'gains' is attainment of the [recluse's] four requisites, such as robes, etc. Verily the envious person cannot endure that gain should be acquired by others, saying, 'What use to this man is this?' 'Honour' is the getting of these well-made and fine requisites. 'Reverence' is the act of making reverence. 'Regard' is the act of loving by the mind. 'Salutation' is the saluting with the fivefold

---

[1] *Vibhanga*, p. 353 *f*. The text does not seem exactly to support Buddhaghosa.

[2] *Dhs*. § 1121.

contact.[1] 'Worship' is worship with scent, flowers, etc. 'Envy' is the act of envying. The mode of envy is called 'envying.' The state of one envying is 'enviousness.' 'Jealousy,' etc., are synonyms of envy. And the grumbling characteristic of this envy is to be understood of both householders and recluses. For instance, suppose that a certain householder by depending on his own work as this or that means of livelihood, such as ploughing, merchandise, etc., gets a splendid conveyance or vehicle, etc., or a gem. Another man not wishing such gain to him is not pleased. He thinks, 'When will he decline from this prosperity and walk about a pauper?' and if for a certain reason the other does decline from that prosperity he is pleased. A certain recluse also being envious at seeing the acquirement of gain, etc., arising from general knowledge, scriptural scholarship, etc., thinks, 'When will this man decline in these acquirements?' etc., and when he sees him, for some reason, decline, then he is glad. Thus envy should be understood to have the characteristic of grumbling at the prosperity of others.

In the exposition of meanness,[2] 'five meannesses,' to wit: 'meanness as regards dwelling,' etc., have been said to show meanness as regards a substance. Herein meanness in a monastery is an instance of the first kind. Similarly with the rest of the terms. The whole monastery, a cell, a single room, and night and day chambers are called dwellings. Those living in such live at ease, get the requisites. A certain bhikkhu does not desire the coming there of a certain dutiful and amiable bhikkhu, and thinks, 'Now that he has come [374] may he go away quickly!' This is called 'meanness in a monastery.' But it is not so in one who is adverse to the arrival there of quarrelsome recluses.

'As regards family'—family, *i.e.*, of servitors as well as of relatives. To one not desiring the approach of another to

---

[1] Touching the ground with knees, hands, forehead.

[2] *Dhs.* § 1122. Meanness (*macchariyaṃ*) is translated avarice in *Dialogues of the Buddha* ii. 55. Buddhaghosa's remarks in the corresponding Commentary may be consulted. (Sum. Vil. on *Mahā Nidāna Sta.*)

that family is 'meanness as regards family.' But it is not so if one does not desire the approach of a bad person. For he, the evil recluse, so behaves as to upset the faith of those families. 'Meanness' lies in not desiring the approach there of the bhikkhu capable of guarding their faith.

'Gains' is the getting of the four requisites. There is meanness as regards gains to one who thinks, "May he not get it," even when it is a virtuous person who gets it. But in the case of a [bhikkhu] who is seen to ruin a gift given in faith, to spoil it by not making use of it, or by making a bad use of it, not to give it to another even when it is about to go rotten [by keeping], there is no meanness in [a giver] who thinks, 'If only this [bhikkhu] may not get it, a virtuous [bhikkhu] might get it and enjoy it.'

'Reputation' refers to personal beauty as well as praise of merits. Here the person who is mean as to beauty of body, wishes not to hear it said that another is worthy of faith and beautiful. One who is mean as to praise of merits does not wish to have [another's] praises sung on account of his virtue, ascetic practice, progress, or behaviour.

'As regards doctrine,' *i.e.*, doctrine of learning and of intuition. Of these, Ariyan disciples are not mean as regards doctrine to be intuited; they desire that intuition for the world, including devas, of doctrines they themselves have intuited. Their desire is, 'May others come to know that intuition.' But 'meanness as regards doctrine' occurs only in respect of textual doctrine. A person endowed with it wishes not to let another know what secret text or commentarial tradition he may know. But he who does not impart it, out of regard for the doctrine, by taking the person into account, or out of regard for the person by taking the doctrine into account, is not mean as regards the doctrine. In the former case the person so considered is frivolous; sometimes it is a recluse, sometimes a brahmin [375], sometimes a Jain. Indeed, the bhikkhu who thinks, 'This person breaks the traditional text, the abstruse, subtle, special doctrine, and will confuse it,' and imparts it not, acts out of regard for the doctrine by taking the person into account. And he who thinks, 'This doctrine is abstruse, subtle. If this person were to acquire it he would perish by making a [false] confession of gnosis,[1] and revealing himself,' and imparts it not, acts out of regard for the person by taking the doctrine into account. But he who thinks, 'If this one were to acquire this doctrine, he would be able to destroy our belief,' and imparts it not, is he who is said to be mean as regards the doctrine.

Among these five meannesses, through meanness, in the first place, as regards a monastery, one becomes a demon, or a Peta, and walks about lifting on to his head the rubbish of that very monastery. Next, one who, seeing his own family making gifts, etc., to others, is mean as to family, and thinks, 'Ruined, alas! is this family of mine'—such an one spits blood from the mouth, dysentery sets in, and his intestines broken into bits come out. Through meanness as regards gains belonging to the Order or to a Chapter, and through using it as though it was meant for individuals, one is born as a demon, or a Peta, or a boa-constrictor. Through meanness as regards personal beauty and praise of merits and doctrine of learning, one who extols his own praises and not those of others; who mentions this and that fault of anyone saying, 'What praise does he deserve?' and does not impart any doctrine of learning to him, becomes ugly, or has a mouth dripping with saliva.[2] Further, owing to the [first, or] monastery-meanness, one is tormented in an iron house. Owing to family-meanness one gets little gain. Owing to meanness over gains one is reborn in the dung-purgatory. Owing to meanness as to reputation one is reborn without beauty or reputation. Owing to meanness as to doctrine one is born in the hot-ash purgatory.

'Stinginess' is the expression of meanness. 'Avariciousness' is the act or mode of being mean. 'Mean spirit' is the state of one endowed with stinginess. 'Let it be for me only and not for another!'—thus wishing not to diffuse all one's own acquisitions one is 'close.'[3] The state of such an one is

---

[1] Aññā, Arahantship.

[2] Read eḷamukho.—*Tr.*

[3] Byāpitum anicchо ti viviccho; byāpitum icchatī ti viccho; na viccho ti viviccho.—*Ṭīkā.*

'avarice,' a synonym for a soft meanness. [376] An ignoble person is churlish. His state is 'ignobleness,' a name for hard stinginess. Verily, a person endowed with it hinders another from giving to others. And this also has been said,

> '*Malicious, miserly, ignoble, wrong . . .*
> *Such men hinder the feeding of the poor . . .*'[1]

A 'niggardly' person seeing mendicants causes his mind to shrink as by sourness. His state is 'niggardliness.' Another way:—'niggardliness' is a 'spoon-feeding.' For when the pot is full to the brim, one takes food from it by a spoon with the edge bent on all sides; it is not possible to get a spoonful; so is the mind of a mean person bent in. When it is bent in, the body also is bent in, recedes, is not diffused—thus stinginess is said to be niggardliness.[2]

'Lack of generosity of heart' is the state of a mind which is shut and gripped, so that it is not stretched out the mode of making gifts, etc., in doing service to others. But because the mean person wishes not to give to others what belongs to himself. and wishes to take what belongs to others, therefore this meanness should be understood to have the characteristic of hiding or seizing one's own property, occurring thus: 'May it be for me and not for another!' The rest in this group is clear in meaning.

It is proper to take these Fetters in the order of the Corruptions, as well as of the Paths. In the order of the Corruptions the Fetters of sensuality and of aversion are put away by the Never-returners' Path; the Fetter of conceit, by the Path of Arahantship; dogmatism, perplexity, observance of mere rule and ritual by the Stream-winners' Path; the Fetter of lust for existence by the Path of Arahantship; envy and meanness by the Stream-winners' Path; ignorance by the Path of Arahantship. In the order of the Paths, dogmatism, perplexity, observance of mere rule and ritual, envy and meanness are put away by the Stream-winners' Path; [377] sensuality and aversion by the Never-returners' Path; conceit, lust for existence and ignorance by the Path of Arahantship.

---

[1] *Kindred Sayings*, i, 120, ll. 2, 3, 7. [2] Cf. *Vis. Mag.*, p. 656.

In the 'Knot-group'[1] the 'bodily Knot' fastens the mental organism[2] in the round of births by way of decease and rebirth. The 'disposition to dogmatize' is thus:—rejecting the word of the Omniscient, he disposes his heart in this way:—The world is eternal; this is true, the other is absurd. But because there is a difference between covetousness and sensuality, therefore in the word-classification of the physical Knot of covetousness, instead of saying, 'That sensual desire, that sensual lust concerning the pleasures of sense,'[3] 'That lust, that infatuation' was said. By means of this, that which has been said above as 'lust of desire which arises for Brahmā's mansions, etc., is not the drug of sensuality, but under the Knot-group it is the physical Knot of covetousness,'[4] was rightly said. And the same in the following Corruption-group.

'Excepting the perversion of mere rule and ritual,'[5] *i.e.*, because one does not dispose the heart in this wise: 'This observance of rule and ritual is true,' but only as 'purity through rules of morality,' therefore rejecting it too as a wrong view, he said, 'excepting,' etc.

In the exposition of sloth and torpor[6] of the Hindrance-group 'mental indisposition' is sickness of mind. For one who is sick is said to be indisposed. It is also said in the Vinaya, 'I am not indisposed, Sir.'[7] 'Unwieldiness' is the mode of unwieldiness called sickness of mind. 'Adhering' is the mode of hanging downwards. The consciousness, namely, when unable to strengthen the postures, hangs like a bat from a tree and like a pot of raw sugar hung to a peg. It is with reference to that mode of consciousness that 'adhering' is said. The second term has been increased by the prefix '*saṃ*.' 'Clinging,' *i.e.*, constricted by non-expansion. The other two signify mode and state. 'Sloth'[8] is density with-

[1] *Dhs.* § 1135.

[2] *Kāyaṃ*, the 'group' composing the individual.

[3] As in the Intoxicant 'sensuality.' *Dhs.* § 1097.

[4] *Dhs.* § 758.

[5] *Dhs.* § 1139.

[6] *Dhs.* § 1156.

[7] Not traced.

[8] Thīna—*B.P.E.* 'stolidity.'

out expansion like that of a lump of butter. 'Stiffening' signifies mode. The state of that is 'rigidity,' that is to say, it is rigidity by way of non-expanding.

[378] 'Of mental factors,'[1] *i.e.*, of the three mental aggregates. 'Indisposition, unwieldiness':—this pair has been mentioned just above. 'Shrouding' means it covers up the mental aggregate as the cloud covers up the sky. 'Enveloping' is covering all round. 'Barricading within' is it obstructs within. To explain: As when a town is taken men shut within are unable to go out, so states shut in by torpor are unable to issue forth by way of diffusion; hence the phrase. 'Torpor' means it oppresses, *i.e.*, it injures by means of unwieldiness. 'Sleep' is that whereby we go to sleep. 'Drowsiness' makes blinking of the eyelashes, etc. 'Slumbering, somnolence'—these two terms signify mode and state. And the reason of the repetition of that term 'sleep' preceding them has been explained. 'This is called the Hindrance of sloth and torpor':—uniting 'this is sloth' and 'this is torpor,' the Hindrance of sloth-torpor is given in the sense of obstructing. That Hindrance of sloth-torpor, which generally rises before and after the sleep of probationers and average men, is completely cut off by the Path of Arahantship. But there is a lapse into the [subconscious] life-continuum (in fatigue) owing to the weakness of the sentient body in Arahants.[2] When this arises unmixed [with thought-process], they sleep. This rest is called their slumber.

Hence it was said by the Blessed One, 'Aggivessana, I recollect spreading the fourfold robe in the last month of the hot season and going off to sleep, mindful and understanding,

---

[1] In *B.P.E.* 'of sense.' *Dhs.* § 1157. The three are 'feeling, perception, and activities' (*sankhārā*).—*Ed.*

[2] Karaja = kāyapasādo. It is also explained as the 'constituted body' (sasambhārakāya); or 'body born of becoming' (karo ti satte nibbattetīti karaṁ; karato jāto karajo. *Madhusāratthadīpanī*). The Commentary on *Dīgha Nikāya II*. takes it to mean the 'body derived from the four great essentials'; while the *Yojanā* gives the last meaning in *Madhusāradīpanī*. The rendering by 'frail body' in *B.P.E.*, p. 213, *n.* 2, is wrong.—*Tr.*

lying on my right side.'[1] And such weakness of the sentient body is not to be killed by the Paths; it is obtained both when grasped-at and when not grasped-at. In the former case, it is obtained when the saint has gone a long journey, or is fatigued after doing some other work. In the latter case, it is obtained in leaves and flowers. For the leaves of some trees spread by means of the sun's heat and contract at night. Lotus flowers, etc., bloom by the sun's heat and contract again at night. [379] But this torpor does not arise in Arahants on account of any immorality.

Here the objection might be raised:—'Torpor is not immoral. Why? It is due to matter. For matter is unmoral, and this torpor is a material quality. Therefore herein the word *kāya* should be [mentally] used as "indisposition, unwieldiness of body."' If this torpor were matter merely by saying 'of kāya,' then states also which are repose, etc., of *kāya* would be material.[2]

[In the passage], 'he experiences bliss by *kāya*, realizes the ultimate truth by *kāya*,' experience of bliss and realization of the ultimate truth would also be by means of the material body. Therefore (owing to the phrase 'of *kāya*' not determining matter) it should not be said that matter is torpor. Here in 'indisposition of *kāya*' *kāya* means the mental *kāya*. If so, then why is 'sleep, drowsiness' said?—for the mental *kaya* does not sleep, does not blink the eyelids. This pair of words has been said as being the result or fruit of that torpor, just as the sexes, etc., are the results of the controlling faculties of femininity and masculinity. For as these sexual forms, etc., such as femininity, etc., are given as the result of the feminine controlling faculty, so sleep, drowsiness, are given as results of the torpor, called sickness, of this mental *kāya*. Indeed when there is torpor, there is also sleep and so on; thus by a figure of speech torpor, though immaterial, has been described as 'sleep, drowsiness, slumbering, somno-

---

[1] *Majjhima* i. 249.

[2] The point lies in the twofold meaning of *kāya*: body and the three mental factors. (Cf. preceding page).—*Ed.*

lence'—drowsiness as causing the movement of eyelids, etc. Thus by this word-definition also, this meaning (of torpor being immaterial) has been accomplished. Thus torpor is not a material quality.

The immaterial nature of torpor has also been shown by 'shrouding,' etc. Indeed matter is not the 'shrouding, enveloping, barricading within' of the mental *kāya*. 'But is not torpor material for this very reason? For that which is non-matter cannot be shrouded,' etc. If the shrouding, etc., of matter were accomplished, and not of non-matter, then (especially as the obstruction of matter is seen in binding bridges, etc.), there would be no obstruction of non-matter. Accordingly, just as immaterial states, such as sensual desire, etc., are called Hindrances in the sense of obstructing, so the shrouding, etc., of torpor also should be understood in the sense of shrouding, etc. Again, because of the expression: 'by removing the five Hindrances which cause the weakening of knowledge and corrupt the mind,'[1] torpor is immaterial. [380] For matter is not the corrupter of mind, nor the weakener of intellect. Why is it not so? Has it not been said, 'Bhikkhus, there are some recluses and brahmins who drink liquor, drink spirituous drink, do not refrain from liquor and drink. Bhikkhus, this drinking habit of recluses and brahmins is the first corruption.'[2] Further it has been said, 'Householder, these are the six dangers from being addicted to wantonness in liquor and strong drink:—present loss of wealth, increase of quarrels, cause of diseases, production of ill-fame, indecent exposure, weakening of wisdom, making the sixth basis.'[3] This meaning is self-evident and accomplished manifestly. Because when spirituous drink goes to the stomach the mind is corrupted, wisdom is weakened, therefore like drink torpor also may corrupt the mind and weaken wisdom.

But spirituous drink is not the corruption itself from merely signifying the cause. For were it so then it would be indicated in such expositions of corruption as, 'By removing these five

---

[1] *Saṃyutta* v. 160. [2] *Aṅguttara* ii. 53. [3] *Digha* iii. 182.

Hindrances which corrupt the mind'; or 'Bhikkhus, likewise there are these five corrupters of mind by which the corrupted mind is not plastic, not wieldy, not brilliant, not altogether radiant, and not concentrated on the destruction of the Intoxicants. Which are the five? Sensual desire is the corrupter of mind';[1] or, 'Bhikkhus, which is the corruption of mind? Covetousness, lawless greed, is the corruption of mind.'[2] And because when liquor is drunk, corruptions arise, corrupting mind and weakening wisdom, therefore from being the cause of corruption and signifying such, liquor is said to be so.

But torpor itself is the corrupting of mind and weakening of wisdom. Therefore it is not a material thing. This is endorsed by the mention of association. For it is said: 'The hindrance of sloth-and-torpor is a hindrance associated with the hindrance of ignorance.'[3] Hence from the mention of association torpor is not a material thing, for matter is not reckoned as an 'associate' [381]. Taking this as stating what is elicited (by reckoning), we may take this also:—just as it is said that we see shell-fish, gravel, potsherds, a shoal of fish stationary or moving—the gravel and potsherds stationary, the rest doing both—so here torpor is stated as a hindrance only, sloth as both hindrance and associate. And combining the two cases, 'both hindrance and hindrance-cum-associate' is stated according as each obtains reckoning.

But [it may be objected] torpor is stationary, it does not move. And being only a hindrance, not an associate, it is only a material thing.

[If it be so, it is not] because you have established its materiality. That the gravel and potsherds are stationary is a fact not created by the Sutta. Hence in the passage quoted, let the meaning be as you say, nevertheless it does not prove that torpor is a material thing. You cannot establish its materiality by that Sutta. Our conclusion holds good, because you have not established the materiality of torpor by what is therein stated to happen. Nay, more:—take the

---

[1] *Anguttara* iii. 16; S. v. 92. [2] Cf. *A.* ii. 67. [3] *Dhs.* § 1170.

passage 'from being abandoned,' etc. in the Vibhanga: it is said:—(he dwells) as one from whom sloth and torpor have departed, that is, inasmuch as they have been abandoned, cast out, there has been a freeing from, elimination of, disengaging, complete extricating from. . . . This consciousness in respect of this sloth and torpor he cleanses, purifies, wholly purifies, releases, delivers, wholly delivers from[1] . . . all this is said because of the casting out. And it is not said with respect to anything material, hence on this account also torpor is not a material quality.

[But, it may be objected], from the passage about the not coming to pass of [the torpor] born of mind—[you have not established your thesis], for torpor is threefold:—mind-born, heat-born, food-born. In the Vibhanga it is stated that, with the different kinds of Jhāna-consciousness, there is a not coming to pass of the torpor that is mind-born. Its immateriality is therefore not established. Torpor is just a material thing.

Nay, it is the materiality that is not established. If it were, we should get it stated [in the Vibhanga] that there is a non-becoming of mind-born torpor. Just this is not established, and torpor is not a material thing. Nay, more:—take the expression 'elimination.' It was said by the Blessed One:—'By eliminating six states, bhikkhus, one is competent [382] to dwell in the attainment of First Jhāna. Which are the six? Sensuous desire, ill-will, sloth and torpor, excitement, worry.[2] He has well seen by right insight the evil in sense desires. Eliminating these five hindrances he will come to know by strong insight his own good. Although the elimination of torpor is mentioned, material qualities are not [included as] that which is to be eliminated. As he said:—'The material aggregate [of personality] is to be understood, comprehended, not to be eliminated, not to be developed.'[3] From these passages on elimination also torpor is immaterial.

[But, it may be objected], texts about elimination refer to both immaterial and material things, for instance, 'Material qualities, bhikkhus, are not yourself. Put them away.'[4]

[1] *Vibh.* p. 254.

[2] *Anguttara* iii. 450.

[3] Cf. *S.* iii. 26, etc.

[4] *Ib.* 33

Here elimination is mentioned of material things as well, hence the reason alleged is not valid.

Nay, it is not invalid by the context. For in this Sutta, where it is said:—' The elimination and repression, bhikkhus, of passionate desire for things material '[1]—that is the elimination here [meant],—the elimination of passionate desire is spoken of as the elimination of matter. Such is the language used in such phrases as ' not having eliminated six states ': ' having eliminated the five Hindrances '[2]—such is the putting away that is meant. And thus by [this and] other contexts, torpor is not a material thing. Hence the language used in such Suttas as ' he having eliminated these five Hindrances . . . the things that defile the mind,' etc.—by these and other Suttas, it is shown that torpor is not a material thing.

Likewise ' states, bhikkhus, which are obstructions, hindrances, overwhelming the mind, weakening insight are five. Which are the five ? Sensual desire . . . sloth and torpor are the obstructions, hindrances, overwhelming the mind, weakening insight ';[3] again :—' Bhikkhus, the hindrance of sloth and torpor brings about darkness, blindness of vision, lack of knowledge, cessation of insight, having its part in adversity,[4] not leading to Nibbāna ';[5] again:—' Brahmin, when he lives with mind possessed by, oppressed by sloth and torpor.[6] . . .' Again :—' Bhikkhus, in one not thinking systematically unrisen sensual desire arises . . . [383] unrisen sloth-and-torpor arises.[7] . . .' Again :—' Bhikkhus, what are the five hindrances but a sheer heap of immorality '[8]—thus such various Suttas have been said exposing the immateriality of torpor.

And because it is immaterial therefore it arises with respect to things immaterial. Thus it is said in the Great Book of the Paṭṭhāna:—' A state of hindrance arises because of a[nother] state of hindrance not in a causal relation to what has gone before.' All that is said in the Vibhanga with respect

---

[1] *S.* iii. 28, etc.

[2] *Anguttara* iii. 64.

[3] *Ibid.*, p. 63; *Saṃyutta* v. 96.

[4] In the Dukkha of the round of rebirth.—*Ṭīkā.*

[5] Cf. *Majjhima* i. 115.

[6] Cf. *Ibid.*, p. 433 *f.*

[7] *Saṃyutta* v. 93.

[8] *Anguttara* iii. 65.

to consciousness of things immaterial being hindered should be expanded by that [formula]:—because of the hindrance of sensuous desire come the hindrances of sloth-torpor, distraction, ignorance.[1] Therefore the conclusion here to be arrived at is that torpor is not a material thing.

In the exposition of worry,[2] 'Thinking what is lawful concerning something that is unlawful' is said to explain worry from the root. By thus imagining an improper thing to be proper, when transgression is committed, when offence against something is done, in one who recollecting it regrets, 'I have done badly,' worry arises by way of after-regret. Therefore it is to show it from the root that the clause was said. Herein if anyone eats unlawful food imagining it to be lawful, unsuitable flesh imagining it to be suitable, bear's flesh to be pork, or leopard's flesh to be venison, eats at a late hour imagining he is in time, eats after the Pavārana, thinking it is not past, eats when dust falls into the bowl imagining that he has got alms, he thus transgresses by imagining what is lawful in something that is unlawful. And he who eats pork thinking it to be bear's flesh, in time thinking it to be behind time, transgresses 'imagining what is unlawful in something that is lawful.' And he who does any faultless thing thinking it to be faulty, and does a fault thinking it to be faultless, and who imagines fault in a faultless thing, and faultlessness in a fault, commits a transgression. And because this worry arises by imagining, when transgression is committed, no fault in faultlessness thus, 'Alas! I have not done well, I have not worked merit, not made a shelter from fear; I have done evil, a barbarous act, a wicked act,'[3] therefore permitting another root or basis of it, [the text] says, 'all this sort . . .' [384] wherein the meaning of the term 'worry' is given. The mode of worrying is 'fidgeting.' The state of one being with worry is 'over-scrupulousness.' In the phrase 'reproach of conscience,'[4] 'reproach' is the approach of the mind towards what is done and undone, faulty

---

[1] Cf. *Vibh.*, pp. 199, 398.

[2] *Dhs.* § 1160.

[3] Cf. *Anguttara* ii. 174.

[4] Cetaso:=of mind, the original English use of the word.—*Ed.*

and faultless. And because one does not [*i.e.*, cannot] undo evil done, or do the good left undone, therefore the returning approach [of conscience] to such things is ugly and weary, or '*re*-proach.' It is of the conscience, not of a being—to intimate this, 'reproach of conscience' has been said. This is its intrinsic nature. And reproach in arising scales the mind, as the point of an awl does a metal bowl; hence 'mental scarifying' has been said. This signifies function.

But that worry which comes in scruples of discipline as, 'Then the venerable Sāriputta did not accept it on account of the scruple that the daily food for guests living in a rest-house had been declined by the Buddha '[1] is not a hindrance. True, there is no such burning regret to the saint as 'By me this evil has been done.' But this worry which resembles a hindrance and is called investigation in this wise, 'Is this proper, or not proper ?' is known as worry respecting discipline.

In the exposition of the expression, 'Which are states that are hindrances and associated with hindrances ?'[2] sloth and torpor do not put away each other. Hence, 'Sloth and torpor are themselves hindrances and associated with the hindrance of ignorance' has been said without making a [special] division. And whereas there may be distraction with worry, this being absent, therefore the two have been spoken of in separate divisions. And any hindrance which does not come into association with any other hindrance is to be understood as not joined.

Now it is proper to take these hindrances in their order as corruptions and also in the order of the Paths. In the former case sensual desire and ill-will are eliminated by the Never-returning Path, sloth and torpor and distraction by the Path of Arahantship, worry and perplexity by the Stream-winning Path, ignorance by the Path of Arahantship. In the latter case, worry and perplexity are eliminated by the Stream-winning Path, sensual desire and ill-will by the Never-returning Path, sloth and torpor, distraction and ignorance by the Path of Arahantship.

---

[1] *Vin.* iv. 70.

[2] *Dhs.* § 1170. *Vinaya* iv. 70.

[385] In the Reversion group the plural number in 'excepting those states'[1] has been made to be consistent with the question 'Which are the states?'

In the exposition of Grasping,[2] 'sensual grasping,' which is both sensuality and grasping, means a clinging to sensuality as a basis. 'Grasping' is a catching hold strongly, the prefix in the word[3] having the meaning of 'strong,' as in 'despair,' 'denounced.' The same holds good in the compound 'opinion-grasping,' *i.e.*, clutching hold of an opinion (or 'view'). In such views as 'the self is eternal,' 'the world is eternal,' the later opinion is clutching hold of the former opinion. So also in rule-and-ritual-grasping:—there is a clutching hold of such. Conforming to bovine habits and bovine usages[4] as means of purification is itself such a mode of grasping. Similarly [in the fourth mode]:—'theory' is a way of declaring; by that there is grasping. What do they declare or grasp? The self (or soul). Thus 'theory-of-self-grasping' is a grasping which is a declaring about self. Or merely a grasping at the word 'self.'[5]

[Reverting to the first of the four modes,[6]] in 'that sensual desire . . . concerning sensual pleasures,' sensual pleasures are taken here as just only desires located in objects of the senses. Hence that the first of the 'Four Graspings' is sensuous desire concerning objects of sense is something actualized even in the Never-Returner, but in him there is never any sensuous lust based thereon.

In the exposition of 'opinion-grasping,'[6] the phrase 'there is no such thing as alms' means that, whereas we know one can give anything to anybody, one grasps the idea that there is no fruit, no result from what is given. A similar meaning attaches to the phrases about a great 'sacrifice' and an 'offering.' We know that there may be offerings by invita-

---

[1] *Dhs.* § 1176.

[2] *Dhs.* §§ 1213-17.

[3] *Upa* in *upādānaṃ*; so *upāyāsa*, *upakuṭṭha*.—*Tr.*

[4] See above, § 1005.

[5] Unable to find the meaning of 'self,' they look upon the mere word as the self.—*Tīkā.*

[6] *Dhs.* § 1215.

tion, to guests, and in marriage-ceremonies, but the opinion here is that there is no fruit, no result to such. In the phrase 'of good or bad deeds,' the ten courses of moral action and the ten courses of immoral action are respectively meant. [386] One knows that they exist, but takes it that they yield no fruit, no result. 'There is no such thing as this world,' *i.e.*, being mentally established in the next world he takes it that there is no present world. 'There is no such thing as the next world,' *i.e.*, being mentally established in this world he takes it that there is no next world. 'There is no such thing as mother or father,' *i.e.*, he knows the existence of mothers and fathers, and takes it that there is no fruit, no ripening on account of anything done to them. 'There are no such beings as spring into birth without parents,' *i.e.*, he takes it that there are no beings who after decease are reborn. 'Righteous and well-behaved,'[1] *i.e.*, he takes it that there are in the world no righteous recluses and brahmins who have observed practice suitable [for Nibbāna]. 'Who having understood and realized, by themselves alone, both this world and the next, make known the same,' *i.e.*, he takes it that there is no omniscient Buddha who, knowing this world and the next by his own special insight, is able to make them known.

It is proper to take these Graspings in due order as Corruptions and of the Paths. In the former case sensual grasping is put away by the four Paths, the remaining three by the Stream-winning Path. In the latter case all but the first are put away by the Stream-winning Path, sensual grasping by the Four Paths.

In the exposition of the Corruptions,[2] these are just bases [seats] of corruption. In other words, persons who have not destroyed the Āsavas, because they are established in greed, hate, and dulness, live in corruption, the corruptions being

---

[1] *B.P.E.*: 'who have reached the highest point, who have attained the height.'

[2] *Dhs.* § 1229. On this almost untranslatable word, see *B.P.E.*, p. 327 *n.* The following sentence is a very strained specimen of exegetic etymology, also unreproducible.—*Ed.*

the bases of persons so established. Because here those corruptions also, which arise by means of such causal relations as contiguity, are said to live (or dwell), therefore they are the dwelling-places of [present] corruptions. Of these ten Corruptions the first 'greed' has been set forth in over a hundred terms in the groups entitled Conditions[1] ('What is greed? That which is lust, infatuation, etc.'), Knots, and in this section. In the groups of Intoxicants, Fetters, Floods,[2] Yokes,[2] Hindrances, Graspings, it has been shown in sets of eight terms. Shown in such detail it may be taken as completed. [387] Of those groups, in those of Conditions, Knots, Hindrances, Graspings, Corruptions, craving which is to be destroyed by the Four Paths forms one portion. In the groups of Intoxicants, Fetters, Floods, Yokes, craving, although it is to be destroyed by the Four Paths, forms two portions. How? In the Intoxicants are two portions: intoxicant of sensuality, intoxicant of rebirth. In the Fetters are two portions: the Fetter of lustful desire, the Fetter of lust for rebirth. In the Floods are two portions: the Flood of sensuality, the Flood of rebirth. In the Yokes are two similar portions.

It is proper to take these bases of corruption in due order of Corruptions and of Paths. In the former case greed is put away by the Four Paths, hate by the Never-returning Path, delusion and conceit by the Path of Arahantship, opinion and perplexity by the Stream-winning Path, sloth, etc., by the Path of Arahantship. In the latter case, opinion and perplexity are put away by the Stream-winning Path, hate by the Never-returning Path, the remaining seven by the Path of Arahantship.

In the exposition of the sensuous realm,[3] 'from beneath' means by the lower portion. 'Waveless deep of woe': *i.e.*, there is here no interval, no break to the fires, to the beings, to painful feeling. And 'deep of woe'[4] means here there is no happiness called ease. Also in the sense of being void

---

[1] *Dhs.* §§ 1053 f. esp. 1059; above, 467 *f.*

[2] *Dhs.* §§ 1151 f.

[3] *Dhs.* § 1280.

[4] Or 'purgatory' (nirayo).

of delight. 'Starting from,' *i.e.*, making this deep of woe called the waveless the limit. 'Above,' *i.e.*, by the upper portion. 'Parinimmitavasavatti devas' are devas usually so designated because of wielding authority in sense-desires created by others. 'Into,' *i.e.*, keeping within. 'Whatever within lies,' *i.e.*, those [states] in this space. 'Has there its range,' *i.e.*, because from having come to be sometime, somewhere, others also traverse within [these limits], therefore not to comprise them, 'has there its range' is said. By this expression those who fare plunged within these limits, who fare, because they have come to be constantly and in all parts of this lower region by proceeding in essentials and derived qualities from the waveless deep of woe upwards, are included. Have their range means that they range about swallowed up in, range about in the lower region. 'Here included':—by this, because there are those who, having here their range, also have their range elsewhere, but are not there included, therefore these also are comprised.

Now to show the nature of the things 'here included' [388] as aggregate, void [of noümenon], and cause, he said the phrase beginning '[whether it be] khandha's,' etc.

In the exposition of the realm of attenuated matter,[1] the Brahma-world means the 'place of Brahma-[devas]' called the plane of First Jhāna. What follows should be understood analogously to the previous paragraph. In the clause 'of one who has attained' and the following, Jhāna of moral, of resultant, and of inoperative thought is to be understood in what is said.

In the exposition of the immaterial realm,[2] 'entrance among the devas of the sphere of infinite space' means entered into that rebirth so. And the same with the second term. The rest should be understood analogously to the foregoing.

In the exposition of the 'harmful' couplet,[3] of the three immoral roots the delusion that [arises] is harmful and associated with greed, and is harmful and associated with

---

[1] *Dhs.* § 1283 (*c*). [2] *Dhs.* § 1285 (*e*).

[3] *Dhs.* § 1294 *f. B.P.E.:* 'concomitant with war.' Cf. *M.* iii. 230 *foll.*

hate. But delusion, when it is associated with perplexity and distraction, is to be understood as harmful, as tainted, because in being eliminated there goes with it the lust and the harm that are associated with false opinions, and are called lust for rebirth in the spheres of attenuated matter and of immateriality.

The Suttanta couplets[1] have been specified and specialized according to their meaning in the discourse on the Table of Contents, and can be well understood by what was there said. Hence the terms will generally be evident in meaning. But there is just a residuum to be explained.

In the first place, taking the couplet on lightning,[2] suppose a man who can see is travelling along a path on a cloudy night. The path is obscured by the darkness. Lightning flashes and dispels the dark. In the absence of darkness the path becomes clear. This happens on a second journey, and again on a third journey. Here like the man who can see setting out on the path is the effort of insight put forth by the Ariyan disciple for the Stream-winning Path. Like the obliteration of the way in darkness is the darkness covering the Truths. Like the moment when lightning flashes and dispels the darkness is the moment when the light of the Stream-winning Path arises and dispels the darkness covering the Truths. Like the manifestation of the way when darkness clears [389] is the time of the manifestation of the four Truths to the Stream-winning Path; and what is manifest in the Path is even manifest to the person who has got it. Like the second journey is the effort of insight to get the Once-returning Path. Like the obliteration of the way in darkness is the darkness covering the Truths. Like the moment of lightning flashing the second time and dispelling darkness is the moment of the light of the Once-returning Path arising and dispelling the darkness covering the Truths. Like the manifestation of the way when darkness clears is the time of the manifestation of the four Truths to the Once-returning Path. And what is manifest in the Path is manifest to the person who has got

[1] *Dhs*. §§ 1296 *f*. Above, p. 68. [2] *Ib*. § 1298; *A*. i. 123 *f*.

it. Like the third journey is the effort of insight to get the Never-returning Path. Like the obliteration of the way in darkness is the darkness covering the Truths. Like the moment of lightning flashing the third time and dispelling darkness is the moment of the light of the Never-returning Path arising and dispelling the darkness covering the Truths. Like the manifestation of the way when darkness clears is the time of the manifestation of the four Truths to the Never-returning Path. And what is manifest in the Path is manifest to the person who has got it.

But there is no rock or gem that cannot be cut by the thunderbolt of Sakka; wherever the thunderbolt falls that place is pierced. The thunderbolt in destroying, destroys without leaving a remainder. And the path taken by it does not regain its original state. So there is no corruption that cannot be destroyed by the Path of Arahantship. It pierces all corruptions. Like the thunderbolt, in destroying the corruptions, it destroys without leaving a remainder. As the path taken by the thunderbolt does not return to its original state, so there is no such thing as the reproduction of the corruptions put away by the Path of Arahantship.

In the exposition of the couplet of 'the fool,'[1] shamelessness and recklessness are manifested in fools; they are also the roots of other states of fools. For a shameless and reckless person is one who leaves nothing immoral undone. Hence these two are taken first and separately. On the 'bright side'[2] also the same method is followed. Likewise, in the following 'dark' couplet.

In the exposition of the couplet of what 'conduces to remorse,'[3] 'remorse' arises from what has been done and what has been left undone. [390] Acts of misconduct burn from commission: acts of good conduct burn from omission. Thus a person feels remorse [lit.: burns] at the thought, 'I have misconducted myself,' 'I have left undone the right act'; 'I have spoken amiss,' . . . 'I have left undone the right

---

[1] *Dhs.* § 1300.
[2] *Dhs.* § 1301; *A.* i. 51.
[3] *Dhs.* § 1304; *A.* i. 49.

thoughts.' Similarly with what does not 'conduce to remorse.' Thus a person doing good does not feel remorse over acts of commission or omission.

In the exposition of the couplet on 'equivalents,'[1] the phrase 'that which is of these or those states' indicates an inclusion of all such states. 'Utterance'[2] is an uttering, the meaning being a predicating. What is it that is predicated? It is I, mine, another, another's, a person, a state, an individual, a man, a youth, Tissa, Datta, a couch, a chair, a mat, a pillow, a monastery, a cell, a door, a window—these are various ways of predicating. 'Designation' is rightly making known. What is designated? Any of the foregoing terms. 'Concept' means a revealing.'[3] 'Current term' means what is commonly said, to wit, any of the foregoing [classes of] terms.

'Name'[4] is fourfold:—that given on a special occasion, that given in virtue of a personal quality, that given by acclamation, that which has spontaneously arisen. Of these, from being chosen and placed by most people among the first world-cycles, the name of the king Mahāsammata is 'name given on a special occasion.' With reference to this it has been said, 'Verily, Vāseṭṭha, "Mahāsammata, Mahāsammata"—thus he was called by the people, and the first of these names was produced.'[5] [391] The name coming through a quality such as Preacher, Ragman, Vinaya-student, Three-piṭaka-man, Faithful, Believer,—such is 'name given in virtue of a personal quality.' The various hundred names of the Tathāgata, such as the Blessed, the Arahant, the Supremely Enlightened, etc., are also such names. Hence it has been said,

'The names won by the virtues of the Sage
Cannot be numbered: thou shalt teach his names
By thousands for his virtues manifold.'

---

[1] *Ib.* § 1306. *B.P.E.:* 'synonymous.' Cf. *S.* iii. 71 *f.*

[2] Saṅkhā.—*B.P.E.:* 'enumeration.'

[3] *B.P.E.:*—'expression.' Paññatti means what the mind both conceives and renders articulate. Cf. *Compendium*, p. 264, etc.—*Ed.*

[4] This and following couplets are from *Dīgha* iii. 212 *f.*; *Anguttara* i. 83 *f.*—*Ed.*

[5] *Dīgha* iii. 93.

On the name-giving day of a baby-boy, the relatives stand round and, having done honour to those worthy of gifts, agree to give the name, saying, 'His name is so-and-so':—this is 'name given by acclamation.' A former concept tallies with a later concept, a former current term with a later one, *e.g.*, the moon in a previous cycle is [what we now call] moon; and there were the sun, ocean, earth, mountains in the past:—this is the 'name spontaneously arisen.' This fourfold kind of name is only the one term 'name.' 'Denomination' is name made. 'Name-assigning' is name established. 'Interpretation' is name-making. 'Distinctive mark' is name showing the meaning, said because this name signifies or indicates meaning. 'Signification'[1] is significant of name.

'All states are processes of equivalent nomenclature' means there is no state which is not such a process. One state fits in with all states and all states coincide with one state. How so? The concept as 'name' is that one state which fits in with all states in any of the four planes. There is no being, nor thing that may not be called by a name. The trees also in the forest, the mountains, etc., are the business of the country folk. For they, on being asked, 'What tree is this?' say the name they know, as 'Cutch,' 'Butea.' Even of the tree the name of which they know not, they say, 'It is the nameless tree.' And that also stands as the established name of that tree.[2] And the same with fishes, tortoises, etc., in the ocean. The other two couplets are of the same meaning as this.

[392] In the couplet of 'name-and-form' (*i.e.*, of mind-matter),[3] 'name' (mind) has the sense of name-making, of bending (*namana*), of causing to bend (*nāmana*). Four of the aggregates are 'name' in the sense of name-making.[4] For

---

[1] Abhilāpo. *B.P.E.*: 'discourse.'

[2] See *B.P.E.*, p. 341, end of *n.* 2.

[3] *Dhs.* § 1309. Nāma-rūpaṃ. Cf. *Compendium*, pp. 192 *f.*, 271 *f.*; *Bud. Psychology*, p. 23. Also *Dialogues of the Buddha*, i. 86; § 83:—'bends down' there is abhinin-nāmeti.

[4] Rūpa (lit. shape, form) is so called because it reveals itself. But nāma being subtle has to depend on a 'name' to make itself known; hence 'making a name.'—*Ṭīkā*.

whereas, from being named by the people, the name of king Mahāsammata was Mahāsammata, and whereas parents by acclamation make a name for their son, 'Let him be called Tissa, Phussa,' and whereas the name comes in virtue of a quality as Preacher, Vinaya-student, such names as 'feeling' come quite otherwise. Feeling and the other [elements of consciousness], like the great earth and other elements, make their own name as they arise. When they arise their name also arises. For no one, when feeling arises, says: 'Be thou called feeling'; there is no function of name-taking. As when the earth appears there is no function of name-taking:—'Be thou called Earth;' and similarly with the world-systems, with Mt. Meru, the moon, sun, stars,—the name is just as it arises, answering to the spontaneously arising concept. So, when it arises the name 'feeling' just arises, answering to the spontaneously arising concept. The same is true for perceptions and the rest [of mind]. For feeling, whether it be in the past, future, or present, is [after all and always] just feeling. And so is perception, so are mental activities, so is consciousness. But Nibbāna, though it be for all time, is always Nibbāna. Such is 'name' in the sense of name-making. The four aggregates are 'name' in the sense of bending, for they bend toward the object [of thought]. In the sense of causing to bend, all [of the foregoing] are 'name.' For the four aggregates cause one another to bend on to the object; and Nibbāna bends faultless states on to itself by means of the causal relation of the dominant influence of object.

'Ignorance and craving for existence'[1] have been taken to show the growth of the roots of the round of rebirths.

'Both the self and world will be'[2]—taking the five aggregates as the self and the world, there is the 'Eternalistic view,'[3] which is laid to heart in the manner of holding that the self and the world will reappear.[4] Secondly, the 'Annihilationistic view'[5] is laid to heart in this way, that the self and the world

---

[1] *Dhs.* §§ 1311-12. [2] *Dhs.* § 1313. [3] *Dhs.* § 1315.
[4] Lit. 'will become.' [5] *Dhs.* § 1316.

will not reappear. [393] 'Referring to the ultimate past,'[1] —eighteen such views which come in the *Brahmajāla Suttanta*[2] with reference to the past are taken. 'Referring to the hereafter':—forty-four such views which come in the same Suttanta with reference to the future are taken.

In the exposition of 'contumacy,'[3] the phrase 'when that which is in accordance with the Law has been said' means that that precept which has been ordained by the Blessed One is said to be in accordance with the Law, showing the basis, and placing the offence thus, 'Thou hast committed this offence. Come, show it, rise from it and make amends.' 'The being surly,' etc., refers to the work of an obstinate person, owing to his retaliation in speech, his want of submissiveness when he is urged. 'Fractiousness' is the abstract form. The other term is just an equivalent. 'Contrariness' is taking the opposite side. A 'captious' person is one who finds it pleasant to take the opposite side. It is an equivalent for one who gets pleasure in the thought, 'I have taken the opposite view and as with a cross-bolt have made him speechless with a single word!' 'Captiousness' is the state of such an one. 'Want of regard' is the state of one who does not accept advice. 'Want of consideration' is an equivalent. 'Truculence' is a mode of this rejection [of advice]. 'Want of reverence' is a state of disrespect arisen in a habitual negation of paying respect where it is owed. 'Want of deference' is a state of habitual negation of showing deference to the seniors with whom one lives. 'This is called,' *i.e.*, such [an attitude] is called 'contumacy'. . . . Actually what is so called is the four aggregates proceeding in this way as the [fifth, the] aggregate of activities.

The answer on 'evil friendship,' etc.,[4] is to be taken by the same method, for 'contumacy,' 'evil friendship,' and the rest are not separate states. [394] 'Unbelievers' are they that have no faith, *i.e.*, no bases of belief such as the Buddha, etc. 'Immoral'[5] really means 'without morals,' for morality

---

[1] *Dhs.* § 1319.

[2] *Dialogues of the Buddha* i. 27 *f*; 46 *f*.

[3] *Dhs.* § 1325.

[4] *Dhs.* § 1326.

[5] *Dus-sīlā*, lit. having bad morality.

cannot be bad. 'Uneducated' means deprived of learning. 'Mean-spirited' refers to those who have the five kinds of selfishness. 'Witless' means without intelligence. 'To resort to' is to follow after. 'To consort with' is to follow vigorously. 'To be taken up with' is to follow in every respect, the term having been intensified by prefixes. The three terms signify just 'following.' 'To be devoted to' is to draw near to, with its variant forms :—' to be engrossed with' (with, in Pali, its intensifying prefix), 'fondness for,' 'enthusiasm for' (also intensified, in Pali, by a prefix). 'To be entangled with' is to be well twisted up with such persons in body and mind. Inclining to them, bent over to them, hanging on them is the meaning.

The exposition of the couplet of gentleness[1] should be understood in a sense opposed to the foregoing.

'The five groups of offences'[2]:—in the exposition of the Pātimokkha Table of Contents these five offences are Pārājika, Saṅghādisesa, Pācittiya, Pāṭidesanīya, Dukkaṭa. 'The seven groups of offences also,' in the Vinaya-exposition, are Pārājika, Saṅghādisesa, Thullaccaya, Pācittiya, Pāṭidesanīya, Dukkaṭa, Dubbhāsita. In these five and seven offences, a knowledge of their limits with their bases or causes is called 'skill in offences.' Knowledge of the limits of emerging from offences, together with the ecclesiastical vote, is 'skill in restoration from offences.'[3] 'Attainment' is because of fitness to attain. Skill in attainment[4] is insight into the stages of ecstasy together with the preamble. The existence of insight as to emerging at a fixed time without fail [from Jhāna] thus, 'I will rise when the moon, sun, or a star reaches such a position' is called 'skill in emerging from attainment in Jhāna.'[5]

[395] Discriminating knowledge in acquiring, attending to, hearing, remembering the eighteen elements is 'proficiency in the elements.'[6] Discriminating knowledge in acquiring, attending to them is 'proficiency in attention.'[7] Discrimi-

---

[1] *Dhs.* § 1327.
[2] *Dhs.* § 1329; *Vin. Texts*, i. 1 *f.*
[3] *Dhs.* § 1330.
[4] *Dhs.* § 1331.
[5] *Dhs.* § 1332.
[6] *Dhs.* § 1333.
[7] *Dhs.* § 1334.

nating knowledge in acquiring, attending to, hearing, remembering the twelve sense-organs is 'skill in sense-organs.'[1] And in these three proficiencies all is proper:—acquiring, attention, hearing, contemplation, penetration, reflection. The hearing, acquiring, and reflection are worldly; penetration is transcendental; contemplation and attention are mixed.

'From ignorance arises kamma,' etc.,[2] will be plain in the *Paṭiccasamuppāda Vibhaṅga.*[3] But the knowledge which knows that, on account of this ignorance as cause, there arises this kamma as effect, is 'skill in the Causal Genesis.' In the exposition of 'skill in affirming, in negating causal conjuncture,'[4] condition and cause are synonyms of each other. The sentient eye making visible matter the object is the condition and also the cause of the arising visual cognition. The sentient ear and the rest are likewise the condition and cause of auditory and other cognition, as mango seeds, *e.g.*, are the condition and cause of mango fruit.

In the second method (the negating of causal conjuncture) the words 'whatever[5] states' indicate causal states that do not fit. The words 'of whatever'[6] indicate resultant states that do not fit. 'Not condition, not cause,' *i.e.*, the sentient eye, when a sound is made the object of thought, is not the condition, is not the cause of the arising auditory cognition. Likewise the sentient ear, etc., are not condition, not cause of the remaining cognitions, just as the mango is not the condition, not the cause of the production of the palmyra.

In the exposition of 'upright,' 'soft,'[7] only the expression 'lowliness of heart' is distinctive. Its meaning is: by the absence of conceit this person's heart is lowly; the state of such a person is 'lowliness of heart.' The rest has come in the word-classification under 'rectitude of thought'[6] and of plasticity of thought.[8]

In the exposition of patience,[9] 'patience' is enduring.

---

[1] *Dhs.* § 1335.

[2] *Lit.* saṅkhārā. *Dhs.* § 1336. Cf. *Compendium*, p. 188, *n.* 2.

[3] *Vibhanga*, p. 135 *f.*

[4] *Dhs.* §§ 1337-38.

[5] *B.P.E.*: 'certain.'

[6] *Dhs.* §§ 1339-40.

[7] *Dhs.* § 51.

[8] *Dhs.* § 45.

[9] *Dhs.* § 1341.

The mode of being patient is 'long-suffering.' By this state they suffer without retaliating. 'Compliance' is to persist without repulsing or opposing. [396] 'Absence of rudeness' is the state of one who is not rude. 'Absence of abruptness,' *i.e.*, from being badly placed or uttered, an ill-spoken word is abrupt. By being opposed to it a good word is not abrupt. Herein the reason has been shown by a figure of speech. 'Complacency of heart,' that is, the mentality itself of the heart as joyous; just the state of one's own mind. The state of not being charged with ill-will is the meaning.[1]

In the exposition of temperance,[2] 'that which is absence of excess in deed' is the threefold bodily good conduct; 'that which is absence of excess in word' is the fourfold good conduct in speech. By the expression, 'in deed and word,' virtue, produced (in these seven ways) at the body-door and the speech-door and, with livelihood as the eighth, is comprised. 'This is called temperance' means that this virtue is called temperance from well avoiding evil. 'Besides, all moral self-restraint' means: because not only in deed and word, but also in thought evil conduct is practised, therefore it is said to show inclusion of virtue in thought.

In the exposition of amity,[3] 'insolent' means, as bosses protrude in a decaying or unhealthy tree, so, owing to faultiness, 'knobs' are produced from words of abusing and slandering, etc. 'Scabrous' means putrid, like a putrid tree. As a putrid tree is scabrous and has trickling, powdery tissue, so such speech is scabrous and enters as though piercing the ear. 'Harsh to others' means bitter to the ears of others, not pleasant to their hearts and productive of hate. 'Vituperative to others' means, as a branch with barbed thorns sticks by penetrating into leather, so it sticks to others and clings on, hindering those who want to go. 'Bordering on anger' means near to anger. 'Not conducive to concentra-

---

[1] Attamanatā. Atta here (cf. Sk. ātta) is not 'self,' 'own,' but 'taken up,' 'uplifted'; hence the word is literally 'exalted-mindedness.' Cf. *Dictionary, Pali Text Soc.*, *s.v.* Atta, *art.* 1. But Buddhaghosa's age had lost sight of this first syllable.—*Ed.*

[2] *Dhs.* § 1342.

[3] *Dhs.* § 1343.

tion' means all these terms not conducive to ecstasy or access are synonyms of the words 'with hate.' 'By putting away such speech,'—this has been said to show that when a man persists in not extirpating harsh speech, [397] even his gentle words, albeit they occur at intervals, are reckoned harsh. Next, hate is noxious (*elaṃ*); amiable speech is innocuous (*nelā*). 'Faultless' is the meaning, as in the passage,

'*Faultless in frame, white-canopied.*'[1]

'Pleasant to the ear,' that is, from sweetness of diction it is pleasant to the ear; it does not produce pain to the ear, like the piercing of a needle. And from the sweetness of sense and meaning not producing ill-temper in the body, it produces affection, and so is called 'affectionate.' That speech which appeals to the heart, which enters the mind easily without striking, we say 'goes to the heart.' 'Urbane' speech is so called because it is full (*purṇa, porī*) of good qualities, and because it is refined like well-bred persons, and because it is of the town (*pura*, urban). It means talk of citizens. For these use appropriate speech and address fatherly men as fathers, and brotherly men as brothers. 'Of much-folk-sweetness' means sweet to many people. 'Of much-folk-pleasantness' means pleasant to many people and making for the growth of mind. 'The speech which there,' that is, in that person, 'is gentle,' *i.e.*, polished, 'friendly,' that is, soft, 'smooth,' that is, not harsh.

In the exposition of courtesy,[2] 'carnal[3] courtesy' is the closing, covering up, by means of bodily needs, the gap which might exist between oneself and others owing to those needs not getting satisfied. 'Spiritual courtesy' is the closing, covering up, by means of the Doctrine, the gap which might exist between oneself and others owing to those needs not getting satisfied. 'He is courteous,' that is, he closes these two gaps in the world; shows courtesy by the twofold courtesy. To be courteous is to leave no [such] interval. The following

---

[1] *Udāna* vii. 5.

[2] *Dhs.* § 1344.

[3] **Āmisena.** Cf. the Christian: 'minister to them in carnal things.' (*Rom.* xv. 27).

discourse explains from the beginning:—'A courteous bhikkhu, on seeing a guest arrive, should meet him [398] and take his bowl and robe, offer him a seat, fan him with palmyra leaf, wash his feet, rub him with oil; if there be butter and syrup he should give him medicine, offer him water, scour the monastery—thus in one part is carnal courtesy shown. Moreover, at eventide—if there be no junior come to pay his respects—the bhikkhu should go to the presence of his guest, sit there and, without asking him irrelevant things, question him on relevant things. He should not ask 'What texts do you recite?' but should ask 'What scriptural text do your teacher and spiritual adviser use?' and should question him on points within his capacities. Should the guest be able to answer, well and good; if not, he himself should give the reply. Thus in one part is spiritual courtesy shown. If the guest stays with him, he should always take him when going his rounds for alms; should he desire to depart, the next day the bhikkhu should take him to a spot which is a favourable point of departure, and having gone about in one village for alms should send him off. But if on the other hand the bhikkhus have been invited, he should go taking the guest, if willing, with him. If he desires not to go, saying such a place is not suitable for him, the bhikkhu should send the rest of the bhikkhus, and with him go for alms; and should give him the carnal things he himself has obtained:—thus is carnal courtesy shown. To whom should the bhikkhu courteous in carnal needs give what he has gained for himself? So far, to the guest. If there be one sick, or one who has not observed Lent, to him also he should give; and also to his teachers and spiritual advisers, also to one who holds his belongings, such as the robe. And the bhikkhu who is fulfilling the precepts should give, beginning from the Elder's seat, his carnal gains every time they are brought, even for a hundred or thousand times. But the courteous bhikkhu should give to him, who has not obtained[1] his carnal needs.

---

[1] Reading aladdhaṃ. With the foregoing cf. *Vin. Texts* iii. 272 *f.*, esp. p. 281 *f.*

On going outside a village and seeing an old or helpless bhikkhu or bhikkhunī he should also give to such an one.

Hereon there is this story: It is said that, just when the village of Guttasāla had been destroyed by bandits, a woman Arahant, emerging from trance and, making a young bhikkhunī carry her baggage, was going along the road together with the people. When at noon they reached the village-gate of Nakulanagara [399] she sat down at the foot of a tree. Just then the Elder, Mahānāga, of Kālavallimaṇḍapa, after going about Nakulanagara village for alms, as he was coming out, saw the sister and offered her a meal. She answered, 'I have no bowl.' He said, 'Use this,' and gave the food with his bowl. She having partaken of the meal, washed the bowl and gave it to the Elder, saying, 'To-day, dear Sir, you will be tired with begging for alms. But from to-day there will be no fatigue to you on account of alms-begging.' And thenceforward never was there to the Elder an alms worth less than a kahapaṇa. This is carnal courtesy. Showing this courtesy, the bhikkhu, with a view to giving help, should speak on the stations of religious exercise to that bhikkhu, cause the text to be recited, dispel worry, perform his present duties, give the *abbhāna, vuṭṭhāna, mānatta, parivāsā,*[1] ordain him who is worthy of ordination, give the full ordination to a worthy one. And it is fit to get a resolution of the Order[2] to a sister also, should she desire ordination of him. This is spiritual courtesy. The bhikkhu courteous in these two ways gains that which he had not, establishes that which has arisen, and guards his own life on any perilous occasion, like the Elder who taking the bowl which he got from king Coranāga[3] by the rim, scattered the food by [shaking] the bowl. But in gaining that which he had not, the story of king Mahānāga[4] should be told. He, travelling from Ceylon to the Indian shore, obtaining favour from the presence of one Elder and coming back, was estab-

---

[1] For these different kinds of probation and penance, see *Vinaya Texts* ii. 397 *ff.*—*Ed.*

[2] Kammavācā

[3] *Mahāvaṃsa* xxxiv. 11.

[4] *Ib.* xxxiii. 45. But neither story is given. In the former presumably there was poison in the bowl.—*Ed.*

lished in the kingdom and made a great gift of medicine in Setambaṅgaṇa as long as he lived. In the matter of establishing what has arisen, the story of thieves who did not plunder the sacred property in Mount Cetiya because of the courtesy they were shown at the hands of Dīghabhāṇaka Abhaya the Elder should be told.

In the exposition of 'having the doors of the controlling faculties unguarded,'[1] the phrase 'sees an object with the eye' means, he sees visible matter by visual cognition which has got the name of eye by way of the cause and is able to see matter. [400] But the Ancients say:—Eye does not see matter. And why? Because it is not consciousness. Consciousness cannot see matter, and why? Because it is not eye. But by the impact of object with door, one sees by consciousness with the sentient organism as the physical basis. And such discourse is said to be supported by its components, as in the phrase 'he pierces by a bow,' etc. Hence 'seeing matter by visual cognition' is the meaning.

'Grasps the general appearance,' *i.e.*, grasps by way of lusting desire a sign such as is of the male, or female, pleasant, etc., and which is the basis of corruption. The stand is taken not merely on what is seen.

'Grasps the details,' *i.e.*, takes the various modes of hands and feet, of smiling, laughing, speaking, looking straight ahead, looking askance, which have earned the name of 'details' from the manifesting, the revealing of the lower nature.

In 'that which might give occasion,' for whatever reason, from whatever conditions of not restraining the controlling faculty of sight, it being not shut by the door-leaf of mindfulness, 'those states,' such as covetousness, always 'follow,' *i.e.*, chase, overwhelm the person 'who lives' with the 'controlling faculty of sight unguarded.'

'He does not set himself to restrain that,' *i.e.*, does not practise in order to shut the controlling faculty of sight with the door-leaf of mindfulness. And such a person is said 'not to keep watch over his controlling-faculty of sight.'

---

[1] *Dhs.* § 1345.

Now in the controlling faculty itself, there is neither restraint nor non-restraint, for neither mindfulness nor lapse of it depends on the sentient eye. Moreover, when the visible object reaches the avenue of sight, then, after two pulsations of the subconscious continuum, consciousness adverting to the five doors functions and ceases, after which visual cognition functions and ceases. After this receptive consciousness arises effecting the function of receiving and ceases. [401] After this examining consciousness arises accomplishing the function of examination and ceases. After this mind-door-adverting consciousness arises accomplishing the function of determination and ceases. Immediately after this apperception takes place. Herein during subconscious life-continuum there is neither restraint nor non-restraint. At one time or another of the advertings there is neither restraint nor non-restraint. But at the moment of apperception there arises either wickedness, forgetfulness, lack of knowledge, of patience or idleness, and there is non-restraint. Nevertheless such non-restraint is called that of the controlling faculty of sight. And why? Because at that apperceptional moment in the existence of non-restraint, the door also is unguarded, the subconscious continuum also is unguarded, and so also are the thought-processes, such as adverting. As, when the four gates of a city are not closed, though the doors of houses, arches, chambers within are well closed, all treasure in the interior of the city is unprotected, unguarded—for thieves entering by the city-gate may do as they please—so when wickedness and so on arise at apperception when there is non-restraint, the door at the apperceptional moment is unguarded, so also is the subconscious continuum, and so are the thought-processes such as adverting.

And the same is true with 'he hears a sound with the ear,' etc.

'That which is of these,' *i.e.*, that non-guarding, non-protecting, non-watching, non-restraint, non-shutting, non-closing of these six controlling faculties of one not having restraint, is the meaning.

In the exposition of immoderation in diet,[1] 'someone

---

[1] *Dhs.* § 1346.

here' means someone in this world of beings; 'through carelessness,' *i.e.*, not knowing, not considering by means of reflecting knowledge; 'unwisely,' *i.e.*, without reason; 'food,' *i.e.*, a thing to be swallowed, such as eatables, etc. 'Takes,' *i.e.*, eats, swallows. 'For sport,' etc.:—this has been said to show the absence of method, for he who eats without method takes food for sport, intoxication, personal decoration, beautification. For the sake of escape from the round of births by food he does not eat.

'That which is his insatiableness,' etc., *i.e.*, the discontent, the dissatisfaction there is in this unwise eating of food. [402] 'Immoderation' is a state of being immoderate, not knowing the limit called measure. 'This is called,' *i.e.*, the practice which arises by way of eating without consideration is called 'immoderation in food.'

In the exposition of 'having the doors of the controlling faculties guarded'[1] 'with the eye' is to be understood by the above-said method. 'Does not grasp the general appearance,' *i.e.*, does not seize by way of lusting desire the sign as described above. So also should the remaining terms be understood by opposition to the said method. And as has been said above—'but at the moment of apperception there arises either wickedness . . . so are the thought-processes such as adverting,'[2] so here also it is said (*substituting* virtue, etc., *for* wickedness, etc., *and the positive for the negative*).

And the same in 'he hears a sound with the ear,' etc.

In the exposition of moderation in diet,[3] 'takes food with reflection and judgment' means eats food with consideration, knowingly, by means of reflecting knowledge.

Now to show that consideration or reason, 'not for sport,' etc., has been said. Herein 'not for sport' means that he eats not for sport. Of such people, actors, acrobats, etc., are said to eat for sport. Indeed they search for and eat unrighteously and unjustly whatever food is favourable to such sport as dancing, singing, composing songs, eulogizing. But the bhikkhu does not eat so. [403] 'Not for intoxication'

---

[1] *Dhs.* § 1347. [2] *See* p. 510. [3] *Dhs.* § 1348.

means that he eats not to swell his pride and manhood. Of such people, kings and kings' ministers are known to eat for intoxication. Indeed these eat lumps of tasty food or excellent food to swell their pride and manhood. But the bhikkhu does not eat so. 'Not for personal charm' means he eats not for bodily decoration. Of such people, women such as are courtezans, who live by physical beauty, and court ladies drink ghee and molasses and eat smooth, soft, sweet food:—'thus our finger-joints will be well shaped and our bodily complexion clear,'—so they eat. But not so the bhikkhu. 'Not for beautifying' means that he eats not for growth of flesh in the body. Of such people, wrestlers and boxers, etc., make the body stout by exceedingly smooth fish, meat, etc.: 'thus our flesh will be filled out, adequate to bear blows,'—so they eat. But not so the bhikkhu.

'So as to suffice' signifies the limit of the result of taking food. 'For the sustenance of this body' means he eats to keep this sentient body[1] going, dependent as it is on the four great essentials. This is the motive of the bhikkhu in eating food, is the meaning. 'For the preservation of' means he eats for the preservation of the life-controlling faculty. In 'for allaying the pangs of hunger,' from not having eaten, the hunger which arises is called 'pang.' He eats for the allaying, the calming of that. In 'for aiding the practice of the higher life,' 'the higher life' comprises the three precepts and all instructions.[2] He eats for the purpose of the glorifying or upholding of that. 'Thus' signifies or indicates the reason. 'For this reason' is the meaning.

In 'I shall subdue the old feeling,' the arisen feeling due to not eating is called the 'old feeling.' He eats so that he will expel such feeling. In 'I shall cause no new feeling to arise,' the feeling arising from over-eating is called 'the new feeling.' He eats so that he will not produce it. Or, the feeling arising from having eaten is called the new feeling. [404] He eats so that he will not produce it.

---

[1] Karajakāya. See p. 485, *n*. 1.

[2] *I.e.*, learning, attainment, penetration.

'And maintenance shall be mine,' *i.e.*, there will be preservation. In 'faultlessness also and comfort,' there is faulty eating and there is faultless eating; wherein all that is unrighteous seeking, unrighteous accepting, unrighteous enjoying is known as faulty; but seeking righteously, accepting righteously, eating with reflections:—all this is known as faultless. Someone makes himself faulty in the partaking of a faultless thing, saying; 'I have obtained it,' he eats to excess, and being unable to digest it suffers from vomiting and purging, so that the bhikkhus in the whole monastery fall to exerting themselves in succouring his body and in seeking medicine. When asked, 'What is the matter?' they reply, 'It is the swollen stomach of so-and-so,' etc., and they blame and censure him:—'This bhikkhu is of this nature at all times; he knows not the capacity of his stomach; he commits a fault where there should be no fault.' Without doing such things, [the good man] eats so that there will be no fault.

As to the term 'comfort,' there is comfort and there is discomfort. The eating of these five brahmins produces discomfort, namely, of the 'lifted-by-hand-er,' the 'enough-for-the-loincloth-er,' the 'there-gyrator,' the 'crowpecked one,' the 'meal-vomiter.' Of these, the first eating much cannot rise by himself, and says, 'Take my hand'; the second has his stomach so swollen that even standing he cannot wrap his loincloth; the third rolls about where he ate unable to rise; the fourth stuffs his mouth so full that crows can peck at it; the fifth can no more fill his mouth, but vomits then and there. When all this is not done [the good man] takes food so that there will be comfort. Comfort is to have a relaxed stomach after four or five mouthfuls. For when so much only is eaten and water drunk, the four postures may go on with ease. Hence the Generalissimo of the Dhamma said:—

[405] *Hath he but eaten mouthfuls four or five,*
Let him drink water—here is sure enough
Refreshment for a bhikkhu filled with zeal.[1]

---

[1] *Psalms of the Brethren*, ver. 983.

Now in this place the items should be collected, for each of these is one:—'not for sport,' 'not for intoxication,' 'not for personal charm,' 'not for beautifying,' 'so as to suffice for the sustenance and preservation of this body,' 'for the allaying of the pangs of hunger and aiding the practice of the holy life,' 'I shall subdue the old feeling and cause no new feeling to arise,' 'and maintenance shall be mine.' 'Faultlessness also and comfort'—herein is the advantage of taking food. But Mahāsīva the Elder says: 'The first four items are called Rejection, and next them the other eight items should be grouped.' Here each of these is one:—'so as to suffice for the sustenance of this body,' 'for its preservation,' 'for the allaying of the pangs of hunger,' 'for aiding the practice of the holy life,' 'I shall subdue the old feeling,' 'I shall cause no new feeling to arise,' 'and maintenance shall be mine,' 'faultlessness also.' And 'comfortable living' is the advantage given by taking food. Thus he whose eating is characterized by the eight items is called knower of measure in food. 'This is called,' *i.e.*, the partaking of food with reflection arising as the knowing what is fit, and measure in search, acceptance, and enjoyment is called 'moderation in diet.'

In the exposition of forgetfulness,[1] 'unmindfulness' is the four [mental] aggregates as devoid of mindfulness. 'Lapse of memory, non-recollection':—these have been enhanced by means of the prefixes.[2] 'Non-remembrance' is the [mental] mode of not remembering; 'not bearing in mind' is inability to bear in mind; for the person endowed therewith has not arrived at noting well, is not fit to commit to memory. 'Superficiality' means floating in the object like gourd-skins in water. 'Oblivion' is ruined, muddled memory. Indeed, the person endowed therewith is like a crow [gazing with eyes fixed] on food, a jackal intent on flesh.

In the exposition of 'culture-strength,'[3] 'of moral states' [406] refers to the (thirty-seven) factors of wisdom. 'Pursuing' means initial pursuit. 'Cultivating' means growth or development. 'Multiplying' means repeated action.

---

[1] *Dhs.* § 1349. Cf. above, p. 150 *f.*

[2] Anu-ssati, paṭi-ssati.

[3] *Dhs.* § 1354.

The exposition of moral failure[1] should be understood as opposed to that of temperance. The exposition of theoretic fallacy[2] should be understood as opposed to that of progress in theories[3] (opinions or views), and this should be understood as opposed to that of grasping after theories.[4]

Though the exposition of purity in morals[5] is the same as that of progress in morals, yet in the latter the morality of Pātimokkha restraint leading to purity has been mentioned. Here, in the former, morality or virtue arrived at purity has been mentioned. And by these six couplets of mindfulness and comprehension, the strengths of reflection and of culture, calm and insight, mark of calm and of support, support and non-distraction, moral progress and progress in theory,[6] worldly and transcendental states of the four planes have been mentioned.

In the exposition of purity in theory[7] 'knowledge of the specific nature of kamma' means the knowledge that *this* moral kamma is one's own, *that* immoral kamma is not one's own. Of these, all immoral kamma, whether done by oneself or another, is not one's own; and why? Because of its destroying good and producing disadvantage. But moral kamma, because it destroys disadvantage and produces advantage, is called one's own. Herein, just as a man of means and money, when on a long journey festivals are proclaimed in village or township, does not think: 'I am a visitor, by whose help can I enjoy the festival?' but enjoys himself just as he pleases, and comes through any difficulty with ease, so these beings, relying on the knowledge as to their own kamma, put forth much action conducive to rebirth, enjoy happiness through happiness,[8] and attain Arahantship in countless numbers.

[407] 'Knowledge in due order of the Truths'[9] is the know-

---

[1] *Dhs.* § 1361. [2] *Dhs.* § 1362. [3] *Dhs.* § 1364. [4] *Dhs.* § 1215.

[5] *Dhs.* § 1365. [6] *Dhs.* §§ 1351-60, 1363-64. [7] *Dhs.* § 1366.

[8] Sukhena sukham. Cf. *Pss. of the Brethren*, ver. 220: *This happiness by happy ways is won*, as different from the ascetic theory, ver. 63; Majjhima i. 93 *f.*:—'happiness is got through suffering.'—*Ed.*

[9] *Dhs.* § 1366.

ledge of insight into that order. 'Knowledge of him who holds the Path' is insight into the Path and Fruition.

In the exposition of the expression 'now purity in theory' by the terms 'that science,' etc., the four insights above, such as knowledge that kamma is one's own, have been classified. In the exposition of the expression 'and as the effort of him who holds certain views,' the energy signified by the expression 'that inception of mental energy,' etc., is similar in course to understanding. And understanding should be understood as worldly on worldly occasions and as transcendental on transcendental occasions.

In the exposition of the couplet of agitation, 'dread of birth' is the knowledge established by seeing birth as perilous. And the same in 'dread of old age and death,' etc. Seeing birth, decay, sickness, and death as perilous by means of the phrase, 'of bad (states) not yet arisen,' describes the reasonable effort of one desirous of escaping from birth, etc. And the meaning of the word-analysis will be plain in the Commentary on the *Vibhaṅga*.[1]

In the exposition of 'And discontent in moral states,'[2] 'further longing' is longing for special excellence. Someone in this world gives first a meal for a party, a meal by tickets, requisites for the Sabbath and for select individuals. Not satisfied with this, he again gives the 'principal meal,'[3] a meal by tickets, a meal for the clergy, robes for Lent, builds a monastery, offers the four requisites. Not satisfied therewith, he takes the refuges, observes the five precepts, etc. Dissatisfied therewith, he becomes a monk and acquires one Nikāya, two Nikāyas, the three Piṭakas, the Buddha's Word,[4] develops the eight attainments, increases insight, acquires Arahantship. When Arahantship is won then comes the Great Content. Thus 'further longing' is longing for special excellence up to Arahantship.

---

[1] *Sammoha-Vinodanī*. The Pali Text Society is about to publish the text.—*Ed.*

[2] *Dhs.* § 1367

[3] Meal taken at a particular house by special invitation.—*Tr.*

[4] Cf. above, p. 32, where 'words' is lit.: 'word.'—*Ed.*

In the exposition of the expression, the phrase 'And the not shrinking back in the effort' means that one who is slack in cultivating the higher moral states in wayside monasteries is said to shrink, recede, step back from such effort; [408] therefore to show that method, 'that which is of moral states,' etc., has been said. Herein 'thorough performance' is thorough work in doing moral deeds; 'persevering performance' is incessant work; 'unresting' is work without break and without stopping; 'absence of stagnation' is absence of stagnated life or occurrence; 'unfaltering conation' is not laying down the will for good; 'unflinching endurance' is not laying down the burden in the work for good.

In 'reminiscent knowledge of one's former living,' 'former lives' are aggregates which have happened, and things [such as garments, village, carriage, etc.] belonging to the aggregates. 'Reminiscent of one's former lives' is that which keeps remembering such former lives. The knowledge associated with such is 'reminiscent knowledge of one's former lives.' The knowledge which pierces the darkness covering the aggregates of past existences is *vijjā*[1] (wisdom). Piercing that darkness it makes the past aggregates plain, manifest—hence *vijjā* is used in the sense of making plain.

'Knowledge of decease-rebirth' is knowledge both of decease and of rebirth. This also pierces the darkness covering the decease and reconception of beings and is *vijjā*. Piercing that darkness it makes plain the decease and reconception of beings—hence *vijjā* here also is used in the sense of making plain.

'Knowledge in the loss of the Intoxicants (or Drugs)' is knowledge at the Ariyan Path-moment of the loss of all corruptions. This also pierces the darkness covering the Four Truths and is *vijjā*. Piercing that darkness it makes plain the Four Truths—hence *vijjā* here also is used in the sense of making plain.

[409] In 'freedom of thought and Nibbāna':—in the sense of being set free on to the object, and of being well freed from

---

[1] A word-play on vidy- (to know) and vijjhati, to pierce.—*Ed.*

opposed states, the eight attainments are known as 'freedom of thought.' Or Nibbāna [is so-called] because it is gone away (*ni*[*r*]-*ggataṃ*) from that jungle (*vānaṃ*) called craving. In the eight attainments and Nibbāna, the former are called 'freedom' because they are free from the self-discarded lower nature; the latter is freedom because of the final release from the lower nature.

'Knowledge of him who holds the path' is the Fourfold Path-knowledge. 'Knowledge of him who holds the Fruition' is the fourfold fruitional knowledge. Of them, the First Path-knowledge when it arises causes the loss, cessation, suppression, and tranquillization of the five corruptions; hence it is known as 'knowledge as to loss.' The Second when it arises causes the loss, etc., of the four corruptions; hence it is known as 'knowledge as to loss.' And the Third likewise. The Fourth when it arises causes the loss, etc., of the eight corruptions; hence it is 'knowledge as to loss.' And the fruitional knowledge of the various paths, arising at the end of the loss, cessation, suppression, tranquillization, non-production, and non-arising of the various corruptions, is known as 'knowledge of non-reproduction.'

End of the explanation of the Chapter of the Summary in the Expositor, the Commentary on the Compendium of States.

BOOK III

DISCOURSE ON THE COMMENTARIAL CHAPTER

Now has arrived the turn of explaining the Commentarial Chapter placed immediately after the chapter of the Summary. But why has this chapter come to be called Commentarial? Because it is established by elucidating the meaning of the three Piṭakas, the Buddha's Word. For the special doctrine which does not come in the three Piṭakas, being defined and determined by the Commentarial Chapter, becomes well determined. It behoves the Abhidhamma student who cannot note the method of procedure in the entire Abhidhamma Piṭaka, the framing of queries, and the numerical series in the Great Book[1] to compare or bring them together from the Commentarial Chapter only.

[410] Whence is its origin? In Sāriputta the Elder. For Sāriputta spoke it and gave it to a pupil of his, who was unable to remember the elucidation in the chapter of the Summary. However, this account has been rejected in the Great Commentary, and the following account has been given:—What is known as Abhidhamma is not the province nor the sphere of a disciple; it is the province, the sphere of the Buddhas. And the Generalissimo of the Dhamma, being questioned by a fellow-student, took him to the Teacher's presence and told him. The Buddha uttered the Commentarial Chapter and gave it to that bhikkhu. How? The Blessed One asked him, 'What states are moral?' That is to say which do you mark as moral states? Then the student remaining silent, he said, 'Have not I, in the method, "Which states are moral? When a moral thought of the sensuous realm arises . . .,"[2] shown moral consciousness as divided

[1] *Paṭṭhāna*.

[2] *Dhs.* § 1.

into planes?'[1] All that moral consciousness in the four planes he arranged point by point, group by group, cluster by cluster by that method: these are the moral states, etc., and gave it to him showing moral states, etc., by way of elucidation.

Herein 'in the four planes' means in the sensuous, material, immaterial realms and the unincluded. 'Moral':—*i.e.*, such as the various kinds of contact, etc.—'these are the moral states,' all these states, such as contact, etc., named in these planes are moral.

But owing to the absence of division *quâ* plane of immoralities, the Blessed One said, 'twelve states of immoral consciousness'[2] wherein 'states' means risings. And this word 'consciousness' is the chief in the discourse. For, as when it is said, the king is come, the coming also of ministers, etc., is implied, so when 'state of consciousness' is said, states associated therewith also are implied. Hence it should be understood that in all places, consciousness together with the associated states has been taken by the expression 'state of consciousness.'

The meaning of all the following triplet and couplet classifiable terms such as 'results in the four planes,'[3] and the non-definition of pleasure, etc., in the feeling triplet, etc., should be tested by the meaning of the Text by the said method and understood. [411] But we shall speak only of what is distinctive.

Among the triplets,[4] first in that of the 'limited object,'[5] there are these twenty-five states of consciousness which have limited objects:—

(1–10) The phrase 'all is result of the sensuous realm' refers to the twice-five cognitions which arise in dependence on the five organs of [special] sense concerning the five varieties of sense-objects. They proceed only by natural law[6] and are divisible into the desired and the undesired.

(11, 12) Two mind-elements, the results of good and of bad

---

[1] *Dhs.* § 1368. [2] *Dhs.* § 1369. [3] *Dhs.* § 1370.
[4] *Dhs.* §§ 1368-1423. [5] *Dhs.* § 1406. [6] Niyamena, niyamato.

conduct severally, arise in dependence on the heart-basis, concerning the five varieties of sense-objects. They proceed by natural law immediately after visual and other sense cognition.

(13) The element of mind-cognition, having no root-conditions, being a result of good conduct and accompanied by joy, proceeds by way of examination in the five doors, and by way of registration in the six doors. It arises by natural law concerning the six varieties of limited objects, namely, sights, sounds, etc.

(14, 15) The two elements of mind-cognition having no root-conditions, being the results of good and bad conduct severally, and accompanied by neutral feeling, arise by way of examination in the five doors and by way of registration in the six doors. They arise by natural law concerning the six varieties of limited objects of sense. Proceeding by way of rebirth they have as mental object limited kamma, kamma-symbol, or tendency-symbol;[1] during life they proceed by way of the subconscious continuum, and at its end by way of decease they have just this as mental object.

(16–23) Eight risings of consciousness, results and with root-conditions, arise by the aforesaid method concerning limited things only, by way of registration and by way of rebirth, subconscious continuum, and decease.

(24) Inoperative[2] mind-element arises in the five doors concerning the five varieties of sense-objects.

(25) Inoperative element of mind-cognition, accompanied by joy, and without root-conditions arises in the six doors concerning such limited objects of sense as are present, and also in the mind-door concerning such as are past and future, making a mode of happiness for Arahants. Such are the twenty-five.

The states of the spheres of infinite consciousness and of neither perception nor non-perception, because they arise by making as object an attainment higher than themselves,

---

[1] Cf. *Compendium*, p. 149 *f.* (*a*, *b*, *c*).

[2] See p. 385.

take 'sublime objects.'[1] [412] Path states and Fruition states, from having Nibbāna as object, take an 'immeasurable object.'[2] Eight states of consciousness dissociated from knowledge, four being moral, four inoperative, occurring to probationers, average persons, and Arahants, concerning such matters of sense-experience as careless[3] giving, reflection, hearing of the Dhamma, take at the time of occurrence limited objects; at the time of considering the first Jhāna, etc., when they are exceedingly fit for practice, they take sublime objects; at the time of considering the concepts such as the device-symbol, etc., they take an undefinable object. Four states of consciousness associated with views as immoral take limited objects at the time when perverting [the truth] there is a being pleased with and delighted at the fifty-five states of sense-experience as implying a 'being' [or fixed entity]. In this way are they sublime in object at the time of occurrence by making the twenty-seven sublime objects the object. And some time they may have undefinable objects as at the time of occurrence with conceptual states as objects. The state of being limited, sublime, undefinable in object should be known as of states which, when they occur, are dissociated from views by virtue of one's being merely pleased with and delighted at those said states, [limited, sublime, and conceptual] as object; of states associated with aversion by virtue of grief; of states associated with doubt by virtue of not arriving at decision; of states accompanied by distraction by virtue of want of balance and calm. And of those [twenty kinds of consciousness] no state is able to arise making transcendental states the object; hence they do not have immeasurable objects.

Eight states of consciousness associated with knowledge, four being moral, four inoperative, have at the time of occurrence limited, sublime, and undefinable objects, by making as their object those aforesaid matters of sense-experience—a careless gift, reflection, hearing of the Dhamma on the part

---

[1] *Dhs.* § 1407. [2] *Dhs.* § 1408.

[3] Asakkacca, since saints have calmed all anxiety, all care.—*Ṭīkā*.

of probationers, average persons, and Arahants. But the state of having an immeasurable object of those eight kinds of consciousness associated with knowledge should be understood at the stage of adoption [in Jhāna], and when considering the transcendental state.

But that Fourth Jhāna of Rūpa-consciousness, as moral and inoperative, is of twelve modes, as follows:—(1) everywhere a vantage-point; (2) space-device; (3) light device; (4) divine states; (5) respiration; [413] (6) varieties of potency; (7) supernormal hearing; (8) thought-reading; (9) knowledge of destiny according to kamma; (10) supernormal sight; (11) reminiscence of former lives; (12) knowledge of the future. Of these (1) is Fourth Jhāna in the eight 'devices.' For inasmuch as Fourth Jhāna is the vantage-point for insight, superknowledge, cessation, the round of rebirth, it is called everywhere a vantage-point. (2) and (3) are vantage-points for insight, superknowledge, and round of rebirth, not for cessation. (4) and (5) are vantage-points for insight and the round of rebirths, but not for superknowledge or cessation.

In this connection the following are said to have an undefinable state as object:—tenfold device-Jhāna because it arises with the device-concept as its object; the divine states of Fourth Jhāna because they arise with the conception of a person as object; and breathing-exercise in Fourth Jhāna because it arises with a symbol as object.

The modes of potency of the Fourth Jhāna have limited and sublime states as objects. How? When one makes the body dependent on the mind, being desirous of going by means of an invisible body, the potency bends the body by the power of mind, inserts, places it in the sublime consciousness; then there is an object of mind obtained by exercise—thus there is a limited object, because the material body is the object. When one makes mind dependent on the body, being desirous of going by means of a visible body, the potency bends mind by the power of body, inserts, places the basic jhāna-consciousness in the material body; then the object of mind is obtained by exercise—thus from being the object of the sublime consciousness it has a sublime object.

Supernormal hearing of the Fourth Jhāna is certainly limited in object because it arises with sound as object.

Knowledge of others' thoughts has the limited, sublime, immeasurable for object. How? [414] It has a limited object at the time of one's knowing the sense-realm thoughts of others, a sublime object at the time of knowing thoughts of the Rūpa and Arūpa realms, and an immeasurable object at the time of knowing the Path and Fruition. And here among average persons, etc., the average man does not know the Stream-winner's thoughts, the Stream-winner does not know the Once-returner's thoughts—and so on up to the Arahant, who knows the thoughts of all beings. The person knows the thoughts of a lower person. Thus should this distinction be understood.

Knowledge of the destiny of one's actions has a limited object at the time of knowing action of the sensuous realm, and a sublime object at the time of knowing action of the Rūpa and Arūpa realms.

Supernormal vision verily has a limited object from having a material object.

Reminiscent knowledge of one's former lives has limited, sublime, immeasurable, undefinable objects. How? It has a limited object at the time of recollecting the aggregates of the sensuous realm, a sublime object at the time of recollecting aggregates of the Rūpa and Arūpa realms, an immeasurable object at the time of recollecting the Path cultivated and the Fruition realized by self or others in the past. 'The Buddhas in the past cultivated the Path, realized the Fruition, and entered Parinibbāna by the element of Nibbāna'—here also is an immeasurable object from reflecting on the Path, Fruition, and Nibbāna of the Buddhas who have cut off the round of rebirths. It has an undefinable object when one is recollecting such things as name, family, earth, sign, etc., in this way:—'In the past there was the Buddha Vipassī; [415] he had the city Bandhumatī. His father was king Bandhumā, his mother was Bandhumatī,' and so on.[1]

---

[1] Cf. *Dialogues of the Buddha* ii. 13 *f.* (*Dīgha* ii. 6 *f.*).

And the same with knowledge of the future. It has a limited object at the time of knowing, *e.g.*, 'in future this man will be born in the sensuous realm,' and a sublime object at the time of knowing 'he will be born in the Rūpa or Arūpa realm,' and an immeasurable object at the time of knowing 'he will cultivate the Path, realize the Fruition, enter Parinibbāna by the element of Nibbāna,' and an undefinable object at the time of knowing name and family in this way:—in future there will be the Buddha Metteyya, his father will be the Brahmin Subrahmā, and his mother will be the Brahmanī Brahmavatī.[1]

The Arūpa realm and loss of the Intoxicants in Fourth Jhāna are to be discussed as they come in the Text.

Mind-door-adverting accompanied by indifference is the precursor of all these classes of moral, immoral, and inoperative consciousness; its variety of objects should be understood by the method given in such consciousness. But it certainly has a limited object at occurrence by virtue of determination being in the five doors. 'Three- and four-fold Jhāna of the Rūpa realm,'[2] etc., have undefinable objects owing to their occurring with the undefinable as limited, etc., for their object. For here Rūpa realms arise in connection with the earth-device, etc.; the sphere of infinite space arises in connection with space separated from any one of the nine devices, and the sphere of nothingness arises in connection with the separation of Arūpa consciousness.

In the triplet of Path-object[3] the eight risings of consciousness associated with knowledge described at the beginning [of this work] have the Path for object when probationers and adepts are themselves reflecting on the Path penetrated. But owing to not being co-existent with the Path they are not conditioned by it; they are dominantly influenced by the Path by virtue of object-dominance when they are reflecting while paying regard to the Path as penetrated by themselves. They should not be said to have the Path for object and for

[1] Cf. *Anāgatavaṃsa*, ver. 96. *JPTS*, 1886, 50.

[2] *Dhs*. § 1408.

[3] *Dhs*. § 1415. To be divided under three heads (in P.T.S. edition).

dominant influence when making any other states than the Path the object of their thought. 'The Four Ariyan Paths' are certainly 'conditioned by the Path' owing to the existence of condition associated with the Path and called the Path. They are 'dominantly influenced by the Path' sometimes by means of the dominant influence of co-existence at the time of cultivating the Path, energy [416] or investigation being made the chief; but they should not be said to be sometime dominantly influenced by the Path at the time of making any other unspecified state in conational consciousness the chief. The nine Jhānas, beginning with that which is everywhere a vantage-point in the twelve kinds of the Fourth Jhāna of the Rūpa realm, have not the Path for object, neither for condition nor for dominant influence. Knowledge of the thoughts of others, of one's former lives, of the future in the Fourth Jhāna has the Path for object at the time of knowing the Path-consciousness of the Ariyans; but from not being co-existent with the Path it is not conditioned by it, and from not arising out of regard for the Path, it is not dominantly influenced by it. And why? Does such knowledge have no regard for the Path? Nay, it is because of their being sublime. For all the world have regard for the king; but his parents do not have regard. For they do not rise from their seat on seeing him, do not raise their hands in homage; they call him just as when he was young. So these three kinds of knowledge, because they themselves are sublime, have no regard for the Path. The mind-door-adverting consciousness has the Path for object from being the precursor of reflection at the time of reflecting on the Path of Ariyans; but from being not co-existent with it, it is not conditioned by the Path, and from not arising out of regard for it, it is not dominantly influenced by the Path. Why does it not have regard? Because it has itself no condition, being base and foolish. Thus the whole world has regard for the king, yet retainers, such as his hunchbacks, dwarfs, and servants, from their own want of knowledge do not have regard like clever men. So this consciousness, because itself has no condition, and is base and foolish, has no regard for the Path. Moral thoughts, etc., dissociated from knowledge, being void of knowledge, and having the transcendental state for object, do not get to the state of having the Path for object, etc.; they have only the undefinable for object.

[417] In the triplet of the past object[1] the states of the sphere of infinite consciousness and that of neither perception nor non-perception, because they arise with the past attainment above for object certainly have the past only for object. 'There are no future objects without connection' means that assuredly an individual or separate consciousness is never known to have a future object. But surely, it may be said, does not knowledge for the future have a future object, and does not knowledge of others' thoughts arise with a future object? They certainly do. But this knowledge of the future and of others' thoughts is never known as one separate consciousness; but, being taken with the Fourth Jhāna of the Rūpa realm, is mixed with other sublime thoughts. Hence it has been said, 'there are no future objects without connection.' Ten cognitions, three mind-elements, from arising about present sense-objects, etc., are known 'to have present objects.'[2]

In the term 'ten states of consciousness,' in the first place, eight have past objects when they occur with reference to kamma or a kamma-symbol at the time of taking conception among devas or men. And the same is true for the time of subconscious continuum and of decease also. But they take present objects at the time of taking conception with reference to the tendency-symbol, and subsequently at the time of subconscious continuum. Likewise when they occur by way of registration at the five doors. But they take past future, or present objects when arising with reference to the object of apperceptions, which in the mind-door are past, future, or present objects. And the same with the element of mind-cognition which is a moral resultant, without root-conditions, and is accompanied by indifference. This is the case in the conception of such as are born-blind among men;

---

[1] *Dhs.* §§ 1417-19. [2] *Dhs.* § 1418.

it has a present object by way of examining at the five doors also. This is the specific distinction here.

But examining accompanied by joy has a present object by way of examining and registration at the five doors, and like the conditioned resultant has past, future, and present objects by virtue of registration at the mind-door. But examining with an immoral resultant, and accompanied by indifference, is similar in course to examining which is a moral resultant, and is accompanied by indifference. [418] For the former only arises to denizens of purgatory by way of rebirth, subconscious continuum, decease. This is the specific distinction here. The mind-door adverting, accompanied by joy, has a present object making laughter at the five sense-doors of Arahants, and has past, future, and present objects when occurring by virtue of causing laughter with reference to states differentiated as past, etc.

In the phrase 'sensuous moral consciousness,' etc., so far four states of consciousness associated with knowledge[1] have, as moral, past, future, and present objects for probationers and average persons when these are contemplating the different kinds of past things such as aggregates, elements, sense-organs, and have undefinable objects at the moment when concepts and Nibbāna are contemplated. And the same is true with states dissociated from knowledge. For there is no consideration of the Path, Fruition, and Nibbāna by them. This is the specific distinction.

In the phrase 'four risings of consciousness associated with opinions,'[2] such states, as immoral, have past, present, future objects when taking pleasure and delight in, and perversely grasping such things, past, present, future, as aggregates, elements, sense-organs. They have undefinable objects when one takes pleasure and delight in, and perversely grasps the term-and-concept of 'person.' This is true also of risings dissociated with opinions; for it is not merely they which perversely seize.

The 'two risings of consciousness associated with aversion'[3]

---

[1] *Dhs.* § 1415. [2] *Dhs.* § 1412. [3] *Ib.*

have past, present, future objects in the case of persons grieved about things in time, and undefinable objects in the case of persons who are grieved about term-and-concept of such objects-in-time.

The phrases, 'associated with doubt,' and 'with distraction,'[1] have past, future, present objects at occurrence owing to their not having reached decision in those states, and owing to excitement. The eight risings of consciousness with root-conditions, as inoperative, are similar in course to moral states of consciousness. Mind-door-adverting accompanied by indifference has a present object at occurrence by way of determining, [419] and past, future, present, undefinable objects at the time of being the precursor to apperceptions having past, future, present objects; it has term-and-concept and Nibbāna as object in the mind-door.

These five, viz., that which is the basis of all, space-device, light-device, divine states, respiration-exercise, in the Jhāna of the Rūpa realm, different kinds of which have been mentioned, have an undefinable object. Variety of potency of the Fourth Jhāna has a past object because of its arising with reference to the past basic Jhāna-consciousness for one who bends his mind by means of the body.

There is a future object to those who are resolving on a future thing, as in the case of such elders as Mahākassapa on disposing of the Buddha's relics. For Mahākassapa the Elder in depositing the Buddha's relics made a resolve, 'For two hundred and eighteen years to come may these perfumes not dry up, these flowers not fade, these lamps not go out';[2] and all happened accordingly. Assagutta the Elder,[3] seeing the clergy at the Vattaniya monastery eating dry food without curry, resolved: 'Daily may the pond before meals be tasty as milk curds'; and it became as the taste of curds before meals and natural after meals. And there is a present object which arises with reference to the body, at the time of going by an invisible body making it dependent on the mind, [or of showing any other miracle].[4]

---

[1] *Dhs.* § 1414.
[2] Cf. *Dialogues* ii. 185.
[3] Cf. *Milinda* i. 11.
[4] P.T.S. ed. omits.

Supernormal hearing of the Fourth Jhāna has a present object when it arises with reference to an actual sound. Knowledge of others' thoughts of the Fourth Jhāna has past and future objects for one who knows the thoughts of others within seven days in the past, within seven days in the future, but is unable to know them when seven days expire, because such knowledge of others' thoughts after seven days is the province of knowledge of the past and of the future. And it has a present object at the time of knowing the present.

[420] This present is threefold: momentary, continuous, durational. Of these, that kind of state which has reached genesis, development, and disruption is the momentary present. That which is included in one or two continuous intervals is the continuous present. This is when an object does not at first become evident to one who goes to the light after having sat in darkness. The [material or immaterial[1]] continuity which occurs until it becomes manifest should be understood as one, or two continuous intervals. Matter also is not manifest at once to one who enters a room after having walked in the light. The [material or immaterial[1]] continuity which occurs until that is manifest should be known as one or two continuous intervals. And to one who stands afar, and who nevertheless sees the change in the hands of dyers, and in the reverberation of bells, drums, etc., the [material or immaterial[1]] continuity which occurs until the sound is heard should be known as one or two continuous intervals. So say the reciters of the Majjhima-Nikāya.

But the reciters of the Saṃyutta-Nikāya, saying that there are two distinct continuities:—(1) the material continuity is when the ripples of the water stepped into by one crossing to the bank have not settled down, or when, after a journey the heat of the body has not subsided, or when to one coming out of the glare into a room, the gloom is not yet dispelled, or when after being occupied with religious exercise in a room, one looks out of the window during the day and the quivering of the eyes has not subsided, but (2) the two or three appercep-

---

[1] P.T.S. ed. omits.

tive intervals are immaterial continuity—maintain that both are a continuous present.

And the kind of state limited by one existence is called the durational present, concerning which it was said [by the Blessed One] in the Bhaddekaratta Sutta:—'Friend, the mind and associated ideas that there are, are both called present; in just that "present," consciousness is bound with passionate desire. Because of consciousness being so bound, mind takes delight in the present. So delighting it is drawn into present things.'[1] [421] The continuous present is accepted in the Commentaries; the durational present, in the Suttas. Of the three presents some say that the momentary present is the object of knowledge of others' thoughts. Why? Because in a person with potency and another person a thought will arise simultaneously.

And this is the simile:—just as a handful of flowers is thrown into the air, one flower-cluster is sure to pierce another, stalk by stalk, so I know another's mind. Thus when people's minds are considered as a group, mind of one is sure to be pierced by another mind at the moment of genesis, development, or disruption. But this has been rejected in the Commentaries as improper, owing to the absence of coincidence in both minds by which one reflects and knows when reflecting even for a hundred and a thousand years, and owing to faultiness in reaching the state of a variety of objects.

And the continuous and the durational present should be known as the object of knowledge of others' thoughts. Of these two, all that consciousness which is another person's at the time of having the measure of two or three apperceptional processes by virtue of the past and future from the existing apperceptional process is called the continuous present.

The saying in the Commentary, that present time should be shown by means of an apperceptional interval has been well said. Wherein this is the explanation: a person of potency desirous of knowing another's mind reflects. The mind-door-adverting consciousness, making the momentary

---

[1] *Majjhima* iii. 197.

present its object together with the other's mind, ceases. Subsequently there takes place four or five apperceptions, the last of which is the potency-consciousness.[1] The remaining [third and fourth apperceptions] are of sensuous-realm consciousness. Of all these that which has ceased is the object, but the others have not different objects; and why ? Because they have a present object by virtue of present time. When there is oneness of object, of all apperceptions the potency-consciousness knows the mind of another, but the others do not. As in the eye-door visual cognition only sees the visible object and other cognition, such as adverting does not see it, so this knowledge of others' thoughts has a present thought by virtue of continuous present and present time. [422] Or, because the continuous present also falls into present time only, therefore by virtue of present time only this knowledge of others' thoughts should be known as having a present object.

Knowledge of one's former lives of the Fourth Jhāna has an undefinable object in the recollection of name and family, and in the consideration of Nibbāna and symbol; it has a past object in the remaining time. Knowledge of the destiny of one's actions of the Fourth Jhāna has a past object. Therein although knowledge of former lives and of others' thoughts also have past objects, yet of them the past aggregates of the former lives and name and family which are bound with the aggregates are not known as object. Indeed, this knowledge of former lives in these past aggregates and states bound therewith is similar in course to omniscience. And of the other knowledge the thought past the limit of seven days is the object. For it does not know another aggregate or what is bound with aggregate. But it is said to have the Path for object by way of explanation from having as object the mind associated with the Path. And only the past volition of knowledge of the destiny of one's actions is the object. This should be known as the specific distinction. This herein is the method of the Commentary. Yet because it

---

[1] *I.e.*, Rūpa-consciousness.—*Ed.*

is said in the *Paṭṭhāna*: 'The moral aggregates are the cause by way of object; causal relation of the knowledge of the varieties of potency, of others' thoughts, of former lives, of the destiny of actions, of the future,' therefore the four aggregates are the object of knowledge of others' thoughts and of the destiny of actions. There also of this last knowledge moralities and immoralities are the object.

Supernormal vision of the Fourth Jhāna has a present object from having for object an actual form or colour.

Knowledge of the future of the Fourth Jhāna has a future object, and indeed in the future aggregate and aggregate-bound is similar in course to omniscient-like knowledge of former lives. Of them although knowledge of others' thoughts has a future object, it makes only the thought arising within seven days the object. [423] This knowledge of the future takes for object the arising thought, aggregates, states bound with aggregates, for one hundred thousand cosmic periods in the future.

The 'threefold and fourfold Jhāna of the Rūpa realm,'[1] because they do not arise with reference to even a single thing in the past, future, or present, have verily an undefinable object.

In the 'personal' triplet,[2] as that state which is bound to the controlling faculty is subjective-personal, even though, in another person's continuity it would be called external, so the [given] state is not in any way personal when not bound to the controlling faculty and external to matter and to Nibbāna. Hence it is said to be external because there is no way of explaining it as subjective-personal, and not because the subjective-personal just does not come to pass. And in this triplet of the 'personal object,'[3] it is with reference to just this not coming to pass of the subjective-personal that the state of having an external object is mentioned. The phrase 'the sphere of nothingness has an undefinable and also a personal object'[4] is said without acquiescence in the personal,

---

[1] *Dhs.* § 1418. [2] Or 'subjective,' etc., triplet. *Dhs.* § 1419.
[3] *Ib.* [4] *Dhs.* § 1420.

external, or personal-external state of the object of the sphere of nothingness merely because the personal state has ceased. Therein not only the Jhāna of the sphere of nothingness has an undefinable object, but also its adverting, its access-thoughts, its object-reconsidering thoughts, its immoral thoughts, proceeding by way of enjoying its object, have undefinable objects. But all these are named along with it, hence they have not been taken separately. How, then, are they taken? This sphere of nothingness, and that consciousness which, as its precursor, arises and proceeds by way of adverting, access, etc., should have one object together with it. All that consciousness is said to have an undefinable object, because [firstly] the undefinable state of the object is *granted* by such a method as this:. 'Sometimes these risings of consciousness said, in the triplet of the "past object," to be the moral consciousness in the realm of sense, the immoral consciousness, the nine states of consciousness as inoperative, the fourth Jhāna of the Rūpa realm may not be said to have even a past object,' and [secondly] because it is *explicitly* stated thus: 'Of the sphere of nothingness the sphere itself, the four unincluded Paths and the four Fruitions—these states have an undefinable past object.'

[424] Now because the undefinableness of the object of the moral consciousness in the realm of sense, etc., has been mentioned above in the triplet of the 'past object'[1] with reference to their having one object together with the sphere of nothingness, therefore this last Jhāna, though spoken of in the triplet of the personal object as single, shows, here also, the undefinableness of the object of the moral consciousness in the realm of sense, etc.[2] For, is there any obstacle to these states of consciousness, which have one object, together with that Jhāna, in having an undefinable object? It is in this way, when this Jhāna is mentioned, that the adverting and other states are implied.

The rest herein is plain in meaning from the Pali. But in the classification according to object, these [two] Jhāna-

---

[1] *Dhs.* § 1417. [2] *Dhs.* § 1419.

spheres: infinite consciousness and neither perception nor non-perception, should be considered as having a personal object because they proceed as moral, resultant, inoperative, with reference to the [next] lower attainment of the six geneses of consciousness, bound up with their own continuity.

Among them the inoperative sphere of infinite space is the object only of the inoperative sphere of infinite consciousness and not of the other [moral, resultant sphere of infinite consciousness]. Why? Because of the absence of a moral resultant sphere of infinite consciousness to one endowed with the inoperative sphere of infinite space. But the moral sphere of infinite space is the object of the threefold sphere of infinite consciousness, moral, resultant, and inoperative. And why? Because of the arising and becoming of the threefold sphere of infinite consciousness above that of the infinite space of one who has produced it. And the resultant sphere of infinite space is not the object of any thought of the sphere of infinite consciousness; and why? Because of the thought not being brought forward after rising from the resultant. And the same with making the sphere of nothingness, moral and inoperative the object of that of neither perception nor non-perception.

All the threefold and fourfold Jhānas of the Rūpa realm, etc., should be considered as having an external object, because they proceed with reference to external earth and other 'devices' (*kasiṇa*) external to the subjective-personal. In connection with the passage 'all sensuous, moral, immoral, unmoral states, the Fourth Jhāna of the Rūpa-realm'[1] . . . four states of consciousness associated with knowledge as moral, have personal objects for one who is reflecting on his own body and mind,[2] external objects for one who is reflecting on another's body and mind, or is reflecting on concepts and Nibbāna, and subjective-external objects for one who is reflecting on both. The same method should be understood in the case of states of consciousness dissociated with knowledge. In none of these is there reflection on Nibbāna [425].

---

[1] *Dhs.* § 1420. [2] Khandhādīni, lit. aggregates, etc.

Four risings of consciousness associated with dogmatism as immoral have personal objects when [the conscious subject] is enjoying, taking delight in, and wrongly handling [the idea of] his own body and mind, external objects when [the idea of] body and mind of another are so enjoyed, etc.; or matter, 'device,' etc., not bound up with the controlling faculty; and subjective-external objects when enjoying, etc., both. And the same method should be understood when the states of consciousness are dissociated with dogmatism. For here there is no wrong handling.

'Two states associated with aversion'[1] have personal objects when the subject is depressed about his own body and mind, external objects when depressed about another's body and mind, or matter, concepts, etc., not bound up with controlling faculty, and subjective-external objects when depressed about both.

'States associated with perplexity and excitement'[2] should be considered as having a personal object; proceeding by way of doubting and wavering among those different kinds already mentioned.

Thirteen risings of consciousness, to wit, twice five [sense-] cognitions and three mental elements, have a personal object when proceeding with reference to their own material qualities, etc., and an external object when the qualities of another are concerned, and a subjective-external object when concerned with both. The element of mind-cognition without root-conditions and accompanied by joy has a personal object when proceeding with reference to its own five material states, etc., by examining, registration at the five doors and to other personal sensuous states by way of registration at the mind-door; it has an external object when proceeding with reference to the states of another person, and a subjective-personal object when referring to both. The same is valid for the twofold element of mind-cognition without root-conditions, a resultant and accompanied by indifference. It is only these [two classes of consciousness] which proceed in happy destiny

[1] *Dhs.* § 1421. [2] *Dhs.* § 1426.

and evil destiny by way of reconception, subconscious continuum, and decease in actions classed as personal, etc. The eight main classes of resultant consciousness are similar in course to these two, but do not proceed solely as examining; they proceed in a happy rebirth by reconception, subconscious continuum, and decease.

Inoperative consciousness without root-conditions accompanied by joy has a personal object when so proceeding as to cause mirth in connection with the subject's own material qualities, etc., at the five sense-doors, [426] an external object when proceeding similarly in connection with those of another; further, it has a personal object when proceeding so as to cause mirth in the Tathāgata in connection with his own kamma, such as his actions when he was the youth Jotipāla, the king Makhādeva, the ascetic Kaṇha,[1] an external object when proceeding in connection with such actions as those of the queen Mallikā,[2] the minister Santatī,[3] the flower-seller Sumana,[4] and a subjective-external object when proceeding in both such connections.

The element of mind-cognition without root-conditions, inoperative and accompanied by indifference, has a personal object when proceeding as determining at the five doors, and as adverting at the mind-door. The eight main classes of inoperative consciousness are similar in the above-named respect to the moral consciousness. But only these eight arise in Arahants; the moral eight arise in probationers and average persons. To this extent is there any difference.

The five Jhānas, having in the way above-stated a vantage-point everywhere in Fourth Jhāna, come also into this triplet, for in device, concept, symbol they have external objects.

The variety of potency of the Fourth Jhāna has a personal object because it makes one's own body and mind the object at the time of bending the mind by body, or body by mind, and at the time of itself creating forms such as a child's; has an external object at the time of manifesting externally

---

[1] See on all three above, p. 387.

[2] *Jātaka*, No. 415.

[3] *Dhammapada Commentary*, iii. 78 *f*.

[4] *Ib*. ii. 40 *f*.

elephants and horses and the like; and has a subjective-external object at procedure, sometimes personal, sometimes external. Supernormal hearing of the Fourth Jhāna has a personal object at the time of hearing its own internal sound and an external object at the time of hearing the sound of others, and a subjective-external object by way of (combining) both. Knowledge of others' thoughts of the Fourth Jhāna has an external object because it has others' thoughts for object; but there is no need for it to know its own thought. Knowledge of one's former lives of the Fourth Jhāna has a personal object when there is a recollecting of one's own individuality,[1] an external object when another's individuality is remembered, or matter not bound up with controlling faculty or the three concepts, and a subjective-external object when remembering in both ways.

[427] Supernormal sight in Fourth Jhāna has a personal object when anything is seen inwardly, an external object when seeing in the ordinary way, and a subjective-external object when seeing in both ways.

Awareness of the future in Fourth Jhāna has a personal object when there is a recollecting of one's own future individuality, an external object when another's future individuality is recollected, or matter not bound up with controlling faculty, and a subjective-external object when recollecting in both ways.

The reason why the sphere of nothingness has an undefinable object has been dealt with above.

In the exposition of the root-condition group,[2] the root-conditions are first shown: 'There are three moral conditions'; then their genesis is shown: 'They arise in the four moral planes.' In this way the explaining of the other groups should be understood.

In 'where two or three Intoxicants arise together'[3] the co-origin of the Intoxicants in three ways should be understood. Therein, the Intoxicant of sensuality arises in one state of

---

[1] Khandhā

[2] *Dhs.* § 1424.

[3] *Dhs.* § 1448.

consciousness in two ways: by virtue of ignorance in the four dissociated from views, and, together with the Intoxicants of views and of ignorance, in those associated with views. The Intoxicant of existence arises in one state of consciousness in one way: together with the Intoxicant of ignorance in the four dissociated from views. And as in this expression the co-origin of Intoxicants is understood, so in 'where two or three Fetters arise together' the co-origin of Fetters may be tenfold.

Herein, 'sensual lust'[1] arises in one state of consciousness in four ways; 'aversion' in three ways; 'conceit' in one way; 'doubt, and lust for existence' arise in one state of consciousness likewise in one way. How? Sensual lust arises in one state of consciousness in four ways—with the Fetters of conceit and of ignorance, of views and of ignorance, of observance of rule and ritual and of ignorance, and of ignorance alone. Aversion arises in one state of consciousness in three ways,—with the Fetters of envy and of ignorance, of meanness and of ignorance, of ignorance alone. Conceit arises in one state of consciousness in one way with the Fetters of lust for existence and of ignorance. [428] And doubt also; for it arises with the Fetter of ignorance. And the same with lust for existence. Thus here two or three fetters arise together in one state of consciousness.

And in the Hindrance-group[2] also in that expression which has been said thus, 'where two or three Hindrances arise together' the co-origin of Hindrances in eight ways should be understood. For among them 'sensual desire' arises in one state of consciousness in two ways, 'ill-will' in four ways, 'excitement' in one way, 'doubt' also in one way. How? Sensual desire arises in one state of consciousness in two ways, with the Hindrances of excitement and of ignorance in classes of automatic consciousness and with the Hindrances of sloth-torpor, of excitement, and of ignorance in voluntary consciousness.

Why was 'two or three' said by way of the above classifica-

---

[1] *Dhs.* § 1460. [2] *Dhs.* § 1486.

tion? Because it is possible for even four Hindrances to arise together in one state of consciousness. 'Ill-will' arises in one state of consciousness in four ways,—with the Hindrances of excitement and of ignorance in automatic consciousness; of sloth-torpor, of excitement and of ignorance in non-automatic consciousness; of excitement, of worry, and of ignorance in automatic; and of sloth-torpor, of excitement, of worry, and of ignorance in non-automatic consciousness. And 'excitement' arises in one way with merely the Hindrance of ignorance. 'Doubt' arises together with the Hindrances of excitement and of ignorance.

In the Corruption-group,[1] in the expression 'where two or three Corruptions arise together,' in various places two or three Corruptions arise together with other Corruptions. Why? Because of the non-production of just two or three Corruptions in a single state of consciousness. Herein the co-origin of the Corruptions is in ten ways. For among them 'greed' arises in one state of consciousness in six ways, 'aversion' in two ways, 'delusion' also in two ways. How? Greed arises in one state of consciousness in six ways,—with delusion, excitement, shamelessness, recklessness of blame in automatic consciousness and in that dissociated from views; with delusion, sloth, excitement, shamelessness, fearlessness of blame in the non-automatic; with delusion, conceit, excitement, shamelessness, fearlessness of blame in the automatic; with delusion, conceit, sloth, excitement, shamelessness, fearlessness of blame in the non-automatic; with delusion, excitement, dogmatism, shamelessness, recklessness of blame in the consciousness associated with dogmatism and automatic; and with delusion, dogmatism, sloth, excitement, shamelessness, recklessness of blame in the non-automatic. And 'aversion' arises in two ways with delusion, excitement, shamelessness, recklessness of blame in the automatic; and with delusion, sloth, excitement, shamelessness, recklessness of blame in the non-automatic. And 'delusion' arises in two ways with doubt, excitement, shamelessness, reckless-

[1] *Dhs.* § 1548.

ness of blame in the doubt-associated; and with excitement, shamelessness, recklessness of blame in the excitement-associated. The rest everywhere is evident in meaning.

End of the explanation of the Commentarial Chapter of the Expositor, the Commentary on the Compendium of States.

Hither the Master of the world attained
Expounding the fair Dhammasaṅgaṇī,
Dividing it according to the names:—
Mind, Matter, Exposition, Summary.
But the interpreting thereof, which I
Began by comprehension of the Truths
Of Abhidhamma, is completed now
And is by name called ATTHASĀLINĪ,
Revealing truths not incompatible.
Through the same merit which I have attained,
Who fashioned it in nine and thirty texts
Of recitations, that the holy Law
May long abide, let all men understand
The Law that bringeth blessing by the grace
Of the Law's King, and let them thus attain
Thro' pure and happy life Nibbāna's bliss
Ineffable, from tears and sorrow free.
Forever may the Law abide, by all
Revered! May rain in its due season fall!
As good kings guarded all mankind of old,
May the king guard mankind as his own son!

This Commentary, called the EXPOSITOR *on the* COMPENDIUM OF STATES, *was made by the Elder, in whom are grouped together the immaculate and gentle virtues of precept and conduct, adorned by pure and exalted faith, understanding and energy, who is capable of diving into the depths of his own and other doctrines, endowed with keen intellect, replete with the ability of unhindered knowledge in the Teacher's religion,—the which is divided into three Piṭakas, together with the commentaries,—*

a great grammarian, gifted with sweetness of speech, full of the virtues of sweetness, nobleness, issuing from the bliss born of the perfection of his acts, an unerring speaker like Sakka's thunderbolt not missing its mark, most excellent of speakers, a great poet, who is the ornament of the lineage of Elders resident at the Great Minster who are lamps in the lineage of the Elders, of well-established intelligence in the Law surpassing human law, and who is attended by analytical knowledge and adorned with such virtues as the sixfold super-knowledge, whose wisdom is very extensive and pure, who bears the name BUDDHAGHOSA *given him by the Elders.*

While Buddha, the great name of the great Sage,
Pure-minded world-chief, in the world abides,
So long may this book live and show the way
Of wisdom's purity to noble sons
Who seek for liberation from the world.

By grace of this, the book I wrote,
Into Metteyya's presence am I come.
Within the Refuges established
Upon the Sāsana I take my stand.
May mother, father, teachers, they who wish me well
And they who do not, give me happy thanks
And long safeguard the merit I have won![1]

May there be success!
May there be welfare!

---

[1] These last seven lines are not in the Burmese texts, but are in the P.T.S. edition, presumably transcribed from the three Siṇhalese MSS. used by the editor. The allusion to Metteyya, as associated by a prophetic utterance with Buddhaghosa in the future (see Buddhaghosuppatti, p. 66) is of interest, and may be compared with the similar envoi at the end of the Visuddhi Magga. It is quite possible that we have here the author's coda to his book, so I have translated and inserted the lines. (The last two sentences are probably additions by a scribe.)—*Ed.*

INDEX

I.—PROPER NAMES

II.—MAIN WORDS AND SUBJECTS

III.—PALI WORDS DEFINED OR DISCUSSED

III.—PALI WORDS DEFINED OR DISCUSSED

IV.—CHIEF SIMILES

[1] In the Indexes we acknowledge with pleasure the kind assistance voluntarily rendered by Mrs. A. Batuwantudave, of Colombo.—*Ed.*